SITY OF

Readings in the Philosophy of Law

second edition

Readings in the Philosophy of Law

second edition

edited by Keith C. Culver

ⓦ BROADVIEW ⓦ
READINGS IN PHILOSOPHY

Library and Archives Canada Cataloguing in Publication

    Readings in the philosophy of law / edited by Keith C. Culver. — 2nd ed.

(Broadview readings in philosophy)
Includes bibliographical references.
ISBN 978-1-55111-810-9

    1. Law—Philosophy. 2. Common law. I. Culver, Keith Charles, 1969- II. Series.

K235.R422 2007   340'.1   C2007-903841-7

Broadview Press is an independent, international publishing house, incorporated in 1985. Broadview believes in shared ownership, both with its employees and with the general public; since the year 2000 Broadview shares have traded publicly on the Toronto Venture Exchange under the symbol BDP.

We welcome comments and suggestions regarding any aspect of our publications—please feel free to contact us at the addresses below or at broadview@broadviewpress.com.

North America
PO Box 1243, Peterborough, Ontario, Canada K9J 7H5
3576 California Road, PO Box 1015, Orchard Park, NY, USA 14127
Tel: (705) 743-8990; Fax: (705) 743-8353
email: customerservice@broadviewpress.com

UK, Ireland, and continental Europe
NBN International, Estover Road, Plymouth, UK PL6 7PY
Tel: 44 (0) 1752 202300; Fax: 44 (0) 1752 202330
Email: enquiries@nbninternational.com

Australia and New Zealand
UNIREPS, University of New South Wales
Sydney, NSW, 2052 Australia
Tel: 61 2 9664 0999; Fax: 61 2 9664 5420
email: info.press@unsw.edu.au

www.broadviewpress.com

Broadview Press acknowledges the financial support of the Government of Canada through the Book Publishing Industry Development Program (BPIDP) for our publishing activities.

Consulting Editor for Philosophy: John Burbidge

PRINTED IN CANADA

This book is printed on paper containing 100% post-consumer fibre.

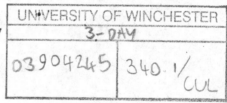

For my teachers in philosophy of law
who showed me how ideas matter:
Wil Waluchow, Joseph Raz, and Neil MacCormick.

CONTENTS

ACKNOWLEDGEMENTS

The second edition of this textbook is the product of many reactions to the first edition. I owe thanks to the instructors and students who used the first edition and shared their satisfaction, concerns, and suggestions. Anonymous reviewers from Broadview Press provided encouragement and requests for modifications, which I have accommodated as much as possible. I owe particular thanks to colleagues who read introductions and further reading lists, and generally helped me to fine tune this edition: Professors Richard Delgado, Brian Leiter, and Neil Mac-Cormick. Professor Michael Giudice, a research assistant in my assembly of the first edition and now a professor himself, read through the entire second edition, providing valuable criticism and commentary. Professor Wil Waluchow deserves thanks for encouraging me to approach Broadview's Company Founder, Don LePan, when I first raised the idea of this textbook, and I thank Don and Broadview for their skill and enthusiasm.

PREFACE

Why use this textbook in philosophy of law?

Accessibility: This textbook is designed to be used by readers with no prior experience of philosophy of law. Brief, easily understood introductions explain the context and key features of the readings, giving readers enough background to enable them to take on the real work of developing their own views regarding the arguments contained in each reading. The introductions are supplemented by a clearly written glossary, study questions and further readings, providing readers with tools for evaluating their own understanding, and a path toward more readings and perspectives on issues introduced in this textbook.

A real debate: Philosophy of law is a living discipline, inhabited by real people thinking about ideas and practices with real consequences for our everyday lives. These ideas have histories, and there are many points of view regarding those histories, so it is sometimes difficult to see the contemporary relevance of philosophy of law when it seems to be preoccupied with its history and diversity. This textbook takes seriously the importance of understanding the interaction between arguments which are in direct conflict, or offer incompatible points of view. Each part of this book is organized to present arguments which clearly compete and conflict with each other in trying to provide the best answer to shared questions and issues. It is up to you, the reader, to decide which arguments are the winners, or whether there is no winner and further investigation is needed.

Understanding what authors themselves said: A sound understanding of the issues and arguments of philosophy of law requires first-hand experience of philosophy of law. This textbook recognizes the importance of each reader coming to his or her own conclusions about what authors in philosophy of law have actually said. There is no substitute for the original text when trying to reach a fair understanding of the best available arguments regarding issues in philosophy of law. The readings contained in this textbook have been edited very lightly, and authors' original references have been left intact wherever possible, to allow this book to serve as a useful resource for further exploration of these arguments.

I look forward to your reaction to this second edition, and hope you find in philosophy of law a rich trove of arguments and insights to contribute to your life as a student, citizen, and perhaps Prime Minister or President.

Keith C. Culver
Fredericton, New Brunswick

INTRODUCTION

Why read this introduction? After all, as any experienced college or university student knows, many textbook introductions are much like sports highlights shows. Readers are expected to ooh and ahh at the great strengths and insights of some area of study, and after the oohing and ahhing is done, it seems to be expected that the reader is captured for life by the area of study. This textbook and introduction are not like that. We will assume that you have your own reasons for choosing a course in philosophy of law—an interesting course description, a good instructor, or a promise to your Mom that you would try something different while at college or university. You likely do not need more convincing to have a look at what philosophy of law is about, and you will choose for yourself whether one course is enough, or whether you want to go further in philosophy of law. What you probably need now is a sense of what it is like to study and do philosophy of law using this textbook. This introduction is intended to be something like a road map or travel guide for your use of this textbook.

Just like a travel guide, this introduction will give you an overview of the kind of place you are going: the group of questions, methods, and arguments which make up philosophy of law. By reading this introduction before you complete the readings your instructor assigns, you will have an idea of what to expect as you approach each reading, and you will have a sense of how each topic and author in the book is related to other topics and authors. Just like a travel guide, the introduction will give you a sense of what to look for in specific readings, and what not to miss.

There is one last, important way this introduction is like a travel guide: introductions and travel guides are never a substitute for the real experience of the journey. If you are to really understand the questions and arguments of philosophy of law you must go right to its heart, in your own reading, working with your instructor, and in thinking and writing about the issues you see in your readings and discuss in class. As you reach beyond the travel guides offered by the introductions, it is also worth remembering that textbooks and travel guides are never entirely up to date. You need to keep your head up, looking at the news and recent developments to see how the changing world of life under law might cause us to look differently at the theories and arguments we use to understand it.

1. What Is "Philosophy of Law"?

Philosophy of law is concerned with the nature and conceptual foundations of law as a distinctive mode of social organization. Philosophy of law asks a wide and widening range of questions about law and legal practices. Some of these questions continue an ancient debate, asking "What is law?" and "What is legal obligation?" Other questions probe the links between law, authority, and morality, asking "What is legitimate authority?" and "Are immoral laws really laws?" Still other questions explore responsibility, restitution, crime, punishment, race, and the border between literary, economic, and political understandings of law. Answers to these questions come from lawyers, philosophers, and others concerned with law and social life. These questions and answers are variously called philosophy of law, legal theory, legal philosophy, or jurisprudence (following the Latin *juris*, meaning law, and *prudentia*, meaning knowledge). We will use these terms interchangeably since they all refer to the same range of questions.

2. How Are These Questions Answered?

Traditionally, philosophy of law has been divided into "analytical" and "normative" areas of inquiry. Analytical jurisprudence has been concerned with *analysis* and *explanation* of legal concepts, asking such general questions as "What is law?" and "What is legal obligation?" Normative jurisprudence has been concerned with *evaluation* and *justification* of law and legal practices, asking such questions as "What is the nature of legitimate legal authority?" and "What justifies legal punishment?" This traditional distinction has recently come under extensive criticism from several directions, some of which are represented in this book. Some writers charge that the traditional distinction ought to be abandoned as invalid or, at best, seriously misleading. Influential writers such as Ronald Dworkin suppose that meaningful legal analysis and evaluation must be carried out simultaneously and focussed on interpretation of a particular legal culture—American, or Canadian, or British, and so forth. Writers from feminist, Critical Legal Studies, Critical Race Theory, and other perspectives are skeptical of the traditional distinction between analytical and normative investigations and argue that it promotes a dangerously distorted understanding of law and legal practices in which important social forces such as gender, race and class are not properly accounted for. Law is fundamentally political and fundamentally attached to particular societies, according to these writers, so broad and general analytical and normative investigations are pointless and misleading. Yet those who are skeptical of the traditional distinction have not succeeded in persuading all legal theorists that the division between analytical and normative investigations ought to be given up as an unfortunate mistake. Many writers continue to defend the value of distinguishing analytical and normative philosophy of law.

As you consider analytical, normative, and other approaches to philosophy of law, it is also important to think about what each approach tries to accomplish. Some are contributions to understanding of what it is to be a human living in a society. Others ask us to take immediate, practical action to fix problems in our legal systems. There is probably a place for a range of approaches to philosophy of law, but they will sometimes conflict and it will not always be an option to try to find a compromise or common ground. Philosophy of law is open to alternative views and new approaches, yet it is not simply a collection of all that has been said about the core questions of philosophy of law. Philosophy of law is above all an attempt to work toward better understanding of life under law, even when that means rejecting particular arguments or entire approaches to law. This book tries to give a concise picture of some of the main contenders in the debate over what philosophy of law is and what it should try to accomplish, and a picture of the results of different theorists' philosophical investigations into law. This book also tries to give you the resources to decide for yourself which perspectives are likely to give the most helpful answers to questions of philosophy of law. You may not arrive at final answers to these questions, but at least you will have some of the tools needed to work toward answers.

3. What Am I Going to Get from Philosophy of Law?

Law pervades our daily lives whether we like it or not, so we all share an immediate practical interest in understanding law. In the longer run, law shapes the general structure of our societies, so we also have a longer-term stake in understanding law. A course in philosophy of law will acquaint you with some of the best answers to date regarding immediate, practical questions with philosophical dimensions, such as the way we ought to understand the wrongdoing involved in an unsuccessful attempt to commit a crime. You will also have an opportunity to examine more abstract, yet equally important philosophical issues regarding the relation between law and justice—issues which may become especially important as you choose how to vote, where you will volunteer your skills in your community, or where you will lend your voice to a protest. As you study some of the arguments philosophers of law have offered in response to questions of philosophy of law, your instructor will show you how to demonstrate understanding of those arguments by explaining them, criticizing them, finding further support for their key claims, and assessing their strength relative to other arguments. Skills in critical analysis and evaluation of arguments in philosophy of law can be an excellent part of preparation for study of law, public service, journalism, business, and life as a private citizen.

4. Am I Ready For This Unfamiliar Discipline?

A new area of study can seem more challenging than it really is. To understand this book you do not need any background in either philosophy or law. In philosophy of law, as in many other areas of study, the main requirement for success at the introductory level and beyond is a willingness to encounter new ideas. It is also important to be prepared to learn about philosophers' and lawyers' special use of certain terms and concepts, and to be ready to read critically and thoroughly. Sometimes this means reading an argument more than once, but this is an ordinary and expected part of reading arguments which have been very carefully and precisely assembled. You may find it helpful to read an assigned reading before a lecture, then again soon after the lecture, taking notes at each stage. As you make notes you should try to identify not only the thesis or central organizing idea, but also the structure and organization of the argument. Make special note of areas you find unclear. If further attention to difficult areas still leaves you uncertain whether you understand an argument, a visit to your instructor or teaching assistant is your next step. Contrary to popular rumour, instructors do not actually eat students for breakfast, and are quite happy to help. Some instructors have a "drop in any time" policy, while others need to schedule specific office hours. Office hours are usually listed on the course outline, on the instructor's office door, or at the main office of your instructor's department.

5. The Structure of This Book: What to Expect

This book focuses on four questions which have concerned legal theorists in the "common law societies" that inherited the structure of the English legal system, as well as in the emerging world of international law. Each question is examined in a separate section. The first section asks "What is law?" In the second section we ask "What limits may justifiably be imposed by law on individual liberty?" The third section asks "How can law justifiably determine what it is to be responsible for legal wrongdoing?" Finally, in the fourth section we ask "What is international law?" Some of the sections include excerpts of cases from various jurisdictions, and so put philosophical arguments into a practical context.

For each section and chapter there are four tools to help you. *Introductions* aimed at first-time readers of legal philosophy discuss some of the main ideas of the section or chapter. Each section and chapter concludes with recommendations for *further reading*, and *study questions* to help you refine your understanding of the arguments you have read. Both the further readings and the study questions will make it possible to find more perspectives on the arguments you read, and provide new ways into the debates we examine. Finally, a *glossary* of legal and philosophical terms forms the last part of the book. This glossary is intended to help you to move between philosophy and law, and to account for the different contexts in which different writers make their arguments.

6. The Content of This Book: An Overview

In the remainder of this general introduction, we will explore very briefly the main ideas of the book. We will do this so that you can begin reading already knowing how the book hangs together as a whole, and how the questions and arguments contained in the book represent an extended exchange of arguments and replies.

6.1 Section I

The first section of the book contains five sets of ideas, each offering an independent answer to the question "What is law?"

The first chapter of Section I begins with natural law theory, a *normative* approach to law. Natural lawyers have traditionally argued that laws must meet certain moral standards if they are to generate genuine obligations. So-called laws which do not meet these standards cannot justifiably demand obedience. Our selections present both a classical natural law theory and a modified, contemporary natural law theory which claims that genuine laws which ought to be obeyed must at least *aim* at morally good goals. We will encounter in this contemporary view the very interesting claim that even immoral laws must sometimes be obeyed if they are only a small part of a system of laws which generally pursues morally justified goals. Since natural law is traditionally thought to set moral standards which laws must meet in order to be real laws, it is perhaps surprising to see a natural law theorist making a purely *analytical* claim that what is treated as a law is in fact a law, even if it does not pursue a morally acceptable goal. Can a natural law theory make this claim and still maintain natural lawyers' ability to distinguish genuine, binding laws from defective laws which ought to be disobeyed? This will be for you to decide.

In the second chapter of this section we turn to what has long been regarded as the view most plainly opposed to natural law theory. Legal positivism traditionally argues that while laws often are morally justified, it is *not necessary* for the existence of law that it have moral merit or even aim at morally justified goals. Legal positivists have instead explained laws as social conventions such as "commands," "social rules," or other norms which are not necessarily moral norms. This *analytical* theory of law allows legal positivists to explain easily how legal systems which pursue different goals in different ways at different times—even systems of morally bad law, such as the law of Nazi-era Germany—are all systems of law. Yet legal positivism has been criticized on several grounds. How, some critics ask, can an entire system of laws pursue morally bad aims and still provide any reason for judges to apply law or for citizens to obey it? Some critics suppose that legal positivists' insistence that laws need not aim at morally good goals is a terrible distortion of what distinguishes life under law from tyranny or a war of all against all. Other critics have objected in a variety of ways to the broad and general scope of legal positivism's picture of law, arguing that this sort of picture has very little value. We meet one of legal positivism's strongest critics in the next chapter.

Chapter 3 contains some of Ronald Dworkin's criticisms of legal positivism and sets out Dworkin's influential replacement view, called "law as integrity." Dworkin answers the question "What is law?" in the context of American legal practices, and argues that law is composed of more than just rules: law also involves an underlying web of moral "principles." Dworkin uses the American case *Riggs v. Palmer* (included here) to show that when judges determine what the law is with respect to a given case, they sometimes need to interpret the particular law in light of the larger legal system and the moral principles which underwrite it. To the extent that Dworkin supposes interpretation of law sometimes requires reference to moral principles which in fact undergird the law, Dworkin's understanding of law is similar to natural law theory. Yet Dworkin does not suppose that the existence of a law is conditional on its passing some test of moral adequacy, so he does not accept what is traditionally regarded as the central idea of natural law theory. Dworkin's answer to the question "What is law?" rejects legal positivists' and natural lawyers' broad and general concerns about the nature of law in favour of an account closely linked to the fact that judges in the common law world sometimes determine the meaning of law through appeal to moral principles which Dworkin sees in the law. It will be for you to evaluate whether Dworkin's insistence on understanding law in the context of a particular legal culture limits the general relevance of his theory, or whether Dworkin's focus on a particular legal culture really is the only way to develop a meaningful theory of law.

In Chapter 4 we encounter a theory of law quite different from the three preceding ideas about law. "Legal realist" writers of the first half of the twentieth century tried to break free of earlier attempts to develop a "scientific" understanding of law as a set of rationally ordered rules whose meaning and proper application could be determined with scientific certainty. Legal realists recognized that there is much more to law than written rules stored in law libraries, and argued that a realistic understanding of law must use a wider array of analytical techniques and take account of what courts in fact do with laws. The legal realists' emphasis on the activities of courts reminded legal theorists that law is a living thing which exists in practice as well as in statutes, codes, and other written documents. This hard-headed realism about the real nature and operation of law goes only so far, however, in an answer to the question "What is law?" Many critics have suggested that legal realists have placed excessive emphasis on explanation of what courts do with law, at the expense of a balanced account of the nature of law both in and out of the courts. These criticisms have been largely accepted, with the result that legal realism is not generally regarded as a viable contemporary theory of law. Yet legal realists' focus on actual prac-

tice has been an important challenge to broad and general theories of law, and the face of jurisprudence has certainly changed as theorists in both analytical and normative camps have attempted to take into account the legal realists' complaint that much legal theory proceeds on misleading versions of the facts about life under law.

In the fifth and final chapter of Section I we consider some influential contemporary criticisms of the dominant analytical and normative theories of law. Feminist and Critical Race Theory writers argue from insights similar to those of legal realists that much orthodox legal theory proceeds on assumptions which must be challenged. These assumptions range from one we noted above—that jurisprudence is either analytical or normative—to assumptions about human nature and the shared experiences, values, and goals of persons living together under law. Many of the critics from these movements are concerned that legal theory's abstract worries about the nature of law have taken attention away from important practical questions of the actual effect of law on social life, and of the strategies required for reform of unjust laws and legal systems. Many feminist legal theorists have focused on normative evaluation of the way women are and have been treated in law, and analysis of the ways law and theories of law bear a masculine bias. Critical Race Theory writers, departing from some insights of the Critical Legal Studies movement, are concerned about the practical effects of law for members of ethnic groups historically distinguished from elites on the basis of the slippery idea of "race." Critical Race Theorists and feminist legal scholars both hold that a dominant group has consciously or unconsciously constructed biased laws and set a biased agenda for thinking about law. Both feminist and Critical Race Theory writers are convinced that the priority given to certain questions about law must be reassessed.

These five kinds of answers to the question "What is law?" are sometimes clearly at odds with one another, as analytical, normative, and skeptical approaches appear to pursue entirely different goals. At other points, it seems possible to borrow the insights of at least parts of analytical and normative theories, while abandoning their weaknesses, to arrive at an acceptable single, comprehensive theory. There are difficulties in either an "all-star" theory made up of analytical and normative insights, or a defence of one particular analytical or normative answer to the question of the nature of law. There are also difficulties with skeptical approaches which deny the traditional distinction between analytical and normative approaches, yet do not offer a better, comprehensive replacement for understanding what law is or what law should become. The ideas provided here and in the suggested further readings can provide a great deal of insight into what the best understanding of law might look like. There is, of course, much more to be said about the nature of law, so it is well worth pursuing answers to the question "What is law?" in the large and rich literature beyond this book.

6.2 Section II

The second section of the book turns to one important aspect of life under law: personal freedom, and its limits. This section may be read independently of Section I, although it is helpful to have in mind the background that Section I provides.

When you think of law, what images immediately come to mind? Courts, police, and bad guys probably appear in the first few thoughts. This is not surprising, given that our lives are filled with fictional TV cops, judges, bad guys, and "reality TV" which shows real car-chases, hold-ups, hostage-taking, and so forth. We are fascinated by the interaction between these groups, and often shocked by what the bad guys have done: in acting "against the law" or "breaking the law" they have used their personal freedom in ways prohibited by law. Here we find an important issue in philosophy of law. In constitutional documents, declarations, and human rights legislation, common law societies are committed to the preservation of the widest possible range of human freedom. Yet we all recognize that freedom needs limits. What should those limits be?

We begin with John Stuart Mill's expression of the classical liberal view that the good of individuals and the good of societies require that laws leave as wide as possible a range of freedoms to individual persons. On this view, society is justified in legislating against only that conduct which harms others. Private conduct which is harmless to others cannot justifiably be limited by law. This view can explain and justify many laws, especially much of the criminal law, yet Mill's arguments have encountered criticism nonetheless. Some of these criticisms appear in the three subsequent articles included here.

The article by Gerald Dworkin in this section explores the idea and justification of *paternalism*—the idea that liberty is sometimes justifiably limited for the good of the person whose liberty is limited. Paternalism has been thought to be inconsistent with personal liberty of the sort sketched above, since paternalism may interfere with private actions which do not harm others. Yet it seems that we are sometimes not the best judges of our own interests, and it is sometimes beneficial to us if our freely carried out private actions are limited for our own good, despite the cost to personal liberty. Can paternalism and genuine freedom co-exist? In what balance? The articles presented here suggest where the borders might reasonably be drawn.

In the last two articles excerpted in this section we will examine a famous debate over the amount and type of liberty a society can tolerate. In the Hart-Devlin debate presented here, the English judge Lord Devlin argued against legalization of homosexual conduct in private between consenting adults, on grounds including the need for a society to have a shared set of values in order to exist. Hart responded with a modified version of Mill's liberal understanding of freedom, and argued in favour of legalization of private homosexual conduct. In this debate some crucial issues of public policy are intertwined with philosophy, and philosophy can be seen as a useful practical tool for resolving some of these issues.

6.3 Section III

From our consideration of liberty and its limits, we move to the idea of responsibility. We sometimes say "with freedom comes responsibility," meaning that our freely chosen actions are ours and ours alone, and we must bear the brunt of criticism or praise for those actions because they are ours—sometimes in the form of suffering significant liberty-limiting punishments. Philosophically interesting questions arrive when we have to say precisely and unambiguously *how* actions are "our own responsibility" in a way worth punishing. This section explores the idea of responsibility in three steps, through two articles and a puzzling case.

In the first article we will explore the idea of being responsible for some state of affairs. What sort of connection must a person's intentions and actions have to some terrible event if we are to be justified in punishing that person? Is responsibility for causing the event enough? Or is the supervisor responsible for the employee who threw the fatal switch? The analysis developed in the first article of this section will help us thread our way through the different senses of responsibility to state clearly what sort of responsibility is required to justify an assessment of wrongdoing—especially voluntary, intentional *criminal* wrongdoing, the type of responsibility with the most serious consequences for the sort of personal liberty explored in Section II. The second article of Section III examines the role of *intention* and *action* in criminal wrongdoing, in an attempt to determine how to characterize the wrongdoing committed in crimes people "meant to do." The difficulty and importance of arriving at a clear and unambiguous understanding of criminal wrongdoing is illustrated at the end of this section with an excerpt from the English criminal case *R v. Shivpuri*. In its decision, the court struggles to understand whether Mr. Shivpuri committed a wrong in his *attempt* to commit a crime. Mr. Shivpuri did not complete his crime and so he was not responsible for causing any obvious harm or damage to the public values with which the criminal law is typically concerned. Yet Mr. Shivpuri clearly *intended* to carry out a criminal action. Should he be allowed to go free simply because he didn't manage to carry out the plan he intended to follow? Or can he be said to have committed a crime even though he did not complete it? Our readings will provide you with the tools to decide.

6.4 Section IV

In Section IV we turn to international law, and the puzzle presented by the development of the European Union. Most of us have a sense of what international law does. It governs such matters as basic human rights which exist in all countries, international borders, and rules of international trade. But does this add up to a *law* of nations, something more than a series of agreements? What are we to make of the fact that international human rights law is frequently ignored, typically with little repercussion against those who ignore it? Does international law really provide binding obligations in the same way the law of individual countries is binding within those countries? The resemblance between these questions and the questions we encountered in Section I is more than skin-deep. Here we ask "What is international law?" and rejoin the debate over the value of analytical and normative approaches to questions in philosophy of law. Our selections include works from analytical and normative perspectives, and an argument from an author who is skeptical both about the existence of international law and about the value of analytical and normative perspectives on international law.

Our selections begin with Hugo Grotius's natural law theory which argues that certain standards of conduct hold universally among all people and all countries. This view captures the widespread sense that there are shared standards which all decent, civilized societies ought to recognize as the basis of international legal order. The second article in this section presents H.L.A. Hart's legal positivist argument that international law remains a possibility which does not yet exist. Hart's argument points to the absence of a settled way to test the validity of what are claimed to be international laws and reminds us that there is an important difference between our aspirations for international law as a way to guide international life and the actual fact of the matter.

The third article of this section, by Martti Koskenniemi, rejects both normative and analytical approaches to understanding international law, arguing that both approaches lack sensitivity to the actual political context of international relations. According to this skeptical argument, there are strong political reasons against the existence of international law in the form theorists have traditionally expected it to take. This skeptical argument claims that purely normative theories of international law lack realism about international relations, and purely analytical theories of law attempt awkwardly to understand international law within the inadequate concepts of domestic law. Koskenniemi's approach goes beyond analytical and normative approaches to law in order to understand law in a broader social and political context, much as the Feminist and Critical Race Theory approaches examined in Section I attempt to go beyond the traditional conception of jurisprudence.

In the final article of this section we arrive at the puzzling case of the European Union. In some ways the European Union looks like the world's next step toward the dream of a truly effective, universally followed system of international law. The European Union brings many states together under a shared parliament, has courts with jurisdiction over individual countries within the European Union, and a wide range of European Union laws apply throughout the countries of the Union. Yet in other respects the European Union looks like little more than a treaty, as each of its members has retained its own armed forces, control over foreign policy, and only some members have chosen to use the European Union's financial currency, known as the "Euro." What should we make of the European Union? Is it the future of international law, a model for international integration which still respects the individuality of member countries?

Once again we arrive at questions of how best to understand this development of what is clearly a kind of legal order, but an order of a new kind, beyond currently available explanations of law and legal system. Does an analytical approach allow the clearest and most precise understanding of these ideas? Or is a normative approach necessary to arrive at an understanding which is useful, meaningful, and appropriately sensitive to political facts? Or must these approaches be abandoned in favour of something completely different, perhaps a wider, political understanding of law, or one which recognizes the biases typical of traditional reasoning about law? The new importance of international law in an age of globalization leads us to look again at competing ways of doing jurisprudence, and the value of the insights delivered by these different approaches.

◆ ◆ ◆ ◆ ◆

FURTHER READINGS

Brian H. Bix, *A Dictionary of Legal Theory*. Oxford: Oxford University Press, 2004.

Jules Coleman and Scott Shapiro, eds. *The Oxford Handbook of Jurisprudence and Philosophy of Law*. Oxford: Oxford University Press, 2002.

Martin Golding and William Edmundson, eds., *The Blackwell Guide to the Philosophy of Law and Legal Theory*. Oxford: Blackwell Publishers, 2004.

Christopher Gray, ed. *The Philosophy of Law: An Encyclopedia*. New York: Garland, 1999.

Dennis Patterson, ed. *A Companion to Philosophy of Law and Legal Theory*. Oxford: Blackwell Publishers, 1999.

SOME ACADEMIC JOURNALS

Canadian Journal of Law and Jurisprudence
Criminal Law and Philosophy
Law and Philosophy
Legal Theory
Oxford Journal of Legal Studies
Ratio Juris
Res Publica

SECTION I

The Idea of Law and Legal Reasoning

CHAPTER 1

Natural Law Theory

INTRODUCTION

This chapter explores the idea of natural law. The range of ideas associated with natural law theory is so wide that it is nearly impossible to avoid excluding one important understanding of natural law while trying to explain another. Here we will explore a general description of natural law theories before discussing the work of two authors whose ideas have been particularly influential.

It is reasonably safe to say that all natural law theorists suppose that certain facts about humans and their world provide the *right* basis for laws with which to guide human conduct. Natural law theorists differ significantly, however, in their understanding of exactly which facts about the world must be taken as guides to law. Some theorists depend on the existence of God and religious texts, inspiration, or divine revelation as the basis for laws. Others rely on an understanding of human nature, human capacity to reason, or human social or biological needs. Yet no matter which facts a particular natural law theorist thinks especially relevant to the basis of law, all natural law theorists argue that their particular set of facts shows that laws cannot have just any content. What we might call "real" laws are those laws which meet certain standards—usually *moral* standards. Those standards are found by looking at the right facts, and using practical reasoning to determine how those facts ought to guide human conduct.

This chapter presents readings from two influential natural law theorists. The first, St. Thomas Aquinas, is the best-known writer of the Roman Catholic natural law tradition. The second, Professor John

Finnis, is the best-known contemporary defender of natural law theory. It might seem at first glance that there can be little in common between a Catholic theologian who studied and wrote in various European centres of learning in the thirteenth century, and a professor of jurisprudence teaching at Oxford University in England in the late twentieth century. In fact, the two share several views, and Finnis makes clear his debt to Aquinas. It is a mark of the persuasiveness of natural law theory that many of its central ideas have survived substantially unchanged from the thirteenth to the twentieth centuries and still appear relevant and compelling. Here we will examine just three of the many areas of agreement between Aquinas and Finnis before turning, in the remainder of this introduction, to the specific features of each author's argument.

1. The Purpose of Law and Legal Theory

Aquinas and Finnis (and many other natural law theorists) agree on the answer to the question "What is the purpose of philosophical investigation of law?" Both authors suppose that the philosophy of law ought to determine how best to order social interaction for the common good—the good of all. Aquinas does not leap out and say explicitly that this is the purpose of the philosophy of law, but we will not have to dig very deeply into his work to find this view. Finnis takes time at the beginning of his book *Natural Law and Natural Rights* (from which our selection is taken) to make clear why he thinks a philosophical investigation of law must do more than simply describe certain features of law. Aquinas and Finnis agree that description is not enough: an adequate philosophy of law must contain the means to distinguish between real laws which impose genuine obligations, and laws which do not impose genuine obligations and are best regarded as defective or degenerate. As Professor Neil MacCormick describes the natural law view, it supposes that "... laws, like other social institutions, are fully intelligible only by reference to the ends or values they ought to realise, and thus by reference to the intentions that those who participate in making them or implementing them must at least purport to have. This does not entail any acceptance of substantive moral criteria as criteria of legal validity, but it does involve acknowledging the moral quality of the relevant ends and values, namely justice and the public good."[1]

2. The Self-Evidence of Basic Goods

Aquinas and Finnis share a further understanding of the way in which we can determine which facts about the world are appropriate guides to the formation of laws. Both writers argue that certain goods (values) are self-evident. Aquinas, writing from a Christian perspective, supposes that certain Christian values are self-evidently good and valuable. Finnis does not appeal to Christian theology. Rather, he argues that careful attention to the requirements of social life and individual fulfilment show that at least some values are good in and of themselves. Laws must advance these values, to best serve the goal of human flourishing. Despite their slightly different starting points, both writers are sympathetic to the famous ancient Greek philosopher Aristotle's view of human

flourishing as involving happiness. This sort of happiness is rather more than a warm and fuzzy feeling of contentment. It involves a deeper sense of fulfilment in several areas of life such as self-development and treating others fairly. Happiness of this sort is self-evidently good, according to Aquinas and Finnis, and laws ought to contribute to this happiness.

3. Practical Reasoning

Aquinas and Finnis both recognize that laws do not make or interpret themselves. Even if it is possible to arrive at a set of general principles which all persons will recognize as the correct basis for laws of human conduct, these general principles must be interpreted and applied by humans to provide specific guidance in specific situations. Consider, for example, the principle that one ought not to harm others. This principle does not contain in itself any guidance regarding its application. Are police officers to be exempt from this principle? If so, under what conditions? To determine how to put this principle into practice in a particular situation, we must use skills of *practical reasoning* to arrive at a law which will guide human conduct in the best possible way.

4. St. Thomas Aquinas

St. Thomas Aquinas (1224–1274) is one of the great thinkers of Western philosophy, and a central figure of Catholic philosophy and theology. Aquinas was born near Naples, Italy, and spent his adult life in several cities in Europe. The source of the selection included in this book is Aquinas's *Summa Theologica*. His *Summa*, as it is called, is a sort of systematic working out of a *theological* view of the world. A theological view of the world accepts the existence of God, and asks what sort of world God has created. Aquinas's concern with the nature of law is understandably influenced by the fact that he views the discussion of law as only part of his larger discussion of the nature of a God-created world. It is

---

1   D. Neil MacCormick, "The Separation of Law and Morals," in R.P. George, ed., *Natural Law Theory: Contemporary Essays* (Oxford: Clarendon Press, 1992), p. 113.

worth noting, however, that Aquinas's theory of law is persuasive to many non-Christians as well: much of his argument can be accepted on rational grounds alone without reference to faith.

Much of the rational, non-religious appeal of Aquinas's arguments can be traced to his philosophical debt to Aristotle. Although Aquinas was certainly a powerful and important original thinker in his own right, his understanding of metaphysics, physics, politics, and ethics is thoroughly Aristotelian. In the thirteenth century, when Aquinas wrote, Aristotle was taken so seriously that he was referred to simply as "The Philosopher." Authors commonly wrote "The Philosopher says ..." in support of their arguments. This was done not simply on the blind assumption that what Aristotle said was true, but on the reasoned, sincerely held belief that Aristotle's views were the most sophisticated, best available views, regardless of the fact that he was not a Christian. To the extent that Aquinas examined law using Aristotle's map of the basic foundations of logical thought, Aquinas's views appeal to both Christians and non-Christians.

In a moment we shall discuss some of Aquinas's main arguments, but first we must examine their packaging. If you have never read the work of a medieval philosopher, Aquinas's style of organization may seem quite odd. Aquinas's discussion of law is given in a form called a "disputatio"—an imitation of a verbal dispute. His work looks a bit like a screenplay with too few indications as to which character should say which line. Yet once the structure of his writing is exposed, we will be able to see that it is actually very carefully and logically organized. The framework is as follows:

1. Aquinas begins by asking a question or series of questions whose answers are a matter of dispute. He encounters each question in turn, each in a unit he calls an "Article."

2. At the beginning of each Article, Aquinas lists a series of objections or possible arguments *against* the view he intends to defend, sometimes mentioning the name of the person known for offering this objection, and sometimes not. Sometimes he does not bother to identify an author of an objection because the view contained in the objection is very well known, or the view is so widely held that there is no need to point to specific persons.

3. After the question and the objections, Aquinas often quotes an authority whose argument disputes the claims of the objections and generally supports Aquinas's own view. He begins this section by saying "on the contrary," to mark the fact that the authority's argument runs contrary to the objection Aquinas has noted. It is worth mentioning again that authorities such as Aristotle are often cited not simply in the blind belief that if an authority said it then it must be true, but in the same way that we rely today on a scientist's expert testimony in court or a physician's expert advice about how to remain healthy.

4. Following his citation of an expert opinion in support of his view, Aquinas offers his own argument. He begins the body or "corpus" of his own argument with the words, "I answer that ..."

5. Aquinas completes consideration of the question by returning to the objections with which he began. He replies to them one by one, restating and expanding parts of the main body of his argument.

It may be tempting to rush past the objections in order to get at the meat of Aquinas's own views. If you do so, you risk misunderstanding precisely why he offers the arguments he does. Aquinas's methodical examination of a question offers in an admittedly artificial format the give-and-take which actually occurs when we attempt to defend a view. Only very rarely will an audience collapse in stunned silence at a speaker's feet, in awe of the speaker's shining intelligence and awesome reasoning. Usually even the most persuasive arguments are met with reasonable objections which must be answered. A full understanding of a speaker's view includes both the body of the speaker's argument and the speaker's responses to objections.

The selections presented here from Aquinas's *Summa Theologica* have been limited to the Questions and Articles most useful to a new reader of Aquinas's philosophy of law. However, in order to leave the door open for your further reading, where Articles have been omitted, their titles have been included for your reference. The selections explore four particular aspects of Aquinas's natural law theory. In this introduction we will begin with (1) his definition of law, and (2) his explanation of what natural law is. We will conclude our discussion of Aquinas with (3) his explanation of the difference between real laws and defective laws, and (4) his explanation of how laws bind their subjects.

4.1 Aquinas's Definition of Law

Aquinas's definition of law states the essence, or fundamental nature, of laws. It is important to recognize that Aquinas was concerned mainly with defining the nature of *laws* rather than the nature of a *legal system*, unlike writers such as Finnis who are concerned as much with the way laws operate in a system as with the nature of *law* more generally. (As you will see in other introductions and readings in this book, there are important differences between explanations of law and of legal systems made up of many laws, much as there are important differences between explanations of a person and of a society, composed of many persons.) Aquinas's definition of law may seem immediately familiar, and that is perhaps a good indication of how thoroughly it has penetrated thought in the Western world. In the body or "corpus" of Question 90, Article 4, Aquinas summarizes the investigation of the question. He writes, "Thus from the four preceding articles, the definition of law may be gathered; and it is nothing else than an ordinance of reason for the common good, made by him who has care of the community, and promulgated." A law, according to Aquinas, is a

result of reasoning about how to reach the common good (the good for everyone). A law is made by a person in authority, and made public or "promulgated" so the law's requirements can be known.

4.2 Natural Law

Armed with an understanding of what Aquinas supposes a law *is*, we can now ask what makes such a law part of natural law? To understand the answer to this question we must first examine Aquinas's understanding of humans. Aquinas accepts that humans were created by God in God's own image, and that God gave humans certain characteristics. The defining characteristic of humans, according to Aquinas, is our possession of *reason*, or *rationality*. We tend naturally to attempt to do good things, mirroring in a limited way God's characteristics as a supremely rational, wholly good being who has created a rationally ordered universe. When we use our God-given powers of reasoning we can see that certain things are self-evidently good, and worth pursuing. Consider, for example, the claim that what is good is to be pursued, and what is bad is to be avoided. Aquinas supposes that this claim is self-evidently true: as rational humans we can see that it is true simply by looking at it. When we use our reasoning correctly as we pursue self-evidently good things and attempt to make laws to achieve the common good, we are said to be using "right reason" and *participating* or *sharing* in God's reasoning and rational ordering of the world. So the natural law is in each person and is discovered by applying reason to general principles whose truth is self-evidently clear. This process results in practical rules for living that best fit our nature as rational persons who are generally good. As Aquinas explains the natural law in the body of Article 2, Question 91, "Wherefore it [the rational creature] has a share of the Eternal Reason, whereby it has a natural inclination to its proper act and end: and this participation of the eternal law in the rational creature is called the natural law."

4.3 Real and Defective Laws

It might seem from this sketch of natural law that there can only be one right way to make a law: either a man-made or "positive" law discovers correctly the reasonable way to achieve the common good, or it doesn't. This is not Aquinas's view. His understanding of natural law is much more subtle and complex. Aquinas recognizes that there may be more than one way to solve a particular social problem and he can accept that different cultures may choose to place different limits on behaviour, as required by different social situations. What is important is that any particular solution meets the general requirements set by the principles which all rational persons must accept. Aquinas divides man-made or positive law into two types: "real" law and "defective" law. (These are not the precise words of Aquinas or his translators, but they represent ideas recognizable in any translation.) Real laws meet the requirements of right reason: they are reasonable standards of conduct which aim at serving the common good. Real laws are "just," because they meet the requirements of justice. Aquinas recognizes, however, that some so-called laws fail in some way to meet the requirements of natural law—they may be unjust, or perhaps they are not promulgated properly. What are we to make of these so-called laws? According to Aquinas, while these failed attempts at laws may in fact be accepted and followed in some particular situation, "such laws do not bind in conscience." These defective laws are justifiably disobeyed. It is arguable, for example, that acts of civil disobedience committed by persons such as Dr. Martin Luther King were justified because the laws Dr. King disobeyed were not binding in conscience, and therefore were not real laws genuinely deserving of obedience.

4.4 How Laws Bind Their Subjects

We may now face the last of our four topics in consideration of the ideas of Aquinas. In his discussion of legal obligations, Aquinas notes that the Latin word for law (*lex*) comes from a word which means "to bind." Many of us in the modern world may feel that this is exactly what our huge and complex bodies of law do to us—laws leave us tightly tied and restrict our options, sometimes for good reasons, and at other times for bad reasons or for reasons which are no longer relevant. Often we continue to obey some law only to avoid being arrested or sued if we ignore that law. For Aquinas, however, police action or other sanctions against disobedience are a last resort and the least important reason to obey the law. According to Aquinas, if a law is real and meets the requirements of natural law, it is *morally* binding. If you are subject to that law, you ought to obey it because the law is for the common good. As a rational person you ought to realize that the common good is a worthwhile goal and you ought to respect law as a reasonable way of achieving that worthwhile goal. You ought also to obey the law because the law is part of God's will, and you are a subject of God. With these weighty considerations supporting the law, police action is left as a tool of last resort. Police action is to be applied to those few persons who for whatever reason fail to realize what they are reasonably required to do or withhold from doing.

You may, after reading all of this, find yourself impressed by the organization of Aquinas's argument and yet still suppose it is not relevant to you. You might, for example, reject the existence of God. Or you might suppose that Aquinas's understanding of God is somehow defective. It may seem that if Aquinas's idea of God is rejected, Aquinas's theory of natural law must be rejected also. It is worth considering, however, whether at least some of the elements of Aquinas's theory can be used in a more modern theory of natural law that does not rely on the existence of God as part of its justification.

5. *Professor Finnis and Natural Law as Practical Reasonableness*

The selections included here from Finnis's book *Natural Law and Natural Rights* are limited to four important topics. We begin with some of Finnis's remarks from his introductory discussion of the purposes of theorizing about law. We will then jump to Finnis's discussion of how we know what is good for humans. In the third part of our selection Finnis discusses "practical reasonableness." The fourth and final part of our excerpt contains Finnis's response to the question of whether an immoral law ought to be obeyed. Throughout these selections, you will find strong similarities between the views of Aquinas and Finnis. Is this evidence that Finnis is not an original thinker? It is likely better to see Finnis as an active participant and developer of an idea and argument which has been refined gradually over several centuries. Far from lacking originality as a philosopher, Finnis is faced with the difficult task of improving arguments which have already benefited from the close attention of some of the best philosophers.

In an earlier section of this introduction, we noted that Aquinas and Finnis agree on the purpose of philosophizing about law. A complete philosophy of law, both agree, is one which helps humans to guide their conduct in a way which promotes the common good. Finnis, with the benefit of several centuries of hindsight, goes further. To simply describe what happens when people make or use laws is not useful at all, according to Finnis. A theory of law which consists merely of a series of descriptions is seriously incomplete. A theorist who lacks an understanding of the *purpose* of law will not know which phenomena to observe or which observations to include in the theory. For Finnis, the key to understanding law is to see law as a *purposeful* activity conducted by generally reasonable humans. To reach this understanding, the theorist must stand inside the law, and understand and participate in achieving the purposes of law. As Finnis puts it, "... A theorist cannot give a theoretical description and analysis of social facts unless he also participates in the work of evaluation, of understanding what is really good for human persons, and what is really required by practical reasonableness."

In our discussion of Aquinas, we noted that theology supplied him with a picture of what is really good for humans. Finnis does not appeal to theology. Instead, Finnis supposes that there are certain basic goods for humans, and that these goods are self-evident upon rational consideration of them. (While Aquinas supposes we are rational and able to perceive goods because God made us rational, Finnis leaves the origin of our rationality largely untreated. What is important for Finnis's theory is that we *are* rational, not whether we are rational because we evolved to be this way or because God made us so.) According to Finnis, there are seven basic forms of good: life, knowledge, play, aesthetic experience, sociability (friendship), practical reasonableness, and "religion," or a desire for a larger explanation of our nature and origin.

Finnis's list of basic goods answers the question "What is really good for humans?" The list does not, however, explain what moral or legal rules must be enacted to help us to achieve these goods. *How* we are to achieve the good for humans is a question of practical reasoning, and Finnis suggests that practical reasoning cannot proceed in just any way. This is the crucial second part of his argument. According to Finnis, proposed moral or legal rules must meet standards of "practical reasonableness" (which is itself a basic human good). Practical reasonableness can be seen as a sort of blend of pure rationality and perception of basic goods. Practical reasonableness is not simply rationality, because what is rationally possible may sometimes be prohibited as unreasonable. Nor is practical reasonableness simply a composite of the six other basic goods. Practical reasonableness is about rationally balancing our pursuit of different goods, while respecting the basic value of each of those goods as necessary ingredients in a good individual and a good society. We shall discuss here just two aspects of practical reasonableness, to give a sense of the sort of procedural standards Finnis thinks are self-evidently good.

Practical reasonableness requires that our attempts to achieve human goods proceed fairly. For example, when we treat persons differently, we must do so for good reasons, and not arbitrarily. Practical reasonableness also requires a certain degree of foresight: we cannot sacrifice certain basic goods simply to achieve consequences which promote some other basic good. So, for example, the basic good of play is not worth having at the cost of life and friendship, as might happen if we ask our friends to stand with apples on their heads as we practice archery. It is important to recognize that the sort of balanced pursuit of human goods which emerges from the requirements of practical reasonableness is simply a weighing of consequences in which achievement of two basic goods outweighs the loss of failing to achieve one basic good. Rather, basic goods are *fundamental* in our thinking about how we ought to conduct ourselves, and we are never justified in sacrificing these goods entirely.

Finnis argues that morality and law are the result of applying the standards of practical reasonableness to questions of how we ought to conduct ourselves, keeping in mind always what is really good for humans—the seven basic goods. Notice that we have said that *both* morality and law are the result of this process of practical reasoning. For Finnis, and for Aquinas and many other natural law theorists, law just *is* a special sort of morality. It is part of the nature of a law that it is morally justified. If a law does not aim at the common good, or fails to meet the requirements of practical reasonableness, that law must be rejected.

Finnis is careful to note that he does not suppose individual citizens are always right to disobey laws which lack moral justification. He observes that there is considerable value in the stability of the rule of law, and allows that there may be an obligation in a larger sense to obey an immoral law for the sake of the rule of law. There is no quick and simple answer to the question "Should I obey this law?"

Is this natural law theory powerful enough to distinguish genuine law from defective law in a practically useful way? Does this natural law theory provide a useful addition to our understanding of life under law? These questions can only be answered after careful consideration of these readings, and comparison of the merits of natural law theory with theories presented in other chapters of the book.

◆ ◆ ◆ ◆ ◆

ST. THOMAS AQUINAS

from "Treatise on Law," *Summa Theologica*

Question 90: Of the Essence of Law (In Four Articles)

... [T]here are four points of inquiry (1) Whether law is something pertaining to reason? (2) Concerning the end of law, (3) Its cause; (4) The promulgation of law.

First Article: Whether Law Is Something Pertaining to Reason?

We proceed thus to the First Article:—

Objection 1. It would seem that law is not something pertaining to reason. For the Apostle says (Rom. vii. 23): *I see another law in my members*, etc. But nothing pertaining to reason is in the members; since the reason does not make use of a bodily organ. Therefore law is not something pertaining to reason.

Obj. 2. Further, in the reason there is nothing else but power, habit, and act. But law is not the power itself of reason. In like manner, neither is it a habit of reason: because the habits of reason are the intellectual virtues of which we have spoken above (Q. 57). Nor again is it an act of reason: because then law would cease, when the act of reason ceases, for instance, while we are asleep. Therefore law is nothing pertaining to reason.

Obj. 3. Further, the law moves those who are subject to it to act aright. But it belongs properly to the will to move to act, as is evident from what has been said above (Q. 9, A. 1). Therefore law pertains, not to the reason, but to the will; according to the words of the Jurist (*Lib.* i. *ff., De Const. Prin.* leg. i): *Whatsoever pleaseth the sovereign, has force of law.*

On the contrary, It belongs to the law to command and to forbid. But it belongs to reason to command, as stated above (Q. 17, A.1). Therefore law is something pertaining to reason.

I answer that, Law is a rule and measure of acts, whereby man is induced to act or is restrained from acting: for *lex* (law) is derived from *ligare* (to bind), because it binds one to act. Now the rule and measure of human acts is the reason, which is the first principle of human acts, as is evident from what has been stated above (Q. 1, A. 1 *ad* 3); since it belongs to the reason to direct to the end, which is the first principle in all matters of action, according to the Philosopher (*Phys.* ii). Now that which is the principle in any genus, is the rule and measure of that genus: for instance, unity in the genus of numbers, and the first movement in the genus of movements. Consequently it follows that law is something pertaining to reason.

Reply Obj. 1. Since law is a kind of rule and measure, it may be in something in two ways. First, as in that which measures and rules: and since this is proper to reason, it follows that, in this way, law is in the reason alone.—Secondly, as in that which is measured and ruled. In this way, law is in all those things that are inclined to something by reason of some

law: so that any inclination arising from a law, may be called a law, not essentially but by participation as it were. And thus the inclination of the members to concupiscence is called the *law of the members.*

Reply Obj. 2. Just as, in external action, we may consider the work and the work done, for instance the work of building and the house built; so in the acts of reason, we may consider the act itself of reason, i.e., to understand and to reason, and something produced by this act. With regard to the speculative reason, this is first of all the definition; secondly, the proposition; thirdly, the syllogism or argument. And since also the practical reason makes use of a syllogism in respect of the work to be done, as stated above (Q. 13, A. 3; Q. 76, A. 1) and as the Philosopher teaches (*Ethic.* vii, 3); hence we find in the practical reason something that holds the same position in regard to operations, as, in the speculative intellect, the proposition holds in regard to conclusions. Such like universal propositions of the practical intellect that are directed to actions have the nature of law. And these propositions are sometimes under our actual consideration, while sometimes they are retained in the reason by means of a habit.

Reply Obj. 3. Reason has its power of moving from the will, as stated above (Q. 17, A. 1): for it is due to the fact that one wills the end, that the reason issues its commands as regards things ordained to the end. But in order that the volition of what is commanded may have the nature of law, it needs to be in accord with some rule of reason. And in this sense is to be understood the saying that the will of the sovereign has the force of law; otherwise the sovereign's will would savor of lawlessness rather than of law.

Second Article: Whether the Law Is Always Something Directed to the Common Good?

We proceed thus to the Second Article:—

Objection 1. It would seem that the law is not always directed to the common good as to its end. For it belongs to law to command and to forbid. But commands are directed to certain individual goods. Therefore the end of the law is not always the common good.

Obj. 2. Further, the law directs man in his actions. But human actions are concerned with particular matters. Therefore the law is directed to some particular good.

Obj. 3. Further, Isidore says (*Etym.* v. 3): *If the law is based on reason, whatever is based on reason will be a law.* But reason is the foundation not only of what is ordained to the common good, but also of that which is directed to private good. Therefore the law is not only directed to the good of all; but also to the private good of an individual.

On the contrary, Isidore says (Etym. v. 21) that *laws are enacted for no private profit, but for the common benefit of the citizens.*

I answer that, As stated above (A. 1), the law belongs to that which is a principle of human acts, because it is their rule and measure. Now as reason is a principle of human acts, so in reason itself there is something which is the principle in respect of all the rest: wherefore to this principle chiefly and mainly law must needs be referred.—Now the first principle in practical matters, which are the object of the practical reason, is the last end: and the last end of human life is bliss or happiness, as stated above (Q. 2, A. 7; Q. 3, A. 1). Consequently the law must needs regard principally the relationship to happiness. Moreover, since every part is ordained to the whole, as imperfect to perfect; and since one man is a part of the perfect community, the law must needs regard properly the relationship to universal happiness. Wherefore, the Philosopher, in the above definition of legal matters mentions both happiness and the body politic: for he says (*Ethic.* v.1) that we call those legal matters *just, which are adapted to produce and preserve happiness and its parts for the body politic:* since the state is a perfect community, as he says in *Polit.* i. 1.

Now in every genus, that which belongs to it chiefly is the principle of the others, and the others belong to that genus in subordination to that thing: thus fire, which is chief among hot things, is the cause of heat in mixed bodies, and these are said to be hot in so far as they have a share of fire. Consequently, since the law is chiefly ordained to the common good, any other precept in regard to some individual work, must needs be devoid of the nature of a law, save in so far as it regards the common good. Therefore every law is ordained to the common good.

Reply Obj. 1. A command denotes an application of a law to matters regulated by the law. Now the order to the common good, at which the law aims, is applicable to particular ends. And in this way commands are given even concerning particular matters.

Reply Obj. 2. Actions are indeed concerned with particular matters: but those particular matters are referable to the common good, not as to a common genus or species, but as to a common final cause, according as the common good is said to be the common end.

Reply Obj. 3. Just as nothing stands firm with regard to the speculative reason except that which is traced back to the first indemonstrable principles, so nothing stands firm with regard to the practical reason, unless it be directed to the last end which is the common good: and whatever stands to reason in this sense, has the nature of a law.

Third Article: Whether the Reason of Any Man Is Competent to Make Laws?

We proceed thus to the Third Article:—

Objection 1. It would seem that the reason of any man is competent to make laws. For the Apostle says (Rom. ii. 14) that *when the Gentiles, who have not the law, do by nature those things that are of the law, ... they are a law to themselves.* Now he says this of all in general. Therefore anyone can make a law for himself.

Obj. 2. Further, as the Philosopher says (*Ethic.* ii. 1), *the intention of the lawgiver is to lead men to virtue.*

But every man can lead another to virtue. Therefore the reason of any man is competent to make laws.

Obj. 3. Further, just as the sovereign of a state governs the state, so every father of a family governs his household. But the sovereign of a state can make laws for the state. Therefore every father of a family can make laws for his household.

On the contrary, Isidore says (*Etym.* v.10): *A law is an ordinance of the people, whereby something is sanctioned by the Elders together with the Commonalty.*

I answer that, A law, properly speaking, regards first and foremost the order to the common good. Now to order anything to the common good, belongs either to the whole people, or to someone who is the viceregent of the whole people. And therefore the making of a law belongs either to the whole people or to a public personage who has care of the whole people: since in all other matters the directing of anything to the end concerns him to whom the end belongs.

Reply Obj. 1. As stated above (A.1 *ad* 1), a law is in a person not only as in one that rules, but also by participation as in one that is ruled. In the latter way each one is a law to himself, in so far as he shares the direction that he receives from one who rules him. Hence the same text goes on: *Who show the work of the law written in their hearts.*

Reply Obj. 2. A private person cannot lead another to virtue efficaciously: for he can only advise, and if his advice be not taken, it has no coercive power, such as the law should have, in order to prove an efficacious inducement to virtue, as the Philosopher says (*Ethic.* x. 9). But this coercive power is vested in the whole people or in some public personage, to whom it belongs to inflict penalties, as we shall state further on (Q. 92, A. 2, *ad* 3; II-II, Q. 64, A. 3). Wherefore the framing of laws belongs to him alone.

Reply Obj. 3. As one man is a part of the household, so a household is a part of the state: and the state is a perfect community, according to *Polit.* i. 1. And therefore, as the good of one man is not the last end, but is ordained to the common good; so too the good of one household is ordained to the good of a single state, which is a perfect community. Consequently he that governs a family, can indeed make certain commands or ordinances, but not such as to have properly the force of law.

Fourth Article: Whether Promulgation Is Essential to a Law?

We proceed thus to the Fourth Article:—

Objection 1. It would seem that promulgation is not essential to a law. For the natural law above all has the character of law. But the natural law needs no promulgation. Therefore it is not essential to a law that it be promulgated.

Obj. 2. Further, it belongs properly to a law to bind one to do or not to do something. But the obligation of fulfilling a law touches not only those in whose presence it is promulgated, but also others. Therefore promulgation is not essential to a law.

Obj. 3. Further, the binding force of a law extends even to the future, since *laws are binding in matters of the future,* as the jurists say (*Cod.* 1., tit. *De lege et constit.* leg. vii). But promulgation concerns those who are present. Therefore it is not essential to a law.

On the contrary, It is laid down in the *Decretals,* dist. 4, *that laws are established when they are promulgated.*

I answer that, As stated above (A. 1), a law is imposed on others by way of a rule and measure. Now a rule or measure is imposed by being applied to those who are to be ruled and measured by it. Wherefore, in order that a law obtain the binding force which is proper to a law, it must needs be applied to the men who have to be ruled by it. Such application is made by its being notified to them by promulgation. Wherefore promulgation is necessary for the law to obtain its force.

Thus from the four preceding articles, the definition of law may be gathered; and it is nothing else than an ordinance of reason for the common good, made by him who has care of the community, and promulgated.

Reply Obj. 1. The natural law is promulgated by the very fact that God instilled it into man's mind so as to be known by him naturally.

Reply Obj. 2. Those who are not present when a law is promulgated, are bound to observe the law, in so far as it is notified or can be notified to them by others, after it has been promulgated.

Reply Obj. 3. The promulgation that takes place now, extends to future time by reason of the durability of written characters, by which means it is continually promulgated. Hence Isidore says (*Etym.* v.3; ii. 10) that *lex* (law) *is derived from legere* (to read) *because it is written.*

Question 91: Of the Various Kinds of Law (In Six Articles)

We must now consider the various kinds of law: under which head there are six points of inquiry: (1) Whether there is an eternal law? (2) Whether there is a natural law? (3) Whether there is a human law? (4) Whether there is a Divine law? (5) Whether there is one Divine law, or several? (6) Whether there is a law of sin? [Ed. note: articles 4–6 are omitted here.]

First Article: Whether There Is an Eternal Law?

We proceed thus to the First Article:—

Objection 1. It would seem that there is no eternal law. Because every law is imposed on someone. But there was not someone from eternity on whom a law could be imposed: since God alone was from eternity. Therefore no law is eternal.

Obj. 2. Further, promulgation is essential to law. But promulgation could not be from eternity: because there was no one to whom it could be promulgated from eternity. Therefore no law can be eternal.

Obj. 3. Further, a law implies order to an end. But nothing ordained to an end is eternal: for the last end alone is eternal. Therefore no law is eternal.

On the contrary, Augustine says (*De Lib. Arb.* i. 6): *That Law which is the Supreme Reason cannot be understood to be otherwise than unchangeable and eternal.*

I answer that, As stated above (Q. 90, A. 1 *ad* 2; AA.3, 4), a law is nothing else but a dictate of practical reason emanating from the ruler who governs a perfect community. Now it is evident, granted that the world is ruled by Divine Providence, as was stated in the First Part (Q. 22, AA. 1,2), that the whole community of the universe is governed by Divine Reason. Wherefore the very Idea of the government of things in God the Ruler of the universe, has the nature of a law. And since the Divine Reason's conception of things is not subject to time but is eternal, according to Prov. viii. 23, therefore it is that this kind of law must be called eternal.

Reply Obj. 1. Those things that are not in themselves, exist with God, inasmuch as they are foreknown and preordained by Him, according to Rom. iv. 17: *Who calls those things that are not, as those that are.* Accordingly the eternal concept of the Divine law bears the character of an eternal law, in so far as it is ordained by God to the government of things foreknown by Him.

Reply Obj. 2. Promulgation is made by word of mouth or in writing; and in both ways the eternal law is promulgated: because both the Divine Word and the writing of the Book of Life are eternal. But the promulgation cannot be from eternity on the part of the creature that hears or reads.

Reply Obj. 3. The law implies order to the end actively, in so far as it directs certain things to the end; but not passively,—that is to say, the law itself is not ordained to the end,—except accidentally, in a governor whose end is extrinsic to him, and to which end his law must needs be ordained. But the end of the Divine government is God Himself, and His law is not distinct from Himself. Wherefore the eternal law is not ordained to another end.

Second Article: Whether There Is in Us a Natural Law?

We proceed thus to the Second Article:—

Objection 1. It would seem that there is no natural law in us. Because man is governed sufficiently by the eternal law: for Augustine says (*De Lib. Arb.* i) that *the eternal law is that by which it is right that all things should be most orderly.* But nature does not abound in superfluities as neither does she fail in necessaries. Therefore no law is natural to man.

Obj. 2. Further, by the law man is directed, in his acts, to the end, as stated above (Q. 90, A. 2). But the directing of human acts to their end is not a function of nature, as is the case in irrational creatures, which act for an end solely by their natural appetite; whereas man acts for an end by his reason and will. Therefore no law is natural to man.

Obj. 3. Further, the more a man is free, the less is he under the law. But man is freer than all the animals, on account of his free-will, with which he is endowed above all other animals. Since therefore other animals are not subject to a natural law, neither is man subject to a natural law.

On the contrary, A gloss on Rom. ii. 14: *When the Gentiles, who have not the law, do by nature those things that are of the law,* comments as follows: *Although they have no written law, yet they have the natural law, whereby each one knows, and is conscious of, what is good and what is evil.*

I answer that, As stated above (Q. 90, A. 1 *ad* 1), law, being a rule and measure, can be in a person in two ways: in one way, as in him that rules and measures; in another way, as in that which is ruled and measured, since a thing is ruled and measured, in so far as it partakes of the rule or measure. Wherefore, since all things subject to Divine providence are ruled and measured by the eternal law, as was stated above (A. 1); it is evident that all things partake somewhat of the eternal law, in so far as, namely, from its being imprinted on them, they derive their respective inclinations to their proper acts and ends. Now among all others, the rational creature is subject to Divine providence in the most excellent way, in so far as it partakes of a share of providence, by being provident both for itself and for others. Wherefore it has a share of the Eternal Reason, whereby it has a natural inclination to its proper act and end: and this participation of the eternal law in the rational creature is called the natural law. Hence the Psalmist after saying (Ps. iv. 6): *Offer up the sacrifice of justice,* as though someone asked what the works of justice are, adds: *Many say, Who showeth us good things?* in answer to which question he says: *The light of Thy countenance, O Lord, is signed upon us:* thus implying that the light of natural reason, whereby we discern what is good and what is evil, which is the function of the natural law, is nothing else than an imprint on us of Divine light. It is therefore evident that the natural law is nothing else than the rational creature's participation of the eternal law.

Reply Obj. 1. This argument would hold, if the natural law were something different from the eternal law: whereas it is nothing but a participation thereof, as stated above.

Reply Obj. 2. Every act of reason and will in us is based on that which is according to nature, as stated above (Q. 10, A. 1): for every act of reasoning is based on principles that are known naturally, and every act of appetite in respect of the means is derived from the natural appetite in respect of the last end. Accordingly the first direction of our acts to their end must needs be in virtue of the natural law.

Reply Obj. 3. Even irrational animals partake in their own way of the Eternal Reason, just as the rational creature does. But because the rational creature partakes thereof in an intellectual and rational manner, therefore the participation of the eternal law in the rational creature is properly called a law, since a law is something pertaining to reason, as stated above (Q. 90, A. 1). Irrational creatures, however, do not partake thereof in a rational manner, wherefore there is no participation of the eternal law in them, except by way of similitude.

Third Article: Whether There Is a Human Law?

We proceed thus to the Third Article:—

Objection 1. It would seem that there is not a human law. For the natural law is a participation of the eternal law, as stated above (A. 2). Now through the eternal law *all things are most orderly*, as Augustine states (*De Lib. Arb.* i. 6). Therefore the natural law suffices for the ordering of all human affairs. Consequently there is no need for a human law.

Obj. 2. Further, a law bears the character of a measure, as stated above (Q. 90, A. 1). But human reason is not a measure of things, but vice versa, as stated in *Metaph.* x, text. 5. Therefore no law can emanate from human reason.

Obj. 3. Further, a measure should be most certain, as stated in *Metaph.* x, text. 3. But the dictates of human reason in matters of conduct are uncertain, according to Wis. ix. 14: *The thoughts of mortal men are fearful, and our counsels uncertain.* Therefore no law can emanate from human reason.

On the contrary, Augustine (*De Lib. Arb.* 1.6) distinguishes two kinds of law, the one eternal, the other temporal, which he calls human.

I answer that, As stated above (Q. 90, A. 1, *ad* 2), a law is a dictate of the practical reason. Now it is to be observed that the same procedure takes place in the practical and in the speculative reason: for each proceeds from principles to conclusions, as stated above (*ibid.*). Accordingly we conclude that just as, in the speculative reason, from naturally known indemonstrable principles, we draw the conclusions of the various sciences, the knowledge of which is not imparted to us by nature, but acquired by the efforts of reason, so too it is from the precepts of the natural law, as from general and indemonstrable principles, that the human reason needs to proceed to the more particular determination of certain matters. These particular determinations, devised by human reason, are called human laws, provided the other essential conditions of law be observed, as stated above (Q. 90, AA. 2, 3, 4). Wherefore Tully says in his *Rhetoric* (*De Invent. Rhet.* ii) *that justice has its source in nature; thence certain things came into custom by reason of their utility; afterwards these things which emanated from nature and were approved by custom, were sanctioned by fear and reverence for the law.*

Reply Obj. 1. The human reason cannot have a full participation of the dictate of the Divine Reason, but according to its own mode, and imperfectly. Consequently, as on the part of the speculative reason, by a natural participation of Divine Wisdom, there is in us the knowledge of certain general principles, but not proper knowledge of each single truth, such as that contained in the Divine Wisdom; so too, on the part of the practical reason, man has a natural participation of the eternal law, according to certain general principles, but not as regards the particular determinations of individual cases, which are, however, contained in the eternal law. Hence the need for human reason to proceed further to sanction them by law.

Reply Obj. 2. Human reason is not, of itself, the rule of things: but the principles impressed on it by nature, are general rules and measures of all things relating to human conduct, whereof the natural reason is the rule and measure, although it is not the measure of things that are from nature.

Reply Obj. 3. The practical reason is concerned with practical matters, which are singular and contingent: but not with necessary things, with which the speculative reason is concerned. Wherefore human laws cannot have that inerrancy that belongs to the demonstrated conclusions of sciences. Nor is it necessary for every measure to be altogether unerring and certain, but according as it is possible in its own particular genus.

• • •

Question 94: Of the Natural Law (In Six Articles)

We must now consider the natural law; concerning which there are six points of inquiry: (1) What is the natural law? (2) What are the precepts of the natural law? (3) Whether all acts of virtue are prescribed by the natural law? (4) Whether the natural law is the same in all? (5) Whether it is changeable? (6) Whether it can be abolished from the heart of man? [*Ed. note*: article 3 is omitted here.]

First Article: Whether the Natural Law Is a Habit?

We proceed thus, to the First Article:—

Objection 1. It would seem that the natural law is a habit. Because, as the Philosopher says (*Ethic.* ii. 5), *there are three things in the soul, power, habit, and passion*. But the natural law is not one of the soul's powers: nor is it one of the passions; as we may see by going through them one by one. Therefore the natural law is a habit.

Obj. 2. Further, Basil says that the conscience or *synderesis is the law of our mind*; which can only apply to the natural law. But the *synderesis* is a habit, as was shown in the First Part (Q. 79, A. 12). Therefore the natural law is a habit.

Obj. 3. Further, the natural law abides in man always, as will be shown further on (A. 6). But man's reason, which the law regards, does not always think about the natural law. Therefore the natural law is not an act, but a habit.

On the contrary, Augustine says (*De Bono Conjug.* xxi) that *a habit is that whereby something is done when necessary*. But such is not the natural law: since it is in infants and in the damned who cannot act by it. Therefore the natural law is not a habit.

I answer that, A thing may be called a habit in two ways. First, properly and essentially: and thus the natural law is not a habit. For it has been stated above (Q. 90, A. 1 *ad* 2) that the natural law is something appointed by reason, just as a proposition is a work of reason. Now that which a man does is not the same as that whereby he does it: for he makes a becoming speech by the habit of grammar. Since then a habit is that by which we act, a law cannot be a habit properly and essentially.

Secondly, the term habit may be applied to that which we hold by a habit: thus faith may mean that which we hold by faith. And accordingly, since the precepts of the natural law are sometimes considered by reason actually, while sometimes they are in the reason only habitually, in this way the natural law may be called a habit. Thus, in speculative matters, the indemonstrable principles are not the habit itself whereby we hold these principles, but are the principles the habit of which we possess.

Reply Obj. 1. The Philosopher proposes there to discover the genus of virtue; and since it is evident that virtue is a principle of action, he mentions only those things which are principles of human acts, viz., powers, habits and passions. But there are other things in the soul besides these three: there are acts; thus to will is in the one that wills; again, things known are in the knower; moreover its own natural properties are in the soul, such as immortality and the like.

Reply Obj. 2. *Synderesis* is said to be the law of our mind, because it is a habit containing the precepts of the natural law, which are the first principles of human actions.

Reply Obj. 3. This argument proves that the natural law is held habitually; and this is granted.

To the argument advanced in the contrary sense we reply that sometimes a man is unable to make use of that which is in him habitually, on account of some impediment: thus, on account of sleep, a man is unable to use the habit of science. In like manner, through the deficiency of his age, a child cannot use the habit of understanding of principles, or the natural law, which is in him habitually.

Second Article: Whether the Natural Law Contains Several Precepts, or One Only?

We proceed thus to the Second Article:—

Objection 1. It would seem that the natural law contains, not several precepts, but one only. For law is a kind of precept, as stated above (Q. 92 A. 2). If therefore there were many precepts of the natural law, it would follow that there are also many natural laws.

Obj. 2. Further, the natural law is consequent to human nature. But human nature, as a whole, is one; though, as to its parts, it is manifold. Therefore, either there is but one precept of the law of nature, on account of the unity of nature as a whole; or there are many, by reason of the number of parts of human nature. The result would be that even things relating to the inclination of the concupiscible faculty belong to the natural law.

Obj. 3. Further, law is something pertaining to reason, as stated above (Q. 90, A. 1). Now reason is but one in man. Therefore there is only one precept of the natural law.

On the contrary, The precepts of the natural law in man stand in relation to practical matters, as the first principles to matters of demonstration. But there are several first indemonstrable principles. Therefore there are also several precepts of the natural law.

I answer that, As stated above (Q. 91, A. 3), the precepts of the natural law are to the practical reason, what the first principles of demonstrations are to the speculative reason; because both are self-evident principles. Now a thing is said to be self-evident in two ways: first, in itself; secondly, in relation to us. Any proposition is said to be self-evident in itself, if its predicate is contained in the notion of the subject: although, to one who knows not the definition of the subject, it happens that such a proposition is not self-evident. For instance, this proposition, *Man is a rational being*, is, in its very nature, self-evident, since who says *man*, says a rational being: and yet to one who knows not what a man is, this proposition is not self-evident. Hence it is that, as Boethius says (*De Hebdom.*), certain axioms or propositions are universally self-evident to all; and such are those propositions whose terms are known to all, as, *Every whole is greater than its part*, and, *Things equal to one and the same are equal to one another*. But some propositions are self-evident only to the wise, who understand the meaning of the terms of such propositions: thus to one who understands that an angel is not a body, it is self-evident that an angel is not circumscriptively in a place: but this is not evident to the unlearned, for they cannot grasp it.

Now a certain order is to be found in those things that are apprehended universally. For that which, before aught else, falls under apprehension, is *being*, the notion of which included in all things whatsoever a man apprehends. Wherefore the first indemonstrable principle is that the *same thing cannot be affirmed and denied at the same time*, which is based on the notion of *being* and *not-being*: and on this principle all others are based, as is stated in *Metaph.* iv, text 9. Now as *being* is the first thing that falls under the apprehension simply, so *good* is the first thing that falls under the apprehension of the practical reason, which is directed to action: since every agent acts for an end under the aspect of good. Consequently the first principle in the practical reason is one founded on the notion of good, viz., *that good is that which all things seek after*. Hence this is the first precept of law, that *good is to be done and pursued, and evil is to be avoided*. All other precepts of the natural law are based upon this: so that whatever the practical reason naturally apprehends as man's good, (or evil) belongs to the precepts of the natural law as something to be done or avoided.

Since, however, good has the nature of an end, and evil, the nature of a contrary, hence it is that all those things to which man has a natural inclination, are naturally apprehended by reason as being good, and consequently as objects of pursuit, and their contraries as evil, and objects of avoidance. Wherefore according to the order of natural inclinations, is the order of the precepts of the natural law. Because in man there is first of all an inclination to good in accordance with the nature which he has in common with all substances: inasmuch as every substance seeks the preservation of its own being, according to its nature: and by reason of this inclination, whatever a means of preserving human life, and warding off its obstacles, belongs to the natural law. Secondly, there is in man an inclination to things that pertain to him more specially, according to that nature which he has in common with other animals: and in virtue of this inclination, those things are said to belong to the natural law, *which nature has taught to all animals*, such as sexual intercourse, education of offspring and so forth. Thirdly, there is in man an inclination to good, according to the nature of his reason, which nature is proper to him: thus man has a natural inclination to know the truth about God, and to live in society: and in this respect, whatever pertains to this inclination belongs to the natural law; for instance, to shun ignorance, to avoid offending those among whom one has to live, and other such things regarding the above inclination.

Reply Obj. 1. All these precepts of the law of nature have the character of one natural law, inasmuch as they flow from one first precept.

Reply Obj. 2. All the inclinations of any parts whatsoever of human nature, e.g., of the concupiscible and irascible parts, in so far as they are ruled by reason, belong to the natural law, and are reduced to one first precept, as stated above: so that the precepts of the natural law are many in themselves, but are based on one common foundation.

Reply Obj. 3. Although reason is one in itself, yet it directs all things regarding man; so that whatever can be ruled by reason, is contained under the law of reason.

• • •

Fourth Article: Whether the Natural Law Is the Same in All Men?

We proceed thus to the Fourth Article:—

Objection 1. It would seem that the natural law is not the same in all. For it is stated in the Decretals (*Dist.* i) that *the natural law is that which is contained in the Law and the Gospel*. But this is not common to all men; because, as it is written (Rom. x. 16), *all do not obey the gospel*. Therefore the natural law is not the same in all men.

Obj. 2. Further, *Things which are according to the law are said to be just*, as stated in *Ethic.* v. But it is stated in the same book that nothing is so universally just as not to be subject to change in regard to some men. Therefore even the natural law is not the same in all men.

Obj. 3. Further, as stated above (AA. 2, 3), to the natural law belongs everything to which a man is inclined according to his nature. Now different men are naturally inclined to different things; some to the desire of pleasures, others to the desire of honors, and other men to other things. Therefore there is not one natural law for all.

On the contrary, Isidore says (*Etym.* v.4): *The natural law is common to all nations.*

I answer that, As stated above (AA. 2, 3), to the natural law belongs those things to which a man is inclined naturally: and among these it is proper to man to be inclined to act according to reason. Now the process of reason is from the common to the proper, as stated in *Phys.* i. The speculative reason, however, is differently situated in this matter, from the practical reason. For, since the speculative reason is busied chiefly with necessary things, which cannot be otherwise than they are, its proper conclusions, like the universal principles, contain the truth without fail. The practical reason, on the other hand, is busied with contingent matters, about which human actions are concerned: and consequently, although there is necessity in the general principles, the more we descend to matters of detail, the more frequently we encounter defects. Accordingly then in speculative matters truth is the same in all men, both as to principles and as to conclusions: although the truth is not known to all as regards the conclusions, but only as regards the principles which are called common notions. But in matters of action, truth or practical rectitude is not the same for all, as to matters of detail, but only as to the general principles: and where there is the same rectitude in matters of detail, it is not equally known to all.

It is therefore evident that, as regards the general principles whether of speculative or of practical reason, truth or rectitude is the same for all, and is equally known by all. As to the proper conclusions of the speculative reason, the truth is the same for all, but is not equally known to all: thus it is true for all that the three angles of a triangle are together equal to two right angles, although it is not known to all. But as to the proper conclusions of the practical reason, neither is the truth or rectitude the same for all, nor, where it is the same, is it equally known by all. Thus it is right and true for all to act according to reason: and from this principle it follows as a proper conclusion, that goods entrusted to another should be restored to their owner. Now this is true for the majority of cases: but it may happen in a particular case that it would be injurious, and therefore unreasonable, to restore goods held in trust; for instance if they are claimed for the purpose of fighting against one's country. And this principle will be found to fail the more, according as we descend further into detail, e.g., if one were to say that goods held in trust should be restored with such and such a guarantee, or in such and such a way; because the greater the number of conditions added, the greater the number of ways in which the principle may fail, so that it be not right to restore or not to restore.

Consequently we must say that the natural law, as to general principles, is the same for all, both as to rectitude and as to knowledge. But as to certain matters of detail, which are conclusions, as it were, of those general principles, it is the same for all in the majority of cases, both as to rectitude and as to knowledge; and yet in some few cases it may fail, both as to rectitude, by reason of certain obstacles (just as natures subject to generation and corruption fail in some few cases on account of some obstacle), and as to knowledge, since in some the reason is perverted by passion, or evil habit, or an evil disposition of nature; thus formerly, theft, although expressly contrary to the natural law, was not considered wrong among the Germans, as Julius Cæsar relates (*De Bello Gall.*vi).

Reply Obj. 1. The meaning of the sentence quoted is not that whatever is contained in the Law and the Gospel belongs to the natural law, since they contain many things that are above nature; but that whatever belongs to the natural law is fully contained in them. Wherefore Gratian, after saying that *the natural law is what is contained in the Law and the Gospel*, adds at once, by way of example, *by which everyone is commanded to do: to others as he would be done by.*

Reply Obj. 2. The saying of the Philosopher is to be understood of things that are naturally just, not as general principles, but as conclusions drawn from them, having rectitude in the majority of cases, but failing in a few.

Reply Obj. 3. As, in man, reason rules and commands the other powers, so all the natural inclinations belonging to the other powers must needs be directed according to reason. Wherefore it is universally right for all men, that all their inclinations should be directed according to reason.

Fifth Article: Whether the Natural Law Can Be Changed?

We proceed thus to the Fifth Article:—

Objection 1. It would seem that the natural law can be changed. Because on Ecclus, xvii. 9, *He gave them instructions, and the law of life*, the gloss says: *He wished the law of the letter to be written, in order to correct the law of nature.* But that which is corrected is changed. Therefore the natural law can be changed.

Obj. 2. Further, the slaying of the innocent, adultery, and theft are against the natural law. But we find these things changed by God: as when God commanded Abraham to slay his innocent son (Gen. xxii. 2); and when he ordered the Jews to borrow and purloin the vessels of the Egyptians (Exod. xii. 35); and when He commanded Osee to take to himself a *wife of fornications* (Osee i. 2). Therefore the natural law can be changed.

Obj. 3. Further, Isidore says (*Etym.* v.4) that *the possession of all things in common, and universal freedom, are matters of natural law.* But these things are seen to be changed by human laws. Therefore it seems that the natural law is subject to change.

On the contrary, It is said in the Decretals (*Dist.* v): *The natural law dates from the creation of the rational creature. It does not vary according to time, but remains unchangeable.*

I answer that, A change in the natural law may be understood in two ways. First, by way of addition. In this sense nothing hinders the natural law from being changed: since many things for the benefit of human life have been added over and above the natural law both by the Divine law and by human laws.

Secondly, a change in the natural law may be understood by way of subtraction, so that what previously was according to the natural law ceases to be so. In this sense, the natural law is altogether unchangeable in its first principles but in its secondary principles, which as we have said (A. 4), are certain detailed proximate conclusions drawn from the first principles, the natural law is not changed so that what it prescribes be not right in most cases. But it may be changed in some particular cases of rare occurrence, through some special causes hindering the observance of such precepts, as stated above (A. 4).

Reply Obj. 1. The written law is said to be given for the correction of the natural law, either because it supplies what was wanting to the natural law; or because the natural law was perverted in the hearts of some men, as to certain matters, so that they es-

teemed those things good which are naturally evil; which perversion stood in need of correction.

Reply Obj. 2. All men alike, both guilty and innocent, die the death of nature which is inflicted by the power of God on account of original sin, according to 1 Kings ii. 6: *The Lord killeth and maketh alive.* Consequently by the command of God, death can be inflicted on any man, guilty or innocent, without any injustice whatever.—In like manner adultery is intercourse with another's wife; who is allotted to him by the law emanating from God. Consequently intercourse with any woman, by the command of God, is neither adultery nor fornication.—The same applies to theft, which is the taking of another's property. For whatever is taken by the command of God, to Whom all things belong, is not taken against the will of its owner, whereas it is in this that theft consists.—Nor is it only in human things, that whatever is commanded by God is right; but also in natural things, whatever is done by God, is, in some way, natural, as stated in the First Part (Q. 105, A. 6 *ad* 1).

Reply Obj. 3. A thing is said to belong to the natural law in two ways. First, because nature inclines thereto: e.g., that one should not do harm to another. Secondly, because nature did not bring in the contrary: thus we might say that for man to be naked is of the natural law, because nature did not give him clothes, but art invented them. In this sense; *the possession of all things in common and universal freedom* are said to be of the natural law, because, to wit, the distinction of possessions and slavery were not brought in by nature, but devised by human reason for the benefit of human life. Accordingly the law of nature was not changed in this respect, except by addition.

Sixth Article: Whether the Law of Nature Can Be Abolished from the Heart of Man?

We proceed thus to the Sixth Article:—

Objection 1. It would seem that the natural law can be abolished from the heart of man. Because on

Rom. ii. 14, *When the Gentiles who have not the law,* etc., a gloss says that *the law of righteousness, which sin had blotted out, is graven on the heart of man when he is restored by grace.* But the law of righteousness is the law of nature. Therefore the law of nature can be blotted out.

Obj. 2. Further, the law of grace is more efficacious than the law of nature. But the law of grace is blotted out by sin. Much more therefore can the law of nature be blotted out.

Obj. 3. Further, that which is established by law is made just. But many things are enacted by men, which are contrary to the law of nature. Therefore the law of nature can be abolished from the heart of man.

On the contrary, Augustine says (*Conf.* ii): *Thy law is written in the hearts of men, which iniquity itself effaces not.* But the law which is written in men's hearts is the natural law. Therefore the natural law cannot be blotted out.

I answer that, As stated above (AA. 4, 5), there belong to the natural law, first, certain most general precepts, that are known to all; and secondly, certain secondary and more detailed precepts; which are, as it were, conclusions following closely from first principles. As to those general principles, the natural law, in the abstract, can nowise be blotted out from men's hearts. But it is blotted out in the case of a particular action, in so far as reason is hindered from applying the general principle to a particular point of practice, on account of concupiscence or some other passion, as stated above (Q. 77, A. 2).—But as to the other, i.e., the secondary precepts, the natural law can be blotted out from the human heart, either by evil persuasions, just as in speculative matters errors occur in respect of necessary conclusions; or by vicious customs and corrupt habits, as among some men, theft, and even unnatural vices, as the Apostle states (Rom. i), were not esteemed sinful.

Reply Obj. 1. Sin blots out the law of nature in particular cases, not universally, except perchance in regard to the secondary precepts of the natural law, in the way stated above.

Reply Obj. 2. Although grace is more efficacious than nature, yet nature is more essential to man, and therefore more enduring.

Reply Obj. 3. This argument is true of the secondary precepts of the natural law, against which some legislators have framed certain enactments which are unjust.

Question 95: Of Human Law (In Four Articles)

We must now consider human law; and (1) this law considered in itself; (2) its power; (3) its mutability. Under the first head there are four points of inquiry: (1) Its utility. (2) Its origin. (3) Its quality. (4) Its division. [*Ed. note*: only Article 2 is included here.]

Second Article: Whether Every Human Law Is Derived from the Natural Law?

We proceed thus to the Second Article:—

Objection 1. It would seem that not every human law is derived from the natural law. For the Philosopher says (*Ethic.* v. 7) *that the legal just is that which originally was a matter of indifference.* But those things which arise from the natural law are not matters of indifference. Therefore the enactments of human laws are not all derived from the natural law.

Obj. 2. Further, positive law is contrasted with natural law, as stated by Isidore (*Etym.* v. 4) and the Philosopher (*Ethic.* v, *loc. cit.*). But those things which flow as conclusions from the general principles of the natural law belong to the natural law, as stated above (Q. 94, A. 4). Therefore that which is established by human law does not belong to the natural law.

Obj. 3. Further, the law of nature is the same for all; since the Philosopher says (*Ethic.* v. 7) that *the natural just is that which is equally valid everywhere.* If therefore human laws were derived from the natural law, it would follow that they too are the same for all: which is clearly false.

Obj. 4. Further, it is possible to give a reason for things which are derived from the natural law. But *it is not possible to give the reason for all the legal enactments of the law-givers*, as the jurist says. Therefore not all human laws are derived from the natural law.

On the contrary, Tully says (*Rhetor.* ii): Things which emanated from nature and were approved by custom, were sanctioned by fear and reverence for the laws.

I answer that, As Augustine says (*De Lib. Arb.* i. 5), *that which is not just seems to be no law at all*: wherefore the force of a law depends on the extent of its justice. Now in human affairs a thing is said to be just, from being right, according to the rule of reason. But the first rule of reason is the law of nature, as is clear from what has been stated above (Q. 91, A. 2 *ad* 2). Consequently every human law has just so much of the nature of law, as it is derived from the law of nature. But if in any point it deflects from the law of nature, it is no longer a law but a perversion of law.

But it must be noted that something may be derived from the natural law in two ways: first, as a conclusion from premises, secondly, by way of determination of certain generalities. The first way is like to that by which, in sciences, demonstrated conclusions are drawn from the principles: while the second mode is likened to that whereby, in the arts, general forms are particularized as to details: thus the craftsman needs to determine the general form of a house to some particular shape. Some things are therefore derived from the general principles of the natural law, by way of conclusions; e.g., that *one must not kill* may be derived as a conclusion from the principle that *one should do harm to no man*: while some are derived therefrom by way of determination; e.g., the law of nature has it that the evil-doer should be punished; but that he be punished in this or that way, is a determination of the law of nature.

Accordingly both modes of derivation are found in the human law. But those things which are derived in the first way, are contained in human law not as emanating therefrom exclusively, but have some force from the natural law also. But those things which are derived in the second way, have no other force than that of human law.

Reply Obj. 1. The Philosopher is speaking of those enactments which are by way of determination or specification of the precepts of the natural law.

Reply Obj. 2. This argument avails for those things that are derived from the natural law, by way of conclusions.

Reply Obj. 3. The general principles of the natural law cannot be applied to all men in the same way on account of the great variety of human affairs: and hence arises the diversity of positive laws among various people.

Reply Obj. 4. These words of the Jurist are to be understood as referring to decisions of rulers in determining particular points of the natural law: on which determinations the judgment of expert and prudent men is based as on its principles; in so far, to wit, as they see at once what is the best thing to decide.

Hence the Philosopher says (*Ethic.* vi. 11) that in such matters, *we ought to pay as much attention to the undemonstrated sayings and opinions of persons who surpass us in experience, age and prudence, as to their demonstrations.*

• • •

Question 96: Of the Power of Human Law (In Six Articles)

We must now consider the power of human law. Under this head there are six points of inquiry: (1) Whether human law should be framed for the community? (2) Whether human law should repress all vices? (3) Whether human law is competent to direct all acts of virtue? (4) Whether it binds man in conscience? (5) Whether all men are subject to human law? (6) Whether those who are under the law may act beside the letter of the law? [*Ed. note*: only Article 4 is included here.]

Fourth Article: Whether Human Law Binds a Man in Conscience?

We proceed thus to the Fourth Article:—

Objection 1. It would seem that human law does not bind a man in conscience. For an inferior power has no jurisdiction in a court of higher power. But the power of man, which frames human law, is beneath the Divine power. Therefore human law cannot impose its precept in a Divine court, such as is the court of conscience.

Obj. 2. Further, the judgment of conscience depends chiefly on the commandments of God. But sometimes God's commandments are made void by human laws, according to Matth. xv. 6: *You have made void the commandment of God for your tradition.* Therefore human law does not bind a man in conscience.

Obj. 3. Further, human laws often bring loss of character and injury on man, according to Isa. x. 1 *et seq.*: *Woe to them that make wicked laws, and when they write, write injustice; to oppress the poor in judgment, and do violence to the cause of the humble of My people.* But it is lawful for anyone to avoid oppression and violence. Therefore human laws do not bind man in conscience.

On the contrary, It is written (1 Pet. ii.19): *This is thankworthy, if for conscience ... a man endure sorrows, suffering wrongfully.*

I answer that, Laws framed by man are either just or unjust. If they be just, they have the power of binding in conscience, from the eternal law whence they are derived, according to Prov. viii. 15: *By Me kings reign; and lawgivers decree just things.* Now laws are said to be just, both from the end, when, to wit, they are ordained to the common good;—and from their author, that is to say, when the law that is made

does not exceed the power of the lawgiver,—and from their form, when, to wit, burdens are laid on the subjects, according to an equality of proportion and with a view to the common good. For, since one man is a part of the community, each man in all that he is and has, belongs to the community; just as a part, in all that it is, belongs to the whole; wherefore nature inflicts a loss on the part, in order to save the whole: so that on this account, such laws as these, which impose proportionate burdens, are just and binding in conscience, and are legal laws.

On the other hand laws may be unjust in two ways: first, by being contrary to human good, through being opposed to the things mentioned above:—either in respect of the end, as when an authority imposes on his subjects burdensome laws, conducive, not to the common good, but rather to his own cupidity or vainglory;—or in respect of the author, as when a man makes a law that goes beyond the power committed to him;—or in respect of the form, as when burdens are imposed unequally on the community, although with a view to the common good. The like are acts of violence rather than laws; because, as Augustine says (*De Lib. Arb.* i. 5), *a law that is not just, seems to be no law at all.* Wherefore such laws do not bind in conscience, except perhaps in order to avoid scandal or disturbance; for which cause a man should even yield his right, according to Matth. v. 40, 41: *If a man take away thy coat, let go thy cloak also unto him; and whosoever will force thee one mile, go with him another two.*

Secondly, laws may be unjust through being opposed to the Divine good: such are the laws of tyrants inducing to idolatry, or to anything else contrary to the Divine law: and laws of this kind must nowise be observed, because, as stated in Acts v.29, *we ought to obey God rather than men.*

Reply Obj. 1. As the Apostle says (Rom. xiii, 1, 2), all human power is from God ... *therefore he that resisteth the power*, in matters that are within its scope, *resisteth the ordinance of God*; so that he becomes guilty according to his conscience.

Reply Obj. 2. This argument is true of laws that are contrary to the commandments of God, which is beyond the scope of (human) power. Wherefore in such matters human law should not be obeyed.

Reply Obj. 3. This argument is true of a law that inflicts unjust hurt on its subjects. The power that man holds from God does not extend to this: wherefore neither in such matters is man bound to obey the law, provided he avoid giving scandal or inflicting a more grievous hurt.

◆ ◆ ◆ ◆ ◆

JOHN FINNIS

from *Natural Law and Natural Rights**

I. Evaluation and the Description of Law

I.1 The Formation of Concepts for Descriptive Social Science

There are human goods that can be secured only through the institutions of human law, and requirements of practical reasonableness that only those institutions can satisfy. It is the object of this book to identify those goods, and those requirements of practical reasonableness, and thus to show how and on what conditions such institutions are justified and the ways in which they can be (and often are) defective.

---

* *Ed. note:* In his argument Finnis frequently refers to parts of his book which are not included in this excerpt; however, these references have been left in the excerpted text in the interest of its completeness as a resource for further exploration of the full text of *Natural Law and Natural Rights.*

It is often supposed that an evaluation of law as a type of social institution, if it is to be undertaken at all, must be preceded by a value-free description and analysis of that institution as it exists in fact. But the development of modern jurisprudence suggests, and reflection on the methodology of any social science confirms, that a theorist cannot give a theoretical description and analysis of social facts, unless he also participates in the work of evaluation, of understanding what is really good for human persons, and what is really required by practical reasonableness.

A social science, such as analytical or sociological jurisprudence, seeks to describe, analyse, and explain some object or subject-matter. This object is constituted by human actions, practices, habits, dispositions and by human discourse. The actions, practices, etc., are certainly influenced by the "natural" causes properly investigated by the methods of the natural sciences, including a part of the science of psychology. But the actions, practices, etc., can be fully understood only by understanding their point, that is to say their objective, their value, their significance or importance, as conceived by the people who performed them, engaged in them, etc. And these conceptions of point, value, significance, and importance will be reflected in the discourse of those same people, in the conceptual distinctions they draw and fail or refuse to draw. Moreover, these actions, practices, etc., and correspondingly these concepts, vary greatly from person to person, from one society to another, from one time and place to other times and places. *How, then, is there to be a general descriptive theory of these varying particulars?*

A theorist wishes to describe, say, law as a social institution. But the conceptions of law (and of *jus, lex, droit, nomos,* ...) which people have entertained, and have used to shape their own conduct, are quite varied. The subject-matter of the theorist's description does not come neatly demarcated from other features of social life and practice. Moreover, this social life and practice bears labels in many languages. The languages can be learned by speakers of other languages, but the principles on which labels are adopted and applied—i.e., the practical concerns and the self-interpretations of the people whose conduct and dispositions go to make up the theorist's subject-matter—are not uniform. Can the theorist do more, then, than list these varying conceptions and practices and their corresponding labels? Even a list requires some principle of selection of items for inclusion in the list. And jurisprudence, like other social sciences, aspires to be more than a conjunction of lexicography with local history, or even than a juxtaposition of all lexicographies conjoined with all local histories....

• • •

I.5 The Theory of Natural Law

Bentham, Austin, Kelsen, Weber, Hart, and Raz all published stern repudiations of what they understood to be the theory of natural law; and Fuller carefully dissociated himself from that theory in its classical forms. But the theoretical work of each of these writers was controlled by the adoption, on grounds left inexplicit and inadequately justified, of some practical viewpoint as the standard of relevance and significance in the construction of his descriptive analysis. A sound theory of natural law is one that explicitly, with full awareness of the methodological situation just described, undertakes a critique of practical viewpoints, in order to distinguish the practically unreasonable from the practically reasonable, and thus to differentiate the really important from that which is unimportant or is important only by its opposition to or unreasonable exploitation of the really important. A theory of natural law claims to be able to identify conditions and principles of practical right-mindedness, of good and proper order among men and in individual conduct. Unless some such claim is justified, analytical jurisprudence in particular and (at least the major part of) all the social sciences in general can have no critically justified criteria for the formation of general concepts,

and must be content to be no more than manifestations of the various concepts peculiar to particular peoples and/or to the particular theorists who concern themselves with those people.

A theory of natural law need not be undertaken primarily for the purpose of thus providing a justified conceptual framework for descriptive social science. It may be undertaken, as this book is, primarily to assist the practical reflections of those concerned to act, whether as judges or as statesmen or as citizens. But in either case, the undertaking cannot proceed securely without a knowledge of the whole range of human possibilities and opportunities, inclinations and capacities, a knowledge that requires the assistance of descriptive and analytical social science. There is thus a mutual though not quite symmetrical interdependence between the project of describing human affairs by way of theory and the project of evaluating human options with a view, at least remotely, to acting reasonably and well. The evaluations are in no way deduced from the descriptions (see II.4); but one whose knowledge of the facts of the human situation is very limited is unlikely to judge well in discerning the practical implications of the basic values. Equally, the descriptions are not deduced from the evaluations; but without the evaluations one cannot determine what descriptions are really illuminating and significant.

• • •

II. Images and Objections

II.1 Natural Law and Theories of Natural Law

What are *principles of natural law*? The sense that the phrase "natural law" has in this book can be indicated in the following rather bald assertions, formulations which will seem perhaps empty or question-begging until explicated in Part Two: There is (i) a set of basic practical principles which indicate the basic forms of human flourishing as goods to be pursued and realized, and which are in one way or another used by everyone who considers what to do, however unsound his conclusions; and (ii) a set of basic methodological requirements of practical reasonableness (itself one of the basic forms of human flourishing) which distinguish sound from unsound practical thinking and which, when all brought to bear, provide the criteria for distinguishing between acts that (always or in particular circumstances) are reasonable-all-things-considered (and not merely relative-to-a-particular purpose) and acts that are unreasonable-all-things-considered, i.e., between ways of acting that are morally right or morally wrong thus enabling one to formulate (iii) a set of general moral standards.

To avoid misunderstandings about the scope of our subject-matter in this book, I should add here that the principles of natural law, thus understood, are traced out not only in moral philosophy or ethics and "individual" conduct, but also in political philosophy and jurisprudence, in political action, adjudication, and the life of the citizen. For those principles justify the exercise of authority in community. They require, too, that that authority be exercised, in most circumstances, according to the manner conveniently labelled the Rule of Law, and with due respect for the human rights which embody the requirements of justice, and for the purpose of promoting a common good in which such respect for rights is a component. More particularly, the principles of natural law explain the obligatory force (in the fullest sense of "obligation") of positive laws, even when those laws cannot be deduced from those principles. And attention to the principles, in the context of these explanations of law and legal obligation, justifies regarding certain positive laws as radically defective, *precisely as laws*, for want of conformity to those principles.

My present purpose, however, is not to anticipate later chapters, but to make some preliminary clarifications. A first essential distinction is that between a theory, doctrine, or account and the subject-matter of that theory, doctrine, or account. There can be a history of theories, doctrines, and accounts of matters that have no history. And principles of natural law, in the sense formulated in the two preceding paragraphs, have no history.

Since I have yet to show that there are indeed any principles of natural law, let me put the point conditionally. Principles of this sort would hold good, as principles, however extensively they were overlooked, misapplied, or defied in practical thinking, and however little they were recognized by those who reflectively theorize about human thinking. That is to say, they would "hold good" just as the mathematical principles of accounting "hold good" even when, as in the medieval banking community, they are unknown or misunderstood. So there could be a history of the varying extent to which they have been used by people, explicitly or implicitly, to regulate their personal activities. And there could be a history of the varying extent to which reflective theorists have acknowledged the sets of principles as valid or "holding good." And there could be a history of the popularity of the various theories offered to explain the place of those principles in the whole scheme of things. But of natural law itself there could, strictly speaking, be no history.

Natural law could not rise, decline, be revived, or stage "eternal returns." It could not have historical achievements to its credit. It could not be held responsible for disasters of the human spirit or atrocities of human practice.

But there is a history of the opinions or set of opinions, theories, and doctrines which assert that there are principles of natural law, a history of origins, rises, declines and falls, revivals and achievements, and of historical responsibilities. Anyone who thinks there really are no such principles will consider that a book about natural law must be a book about mere opinions, and that the principal interest of those opinions is their historical causes and effects. But anyone who considers that there are principles of natural law, in the sense already outlined, ought to see the importance of maintaining a distinction between discourse about natural law and discourse about a doctrine or doctrines of natural law. Unhappily, people often fail to maintain the distinction.[1]

This is a book about natural law. It expounds or sets out a theory of natural law, but is not *about* that theory. Nor is it about other theories. It refers to other theories only to illuminate the theory expounded here, or to explain why some truths about natural law have at various times and in various ways been overlooked or obscured. The book does not enter into discussions about whether natural law doctrines have exerted a conservative or radical influence on Western politics, or about the supposed psychological (infantile)[2] origins of such doctrines, or about the claim that some or all specific natural law doctrines are asserted hypocritically,[3] arrogantly,[4] or as a disguise or vehicle for expressions of ecclesiastical faith. For none of these discussions has any real bearing on the question whether there is a natural law and, if so, what its content is. Equally irrelevant to that question is the claim that disbelief in natural law yields bitter fruit. Nothing in this book is to be interpreted as either advancing or denying such claims; the book simply prescinds from all such matters.

II.2 Legal Validity and Morality

The preceding section treated theories of natural law as theories of the rational foundations for moral judgment, and this will be the primary focus of subsequent sections of this chapter. But in the present section I consider the more restricted and juristic understanding of "natural law" and "natural law doctrine(s)."

Here we have to deal with the image of natural law entertained by jurists such as Kelsen, Hart, and Raz. This image should be reproduced in their own words, since they themselves scarcely identify, let alone quote from, any particular theorist as defending the view that they describe as the view of natural law doctrine. Joseph Raz usefully summarizes and adopts Kelsen's version of this image:

> Kelsen correctly points out that according to natural law theories there is no specific notion of legal validity. The only concept of validity is validity according to natural law, i.e., moral validity. Natural lawyers can only judge a law as morally valid, that is, just or morally invalid, i.e., wrong. They cannot say of a law that it is legally valid but morally wrong. If it is wrong and unjust, it is also invalid in the only sense of validity they recognise.[5]

In his own terms, Raz later defines "Natural Law theorists" as "those philosophers who think it a criterion of adequacy for theories of law that they show ... that it is a necessary truth that every law has moral worth.[6]

---

1   Notable examples of this failure include A.P. D'Entrèves, *Natural Law* (London:1951, rev. ed. 1970), e.g., pp. 13, 18, 22, etc.; Julius Stone, *Human Law and Human Justice* (London: 1965), chs. 2 and 7.

2   See Alf Ross, *On Law and Justice* (London: 1958), pp. 258, 262-63.

3   See Wolfgang Friedmann, letter (1953) 31 *Canadian Bar Rev.* 1074 at 1075.

4   See Wolfgang Friedmann, review (1958) 3 *Nat. L.F.* 208 at 210; also Hans Kelsen, *Allgemeine Staatslehre* (Berlin: 1925), p. 335, on "natural law naivety or arrogance" (in the passage, omitted from the 1945 English translation (*General Theory*, cf. p. 300), about the fully legal character of despotism).

5   Raz, "Kelsen's Theory of the Basic Norm" (1974)19 *Am. J. Juris.* 94 at p. 100.

6   *Practical Reason*, p. 162. This formulation corresponds to the contradictory of the characterization of "Legal Positivism" constructed by Hart in order to define "the issue between Natural Law and Legal Positivism": *Concept of Law*, p. 181. See also *Practical Reason*, pp. 155, 162; all these formulations seem to be intended by Raz to apply

For my part, I know of no philosopher who fits, or fitted, such a description, or who would be committed to trying to defend that sort of theoretical or meta-theoretical proposal.

• • •

[*Ed. note*: Having rejected Raz's characterization of natural law theory, Finnis explains his understanding of natural law. The next excerpt demonstrates demonstrates the style of his reasoning about the basic good of "knowledge." What is important here is that Finnis supposes "knowledge" is *self-evidently* good and so is a "given" in deliberations about conduct. We will not examine Finnis's full discussion of the seven basic forms of the human good: life, knowledge, play, aesthetic experience, friendship, practical reasonableness, and "religion." We will turn instead to Finnis's discussion of what "practical reasonableness" requires us to do as we pursue these basic goods.]

III. A Basic Form of Good: Knowledge

III.1 An Example

Neither this chapter nor the next makes or presupposes any moral judgments. Rather, these two chapters concern the evaluative substratum of all moral judgments. That is to say, they concern the acts of practical understanding in which we grasp the basic values of human existence and thus, too, the basic principles of all practical reasoning.

The purpose of this chapter, in particular, is to illustrate (i) what I mean by "basic value" and "basic practical principle," (ii) how such values and principles enter into any consideration of good reasons for

equally to "definitional" and "derivative" approach theories of natural law. (Since no one uses the "definitional" approach, there is no need to inquire into the value of the supposed distribution between "definitional" and "derivative" approaches.)

action and any full description of human conduct, and (iii) the sense in which such basic values are obvious ("self-evident"), and even unquestionable. For this purpose, I discuss only one basic value, leaving to the next chapter the identification of the other forms of human good that, so far as I can see, are likewise irreducibly basic.

The example of a basic value to be examined now is: knowledge. Perhaps it would be more accurate to call it "speculative knowledge," using the term "speculative" here, not to make the Aristotelian distinction between the *theoretike* and the *praktike*, but to distinguish knowledge as sought for its own sake from knowledge as sought only instrumentally, i.e., as useful in the pursuit of some other objective, such as survival, power, popularity, or a money-saving cup of coffee. Now "knowledge," unlike "belief," is an achievement-word; there are true beliefs and false beliefs, but knowledge is of truth. So one could speak of truth as the basic good with which we are here concerned, for one can just as easily speak of "truth for its own sake" as of "knowledge for its own sake." In any event, truth is not a mysterious abstract entity; we want the truth when we want the judgments in which we affirm or deny propositions to be true judgments, or (what comes to the same) want the propositions affirmed or denied, or to be affirmed or denied, to be true propositions. So, to complete the explanation of what is meant by the knowledge under discussion here, as distinct from instrumental knowledge, I can add that the distinction I am drawing is not between one set of propositions and another. It is not a distinction between fields of knowledge. Any proposition, whatever its subject-matter, can be inquired into (with a view to affirming or denying it) in either of the two distinct ways, (i) instrumentally or (ii) out of curiosity, the pure desire to know, to find out the truth about it simply out of an interest in or concern for truth and a desire to avoid ignorance or error as such.

This chapter, then, is an invitation to reflect on one form of human activity, the activity of trying to find out, to understand, and to judge matters correctly. This is not, perhaps, the easiest activity to understand; but it has the advantage of being the activity which the reader himself is actually engaged in. But if it seems too abstruse and tricky to try to understand this form of activity reflectively (i.e., by reflecting on one's attempt to understand and assess the truth of this chapter itself), one can reflect on any other exercise of curiosity. One could consider, for example, the wide-ranging effort of historical inquiry involved in discovering the actual intentions of the principal authors of the Statute of Uses (1536) or of the Fourteenth Amendment of the US Constitution (1866). Or something more humble (like weighing the truth of some gossipy rumour), or more "scientific"—it makes no difference, for present purposes.

• • •

V. The Basic Requirements of Practical Reasonableness

V.1 The Good of Practical Reasonableness Structures Our Pursuit of Goods

There is no reason to doubt that each of the basic aspects of human well-being is worth seeking to realize. But there are many such basic forms of human good; I identified seven. And each of them can be participated in, and promoted, in an inexhaustible variety of ways and with an inexhaustible variety of combinations of emphasis, concentration, and specialization. To participate thoroughly in any basic value calls for skill, or at least a thoroughgoing commitment. But our life is short.

By disclosing a horizon of attractive possibilities for us, our grasp of the basic values thus creates, not answers, the problem for intelligent decision: What is to be done? What may be left undone? What is not to be done? We have, in the abstract, no reason to leave any of the basic goods out of account. But we do have good reason to choose commitments, pro-

jects, and actions, knowing that choice effectively rules out many alternative reasonable or possible commitment(s), project(s), and action(s).

To have this choice between commitment to concentration upon one value (say, speculative truth) and commitment to others, and between one intelligent and reasonable project (say, understanding this book) and other eligible projects for giving definite shape to one's participation in one's selected value, and between one way of carrying out that project and other appropriate ways, is the primary respect in which we can call ourselves both free and responsible.

For amongst the basic forms of good that we have no good reason to leave out of account is the good of practical reasonableness, which is participated in precisely by shaping one's participation in the other basic goods, by guiding one's commitments, one's selection of projects, and what one does in carrying them out.

The principles that express the general ends of human life do not acquire what would nowadays be called a "moral" force until they are brought to bear upon definite ranges of project, disposition, or action, or upon particular projects, dispositions, or actions. How they are thus to be brought to bear is the problem for practical reasonableness. "Ethics," as classically conceived, is simply a recollectively and/ or prospectively reflective expression of this problem and of the general lines of solutions which have been thought reasonable.

How does one tell that a decision is practically reasonable? This question is the subject-matter of the present chapter. The classical exponents of ethics (and of theories of natural law) were well aware of this problem of criteria and standards of judgment. They emphasize that an adequate response to that problem can be made only by one who has experience (both of human wants and passions and of the conditions of human life) and intelligence and a desire for reasonableness stronger than the desires that might overwhelm it. Even when, later, Thomas

Aquinas clearly distinguished a class of practical principles which he considered self-evident to anyone with enough experience and intelligence to understand the words by which they are formulated, he emphasized that moral principles such as those in the Ten Commandments are *conclusions from* the primary self-evident principles, that reasoning to such conclusions requires good judgment, and that there are many other more complex and particular moral norms to be followed and moral judgments and decisions to be made, all requiring a degree of practical wisdom which (he says) few men in fact possess: II.3, above.

Now, you may say, it is all very well for Aristotle to assert that ethics can be satisfactorily expounded only by and to those who are experienced and wise and indeed of good habits,[7] and that these characteristics are only likely to be found in societies that already have sufficiently sound standards of conduct,[8] and that the popular morality of such societies (as crystallized and detectable in their language of praise and blame, and their lore) is a generally sound pointer in the elaboration of ethics.[9] He may assert that what is right and morally good is simply *seen* by the man (the *phronimos*, or again the *spoudaios*) who is right minded and morally good,[10] and that what such a man thinks and does *is* the criterion of sound terminology and correct conclusions in ethics (and politics).[11] Such assertions can scarcely be denied. But they are scarcely helpful to those who are wondering whether their own view of what is to be done is a reasonable view *or not*. The notion of "the mean," for which Aristotle is perhaps too well known, seems likewise to be accurate but not very helpful (though

its classification of value-words doubtless serves as a reminder of the dimensions of the moral problem). For what is "the mean and best, that is characteristic of virtue"? It is "to feel [anger, pity, appetite, etc.] when one ought to, and in relation to the objects and persons that one ought to, and with the motives and in the manner that one ought to...."[12] Have we no more determinate guide than this?

In the two millennia since Plato and Aristotle initiated formal inquiry into the content of practical reasonableness, philosophical reflection has identified a considerable number of requirements of *method* in practical reasoning. Each of these requirements has, indeed, been treated by some philosopher with exaggerated respect, as if it were the exclusive controlling and shaping requirement. For, as with each of the basic forms of good, each of these requirements is fundamental, underived, irreducible, and hence is capable when focused upon of seeming the most important.

Each of these requirements concerns what one *must* do, or think, or be if one is to participate in the basic value of practical reasonableness. Someone who lives up to these requirements is thus Aristotle's *phronimos*; he has Aquinas's *prudentia*; they are requirements of reasonableness or practical wisdom, and to fail to live up to them is irrational. But, secondly, reasonableness both *is* a basic aspect of human well-being and *concerns* one's participation in all the (other) basic aspects of human well-being. Hence its requirements concern fullness of well-being (in the measure in which any one person can enjoy such fullness of well-being in the circumstances of his lifetime) So someone who lives up to these requirements is also Aristotle's *spoudaios* (mature man), his life is *eu zen* (well-living) and, unless circumstances are quite against him, we can say that he has Aristotle's *eudaimonia* (the inclusive all-round flourishing or well-being—not safely translated as "happiness"). But, thirdly, the basic forms of good

7   *Nic. Eth.* I, 3: 1095a7-11; 4: 1095b5-13; X, 9: 1179b27-30.

8   *Nic. Eth.* X, 9: 1179b27-1180a5.

9   See *Nic. Eth.* VI, 5: 1140a24-25; II, 5: 1105b30-31; III, 6: 1115a20; III, 10:1117b32; cf. X, 2: 1173a1.

10 *Nic. Eth.* VI, 11: 1143a35-1143b17.

11 *Nic. Eth.* X, 10: 1176a17-18; cf. III, 6: 1113a33; IX, 4: 1166a12-13: see also I.4, above.

12 *Nic. Eth.* II, 6: 1106b21-24.

are opportunities of *being*; the more fully a man participates in them the more he is what he can be. And for this state of being fully what one can be, Aristotle appropriated the word *physis*, which was translated into Latin as *natura* (cf. XIII.l, below). So Aquinas will say that these requirements are requirements not only of reason, and of goodness, but also (by entailment) of (human) nature: II.4, above.

Thus, speaking very summarily, we could say that the requirements to which we now turn express the "natural law method" of working out the (moral) "natural law" from the first (pre-moral) "principles of natural law." Using only the modern terminology (itself of uncertain import) of "morality," we can say that the following sections of this chapter concern the sorts of reasons why (and thus the ways in which) there are things that morally ought (not) to be done.

V.2 A Coherent Plan of Life

First, then, we should recall that, though they correspond to urges and inclinations which can make themselves felt prior to any intelligent consideration of what is worth pursuing, the basic aspects of human well-being are discernible only to one who thinks about his opportunities, and thus are realizable only by one who intelligently directs, focuses, and controls his urges, inclinations, and impulses. In its fullest form, therefore, the first requirement of practical reasonableness is what John Rawls calls a rational plan of life.[13] Implicitly or explicitly one must have a harmonious set of purposes and orientations, not as the "plans" or "blueprints" of a pipe-dream, but as effective commitments. (Do not confuse the adoption of a set of basic personal or social commitments with the process, imagined by some contemporary philosophers, of "choosing basic values"!) It is unreasonable to live merely from moment to moment, following immediate cravings, or just drifting. It is also irrational to devote one's attention exclusively to specific projects which can be carried out completely by simply deploying defined means to defined objectives. Commitment to the practice of medicine (for the sake of human life), or to scholarship (for the sake of truth), or to any profession, or to a marriage (for the sake of friendship and children) ... all require both direction and control of impulses, and the undertaking of specific projects; but they also require the redirection of inclinations, the reformation of habits, the abandonment of old and adoption of new projects, as circumstances require, and, overall, the harmonization of all one's deep commitments for which there is no recipe or blueprint, since basic aspects of human good are not like the definite objectives of particular projects, but are *participated in* (see III.3, above).

As Rawls says, this first requirement is that we should "see our life as one whole, the activities of one rational subject spread out in time. Mere temporal position, or distance from the present, is not a reason for favouring one moment over another."[14] But since human life is in fact subject to all manner of unforeseeable contingencies, this effort to "see" our life as one whole is a rational effort only if it remains on the level of general commitments, and the harmonizing of them. Still, generality is not emptiness (as one can confirm for oneself by contrasting any of the basic forms of good, which as formulated in the "substantive" practical principles are quite general, with their opposites). So, in every age, wise men have counselled "in whatever you do remember your last days" (Ecclesiasticus 7:36), not so much to emphasize the importance of the hour of death in relation to a life hereafter, but rather to establish the proper perspective for choosing how to live one's present life. For, from the imagined and heuristically postulated standpoint of the still unknown time of

---

13 *Theory of Justice*, pp. 408-23, adopting the terminology of W. F. R. Hardie, "The Final Good in Aristotle's Ethics" (1965) 60 *Philosophy* 277.

14 *Theory of Justice*, p. 420.

one's death, one can see that many sorts of choices would be irrational, a waste of opportunities, meaningless, a failure, a shame. So the Christian parable of the man who devoted all his energies to gathering riches, with a view to nothing more than drinking and eating them up, makes its "moral" point by appealing to the intelligence by which we discern folly: "*You fool!* This night your life shall be required of you. Then whose shall that wealth be which you have heaped together?" (Luke 12:20.)

The content and significance of this first requirement will be better understood in the light of the other requirements. For indeed, all the requirements are interrelated and capable of being regarded as aspects one of another.

V.3 No Arbitrary Preferences Amongst Values

Next, there must be no leaving out of account, or arbitrary discounting or exaggeration, of any of the basic human values. Any commitment to a coherent plan of life is going to involve some degree of concentration on one or some of the basic forms of good, at the expense, temporarily or permanently, of other forms of good: IV.4. But the commitment will be rational only if it is on the basis of one's assessment of one's capacities, circumstances, and even of one's tastes. It will be unreasonable if it is on the basis of a devaluation of any of the basic forms of human excellence, or if it is on the basis of an over-evaluation of such merely derivative and supporting or instrumental goods as wealth or "opportunity" or of such merely; secondary and conditionally valuable goods as reputation or (in a different sense of secondariness) pleasure.

A certain scholar may have little taste or capacity for friendship, and may feel that life for him would have no savour if he were prevented from pursuing his commitment to knowledge. None the less, it would be unreasonable for him to deny that, objectively, human life (quite apart from truthseeking and

knowledge) and friendship are good in themselves. It is one thing to have little capacity and even no "taste" for scholarship, or friendship, or physical heroism, or sanctity; it is quite another thing, and stupid or arbitrary, to think or speak or act as if these were not real forms of good.

So, in committing oneself to a rational plan of life, and in interacting with other people (with their own plans of life), one must not use Rawls's "thin theory of the good." For the sake of a "democratic"[15] impartiality between differing conceptions of human good, Rawls insists that, in selecting principles of justice, one must treat as primary goods only liberty, opportunity, wealth, and self-respect, and that one must not attribute intrinsic value to such basic forms of good as truth, or play, or art, or friendship. Rawls gives no satisfactory reason for this radical emaciation of human good, and no satisfactory reason is available: the "thin theory" is arbitrary. It is quite reasonable for many men to choose not to commit themselves to any real pursuit of knowledge, and it is quite unreasonable for a scholar-statesman or scholar-father to demand that all his subjects or children should conform themselves willy-nilly to the modes and standards of excellence that he chooses and sets for himself. But it is even more unreasonable for anyone to deny that knowledge *is* (and is to be treated as) a form of excellence, and that error, illusion, muddle, superstition, and ignorance are evils that no one should wish for, or plan for, or encourage in himself or in others. If a statesman (VIII.5) or father or any self-directing individual treats truth or friendship or play or any of the other basic forms of good as of no account, and never asks himself whether his life-plan(s) makes reasonable allowance for participation in those intrinsic human values (and for avoidance of their opposites), then he can be properly accused both of irrationality and of stunting or mutilating himself and those in his care.

---

15 Cf. *Theory of Justice*, p. 527.

V.4 No Arbitrary Preferences Amongst Persons

Next, the basic goods are human goods, and can in principle be pursued, realized, and participated in by any human being. Another person's survival, his coming to know, his creativity, his all-round flourishing, may not interest me, may not concern me, may in any event be beyond my power to affect. But have I any *reason* to deny that they are really good, or that they are fit matters of interest, concern, and favour by that man and by all those who have to do with him? The questions of friendship, collaboration, mutual assistance, and justice are the subject of the next chapters. Here we need not ask just who is responsible for whose well-being: see VII.4. But we can add, to the second requirement of fundamental impartiality of recognition of each of the basic forms of good, a third requirement: of fundamental impartiality among the human subjects who are or may be partakers of those goods.

My own well-being (which, as we shall see, includes a concern for the well-being of others, my friends: VI.4; but ignore this for the moment) is reasonably the first claim on my interest, concern, and effort. Why can I so regard it? Not because it is of more value than the well-being of others, simply because it is mine: intelligence and reasonableness can find no basis in the mere fact that A is A and is not B (that I am I and am not you) for evaluating his (our) well-being differentially. No: the only *reason* for me to prefer my well-being is that it is through *my* self-determined and self-realizing participation in the basic goods that I can do what reasonableness suggests and requires, viz. favour and realize the forms of human good indicated in the first principles of practical reason.

There is, therefore, reasonable scope for self-preference. But when all allowance is made for that, this third requirement remains, a pungent critique of selfishness, special pleading, double standards, hypocrisy, indifference to the good of others whom one could easily help ("passing by on the other side"), and all the other manifold forms of egoistic and group bias. So much so that many have sought to found ethics virtually entirely on this principle of impartiality between persons. In the modern philosophical discussion, the principle regularly is expressed as a requirement that one's moral judgments and preferences be *universalizable*.

The classical non-philosophical expression of the requirement is, of course, the so-called Golden Rule formulated not only in the Christian gospel but also in the sacred books of the Jews, and not only in didactic formulae but also in the moral appeal of sacred history and parable. It needed no drawing of the moral, no special traditions of moral education, for King David (and every reader of the story of his confrontation with Nathan the prophet) to feel the rational conclusiveness of Nathan's analogy between the rich man's appropriation of the poor man's ewe and the King's appropriation of Uriah the Hittite's wife, and thus the rational necessity for the King to extend his condemnation of the rich man to himself. "You are the man" (2 Samuel 12:7).

"Do to (or for) others what you would have them do to (or for) you." Put yourself in your neighbour's shoes. Do not condemn others for what you are willing to do yourself. Do not (without special reason) prevent others getting for themselves what you are trying to get for yourself. These are requirements of reason, because to ignore them is to be arbitrary as between individuals.

But what are the bounds of reasonable self-preference, of reasonable discrimination in favour of myself, my family, my group(s)? In the Greek, Roman, and Christian traditions of reflection, this question was approached via the heuristic device of adopting the viewpoint, the standards, the principles of justice, of one who sees the whole arena of human affairs and who has the interests of each participant in those affairs equally at heart and equally in mind—the "ideal observer." Such an impartially benevolent "spectator" would condemn some but not all forms of self-preference, and some but not all forms of competition: VII.3-4, below. The heuristic device helps one to attain impartiality as between the possible subjects of human well-being (persons) and to exclude mere bias in one's practical reasoning. It permits one to be impartial, too, among inexhaustibly many of the life-plans that differing individuals may choose. But, of course, it does not suggest "impartiality" about the basic aspects of human good. It does not authorize one to set aside the second requirement of practical reason by indifference to death and disease, by preferring trash to art, by favouring the comforts of ignorance and illusion, by repressing all play as unworthy of man, by praising the ideal of self-aggrandizement and contemning the ideal of friendship, or by treating the search for the ultimate source and destiny of things as of no account or as an instrument of statecraft or a plaything reserved for leisured folk ...

Therein lies the contrast between the classical heuristic device of the benevolently divine viewpoint and the equivalent modern devices for eliminating mere bias, notably the heuristic concept of the social contract. Consider Rawls's elaboration of the social contract strategy, an elaboration which most readily discloses the purpose of that strategy as a measure and instrument of practical reason's requirement of interpersonal impartiality. Every feature of Rawls's construction is designed to guarantee that if a supposed principle of justice is one that would be unanimously agreed on, behind the "veil of ignorance," in the "Original Position," then it must be a principle that is fair and unbiased as between persons. Rawls's heuristic device is thus of some use to anyone who is concerned for the third requirement of practical reasonableness, and in testing its implications. Unfortunately, Rawls disregards the second requirement of practical reasonableness, viz. that each basic or intrinsic human good be treated as a basic and intrinsic good. The conditions of the Original Position are designed by Rawls to guarantee that no principle of justice will systematically favour any life-plan simply because that life-plan participates more fully in human well-being in any or all of its basic aspects (e.g., by favouring knowledge over ignorance and illusion, art over trash, etc.).

And it simply does not follow, from the fact that a principle chosen in the Original Position would be unbiased and fair as between individuals, that a principle which would *not* be chosen in the Original Position must be unfair or not a proper principle of justice in the real world. For in the real world, as Rawls himself admits, intelligence can discern intrinsic basic values and their contraries.[16] Provided we make the distinctions mentioned in the previous section, between basic practical principles and mere matters of taste, inclination, ability, etc., we are able (and are required in reason) to favour the basic forms of good and to avoid and discourage their contraries. In doing so we are showing no improper favour to individuals as such, no unreasonable "respect of persons," no egoistic or group bias, no partiality opposed to the Golden Rule or to any other aspect of this third requirement of practical reason: see VIII.5-6, below.

V.5 Detachment and Commitment

The fourth and fifth requirements of practical reasonableness are closely complementary both to each other and to the first requirement of adopting a coherent plan of life, order of priorities, set of basic commitments.

In order to be sufficiently open to all the basic forms of good in all the changing circumstances of a lifetime, and in all one's relations, often unforeseeable, with other persons, and in all one's opportunities of effecting their well-being or relieving hardship, one must have a certain detachment from all the specific and limited projects which one undertakes. There is no good reason to take up an attitude to any of one's particular objectives, such that if one's project failed and one's objective eluded

---

16 *Theory of Justice*, p. 328.

one, one would consider one's life drained of meaning. Such an attitude irrationally devalues and treats as meaningless the basic human good of authentic and reasonable self-determination, a good in which one meaningfully participates simply by trying to do something sensible and worthwhile, whether or not that sensible and worthwhile project comes to nothing. Moreover, there are often straightforward and evil consequences of succumbing to the temptation to give one's particular project the overriding and unconditional significance which only a basic value and a general commitment can claim: they are the evil consequences that we call to mind when we think of fanaticism. So the fourth requirement of practical reasonableness can be called detachment.

The fifth requirement establishes the balance between fanaticism and dropping out, apathy, unreasonable failure or refusal to "get involved" with anything. It is simply the requirement that having made one's general commitments one must not abandon them lightly (for to do so would mean, in the extreme case, that one would fail ever to really participate in any of the basic values). And this requirement of fidelity has a positive aspect. One should be looking creatively for new and better ways of carrying out one's commitments, rather than restricting one's horizon and one's effort to the projects, methods, and routines with which one is familiar. Such creativity and development shows that a person, or a society, is really living on the level of practical *principle*, not merely on the level of conventional rules of conduct, rules of thumb, rules of method, etc., whose real appeal is not to reason (which would show up their inadequacies) but to the sub-rational complacency of habit, mere urge to conformity, etc.

V.6 The (Limited) Relevance of Consequences: Efficiency, Within Reason

The sixth requirement has obvious connections with the fifth, but introduces a new range of problems for practical reason, problems which go to the heart of morality. For this is the requirement that one bring about good in the world (in one's own life and the lives of others) by actions that are efficient for their (reasonable) purpose(s). One must not waste one's opportunities by using inefficient methods. One's actions should be judged by their effectiveness, by their fitness for their purpose, by their utility, their consequences ...

There is a wide range of contexts in which it is possible and only reasonable to calculate, measure, compare, weigh, and assess the consequences of alternative decisions. Where a choice must be made it is reasonable to prefer human good to the good of animals. Where a choice must be made it is reasonable to prefer basic human goods (such as life) to merely instrumental goods (such as property). Where damage is inevitable, it is reasonable to prefer stunning to wounding, wounding to maiming, maiming to death: i.e., lesser rather than greater damage to one-and-the-same basic good in one-and-the-same instantiation. Where one way of participating in a human good includes *both* all the good aspects and effects of its alternative, *and* more, it is reasonable to prefer that way: a remedy that both relieves pain and heals is to be preferred to the one that merely relieves pain. Where a person or a society has created a personal or social hierarchy of practical norms and orientations, through reasonable choice of commitments, one can in many cases reasonably measure the benefits and disadvantages of alternatives. (Consider a man who has decided to become a scholar, or a society that has decided to go to war.) Where one is considering objects or activities in which there is reasonably a market, the market provides a common denominator (currency) and enables a comparison to be made of prices, costs, and profits. Where there are alternative techniques or facilities for achieving definite objectives, cost-benefit analysis will make possible a certain range of reasonable comparisons between techniques or facilities. Over a wide range of preferences and wants, it is reasonable for an individual or society to seek to maximize the satisfaction of those preferences or wants.

But this sixth requirement is only one requirement among a number. The first, second, and third requirements require that in seeking to maximize the satisfaction of preferences one should discount the preferences of for example, sadists (who follow the impulses of the moment, and/or do not respect the value of life, and/or do not universalize their principles of action with impartiality). The first, third, and (as we shall see) seventh and eighth requirements require that cost-benefit analysis be contained within a framework that excludes any project involving certain intentional killings, frauds, manipulations of personality, etc. And the second requirement requires that one recognize that each of the basic aspects of human well-being is equally basic, that none is objectively more important than any of the others, and thus that none can provide a common denominator or single yardstick for assessing the utility of all projects: they are incommensurable, and any calculus of consequences that pretends to commensurate them is irrational.

• • •

V.7 Respect for Every Basic Value in Every Act

The seventh requirement of practical reasonableness can be formulated in several ways. A first formulation is that one should not choose to do any act which *of itself does nothing but* damage or impede a realization or participation of any one or more of the basic forms of human good. For the only "reason" for doing such an act, other than the non-reason of some impelling desire, could be that the good *consequences* of the act *outweigh* the damage done in and through the act itself. But, outside merely technical contexts, consequentialist "weighing" is always and necessarily arbitrary and delusive for the reasons indicated in the preceding section. [*Ed. note*: This argument has been omitted.]

Now an act of the sort we are considering will always be done (if it is done intelligently at all) as a means of promoting or protecting, directly or indirectly, one or more of the basic goods, in one or more of their aspects. For anyone who rises above the level of impulse and acts deliberately must be seeking to promote some form of good (even if only the good of authentically powerful self-expression and self-integration which he seeks through sadistic assaults or through malicious treachery or deception, with "no ulterior motives"). Hence, if consequentialist reasoning were reasonable, acts which themselves do nothing but damage or impede a human good could often be justified as parts of, or steps on the way to carrying out, some project for the promotion or protection of some form(s) of good. For example, if consequentialist reasoning were reasonable, one might sometimes reasonably kill some innocent person to save the lives of some hostages. But consequentialist reasoning is arbitrary and senseless, not just in one respect but in many. So we are left with the fact that such a killing is an act which of itself does nothing but damage the basic value of life. The goods that are expected to be secured in and through the consequential release of the hostages (if it takes place) would be secured not in or as an aspect of the killing of the innocent man but in or as an aspect of a distinct, subsequent act, an act which would be one "consequence" amongst the innumerable multitude of incommensurable consequences of the act of killing. Once we have excluded consequentialist reasoning, with its humanly understandable but in truth naively arbitrary limitation of focus to the purported calculus "one life versus many," the seventh requirement is self-evident.

• • •

V.8 The Requirements of the Common Good

Very many, perhaps even most, of our concrete moral responsibilities, obligations, and duties have their basis in the eighth requirement. We can label this the requirement of favouring and fostering the common good of one's communities. The sense and implications of this requirement are complex and manifold: see especially VI.8, VII.2-5, IX.l, XI.2, XII.2-3.

V.9 Following One's Conscience

The ninth requirement might be regarded as a particular aspect of the seventh (that no basic good may be directly attacked in any act), or even as a summary of all the requirements. But it is quite distinctive. It is the requirement that one should not do what one judges or thinks or "feels"-all-in-all should not be done. That is to say one must act "in accordance with one's conscience."

This chapter has been in effect a reflection on the workings of conscience. If one were by inclination generous, open, fair, and steady in one's love of human good, or if one's milieu happened to have settled on reasonable *mores*, then one would be able, without solemnity, rigmarole, abstract reasoning, or casuistry, to make the particular practical judgments (i.e., judgments of conscience) that reason requires. If one is not so fortunate in one's inclinations or upbringing, then one's conscience will mislead one, unless one strives to be reasonable and is blessed with a pertinacious intelligence alert to the forms of human good yet undeflected by the sophistries which intelligence so readily generates to rationalize indulgence, time-serving, and self-love. (The stringency of these conditions is the permanent ground for the possibility of authority in morals, i.e., of authoritative guidance, by one who meets those conditions, acknowledged willingly by persons of conscience.)

The first theorist to formulate this ninth requirement in all its unconditional strictness seems to have been Thomas Aquinas: if one chooses to do what one judges to be in the last analysis unreasonable, or if one chooses not to do what one judges to be in the last analysis required by reason, then one's choice

is unreasonable (wrongful), however erroneous one's judgments of conscience may happen to be. (A *logically* necessary feature of such a situation is, of course, that one is ignorant of one's mistake.)

This dignity of even the mistaken conscience is what is expressed in the ninth requirements. It flows from the fact that practical reasonableness is not simply a mechanism for producing correct judgments, but an aspect of personal full-being, to be respected (like all the other aspects) in every act as well as "over-all"—whatever the consequences.

V.10 The Product of These Requirements: Morality

Now we can see why some philosophers have located the essence of "morality" in the reduction of harm, others in the increase of well-being, some in social harmony, some in universalizability of practical judgment, some in the all-round flourishing of the individual, others in the preservation of freedom and personal authenticity. Each of these has a place in rational choice of commitments, projects, and particular actions. Each, moreover, contributes to the sense, significance, and force of terms such as "moral," "[morally] ought," and "right"; not every one of the nine requirements has a direct role in every moral judgment, but some moral judgments do sum up the bearing of each and all of the nine on the questions in hand, and every moral judgment sums up the bearing of one or more of the requirements.

• • •

XII Unjust Laws

XII.1 A Subordinate Concern of Natural Law Theory

The long haul through the preceding chapters will perhaps have convinced the reader that a theory of natural law need not have as its principal concern, either theoretical or pedagogical, the affirmation that "unjust laws are not law." Indeed, I know of no theory of natural law in which that affirmation, or anything like it, is more than a subordinate theorem. The principal concern of a theory of natural law is to explore the requirements of practical reasonableness in relation to the good of human beings who, because they live in community with one another, are confronted with problems of justice and rights, of authority, law, and obligation. And the principal jurisprudential concern of a theory of natural law is thus to identify the principles and limits of the Rule of Law (X.4), and to trace the ways in which sound laws, in all their positivity and mutability, are to be derived (not, usually, deduced: X.7) from unchanging principles—principles that have their force from their reasonableness, not from any originating acts or circumstances. Still, even the reader who has not been brought up to believe that "natural law" can be summed up in the slogan "*lex injusta non est lex*" [*Ed. note*: "unjust laws are not laws"] will wish a little more to be said about that slogan and about the effect of unjust exercises of authority upon our responsibilities as reasonable persons.

The ultimate basis of a ruler's authority is the fact that he has the opportunity, and thus the responsibility, of furthering the common good by stipulating solutions to a community's co-ordination problems: IX.4. Normally, though not necessarily, the immediate source of this opportunity and responsibility is the fact that he is designated by or under some authoritative rule as bearer of authority in respect of certain aspects of those problems: IX.4, X.3. In any event, authority is useless for the common good unless the stipulations of those in authority (or which emerge through the formation of authoritative customary rules) are treated as exclusionary reasons, i.e., as sufficient reason for acting notwithstanding that the subject would not himself have made the same stipulation and indeed considers the actual stipulation to be in some respect(s) unreasonable, not fully appropriate for the common good ...: IX.1, IX.2. The

principles set out in the preceding three sentences control our understanding both of the types of injustice in the making and administration of law, and of the consequences of such injustice.

XII.2 Types of Injustice in Law

First, since authority is derived solely from the needs of the common good, a ruler's use of authority is radically defective if he exploits his opportunities by making stipulations intended by him not for the common good but for his own or his friends' or party's or faction's advantage, or out of malice against some person or group. In making this judgment, we should not be deflected by the fact that most legal systems do not permit the exercise of "constitutional" powers to be challenged on the ground that that exercise was improperly motivated. These restrictions on judicial review are justified, if at all, either by pragmatic considerations or by a principle of separation of powers. In either case, they have no application to the reasonable man assessing the claims of authority upon him. On the other hand, it is quite possible that an improperly motivated law may happen to be in its contents compatible with justice and even promote the common good.

Secondly, since the location of authority is normally determined by authoritative rules dividing up authority and jurisdiction amongst separate office-holders, an office-holder may wittingly or unwittingly exploit his opportunity to affect people's conduct, by making stipulations which stray beyond his authority. Except in "emergency" situations (X.5) in which the law (even the constitution) should be bypassed and in which the source of authority reverts to its ultimate basis (IX.4), an *ultra vires* act is an abuse of power and an injustice to those treated as subject to it. (The injustice is "distributive" inasmuch as the official improperly assumes to himself an excess of authority, and "commutative" inasmuch as the official improperly seeks to subject others to his own decisions.) Lawyers sometimes are surprised to hear the *ultra vires* actions of an official categorized as abuse of power, since they are accustomed to thinking of such actions as "void and of no effect" in law. But such surprise is misplaced; legal rules about void and voidable acts are "deeming" rules, directing judges to treat actions, which are empirically more or less effective, *as if* they had not occurred (at least, as juridical acts), or *as if* from a certain date they had been overridden by an *intra vires* act of repeal or annulment. Quite reasonably, purported juridical acts of officials are commonly presumed to be lawful, and are treated as such by both fellow officials and laymen, unless and until judicially held otherwise. Hence, *ultra vires* official acts, even those which are not immune-for-procedural-or-pragmatic-reasons from successful challenge, will usually subject persons to effects which cannot afterwards be undone; and the bringing about of (the likelihood of) such effects is an abuse of power and an unjust imposition.

Thirdly, the exercise of authority in conformity with the Rule of Law normally is greatly to the common good (even when it restricts the efficient pursuit of other objectives); it is an important aspect of the commutative justice of treating people as entitled to the dignity of self-direction (X.4), and of the distributive justice of affording all an equal opportunity of understanding and complying with the law. Thus the exercise of legal authority otherwise than in accordance with due requirements of manner and form is an abuse and an injustice, unless those involved consent, or ought to consent, to an accelerated procedure in order to cut out "red tape" which in the circumstances would prejudice substantial justice (cf. VII.7).

Fourthly, what is stipulated may suffer from none of these defects of intention, author, and form, and yet be substantively unjust. It may be distributively unjust, by appropriating some aspect of the common stock, or some benefit of common life or enterprise, to a class not reasonably entitled to it on any of the criteria of distributive justice, while denying it to other persons; or by imposing on some a burden from which others are, on no just criterion, exempt. It may be commutatively unjust, by denying to one, some, or everyone an absolute human right, or a human right the exercise of which is in the circumstances possible, consistent with the reasonable requirements of public order, public health, etc., and compatible with the due exercise both of other human rights and of the same human rights by other persons (VII.4-5, VIII.7).

XII.3 Effects of Injustice on Obligation

How does injustice, of any of the foregoing sorts, affect the obligation to obey the law?

It is essential to specify the exact sense of this question. Any sound jurisprudence will recognize that someone uttering the question might conceivably mean by "obligation to obey the law" either (i) empirical liability to be subjected to sanction in event of non-compliance; or (ii) legal obligation in the intra-systemic sense ("legal obligation in the legal sense") in which the practical premiss that conformity to law is socially necessary is a framework principle insulated from the rest of practical reasoning; or (iii) legal obligation in the moral sense (i.e., the moral obligation that presumptively is entailed by legal obligation in the intra-systemic or legal sense); or (iv) moral obligation deriving not from the legality of the stipulation-of-obligation but from some "collateral" source (to be explained shortly). None of these interpretations is absurd, and a sound jurisprudence will show to what extent the answers to each will differ and to what extent they are interrelated.

An unsound jurisprudential method will seek to banish the question, in some of its senses, to "another discipline,"[17] or even declare those senses to be nonsense. Thus John Austin:

> Now, to say that human laws which conflict with the divine law are not binding, that is to say, are not laws, *is to talk stark nonsense.*

17 Cf. Hart, *Concept of Law*, p. 205.

The most pernicious laws, and therefore those which are most opposed to the will of God, have been and are continually enforced as laws by judicial tribunals. Suppose an act innocuous, or Positively beneficial, be prohibited by the sovereign under the penalty of death; if I commit this act, I shall be tried and condemned, and if object to the sentence, that it is contrary to the law of God, who has commanded that human lawgivers shall not prohibit acts which have no evil consequences, the Court of Justice will demonstrate the inconclusiveness of my reasoning by hanging me up, in pursuance of the law of which I have impugned the validity.[18]

I need not comment on the tone of this treatment of unjust law and conscientious objection. What concerns us is the methodological obtuseness of the words here italicized, the failure to allow that one and the same verbal formulation may bear differing though not necessarily unrelated meanings and express questions whose interrelations and differences can fruitfully be explored.

The first of the four conceivable senses of the question listed above is the least likely, in practice, to be intended by anyone raising the question. (Nevertheless, it is the only sense which Austin explicitly recognizes.) Someone who asks how injustice affects his obligation to conform to law is not likely to be asking for information on the practically important but theoretically banal point of fact, "Am I or am I not likely to be hanged for non-compliance with this law?"

The second of the four listed senses of the question of obligation might seem, at first glance, to be empty. For what is the point of asking whether there is a legal obligation in the legal sense to conform to a stipulation which is in the legal sense obligatory? This objection is, however, too hasty. In my discus-

sion of the formal features of legal order (X.3), of the Rule of Law (X.4), and of legal obligation (XI.4), I emphasized the way in which the enterprise of exercising authority through law proceeds by positing a system of rules which derive their authority not from the intrinsic appropriateness of their content but from the fact of stipulation in accordance with rules of stipulation. I emphasized the degree to which the resulting system is conceived of, in legal thought, as internally complete ("gapless") and coherent, and thus as sealed off (so to speak) from the unrestricted flow of practical reasoning about what is just and for the common good. I treated these "model" features of legal system and legal thought not as mere items in some "legal logic" (which as a matter of logic could certainly differ widely from that model!), but as practically reasonable responses to the need for security and predictability, a need which is indeed a matter of justice and human right. But all this should not disguise the extent to which legal thought in fact (and reasonably) does allow the system of rules to be permeated by principles of practical reasonableness which derive their authority from their appropriateness (in justice and for the common good) and not, or not merely, from their origin in some past act of stipulation or some settled usage. The legal system, even when conceived strictly as a set of normative meaning-contents (in abstraction from institutions, processes, personnel, and attitudes), is more open than the model suggests—open, that is to say, to the unrestricted flow of practical reasoning, in which a stipulation, valid according to the system's formal criteria of validity ("rules of recognition"), may be judged to be, or to have become, unjust and, therefore, after all, wholly or partially inapplicable.

In some legal systems this openness to unvarnished claims about the injustice of an existing or purported law is particularly evident, as in the United States of America. In others, as in English law, it is less obvious but still is familiar to lawyers, for example from the "golden rule" that statutes are to be interpreted so as to avoid "absurdity" or

---

18 *Province*, p. 185 (emphasis added).

injustice, and from the debates, quite frequent in the highest courts, about the propriety of amending or abandoning even well-established rules or "doctrines" of common law. Those who doubt or minimize the presence of open-ended principles of justice in professional legal thought will usually be found, on close examination, to be making a constitutional claim, viz. that the judiciary ought to leave change and development of law to the legislature. Conversely, those who stress the pervasiveness of such principles and minimize the coverage of practical problems by black-and-white rules will usually be found to be advancing the contradictory constitutional claim. In other words, what is presented[19] as a dispute about the "legal system" *qua* set of normative meaning-contents is in substance, typically, a dispute about the "legal system" *qua* constitutional order of institutions.

In short, even in well-developed legal orders served by a professional caste of lawyers, there are (and reasonably) quite a few opportunities of raising "intra-systemically," for example before a court of law, the question whether what would otherwise be an indubitable legal obligation is in truth not (*legally*) obligatory because it is unjust. On the other hand, since there is little point in meditating about the legal-obligation-imposing force of normative meaning-contents which are not treated as having legal effect in the principal legal institutions of a community (viz. the courts), it is idle to go on asking the question in this sense (the second of the four listed) after the highest court has ruled that in its judgment the disputed law is not unjust or, if unjust, is none the less law, legally obligatory, and judicially enforceable. It is not conducive to clear thought, or to any good practical purpose, to smudge the positivity of law by denying the legal obligatoriness *in the legal or intra-sytematic sense* of a rule recently affirmed as legally valid and obligatory by the highest institution

of the "legal system." (Austin's concern to make this point, in the "hanging me up" passage, was quite reasonable. What was unreasonable was his failure to acknowledge (a) the limited relevance of the point, and (b) the existence of questions which may be expressed in the same language but which are not determinately answerable intra-systemically).

The question in its *third* sense therefore arises in clear-cut form when one is confident that the legal institutions of one's community will not accept that the law in question is affected by the injustice one discerns in it. The question can be stated thus: Given that legal obligation presumptively entails a moral obligation, and that the legal system is by and large just, does a particular unjust law impose upon me any moral obligation to conform to it?

Notoriously, many people (let us call them "positivists") propose that this question should not be tackled in "jurisprudence" but should be left to "another discipline," no doubt "political philosophy" or "ethics." Now it is not a purpose of this book to conduct a polemic against anybody's conception of the limits of jurisprudence. Suffice it to mention some disadvantages of this proposal. Firstly, the proposed division is artificial to the extent that the arguments and counter-arguments which it is proposed to expel from jurisprudence are in fact (as we observed in the preceding paragraphs) to be found on the lips of lawyers in court and of judges giving judgment. Of course, the arguments about justice and obligation that find favor in the courts of a given community at a given time may be arguments that would be rejected by a sound and critical ethics or political philosophy. But they are part of the same realm of discourse. One will not understand either the "logic" or the "sociology" of one's own or anyone else's legal system unless one is aware (not merely in the abstract but in detail) how both the arguments in the courts, and the formulation of norms by "theoretical" jurists, are affected, indeed permeated, by the vocabulary, the syntax, and the principles of the "ethics" and "political philosophy" of that community, or of its

---

19 As in Dworkin, *Taking Rights Seriously* (London: 1977), chs. 2-4.

elite or professional caste. In turn, one will not well understand the ethics or political philosophy of that community or caste unless one has reflected on the *intrinsic* problems of "ethic" and "political philosophy," i.e., on the basic aspects of human well-being and the methodological requirements of practical reasonableness. Finally, one will not well understand these intrinsic problems and principles unless one is aware of the extent to which the language in which one formulates them for oneself, and the concepts which one "makes one's own" are themselves the symbols and concepts of a particular human civilization, a civilization which has worked itself out, as much as anywhere, in its law courts and law schools. This set of considerations affords the first reason why I would not myself accept the proposal to banish to some "other discipline" the question of the moral obligation of an unjust law.

The second reason, not unconnected with the first, is to be found in the argument, developed in my first chapter and not to be repeated here, that a jurisprudence which aspires to be more than the lexicography of a particular culture cannot solve its theoretical problems of definition or concept-formation unless it draws upon at least some of the considerations of values and principles of practical reasonableness which are the subject-matter of "ethics" (or "political philosophy"). Since there can be no sharp distinction between the "two disciplines" at that basic level, it is not clear why the distinction, if such there be, should be thought so very important at other levels.

The third reason is that (not surprisingly, in view of what I have just said) the programme of separating off from jurisprudence all questions or assumptions about the moral significance of law is not consistently carried through by those who propose it. Their works are replete with more or less undiscussed assumptions such as that the formal features of legal order contribute to the practical reasonableness of making, maintaining, and obeying law; that these formal features have some connection with the

concept of justice and that, conversely, lawyers are justified in thinking of certain principles of justice as principles of *legality*;[20] and that the fact that a stipulation is *legally* valid gives some reason, albeit not conclusive, for treating it as *morally* obligatory or *morally* permissible to act in accordance with it.[21] But none of these assumptions can be shown to be warranted, or could even be discussed, without transgressing the proposed boundary between jurisprudence and moral or political philosophy—in the way that I have systematically "transgressed" it in the preceding five chapters. Thus the state of the scholarly literature testifies, so to speak, to what a sound philosophy of practical reason establishes abstractly: the principles of practical reasonableness and their requirements form one unit of inquiry which can be subdivided into "moral," "political," and "jurisprudential" only for a pedagogical or expository convenience which risks falsifying the understanding of all three.

What, then, are we to say in reply to the question whether an unjust law creates a moral obligation *in the way* that just law *of itself* does? The right response begins by recalling that the stipulations of those in authority have presumptive obligatory force (in the eyes of the reasonable person thinking unrestrictedly about what to do) only because of what is needed if the common good is to be secured and realized.

All my analyses of authority and obligation can be summed up in the following theorem: the ruler has, very strictly speaking, no right to be obeyed (XI.7); but he has the authority to give directions and make laws that are morally obligatory and that he has the responsibility of enforcing. He has this authority for the sake of the common good (the needs of which can also, however, make authoritative the opinions—as in custom—or stipulations of men who have no authority). Therefore, if he uses his authority to make stipulations against the com-

---

20 See Hart, *Concept of Law*, pp. 156-57, 202.
21 See ibid., pp. 206-07.

mon good, or against any of the basic principles of practical reasonableness, those stipulations altogether lack the authority they would otherwise have *by virtue of being his*. More precisely, stipulations made for partisan advantage, or (without emergency justification) in excess of legally defined authority, or imposing inequitable burdens on their subjects, or directing the doing of things that should never be done, simply fail, of themselves, to create any moral obligation whatever.

This conclusion should be read with precision. Firstly, it should not be concluded that an enactment which itself is for the common good and compatible with justice is deprived of its moral authority by the fact that the act of enacting it was rendered unjust by the partisan motives of its author. Just as we should not be deflected from adjudging the act of enactment unjust by the fact that improper motivation is not, in a given system, ground for judicial review, so we should not use the availability of judicial review for that ground, in certain other systems of law, as a sufficient basis for concluding that a private citizen (to whom is not entrusted the duty of disciplining wayward officials or institutions) is entitled to treat the improper motives of the authors of a just law as exempting him from his moral duty of compliance. Secondly, it should not be concluded that the distributive injustice of a law exempts from its moral obligation those who are *not* unjustly burdened by it.

Understood with those precisions, my response to the question in its third sense corresponds to the classical position: viz. that for the purpose of assessing one's legal obligations in the moral sense, one is entitled to discount laws that are "unjust" in any of the ways mentioned. Such laws lack the moral authority that in other cases comes simply from their origin, "pedigree," or formal source. In this way, then, *lex injusta non est lex* and *virtutem obligandi non habet*,[22] whether or not it is "legally valid" and

"legally obligatory" in the restricted sense that it (i) emanates from a legally authorized source, (ii) will in fact be enforced by courts and/or other officials, and/or (iii) is commonly spoken of as a law like other laws.

But at the same time I must add that the last-mentioned facts, on which the lawyer *qua* lawyer (normally but, as I have noted, not exclusively) may reasonably concentrate, are not irrelevant to the moralist, the reasonable man with his unrestricted perspective.

At this point there emerges our question in the *fourth* of the senses I listed at the beginning of this section. It may be the case, for example, that if I am *seen* by fellow citizens to be disobeying or disregarding this "law," the effectiveness of other laws, and/or the general respect of citizens for the authority of a generally desirable ruler or constitution, will probably be weakened, with probable bad consequences for the common good. Does not this collateral fact create a moral obligation? The obligation is to comply with the law, but it should not be treated as an instance of what I have called "legal obligation in the moral sense." For it is not based on the good of *being* law-abiding, but only on the desirability of not rendering ineffective the just parts of the legal system. Hence it will not require compliance with

22 Aquinas, *S.T.* I-II. q.96, a. 6c; he is referring back to the discussion in a. 4, which (having quoted Augustine's remark (see XII.4, below) about unjust laws not seeming to be law) concludes: "So such [unjust] laws do not oblige in the forum of conscience (except perhaps where the giving of a corrupting example [*scandalum*] or the occasioning of civil disorder [*turbationem*] are to be avoided—for to avoid these, a man ought to yield his right). He adds that the last-mentioned "exceptional" source or form of obligation to obey the law does not obtain where the injustice of the law is that it promotes something which ought never to be done (forbidden by divine law). Later he speaks similarly of unjust judgments of courts (for "the sentence of the judge is like a particular law for a particular case": II-II, q. 67, a. 1c): e.g., II-II, q. 69, a. 4c, mentioning again *scandalum* and *turbatio*. See also II-II, q. 70, a. 1 ad 2 (the obligation *de jure naturali* to keep a secret may prevail over human law compelling testimony).

unjust laws according to their tenor or "legislative intent," but only such degree of compliance as is necessary to avoid bringing "the law" (as a whole) "into contempt." This degree of compliance will vary according to time, place, and circumstance; in some limiting cases (e.g., of judges or other officials administering the law) the morally required degree of compliance may amount to full or virtually full compliance, just *as if* the law in question had been a just enactment.

So, if an unjust stipulation is, in fact, homogeneous with other laws in its formal source, in its reception by courts and officials, and in its common acceptance, the good citizen may (not always) be morally required to conform to that stipulation to the extent necessary to avoid weakening "the law," the legal system (of rules, institutions, and dispositions) as a whole. The ruler still has the responsibility of repealing rather than enforcing his unjust law, and in this sense has no right that it should be conformed to. But the citizen, or official, may meanwhile have the diminished, collateral, and in an important sense extra-legal, obligation to obey it.

The foregoing paragraphs oversimplify the problems created for the conscience of reasonable citizens by unreasonableness in lawmaking. They pass over the problems of identifying inequity in distribution of burdens, or excessive or wrongly motivated exercise of authority. They pass over the dilemmas faced by conscientious officials charged with the administration of unjust laws. They pass over all questions about the point at which it may be for the common good to replace a persistently unjust lawmaker, by means that are prohibited by laws of a type normally justified both in their enactment and in their application. They pass over the question whether, notwithstanding the normal impropriety of bringing just laws into contempt, there may be circumstances in which it is justified to use one's public disobedience, whether to an unjust law itself or to a law itself quite just, as an instrument for effecting reform of unjust laws. And they pass over the

question whether, in the aftermath of an unjust regime, the responsibility for declaring its unjust laws unjust and for annulling and undoing their legal and other effects should be undertaken by *courts* (on the basis that a court of justice-according-to-law ought not to be required to attribute legal effect to radically unjust laws), or by retrospective *legislation* (on the basis that the change from one legal regime to the other ought to be explicit).

Much can be said on such questions, but little that is not highly contingent upon social, political, and cultural variables. It is universally true that one has an absolute (liberty-) right not to perform acts which anyone has an absolute (claim-) right that one should not perform (VIII.7). But beyond this, one should not expect generally usable but precise guides for action in circumstances where the normally authoritative sources of precise guidance have partially broken down.

• • •

Notes I

Notes I.1

Description of human institutions and practices requires identification of their point ... See Max Weber, *Theory of Social and Economic Organization* (ed. T. Parsons, New York and London:1947), pp. 88-126; On Law, pp. 1-10; Alfred Schütz, "Concept and Theory Formation in the Social Sciences" (1954) 5 *J. of Philosophy* reprinted in his *Collected Papers*, vol. I (ed. M. Natanson, The Hague: 1967), 48 at pp. 58-59; Eric Voegelin, *The New Science of Politics* (Chicago and London: 1952), pp. 27-29.

Bentham on definition of law ... See also Bentham, *Collected Works* (ed. J. Bowring, Edinburgh: 1863), vol. IV, p.483; and excursus to XI.8 (notes), below.

Kelsen's technique of definition ... See also Hans Kelsen, *Pure Theory of Law* (Berkeley and Los Angeles: 1967), pp. 30-31.

Description of social institutions, such as law, requires identification of their point or function(s) ... See also J. Raz, "On the Functions of the Law," in *Oxford Essays II*, pp. 278-304, at 278; *Legal System*, p. 145.

Raz on the criterion of law ... Raz is clear that any theorist seeking to describe law must decide between different theoretical concepts, and that "the explicit formulation of meta-theoretical criteria is a condition for a rational and reasoned comparison of theories": Raz, *Legal System*, p. 146. Central to his own account of meta-theoretical criteria is his decision that legal theory should explicate "common sense and professional opinion": p.201. In *Legal System*, he offers a "jurisprudential criterion" (p.200): viz. that "a momentary legal system contains all, and only all, the laws recognized by a primary law-applying organ which it institutes" (p. 192). He underlines that this criterion "is concerned with the actual behaviour of primary organs, not with what they ought to do ... (p. 198). But in *Practical Reason* he criticizes those legal theorists "who concluded that the law consists of all the standards which the courts do apply. This ... confuses institutionalized systems with systems of absolute discretion" (p. 142). So his new criterion is: a legal system contains "only those norms which its primary organs are bound to obey" (p. 142: also p. 148). This shift in Raz's jurisprudential criterion for membership of a legal system is to be traced to his shift from a concern to reproduce the rather undifferentiated "ordinary man's" point of view to a concern to reproduce the "legal point of view, the view of one (paradigmatically a judge, or an "ideal law-abiding citizen") who believes that people are in some way *justified* in following the rules of the system: pp. 139, 143, 171.

Notes II
Notes II.1

History of theories of natural law, and of their influence ... An informative study (rather wider than its subtitle) is C.G. Haines, *The Revival of Natural Law: A study of the establishment and of the interpretation of limits on legislatures with special reference to the development of certain phases of American constitutional law* (Cambridge, Mass.: 1930).

Natural law has no history ... "But what about changes in human nature?" "What about the fact that man is a historical being?" "Does this thesis derive from a theory of eternal or a historical essences?" Well, the thesis in the text concerns the basic forms of human flourishing, and the basic requirements of practical reasonableness. So if someone wishes to propose that what, in Chapters III-IV, I identify as basic forms of human flourishing would not have been flourishing for human beings of some epoch, or that what, in Chapters V-VI, I identify as basic requirements of practical reasonableness would not have been applicable to such other human beings (because of some difference between their condition and ours), the onus is on him to show us these beings and those differences. I have read countless proclamations of the historicity, etc., of man, but no serious attempt to meet this challenge. Abstract discussions of the mutability or immutability of human nature are beside the point: the argument of this book does not rely, even implicitly, on the term "human nature."

Notes II.2

Natural law theory and legal validity ... Kelsen, Hart, and Raz, to validate their image of natural law theory could point to Blackstone, I *Comm.* 41: "... no human laws are of any validity, if contrary to this [sc. natural law]." But Blackstone simply does not mean what he there says; on the very next page, he is saying ".... no human laws should be suffered to contradict these [sc. the law of nature and the law of revelation] ... Nay, if any human law should allow or injoin us to commit it [sc. murder, demonstrably forbidden by the natural law], we are bound to transgress *that human law* ..." (emphasis added). The truth is that, though they are not negligible for an understanding of the *Commentaries* (see Finnis, "Blackstone's Theoretical Intentions" (1967) 12 *Nat. L.F.* 163), Blackstone's remarks in this Introduction to his work cannot be dignified with the title "a theory."

"Natural law" and the notion that statutes are merely declaratory ... The mistaken idea that mainstream natural law theories taught that just enactments must be merely declaratory of natural law (or: cannot be identified as enactments without some moral reasoning about their content) has engendered very serious misunderstandings of the history of Western (not least English) law and legal thought. Morris Arnold, "Statutes as Judgments: the Natural Law Theory of Parliamentary Activity in Medieval England" (1977) 126 *U. Pa. L. Rev.* 329, identifies and refutes the bad history, but not the bad jurisprudence underlying it.

Notes V

Notes V.1

Freedom of choice.... The notion of freedom of choice, as the matrix in which human responsibility for good is set, first becomes an explicit theme in Christian writings. It is given great prominence by Thomas Aquinas, who opens the part of his *Summa Theologiae* which deals with human action and morality by stating: "Man is made in the image of God, and this implies, as St. John of Damascus said, that man is intelligent and free in judgment and master of himself. So having considered both the exemplar of that image, namely God, and the things that pro-

ceed by divine power and the will of God, it remains for us now to consider the image itself, i.e., man, precisely insofar as he is the source of his own actions and has freedom of judgment and power over his own works and deeds": *S. T.* I-II, Prologue. For a vindication of the reality of freedom of choice, see J. Boyle, G. Grisez, and O. Tollefsen, *Free Choice: A Self-Referential Argument* (Notre Dame and London: 1976).

Ethics as the reflective account of practical reasonableness ... There is no clearly settled meaning of "ethics" in modern philosophical discussion. But there is substantial agreement that one can usefully distinguish between (i) descriptive empirical enquiries about people's moral judgments, (ii) "moral," "normative," or (practically) "critical" questions, for one's own judgment, about what is to be done, and (iii) "analytical," "meta-ethical" (theoretically) "critical" questions about the language and logic used in discourse of the two preceding kinds. Still, "meta-ethics" cannot well proceed without assuming that some "normative" judgments are more worthy of attention than others, while normative moral judgment cannot be made with full rationality without critical reflection on itself to clarify its terms and its logic. Hence there is no good reason to separate (ii) from (iii); the classical conjunction of the two, as "ethics" or "moral philosophy," was fully justified. For modern discussion, see e.g., R.M. Hare, "Ethics" in his *Essays on the Moral Concepts* (London: 1972), pp. 39-40; William K. Frankena, *Ethics* (2nd ed., Englewood Cliffs, New Jersey: 1973), pp. 4-5 (taking "the more traditional view" that "ethics" should rightly include both "meta-ethics" and "normative ethics").

"Moral principles" are conclusions from primary practical principles ... In Aquinas's view, most of the Ten Commandments are (a) moral principles, and (b) secondary principles of natural law, *conclusions* drawn from the primary principles by a rational elaboration which most men find easy but which can be perverted by passion and convention: *S. T.* I-II, q.

10, a. 3c and ad 1; a. 6c; a. 11c and ad 1; cf. also q. 94, a. 5c: a. 6c and ad 3; and see next note.

Elaboration of moral principles, and particular moral decisions, both require wisdom that is far from universal ... see, e.g., *S.T.* I-II, q. 100, aa. 1, 3, 11; this wisdom is *prudentia* (II-II, q. 47, a. 2c and ad 1; aa. 6, 15; and notes to II.3 above). On the folly of the many see I-II, q. 9, a. 5 ad 3; q. 14, a. 1 ad 3. On the corruption of practical reasonableness in various cultures and people(s), see I, q. 113, a. 1; I-II, q. 58, a. 5; q. 94, a. 4; q. 99, a. 2 and 2; and II.3 above, and p. 225 n. 28 below.

"The mean" ... Aristotle's account is circular: right action is action according to right principle (or right reason) (*Nic. Eth.* II, 2: 1103b31-32); the criterion of right principle is the mean between the vices of excess and deficiency (*Nic. Eth.* II, 2: 1104a12-27; II,6: 1106a25-1107a8); but the mean is itself determined by reference to the practical wisdom of the *phronimos* [as to whom see the next note, below] and (which comes to the same thing) to the right principle (*Nic. Eth.* II, 6: 1107a1; VI, 1: 1133b20 . The importance of this idea of the mean in Aristotle's ethics is often exaggerated.

The "*phronimos*" in Aristotle ... He is the man who has *phronesis,* practical wisdom, full reasonableness (in the Latin writings, *prudentia*). He *is* the norm of action: *Nic. Eth.* II, 6: 1107a1: VI, 11: 1143b15. "Men like Pericles are considered to be phronimoi because they have the faculty of discerning what things are good for themselves and for mankind": *Nic. Eth.* VI, 5: 1140b8-10. *Phronesis* is "a truth-attaining rational quality, concerned with action in relation to things that are good and bad for human beings": *Nic. Eth.* VI, 5: 1140b6-8.

Aquinas's notion of "prudentia" ... For Aquinas, the virtue of *prudentia* is what enables one to reason well towards choice of commitments, projects, and actions, to apply the most general practical principles concretely, to choose rightly, to find the right mean, to be virtuous, to be a good man: *S.T.* II-II, q. 47, aa. 1—7: notes to II.3 above.

The "spoudaios" in Aristotle ... The term is often translated "good man" or "virtuous man." But a richer translation is "mature man" (by contrast with the young and inexperienced who can scarcely, if at all, do ethics: *Nic. Eth.* I, 3: 1095a3). He it is who judges practical affairs correctly, and he it is "who is the standard and measure [*kanon kai metron*, in Latin *regula et mensura*: Aquinas will take these terms into the heart of his definition of lex, law: *S.T.* I-II, q. 90, a. 1c] of what is noble [or upright: *kalon*] and pleasant": *Nic. Eth.* III, 5: 1113a32. What the *spoudaios* does is done well and properly: I.7: 1098a15. " Those things are actually valuable and pleasant which appear so to the *spoudaios*": X, 6: 1176b26. So the central case of friendship is the friendship of *spoudaioi*, who can reasonably find each other lovable simply as such (IX, 9: 1170a13-15; cf. IX, 4: 1166a13) and the central case of the polis is the *spoudaia polis* (*Pol.* VII, 12: 1332a33). See 1.4 above XII. 4 below.

Aristotle's notion of "eudaimonia" ... See John M. Cooper, *Reason and Human Good in Aristotle* (Cambridge, Mass., and London: 1975), and note to V.2, below, on "rational plans of life."

"Physis" and "natura" as fullness of being ... See Aristotle, *Meta.* XII, 3: 1070a12; V.4: 1015a14-15.

Morality, for Aquinas, is fullness of reasonableness, goodness, and human nature ... See especially *S.T.* I-II, q. 18, a. 1c; q. 71, a. 2.

The modern notion(s) of morality ... "Morality" and cognate words have connotations and overtones that no single word (or standard set of words)" has either in Plato and Aristotle's Greek or in Aquinas's Latin (though for examples of a use similar to the modern, see *S.T.* I-II, q. 18; q. 99, a. 2; q. 100). A useful description of aspects of the modern concept is Hart, *Concept of Law*, pp. 163-76.

The basic requirements of practical reasonableness ... The differentiation and analysis of these requirements is largely the work of Germain Grisez, and marks a major advance in the philosophical analysis of natural law. He calls these guidelines "modes of obligation" ("Methods of Ethical Inquiry" (1967) 41 *Proc. Amer. Cath. Philosophical Ass.* 160) or "modes of responsibility" *Beyond the New Morality: The Responsibilities of Freedom*, Notre Dame and London, 1974, pp.108-36, 213). His list numbers eight, rather than nine, and differs in some details.

Notes V.2

Rational plans of life ... Besides Rawls, *Theory of Justice*, pp. 408-23, see Charles Fried, *An Anatomy of Values: Problems of Personal and Social Choice* (Cambridge. Mass.: 1970), pp. 97-101 (the "life plan"). Like Grisez, both Rawls and Fried are drawing on Josiah Royce, *The Philosophy of Loyalty* (New York: 1908), who argued, at p. 168. that "a person, an individual self, may be defined as a human life lived according to a plan" (a definition which makes its point by the paradox of metonymy). The term "plan" has the serious drawback that it suggests, too much, that participation in human fullness and reasonableness is just like pursuit of a definite objective, and that commitments basic values "for good" (i.e., with a view to a lifetime, or "indefinitely")" are just like settling on particular concrete projects and taking efficient steps to carry them out. Nevertheless, the idea of a plan of life expresses in modern terms the rational requirement (viz. of an over-all *unity* and harmony of purpose, of an *integration* of commitments, projects, actions, habits, feelings) that the ancients preferred to express in terms of a unity of *end*. This notion ("end") has much the same drawbacks as its modern counterpart, "plan"; hence the constant temptation to treat what is really an "inclusive end" as if it were a "dominant end," a temptation which not only Aristotle's interpreters (often) but also Aris-

totle himself (occasionally) find hard to resist. See J.L. Ackrill, "Aristotle on *Eudaimonia*" (1975) 60 *Proc. Brit. Acad.* 339, and notes to III.3, above; and further, below, notes to V.7, concerning "dominant end" theories. In any event, Cooper, *Reason and Human Good in Aristotle*, pp. 96-97, 121-25, and *passim*, has suggested that in Aristotle *eudaimonia* can be regarded as the effective possession-in-action of a rational over-all plan of life. If the matter were further investigated I think it would emerge that Aristotle's implicit conception of *eudaimonia* is of that condition in which a man is (or tends to be: see next note) when he satisfies-in-action not merely this first requirement of practical reasonableness but all nine requirements traced in this chapter.

Unforseeable contingencies in human life ... The subjection of human reasonableness and fulfilment to chance and hazard is emphasized by Aristotle: see P. Aubenque, *La Prudence chez Aristotle* (Paris: 1963), pp. 64-91. Christian, like Stoic, reflection, introduced the notion of providence rejected by Aristotle (but not by Plato: see *Laws* X, 903-04): human affairs are subject to divine *prudentia*, which makes everything contribute to the good of the universe: Aquinas, *S.T.* I, q. 22, aa. 1, 2; I-II, q. 19, a. loc; XIII.3 below. But: that "we *do not know* what God concretely [or in particular] wills" remains a central tenet of Aquinas's theory of natural law: I-II, q. 19, a. 10 ad 1; q. 91, a. 3 ad 1; XIII.5 below; so we have to cling to the general principles of reason, the general forms of good, the general structure of our nature: I-II, q. 19, a. 10 ad 1 and ad 2. Moreover, on the view of Aquinas (unlike both Aristotle and the Stoics), the good of the universe includes and is in part realized by the good of creatures "made in God's image," i.e., creatures whose good includes and is realized by their own intelligent creativity and free self-determination: I-II, prol. (quoted in notes to V.1, above). Divine providence, on this view, works itself out through, *inter alia*, human choices that are really free and self-constituting (not merely blind).

Seeing one's life from the imagined standpoint of one's death ... So Plato's Socrates teaches that philosophy (which for him is always contemplatively practical); is the practice of dying: *Phaedo* 64a.

Notes V.3

Wealth, reputation, "opportunity" (power) , and pleasure as secondary forms of good ... See Aristotle, *Nic. Eth.* 1, 5; X, 1-3; Aquinas, *S.T.* I-II, q. 2. aa. 1-6; notes to IV.3 above. Cf. the notes on Rawls's "primary goods," below.

Rawls's "thin theory" of good ... Good, in this "thin" sense, is what it is rational for any man to want *whatever else* his preferences, wants, aims, etc. See *Theory of Justice*, pp. 396-407, 433-34.

Rawls's "primary goods" ... These are the goods which "it is rational to want ... whatever else is wanted, since they are in general necessary for the framing and the execution of a rational plan of life," and are "liberty and opportunity, income and wealth, and above all self-respect": *Theory of Justice*, p.433: also 253, 260, 328. Rawls will not permit a theorist of justice to treat real primary goods (in our sense), such as truth, art, culture, religion, or friendship, as having an *intrinsic* value or as being *objective* final ends of human life (see ibid., pp.419, 527): to do so would be out of line with his "rejection of the principle of perfection and the acceptance of democracy in the assessment of one another's excellences": ibid., p.527.

Rawls on intrinsic goods, excellences, and perfections ... Rawls expressly does *not* contend that "criteria of excellence lack a rational basis from the standpoint of every day life," and he grants that "the freedom and well-being of individuals, when measured by the excellence of their activities and works, is vastly different in value" and that "comparisons of intrinsic value can obviously be made": *Theory of Justice*, pp. 328, 329. But he will not allow such differentiations (e.g., of the intrinsic value of [having] true beliefs

and the intrinsic disvalue of [having] false beliefs) to enter at all into the rational determination of the basic principles of justice: see ibid., pp. 327-32.

Notes V.4

The rationality of priority of concern for one's own good ... On the proper priority of self-love—a principle that must be understood with precision—see *Nic. Eth.* IX, 4:1166a1-1166b29;" *S.T.* II-II, q. 26, aa. 3-5; VI.l, VI.4, and XIII.5, below.

"Passing by on the other side" ... See Luke 10:32. On the "Good Samaritan" principle in modern societies, see James Ratcliffe (ed.), *The Good Samaritan and the Law* (New York: 1966).

The Golden Rule ... See Tobit 4:16; Matthew 7:12; Luke 6:31. Kelsen's contention (*What is Justice?* Berkeley: 1957, pp. 16-18) that the Golden Rule is empty overlooks the fact that it is only one amongst (say) nine basic requirements of practical reason, which itself is only one amongst (say) seven basic practical principles. In fact, the Golden Rule is a potent solvent and determinant in moral matters.

The heuristic device of the "ideal observer" ... Plato's formulation is implicit, but central to his thought: both the Myth of the Cave (*Rep.* VII: 514a-521b) and the image of the divine puppet-master whose tug we are to follow (*Laws*, VII: 804b; see XIII.5, below) are to be understood as insisting on the need to raise one's mind's eye to this viewpoint in judging human affairs. For the modern discussion, initiated by David Hume and elaborated by Adam Smith see e.g., D.D. Raphael, "The Impartial Spectator" (1972) 58 *Proc. Brit. Acad.* 335.

"The social contract" as a heuristic device for excluding bias ... Rawls is particularly clear what his notion of the Original Position (which includes a requirement that the parties in it agree together, i.e., "contract," on principles of justice) is a device for excluding bias, for guaranteeing objectivity, and for seeing the whole human situation *sub specie aeternitatis*: see especially the last page of *Theory of Justice*, p. 587; also p. 516.

Notes V.5

The requirement of reasonable detachment ... Epictetus "version of Stoicism" (c.AD 100) elevates this requirement to a dominant position: see especially Arrian's *Encheiridion of Epictetus, passim*. For balance, see Josiah Royce, *The Philosophy of Loyalty* (New York: 1908), especially Lecture V, sec.1.

The requirement of "commitment" ... See Gabriel Marcel (much influenced by Royce), e.g., *Homo Viator* (London: 1951), pp. 125-34, 155-56.

Notes V.6

The rational limitations of cost-benefit analysis ... See E.J. Mishan, *Cost-Benefit Analysis: An Introduction* (London: 1971), pp. 108, 307-21.

Problems of utilitarianism or consequentialism ... See D.H. Hodgson, *Consequences of Utiltiarianism* (Oxford: 1967), chs. II-III; Dan W. Brock, "Recent Work in Utilitarianism" (1973) 10 *Amer. Philosophical Q.* 245; Germain Grisez, "Against Consequentialism" (1978). 23 *Am. J. Juris.* 21. Notice that what I describe as irrational is consequentialism as a general method in ethics i.e., in open-ended practical reasoning), and *not* what Neil MacCormick, *Legal Reasoning and Legal Theory* (Oxford: 1978), pp. 10-56 and ch.VI. calls "consequentialist" reasoning by judges, viz. (to summarize his valuable analysis) (i) examining the *types* of decision which would "have to be given" in other cases if a certain decision is given in the case before them, and (ii) asking about the acceptability or unacceptability of such "consequences" of the proposed decision in that case. As MacCormick notes (ibid., p. 105), "there is ... no

reason to assume that [this mode of argument] involves evaluation in terms of a single scale...." In fact, the evaluation will be by reference to the established commitments of a society.

Consequentialism: irrational and arbitrary, or merely "unworkable"? ... G.J. Warnock, *The Object of Morality* (London: 1971), pp. 28-30, recites some objections to utilitarianism, not explicitly distinguishing "practical" difficulties of unworkability from problems that go to the very sense (intelligibility) of the utilitarian method. He remarks that objections "of this sort are not really, I think, all that impressive." For moral problems *are* difficult, "And as to the difficulty in comparison and computation of "happinesses," it is at any rate clear that such comparisons do somehow get made ..." Warnock thus misses the point; some approximate commensuration of some goods is, of course, possible and commonplace within a "moral" framework established by commitments, relationships, etc., which have been adopted reasonably-in-terms-of-the-nine-requirements-of-practical-reasonableness: just as some more precise commensuration of costs with benefits is possible in relation to some concrete operational goal. The trouble with utilitarianism is that it offers to replace the nine criteria of practical reasonableness with one that is in truth rationally applicable only in a subordinate, contained element of practical thinking: the recommendation could be called a sort of category mistake.

Critique of "dominant end" theories of ethics ... See Rawls, *Theory of Justice*, pp. 548-60, esp. 554; see also Cooper, *Reason and Human Good in Aristotle,* pp. 94-100.

"Every desire has an equal claim to satisfaction" ... See William James, *The Will to Believe* (New York: 1897), pp. 195 ff.; Bertrand Russell, *Human Society in Ethics and Politics* (London: 1954), pp. 56-59, 84. For the importation of this view into jurisprudence by Roscoe Pound, see VII.6, below. In a muted form this view, at least as a methodological postulate, lies at the root of Rawls's *Theory of Justice*. In a more or less straightforward way it underpins most modern versions of utilitarianism and indeed most modern ethics. John Stuart Mill rebelled against Jeremy Bentham's version of it: *Utilitarianism* (1863), ch. 1. But the utilitarian has no choice but to adopt either a strict dominant end theory or a strict equality of desires (or preferences) theory. Hence Mill's utilitarian criterion is incoherent, as is shown e.g., by Anthony Quinton, *Utilitarian Ethics* (London: 1973), pp. 39-47.

Maximization of good (pleasure) or minimization of evil (pain)? ... See the vigorous exploration of the problem by Cicero, *De Finibus*, II, 6-25, esp. 17. For critique of the view that pain and pleasure are commensurable, see Robinson A. Grover, "The Ranking Assumption" (1974) 4 *Theory and Decision* 277-99.

"Greatest good of the greatest number" ... For the logical problems caused by the double superlative, see P.T. Geach, *The Virtues* (Cambridge: 1977), pp. 91-94.

Notes V.7

The seventh requirement ... This is clearly and variously formulated in Germain Grisez's works, e.g., (with R. Shaw), *Beyond the New Morality*, ch. 13; *Contraception and the Natural Law* (Milwaukee: 1964) , pp. 68-71, 110-14: *Abortion: the Myths, the Realities, and the Arguments* (New York: 1970), pp. 318-19. For the classic formulation, see Romans 3:8.

"Intention" and the characterization of action ... See Germain Grisez, "Toward a Consistent Natural-Law Ethics of Killing" (1970) 15 *Am. J. Juris.* 64; J.M. Finnis, "The Rights and Wrongs of Abortion: A Reply to Judith Thomson" (1973) 2 *Phil. Pub. Aff.* 117-45 (reprinted in, e.g., Dworkin, *Philosophy of Law*, Oxford: 1977); H.L.A. Hart, *Punishment and Responsibility* (Oxford: 1968), ch. 5; G.E.M. Anscombe, "War and Murder" in W. Stein (ed.), *Nuclear Weapons and Christian Conscience* (London: 1961), pp 57-59; Charles Fried, "Right and Wrong—Preliminary Considerations" (1976) 5 *J. Legal Studies* 165-200.

The "doctrine" of "double-effect" ... See, e.g., J.T. Mangan, "An Historical Account of the Principle of the Double Effect" (1949) 10 *Theological Studies* 40-61.

"Natural Law" in Roman Catholic pronouncements of strict negative principles ... A recent example is Vatican Council II's declaration that it is a "principle of universal natural law" that "every act of war which tends indiscriminately to the destruction of entire cities or extensive areas along with their population is a crime": Pastoral Constitution *Gaudium et Spes* (1965) 79, 80. As to some of the ecclesiastically recognized implications of the seventh requirement, briefly listed in the text, see Finnis, "Natural Law—and Unnatural Acts" (1970) 11 *Heythrop J.* 365; "The Rights and Wrongs of Abortion: A Reply to Judith Thomson" (1973) 2 *Phil. Pub. Aff.* 117-45.

Notes V.9

Conscience (practical reasonableness) and the obligation to follow it ... See Eric D'Arcy, *Conscience and its Right to Freedom* (London: 1961), pp. 76-125. Aquinas's discussion is clear: *S.T.* I-II, q. 19, a. 5. It scarcely needs to be added that (i) if my conscience is erroneous, what I do will be unreasonable, and (ii) if my conscience is erroneous because of my negligence and indifference in forming it, in doing what I do I will be acting culpably (notwithstanding that I am required by the ninth requirement of practical reasonableness to do it), see *S.T.* I-II, q. 19, a. 6; and (iii) that if I am aware that I have formed my practical judgment inadequately it will be reasonable of me to bow to contrary advice or instructions or norms.

Of course, it by no means follows (as D'Arcy's own argument too easily assumed) that if, because of this ninth requirement, I have an obligation to Φ others have no liberty to prevent me from doing Φ, or to punish me from doing Φ; indeed, often enough they have not only the liberty but also an obligation to do so: see X.1, below.

Notes XII

Notes XII.2

Types of Injustice laws.... See Aquinas, *S.T.* I-II, q. 96, a. 4c; St. German, *Doctor and Student*, First Dial., c. 4; Suarez, *De Legibus*, Book I, c. 9, paras. 12-16.

Notes XII.3

Consequences of injustice of laws ... See Suarez, *De Legibus*, Book I. c. 9. paras. 11-12, 20.

Unjust legislative motives may be disregarded if the enactment itself is reasonable ... See *De Legibus*, loc. cit.; *Doctor and Student*, I, c.26.

Collateral moral obligation to obey the law ... See *S.T.* I-II, q. 96. a. 4. Such an obligation may arise from quite different sorts of reasons; e.g., from one's duty to one's family to avoid the punishment that would come from breaking the law.

Undoing the effects of unjust laws ... The celebrated debate between Hart and Fuller on this point comes down to a question of constitutional niceties, of purely symbolic implications, and of convenience in settling details: cf. (1958) 71 *Harv. L. Rev.* at pp. 618-21 (Hart) and 655 (Fuller); Fuller, *Morality of Law.* Appendix.

◆ ◆ ◆ ◆ ◆

STUDY QUESTIONS

1. Is practical reason of the type discussed by Aquinas and Finnis relative to particular times, places, or cultures?

2. How persuasive is Finnis's account of situations in which legal obligations are properly rejected and disobeyed? Can Finnis's account be made more precise or thorough?

3. What implications does natural law theory have for tolerance of diverse ways of life?

4. How persuasive is Finnis's argument that descriptive jurisprudence is not useful unless it proceeds with the goals of prescription or reform in mind?

5. Are "basic goods" of the kind discussed by Finnis really universal for all humans, or do these goods reflect a male-centred or other kind of elite view of our lives and needs?

◆ ◆ ◆ ◆ ◆

FURTHER READINGS

American Journal of Jurisprudence

Aristotle, *Nicomachean Ethics*, trans. T. Irwin. Indianapolis: Hackett Publishing, 1985.

John Finnis, ed. *Natural Law* (2 vols.). Aldershot: Ashgate, 1991.

Lon L. Fuller, *The Morality of Law.* New Haven: Yale University Press, 1969.

Robert P. George, ed. *Natural Law Theory: Contemporary Essays.* Oxford: Oxford University Press, 1992.

Robert P. George, *In Defense of Natural Law.* Oxford: Clarendon Press, 1999.

Mark. C. Murphy, *Natural Law in Jurisprudence and Politics.* Cambridge: Cambridge University Press, 2006.

CHAPTER 2

Legal Positivism

INTRODUCTION

This chapter presents the work of writers who defend the idea called legal positivism. Most simply put, legal positivists argue that there is no necessary connection between law and morality. Our readings begin with the work of the Victorian-era lawyer and theorist John Austin (1790–1859). Austin trained and practiced briefly as a lawyer, but found his abilities lay in directions other than practice. Through the efforts of Utilitarian philosopher Jeremy Bentham and other prominent thinkers, Austin was the first person to hold the Chair in Jurisprudence and the Law of Nations at the University of London. There he gave the lectures leading to *The Province of Jurisprudence Determined*, in which he argued that we must distinguish "law as it is from law as it ought to be."[1]

This introduction will focus on the English legal philosopher H.L.A. Hart, the best-known modern defender of legal positivism. For many years his work was regarded as "the ruling theory of law," even by his critics.[2] Professor Hart was a successful lawyer before World War II (1939–45), and in 1948 he became Professor of Jurisprudence in Oxford University where he spent the remainder of his long career until his death in 1992. Professor Hart is most famous for his new defence of the central idea of legal positivism in his book *The Concept of Law*. The articles included in this chapter contain Austin's argument for legal positivism and Hart's proposed modifications.

This introduction also explores the first part of one of the many long-running debates in which Hart took part. In the articles in this chapter we shall see the beginning of the debate between Hart and R.M. Dworkin over the nature of law and judges' interpretation of it. This debate began in earnest with the publication of *The Concept of Law* in 1961, which seemed to offer the best account of law. Since then, however, Ronald Dworkin has offered widely accepted arguments against Hart's view, and positivism is no longer clearly the ruling theory of law. As the consequences of the Hart-Dworkin debate have been explored by legal theorists, new positivist theories are being developed by some of the authors listed in the "Further Readings" for this chapter.

1. Why Separate Law and Morality?

It is important to understand the social context of Hart's defence of legal positivism. Hart's appointment at Oxford came in 1948, in a world recovering from the physical destruction of war and the shock of discovering the extent of the Holocaust. At the Nuremberg Trials in Germany beginning in 1946, many Germans accused of horrible crimes against humanity offered the defence that they were only following orders and so could not be held responsible for their actions. Prosecutors, and eventually judges, op-

---

1   John Austin, *The Province of Jurisprudence Determined*.
2   Ronald Dworkin, *Taking Rights Seriously*. Preface, i.

posed this argument, and argued that certain orders require such terrible actions that those orders must be rejected and disobeyed. The judges at Nuremberg appeared to accept that there can only be obligation to obey laws which are morally justified. The judges accepted the argument that the so-called laws allowing and sometimes requiring certain horrible actions were in fact never genuine laws, therefore there never was a genuine obligation to obey. So holding persons responsible for war crimes was not simply imposing the will of the victor on the helpless loser. Rather, war crimes trials were justified because the judges simply applied the real law which existed all along. At the time of the Nuremberg Trials, this seemed to be the best and perhaps the only way to hold war criminals responsible for actions which were legally justified at the time they were committed.

In this context, Hart's defence of legal positivism was shocking and unusual. Why claim that law and morality have no necessary connection when it seems so completely clear that law and morality *must* be connected if justice is to be done? The simplest positivist answer to this question can be summarized in a single word: *clarity*. By recognizing that laws can be used for many different purposes, both good and bad, we gain a clearer picture of the possibilities and limits of law as a tool for guiding behaviour. Hart worried that if we deny that laws can be morally bad but still be laws, we ignore the fact that there are important similarities of function between all laws, morally good or bad. Our picture of law as it is may not present an attractive view of humans, but clarity about the nature of law requires that we include in our picture all relevant evidence, attractive or not. Clarity of this sort is valuable for more than its own sake: a clear understanding of the nature of law can be very useful to those who wish to reform law rationally and efficiently.

The importance of Hart's work comes from more than his defence of an unpopular yet important view. Hart's enduring importance lies in his new ideas for analysis of law. At the beginning of *The*

Concept of Law Hart uses a phrase which indicates the direction of his analysis, calling *The Concept of Law* an "essay in descriptive sociology."[3] The precise meaning of this phrase has puzzled Hart's admirers and his critics. However, it is possible to explain at least partially what Hart seems to mean by saying that his investigation of law is "descriptive" and in some sense "sociological." Throughout his legal philosophy, Hart supposes that description of a thing *adds* to our understanding of that thing. So when we are concerned with law, we describe laws and law-following as part of our development of a broader picture of law as a social phenomenon. It is important to note also that by using "description" Hart means to exclude assessing the value of a thing at the same time as we describe it. According to Hart, we can reduce unhelpful obscurity and vagueness in our understanding of a thing if we describe it first, and later evaluate it. This sense of description appears to be compatible with an understanding of sociology as a discipline concerned with *observation* of social phenomena. As we shall see in a moment, one of Hart's most important contributions to the philosophy of law is borrowed from a sociological understanding of what can be learned about the idea of law from observation of situations where what is said to be "law" exists.

2. The Idea of Rules

Hart borrows from sociology the idea of a "social rule." We are all familiar with some of the general characteristics of rules. We follow rules every day as we play sports, borrow things from friends, and wait our turn. One of Hart's special insights into law comes with his description of the way what is said to be "law" involves special types of social rules. According to Hart, law, where it is said to exist, is typically found in the form of a system made up of two types of rules. The first type, called "primary

---

3   H.L.A. Hart, *The Concept of Law*, Preface, i.

rules," make certain conduct non-optional. For example, we might devise a rule which says, "Club members who use club equipment *must* return it to the equipment shed." Here the use of the word "must" shows that the rule is non-optional. Primary rules are made, changed, and eliminated by use of "secondary rules." Let us work through an example. Suppose a new and slightly obnoxious member of our club protests that our rule is well-suited to the needs of people with the attention span of a young wombat, but not to the needs of a modern sports club. If our club's organization includes secondary rules, we may have a clear way of coping with the new member's protest. We point to a secondary rule of our club, which might say, "Any member who wishes to introduce, protest and change, or remove a club rule may do so at any club meeting attended by at least two thirds of the club's members." This secondary rule explains both what can be done to primary rules (introduction, change, elimination), and how to do it.

The idea of primary and secondary rules is at the core of Hart's understanding of law. However, the picture is not yet complete. Suppose the new member of the club hears our explanation of the secondary rules used to change the primary rules and says, "That's all very interesting, but irrelevant, since I've decided that the rule I dislike doesn't apply to me, so my problem is solved." This response to our claim that the new member is bound by some rule raises an interesting problem. How are we to determine with certainty what the law is in some situation, and who is subject to the law? The answer to this question is the idea of a "rule of recognition." The rule of recognition shows the characteristics of valid rules of the system—the rules "recognized" by judges and other officials as the rules of the system. The rule of recognition is sometimes called the "master rule" to mark its special status as the most important of the secondary rules. A rule of recognition can be a written document, such as a constitution, or perhaps a list of all valid rules in a particular legal system. It is

best, however, to see the rule of recognition as something *shown* by the officials of the system. By using and applying certain rules to themselves and others, officials such as judges show everyone in the system which rules are regarded as valid by the officials.

Suppose the new member of our club hears all of this and rejects our patient and reasonable explanation of how we know that certain rules of the club apply to him. Suppose he quickly kicks each of us in the shins and races off with club equipment while we clutch our shins in agony and wonder why he has behaved so oddly. We soon realize that there is a fundamental difference between the new member of the club and the rest of us. We *accept* the rules of the club while he does not. Hart has an interesting and controversial way of explaining this difference. Those who accept the rules have what Hart calls the "internal point of view" to the rules. Those who do not accept the rules take the "external point of view." So how can we know that the new member of our club is properly said to take the external point of view to the club's rules?

Hart supposes that people who accept rules both physically obey those rules and use those rules as a basis for criticism and direction of social pressure against those who disobey the rules. Those with the internal point of view to the rules speak of them in a particular way, sometimes pointing to conduct as wrong without needing to refer explicitly to the rule because the rule is so widely known. Consider, for example, the well-known legal rule that vehicles must stop at red lights. Those who know and accept the rule might criticize its violation by saying, "Stop! The light is red!" Or, "You nitwit! That light was red! You ought to have stopped!" In each case, the rule is not stated because it is so well known, and the speaker refers implicitly to the rule. Yet even if the rule is not known to the person about to break it, if that person generally has the internal point of view to the rules, the mere mention of the rule typically gives the person a reason to act as the rule requires. Consider again the example of the rules of a club.

One member might say to another "You can't leave those there—they must be hung up properly, as the rules require." An ordinary response from another club member might be, "Sorry, I didn't realize that was the rule. I'll hang them up." Those who have the internal point of view take the existence of a rule as a good reason for acting in the way the rule requires. Often the specific identity of the rule is not at issue, although a club member might, after a reprimand, find a copy of the club rules to refresh his or her memory.

On the other hand, those with the external point of view typically speak quite differently about the rules. The shin-kicking new member of the club indicates by his actions that he does not accept the club's rules. We might find further evidence of his external point of view if we were to overhear him telling an acquaintance about the club and its rules: "The fools who are members of the club I joined have made a useless rule about the use of club equipment—but why should I care? I've taken what I want, and I'll return it if and when it suits me." The new member of the club shows us, in his speaking of club rules as something *others* hold, that he does not accept the rules of the club as binding on *him*. As members of a club, we do not have many options when we consider what we ought to do about the new member's rule-breaking. We may visit him or write a letter to demand the return of club equipment, or we might change the locks at the club and decide to terminate his membership. We may not, however, hire an assassin, or attack the outcast former club member with pointy garden tools.

3. Legal Obligation and Coercion

Here the analogy between a club and a legal system breaks down. Both involve rule-following, but only the legal system claims a *monopoly* on legitimate use of force. Hart's most important improvement over Austin comes with Hart's attempt to give a realistic understanding of the relationship between coercion and law. Austin argued that at the core of the idea of law we find orders backed by threats. As you will see in Hart's revised argument for legal positivism, Hart supposes that orders and threats are only *part* of an accurate description of what is said to be law and legal obligation. Legal obligations, according to Hart, are something more complex than "the gunman situation writ large." Hart explains the difference between legal obligation and the gunman situation in terms which may now sound odd to North Americans, and to many in Britain as well. Hart writes that there is a difference between the statement that someone "was obliged to do something and the assertion that he had an obligation to do it."[4] This way of using "obliged" is no longer common, but Hart's meaning is still clear enough. When a gunman places a loaded weapon at the base of your skull and murmurs orders in your ear, we do not suppose you have made a free choice when you obey the gunman's orders. We say, Hart observes, that the gunman has "obliged" you to do as he wishes. Note also that we do not usually hold persons accountable for what they have been coerced to do. We do, however, hold persons accountable for what they have an obligation to do. If you have an obligation, you may choose to act as the obligation requires or you may break that obligation. Either way, we hold you responsible for your actions as freely chosen, and praise or criticize you accordingly. To have an obligation is therefore not simply to follow orders backed by threats, but to be subject to a social situation in which a rule is generally accepted as providing a very strong reason for acting in a certain way. As Hart explains it, "Rules are conceived and spoken of as imposing obligations when the general demand for conformity is

---

4   Hart, "Law as the Union of Primary and Secondary Rules."

insistent and the social pressure brought to bear on those who deviate or threaten to deviate is great."[5]

Hart's new explanation of legal obligation captures the fact that we obey the law and *use* the law as a standard of behaviour even when the law poses no threat through giving us a reason to be afraid to disobey. We may each have different reasons for obeying the law, according to Hart, but typically at least some of the time those reasons do not include fear of coercion. Some of the time, we agree to some particular way of doing things as a matter of co-ordination for mutual gain, and no threats are needed to get us to do things that way. For example, a threat of coercion is not needed to convince people to drive on one side of the road rather than the other, since there are obvious mutual gains to be had (predictability and safety in driving) by agreeing to drive on one side. In this instance, a legal obligation to drive on the right (as in North America) is generally accepted for commonsensical reasons exclusive of fear of coercion.

Hart's positivist explanation of legal obligation fits neatly with the remainder of his descriptive, morally neutral account of law. Hart supposes that in the typical place where "law" and "legal obligation" are said to exist, there is an accepted system of primary and secondary rules, and a rule of recognition. Hart admits that many laws aim to achieve morally good purposes, but he insists that it is not *necessary* for laws to have morally good purposes. According to Hart, so long as the goal of the law is *thought* to be important, it does not matter to the law's status as a law whether the goal is morally good, bad, or indifferent. Hart recognizes that various societies in the world use law to promote very different visions of the best way to live.

4. *The Idea of Law, and the Idea of Adjudication*

So far we have examined Hart's answer to the question "What does it mean to say that "law" exists in some social situation?" Hart's answer, as we have seen, involves primary and secondary rules (including a rule of recognition), and acceptance of those rules. Yet this examination of law obviously does not answer all possible questions we might have about law. Again, Hart leaves for others, or at least for another day, the question of the ingredients of a truly just society in which citizens may find genuine happiness. As Hart's views have been presented so far, we are also left without any explanation of the importance of courts to the existence of law. We shall turn to that question now.

In the common law system shared by all nations which borrowed the bases of their legal systems from the English model, judges play an extremely important role in development of the law. The precedents set by judges guide the way lawyers, private citizens, and other judges interpret and use the law. Hart offers an interesting explanation of the way judges interpret law. It is a matter of debate whether this explanation is part of or separate from his broader positivist account of law, yet regardless of this debate, it is important to understand Hart's explanation of judges' interpretation of law in order to understand why Dworkin disagrees with that explanation.

According to Hart's view, much of the time judges interpret and apply laws whose meaning is reasonably clear. In what might be called a "standard" instance of the way a judge reaches a decision, roughly the following steps are taken: a judge examines the text of the legal rule which governs the dispute the judge must resolve, the judge considers the facts of the case, and the judge applies the legal rule found in the law to reach a decision. In this standard instance of a judge's use of the legal rule, the facts of the case at hand fall within the accepted

---

5   Ibid.

"core" meaning of the legal rule. Hart uses the example of a legal rule which says, "No vehicles shall be allowed in public parks." If someone is charged with illegally driving a car through the park, it is clear that "car" falls within the core meaning of "vehicle" and so the driver of the car is rightly held responsible for breach of his or her legal obligation. Trouble arrives when there is no clear correspondence between a legal rule and the facts. Consider, for example, a person using a wheelchair in a park. Is this a vehicle? Is a motorized wheelchair a vehicle? It is nearly impossible for law-makers to anticipate every possible application of the law they write, so they frequently use terms such as "vehicle" which have a reasonably certain core meaning. Yet in difficult cases, the meaning of terms such as "vehicle" is not clear. Hart calls these difficult cases "problems of the penumbra," and he distinguishes between "core" and "penumbral" meanings of legal terms and rules. The penumbra refers to the fuzzy edges of the meaning of a legal term or rule, where argument is needed to demonstrate that it is appropriate to interpret the term or rule in a particular way. Much of the dispute between Hart and Dworkin centres on the type of argument used to fill out the penumbral meaning of legal terms. Hart and Dworkin agree that where the accepted core meaning of a legal term or rule ends, judicial discretion begins. But what is "discretion"?

According to Hart, judges use discretion when they go outside the accepted meaning of legal terms to reach an interpretation of law with which a dispute can be resolved. In a discretionary ruling, a judge examines the text of the law which governs the dispute the judge must resolve, the judge examines the facts of the case, and the judge finds that the law as it stands does not clearly apply to the facts of the case. The judge exercises discretion by interpreting the law in a way which gives a new, or extended meaning to the law. It is tempting to suppose that judges simply reach into their private views, or simply act as they feel is right when they

expand the meaning of a legal rule and flesh out its unclear penumbra. Yet, according to Hart, this is not what, as a matter of fact, usually occurs. Rather, judges typically examine the underlying purpose of the unclear legal rule, examine its language, and expand its meaning in a way which serves the underlying purpose of the law. As Hart puts it, "We can say laws are incurably incomplete and we must decide penumbral cases rationally by reference to social aims."[6] It is again important to see the positivist element in this explanation of what judges do. As Hart describes judges' practice, judges typically interpret the law in a morally neutral way, and do not attempt to inject law with a moral purpose. Hart writes, "The point here is that intelligent decisions ... are not necessarily identical with decisions defensible on moral grounds. We may say of a decision: "Yes, that is right; that is as it ought to be," and we may mean only that some accepted purpose or policy has been thereby advanced; we may not mean to endorse the moral propriety of the policy or the decision."[7] According to Hart, there is an important difference between saying that a discretionary decision is appropriate in light of general social policy, and saying that a discretionary decision extends the meaning of some legal rule in a morally good way. Hart admits that discretionary decisions often do advance morally justifiable policies, but insists, as a positivist, that a decision need not do so.

As you will see in Chapter 3 in the introduction to the work of R.M. Dworkin, Professor Dworkin disagrees strongly with Professor Hart's account of discretion. According to Dworkin, judges do in fact use moral reasoning in discretionary decisions, and, further, they are right to do so. While reading this debate between Hart and Dworkin, bear in mind that their debate is not a "winner takes all" matter. If

---

6   Hart, "Positivism and the Separation of Law and Morals."

7   Ibid.

the Legal Realists discussed in Chapter 4, or Critical Race Theory writers of Chapter 5 are right about law, it may be that both Hart and Dworkin offer misleading views of law.

◆ ◆ ◆ ◆ ◆

JOHN AUSTIN

from *The Province of Jurisprudence Determined*

Lecture I

The matter of jurisprudence is positive law: law, simply and strictly so called: or law set by political superiors to political inferiors. But positive law (or law, simply and strictly so called) is often confounded with objects to which it is related by *resemblance*, and with objects to which it is related in the way of *analogy*: with objects which are *also* signified, *properly* and *improperly*, by the large and vague expression *law*. To obviate the difficulties springing from that confusion, I begin my projected Course with determining the province of jurisprudence, or with distinguishing the matter of jurisprudence from those various related objects: trying to define the subject of which I intend to treat, before I endeavour to analyse its numerous and complicated parts.

[A law, in the most general and comprehensive acceptation in which the term, in its literal meaning, is employed, may be said to be a rule laid down for the guidance of an intelligent being by an intelligent being having power over him. Under this definition are included, and without impropriety, several species. It is necessary to define accurately the line of demarcation which separates these species from one another, as much mistiness and intricacy has been infused into the science of jurisprudence by their being confounded or not clearly distinguished. In

the comprehensive sense above indicated, or in the largest meaning which it has, without extension by metaphor or analogy,]* the term *law* embraces the following objects:—Laws set by God to his human creatures, and laws set by men to men.

The whole or a portion of the laws set by God to men is frequently styled the law of nature, or natural law: being, in truth, the only natural law of which it is possible to speak without a metaphor, or without a blending of objects which ought to be distinguished broadly. But, rejecting the appellation Law of Nature as ambiguous and misleading, I name those laws or rules, as considered collectively or in a mass, the *Divine law*, or the *law of God*.

Laws set by men to men are of two leading or principal classes: classes which are often blended, although they differ extremely; and which, for that reason, should be severed precisely, and opposed distinctly and conspicuously.

Of the laws or rules set by men to men, some are established by *political* superiors, sovereign and subject: by persons exercising supreme and subordinate *government*, in independent nations, or independent political societies. The aggregate of the rules thus established, or some aggregate forming a portion of that aggregate, is the appropriate matter of jurisprudence, general or particular. To the aggregate

---

* "The *PJD* underwent five editions from 1832 to 1885. The third (1869), fourth (1873), and fifth (1885) editions, however, were not published as separate books. Instead, they were incorporated into the first of the two volumes of Robert Campbell's editions of Austin's *LJ* [*Lectures on Jurisprudence*, published posthumously in 1885]. The present Cambridge edition of the *PJD* contains the complete and unabridged text of the fifth edition (including Austin's footnotes). The large number of passages that Campbell inserted into the text, however, have been placed within square brackets. This editorial innovation indicates, for the first time, exactly how much material he added to the second edition.... I have also followed the precedent set by H.L.A. Hart and deleted the footnotes of the previous editors (he retained only two of Campbell's notes)." [Note by W.E. Rumble, Cambridge edition, 1995, p. xxv.]

of the rules thus established, or to some aggregate forming a portion of that aggregate, the term *law*, as used simply and strictly, is exclusively applied. But, as contradistinguished to *natural* law, or to the law of *nature* (meaning, by those expressions, the law of God), the aggregate of the rules, established by political superiors, is frequently styled *positive* law, or law existing *by position*. As contradistinguished to the rules which I style *positive morality*, and on which I shall touch immediately, the aggregate of the rules, established by political superiors, may also be marked commodiously with the name of *positive law*. For the sake, then, of getting a name brief and distinctive at once, and agreeably to frequent usage, I style that aggregate of rules, or any portion of that aggregate, *positive law*: though rules, which are *not* established by political superiors, are also *positive*, or exist *by position*, if they be rules or laws, in the proper signification of the term.

Though *some* of the laws or rules, which are set by men to men, are established by political superiors, others are *not* established by political superiors, or are not established by political superiors, in that capacity or character.

[Closely analogous to human laws of this second class, are a set of objects frequently but *improperly* termed *laws*, being rules set and enforced by *mere opinion*, that is, by the opinions or sentiments held or felt by an indeterminate body of men in regard to human conduct. Instances of such a use of the term *law* are the expressions—"The law of honour;" "The law set by fashion;" and rules of this species constitute much of what is usually termed "International law."

The aggregate of human laws properly so called belonging to the second of the classes above mentioned, with the aggregate of objects *improperly* but by *close analogy* termed laws, I place together in a common class, and denote them by the term] *positive morality*. The name *morality* severs them from *positive law*, while the epithet *positive* disjoins them from the *law of God*. And to the end of obviating confusion, it is necessary or expedient that they *should* be disjoined from the latter by that distinguishing epithet. For the name *morality (or morals)*, when standing unqualified or alone, denotes indifferently either of the following objects: namely, positive morality *as it is*, or without regard to its merits; and positive morality *as it would be*, if it conformed to the law of God, and were, therefore, deserving of *approbation*.

[Besides the various sorts of rules which are included in the literal acceptation of the term law, and those which are by a close and striking analogy, though improperly, termed laws, there are numerous applications of the term law, which] rest upon a slender analogy and are merely metaphorical or figurative. Such is the case when we talk of *laws* observed by the lower animals; of *laws* regulating the growth or decay of vegetables; of *laws* determining the movements of inanimate bodies or masses. For where *intelligence* is not, or where it is too bounded to take the name of *reason*, and, therefore, is too bounded to conceive the purpose of a law, there is not the *will* which law can work on, or which duty can incite or restrain. Yet through these misapplications of a *name*, flagrant as the metaphor is, has the field of jurisprudence and morals been deluged with muddy speculation.

[Having] suggested the *purpose* of my attempt to determine the province of jurisprudence: to distinguish positive law, the appropriate matter of jurisprudence, from the various objects to which it is related by resemblance, and to which it is related, nearly or remotely, by a strong or slender analogy: I shall [now] state the essentials of a *law* or *rule* (taken with the largest signification which can be given to the term *properly*).

Every *law* or *rule* (taken with the largest signification which can be given to the term *properly*) is a *command*. Or, rather, laws or rules, properly so called, are a *species* of commands. Now, since the term *command* comprises the term *law*, the first is the simpler as well as the larger of the *two*. But, simple as it is, it admits of explanation. And, since it is the *key* to the sciences of jurisprudence and morals, its meaning should be analysed with precision.

Accordingly, I shall endeavour, in the first instance, to analyse the meaning of "*command:*" an analysis which, I fear, will task the patience of my hearers, but which they will bear with cheerfulness, or, at least, with resignation, if they consider the difficulty of performing it. The elements of a science are precisely the parts of it which are explained least easily. Terms that are the largest, and, therefore, the simplest of a series, are without equivalent expressions into which we can resolve them *concisely.* And when we endeavour to *define* them, or to translate them into terms which we suppose are better understood, we are forced upon awkward and tedious circumlocutions.

If you express or intimate a wish that I shall do or forbear from some act, and if you will visit me with an evil in case I comply not with your wish, the *expression* or *intimation* of your wish is a *command.* A command is distinguished from other significations of desire, not by the style in which the desire is signified, but by the power and the purpose of the party commanding to inflict an evil or pain in case the desire be disregarded. If you cannot or will not harm me, in case I comply not with your wish, the expression of your wish is not a command, although you utter your wish in imperative phrase. If you are able and willing to harm me in case I comply not with your wish, the expression of your wish amounts to a command, although you are prompted by a spirit of courtesy to utter it in the shape of a request. "*Preces erant, sed quibus contradici non posset.*" [*Ed. note*: "These were only requests, but they could not be denied."] Such is the language of Tacitus, when speaking of a petition by the soldiery to a son and lieutenant of Vespasian.

A command, then, is a signification of desire. But a command is distinguished from other significations of desire by this peculiarity: that the party to whom it is directed is liable to evil from the other in case he comply not with the desire.

Being liable to evil from you if I comply not with a wish which you signify, I am *bound* or *obliged* by your command, or I lie under a *duty* to obey it. If, in spite of that evil in prospect, I comply not with the wish which you signify, I am said to disobey your command, or to violate the duty which it imposes.

Command and duty are, therefore, correlative terms: the meaning denoted by each being implied or supposed by the other. Or (changing the expression) wherever a duty lies, a command has been signified; and whenever a command is signified, a duty is imposed.

Concisely expressed, the meaning of the correlative expressions is this. He who will inflict an evil in case his desire be disregarded, utters a command by expressing or intimating his desire: He who is liable to the evil in case he disregard the desire, is bound or obliged by the command.

The evil which will probably be incurred in case a command be disobeyed or (to use an equivalent expression) in case a duty be broken, is frequently called a *sanction*, or an *enforcement of obedience.* Or (varying the phrase) the command or the duty is said to be *sanctioned* or *enforced* by the chance of incurring the evil.

Considered as thus abstracted from the command and the duty which it enforces, the evil to be incurred by disobedience is frequently styled a *punishment.* But, as punishments, strictly so called, are only a *class* of sanctions, the term is too narrow to express the meaning adequately.

I observe that Dr. Paley, in his analysis of the term *obligation*, lays much stress upon the *violence* of the motive to compliance. In so far as I can gather a meaning from his loose and inconsistent statement, his meaning appears to be this: that unless the motive to compliance be *violent* or *intense*, the expression or intimation of a wish is not a *command*, nor does the party to whom it is directed lie under a *duty* to regard it.

If he means, by a *violent* motive, a motive operating with certainty, his proposition is manifestly false.

The greater the evil to be incurred in case the wish be disregarded, and the greater the *chance* of incurring it on that same event, the greater, no doubt, is the chance that the wish will *not* be disregarded. But no conceivable motive will *certainly* determine to compliance, or no conceivable motive will render obedience inevitable. If Paley's proposition be true, in the sense which I have now ascribed to it, commands and duties are simply impossible. Or, reducing his proposition to absurdity by a consequence as manifestly false, commands and duties are possible, but are never disobeyed or broken.

If he means by a *violent* motive, an evil which inspires fear, his meaning is simply this: that the party bound by a command is bound by the prospect of an evil. For that which is not feared is not apprehended as an evil; or (changing the shape of the expression) is not an evil in prospect.

The truth is, that the magnitude of the eventual evil, and the magnitude of the chance of incurring it, are foreign to the matter in question. The greater the eventual evil, and the greater the chance of incurring it, the greater is the efficacy of the command, and the greater is the strength of the obligation: Or (substituting expressions exactly equivalent), the greater is the chance that the command will be obeyed, and that the duty will not be broken. But where there is the smallest *chance* of incurring the smallest evil, the expression of a wish amounts to a command, and, therefore, imposes a duty. The sanction, if you will, is feeble or insufficient; but still there *is* a sanction, and, therefore, a duty and a command.

By some celebrated writers (by Locke, Bentham, and, I think, Paley), the term *sanction*, or *enforcement of obedience*, is applied to conditional good as well as to conditional evil: to reward as well as to punishment. But, with all my habitual veneration for the names of Locke and Bentham, I think that this extension of the term is pregnant with confusion and perplexity.

Rewards are, indisputably, *motives* to comply with the wishes of others. But to talk of commands and duties as *sanctioned* or *enforced* by rewards, or to talk of rewards as *obliging* or *constraining* to obedience, is surely a wide departure from the established meaning of the terms.

If *you* expressed a desire that I should render a service, and if you proffered a reward as the motive or inducement to render it, *you* would scarcely be said to *command* the service, nor should *I*, in ordinary language, be *obliged* to render it. In ordinary language, *you* would *promise* me a reward, on condition of my rendering the service, whilst *I* might be *incited* or *persuaded* to render it by the hope of obtaining the reward.

Again: If a law hold out a *reward*, as an inducement to do some act, an eventual *right* is conferred, and not an *obligation* imposed, upon those who shall act accordingly: The *imperative* part of the law being addressed or directed to the party whom it requires to *render* the reward.

In short, I am determined or inclined to comply with the wish of another, by the fear of disadvantage or evil. I am also determined or inclined to comply with the wish of another, by the hope of advantage or good. But it is only by the chance of incurring evil, that I am *bound* or *obliged* to compliance. It is only by conditional *evil*, that duties are *sanctioned* or *enforced*. It is the power and the purpose of inflicting eventual *evil*, and *not* the power and the purpose of imparting eventual *good*, which gives to the expression of a wish the name of a *command*.

If we put *reward* into the import of the term *sanction*, we must engage in a toilsome struggle with the current of ordinary speech; and shall often slide unconsciously, notwithstanding our efforts to the contrary, into the narrower and customary meaning.

It appears, then, from what has been premised, that the ideas or notions comprehended by the term *command* are the following.

1. A wish or desire conceived by a rational being, that another rational being shall do or forbear. 2. An

evil to proceed from the former, and to be incurred by the latter, in case the latter comply not with the wish. 3. An expression or intimation of the wish by words or other signs.

It also appears from what has been premised, that *command*, *duty*, and *sanction* are inseparably connected terms: that each embraces the same ideas as the others, though each denotes those ideas in a peculiar order or series.

"A wish conceived by one, and expressed or intimated to another, with an evil to be inflicted and incurred in case the wish be disregarded," are signified directly and indirectly by each of the three expressions. Each is the name of the same complex notion.

But when I am talking *directly* of the expression or intimation of the wish, I employ the term *command*: The expression or intimation of the wish being presented *prominently* to my hearer; whilst the evil to be incurred, with the chance of incurring it, are kept (if I may so express myself) in the background of my picture.

When I am talking *directly* of the chance of incurring the evil, or (changing the expression) of the liability or obnoxiousness to the evil, I employ the term *duty*, or the term *obligation*: The liability or obnoxiousness to the evil being put foremost, and the rest of the complex notion being signified implicitly.

When I am talking *immediately* of the evil itself, I employ the term *sanction*, or a term of the like import: The evil to be incurred being signified directly; whilst the obnoxiousness to that evil, with the expression or intimation of the wish, are indicated indirectly or obliquely.

To those who are familiar with the language of logicians (language unrivalled for brevity, distinctness, and precision), I can express my meaning accurately in a breath.—Each of the three terms *signifies* the same notion; but each *denotes* a different part of that notion, and *connotes* the residue.

Commands are of two species. Some are *laws* or *rules*. The others have not acquired an appropriate name, nor does language afford an expression which will mark them briefly and precisely. I must, therefore, note them as well as I can by the ambiguous and inexpressive name of "*occasional* or *particular* commands."

The term *laws* or *rules* being not unfrequently applied to occasional or particular commands, it is hardly possible to describe a line of separation which shall consist in every respect with established forms of speech. But the distinction between laws and particular commands may, I think, be stated in the following manner.

By every command, the party to whom it is directed is obliged to do or to forbear.

Now where it obliges *generally* to acts or forbearances of a *class*, a command is a law or rule. But where it obliges to a *specific* act or forbearance, or to acts or forbearances which it determines *specifically* or *individually*, a command is occasional or particular.

In other words, a class or description of acts is determined by a law or rule, and acts of that class or description are enjoined or forbidden generally. But where a command is occasional or particular, the act or acts, which the command enjoins or forbids, are assigned or determined by their specific or individual natures as well as by the class or description to which they belong.

The statement which I have given in abstract expressions I will now endeavour to illustrate by apt examples.

If you command your servant to go on a given errand, or *not* to leave your house on a given evening, or to rise at such an hour on such a morning, or to rise at that hour during the next week or month, the command is occasional or particular. For the act or acts enjoined or forbidden are specially determined or assigned.

But if you command him *simply* to rise at that hour, or to rise at that hour *always*, or to rise at that hour *till further orders*, it may be said, with propriety, that you lay down a *rule* for the guidance of your servant's conduct. For no specific act is assigned by the command, but the command obliges him generally to acts of a determined class.

If a regiment be ordered to attack or defend a post, or to quell a riot, or to march from their present quarters, the command is occasional or particular. But an order to exercise daily till further orders shall be given would be called a *general* order, and *might* be called a *rule*.

If Parliament prohibited simply the exportation of corn, either for a given period or indefinitely, it would establish a law or rule: a *kind* or *sort* of acts being determined by the command, and acts of that kind or sort being *generally* forbidden. But an order issued by Parliament to meet an impending scarcity, and stopping the exportation of corn *then shipped and in port,* would not be a law or rule, though issued by the sovereign legislature. The order regarding exclusively a specified quantity of corn, the negative acts or forbearances, enjoined by the command, would be determined specifically or individually by the determinate nature of their subject.

As issued by a sovereign legislature, and as wearing the form of a law, the order which I have now imagined would probably be *called* a law. And hence the difficulty of drawing a distinct boundary between laws and occasional commands.

Again: An act which is not an offence, according to the existing law, moves the sovereign to displeasure: and, though the authors of the act are legally innocent or unoffending, the sovereign commands that they shall be punished. As enjoining a specific punishment in that specific case, and as not enjoining generally acts or forbearances of a class, the order uttered by the sovereign is not a law or rule.

Whether such an order would be *called* a law, seems to depend upon circumstances which are purely immaterial: immaterial, that is, with reference to the present purpose, though material with reference to others. If made by a sovereign assembly deliberately, and with the forms of legislation, it would probably be called a law. If uttered by an absolute monarch, without deliberation or ceremony, it would scarcely be confounded with acts of legislation, and would be styled an arbitrary command. Yet, on either of these suppositions, its nature would be the same. It would not be a law or rule, but an occasional or particular command of the sovereign One or Number.

To conclude with an example which best illustrates the distinction, and which shows the importance of the distinction most conspicuously, *judicial commands* are commonly occasional or particular, although the commands which they are calculated to enforce are commonly laws or rules.

For instance, the lawgiver commands that thieves shall be hanged. A specific theft and a specified thief being given, the judge commands that the thief shall be hanged, agreeably to the command of the lawgiver.

Now the lawgiver determines a class or description of acts; prohibits acts of the class generally and indefinitely; and commands, with the like generality, that punishment shall follow transgression. The command of the lawgiver is, therefore, a law or rule. But the command of the judge is occasional or particular. For he orders a specific punishment, as the consequence of a specific offence.

According to the line of separation which I have now attempted to describe, a law and a particular command are distinguished thus.—Acts or forbearances of a class are enjoined *generally* by the former. Acts *determined specifically*, are enjoined or forbidden by the latter.

A different line of separation has been drawn by Blackstone and others. According to Blackstone and others, a law and a particular command are distinguished in the following manner.—A law obliges *generally* the members of the given community, or a law obliges *generally* persons of a given class. A particular command obliges a *single* person, or persons whom it determines *individually*.

That laws and particular commands are not to be distinguished thus, will appear on a moment's reflection.

For, *first*, commands which oblige generally the members of the given community, or commands which oblige generally persons of given classes, are not always laws or rules. [Thus, in the case already supposed; that in which the sovereign commands that all corn actually shipped for exportation be stopped and detained; the command is obligatory upon the whole community, but as it obliges them only to a set of acts individually assigned, it is not a law. Again, suppose the sovereign to issue an order, enforced by penalties, for a general mourning,] on occasion of a public calamity. Now, though it is addressed to the community at large, the order is scarcely a rule, in the usual acceptation of the term. For, though it obliges generally the members of the entire community, it obliges to acts which it assigns specifically, instead of obliging generally to acts or forbearances of a class. If the sovereign commanded that *black* should be the dress of his subjects, his command would amount to a law. But if he commanded them to wear it on a specified occasion, his command would be merely particular.

And, *secondly*, a command which obliges exclusively persons individually determined, may amount, notwithstanding, to a law or rule.

For example, A father may set a *rule* to his child or children: a guardian, to his ward: a master, to his slave or servant. And certain of God's *laws* were as binding on the first man, as they are binding at this hour on the millions who have sprung from his loins.

Most, indeed, of the laws which are established by political superiors, or most of the laws which are simply and strictly so called, oblige generally the members of the political community, or oblige generally persons of a class. To frame a system of duties for every individual of the community, were simply impossible: and if it were possible, it were utterly useless. Most of the laws established by political su-

periors are, therefore, *general* in a twofold manner: as enjoining or forbidding generally acts of kinds or sorts; and as binding the whole community, or, at least, whole classes of its members.

But if we suppose that Parliament creates and grants an office, and that Parliament binds the grantee to services of a given description, we suppose a law established by political superiors, and yet exclusively binding a specified or determinate person.

Laws established by political superiors, and exclusively binding specified or determinate persons, are styled, in the language of the Roman jurists, *privilegia*. Though that, indeed, is a name which will hardly denote them distinctly: for, like most of the leading terms in actual systems of law, it is not the name of a definite class of objects, but of a heap of heterogeneous objects.[1]

It appears, from what has been premised, that a law, properly so called, may be defined in the following manner.

A law is a command which obliges a person or persons.

But, as contradistinguished or opposed to an occasional or particular command, a law is a command which obliges a person or persons, and obliges *generally* to acts or forbearances of a *class*.

In language more popular but less distinct and precise, a law is a command which obliges a person or persons to a *course* of conduct.

---

1   Where a *privilegium* merely imposes a duty, it exclusively obliges a determinate person or persons. But where a *privilegium* confers a right, and the right conferred *avails against the world at large*, the law is *privilegium* as viewed from a certain aspect, but is also *a general law* as viewed from another aspect. In respect of the right conferred, the law exclusively regards a determinate person, and, therefore, is *privilegium*. In respect of the duty imposed, and corresponding to the right conferred, the law regards generally the members of the entire community.

This I shall explain particularly at a subsequent point of my Course, when I consider the peculiar nature of so-called *privilegia*, or of so-called *private laws*.

Laws and other commands are said to proceed from *superiors*, and to bind or oblige *inferiors*. I will, therefore, analyse the meaning of those correlative expressions; and will try to strip them of a certain mystery, by which that simple meaning appears to be obscured.

Superiority is often synonymous with *precedence* or *excellence*. We talk of superiors in rank; of superiors in wealth; of superiors in virtue: comparing certain persons with certain other persons; and meaning that the former precede or excel the latter in rank, in wealth, or in virtue.

But, taken with the meaning wherein I here understand it, the term *superiority* signifies *might*: the power of affecting others with evil or pain, and of forcing them, through fear of that evil, to fashion their conduct to one's wishes.

For example, God is emphatically the *superior* of Man. For his power of affecting us with pain, and of forcing us to comply with his will, is unbounded and resistless.

To a limited extent, the sovereign One or Number is the superior of the subject or citizen: the master, of the slave or servant: the father, of the child.

In short, whoever can *oblige* another to comply with his wishes, is the *superior* of that other, so far as the ability reaches: The party who is obnoxious to the impending evil, being, to that same extent, the *inferior*.

The might or superiority of God is simple or absolute. But in all or most cases of human superiority, the relation of superior and inferior, and the relation of inferior and superior, are reciprocal. Or (changing the expression) the party who is the superior as viewed from one aspect, is the inferior as viewed from another.

For example, To an indefinite, though limited extent, the monarch is the superior of the governed: his power being commonly sufficient to enforce compliance with his will. But the governed, collectively or in mass, are also the superior of the monarch: who is checked in the abuse of his might by his fear of exciting their anger; and of rousing to active resistance the might which slumbers in the multitude.

A member of a sovereign assembly is the superior of the judge: the judge being bound by the law which proceeds from that sovereign body. But, in his character of citizen or subject, he is the inferior of the judge: the judge being the minister of the law, and armed with the power of enforcing it.

It appears, then, that the term *superiority* (like the terms *duty* and *sanction*) is implied by the term command. For superiority is the power of enforcing compliance with a wish: and the expression or intimation of a wish, with the power and the purpose of enforcing it, are the constituent elements of a command.

"That *laws* emanate from *superiors*" is, therefore, an identical proposition. For the meaning which it affects to impart is contained in its subject.

If I mark the peculiar source of a given law, or if I mark the peculiar source of laws of a given class, it is possible that I am saying something which may instruct the hearer. But to affirm of laws universally "that they flow from *superiors*," or to affirm of laws universally "that *inferiors* are bound to obey them," is the merest tautology and trifling.

Like most of the leading terms in the science of jurisprudence and morals, the term *laws* is extremely ambiguous. Taken with the largest signification which can be given to the term properly, *laws* are a species of *commands*. But the term is improperly applied to various objects which have nothing of the imperative character: to objects which are *not* commands; and which, therefore, are *not* laws, properly so called.

Accordingly, the proposition "that laws are commands" must be taken with limitations. Or, rather, we must distinguish the various meanings of the term *laws*; and must restrict the proposition to that class of objects which is embraced by the largest signification that can be given to the term properly.

[I have already indicated, and shall hereafter more fully describe, the objects improperly termed laws, which are *not* within the province of juris-prudence (being either rules enforced by opinion and closely analogous to laws properly so called, or being laws so called by a metaphorical application of the term merely). There are other objects improperly termed laws (not being commands) which yet may properly be included within the province of jurisprudence. These I shall endeavour to particularise:—]

1. Acts on the part of legislatures to *explain* positive law, can scarcely be called laws, in the proper signification of the term. Working no change in the actual duties of the governed, but simply declaring what those duties are, they properly are acts of *interpretation* by legislative authority. Or, to borrow an expression from the writers on the Roman Law, they are acts of *authentic* interpretation.

But, this notwithstanding, they are frequently styled laws; *declaratory* laws, or declaratory statutes. They must, therefore, be noted as forming an exception to the proposition "that laws are a species of commands."

It often, indeed, happens (as I shall show in the proper place), that laws declaratory in name are imperative in effect: Legislative, like judicial interpretation, being frequently deceptive; and establishing new law, under guise of expounding the old.

2. Laws to repeal laws, and to release from existing duties, must also be excepted from the proposition "that laws are a species of commands." In so far as they release from duties imposed by existing laws, they are not commands, but revocations of commands. They authorize or permit the parties, to whom the repeal extends, to do or to forbear from acts which they were commanded to forbear from or to do. And, considered with regard to *this*, their immediate or direct purpose, they are often named *permissive laws*, or, more briefly and more properly, *permissions*.

Remotely and indirectly, indeed, permissive laws are often or always imperative. For the parties released from duties are restored to liberties or rights:

and duties answering those rights are, therefore, created or revived.

But this is a matter which I shall examine with exactness, when I analyse the expressions "legal right," "permission by the sovereign or state," and "civil or political liberty."

3. Imperfect laws, or laws of imperfect obligation, must also be excepted from the proposition "that laws are a species of commands."

An imperfect law (with the sense wherein the term is used by the Roman jurists) is a law which wants a sanction, and which therefore, is not binding. A law declaring that certain acts are crimes, but annexing no punishment to the commission of acts of the class, is the simplest and most obvious example.

Though the author of an imperfect law signifies a desire, he manifests no purpose of enforcing compliance with the desire. But where there is not a purpose of enforcing compliance with the desire, the expression of a desire is not a command. Consequently, an imperfect law is not so properly a law, as counsel, or exhortation, addressed by a superior to inferiors.

Examples of imperfect laws are cited by the Roman jurists. But with us in England, laws professedly imperative are always (I believe) perfect or obligatory. Where the English legislature affects to command, the English tribunals not unreasonably presume that the legislature exacts obedience. And, if no specific sanction be annexed to a given law, a sanction is supplied by the courts of justice, agreeably to a general maxim which obtains in cases of the kind.

The imperfect laws, of which I am now speaking, are laws which are imperfect, in the sense of *the Roman jurists*: that is to say, laws which speak the desires of political superiors, but which their authors (by oversight or design) have not provided with sanctions. Many of the writers on *morals*, and on the so called *law of nature*, have annexed a different meaning to the term *imperfect*. Speaking of imperfect obligations, they commonly mean duties which are *not legal*: duties imposed by commands of God, or duties imposed by positive morality, as contradistinguished to duties imposed by positive law. An *imperfect* obligation, in the sense of the Roman jurists, is exactly equivalent to no obligation at all. For the term *imperfect* denotes simply, that the law wants the sanction appropriate to laws of the kind. An imperfect obligation, in the other meaning of the expression, is a religious or a moral obligation. The term imperfect does not denote that the law imposing the duty wants the appropriate sanction. It denotes that the law imposing the duty is *not* a law established by a political superior: that it wants that *perfect*, or that surer or more cogent sanction, which is imparted by the sovereign or state.

I believe that I have now reviewed all the classes of objects, to which the term *laws* is improperly applied. The laws (improperly so called) which I have here lastly enumerated, are (I think) the only laws which are not commands, and which yet may be properly included within the province of jurisprudence. But though these, with the so called laws set by opinion and the objects metaphorically termed laws, are the only laws which *really* are not commands, there are certain laws (properly so called) which may *seem* not imperative. Accordingly, I will subjoin a few remarks upon laws of this dubious character.

1. There are laws, it may be said, which *merely* create *rights*: And, seeing that every command imposes a *duty*, laws of this nature are not imperative.

But, as I have intimated already, and shall show completely hereafter, there are no laws *merely* creating *rights*. There are *laws*, it is true, which *merely* create *duties*: duties not correlating with correlating rights, and which, therefore may be styled *absolute*.

But every law, really conferring a right, imposes expressly or tacitly a *relative* duty, or a duty correlating with the right. If it specify the remedy to be given, in case the right shall be infringed, it imposes the relative duty expressly. If the remedy to be given be not specified, it refers tacitly to pre-existing law, and clothes the right which it purports to create with a remedy provided by that law. Every law, really conferring a right, is, therefore, imperative: as imperative, as if its only purpose were the creation of a duty, or as if the relative duty, which it inevitably imposes, were merely absolute.

The meanings of the term *right*, are various and perplexed; taken with its proper meaning, it comprises ideas which are numerous and complicated; and the searching and extensive analysis, which the term, therefore, requires, would occupy more room than could be given to it in the present lecture: It is not, however, necessary, that the analysis should be performed here. I propose, in my earlier lectures, to determine the province of jurisprudence; or to distinguish the laws established by political superiors, from the various laws, proper and improper, with which they are frequently confounded. And this I may accomplish exactly enough, without a nice inquiry into the import of the term *right*.

2. According to an opinion which I must notice *incidentally* here, though the subject to which it relates will be treated *directly* hereafter, *customary laws* must be excepted from the proposition "that laws are a species of commands."

By many of the admirers of customary laws (and, especially, of their German admirers), they are thought to oblige legally (independently of the sovereign or state), *because* the citizens or subjects have observed or kept them. Agreeably to this opinion, they are not the *creatures* of the sovereign or state, although the sovereign or state may abolish them at pleasure. Agreeably to this opinion, they are positive law (or law, strictly so called), inasmuch as they are enforced by the courts of justice: But, that notwithstanding, they exist *as positive law* by the spontaneous adoption of the governed, and not by position or establishment on the part of political superiors. Consequently, customary laws, considered as positive law, are not commands. And, consequently, customary laws, considered as positive law, are not laws or rules properly so called.

An opinion less mysterious, but somewhat allied to this, is not uncommonly held by the adverse party: by the party which is strongly opposed to customary law; and to all law made judicially, or in the way of judicial legislation. According to the latter opinion, all judge-made law, or all judge-made law established by *subject* judges, is purely the creature of the judges by whom it is established immediately. To impute it to the sovereign legislature, or to suppose that it speaks the will of the sovereign legislature, is one of the foolish or knavish *fictions* with which lawyers, in every age and nation, have perplexed and darkened the simplest and clearest truths.

I think it will appear, on a moment's reflection, that each of these opinions is groundless: that customary law is *imperative*, in the proper signification of the term; and that all judge-made law is the creature of the sovereign or state.

At its origin, a custom is a rule of conduct which the governed observe spontaneously, or not in pursuance of a law set by a political superior. The custom is transmuted into positive law, when it is adopted as such by the courts of justice, and when the judicial decisions fashioned upon it are enforced by the power of the state. But before it is adopted by the courts, and clothed with the legal sanction, it is merely a rule of positive morality: a rule generally observed by the citizens or subjects; but deriving the only force, which it can be said to possess, from the general disapprobation falling on those who transgress it.

Now when judges transmute a custom into a legal rule (or make a legal rule not suggested by a custom), the legal rule which they establish is established by the sovereign legislature. A subordinate or subject judge is merely a minister. The portion of the sovereign power which lies at his disposition is merely delegated. The rules which he makes derive their legal force from authority given by the state: an authority which the state may confer expressly, but which it commonly imparts in the way of acquiescence. For, since the state may reverse the rules which he makes, and yet permits him to enforce them by the power of the political community, its sovereign will "that his rules shall obtain as law" is clearly evinced by its conduct, though not by its express declaration.

The admirers of customary law love to trick out their idol with mysterious and imposing attributes. But to those who can see the difference between positive law and morality, there is nothing of mystery about it. Considered as rules of positive morality, customary laws arise from the consent of the governed, and not from the position or establishment of political superiors. But, considered as moral rules turned into positive laws, customary laws are established by the state: established by the state directly, when the customs are promulged in its statutes; established by the state circuitously, when the customs are adopted by its tribunals.

The opinion of the party which abhors judge-made laws, springs from their inadequate conception of the nature of commands.

Like other significations of desire, a command is express or tacit. If the desire be signified by *words* (written or spoken), the command is express. If the desire be signified by conduct (or by any signs of desire which are *not* words), the command is tacit.

Now when customs are turned into legal rules by decisions of subject judges, the legal rules which emerge from the customs are tacit commands of the sovereign legislature. The state, which is able to abolish, permits its ministers to enforce them: and it, therefore, signifies its pleasure, by that its voluntary acquiescence, "that they shall serve as a law to the governed."

My present purpose is merely this: to prove that the positive law styled *customary* (and all positive law made judicially) is established by the state directly or circuitously, and, therefore, is *imperative*. I am far from disputing, that law made judicially (or in the way of improper legislation) and law made by statute (or in the properly legislative manner) are distinguished by weighty differences. I shall inquire, in future lectures, what those differences are; and why subject judges, who are properly ministers of the law, have commonly shared with the sovereign in the business of making it.

I assume, then, that the only laws which are not imperative, [and which belong to the subject-matter of jurisprudence,] are the following—1. Declaratory laws, or laws explaining the import of existing positive law. 2. Laws abrogating or repealing existing positive law. 3. Imperfect laws, or laws of imperfect obligation (with the sense wherein the expression is used by the Roman jurists).

But the space occupied in the science by these improper laws is comparatively narrow and insignificant. Accordingly, although I shall take them into account so often as I refer to them directly, I shall throw them out of account on other occasions. Or (changing the expression) I shall limit the term *law* to laws which are imperative, unless I extend it expressly to laws which are not.

• • •

[*Ed. note*: The following material excerpted from Chapter V of *The Province of Jurisprudence Determined* examines the relationship between law and morality and contains some of Austin's arguments for the conceptual separation of law and legal obligation from morality and moral obligation.]

Lecture V

... The existence of law is one thing; its merit or demerit is another. Whether it be or be not is one enquiry; whether it be or be not conformable to an assumed standard, is a different enquiry. A law, which actually exists, is a law, though we happen to dislike it, or though it vary from the text, by which we regulate our approbation and disapprobation. This truth, when formally announced as an abstract proposition, is so simple and glaring that it seems idle to insist upon it. But simple and glaring as it is, when enunciated in abstract expressions the enum-

eration of the instances in which it has been forgotten would fill a volume.

Sir William Blackstone, for example, says in his "Commentaries," that the laws of God are superior in obligation to all other laws; that no human laws should be suffered to contradict them; that human laws are of no validity if contrary to them; and that all valid laws derive their force from that Divine original.

Now, he *may* mean that all human laws ought to conform to the Divine laws. If this be his meaning, I assent to it without hesitation. The evils which we are exposed to suffer from the hands of God as a consequence of disobeying His commands are the greatest evils to which we are obnoxious; the obligations which they impose are consequently paramount to those imposed by any other laws, and if human commands conflict with the Divine law, we ought to disobey the command which is enforced by the less powerful sanction; this is implied in the term *ought*: the proposition is identical, and therefore perfectly indisputable—it is our interest to choose the smaller and more uncertain evil, in preference to the greater and surer. If this be Blackstone's meaning, I assent to his proposition, and have only to object to it, that it tells us just nothing.

Perhaps, again, he means that human lawgivers are themselves obliged by the Divine laws to fashion the laws which they impose by that ultimate standard, because if they do not, God will punish them. To this also I entirely assent: for if the index to the law of God be the principle of utility, that law embraces the whole of our voluntary actions in so far as motives applied from without are required to give them a direction conformable to the general happiness.

But the meaning of this passage of Blackstone, if it has a meaning, seems rather to be this: that no human law which conflicts with the Divine law is obligatory or binding; in other words, that no human law which conflicts with the Divine law *is a law*, for a law without an obligation is a contradiction in terms. I suppose this to be his meaning, because when we say of any transaction that it is invalid or void, we mean that it is not binding: as, for example, if it be a contract, we mean that the political law will not lend its sanction to enforce the contract.

Now, to say that human laws which conflict with the Divine law are not binding, that is to say, are not laws, is to talk stark nonsense. The most pernicious laws, and therefore those which are most opposed to the will of God, have been and are continually enforced as laws by judicial tribunals. Suppose an act innocuous, or positively beneficial, be prohibited by the sovereign under the penalty of death; if I commit this act, I shall be tried and condemned, and if I object to the sentence, that it is contrary to the law of God, who has commanded that human lawgivers shall not prohibit acts which have no evil consequences, the Court of Justice will demonstrate the inconclusiveness of my reasoning by hanging me up, in pursuance of the law of which I have impugned the validity. An exception, demurrer, or plea, founded on the law of God was never heard in a Court of Justice, from the creation of the world down to the present moment.

But this abuse of language is not merely puerile, it is mischievous. When it is said that a law ought to be disobeyed, what is meant is that we are urged to disobey it by motives more cogent and compulsory than those by which it is itself sanctioned. If the laws of God are certain, the motives which they hold out to disobey any human command which is at variance with them are paramount to all others. But the laws of God are not always certain. All divines, at least all reasonable divines, admit that no scheme of duties perfectly complete and unambiguous was ever imparted to us by revelation. As an index to the Divine will, utility is obviously insufficient. What appears pernicious to one person may appear beneficial to another. And as for the moral sense, innate practical principles, conscience they are merely convenient cloaks for ignorance or sinister interest: they mean either that I hate the law to which I object and cannot tell why, or that I hate the law, and that the cause of my hatred is one which I find it incommodious to avow. If I say openly, I hate the law, *ergo*, it is not binding and ought to be disobeyed, no one will listen to me; but by calling my hate my conscience or my moral sense, I urge the same argument in another and a more plausible form: I seem to assign a reason for my dislike, when in truth I have only given it a sounding and specious name. In times of civil discord the mischief of this detestable abuse of language is apparent. In quiet times the dictates of utility are fortunately so obvious that the anarchical doctrine sleeps, and men habitually admit the validity of laws which they dislike. To prove by pertinent reasons that a law is pernicious is highly useful, because such process may lead to the abrogation of the pernicious law. To incite the public to resistance by determinate views of *utility* may be useful, for resistance, grounded on clear and definite prospects of good, is sometimes beneficial. But to proclaim generally that all laws which are pernicious or contrary to the will of God are void and not to be tolerated, is to preach anarchy, hostile and perilous as much to wise and benign rule as to stupid and galling tyranny.

In another passage of his "Commentaries," Blackstone enters into an argument to prove that a master cannot have a right to the labour of his slave. Had he contented himself with expressing his *disapprobation*, a very well-grounded one certainly, of the institution of slavery, no objection could have been made to his so expressing himself. But to dispute the existence or the possibility of the right is to talk absurdly. For in every age, and in almost every nation, the right has been given by positive law, whilst that pernicious disposition of positive law has been backed by the positive morality of the free or master classes.

• • •

[*Ed. note*: The following material excerpted from Chapter VI of *The Province of Jurisprudence* Determined examines the idea of sovereignty.]

Chapter VI

... I shall analyse the expression *sovereignty*, the correlative expression *subjection*, and the inseparably connected expression *independent political society*. With the ends or final causes for which governments *ought* to exist, or with their different degrees of fitness to attain or approach those ends, I have no concern. I examine the notions of *sovereignty* and *independent political society*, in order that I may finish the purpose to which I have adverted above: in order that I may distinguish completely the appropriate province of jurisprudence from the regions which lie upon its confines, and by which it is encircled. It is necessary that I should examine those notions, in order that I may finish that purpose. For the essential difference of a positive law (or the difference that severs it from a law which is not a positive law) may be stated thus. Every positive law, or every law simply and strictly so called, is set by a sovereign person, or a sovereign body of persons, to a member or members of the independent political society wherein that person or body is sovereign or supreme. Or (changing the expression) it is set by a monarch, or sovereign number, to a person or persons in a state of subjection to its author. Even though it sprung directly from another fountain or source, it *is* a positive law, or a law strictly so called, by the institution of that present sovereign in the character of political superior. Or (borrowing the language of Hobbes) "the legislator is he, not by whose authority the law was first made, but by whose authority it continues to be a law."

Having stated the topic or subject appropriate to my present discourse, I proceed to distinguish sovereignty from other superiority or might, and to distinguish society political and independent from society of other descriptions.

The superiority which is styled sovereignty, and the independent political society which sovereignty implies, is distinguished from other superiority, and from other society, by the following marks or characters.—1. The *bulk* of the given society are in a *habit* of obedience or submission to a *determinate* and *common* superior: let that common superior be a certain individual person, or a certain body or aggregate of individual persons. 2. That certain individual or that certain body of individuals, is *not* in a habit of obedience to a determinate human superior. Laws (improperly so called) which opinion sets or imposes, may permanently affect the conduct of that certain individual or body. To express or tacit commands of other determinate parties, that certain individual or body may yield occasional submission. But there is no determinate person, or determinate aggregate of persons, to whose commands, express or tacit, that certain individual or body renders habitual obedience.

Or the notions of sovereignty and independent political society may be expressed concisely thus.— If a *determinate* human superior, *not* in a habit of obedience to a like superior, receive *habitual* obedience from the *bulk* of a given society, that determinate superior is sovereign in that society, and the society (including the superior) is a society political and independent.

To that determinate superior, the other members of the society are *subject*: or on that determinate superior, the other members of the society are *dependent*. The position of its other members towards that determinate superior, is a *state of subjection*, or *a state of dependence*. The mutual relation which subsists between that superior and them, may be styled the *relation of sovereign and subject*, or *the relation of sovereignty and subjection*.

Hence it follows, that it is only through an ellipsis, or an abridged form of expression, that the *society* is styled *independent*. The party truly independent (independent, that is to say, of a determinate human superior), is not the society, but the sovereign portion of the society: that certain member of the society, or that certain body of its members, to whose commands, expressed or intimated, the generality or bulk of its members render habitual obedience. Upon that certain person, or certain body of persons, the other members of the society are *dependent*: or to that certain person, or certain body of persons, the other members of the society are *subject*. By "an independent political society," or "an independent and sovereign nation," we mean a political society consisting of a sovereign and subjects, as opposed to a political society which is merely subordinate: that is to say, which is merely a limb or member of another political society, and which therefore consists entirely of persons in a state of subjection.

In order that a given society may form a society political and independent, the two distinguishing marks which I have mentioned above must unite. The *generality* of the given society must be in the *habit* of obedience to a *determinate* and *common* superior: whilst that determinate person, or determinate body of persons must *not* be habitually obedient to a determinate person or body. It is the union of that positive, with this negative mark, which renders that certain superior sovereign or supreme, and which renders that given society (including that certain superior) a society political and independent.

To show that the union of those marks renders a given society a society political and independent, I call your attention to the following positions and examples.

1. In order that a given society may form a society political, the generality or bulk of its members must be in a *habit* of obedience to a determinate and common superior.

In case the generality of its members obey a determinate superior, but the obedience be rare or transient and not habitual or permanent, the relation of sovereignty and subjection is not created thereby between that certain superior and the members of that given society. In other words, that determinate superior and the members of that given society do not become thereby an independent political society. Whether that given society be political and independent or not, it is not an independent political society whereof that certain superior is the sovereign portion.

For example: In 1815 the allied armies occupied France; and so long as the allied armies occupied France, the commands of the allied sovereigns were obeyed by the French government, and, through the French government, by the French people generally. But since the commands and the obedience were comparatively rare and transient, they were not sufficient to constitute the relation of sovereignty and subjection between the allied sovereigns and the members of the invaded nation. In spite of those commands, and in spite of that obedience, the French government was sovereign or independent. Or in spite of those commands and in spite of that obedience, the French government and its subjects were an independent political society whereof the allied sovereigns were not the sovereign portion.

Now if the French nation, before the obedience to those sovereigns, had been an independent society in a state of nature or anarchy, it would not have been changed by the obedience into a society political. And it would not have been changed by the obedience into a society political, because the obedience was not habitual. For, inasmuch as the obedience was not habitual, it was not changed by the obedience from a society political and independent, into a society political but subordinate.—A given society, therefore, is not a society political, unless the generality of its members be in a *habit* of obedience to a determinate and common superior.

Again: A feeble state holds its independence precariously, or at the will of the powerful states to whose aggressions it is obnoxious. And since it is obnoxious to their aggressions, it and the bulk of its subjects render obedience to commands which they occasionally express or intimate. Such, for instance, is the position of the Saxon government and its subjects in respect of the conspiring sovereigns who form the Holy Alliance. But since the commands and the obedience are comparatively few and rare, they are not sufficient to constitute the relation of sovereignty and subjection between the powerful states and the feeble state with its subjects. In spite of those commands, and in spite of that obedience, the feeble state is sovereign or independent. Or in spite of those commands, and in spite of that obedience, the feeble state and its subjects are an independent political society whereof the powerful states are not the sovereign portion. Although the powerful states are permanently *superior*, and although the feeble state is permanently *inferior*, there is neither a *habit* of command on the part of the former, nor a *habit* of obedience on the part of the latter. Although the latter is unable to defend and maintain its independence, the latter is independent of the former in fact or practice.

From the example now adduced, as from the example adduced before, we may draw the following inference: that a given society is not a society political, unless the generality of its members be in the *habit* of obedience to a determinate and common superior.—By the obedience to the powerful states, the feeble state and its subjects are not changed from an independent, into subordinate political society. And they are not changed by the obedience into subordinate political society, because the obedience is not habitual. Consequently, if they were a natural society (setting that obedience aside), they would not be changed by that obedience into a society political.

2. In order that a given society may form a society political, habitual obedience must be rendered, by the *generality* or *bulk* of its members, to a determinate and *common* superior. In other words, habitual obedience must be rendered, by the *generality* or *bulk* of its members, to *one and the same* determinate person, or determinate, body of persons.

Unless habitual obedience be rendered by the *bulk* of its members, and be rendered by the bulk of its members to *one and the same* superior, the given society is either in a state of nature, or is split into two or more independent political societies.

For example: In case a given society be torn by intestine war, and in case the conflicting parties be nearly balanced, the given society is in one of the two positions which I have now supposed.—As there is no common superior to which the bulk of its members render habitual obedience, it is not a political society single or undivided.—If the bulk of each of the parties be in a habit of obedience to its head, the given society is broken into two or more societies, which, perhaps, may be styled independent political societies.—If the bulk of each of the parties be not in that habit of obedience, the given society is simply or absolutely in a state of nature or anarchy. It is either resolved or broken into its individual elements, or into numerous societies of an extremely limited size: of a size so extremely limited, that they could hardly be styled societies independent and *political*. For, as I shall show hereafter, a given independent society would hardly be styled *political*, in case it fell short of a *number* which cannot be fixed with precision, but which may be called considerable, or not extremely minute.

3. In order that a given society may form a society political, the generality or bulk of its members must habitually obey a superior *determinate* as well as common.

On this position I shall not insist here. For I have shown sufficiently in my fifth lecture, that no indeterminate party can command expressly or tacitly, or can receive obedience or submission: that no indeterminate body is capable of corporate conduct, or is capable, as a body, of positive or negative deportment.

4. It appears from what has preceded, that, in order that a given society may form a society political, the bulk of its members must be in a habit of obedience to a certain and common superior. But, in order that the given society may form a society political and independent, that certain superior must not be habitually obedient to a determinate human superior.

◆ ◆ ◆ ◆ ◆

H.L.A. HART

"Positivism and the Separation of Law and Morals"

In this article I shall discuss and attempt to defend a view which Mr. Justice Holmes, among others, held and for which he and they have been much criticized. But I wish first to say why I think that Holmes, whatever the vicissitudes of his American reputation may be, will always remain for Englishmen a heroic figure in jurisprudence. This will be so because he magically combined two qualities: one of them is imaginative power, which English legal thinking has often lacked; the other is clarity, which English legal thinking usually possesses. The English lawyer who turns to read Holmes is made to see that what he had taken to be settled and stable is really always on the move. To make this discovery with Holmes is to be with a guide whose words may leave you unconvinced, sometimes even repelled, but never mystified. Like our own Austin, with whom Holmes shared many ideals and thoughts, Holmes was sometimes clearly wrong; but again like Austin, when this was so he was always wrong clearly. This surely is a sovereign virtue in jurisprudence. Clarity I know is said not to be enough; this may be true, but there are still questions in jurisprudence where the issues are confused because they are discussed in a style which Holmes would have spurned for its obscurity. Perhaps this is inevitable: jurisprudence trembles so uncertainly on the margin of many subjects that there will always be need for someone, in Bentham's phrase, "to pluck the mask of Mystery" from its face.[1] This is true, to a pre-eminent degree, of the subject of this article. Contemporary voices tell us we must recognize something obscured by the legal "positivists" whose day is now over: that there is a "point of intersection between law and morals,"[2] or that what *is* and what *ought* to be are somehow indissolubly fused or inseparable,[3] though the positivists denied it. What do these phrases mean? Or rather which of the many things that they *could* mean, *do* they mean? Which of them do "positivists" deny and why is it wrong to do so?

I.

I shall present the subject as part of the history of an idea. At the close of the eighteenth century and the beginning of the nineteenth the most earnest thinkers in England about legal and social problems and the architects of great reforms were the great Utilitarians. Two of them, Bentham and Austin, constantly insisted on the need to distinguish, firmly and with the maximum of clarity, law as it is from law as it ought to be. This theme haunts their work, and they condemned the natural-law thinkers precisely because they had blurred this apparently simple but vital distinction. By contrast, at the present time in this country and to a lesser extent in England, this separation between law and morals is held to be superficial and wrong. Some critics have thought that it blinds men to the true nature of law and its roots in social life.[4] Others have thought it not only

---

1 Bentham, *A Fragment on Government,* in I *Works* 221, 235 (Bowring ed. 1859) (preface, 41st para.).

2 D'Entrèves, *Natural Law* 116 (2d ed. 1952).

3 Fuller, *The Law in Quest for Itself* 12 (1940); Brecht, *The Myth of Is and Ought,* 54 Harv. L. Rev. 811 (1941); Fuller, *Human Purpose and Natural Law,* 53 *J. Philos.* 697 (1953).

4 See Friedmann, *Legal Theory* 154, 294-95 (3d ed. 1953). Friedmann also says of Austin that "by his sharp distinction between the science of legislation and the science of law," he "inaugurated an era of legal positivism and self-sufficiency which enabled the rising national State to assert its authority undisturbed by juristic doubts." *Id.* at 416. Yet, "the existence of a highly organised State which claimed sovereignty and unconditional obedience of the citizen" is said to be "the political condition which makes analytical positivism possible." *Id.* at 163. There is

intellectually misleading but corrupting in practice, at its worst apt to weaken resistance to state tyranny or absolutism,[5] and at its best apt to bring law into disrespect. The nonpejorative name "Legal Positivism," like most terms which are used as missiles in intellectual battles, has come to stand for a baffling multitude of different sins. One of them is the sin, real or alleged, of insisting, as Austin and Bentham did, on the separation of law as it is and law as it ought to be.

How then has this reversal of the wheel come about? What are the theoretical errors in this distinction? Have the practical consequences of stressing the distinction as Bentham and Austin did been bad? Should we now reject it or keep it? In considering these questions we should recall the social philosophy which went along with the Utilitarians' insistence on this distinction. They stood firmly but on their own utilitarian ground for all the principles of liberalism in law and government. No one has ever combined, with such even-minded sanity as the Utilitarians, the passion for reform with respect for law together with a due recognition of the need to control the abuse of power even when power is in the hands of reformers. One by one in Bentham's works you can identify the elements of the *Rechtstaat* and all the principles for the defense of which the terminology of natural law has in our day been revived. Here are liberty of speech, and of press, the right of

association,[6] the need that laws should be published and made widely known before they are enforced,[7] the need to control administrative agencies,[8] the insistence that there should be no criminal liability without fault,[9] and the importance of the principle of legality, *nulla poena sine lege*.[10] Some, I know, find the political and moral insight of the Utilitarians a very simple one, but we should not mistake this simplicity for superficiality nor forget how favorably their simplicities compare with the profundities of other thinkers. Take only one example: Bentham on slavery. He says the question at issue is not whether those who are held as slaves can reason, but simply whether they suffer.[11] Does this not compare well with the discussion of the question in terms of whether or not there are some men whom Nature has fitted only to be the living instruments of others? We owe it to Bentham more than anyone else that we have stopped discussing this and similar questions of social policy in that form.

So Bentham and Austin were not dry analysts fiddling with verbal distinctions while cities burned, but were the vanguard of a movement which la-

---

therefore some difficulty in determining which, in this account, is to be hen and which egg (analytical positivism or political condition). Apart from this, there seems to be little evidence that any national State rising in or after 1832 (when the *Province of Jurisprudence Determined* was first published) was enabled to assert its authority by Austin's work or "the era of legal positivism" which he "inaugurated."

5   See Radbruch, *Die Erneuerung des Rechts*, 2 *Die Wandlung* 8 (Germany1947); Radbruch, *Gesetzliches Unrecht und Übergesetzliches Recht*, 1 *Süddeutsche Juristen-Zeitung* 105 (Germany 1946) (reprinted in Radbruch, *Rechtsphilosophie* 347 (4th ed. 1950)). Radbruch's views are discussed at pp. 617-21 *infra*.

6   Bentham, *A Fragment on Government*, in 1 *Works* 221, 230 (Bowring ed. 1859) (preface, 16th para.); Bentham, *Principles of Penal Law*, in 1 *Works* 365, 574-75, 576-78 (Bowring ed. 1859) (pt. III, c. XXI, 8th para., 12th para.).

7   Bentham, *Of Promulgation of the Laws*, in 1 *Works* 155 (Bowring ed. 1859); Bentham, *Principles of the Civil Code*, in 1 *Works* 297, 323 (Bowring ed. 1859) (pt. I, c. XVII, 2d para.); Bentham, *A Fragment on Government*, in 1 *Works* 221, 233 n.[m] (Bowring ed. 1859) (preface, 35th para.).

8   Bentham, *Principles of Penal Law*, in 1 *Works* 365, 576 (Bowring ed. 1859) (pt. III, c. XXI, 10th para., 11th para.).

9   Bentham, *Principles of Morals and Legislation*, in 1 *Works* 1, 84 (Bowring ed. 1859) (c. XIII).

10   Bentham, *Anarchical Fallacies*, in 2 *Works* 489, 511-12 (Bowring ed. 1859) (art. VIII); Bentham, *Principles of Morals and Legislation*, in 1 *Works* 1, 144 (Bowring ed. 1859) (c. XIX, 11th para.).

11   *Id.* at 142 n.§ (c. XIX, 4th para. n.§).

boured with passionate intensity and much success to bring about a better society and better laws. Why then did they insist on the separation of law as it is and law as it ought to be? What did they mean? Let us first see what they said. Austin formulated the doctrine:

> The existence of law is one thing; its merit or demerit is another. Whether it be or be not is one enquiry; whether it be or be not conformable to an assumed standard, is a different enquiry. A law, which actually exists, is a law, though we happen to dislike it, or though it vary from the text, by which we regulate our approbation and disapprobation. This truth, when formally announced as an abstract proposition, is so simple and glaring that it seems idle to insist upon it. But simple and glaring as it is, when enunciated in abstract expressions the enumeration of the instances in which it has been forgotten would fill a volume.

> Sir William Blackstone, for example, says in his "Commentaries," that the laws of God are superior in obligation to all other laws; that no human laws should be suffered to contradict them; that human laws are of no validity if contrary to them; and that all valid laws derive their force from that Divine original.

> Now, he *may* mean that all human laws ought to conform to the Divine laws. If this be his meaning, I assent to it without hesitation.... Perhaps, again, he means that human lawgivers are themselves obliged by the Divine laws to fashion the laws which they impose by that ultimate standard, because if they do not, God will punish them. To this also I entirely assent ...

> But the meaning of this passage of Blackstone, if it has a meaning, seems rather to be this: that no human law which conflicts with the Divine law is obligatory or binding; in other words, that no human law which conflicts with the Divine law *is a law*....[12]

Austin's protest against blurring the distinction between what law is and what it ought to be is quite general: it is a mistake, whatever our standard of what ought to be, whatever "the text by which we regulate our approbation or disapprobation." His examples, however, are always a confusion between law as it is and law as morality would require it to be. For him, it must be remembered, the fundamental principles of morality were God's commands, to which utility was an "index": besides this there was the actual accepted morality of a social group or "positive" morality.

Bentham insisted on this distinction without characterizing morality by reference to God but only, of course, by reference to the principles of utility. Both thinkers' prime reason for this insistence was to enable men to see steadily the precise issues posed by the existence of morally bad laws, and to understand the specific character of the authority of a legal order. Bentham's general recipe for life under the government of laws was simple: it was "*to obey punctually; to censure freely*."[13] But Bentham was especially aware, as an anxious spectator of the French revolution, that this was not enough: the time might come in any society when the law's commands were so evil that the question of resistance had to be faced, and it was then essential that the issues at stake at this point should neither be oversimplified nor obscured.[14] Yet, this was precisely what the confusion

---

12 Austin, *The Province of Jurisprudence Determined* 184-85 (Library of Ideas ed. 1954).

13 Bentham, *A Fragment on Government*, in I *Works* 221, 230 (Bowring ed. 1859) (preface, fifth para.).

14 See Bentham, *Principles of Legislation*, in *The Theory of Legislation* I, 65 n.* (Ogden ed. 1931) (c. XII, 2d para. n.*).

    Here we touch upon the most difficult of questions. If the law is not what it ought to be; if

between law and morals had done and Bentham found that the confusion had spread symmetrically in two different directions. On the one hand Bentham had in mind the anarchist who argues thus: "This ought not to be the law, therefore it is not and I am free not merely to censure but to disregard it." On the other hand he thought of the reactionary who argues: "This is the law, therefore it is what it ought to be," and thus stifles criticism at its birth. Both errors, Bentham thought, were to be found in Blackstone: there was his incautious statement that human laws were invalid if contrary to the law of God,[15] and "that spirit of obsequious *quietism* that seems constitutional in our Author" which "will scarce ever let him recognise a difference" between what is and what ought to be.[16] This indeed was for Bentham the occupational disease of lawyers: "[I]n the eyes of lawyers—not to speak of their dupes— that is to say, as yet, the generality of non-lawyers the *is* and *ought to be* ... were one and indivisible."[17] There are therefore two dangers between which in-

sistence on this distinction will help us to steer: the danger that law and its authority may be dissolved in man's conceptions of what law ought to be and the danger that the existing law may supplant morality as a final test of conduct and so escape criticism.

In view of later criticisms it is also important to distinguish several things that the Utilitarians did not mean by insisting on their separation of law and morals. They certainly accepted many of the things that might be called "the intersection of law and morals." First, they never denied that, as a matter of historical fact, the development of legal systems had been powerfully influenced by moral opinion, and, conversely, that moral standards had been profoundly influenced by law, so that the content of many legal rules mirrored moral rules or principles. It is not in fact always easy to trace this historical causal connection, but Bentham was certainly ready to admit its existence; so too Austin spoke of the "frequent coincidence"[18] of positive law and morality and attributed the confusion of what law is with what law ought to be to this very fact.

Secondly, neither Bentham nor his followers denied that by explicit legal provisions moral principles might at different points be brought into a legal system and form part of its rules or that courts might be legally bound to decide in accordance with what they thought just or best. Bentham indeed recognized, as Austin did not, that even the supreme legislative power might be subjected to legal restraints by a constitution[19] and would not have denied that moral principles, like those of the fifth amendment, might form the content of such legal constitutional restraints. Austin differed in thinking that restraints on the supreme legislative power could not have the force of law, but would remain merely political or moral checks;[20] but of course he would have recognized that a statute, for example, might confer a

---

it openly combats with the principle of utility; ought we to obey it? Ought we to violate it? Ought we to remain neuter between the law which commands an evil, and morality which forbids it?
See also Bentham, *A Fragment on Government*, in I *Works* 221, 287-88 (Bowring ed. 1859) (c. IV, 20th-25th paras.).

15   1 Blackstone, *Commentaries* *41. Bentham criticized "this dangerous maxim," saying "the natural tendency of such a doctrine is to impel a man, by the force of conscience, to rise up in arms against any law whatever that he happens not to like." Bentham, *A Fragment on Government*, in I *Works* 221, 287 (Bowring ed. 1859) (c. IV, 19th para.). See also Bentham, *A Comment on the Commentaries* 49 (1928) (c. III). For an expression of a fear lest anarchy result from such a doctrine, combined with a recognition that resistance may be justified on grounds of utility, see Austin, *op. cit. supra* note 12, at 186.

16   Bentham, *A Fragment on Government*, in I *Works* 221, 294 (Bowring ed. 1859) (c. V, 10th para.).

17   Bentham, *A Commentary on Humphrey's Real Property Code*, in 5 *Works* 389 (Bowring ed. 1843).

18   Austin, *op. cit. supra* note 12, at 162.

19   Bentham, *A Fragment on Government*, in I *Works* 221, 289-90 (Bowring ed. 1859) (c. IV, 33d-34th paras.).

20   See Austin, *op. cit. supra* note 12, at 231.

delegated legislative power and restrict the area of its exercise by reference to moral principles.

What both Bentham and Austin were anxious to assert were the following two simple things: first, in the absence of an expressed constitutional or legal provision, it could not follow from the mere fact that a rule violated standards of morality that it was not a rule of law; and conversely, it could not follow from the mere fact that a rule was morally desirable that it was a rule of law.

The history of this simple doctrine in the nineteenth century is too long and too intricate to trace here. Let me summarize it by saying that after it was propounded to the world by Austin it dominated English jurisprudence and constitutes part of the framework of most of those curiously English and perhaps unsatisfactory productions—the omnibus surveys of the whole field of jurisprudence. A succession of these were published after a full text of Austin's lectures finally appeared in 1863. In each of them the utilitarian separation of law and morals is treated as something that enables lawyers to attain a new clarity. Austin was said by one of his English successors, Amos, "to have delivered the law from the dead body of morality that still clung to it";[21] and even Maine, who was critical of Austin at many points, did not question this part of his doctrine. In the United States men like N. St. John Green,[22] Gray, and Holmes considered that insistence on this

distinction had enabled the understanding of law as a means of social control to get off to a fruitful new start; they welcomed it both as self-evident and as illuminating as a revealing tautology. This distinction is, of course, one of the main themes of Holmes' most famous essay "The Path of the Law,"[23] but the place it had in the estimation of these American writers is best seen in what Gray wrote at the turn of the century in *The Nature and Sources of the Law.* He said:

> The great gain in its fundamental conceptions which Jurisprudence made during the last century was the recognition of the truth that the Law of a State ... is not an ideal, but something which actually exists.... [I]t is not that which ought to be, but that which is. To fix this definitely in the Jurisprudence of the Common Law, is the feat that Austin accomplished.[24]

II.

So much for the doctrine in the heyday of its success. Let us turn now to some of the criticisms. Undoubtedly, when Bentham and Austin insisted on the distinction between law as it is and as it ought to be, they had in mind *particular* laws the meanings of which were clear and so not in dispute, and they were concerned to argue that such laws, even if morally outrageous, were still laws. It is, however, necessary, in considering the criticisms which later developed, to consider more than those criticisms which were directed to this particular point if we are to get at the root of the dissatisfaction felt; we must also take account of the objection that, even if what the Utilitarians said on this particular point were true, their insistence on it, in a terminology suggesting a general cleavage between what is and ought to

---

21 Amos, *The Science of Law* 4 (5th ed. 1881). See also Markby, *Elements of Law* 4-5 (5th ed. 1896):
Austin, by establishing the distinction between positive law and morals, not only laid the foundation for a science of law, but cleared the conception of law ... of a number of pernicious consequences to which ... it had been supposed to lead. Positive laws, as Austin has shown, must be legally binding, and yet a law may be unjust.... He has admitted that law itself may be immoral, in which case it may be our moral duty to disobey it....
Cf. Holland, *Jurisprudence* 1-20 (1880).
22 See Green, Book Review, 6 *Am. L. Rev.* 57, 61 (1871) (reprinted in Green, *Essays and Notes on the Law of Tort and Crime* 31, 35 (1933)).

23 10 *Harv. L. Rev.* 457 (1897).
24 Gray, *The Nature and Sources of the Law* 94 (1st ed. 1909) (§213).

be law, obscured the fact that at other points there is an essential point of contact between the two. So in what follows I shall consider not only criticisms of the particular point which the Utilitarians had in mind, but also the claim that an essential connection between law and morals emerges if we examine how laws, the meanings of which are in dispute, are interpreted and applied in concrete cases; and that this connection emerges again if we widen our point of view and ask, not whether every particular rule of law must satisfy a moral minimum in order to be a law, but whether a system of rules which altogether failed to do this could be a legal system.

There is, however, one major initial complexity by which criticism has been much confused. We must remember that the Utilitarians combined with their insistence on the separation of law and morals two other equally famous but distinct doctrines. One was the important truth that a purely analytical study of legal concepts, a study of the meaning of the distinctive vocabulary of the law, was as vital to our understanding of the nature of law as historical or sociological studies, though of course it could not supplant them. The other doctrine was the famous imperative theory of law—that law is essentially a command.

These three doctrines constitute the utilitarian tradition in jurisprudence; yet they are distinct doctrines. It is possible to endorse the separation between law and morals and to value analytical inquiries into the meaning of legal concepts and yet think it wrong to conceive of law as essentially a command. One source of great confusion in the criticism of the separation of law and morals was the belief that the falsity of any one of these three doctrines in the utilitarian tradition showed the other two to be false; what was worse was the failure to see that there were three quite separate doctrines in this tradition. The indiscriminate use of the label "positivism" to designate ambiguously each one of these three separate doctrines (together with some others which the Utilitarians never professed) has

perhaps confused the issue more than any other single factor.[25] Some of the early American critics of the Austinian doctrine were, however, admirably clear on just this matter. Gray, for example, added at the end of the tribute to Austin, which I have already quoted, the words, "He may have been wrong in treating the Law of the State as being the command of the sovereign"[26] and he touched shrewdly on many points where the command theory is defective. But other critics have been less clearheaded and have thought that the inadequacies of the command theory which gradually came to light were sufficient to demonstrate the falsity of the separation of law and morals.

---

25 It may help to identify five (there may be more) meanings of "positivism" bandied about in contemporary jurisprudence:

(1) the contention that laws are commands of human beings, see pp. 602-06 *infra*,

(2) the contention that there is no necessary connection between law and morals or law as it is and ought to be, see pp. 594-600 *supra*,

(3) the contention that the analysis (or study of the meaning) of legal concepts is (a) worth pursuing and (b) to be distinguished from historical inquiries into the causes or origins of laws, from sociological inquiries into the relation of law and other social phenomena, and from the criticism or appraisal of law whether in terms of morals, social aims, "functions," or otherwise, see pp. 624-26 *infra*,

(4) the contention that a legal system is a "closed logical system" in which correct legal decisions can be deduced by logical means from predetermined legal rules without reference to social aims, policies, moral standards, see pp. 608-10 *infra*, and

(5) the contention that moral judgments cannot be established or defended, as statements of facts can, by rational argument, evidence, or proof ("noncognitivism" in ethics), see pp. 624-26 *infra*.

Bentham and Austin held the views described in (1), (2), and (3) but not those in (4) and (5). Opinion (4) is often ascribed to analytical jurists, see pages pp. 608–10 infra, but I know of no "analyst" who held this view.

26 Gray, *The Nature and Sources of the Law* 94-95 (2d ed. 1921).

This was a mistake, but a natural one. To see how natural it was we must look a little more closely at the command idea. The famous theory that law is a command was a part of a wider and more ambitious claim. Austin said that the notion of a command was "the *key* to the sciences of jurisprudence and morals,"[27] and contemporary attempts to elucidate moral judgments in terms of "imperative" or "prescriptive" utterances echo this ambitious claim. But the command theory, viewed as an effort to identify even the quintessence of law, let alone the quintessence of morals, seems breathtaking in its simplicity and quite inadequate. There is much, even in the simplest legal system, that is distorted if presented as a command. Yet the Utilitarians thought that the essence of a legal system could be conveyed if the notion of a command were supplemented by that of a habit of obedience. The simple scheme was this: What is a command? It is simply an expression by one person of the desire that another person should do or abstain from some action, accompanied by a threat of punishment which is likely to follow disobedience. Commands are laws if two conditions are satisfied: first, they must be general; second, they must be commanded by what (as both Bentham and Austin claimed) exists in every political society whatever its constitutional form, namely, a person or a group of persons who are in receipt of habitual obedience from most of the society but pay no such obedience to others. These persons are its sovereign. Thus law is the command of the uncommanded commanders of society—the creation of the legally untrammelled will of the sovereign who is by definition outside the law.

It is easy to see that this account of a legal system is thread-bare. One can also see why it might seem that its inadequacy is due to the omission of some essential connection with morality. The situation which the simple trilogy of command, sanction, and sovereign avails to describe, if you take these notions

at all precisely, is like that of a gunman saying to his victim, "Give me your money or your life." The only difference is that in the case of a legal system the gunman says it to a large number of people who are accustomed to the racket and habitually surrender to it. Law surely is not the gunman situation writ large, and legal order is surely not to be thus simply identified with compulsion.

This scheme, despite the points of obvious analogy between a statute and a command, omits some of the most characteristic elements of law. Let me cite a few. It is wrong to think of a legislature (and a fortiori an electorate) with a changing membership, as a group of persons habitually obeyed: this simple idea is suited only to a monarch sufficiently long-lived for a "habit" to grow up. Even if we waive this point, nothing which legislators do makes law unless they comply with fundamental accepted rules specifying the essential lawmaking procedures. This is true even in a system having a simple unitary constitution like the British. These fundamental accepted rules specifying what the legislature must do to legislate are not commands habitually obeyed, nor can they be expressed as habits of obedience to persons. They lie at the root of a legal system, and what is most missing in the utilitarian scheme is an analysis of what it is for a social group and its officials to accept such rules. This notion, not that of a command as Austin claimed, is the "key to the science of jurisprudence," or at least one of the keys.

Again, Austin, in the case of a democracy, looked past the legislators to the electorate as "the sovereign" (or in England as part of it). He thought that in the United States the mass of the electors to the state and federal legislatures were the sovereign whose commands, given by their "agents" in the legislatures, were law. But on this footing the whole notion of the sovereign outside the law being "habitually obeyed" by the "bulk" of the population must go: for in this case the "bulk" obeys the bulk, that is, it obeys itself. Plainly the general acceptance of the authority of a lawmaking procedure, irrespec-

---

27 Austin, *op. cit. supra* note 12, at 13.

tive of the changing individuals who operate it from time to time, can be only distorted by an analysis in terms of mass habitual obedience to certain persons who are by definition outside the law, just as the cognate but much simpler phenomenon of the general social acceptance of a rule, say of taking off the hat when entering a church, would be distorted if represented as habitual obedience by the mass to specific persons.

Other critics dimly sensed a further and more important defect in the command theory, yet blurred the edge of an important criticism by assuming that the defect was due to the failure to insist upon some important connection between law and morals. This more radical defect is as follows. The picture that the command theory draws of life under law is essentially a simple relationship of the commander to the commanded, of superior to inferior, of top to bottom; the relationship is vertical between the commanders or authors of the law conceived of as essentially outside the law and those who are commanded and subject to the law. In this picture no place, or only an accidental or subordinate place, is afforded for a distinction between types of legal rules which are in fact radically different. Some laws require men to act in certain ways or to abstain from acting whether they wish to or not. The criminal law consists largely of rules of this sort: like commands they are simply "obeyed" or "disobeyed." But other legal rules are presented to society in quite different ways and have quite different functions. They provide facilities more or less elaborate for individuals to create structures of rights and duties for the conduct of life within the coercive framework of the law. Such are the rules enabling individuals to make contracts, wills, and trusts, and generally to mould their legal relations with others. Such rules, unlike the criminal law, are not factors designed to obstruct wishes and choices of an antisocial sort. On the contrary, these rules provide facilities for the realization of wishes and choices. They do not say (like commands) "do this whether you wish it or not," but rather "if you wish to do this, here is the way to do it." Under these rules we exercise powers, make claims, and assert rights. These phrases mark off characteristic features of laws that confer rights and powers; they are laws which are, so to speak, put at the disposition of individuals in a way in which the criminal law is not. Much ingenuity has gone into the task of "reducing" laws of this second sort to some complex variant of laws of the first sort. The effort to show that laws conferring rights are "really" only conditional stipulations of sanctions to be exacted from the person ultimately under a legal duty characterizes much of Kelsen's work.[28] Yet to urge this is really just to exhibit dogmatic determination to suppress one aspect of the legal system in order to maintain the theory that the stipulation of a sanction, like Austin's command, represents the quintessence of law. One might as well urge that the rules of baseball were "really" only complex conditional directions to the scorer and that this showed their real or "essential" nature.

One of the first jurists in England to break with the Austinian tradition, Salmond, complained that the analysis in terms of commands left the notion of a right unprovided with a place.[29] But he confused the point. He argued first, and correctly, that if laws are merely commands it is inexplicable that we should have come to speak of legal rights and powers as conferred or arising under them, but then wrongly concluded that the rules of a legal system must necessarily be connected with moral rules or principles of justice and that only on this footing could the phenomenon of legal rights be explained.

---

28 See, e.g., Kelsen, *General Theory of Law and State* 58-61, 143-44 (1945). According to Kelsen, all laws, not only those conferring rights and powers, are reducible to such "primary norms" conditionally stipulating sanctions.

29 Salmond, *The First Principles of Jurisprudence* 97-98 (1893). He protested against "the creed of what is termed the English school of jurisprudence," because it "attempted to deprive the idea of law of that ethical significance which is one of its most essential elements." *Id.* at 9, 10.

Otherwise, Salmond thought, we would have to say that a mere "verbal coincidence" connects the concepts of legal and moral right. Similarly, continental critics of the Utilitarians, always alive to the complexity of the notion of a subjective right, insisted that the command theory gave it no place. Hägerström insisted that if laws were merely commands the notion of an individual's right was really inexplicable, for commands are, as he said, something which we either obey or we do not obey; they do not confer rights.[30] But he, too, concluded that moral, or, as he put it, common-sense, notions of justice must therefore be necessarily involved in the analysis of any legal structure elaborate enough to confer rights.[31]

Yet, surely these arguments are confused. Rules that confer rights, though distinct from commands, need not be moral rules or coincide with them. Rights, after all, exist under the rules of ceremonies, games, and in many other spheres regulated by rules which are irrelevant to the question of justice or what the law ought to be. Nor need rules which confer rights be just or morally good rules. The rights of a master over his slaves show us that. "Their merit or demerit," as Austin termed it, depends on how rights are distributed in society and over whom or what they are exercised. These critics indeed revealed the inadequacy of the simple notions of command and habit for the analysis of law; at many points it is apparent that the social acceptance of a rule or standard of authority (even if it is motivated only by fear or superstition or rests on inertia) must be brought into the analysis and can-

not itself be reduced to the two simple terms. Yet nothing in this showed the utilitarian insistence on the distinction between the existence of law and its "merits" to be wrong.

III.

I now turn to a distinctively American criticism of the separation of the law that is from the law that ought to be. It emerged from the critical study of the judicial process with which American jurisprudence has been on the whole so beneficially occupied. The most skeptical of these critics—the loosely named "Realists" of the 1930's—perhaps too naïvely accepted the conceptual framework of the natural sciences as adequate for the characterization of law and for the analysis of rule-guided action of which a living system of law at least partly consists. But they opened men's eyes to what actually goes on when courts decide cases, and the contrast they drew between the actual facts of judicial decision and the traditional terminology for describing it as if it were a wholly logical operation was usually illuminating; for in spite of some exaggeration the "Realists" made us acutely conscious of one cardinal feature of human language and human thought, emphasis on which is vital not only for the understanding of law but in areas of philosophy far beyond the confines of jurisprudence. The insight of this school may be presented in the following example. A legal rule forbids you to take a vehicle into the public park. Plainly this forbids an automobile, but what about bicycles, roller skates, toy automobiles? What about airplanes? Are these, as we say, to be called "vehicles" for the purpose of the rule or not? If we are to communicate with each other at all, and if, as in the most elementary form of law, we are to express our intentions that a certain type of behavior be regulated by rules, then the general words we use—like "vehicle" in the case I consider—must have, some standard instance in which no doubts are felt about its application.

---

30 Hägerström, *Inquiries into the Nature of Law and Morals* 217 (Olivecrona ed. 1953): "[T]he whole theory of the subjective rights of private individuals is incompatible with the imperative theory." See also *id.* at 221:

The description of them [claims to legal protection] as rights is wholly derived from the idea that the law which is concerned with them is a true expression of rights and duties in the sense in which the popular notion of justice understands these terms.

31 *Id.* at 218.

There must be a core of settled meaning, but there will be, as well, a penumbra of debatable cases in which words are neither obviously applicable nor obviously ruled out. These cases will each have some features in common with the standard case; they will lack others or be accompanied by features not present in the standard case. Human invention and natural processes continually throw up such variants on the familiar, and if we are to say that these ranges of facts do or do not fall under existing rules, then the classifier must make a decision which is not dictated to him, for the facts and phenomena to which we fit our words and apply our rules are as it were *dumb*. The toy automobile cannot speak up and say, "I am a vehicle for the purpose of this legal rule," nor can the roller skates chorus, "We are not a vehicle." Fact situations do not await us neatly labeled, creased, and folded, nor is their legal classification written on them to be simply read off by the judge. Instead, in applying legal rules, someone must take the responsibility of deciding that words do or do not cover some case in hand with all the practical consequences involved in this decision.

We may call the problems which arise outside the hard core of standard instances or settled meaning "problems of the penumbra"; they are always with us whether in relation to such trivial things as the regulation of the use of the public park or in relation to the multidimensional generalities of a constitution. If a penumbra of uncertainty must surround all legal rules, then their application to specific cases in the penumbral area cannot be a matter of logical deduction, and so deductive reasoning, which for generations has been cherished as the very perfection of human reasoning, cannot serve as a model for what judges, or indeed anyone, should do in bringing particular cases under general rules. In this area men cannot live by deduction alone. And it follows that if legal arguments and legal decisions of penumbral questions are to be rational, their rationality must lie in something other than a logical relation to premises. So if it

is rational or "sound" to argue and to decide that for the purposes of this rule an airplane is not a vehicle, this argument must be sound or rational without being logically conclusive. What is it then that makes such decisions correct or at least better than alternative decisions? Again, it seems true to say that the criterion which makes a decision sound in such cases is some concept of what the law ought to be; it is easy to slide from that into saying that it must be a moral judgment about what law ought to be. So here we touch upon a point of necessary "intersection between law and morals" which demonstrates the falsity or, at any rate, the misleading character of the Utilitarians' emphatic insistence on the separation of law as it is and ought to be. Surely, Bentham and Austin could only have written as they did because they misunderstood or neglected this aspect of the judicial process, because they ignored the problems of the penumbra.

The misconception of the judicial process which ignores the problems of the penumbra and which views the process as consisting pre-eminently in deductive reasoning is often stigmatized as the error of "formalism" or "literalism." My question now is, how and to what extent does the demonstration of this error show the utilitarian distinction to be wrong or misleading? Here there are many issues which have been confused, but I can only disentangle some. The charge of formalism has been leveled both at the "positivist" legal theorist and at the courts, but of course it must be a very different charge in each case. Leveled at the legal theorist, the charge means that he has made a theoretical mistake about the character of legal decision; he has thought of the reasoning involved as consisting in deduction from premises in which the judges' practical choices or decisions play no part. It would be easy to show that Austin was guiltless of this error: only an entire misconception of what analytical jurisprudence is and why he thought it important has led to the view that he, or any other analyst, believed that the law was a closed logical system in which judges deduced their decisions from premises.[32] On the contrary, he was very much alive to the character of language, to its vagueness or open character;[33] he thought that in the penumbral situation judges must necessarily legislate,[34] and, in accents that sometimes recall those of the late Judge Jerome Frank, he berated the common-law judges for legislating feebly and timidly and for blindly relying on real or fancied analogies with past cases instead of adapting their decisions to the growing needs of society as revealed by the moral standard of utility.[35] The villains of this piece, responsible for the conception of the judge as an automaton, are not the Utilitarian thinkers. The responsibility, if it is to be laid at the door of any theorist, is with thinkers like Blackstone and, at an earlier stage, Montesquieu. The root of this evil is preoccupation with the separation of powers and Blackstone's "childish fiction" (as Austin termed it) that judges only "find," never "make," law.

But we are concerned with "formalism" as a vice not of jurists but of judges. What precisely is it for a judge to commit this error, to be a "formalist," "automatic," a "slot machine"? Curiously enough the literature which is full of the denunciation of

---

32 This misunderstanding of analytical jurisprudence is to be found in, among others, Stone, *The Province and Function of Law* 141 (1950):

> In short, rejecting the implied assumption that all propositions of all parts of the law must be logically consistent with each other and proceed on a single set of definitions ... he [Cardozo, J.,] denied that the law is actually what the analytical jurist, *for his limited purposes*, assumes it to be.

See also *id.* at 49, 52, 138, 140; Friedmann, *Legal Theory* 209 (3rd ed. 1953). This misunderstanding seems to depend on the unexamined and false belief that analytical studies of the meaning of legal terms would be impossible or absurd if, to reach sound decisions in particular cases, more than a capacity for formal logical reasoning from unambiguous and clear predetermined premises is required.

33 See the discussion of vagueness and uncertainty in law, in Austin, *op. cit. supra* note 12, at 202-05, 207, in which Austin recognized that, in consequence of this vagueness, often only "fallible tests" can be provided for determining whether particular cases fall under general expressions.

34 See Austin, *op. cit. supra* note 12, at 191: "I cannot understand how any person who has considered the subject can suppose that society could possibly have gone on if judges had not legislated...." As a corrective to the belief that the analytical jurist must take a "slot machine" or "mechanical" view of the judicial process it is worth noting the following observations made by Austin:

(1) Whenever law has to be applied, the "'competition of opposite analogies'" may arise, for the case "may resemble in some of its points" cases to which the rule has been applied in the past and in other points "cases from which the application of the law has been withheld." 2 Austin, *Lectures on Jurisprudence* 633 (5th ed. 1885).

(2) Judges have commonly decided cases and so derived new rules by "building" on a variety of grounds including sometimes (in Austin's opinion too rarely) their views of what law ought to be. Most commonly they have derived law from preexisting law by "consequence founded on analogy," i.e., they have made a new rule "in *consequence* of the existence of a similar rule applying to subjects which are *analogous*.... 2 *id.* at 638-39.

(3) "[I]f every rule in a system of law were perfectly definite or precise," these difficulties incident to the application of law would not arise. "But the ideal completeness and correctness I now have imagined is not attainable in fact.... though the system had been built and ordered with matchless solicitude and skill." 2 *id.* at 997-98. Of course he thought that much could and should be done by codification to eliminate uncertainty. See 2 *id.* at 662-81.

35 2 *id.* at 641:

Nothing, indeed, can be more natural, than that legislators, direct or judicial (especially if they be narrow-minded, timid and unskillful), should lean as much as they can on the examples set by their predecessors.

See also 2 *id.* at 647:

But it is much to be regretted that Judges of capacity, experience and weight, have not seized every opportunity of introducing a new rule (a rule beneficial for the future).... This is the reproach I should be inclined to make against Lord Eldon.... [T]he judges of the Common Law Courts would not do what they ought to have done, namely to model their rules of law and of procedure to the growing exigencies of society, instead of stupidly and sulkily adhering to the old and barbarous usages.

these vices never makes this clear in concrete terms; instead we have only descriptions which cannot mean what they appear to say: it is said that in the formalist error courts make an excessive use of logic, take a thing to "a dryly logical extreme,"[36] or make an excessive use of analytical methods. But just how in being a formalist does a judge make an excessive use of logic? It is clear that the essence of his error is to give some general term an interpretation which is blind to social values and consequences (or which is in some other way stupid or perhaps merely disliked by critics). But logic does not prescribe interpretation of terms; it dictates neither the stupid nor intelligent interpretation of any expression. Logic only tells you hypothetically that *if* you give a certain term a certain interpretation then a certain conclusion follows. Logic is silent on how to classify particulars—and this is the heart of a judicial decision. So this reference to logic and to logical extremes is a misnomer for something else, which must be this. A judge has to apply a rule to a concrete case—perhaps the rule that one may not take a stolen "vehicle" across state lines, and in this case an airplane has been taken.[37] He either does not see or pretends not to see that the general terms of this rule are susceptible of different interpretations and that he has a choice left open uncontrolled by linguistic conventions. He ignores, or is blind to, the fact that he is in the area of the penumbra and is not dealing with a standard case. Instead of choosing in the light of social aims, the judge fixes the meaning in a different way. He either takes the meaning that the word most obviously suggests in its ordinary nonlegal context to ordinary men, or one which the word has been given in some other legal context, or, still worse, he thinks of a standard case and then arbitrarily identifies certain features in it—for example, in the case of a vehicle,

(1) normally used on land, (2) capable of carrying a human person, (3) capable of being self-propelled— and treats these three as always necessary and always sufficient conditions for the use in all contexts of the word "vehicle," irrespective of the social consequences of giving it this interpretation. This choice, not "logic," would force the judge to include a toy motor car (if electrically propelled) and to exclude bicycles and the airplane. In all this there is possibly great stupidity but no more "logic," and no less, than in cases in which the interpretation given to a general term and the consequent application of some general rule to a particular case is consciously controlled by some identified social aim.

Decisions made in a fashion as blind as this would scarcely deserve the name of decisions; we might as well toss a penny in applying a rule of law. But it is at least doubtful whether any judicial decisions (even in England) have been quite as automatic as this. Rather, either the interpretations stigmatized as automatic have resulted from the conviction that it is fairer in a criminal statute to take a meaning which would jump to the mind of the ordinary man at the cost even of defeating other values, and this itself is a social policy (though possibly a bad one); or much more frequently, what is stigmatized as "mechanical" and "automatic" is a determined choice made indeed in the light of a social aim but of a conservative social aim. Certainly many of the Supreme Court decisions at the turn of the century which have been so stigmatized[38] represent clear choices in the penumbral area to give effect to a policy of a conservative type. This is peculiarly true of Mr. Justice Peckham's opinions defining the spheres of police power and due process.[39]

---

36 Hynes v. New York Cent. R.R., 231 N.Y. 229, 235, 131 N.E. 898, 900 (1921); see Pound, *Interpretations of Legal History* 123 (2d ed. 1930); Stone, *op. cit. supra* note 32, at 140-41.

37 See McBoyle v. United States, 283 U.S. 25 (1931).

38 See, e.g., Pound, *Mechanical Jurisprudence, 8 Colum. L. Rev.* 605, 615-16 (1908).

39 See, e.g., Lochner v. New York, 198 U.S. 45 (1905). Justice Peckham's opinion that there were no reasonable grounds for interfering with the right of free contract by determining the hours of labour in the occupation of a baker may indeed be a wrongheaded piece of con-

But how does the wrongness of deciding cases in an automatic and mechanical way and the rightness of deciding cases by reference to social purposes show that the utilitarian insistence on the distinction between what the law is and what it ought to be is wrong? I take it that no one who wished to use these vices of formalism as proof that the distinction between what is and what ought to be is mistaken would deny that the decisions stigmatized as automatic are law; nor would he deny that the system in which such automatic decisions are made is a legal system. Surely he would say that they are law, but they are bad law, they ought not to be law. But this would be to use the distinction, not to refute it; and of course both Bentham and Austin used it to attack judges for failing to decide penumbral cases in accordance with the growing needs of society.

Clearly, if the demonstration of the errors of formalism is to show the utilitarian distinction to be wrong, the point must be drastically restated. The point must be not merely that a judicial decision to be rational must be made in the light of some conception of what ought to be, but that the aims, the social policies and purposes to which judges should appeal if their decisions are to be rational, are themselves to be considered as part of the law in some suitably wide sense of "law" which is held to be more illuminating than that used by the Utilitarians. This restatement of the point would have the following consequence: instead of saying that the recurrence of penumbral questions shows us that legal rules are essentially incomplete, and that, when they fail to determine decisions, judges must legislate and so exercise a creative choice between alternatives, we shall say that the social policies which guide the judges' choice are in a sense there for them to discover; the judges are only "drawing out" of the rule what, if it is properly understood, is "latent" within it. To call this judicial legislation is to obscure some

servatism but there is nothing automatic or mechanical about it.

essential continuity between the clear cases of the application and the penumbral decisions. I shall question later whether this way of talking is salutary, but I wish at this time to point out something obvious, but likely, if not stated, to tangle the issues. It does not follow that, because the opposite of a decision reached blindly in the formalist or literalist manner is a decision intelligently reached by reference to some conception of what ought to be, we have a junction of law and morals. We must, I think, beware of thinking in a too simple-minded fashion about the word "ought." This is not because there is no distinction to be made between law as it is and ought to be. Far from it. It is because the distinction should be between what is and what from many different points of view ought to be. The word "ought" merely reflects the presence of some standard of criticism; one of these standards is a moral standard but not all standards are moral. We say to our neighbour, "You ought not to lie," and that may certainly be a moral judgment, but we should remember that the baffled poisoner may say, "I ought to have given her a second dose." The point here is that intelligent decisions which we oppose to mechanical or formal decisions are not necessarily identical with decisions defensible on moral grounds. We may say of many a decision: "Yes, that is right; that is as it ought to be," and we may mean only that some accepted purpose or policy has been thereby advanced; we may not mean to endorse the moral propriety of the policy or the decision. So the contrast between the mechanical decision and the intelligent one can be reproduced inside a system dedicated to the pursuit of the most evil aims. It does not exist as a contrast to be found only in legal systems which, like our own, widely recognize principles of justice and moral claims of individuals.

An example may make this point plainer. With us the task of sentencing in criminal cases is the one that seems most obviously to demand from the judge the exercise of moral judgment. Here the factors to be weighed seem clearly to be moral factors:

society must not be exposed to wanton attack; too much misery must not be inflicted on either the victim or his dependents; efforts must be made to enable him to lead a better life and regain a position in the society whose laws he has violated. To a judge striking the balance among these claims, with all the discretion and perplexities involved, his task seems as plain an example of the exercise of moral judgment as could be; and it seems to be the polar opposite of some mechanical application of a tariff of penalties fixing a sentence careless of the moral claims which in our system have to be weighed. So here intelligent and rational decision is guided however uncertainly by moral aims. But we have only to vary the example to see that this need not necessarily be so and surely, if it need not necessarily be so, the Utilitarian point remains unshaken. Under the Nazi regime men were sentenced by courts for criticism of the regime. Here the choice of sentence might be guided exclusively by consideration of what was needed to maintain the state's tyranny effectively. What sentence would both terrorize the public at large and keep the friends and family of the prisoner in suspense so that both hope and fear would cooperate as factors making for subservience? The prisoner of such a system would be regarded simply as an object to be used in pursuit of these aims. Yet, in contrast with a mechanical decision, decision on these grounds would be intelligent and purposive, and from one point of view the decision would be as it ought to be. Of course, I am not unaware that a whole philosophical tradition has sought to demonstrate the fact that we cannot correctly call decisions or behavior truly rational unless they are in conformity with moral aims and principles. But the example I have used seems to me to serve at least as a warning that we cannot use the errors of formalism as something which per se demonstrates the falsity of the utilitarian insistence on the distinction between law as it is and law as *morally* it ought to be.

We can now return to the main point. If it is true that the intelligent decision of penumbral ques-

tions is one made not mechanically but in the light of aims, purposes, and policies, though not necessarily in the light of anything we would call moral principles, is it wise to express this important fact by saying that the firm utilitarian distinction between what the law is and what it ought to be should be dropped? Perhaps the claim that it is wise cannot be theoretically refuted for it is, in effect, an *invitation* to revise our conception of what a legal rule is. We are invited to include in the "rule" the various aims and policies in the light of which its penumbral cases are decided on the ground that these aims have, because of their importance, as much right to be called law as the core of legal rules whose meaning is settled. But though an invitation cannot be refuted, it may be refused and I would proffer two reasons for refusing this invitation. First, everything we have learned about the judicial process can be expressed in other less mysterious ways. We can say laws are incurably incomplete and we must decide the penumbral cases rationally by reference to social aims. I think Holmes, who had such a vivid appreciation of the fact that "general propositions do not decide concrete cases," would have put it that way. Second, to insist on the utilitarian distinction is to emphasize that the hard core of settled meaning is law in some centrally important sense and that even if there are borderlines, there must first be lines. If this were not so the notion of rules controlling courts' decisions would be senseless as some of the "Realists"—in their most extreme moods, and, I think, on bad grounds—claimed.[40]

---

40 One recantation of this extreme position is worth mention in the present context. In the first edition of *The Bramble Bush*, Professor Llewellyn committed himself wholeheartedly to the view that "what these officials do about disputes is, to my mind, the law itself" and that "*rules* ... are important so far as they help you ... predict what judges will do.... That is all their importance, except as pretty playthings." Llewellyn, *The Bramble Bush* 3, 5 (1st ed. 1930). In the second edition he said that these were "unhappy words when not more fully developed, and they are plainly at best a very partial statement of

By contrast, to soften the distinction, to assert mysteriously that there is some fused identity between law as it is and as it ought to be, is to suggest that all legal questions are fundamentally like those of the penumbra. It is to assert that there is no central element of actual law to be seen in the core of central meaning which rules have, that there is nothing in the nature of a legal rule inconsistent with *all* questions being open to reconsideration in the light of social policy. Of course, it is good to be occupied with the penumbra. Its problems are rightly the daily diet of the law schools. But to be occupied with the penumbra is one thing, to be preoccupied with it another. And preoccupation with the penumbra is, if I may say so, as rich a source of confusion in the American legal tradition as formalism in the English. Of course we might abandon the notion that rules have authority; we might cease to attach force or even meaning to an argument that a case falls clearly within a rule and the scope of a precedent. We might call all such reasoning "automatic" or "mechanical," which is already the routine invective of the courts. But until we decide that this *is* what we want, we should not encourage it by obliterating the Utilitarian distinction.

IV.

The third criticism of the separation of law and morals is of a very different character; it certainly is less an intellectual argument against the Utilitarian distinction than a passionate appeal supported not by detailed reasoning but by reminders of a terrible experience. For it consists of the testimony of those who have descended into Hell, and, like Ulysses or Dante, brought back a message for human beings.

Only in this case the Hell was not beneath or beyond earth, but on it; it was a Hell created on earth by men for other men.

This appeal comes from those German thinkers who lived through the Nazi regime and reflected upon its evil manifestations in the legal system. One of these thinkers, Gustav Radbruch, had himself shared the "positivist" doctrine until the Nazi tyranny, but he was converted by this experience and so his appeal to other men to discard the doctrine of the separation of law and morals has the special poignancy of a recantation. What is important about this criticism is that it really does confront the particular point which Bentham and Austin had in mind in urging the separation of law as it is and as it ought to be. These German thinkers put their insistence on the need to join together what the Utilitarians separated just where this separation was of most importance in the eyes of the Utilitarians; for they were concerned with the problem posed by the existence of morally evil laws.

Before his conversion Radbruch held that resistance to law was a matter for the personal conscience, to be thought out by the individual as a moral problem, and the validity of a law could not be disproved by showing that its requirements were morally evil or even by showing that the effect of compliance with the law would be more evil than the effect of disobedience. Austin, it may be recalled, was emphatic in condemning those who said that if human laws conflicted with the fundamental principles of morality then they cease to be laws, as talking "stark nonsense."

> The most pernicious laws, and therefore those which are most opposed to the will of God, have been and are continually enforced as laws by judicial tribunals. Suppose an act innocuous, or positively beneficial, be prohibited by the sovereign under the penalty of death; if I commit this act, I shall be tried and condemned, and if I object to

---

the whole truth.... [O]ne office of law is to control officials in some part, and to guide them even ... where no thoroughgoing control is possible, or is desired.... [T]he words fail to take proper account ... of the office of the institution of law as an instrument of conscious shaping...." Llewellyn, *The Bramble Bush* 9 (2d ed. 1951).

the sentence, that it is contrary to the law of God ... the court of justice will demonstrate the inconclusiveness of my reasoning by hanging me up, in pursuance of the law of which I have impugned the validity. An exception, demurrer, or plea, founded on the law of God was never heard in a Court of Justice, from the creation of the world down to the present moment.[41]

These are strong, indeed brutal words, but we must remember that they went along—in the case of Austin and, of course, Bentham—with the conviction that if laws reached a certain degree of iniquity then there would be a plain moral obligation to resist them and to withhold obedience. We shall see, when we consider the alternatives, that this simple presentation of the human dilemma which may arise has much to be said for it.

Radbruch, however, had concluded from the ease with which the Nazi regime had exploited subservience to mere law—or expressed, as he thought, in the "positivist" slogan "law as law" (*Gesetz als Gesetz*)—and from the failure of the German legal profession to protest against the enormities which they were required to perpetrate in the name of law, that "positivism" (meaning here the insistence on the separation of law as it is from law as it ought to be) had powerfully contributed to the horrors. His considered reflections led him to the doctrine that the fundamental principles of humanitarian morality were part of the very concept of *Recht* or Legality and that no positive enactment or statute, however clearly it was expressed and however clearly it conformed with the formal criteria of validity of a given legal system, could be valid if it contravened basic principles of morality. This doctrine can be appreciated fully only if the nuances imported by the German word *Recht* are grasped. But it is clear that the doctrine meant that every lawyer and judge should denounce statutes that transgressed the fundamental principles not as merely immoral or wrong but as having no legal character, and enactments which on this ground lack the quality of law should not be taken into account in working out the legal position of any given individual in particular circumstances. The striking recantation of his previous doctrine is unfortunately omitted from the translation of his works, but it should be read by all who wish to think afresh on the question of the interconnection of law and morals.[42]

It is impossible to read without sympathy Radbruch's passionate demand that the German legal conscience should be open to the demands of morality and his complaint that this has been too little the case in the German tradition. On the other hand there is an extraordinary naïveté in the view that insensitiveness to the demands of morality and subservience to state power in a people like the Germans should have arisen from the belief that law might be law though it failed to conform with the minimum requirements of morality. Rather this terrible history prompts inquiry into why emphasis on the slogan "law is law," and the distinction between law and morals, acquired a sinister character in Germany, but elsewhere, as with the Utilitarians themselves, went along with the most enlightened liberal attitudes. But something more disturbing than naïveté is latent in Radbruch's whole presentation of the issues to which the existence of morally iniquitous laws give rise. It is not, I think, uncharitable to say that we can see in his argument that he has only half digested the spiritual message of liberalism which

---

41 Austin, *The Province of Jurisprudence Determined* 185 (Library of Ideas ed. 1954).

42 See Radbruch, *Gesetzliches Unrecht und Übergesetzliches Recht*, 1 *Süddeutsche Juristen-Zeitung* 105 (Germany 1946) (reprinted in Radbruch, *Rechtsphilosophie* 347 [4th ed. 1950]). I have used the translation of part of this essay and of Radbruch, *Die Erneurung des Rechts*, 2. *Die Wandlung* 8 (Germany, 1947), prepared by Professor Lon Fuller of the Harvard Law School as a mimeographed supplement to the readings in jurisprudence used in his course at Harvard.

he is seeking to convey to the legal profession. For everything that he says is really dependent upon an enormous overvaluation of the importance of the bare fact that a rule may be said to be a valid rule of law, as if this, once declared, was conclusive of the final moral question: "Ought this rule of law to be obeyed?" Surely the truly liberal answer to any sinister use of the slogan "law is law" or of the distinction between law and morals is, "Very well, but that does not conclude the question. Law is not morality; do not let it supplant morality."

However, we are not left to a mere academic discussion in order to evaluate the plea which Radbruch made for the revision of the distinction between law and morals. After the war Radbruch's conception of law as containing in itself the essential moral principle of humanitarianism was applied in practice by German courts in certain cases in which local war criminals, spies, and informers under the Nazi regime were punished. The special importance of these cases is that the persons accused of these crimes claimed that what they had done was not illegal under the laws of the regime in force at the time these actions were performed. This plea was met with the reply that the laws upon which they relied were invalid as contravening the fundamental principles of morality. Let me cite briefly one of these cases.[43]

In 1944 a woman, wishing to be rid of her husband, denounced him to the authorities for insulting remarks he had made about Hitler while home on leave from the German army. The wife was under no legal duty to report his acts, though what he had said was apparently in violation of statutes making it illegal to make statements detrimental to the government of the Third Reich or to impair by any means the military defense of the German people. The husband was arrested and sentenced to death,

apparently pursuant to these statutes, though he was not executed but was sent to the front. In 1949 the wife was prosecuted in a West German court for an offense which we would describe as illegally depriving a person of his freedom (*rechtswidrige Freiheitsberaubung*). This was punishable as a crime under the German Criminal Code of 1871 which had remained in force continuously since its enactment. The wife pleaded that her husband's imprisonment was pursuant to the Nazi statutes and hence that she had committed no crime. The court of appeal to which the case ultimately came held that the wife was guilty of procuring the deprivation of her husband's liberty by denouncing him to the German courts, even though he had been sentenced by a court for having violated a statute, since, to quote the words of the court, the statute "was contrary to the sound conscience and sense of justice of all decent human beings." This reasoning was followed in many cases which have been hailed as a triumph of the doctrines of natural law and as signaling the overthrow of positivism. The unqualified satisfaction with this result seems to me to be hysteria. Many of us might applaud the objective—that of punishing a woman for an outrageously immoral act—but this was secured only by declaring a statute established since 1934 not to have the force of law, and at least the wisdom of this course must be doubted. There were, of course, two other choices. One was to let the woman go unpunished; one can sympathize with and endorse the view that this might have been a bad thing to do. The other was to face the fact that if the woman were to be punished it must be pursuant to the introduction of a frankly retrospective law and with a full consciousness of what was sacrificed in securing her punishment in this way. Odious as retrospective criminal legislation and punishment may be, to have pursued it openly in this case would at least have had the merits of candour. It would have made plain that in punishing the woman a choice had to be made between two evils, that of leaving her unpunished and that of sacrificing a very precious principle of

43 Judgment of July 27, 1949, Oberlandesgericht, Bamberg, 5 *Süddeutsche Juristen-Zeitung* 207 (Germany, 1950), 64 *Harv. L. Rev.* 1005 (1951); see Friedmann, *Legal Theory* 457 (3rd ed. 1953).

morality endorsed by most legal systems. Surely if we have learned anything from the history of morals it is that the thing to do with a moral quandary is not to hide it. Like nettles, the occasions when life forces us to choose between the lesser of two evils must be grasped with the consciousness that they are what they are. The vice of this use of the principle that, at certain limiting points, what is utterly immoral cannot be law or lawful is that it will serve to cloak the true nature of the problems with which we are faced and will encourage the romantic optimism that all the values we cherish ultimately will fit into a single system, that no one of them has to be sacrificed or compromised to accommodate another.

> "All Discord Harmony not understood,
> All Partial Evil Universal Good"

This is surely untrue and there is an insincerity in any formulation of our problem which allows us to describe the treatment of the dilemma as if it were the disposition of the ordinary case.

It may seem perhaps to make too much of forms, even perhaps of words, to emphasize one way of disposing of this difficult case as compared with another which might have led, so far as the woman was concerned, to exactly the same result. Why should we dramatize the difference between them? We might punish the woman under a new retrospective law and declare overtly that we were doing something inconsistent with our principles as the lesser of two evils; or we might allow the case to pass as one in which we do not point out precisely where we sacrifice such a principle. But candour is not just one among many minor virtues of the administration of law, just as it is not merely a minor virtue of morality. For if we adopt Radbruch's view, and with him and the German courts make our protest against evil law in the form of an assertion that certain rules cannot be law because of their moral iniquity, we confuse one of the most powerful, because it is the simplest, forms of moral criticism. If with the Utilitarians we speak plainly, we say that laws may be law but too

evil to be obeyed. This is a moral condemnation which everyone can understand and it makes an immediate and obvious claim to moral attention. If, on the other hand, we formulate our objection as an assertion that these evil things are not law, here is an assertion which many people do not believe, and if they are disposed to consider it at all, it would seem to raise a whole host of philosophical issues before it can be accepted. So perhaps the most important single lesson to be learned from this form of the denial of the Utilitarian distinction is the one that the Utilitarians were most concerned to teach: when we have the ample resources of plain speech we must not present the moral criticism of institutions as propositions of a disputable philosophy.

V.

I have endeavored to show that, in spite of all that has been learned and experienced since the Utilitarians wrote, and in spite of the defects of other parts of their doctrine, their protest against the confusion of what is and what ought to be law has a moral as well as an intellectual value. Yet it may well be said that, though this distinction is valid and important if applied to any particular law of a system, it is at least misleading if we attempt to apply it to "law," that is, to the notion of a legal system, and that if we insist, as I have, on the narrower truth (or truism), we obscure a wider (or deeper) truth. After all, it may be urged, we have learned that there are many things which are untrue of laws taken separately, but which are true and important in a legal system considered as a whole. For example, the connection between law and sanctions and between the existence of law and its "efficacy" must be understood in this more general way. It is surely not arguable (without some desperate extension of the word "sanction" or artificial narrowing of the word "law") that every law in a municipal legal system must have a sanction, yet it is at least plausible to argue that a legal system must, to be a legal system, provide sanctions for certain of its rules. So too, a rule of law may be said to exist though enforced or obeyed in only a minority of cases, but this could not be said of a legal system as a whole. Perhaps the differences with respect to laws taken separately and a legal system as a whole are also true of the connection between moral (or some other) conceptions of what law ought to be and law in this wider sense.

This line of argument, found (at least in embryo form) in Austin, where he draws attention to the fact that every developed legal system contains certain fundamental notions which are "necessary" and "bottomed in the common nature of man,"[44] is worth pursuing—up to a point—and I shall say briefly why and how far this is so.

We must avoid, if we can, the arid wastes of inappropriate definition, for, in relation to a concept as many-sided and vague as that of a legal system, disputes about the "essential" character, or necessity to the whole, of any single element soon begin to look like disputes about whether chess could be "chess" if played without pawns. There is a wish, which may be understandable, to cut straight through the question whether a legal system, to be a legal system, must measure up to some moral or other standard with simple statements of fact: for example, that no system which utterly failed in this respect has ever existed or could endure; that the normally fulfilled assumption that a legal system aims at some form of justice colours the whole way in which we interpret specific rules in particular cases, and if this normally fulfilled assumption were not fulfilled no one would have any reason to obey except fear (and probably not that) and still less, of course, any moral obligation to obey. The connection between law and moral standards and principles of justice is therefore as little arbitrary and as "necessary" as the connection between law and sanctions, and the pur-

suit of the question whether this necessity is logical (part of the "meaning" of law) or merely factual or causal can safely be left as an innocent pastime for philosophers.

Yet in two respects I should wish to go further (even though this involves the use of a philosophical fantasy) and show what could intelligibly be meant by the claim that certain provisions in a legal system are "necessary." The world in which we live, and we who live in it, may one day change in many different ways; and if this change were radical enough not only would certain statements of fact now true be false and vice versa, but whole ways of thinking and talking which constitute our present conceptual apparatus, through which we see the world and each other, would lapse. We have only to consider how the whole of our social, moral, and legal life, as we understand it now, depends on the contingent fact that though our bodies do change in shape, size, and other physical properties they do not do this so drastically nor with such quicksilver rapidity and irregularity that we cannot identify each other as the same persistent individual over considerable spans of time. Though this is but a contingent fact which may one day be different, on it at present rest huge structures of our thought and principles of action and social life. Similarly, consider the following possibility (not because it is more than a possibility but because it reveals why we think certain things necessary in a legal system and what we mean by this): suppose that men were to become invulnerable to attack by each other, were clad perhaps like giant land crabs with an impenetrable carapace, and could extract the food they needed from the air by some internal chemical process. In such circumstances (the details of which can be left to science fiction) rules forbidding the free use of violence and rules constituting the minimum form of property—with its rights and duties sufficient to enable food to grow and be retained until eaten—would not have the necessary nonarbitrary status which they have for us, constituted as we are in a world like ours. At present,

44 Austin, *Uses of the Study of Jurisprudence*, in *The Province of Jurisprudence Determined* 365, 373, 367-69 (Library of Ideas ed. 1954).

and until such radical changes supervene, such rules are so fundamental that if a legal system did not have them there would be no point in having any other rules at all. Such rules overlap with basic moral principles vetoing murder, violence, and theft; and so we can add to the factual statement that all legal systems in fact coincide with morality at such vital points, the statement that this is, in this sense, necessarily so. And why not call it a "natural" necessity?

Of course even this much depends on the fact that in asking what content a legal system must have we take this question to be worth asking only if we who consider it cherish the humble aim of survival in close proximity to our fellows. Natural-law theory, however, in all its protean guises, attempts to push the argument much further and to assert that human beings are equally devoted to and united in their conception of aims (the pursuit of knowledge, justice to their fellow men) other than that of survival, and these dictate a further necessary content to a legal system (over and above my humble minimum) without which it would be pointless. Of course we must be careful not to exaggerate the differences among human beings, but it seems to me that above this minimum the purposes men have for living in society are too conflicting and varying to make possible much extension of the argument that some fuller overlap of legal rules and moral standards is "necessary" in this sense.

Another aspect of the matter deserves attention. If we attach to a legal system the minimum meaning that it must consist of general rules—general both in the sense that they refer to courses of action, not single actions, and to multiplicities of men, not single individuals—this meaning connotes the principle of treating like cases alike, though the criteria of when cases are alike will be, so far, only the general elements specified in the rules. It is, however, true that *one* essential element of the concept of justice is the principle of treating like cases alike. This is justice in the administration of the law, not justice of the law. So there is, in the very notion of law consisting

of general rules, something which prevents us from treating it as if morally it is utterly neutral, without any necessary contact with moral principles. Natural procedural justice consists therefore of those principles of objectivity and impartiality in the administration of the law which implement just this aspect of law and which are designed to ensure that rules are applied only to what are genuinely cases of the rule or at least to minimize the risks of inequalities in this sense.

These two reasons (or excuses) for talking of a certain overlap between legal and moral standards as necessary and natural, of course, should not satisfy anyone who is really disturbed by the Utilitarian or "positivist" insistence that law and morality are distinct. This is so because a legal system that satisfied these minimum requirements might apply, with the most pedantic impartiality as between the persons affected, laws which were hideously oppressive, and might deny to a vast rightless slave population the minimum benefits of protection from violence and theft. The stink of such societies is, after all, still in our nostrils and to argue that they have (or had) no legal system would only involve the repetition of the argument. Only if the rules failed to provide these essential benefits and protection for anyone—even for a slave-owning group—would the minimum be unsatisfied and the system sink to the status of a set of meaningless taboos. Of course no one denied those benefits would have any reason to obey except fear and would have every moral reason to revolt.

VI.

I should be less than candid if I did not, in conclusion, consider something which, I suspect, most troubles those who react strongly against "legal positivism." Emphasis on the distinction between law as it is and law as it ought to be may be taken to depend upon and to entail what are called "subjectivist" and "relativist" or "noncognitive" theories concerning the very nature of moral judgments, moral distinctions, or "values." Of course the Utilitarians themselves (as distinct from later positivists like Kelsen) did not countenance any such theories: however unsatisfactory their moral philosophy may appear to us now. Austin thought ultimate moral principles were the command of God, known to us by revelation or through the "index" of utility, and Bentham thought they were verifiable propositions about utility. Nonetheless I think (though I cannot prove) that insistence upon the distinction between law as it is and ought to be has been, under the general head of "positivism," confused with a moral theory according to which statements of what is the case ("statements of fact") belong to a category or type radically different from statements of what ought to be ("value statements"). It may therefore be well to dispel this source of confusion.

There are many contemporary variants of this type of moral theory: according to some, judgments of what ought to be, or ought to be done, either are or include as essential elements expressions of "feeling," "emotion," or "attitudes" or "subjective preferences"; in others such judgments both express feelings or emotions or attitudes and enjoin others to share them. In other variants such judgments indicate that a particular case falls under a general principle or policy of action which the speaker has "chosen" or to which he is "committed" and which is itself not a recognition of what is the case but analogous to a general "imperative" or command addressed to all including the speaker himself. Common to all these variants is the insistence that judgments of what ought to be done, because they contain such "non-cognitive" elements, cannot be argued for or established by rational methods as statements of fact can be, and cannot be shown to follow from any statement of fact but only from other judgments of what ought to be done in conjunction with some statement of fact. We cannot, on such a theory, demonstrate, e.g., that an action was wrong, ought not to have been done, merely by showing that it consisted of the deliberate infliction

of pain solely for the gratification of the agent. We only show it to be wrong if we add to those verifiable "cognitive" statements of fact a general principle not itself verifiable or "cognitive" that the infliction of pain in such circumstances is wrong, ought not to be done. Together with this general distinction between statements of what is and what ought to be go sharp parallel distinctions between statements about means and statements of moral ends. We can rationally discover and debate what are appropriate means to given ends, but ends are not rationally discoverable or debatable; they are "fiats of the will," expressions of "emotions," "preferences," or "attitudes."

Against all such views (which are of course far subtler than this crude survey can convey) others urge that all these sharp distinctions between is and ought, fact and value, means and ends, cognitive and noncognitive, are wrong. In acknowledging ultimate ends or moral values we are recognizing something as much imposed upon us by the character of the world in which we live, as little a matter of choice, attitude, feeling, emotion as the truth of factual judgments about what is the case. The characteristic moral argument is not one in which the parties are reduced to expressing or kindling feelings or emotions or issuing exhortations or commands to each other but one by which parties come to acknowledge after closer examination and reflection that an initially disputed case falls within the ambit of a vaguely apprehended principle (itself no more "subjective," no more a "fiat of our will" than any other principle of classification) and this has as much title to be called "cognitive" or "rational" as any other initially disputed classification of particulars.

Let us now suppose that we accept this rejection of "non-cognitive" theories of morality and this denial of the drastic distinction in type between statements of what is and what ought to be, and that moral judgments are as rationally defensible as any other kind of judgments. What would follow from this as to the nature of the connection between law as it is and law as it ought to be? Surely, from this alone, nothing. Laws, however morally iniquitous, would still (so far as this point is concerned) be laws. The only difference which the acceptance of this view of the nature of moral judgments would make would be that the moral iniquity of such laws would be something that could be demonstrated; it would surely follow merely from a statement of what the rule required to be done that the rule was morally wrong and so ought not to be law or conversely that it was morally desirable and ought to be law. But the demonstration of this would not show the rule not to be (or to be) law. Proof that the principles by which we evaluate or condemn laws are rationally discoverable, and not mere "fiats of the will," leaves untouched the fact that there are laws which may have any degree of iniquity or stupidity and still be laws. And conversely there are rules that have every moral qualification to be laws and yet are not laws.

Surely something further or more specific must be said if disproof of "noncognitivism" or kindred theories in ethics is to be relevant to the distinction between law as it is and law as it ought to be, and to lead to the abandonment at some point or some softening of this distinction. No one has done more than Professor Lon Fuller of the Harvard Law School in his various writings to make clear such a line of argument and I will end by criticising what I take to be its central point. It is a point which again emerges when we consider not those legal rules or parts of legal rules the meanings of which are clear and excite no debate but the interpretation of rules in concrete cases where doubts are initially felt and argument develops about their meaning. In no legal system is the scope of legal rules restricted to the range of concrete instances which were present or are believed to have been present in the minds of legislators; this indeed is one of the important differences between a legal rule and a command. Yet, when rules are recognized as applying to instances beyond any that legislators did or could have considered, their extension to such new cases often presents itself not as a deliberate choice or fiat on the part of those who so interpret the rule. It appears neither as a decision to give the rule a new or extended meaning nor as a guess as to what legislators, dead perhaps in the eighteenth century, would have said had they been alive in the twentieth century. Rather, the inclusion of the new case under the rule takes its place as a natural elaboration of the rule, as something implementing a "purpose" which it seems natural to attribute (in some sense) to the rule itself rather than to any particular person dead or alive. The Utilitarian description of such interpretative extension of old rules to new cases as judicial legislation fails to do justice to this phenomenon; it gives no hint of the differences between a deliberate fiat or decision to treat the new case in the same way as past cases and a recognition (in which there is little that is deliberate or even voluntary) that inclusion of the new case under the rule will implement or articulate a continuing and identical purpose, hitherto less specifically apprehended.

Perhaps many lawyers and judges will see in this language something that precisely fits their experience; others may think it a romantic gloss on facts better stated in the Utilitarian language of judicial "legislation" or in the modern American terminology of "creative choice."

To make the point clear Professor Fuller uses a nonlegal example from the philosopher Wittgenstein which is, I think, illuminating.

> Someone says to me: "Show the children a game." I teach them gaming with dice and the other says "I did not mean that sort of game." Must the exclusion of the game with dice have come before his mind when he gave me the order?[45]

Something important does seem to me to be touched on in this example. Perhaps there are the following (distinguishable) points. First, we nor-

---

45 Fuller, *Human Purpose and Natural Law*, 53 *J. Philos.* 697, 700 (1956).

mally do interpret not only what people are trying to do but what they say in the light of assumed common human objectives so that unless the contrary were expressly indicated we would not interpret an instruction to show a young child a game as a mandate to introduce him to gambling even though in other contexts the word "game" would be naturally so interpreted. Second, very often, the speaker whose words are thus interpreted might say: "Yes, that's what I mean [or "that's what I meant all along"] though I never thought of it until you put this particular case to me." Third, when we thus recognize, perhaps after argument or consultation with others, a particular case not specifically envisaged beforehand as falling within the ambit of some vaguely expressed instruction, we may find this experience falsified by description of it as a mere decision on our part so to treat the particular case, and that we can only describe this faithfully as coming to realize and to articulate what we "really" want or our "true purpose"—phrases which Professor Fuller uses later in the same article.[46]

I am sure that many philosophical discussions of the character of moral argument would benefit from attention to cases of the sort instanced by Professor Fuller. Such attention would help to provide a corrective to the view that there is a sharp separation between "ends" and "means" and that in debating "ends" we can only work on each other nonrationally, and that rational argument is reserved for discussion of "means." But I think the relevance of his point to the issue whether it is correct or wise to insist on the distinction between law as it is and law as it ought to be is very small indeed. Its net effect is that in interpreting legal rules there are some cases which we find after reflection to be so natural an elaboration or articulation of the rule that to think of and refer to this as "legislation," "making law," or a "fiat" on our part would be misleading. So, the argument must be, it would be misleading to dis-

tinguish in such cases between what the rule is and what it ought to be—at least in some sense of ought. We think it ought to include the new case and come to see after reflection that it really does. But even if this way of presenting a recognizable experience as an example of a fusion between is and ought to be is admitted, two caveats must be borne in mind. The first is that "ought" in this case need have nothing to do with morals for the reasons explained already in section III: there may be just the same sense that a new case will implement and articulate the purpose of a rule in interpreting the rules of a game or some hideously immoral code of oppression whose immorality is appreciated by those called in to interpret it. They too can see what the "spirit" of the game they are playing requires in previously unenvisaged cases. More important is this: after all is said and done we must remember how rare in the law is the phenomenon held to justify this way of talking, how exceptional is this feeling that one way of deciding a case is imposed upon us as the only natural or rational elaboration of some rule. Surely it cannot be doubted that, for most cases of interpretation, the language of choice between alternatives, "judicial legislation" or even "fiat" (though not arbitrary fiat), better conveys the realities of the situation.

Within the framework of relatively well-settled law there jostle too many alternatives too nearly equal in attraction between which judge and lawyer must uncertainly pick their way to make appropriate here language which may well describe those experiences which we have in interpreting our own or others' principles of conduct, intention, or wishes, when we are not conscious of exercising a deliberate choice, but rather of recognising something awaiting recognition. To use in the description of the interpretation of laws the suggested terminology of a fusion or inability to separate what is law and ought to be will serve (like earlier stories that judges only find, never make, law) only to conceal the facts, that here if anywhere we live among uncertainties between which we have to choose, and that the exist-

---

46 *Id.* at 701, 702.

ing law imposes only limits on our choice and not the choice itself.

◆ ◆ ◆ ◆ ◆

H.L.A. HART

"Law as the Union of Primary and Secondary Rules" from *The Concept of Law*

1. A Fresh Start

In the last three chapters [of *The Concept of Law*] we have seen that, at various crucial points, the simple model of law as the sovereign's coercive orders failed to reproduce some of the salient features of a legal system. To demonstrate this, we did not find it necessary to invoke (as earlier critics have done) international law or primitive law which some may regard as disputable or borderline examples of law; instead we pointed to certain familiar features of municipal law in a modern state, and showed that these were either distorted or altogether unrepresented in this over-simple theory.

The main ways in which the theory failed are instructive enough to merit a second summary. First, it became clear that though of all the varieties of law, a criminal statute, forbidding or enjoining certain actions under penalty, most resembles orders backed by threats given by one person to others, such a statute none the less differs from such orders in the important respect that it commonly applies to those who enact it and not merely to others. Secondly, there are other varieties of law, notably those conferring legal powers to adjudicate or legislate (public powers) or to create or vary legal relations (private powers) which cannot, without absurdity, be construed as orders backed by threats. Thirdly, there are legal rules which differ from orders in their mode of origin, because they are not brought into being by anything analogous to explicit prescription. Finally, the analysis of law in terms of the sovereign, habitually obeyed and necessarily exempt from all legal limitation, failed to account for the continuity of legislative authority characteristic of a modern legal system, and the sovereign person or persons could not be identified with either the electorate or the legislature of a modern state.

It will be recalled that in thus criticizing the conception of law as the sovereign's coercive orders we considered also a number of ancillary devices which were brought in at the cost of corrupting the primitive simplicity of the theory to rescue it from its difficulties. But these too failed. One device, the notion of a *tacit* order, seemed to have no application to the complex actualities of a modern legal system, but only to very much simpler situations like that of a general who deliberately refrains from interfering with orders given by his subordinates. Other devices, such as that of treating power-conferring rules as mere fragments of rules imposing duties, or treating all rules as directed only to officials, distort the ways in which these are spoken of, thought of, and actually used in social life. This had no better claim to our assent than the theory that all the rules of a game are "really" directions to the umpire and the scorer. The device, designed to reconcile the self-binding character of legislation with the theory that a statute is an order given to *others*, was to distinguish the legislators acting in their official capacity, as *one* person ordering *others* who include themselves in their private capacities. This device, impeccable in itself, involved supplementing the theory with something it does not contain: this is the notion of a rule defining what must be done to legislate; for it is only in conforming with such a rule that legislators have an official capacity and a separate personality to be contrasted with themselves as private individuals.

The last three chapters are therefore the record of a failure and there is plainly need for a fresh start. Yet the failure is an instructive one, worth the detailed consideration we have given it, because at each point where the theory failed to fit the facts it was possible to see at least in outline why it was bound to fail and what is required for a better account. The root cause of failure is that the elements out of which the theory was constructed, viz. the ideas of orders, obedience, habits, and threats, do not include, and cannot by their combination yield, the idea of a rule, without which we cannot hope to elucidate even the most elementary forms of law. It is true that the idea of a rule is by no means a simple one: we have already seen in Chapter III the need, if we are to do justice to the complexity of a legal system, to discriminate between two different though related types. Under rules of the one type, which may well be considered the basic or primary type, human beings are required to do or abstain from certain actions, whether they wish to or not. Rules of the other type are in a sense parasitic upon or secondary to the first; for they provide that human beings may by doing or saying certain things introduce new rules of the primary type, extinguish or modify old ones, or in various ways determine their incidence or control their operations. Rules of the first type impose duties; rules of the second type confer powers, public or private. Rules of the first type concern actions involving physical movement or changes; rules of the second type provide for operations which lead not merely to physical movement or change, but to the creation or variation of duties or obligations.

We have already given some preliminary analysis of what is involved in the assertion that rules of these two types exist among a given social group, and in this chapter we shall not only carry this analysis a little farther but we shall make the general claim that in the combination of these two types of rule there lies what Austin wrongly claimed to have found in the notion of coercive orders, namely, "the key to the science of jurisprudence." We shall not indeed claim that wherever the word "law" is "properly" used this combination of primary and secondary rules is to be found; for it is clear that the diverse range of cases of which the word "law" is used are not linked by any such simple uniformity, but by less direct relations—often of analogy of either form or content—to a central case. What we shall attempt to show, in this and the succeeding chapters, is that most of the features of law which have proved most perplexing and have both provoked and eluded the search for definition can best be rendered clear, if these two types of rule and the interplay between them are understood. We accord this union of elements a central place because of their explanatory power in elucidating the concepts that constitute the framework of legal thought. The justification for the use of the word "law" for a range of apparently heterogeneous cases is a secondary matter which can be undertaken when the central elements have been grasped.

2. *The Idea of Obligation*

It will be recalled that the theory of law as coercive orders, notwithstanding its errors, started from the perfectly correct appreciation of the fact that where there is law, there human conduct is made in some sense non-optional or obligatory. In choosing this starting-point the theory was well inspired, and in building up a new account of law in terms of the interplay of primary and secondary rules we too shall start from the same idea. It is, however, here, at this crucial first step, that we have perhaps most to learn from the theory's errors.

Let us recall the gunman situation. A orders B to hand over his money and threatens to shoot him if he does not comply. According to the theory of coercive orders this situation illustrates the notion of obligation or duty in general. Legal obligation is to be found in this situation writ large; A must be the sovereign habitually obeyed and the orders must be general, prescribing courses of conduct not single actions. The plausibility of the claim that the gunman situation displays the meaning of obligation lies in the fact that it is certainly one in which we would say that B, if he obeyed, was "obliged" to hand over his money. It is, however, equally certain that we should misdescribe the situation if we said, on these facts, that B "had an obligation" or a "duty" to hand over the money. So from the start it is clear that we need something else for an understanding of the idea of obligation. There is a difference, yet to be explained, between the assertion that someone *was obliged* to do something and the assertion that he *had an obligation* to do it. The first is often a statement about the beliefs and motives with which an action is done: B was obliged to hand over his money may simply mean, as it does in the gunman case, that he believed that some harm or other unpleasant consequences would befall him if he did not hand it over and he handed it over to avoid those consequences. In such cases the prospect of what would happen to the agent if he disobeyed has rendered something he would otherwise have preferred to have done (keep the money) less eligible.

Two further elements slightly complicate the elucidation of the notion of being obliged to do something. It seems clear that we should not think of B as obliged to hand over the money if the threatened harm was, according to common judgments, trivial in comparison with the disadvantage or serious consequences, either for B or for others, of complying with the orders, as it would be, for example, if A merely threatened to pinch B. Nor perhaps should we say that B was obliged, if there were no reasonable grounds for thinking that A could or would probably implement his threat of relatively serious harm. Yet, though such references to common judgments of comparative harm and reasonable estimates of likelihood, are implicit in this notion, the statement that a person was obliged to obey someone is, in the main, a psychological one referring to the beliefs and motives with which an action was done. But the statement that someone *had an obligation*

to do something is of a very different type and there are many signs of this difference. Thus not only is it the case that the facts about B's action and his beliefs and motives in the gunman case, though sufficient to warrant the statement that B was obliged to hand over his purse, are *not sufficient* to warrant the statement that he had an obligation to do this; it is also the case that facts of this sort, i.e., facts about beliefs and motives, are *not necessary* for the truth of a statement that a person had an obligation to do something. Thus the statement that a person had an obligation, e.g., to tell the truth or report for military service, remains true even if he believed (reasonably or unreasonably) that he would never be found out and had nothing to fear from disobedience. Moreover, whereas the statement that he had this obligation is quite independent of the question whether or not he in fact reported for service, the statement that someone was obliged to do something, normally carries the implication that he actually did it.

Some theorists, Austin among them, seeing perhaps the general irrelevance of the person's beliefs, fears, and motives to the question whether he had an obligation to do something, have defined this notion not in terms of these subjective facts, but in terms of the *chance* or *likelihood* that the person having the obligation will suffer a punishment or "evil" at the hands of others in the event of disobedience. This, in effect, treats statements of obligation not as psychological statements but as predictions or assessments of chances of incurring punishment or "evil." To many later theorists this has appeared as a revelation, bringing down to earth an elusive notion and restating it in the same clear, hard, empirical terms as are used in science. It has, indeed, been accepted sometimes as the only alternative to metaphysical conceptions of obligation or duty as invisible objects mysteriously existing "above" or "behind" the world of ordinary, observable facts. But there are many reasons for rejecting this interpretation of statements of obligation as predictions, and it is not, in fact, the only alternative to obscure metaphysics.

The fundamental objection is that the predictive interpretation obscures the fact that, where rules exist, deviations from them are not merely grounds for a prediction that hostile reactions will follow or that a court will apply sanctions to those who break them, but are also a reason or justification for such reaction and for applying the sanctions. We have already drawn attention in Chapter IV to this neglect of the internal aspect of rules and we shall elaborate it later in this chapter.

There is, however, a second, simpler, objection to the predictive interpretation of obligation. If it were true that the statement that a person had an obligation meant that *he* was likely to suffer in the event of disobedience, it would be a contradiction to say that he had an obligation, e.g., to report for military service but that, owing to the fact that he had escaped from the jurisdiction, or had successfully bribed the police or the court, there was not the slightest chance of his being caught or made to suffer. In fact, there is no contradiction in saying this, and such statements are often made and understood.

It is, of course, true that in a normal legal system, where sanctions are exacted for a high proportion of offences, an offender usually runs a risk of punishment; so, usually the statement that a person has an obligation and the statement that he is likely to suffer for disobedience will both be true together. Indeed, the connection between these two statements is somewhat stronger than this: at least in a municipal system it may well be true that, unless *in general* sanctions were likely to be exacted from offenders, there would be little or no point in making particular statements about a person's obligations. In this sense, such statements may be said to presuppose belief in the continued normal operation of the system of sanctions much as the statement "he is out" in cricket presupposes, though it does not assert, that players, umpire, and scorer will probably take the usual steps. None the less, it is crucial for the understanding of the idea of obligation to see that in individual cases the statement that a person

has an obligation under some rule and the prediction that he is likely to suffer for disobedience may diverge.

It is clear that obligation is not to be found in the gunman situation, though the simpler notion of being obliged to do something may well be defined in the elements present there. To understand the general idea of obligation as a necessary preliminary to understanding it in its legal form, we must turn to a different social situation which, unlike the gunman situation, includes the existence of social rules; for this situation contributes to the meaning of the statement that a person has an obligation in two ways. First, the existence of such rules, making certain types of behaviour a standard, is the normal, though unstated, background or proper context for such a statement; and, secondly, the distinctive function of such a statement is to apply such a general rule to a particular person by calling attention to the fact that his case falls under it. We have already seen in Chapter IV that there is involved in the existence of any social rules a combination of regular conduct with a distinctive attitude to that conduct as a standard. We have also seen the main ways in which these differ from mere social habits, and how the varied normative vocabulary ("ought," "must," "should") is used to draw attention to the standard and to deviations from it, and to formulate the demands, criticisms, or acknowledgements which may be based on it. Of this class of normative words the words "obligation" and "duty" form an important sub-class, carrying with them certain implications not usually present in the others. Hence, though a grasp of the elements generally differentiating social rules from mere habits is certainly indispensable for understanding the notion of obligation or duty, it is not sufficient by itself.

The statement that someone has or is under an obligation does indeed imply the existence of a rule; yet it is not always the case that where rules exist the standard of behaviour required by them is conceived of in terms of obligation. "He ought to have" and "He had an obligation to" are not always interchangeable expressions, even though they are alike in carrying an implicit reference to existing standards of conduct or are used in drawing conclusions in particular cases from a general rule. Rules of etiquette or correct speech are certainly rules: they are more than convergent habits or regularities of behaviour; they are taught and efforts are made to maintain them; they are used in criticizing our own and other people's behaviour in the characteristic normative vocabulary. "You ought to take your hat off," "It is wrong to say 'you was.'" But to use in connection with rules of this kind the words "obligation" or "duty" would be misleading and not merely stylistically odd. It would misdescribe a social situation; for though the line separating rules of obligation from others is at points a vague one, yet the main rationale of the distinction is fairly clear.

Rules are conceived and spoken of as imposing obligations when the general demand for conformity is insistent and the social pressure brought to bear upon those who deviate or threaten to deviate is great. Such rules may be wholly customary in origin: there may be no centrally organized system of punishments for breach of the rules; the social pressure may take only the form of a general diffused hostile or critical reaction which may stop short of physical sanctions. It may be limited to verbal manifestations of disapproval or of appeals to the individuals' respect for the rule violated; it may depend heavily on the operation of feelings of shame, remorse, and guilt. When the pressure is of this last-mentioned kind we may be inclined to classify the rules as part of the morality of the social group and the obligation under the rules as moral obligation. Conversely, when physical sanctions are prominent or usual among the forms of pressure, even though these are neither closely defined nor administered by officials but are left to the community at large, we shall be inclined to classify the rules as a primitive or rudimentary form of law. We may, of course, find both these types of serious social pressure behind what is,

in an obvious sense, the same rule of conduct; sometimes this may occur with no indication that one of them is peculiarly appropriate as primary and the other secondary, and then the question whether we are confronted with a rule of morality or rudimentary law may not be susceptible of an answer. But for the moment the possibility of drawing the line between law and morals need not detain us. What is important is that the insistence on importance or *seriousness* of social pressure behind the rules is the primary factor determining whether they are thought of as giving rise to obligations.

Two other characteristics of obligation go naturally together with this primary one. The rules supported by this serious pressure are thought important because they are believed to be necessary to the maintenance of social life or some highly prized feature of it. Characteristically, rules so obviously essential as those which restrict the free use of violence are thought of in terms of obligation. So too rules which require honesty or truth or require the keeping of promises, or specify what is to be done by one who performs a distinctive role or function in the social group are thought of in terms of either "obligation" or perhaps more often "duty." Secondly, it is generally recognized that the conduct required by these rules may, while benefiting others, conflict with what the person who owes the duty may wish to do. Hence obligations and duties are thought of as characteristically involving sacrifice or renunciation, and the standing possibility of conflict between obligation or duty and interest is, in all societies, among the truisms of both the lawyer and the moralist.

The figure of a *bond* binding the person obligated, which is buried in the word "obligation," and the similar notion of a debt latent in the word "duty" are explicable in terms of these three factors, which distinguish rules of obligation or duty from other rules. In this figure, which haunts much legal thought, the social pressure appears as a chain binding those who have obligations so that they are not free to do what they want. The other end of the chain is sometimes held by the group or their official representatives, who insist on performance or exact the penalty: sometimes it is entrusted by the group to a private individual who may choose whether or not to insist on performance or its equivalent in value to him. The first situation typifies the duties or obligations of criminal law and the second those of civil law where we think of private individuals having rights correlative to the obligations.

Natural and perhaps illuminating though these figures or metaphors are, we must not allow them to trap us into a misleading conception of obligation as essentially consisting in some feeling of pressure or compulsion experienced by those who have obligations. The fact that rules of obligation are generally supported by serious social pressure does not entail that to have an obligation under the rules is to experience feelings of compulsion or pressure. Hence there is no contradiction in saying of some hardened swindler, and it may often be true, that he had an obligation to pay the rent but felt no pressure to pay when he made off without doing so. To *feel* obliged and to have an obligation are different though frequently concomitant things. To identify them would be one way of misinterpreting, in terms of psychological feelings, the important internal aspect of rules to which we drew attention in Chapter III.

Indeed, the internal aspect of rules is something to which we must again refer before we can dispose finally of the claims of the predictive theory. For an advocate of that theory may well ask why, if social pressure is so important a feature of rules of obligation, we are yet so concerned to stress the inadequacies of the predictive theory; for it gives this very feature a central place by defining obligation in terms of the likelihood that threatened punishment or hostile reaction will follow deviation from certain lines of conduct. The difference may seem slight between the analysis of a statement of obligation as a prediction, or assessment of the chances, of hostile reaction to deviation, and our own contention that though this statement presupposes a background

in which deviations from rules are generally met by hostile reactions, yet its characteristic use is not to predict this but to say that a person's case falls under such a rule. In fact, however, this difference is not a slight one. Indeed, until its importance is grasped, we cannot properly understand the whole distinctive style of human thought, speech, and action which is involved in the existence of rules and which constitutes the normative structure of society.

The following contrast again in terms of the "internal" and "external" aspect of rules may serve to mark what gives this distinction its great importance for the understanding not only of law but of the structure of any society. When a social group has certain rules of conduct, this fact affords an opportunity for many closely related yet different kinds of assertion; for it is possible to be concerned with the rules, either merely as an observer who does not himself accept them, or as a member of the group which accepts and uses them as guides to conduct. We may call these respectively the "external" and the "internal" points of view. Statements made from the external point of view may themselves be of different kinds. For the observer may, without accepting the rules himself, assert that the group accepts the rules, and thus may from outside refer to the way in which *they* are concerned with them from the internal point of view. But whatever the rules are, whether they are those of games, like chess or cricket, or moral or legal rules, we can if we choose occupy the position of an observer who does not even refer in this way to the internal point of view of the group. Such an observer is content merely to record the regularities of observable behaviour in which conformity with the rules partly consists and those further regularities, in the form of the hostile reaction, reproofs, or punishments, with which deviations from the rules are met. After a time the external observer may, on the basis of the regularities observed, correlate deviation with hostile reaction, and be able to predict with a fair measure of success, and to assess the chances that a deviation from the group's normal behaviour will meet with hostile reaction or punishment. Such knowledge may not only reveal much about the group, but might enable him to live among them without unpleasant consequences which would attend one who attempted to do so without such knowledge.

If, however, the observer really keeps austerely to this extreme external point of view and does not give any account of the manner in which members of the group who accept the rules view their own regular behaviour, his description of their life cannot be in terms of rules at all, and so not in the terms of the rule-dependent notions of obligation or duty. Instead, it will be in terms of observable regularities of conduct, predictions, probabilities, and signs. For such an observer, deviations by a member of the group from normal conduct will be a sign that hostile reaction is likely to follow, and nothing more. His view will be like the view of one who, having observed the working of a traffic signal in a busy street for some time, limits himself to saying that when the light turns red there is a high probability that the traffic will stop. He treats the light merely as a natural *sign that* people will behave in certain ways, as clouds are a *sign that* rain will come. In so doing he will miss out a whole dimension of the social life of those whom he is watching, since for them the red light is not merely a sign that others will stop: they look upon it as a *signal for* them to stop, and so a reason for stopping in conformity to rules which make stopping when the light is red a standard of behaviour and an obligation. To mention this is to bring into the account the way in which the group regards its own behaviour. It is to refer to the internal aspect of rules seen from their internal point of view.

The external point of view may very nearly reproduce the way in which the rules function in the lives of certain members of the group, namely those who reject its rules and are only concerned with them when and because they judge that unpleasant consequences are likely to follow violation.

Their point of view will need for its expression, "I was obliged to do it," "I am likely to suffer for it if ...," "You will probably suffer for it if ...," "They will do that to you if...." But they will not need forms of expression like "I had an obligation" or "You have an obligation" for these are required only by those who see their own and other persons' conduct from the internal point of view. What the external point of view, which limits itself to the observable regularities of behaviour, cannot reproduce is the way in which the rules function as rules in the lives of those who normally are the majority of society. These are the officials, lawyers, or private persons who use them, in one situation after another, as guides to the conduct of social life, as the basis for claims, demands, admissions, criticism, or punishment, viz., in all the familiar transactions of life according to rules. For them the violation of a rule is not merely a basis for the prediction that a hostile reaction will follow but a *reason* for hostility.

At any given moment the life of any society which lives by rules, legal or not, is likely to consist in a tension between those who, on the one hand, accept and voluntarily co-operate in maintaining the rules, and so see their own and other persons' behaviour in terms of the rules, and those who, on the other hand, reject the rules and attend to them only from the external point of view as a sign of possible punishment. One of the difficulties facing any legal theory anxious to do justice to the complexity of the facts is to remember the presence of both these points of view and not to define one of them out of existence. Perhaps all our criticisms of the predictive theory of obligation may be best summarized as the accusation that this is what it does to the internal aspect of obligatory rules.

3. The Elements of Law

It is, of course, possible to imagine a society without a legislature, courts, or officials of any kind. Indeed, there are many studies of primitive communities which not only claim that this possibility is realized but depict in detail the life of a society where the only means of social control is that general attitude of the group towards its own standard modes of behaviour in terms of which we have characterized rules of obligation. A social structure of this kind is often referred to as one of "custom;" but we shall not use this term, because it often implies that the customary rules are very old and supported with less social pressure than other rules. To avoid these implications we shall refer to such a social structure as one of primary rules of obligation. If a society is to live by such primary rules alone, there are certain conditions which, granted a few of the most obvious truisms about human nature and the world we live in, must clearly be satisfied. The first of these conditions is that the rules must contain in some form restrictions on the free use of violence, theft, and deception to which human beings are tempted but which they must, in general, repress, if they are to coexist in close proximity to each other. Such rules are in fact always found in the primitive societies of which we have knowledge, together with a variety of others imposing on individuals various positive duties to perform services or make contributions to the common life. Secondly, though such a society may exhibit the tension, already described, between those who accept the rules and those who reject the rules except where fear of social pressure induces them to conform, it is plain that the latter cannot be more than a minority, if so loosely organized a society of persons, approximately equal in physical strength, is to endure: for otherwise those who reject the rules would have too little social pressure to fear. This too is confirmed by what we know of primitive communities where, though there are dissidents and malefactors, the majority live by the rules seen from the internal point of view.

More important for our present purpose is the following consideration. It is plain that only a small community closely knit by ties of kinship, common sentiment, and belief, and placed in a stable environ-ment, could live successfully by such a regime of un-official rules. In any other conditions such a simple form of social control must prove defective and will require supplementation in different ways. In the first place, the rules by which the group lives will not form a system, but will simply be a set of separate standards, without any identifying or common mark, except of course that they are the rules which a particular group of human beings accepts. They will in this respect resemble our own rules of etiquette. Hence if doubts arise as to what the rules are or as to the precise scope of some given rule, there will be no procedure for settling this doubt, either by reference to an authoritative text or to an official whose declarations on this point are authoritative. For, plainly, such a procedure and the acknowledgement of either authoritative text or persons involve the existence of rules of a type different from the rules of obligation or duty which *ex hypothesi* are all that the group has. This defect in the simple social structure of primary rules we may call its *uncertainty*.

A second defect is the *static* character of the rules. The only mode of change in the rules known to such a society will be the slow process of growth, whereby courses of conduct once thought optional become first habitual or usual, and then obligatory, and the converse process of decay, when deviations, once severely dealt with, are first tolerated and then pass unnoticed. There will be no means, in such a society, of deliberately adapting the rules to changing circumstances, either by eliminating old rules or introducing new ones: for, again, the possibility of doing this presupposes the existence of rules of a different type from the primary rules of obligation by which alone the society lives. In an extreme case the rules may be static in a more drastic sense. This, though never perhaps fully realized in any actual community, is worth considering because the remedy for it is something very characteristic of law. In this extreme case, not only would there be no way of deliberately changing the general rules, but the obligations which arise under the rules in particular cases could not be varied or modified by the deliberate choice of any individual. Each individual would simply have fixed obligations or duties to do or abstain from doing certain things. It might indeed very often be the case that others would benefit from the performance of these obligations; yet if there are only primary rules of obligation they would have no power to release those bound from performance or to transfer to others the benefits which would accrue from performance. For such operations of release or transfer create changes in the initial positions of individuals under the primary rules of obligation, and for these operations to be possible there must be rules of a sort different from the primary rules.

The third defect of this simple form of social life is the *inefficiency* of the diffuse social pressure by which the rules are maintained. Disputes as to whether an admitted rule has or has not been violated will always occur and will, in any but the smallest societies, continue interminably, if there is no agency specially empowered to ascertain finally, and authoritatively, the fact of violation. Lack of such final and authoritative determinations is to be distinguished from another weakness associated with it. This is the fact that punishments for violations of the rules, and other forms of social pressure involving physical effort or the use of force, are not administered by a special agency but are left to the individuals affected or to the group at large. It is obvious that the waste of time involved in the group's unorganized efforts to catch and punish offenders, and the smouldering vendettas which may result from self-help in the absence of an official monopoly of "sanctions," may be serious. The history of law does, however, strongly suggest that the lack of official agencies to determine authoritatively the fact of violation of the rules is a much more serious defect; for many societies have remedies for this defect long before the other.

The remedy for each of these three main defects in this simplest form of social structure consists in supplementing the *primary* rules of obligation with *secondary* rules which are rules of a different kind.

The introduction of the remedy for each defect might, in itself, be considered a step from the pre-legal into the legal world; since each remedy brings with it many elements that permeate law: certainly all three remedies together are enough to convert the regime of primary rules into what is indisputably a legal system. We shall consider in turn each of these remedies and show why law may most illuminatingly be characterized as a union of primary rules of obligation with such secondary rules. Before we do this, however, the following general points should be noted. Though the remedies consist in the introduction of rules which are certainly different from each other; as well as from the primary rules of obligation which they supplement, they have important features in common and are connected in various ways. Thus they may all be said to be on a different level from the primary rules, for they are all *about* such rules; in the sense that while primary rules are concerned with the actions that individuals must or must not do, these secondary rules are all concerned with the primary rules themselves. They specify the ways in which the primary rules may be conclusively ascertained, introduced, eliminated, varied, and the fact of their violation conclusively determined.

The simplest form of remedy for the *uncertainty* of the regime of primary rules is the introduction of what we shall call a "rule of recognition." This will specify some feature or features possession of which by a suggested rule is taken as a conclusive affirmative indication that it is a rule of the group to be supported by the social pressure it exerts. The existence of such a rule of recognition may take any of a huge variety of forms, simple or complex. It may, as in the early law of many societies, be no more than that an authoritative list or text of the rules is to be found in a written document or carved on some public monument. No doubt as a matter of history this step from the pre-legal to the legal may be accomplished in distinguishable stages, of which the first is the mere reduction to writing of hitherto unwritten rules. This is not itself the crucial step, though it is a very important one: what is crucial is the acknowledgement of reference to the writing or inscription as *authoritative*, i.e., as the *proper* way of disposing of doubts as to the existence of the rule. Where there is such an acknowledgement there is a very simple form of secondary rule: a rule for conclusive identification of the primary rules of obligation.

In a developed legal system the rules of recognition are of course more complex; instead of identifying rules exclusively by reference to a text or list they do so by reference to some general characteristic possessed by the primary rules. This may be the fact of their having been enacted by a specific body, or their long customary practice, or their relation to judicial decisions. Moreover, where more than one of such general characteristics are treated as identifying criteria, provision may be made for their possible conflict by their arrangement in an order of superiority, as by the common subordination of custom or precedent to statute, the latter being a superior source of law. Such complexity may make the rules of recognition in a modern legal system seem very different from the simple acceptance of an authoritative text: yet even in this simplest form, such a rule brings with it many elements distinctive of law. By providing an authoritative mark it introduces, although in embryonic form, the idea of a legal system: for the rules are now not just a discrete unconnected set but are, in a simple way, unified. Further, in the simple operation of identifying a given rule as possessing the required feature of being an item on an authoritative list of rules we have the germ of the idea of legal validity.

The remedy for the *static* quality of the regime of primary rules consists in the introduction of what we shall call "rules of change." The simplest form of such a rule is that which empowers an individual or body of persons to introduce new primary rules for the conduct of the life of the group, or of some class within it, and to eliminate old rules. As we have already argued in Chapter IV it is in terms of such a rule, and not in terms of orders backed by threats, that the ideas of legislative enactment and repeal are to be understood. Such rules of change may be very simple or very complex: the powers conferred may be unrestricted or limited in various ways: and the rules may, besides specifying the persons who are to legislate, define in more or less rigid terms the procedure to be followed in legislation. Plainly, there will be a very close connection between the rules of change and the rules of recognition: for where the former exists the latter will necessarily incorporate a reference to legislation as an identifying feature of the rules, though it need not refer to all the details of procedure involved in legislation. Usually some official certificate or official copy will, under the rules of recognition, be taken as a sufficient proof of due enactment. Of course if there is a social structure so simple that the only "source of law" is legislation, the rule of recognition will simply specify enactment as the unique identifying mark or criterion of validity of the rules. This will be the case for example in the imaginary kingdom of Rex I depicted in Chapter IV: there the rule of recognition would simply be that whatever Rex I enacts is law.

We have already described in some detail the rules which confer on individuals power to vary their initial positions under the primary rules. Without such private power-conferring rules society would lack some of the chief amenities which law confers upon it. For the operations which these rules make possible are the making of wills, contracts, transfers of property, and many other voluntarily created structures of rights and duties which typify life under law, though of course an elementary form of power-conferring rule also underlies the moral institution of a promise. The kinship of these rules with the rules of change involved in the notion of legislation is clear, and as recent theory such as Kelsen's has shown, many of the features which puzzle us in the institutions of contract or property are clarified by thinking of the operations of making a contract or transferring property as the exercise of limited legislative powers by individuals.

The third supplement to the simple regime of primary rules, intended to remedy the *inefficiency* of its diffused social pressure, consists of secondary rules empowering individuals to make authoritative determinations of the question whether, on a particular occasion, a primary rule has been broken. The minimal form of adjudication consists in such determinations, and we shall call the secondary rules which confer the power to make them "rules of adjudication." Besides identifying the individuals who are to adjudicate, such rules will also define the procedure to be followed. Like the other secondary rules these are on a different level from the primary rules: though they may be reinforced by further rules imposing duties on judges to adjudicate, they do not impose duties but confer judicial powers and a special status on judicial declarations about the breach of obligations. Again these rules, like the other secondary rules, define a group of important legal concepts: in this case the concepts of judge or court, jurisdiction and judgment. Besides these resemblances to the other secondary rules, rules of adjudication have intimate connections with them. Indeed, a system which has rules of adjudication is necessarily also committed to a rule of recognition of an elementary and imperfect sort. This is so because, if courts are empowered to make authoritative determinations of the fact that a rule has been broken, these cannot avoid being taken as authoritative determinations of what the rules are. So the rule which confers jurisdiction will also be a rule of recognition, identifying the primary rules through the judgments of the courts and these judgments will become a "source" of law. It is true that this form of rule of recognition, inseparable from the minimum form of jurisdiction, will be very imperfect. Unlike an authoritative text or a statute book, judgments may not be couched in general terms and their use as authoritative guides to the rules depends on a somewhat shaky inference from particular decisions, and the reliability of this must fluctuate both with the skill of the interpreter and the consistency of the judges.

It need hardly be said that in few legal systems are judicial powers confined to authoritative determinations of the fact of violation of the primary rules. Most systems have, after some delay, seen the advantages of further centralization of social pressure, and have partially prohibited the use of physical punishments or violent self help by private individuals. Instead they have supplemented the primary rules of obligation by further secondary rules, specifying or at least limiting the penalties for violation, and have conferred upon judges, where they have ascertained the fact of violation, the exclusive power to direct the application of penalties by other officials. These secondary rules provide the centralized official "sanctions" of the system.

If we stand back and consider the structure which has resulted from the combination of primary rules of obligation with the secondary rules of recognition, change and adjudication, it is plain that we have here not only the heart of a legal system, but a most powerful tool for the analysis of much that has puzzled both the jurist and the political theorist.

Not only are the specifically legal concepts with which the lawyer is professionally concerned, such as those of obligation and rights, validity and source of law, legislation and jurisdiction, and sanction, best elucidated in terms of this combination of elements. The concepts (which bestride both law and political theory) of the state, of authority, and of an official require a similar analysis if the obscurity which still lingers about them is to be dissipated. The reason why an analysis in these terms of primary and secondary rules has this explanatory power is not far to seek. Most of the obscurities and distortions surrounding legal and political concepts arise from the fact that these essentially involve reference to what we have called the internal point of view: the view of those who do not merely record and predict behaviour conforming to rules, but *use* the rules as standards for the appraisal of their own and others' behaviour. This requires more detailed attention in the analysis of legal and political concepts than it has usually received. Under the simple regime of primary rules the internal point of view is manifested in its simplest form, in the use of those rules as the basis of criticism, and as the justification of demands for conformity, social pressure, and punishment. Reference to this most elementary manifestation of the internal point of view is required for the analysis of the basic concepts of obligation and duty. With the addition to the system of secondary rules, the range of what is said and done from the internal point of view is much extended and diversified. With this extension comes a whole set of new concepts and they demand a reference to the internal point of view for their analysis. These include the notions of legislation, jurisdiction, validity, and, generally, of legal powers, private and public. There is a constant pull towards an analysis of these in the terms of ordinary or "scientific," fact-stating or predictive discourse. But this can only reproduce their external aspect: to do justice to their distinctive, internal aspect we need to see the different ways in which the law-making operations of the legislator, the adjudication of a court, the exercise of private or official powers, and other "acts-in-the-law" are related to secondary rules.

In the next chapter we shall show how the ideas of the validity of law and sources of law, and the truths latent among the errors of the doctrines of sovereignty may be rephrased and clarified in terms of rules of recognition. But we shall conclude this chapter with a warning: though the combination of primary and secondary rules merits, because it explains many aspects of law, the central place assigned to it, this cannot by itself illuminate every problem. The union of primary and secondary rules is at the centre of a legal system; but it is not the whole, and as we move away from the centre we shall have to accommodate, in ways indicated in later chapters, elements of a different character.

♦ ♦ ♦ ♦ ♦

H.L.A. HART

from "The Foundations of a Legal System" from *The Concept of Law*

1. Rule of Recognition and Legal Validity

According to the theory criticized in Chapter IV the foundations of a legal system consist of the situations in which the majority of a social group habitually obey the orders backed by threats of the sovereign person or persons, who themselves habitually obey no one. This social situation is, for this theory, both a necessary and a sufficient condition for the existence of law. We have already exhibited in some detail the incapacity of this theory to account for some of the salient features of a modern municipal legal system: yet nonetheless, as its hold over the minds of many thinkers suggests, it does contain, though in a blurred and misleading form, certain truths about certain important aspects of law. These truths can, however, only be clearly presented, and their importance rightly assessed, in terms of the more complex social situation where a secondary rule of recognition is accepted and used for the identification of primary rules of obligation. It is this situation which deserves, if anything does, to be called the foundations of a legal system. In this chapter we shall discuss various elements of this situation which have received only partial or misleading expression in the theory of sovereignty and elsewhere.

Wherever such a rule of recognition is accepted, both private persons and officials are provided with authoritative criteria for identifying primary rules of obligation. The criteria so provided may, as we have seen, take any one or more of a variety of forms: these include reference to an authoritative text; to legislative enactment; to customary practice; to general declarations of specified persons, or to past judicial decisions in particular cases. In a very simple system like the world of Rex I depicted in Chapter IV, where only what he enacts is law and no legal limitations upon his legislative power are imposed by customary rule or constitutional document, the sole criterion for identifying the law will be a simple reference to the fact of enactment by Rex I. The existence of this simple form of rule of recognition will be manifest in the general practice, on the part of officials or private persons, of identifying the rules by this criterion. In a modern legal system where there are a variety of "sources" of law, the rule of recognition is correspondingly more complex: the criteria for identifying the law are multiple and commonly include a written constitution, enactment by a legislature, and judicial precedents. In most cases, provision is made for possible conflict by ranking these criteria in an order of relative subordination and primacy. It is in this way that in our system "common law" is subordinate to "statute."

It is important to distinguish this relative *subordination* of one criterion to another from *derivation*, since some spurious support for the view that all law is essentially or "really" (even if only "tacitly") the product of legislation, has been gained from confusion of these two ideas. In our own system, custom and precedent are subordinate to legislation since customary and common law rules may be deprived of their status as law by statute. Yet they owe their status of law, precarious as this may be, not to a "tacit" exercise of legislative power but to the acceptance of a rule of recognition which accords them this independent though subordinate place. Again, as in the simple case, the existence of such a complex rule of recognition with this hierarchical ordering of distinct criteria is manifested in the general practice of identifying the rules by such criteria.

In the day-to-day life of a legal system its rule of recognition is very seldom expressly formulated

as a rule; though occasionally, courts in England may announce in general terms the relative place of one criterion of law in relation to another, as when they assert the supremacy of Acts of Parliament over other sources or suggested sources of law. For the most part the rule of recognition is not stated, but its existence is *shown* in the way in which particular rules are identified, either by courts or other officials or private persons or their advisers. There is, of course, a difference in the use made by courts of the criteria provided by the rule and the use of them by others: for when courts reach a particular conclusion on the footing that a particular rule has been correctly identified as law, what they say has a special authoritative status conferred on it by other rules. In this respect, as in many others, the rule of recognition of a legal system is like the scoring rule of a game. In the course of the game the general rule defining the activities which constitute scoring (runs, goals, &c.) is seldom formulated; instead it is *used* by officials and players in identifying the particular phases which count towards winning. Here too, the declarations of officials (umpire or scorer) have a special authoritative status attributed to them by other rules. Further, in both cases there is the possibility of a conflict between these authoritative applications of the rule and the general understanding of what the rule plainly requires according to its terms. This, as we shall see later, is a complication which must be catered for in any account of what it is for a system of rules of this sort to exist.

The use of unstated rules of recognition, by courts and others, in identifying particular rules of the system is characteristic of the internal point of view. Those who use them in this way thereby manifest their own acceptance of them as guiding rules and with this attitude there goes a characteristic vocabulary different from the natural expressions of the external point of view. Perhaps the simplest of these is the expression, "It is the law that...," which we may find on the lips not only of judges, but of ordinary men living under a legal system, when they identify a given rule of the system. This, like the expression "Out" or "Goal," is the language of one assessing a situation by reference to rules which he in common with others acknowledges as appropriate for this purpose. This attitude of shared acceptance of rules is to be contrasted with that of an observer who records *ab extra* the fact that a social group accepts such rules but does not himself accept them. The natural expression of this external point of view is not "It is the law that ..." but "In England they recognize as law ... whatever the Queen in Parliament enacts...." The first of these forms of expression we shall call an *internal statement* because it manifests the internal point of view and is naturally used by one who, accepting the rule of recognition and without stating the fact that it is accepted, applies the rule in recognizing some particular rule of the system as valid. The second form of expression we shall call an *external statement* because it is the natural language of an external observer of the system who, without himself accepting its rule of recognition, states the fact that others accept it.

If this use of an accepted rule of recognition in making internal statements is understood and carefully distinguished from an external statement of fact that the rule is accepted, many obscurities concerning the notion of legal "validity" disappear. For the word "valid" is most frequently, though not always, used, in just such internal statements, applying to a particular rule of a legal system, an unstated but accepted rule of recognition. To say that a given rule is valid is to recognize it as passing all the tests provided by the rule of recognition and so as a rule of the system. We can indeed simply say that the statement that a particular rule is valid means that it satisfies all the criteria provided by the rule of recognition. This is incorrect only to the extent that it might obscure the internal character of such statements; for, like the cricketers' "Out," these statements of validity normally apply to a particular case a rule of recognition accepted by the speaker and others, rather than expressly state that the rule is satisfied.

Some of the puzzles connected with the idea of legal validity are said to concern the relation between the validity and the "efficacy" of law. If by "efficacy" is meant that the fact that a rule of law which requires certain behaviour is obeyed more often than not, it is plain that there is no necessary connection between the validity of any particular rule and *its* efficacy, unless the rule of recognition of the system includes among its criteria, as some do, the provision (sometimes referred to as a rule of obsolescence) that no rule is to count as a rule of the system if it has long ceased to be efficacious.

From the inefficacy of a particular rule, which may or may not count against its validity, we must distinguish a general disregard of the rules of the system. This may be so complete in character and so protracted that we should say, in the case of a new system, that it had never established itself as the legal system of a given group, or, in the case of a once-established system, that it had ceased to be the legal system of the group. In either case, the normal context or background for making any internal statement in terms of the rules of the system is absent. In such cases it would be generally *pointless* either to assess the rights and duties of particular persons by reference to the primary rules of a system or to assess the validity of any of its rules by reference to its rules of recognition. To insist on applying a system of rules which had either never actually been effective or had been discarded would, except in special circumstances mentioned below, be as futile as to assess the progress of a game by reference to a scoring rule which had never been accepted or had been discarded.

One who makes an internal statement concerning the validity of a particular rule of a system may be said to *presuppose* the truth of the external statement of fact that the system is generally efficacious. For the normal use of internal statements is in such a context of general efficacy. It would however be wrong to say that statements of validity mean that the system is generally efficacious. For though it is normally pointless or idle to talk of the validity of a rule of a system which has never established itself or has been discarded, none the less it is not meaningless nor is it always pointless. One vivid way of teaching Roman Law is to speak *as if* the system were efficacious still and to discuss the validity of particular rules and solve problems in their terms; and one way of nursing hopes for the restoration of an old social order destroyed by revolution, and rejecting the new, is to cling to the criteria of legal validity of the old regime. This is implicitly done by the White Russian who still claims property under some rule of descent which was a valid rule of Tsarist Russia.

A grasp of the normal contextual connection between the internal statement that a given rule of a system is valid and the external statement of fact that the system is generally efficacious, will help us see in its proper perspective the common theory that to assert the validity of a rule is to predict that it will be enforced by courts or some other official action taken. In many ways this theory is similar to the predictive analysis of obligation which we considered and rejected in the last chapter. In both cases alike the motive for advancing this predictive theory is the conviction that only thus can metaphysical interpretations be avoided: that either a statement that a rule is valid must ascribe some mysterious property which cannot be detected by empirical means or it must be a prediction of future behaviour of officials. In both cases also the plausibility of the theory is due to the same important fact: that the truth of the external statement of fact, which an observer might record, that the system is generally efficacious and likely to continue so, is normally presupposed by anyone who accepts the rules and makes an internal statement of obligation or validity. The two are certainly very closely associated. Finally, in both cases alike the mistake of the theory is the same: it consists in neglecting the special character of the internal statement and treating it as an external statement about official action.

This mistake becomes immediately apparent when we consider how the judge's own statement that a particular rule is valid functions in judicial decision; for, though here too, in making such a statement, the judge presupposes but does not state the general efficacy of the system, he plainly is not concerned to predict his own or others' official action. His statement that a rule is valid is an internal statement recognizing that the rule satisfies the tests for identifying what is to count as law in his court, and constitutes not a prophecy of but part of the *reason* for his decision. There is indeed a more plausible case for saying that a statement that a rule is valid is a prediction when such a statement is made by a private person; for in the case of conflict between unofficial statements of validity or invalidity and that of a court in deciding a case, there is often good sense in saying that the former must then be withdrawn. Yet even here, as we shall see when we come in Chapter VII to investigate the significance of such conflicts between official declarations and the plain requirements of the rules, it may be dogmatic to assume that it is withdrawn as a statement now shown to be *wrong*, because it has falsely *predicted* what a court would say. For there are more reasons for withdrawing statements than the fact that they are wrong, and also more ways of being wrong than this allows.

The rule of recognition providing the criteria by which the validity of other rules of the system is assessed is in an important sense, which we shall try to clarify, an *ultimate* rule: and where, as is usual, there are several criteria ranked in order of relative subordination and primacy one of them is *supreme*. These ideas of the ultimacy of the rule of recognition and the supremacy of one of its criteria merit some attention. It is important to disentangle them from the theory, which we have rejected, that somewhere in every legal system, even though it lurks behind legal forms, there must be a sovereign legislative power which is legally unlimited.

Of these two ideas, supreme criterion and ultimate rule, the first is the easiest to define. We may say that a criterion of legal validity or source of law is supreme if rules identified by reference to it are still recognized as rules of the system, even if they conflict with rules identified by reference to the other criteria, whereas rules identified by reference to the latter are not so recognized if they conflict with the rules identified by reference to the supreme criterion. A similar explanation in comparative terms can be given of the notions of "superior" and "subordinate" criteria which we have already used. It is plain that the notions of a superior and a supreme criterion merely refer to a *relative* place on a scale and do not import any notion of legally *unlimited* legislative power. Yet "supreme" and "unlimited" are easy to confuse—at least in legal theory. One reason for this is that in the simpler forms of legal system the ideas of ultimate rule of recognition, supreme criterion, and legally unlimited legislature seem to converge. For where there is a legislature subject to no constitutional limitations and competent by its enactment to deprive all other rules of law emanating from other sources of their status as law, it is part of the rule of recognition in such a system that enactment by that legislature is the supreme criterion of validity. This is, according to constitutional theory, the position in the United Kingdom. But even systems like that of the United States in which there is no such legally unlimited legislature may perfectly well contain an ultimate rule of recognition which provides a set of criteria of validity, one of which is supreme. This will be so, where the legislative competence of the ordinary legislature is limited by a constitution which contains no amending power, or places some clauses outside the scope of that power. Here there is no legally unlimited legislature, even in the widest interpretation of "legislature;" but the system of course contains an ultimate rule of recognition and, in the clauses of its constitution, a supreme criterion of validity.

The sense in which the rule of recognition is the *ultimate* rule of a system is best understood if we pursue a very familiar chain of legal reasoning. If the question is raised whether some suggested rule is legally valid, we must, in order to answer the question, use a criterion of validity provided by some other rule. Is this purported by-law of the Oxfordshire County Council valid? Yes: because it was made in exercise of the powers conferred, and in accordance with the procedure specified, by a statutory order made by the Minister of Health. At this first stage the statutory order provides the criteria in terms of which the validity of the by-law is assessed. There may be no practical need to go farther; but there is a standing possibility of doing so. We may query the validity of the statutory order and assess its validity in terms of the statute empowering the minister to make such orders. Finally, when the validity of the statute has been queried and assessed by reference to the rule that what the Queen in Parliament enacts is law, we are brought to a stop in inquiries concerning validity: for we have reached a rule which, like the intermediate statutory order and statute, provides criteria for the assessment of the validity of other rules; but it is also unlike them in that there is no rule providing criteria for the assessment of its own legal validity.

There are, indeed, many questions which we can raise about this ultimate rule. We can ask whether it is the practice of courts, legislatures, officials, or private citizens in England actually to use this rule as an ultimate rule of recognition. Or has our process of legal reasoning been an idle game with the criteria of validity of a system now discarded? We can ask whether it is a satisfactory form of legal system which has such a rule at its root. Does it produce more good than evil? Are there prudential reasons for supporting it? Is there a moral obligation to do so? These are plainly very important questions; but, equally plainly, when we ask them about the rule of recognition, we are no longer attempting to answer the same kind of question about it as those which we answered about other rules with its aid. When we move from saying that a particular enactment is valid, because it satisfies the rule that what the Queen in Parliament enacts is law, to saying that in

England this last rule is used by courts, officials, and private persons as the ultimate rule of recognition, we have moved from an internal statement of law asserting the validity of a rule of the system to an external statement of fact which an observer of the system might make even if he did not accept it. So too when we move from the statement that a particular enactment is valid, to the statement that the rule of recognition of the system is an excellent one and the system based on it is one worthy of support, we have moved from a statement of legal validity to a statement of value.

Some writers, who have emphasized the legal ultimacy of the rule of recognition, have expressed this by saying that, whereas the legal validity of other rules of the system can be demonstrated by reference to it, its own validity cannot be demonstrated but is "assumed" or "postulated" or is a "hypothesis." This may, however, be seriously misleading. Statements of legal validity made about particular rules in the day-to-day life of a legal system whether by judges, lawyers, or ordinary citizens do indeed carry with them certain presuppositions. They are internal statements of law expressing the point of view of those who accept the rule of recognition of the system and, as such, leave unstated much that could be stated in external statements of fact about the system. What is thus left unstated forms the normal background or context of statements of legal validity and is thus said to be "presupposed" by them. But it is important to see precisely what these presupposed matters are, and not to obscure their character. They consist of two things. First, a person who seriously asserts the validity of some given rule of law, say a particular statute, himself makes use of a rule of recognition which he accepts as appropriate for identifying the law. Secondly, it is the case that this rule of recognition, in terms of which he assesses the validity of a particular statute, is not only accepted by him but is the rule of recognition actually accepted and employed in the general operation of the system. If the truth of this presupposition were doubted, it could

be established by reference to actual practice: to the way in which courts identify what is to count as law, and to the general acceptance of or acquiescence in these identifications.

Neither of these two presuppositions are well described as "assumptions" of a "validity" which cannot be demonstrated. We only need the word "validity," and commonly only use it, to answer questions which arise *within* a system of rules where the status of a rule as a member of the system depends on its satisfying certain criteria provided by the rule of recognition. No such question can arise as to the validity of the very rule of recognition which provides the criteria; it can neither be valid nor invalid but is simply accepted as appropriate for use in this way. To express this simple fact by saying darkly that its validity is "assumed but cannot be demonstrated," is like saying that we assume, but can never demonstrate, that the standard metre bar in Paris which is the ultimate test of the correctness of all measurement in metres, is itself correct.

A more serious objection is that talk of the "assumption" that the ultimate rule of recognition is valid conceals the essentially factual character of the second presupposition which lies behind the lawyers' statement of validity. No doubt the practice of judges, officials, and others, in which the actual existence of a rule of recognition consists, is a complex matter. As we shall see later, there are certainly situations in which questions as to the precise content and scope of this kind of rule, and even as to its existence, may not admit of a clear or determinate answer. None the less it is important to distinguish "assuming the validity" from "presupposing the existence" of such a rule; if only because failure to do this obscures what is meant by the assertion that such a rule *exists*.

In the simple system of primary rules of obligation sketched in the last chapter, the assertion that a given rule existed could only be an external statement of fact such as an observer who did not accept the rules might make and verify by ascertaining whether or not, as a matter of fact, a given mode of behaviour was generally accepted as a standard and was accompanied by those features which, as we have seen, distinguish a social rule from mere convergent habits. It is in this way also that we should now interpret and verify the assertion that in England a rule—though not a legal one—exists that we must bare the head on entering a church. If such rules as these are found to exist in the actual practice of a social group, there is no separate question of their validity to be discussed, though of course their value or desirability is open to question. Once their existence has been established as a fact we should only confuse matters by affirming or denying that they were valid or by saying that "we assumed" but could not show their validity. Where, on the other hand, as in a mature legal system, we have a system of rules which includes a rule of recognition so that the status of a rule as a member of the system now depends on whether it satisfies certain criteria provided by the rule of recognition, this brings with it a new application of the word "exist." The statement that a rule exists may now no longer be what it was in the simple case of customary rules—an external statement of the *fact* that a certain mode of behaviour was generally accepted as a standard in practice. It may now be an internal statement applying an accepted but unstated rule of recognition and meaning (roughly) no more than "valid given the system's criteria of validity." In this respect, however, as in others a rule of recognition is unlike other rules of the system. The assertion that it exists can only be an external statement of fact. For whereas a subordinate rule of a system may be valid and in that sense "exist" even if it is generally disregarded, the rule of recognition exists only as a complex, but normally concordant, practice of the courts, officials, and private persons in identifying the law by reference to certain criteria. Its existence is a matter of fact.

2. New Questions

Once we abandon the view that the foundations of a legal system consist in a habit of obedience to a legally unlimited sovereign and substitute for this the conception of an ultimate rule of recognition which provides a system of rules with its criteria of validity, a range of fascinating and important questions confronts us. They are relatively new questions; for they were veiled so long as jurisprudence and political theory were committed to the older ways of thought. They are also difficult questions, requiring for a full answer, on the one hand a grasp of some fundamental issues of constitutional law and on the other an appreciation of the characteristic manner in which legal forms may silently shift and change. We shall therefore investigate these questions only so far as they bear upon the wisdom or unwisdom of insisting, as we have done, that a central place should be assigned to the union of primary and secondary rules in the elucidation of the concept of law.

The first difficulty is that of classification; for the rule which, in the last resort, is used to identify the law escapes the conventional categories used for describing a legal system, though these are often taken to be exhaustive. Thus, English constitutional writers since Dicey have usually repeated the statement that the constitutional arrangements of the United Kingdom consist partly of laws strictly so called (statutes, orders in council, and rules embodied in precedents) and partly of conventions which are mere usages, understandings, or customs. The latter include important rules such as that the Queen may not refuse her consent to a bill duly passed by Peers and Commons; there is, however, no legal duty on the Queen to give her consent and such rules are called conventions because the courts do not recognize them as imposing a legal duty. Plainly the rule that what the Queen in Parliament enacts is law does not fall into either of these categories. It is not a convention, since the courts are most intimately concerned with it and they use it in identifying the law; and it is not a rule on the same level as the "laws strictly so called" which it is used to identify. Even if it were enacted by statute, this would not reduce it to the level of a statute; for the legal status of such an enactment necessarily would depend on the fact that the rule existed antecedently to and independently of the enactment. Moreover, as we have shown in the last section, its existence, unlike that of a statute, must consist in an actual practice.

This aspect of things extracts from some a cry of despair: how can we show that the fundamental provisions of a constitution which are surely law are really law? Others reply with the insistence that at the base of legal systems there is something which is "not law," which is "pre-legal," "metalegal," or is just "political fact." This uneasiness is a sure sign that the categories used for the description of this most important feature in any system of law are too crude. The case for calling the rule of recognition "law" is that the rule providing criteria for the identification of other rules of the system may well be thought a defining feature of a legal system, and so itself worth calling "law;" the case for calling it "fact" is that to assert that such a rule exists is indeed to make an external statement of an actual fact concerning the manner in which the rules of an "efficacious" system are identified. Both these aspects claim attention but we cannot do justice to them both by choosing one of the labels "law" or "fact." Instead, we need to remember that the ultimate rule of recognition may be regarded from two points of view: one is expressed in the external statement of fact that the rule exists in the actual practice of the system; the other is expressed in the internal statements of validity made by those who use it in identifying the law.

A second set of questions arises out of the hidden complexity and vagueness of the assertion that a legal system *exists* in a given country or among a given social group. When we make this assertion we in fact refer in compressed, portmanteau form to a number of heterogeneous social facts, usually concomitant. The standard terminology of legal and political thought, developed in the shadow of a misleading theory, is apt to oversimplify and obscure the facts. Yet when we take off the spectacles constituted by this terminology and look at the facts, it

becomes apparent that a legal system, like a human being, may at one stage be unborn, at a second not yet wholly independent of its mother, then enjoy a healthy independent existence, later decay and finally die. These halfway stages between birth and normal, independent existence and, again, between that and death, put out of joint our familiar ways of describing legal phenomena. They are worth our study because, baffling as they are, they throw into relief the full complexity of what we take for granted when, in the normal case, we make the confident and true assertion that in a given country a legal system exists.

One way of realizing this complexity is to see just where the simple, Austinian formula of a general habit of obedience to orders fails to reproduce or distorts the complex facts which constitute the minimum conditions which a society must satisfy if it is to have a legal system. We may allow that this formula does designate one necessary condition: namely, that where the laws impose obligations or duties these should be generally obeyed or at any rate not generally disobeyed. But though essential, this only caters for what we may term the "end product" of the legal system, where it makes its impact on the private citizen; whereas its day-to-day existence consists also in the official creation, the official identification, and the official use and application of law. The relationship with law involved here can be called "obedience" only if that word is extended so far beyond its normal use as to cease to characterize informatively these operations. In no ordinary sense of "obey" are legislators obeying rules when, in enacting laws, they conform to the rules conferring their legislative powers, except of course when the rules conferring such powers are reinforced by rules imposing a duty to follow them. Nor, in failing to conform with these rules do they "disobey" a law, though they may fail to make one. Nor does the word "obey" describe well what judges do when they apply the system's rule of recognition and recognize a statute as valid law and use it in the determination of disputes. We can of course, if we wish, preserve the simple terminology of "obedience" in face of the facts by many devices. One is to express, e.g., the use made by judges of general criteria of validity in recognizing a statute, as a case of obedience to orders given by the "Founders of the Constitution," or (where there are no "Founders") as obedience to a "depsychologized command" i.e., a command without a commander. But this last should perhaps have no more serious claims on our attention than the notion of a nephew without an uncle. Alternatively we can push out of sight the whole official side to law and forgo the description of the use of rules made in legislation and adjudication, and instead, think of the whole official world as one person (the "sovereign") issuing orders, through various agents or mouthpieces, which are habitually obeyed by the citizen. But this is either no more than a convenient shorthand for complex facts which still await description, or a disastrously confusing piece of mythology.

It is natural to react from the failure of attempts to give an account of what it is for a legal system to exist, in the agreeably simple terms of the habitual obedience which is indeed characteristic of (though it does not always exhaustively describe) the relationship of the ordinary citizen to law, by making the opposite error. This consists in taking what is characteristic (though again not exhaustive) of the official activities, especially the judicial attitude or relationship to law, and treating this as an adequate account of what must exist in a social group which has a legal system. This amounts to replacing the simple conception that the bulk of society habitually obey the law with the conception that they must generally share, accept, or regard as binding the ultimate rule of recognition specifying the criteria in terms of which the validity of laws are ultimately assessed. Of course we can imagine, as we have done in Chapter III, a simple society where knowledge and understanding of the sources of law are widely diffused. There the "constitution" was so simple that no fiction would be involved in attributing knowledge

and acceptance of it to the ordinary citizen as well as to the officials and lawyers. In the simple world of Rex I we might well say that there was more than mere habitual obedience by the bulk of the population to his word. There it might well be the case that both they and the officials of the system "accepted," in the same explicit, conscious way, a rule of recognition specifying Rex's word as the criterion of valid law for the whole society, though subjects and officials would have different roles to play and different relationships to the rules of law identified by this criterion. To insist that this state of affairs, imaginable in a simple society, always or usually exists in a complex modern state would be to insist on a fiction. Here surely the reality of the situation is that a great proportion of ordinary citizens—perhaps a majority—have no general conception of the legal structure or of its criteria of validity. The law which he obeys is something which he knows of only as "the law." He may obey it for a variety of different reasons and among them may often, though not always, be the knowledge that it will be best for him to do so. He will be aware of the general likely consequences of disobedience: that there are officials who may arrest him and others who will try him and send him to prison for breaking the law. So long as the laws which are valid by the system's tests of validity are obeyed by the bulk of the population this surely is all the evidence we need in order to establish that a given legal system exists.

But just because a legal system is a complex union of primary and secondary rules, this evidence is not all that is needed to describe the relationships to law involved in the existence of a legal system. It must be supplemented by a description of the relevant relationship of the officials of the system to the secondary rules which concern them as officials. Here what is crucial is that there should be a unified or shared official acceptance of the rule of recognition containing the system's criteria of validity. But it is just here that the simple notion of general obedience, which was adequate to characterize the indispensable minimum in the case of ordinary citizens, is inadequate. The point is not, or not merely, the "linguistic" one that "obedience" is not naturally used to refer to the way in which these secondary rules are respected as rules by courts and other officials. We could find, if necessary, some wider expression like "follow," "comply," or "conform to" which would characterize both what ordinary citizens do in relation to law when they report for military service and what judges do when they identify a particular statute as law in their courts, on the footing that what the Queen in Parliament enacts is law. But these blanket terms would merely mask vital differences which must be grasped if the minimum conditions involved in the existence of the complex social phenomenon which we call a legal system is to be understood.

What makes "obedience" misleading as a description of what legislators do in conforming to the rules conferring their powers, and of what courts do in applying an accepted ultimate rule of recognition, is that obeying a rule (or an order) *need* involve no thought on the part of the person obeying that what he does is the right thing both for himself and for others to do: he need have no view of what he does as a fulfilment of a standard of behaviour for others of the social group. He need not think of his conforming behaviour as "right," "correct," or "obligatory." His attitude, in other words, need not have any of that critical character which is involved whenever social rules are accepted and types of conduct are treated as general standards. He need not, though he may, share the internal point of view accepting the rules as standards for all to whom they apply. Instead, he may think of the rule only as something demanding action from *him* under threat of penalty; he may obey it out of fear of the consequences, or from inertia, without thinking of himself or others as having an obligation to do so and without being disposed to criticize either himself or others for deviations. But this merely personal concern with the rules, which is all the ordinary citizen *may* have in obeying them, cannot characterize the attitude of the

courts to the rules with which they operate as courts. This is most patently the case with the ultimate rule of recognition in terms of which the validity of other rules is assessed. This, if it is to exist at all, must be regarded from the internal point of view as a public, common standard of correct judicial decision, and not as something which each judge merely obeys for his part only. Individual courts of the system though they may, on occasion, deviate from these rules must, in general, be critically concerned with such deviations as lapses from standards, which are essentially common or public. This is not merely a matter of the efficiency or health of the legal system, but is logically a necessary condition of our ability to speak of the existence of a single legal system. If only some judges acted "for their part only" on the footing that what the Queen in Parliament enacts is law, and made no criticisms of those who did not respect this rule of recognition, the characteristic unity and continuity of a legal system would have disappeared. For this depends on the acceptance, at this crucial point, of common standards of legal validity. In the interval between these vagaries of judicial behaviour and the chaos which would ultimately ensue when the ordinary man was faced with contrary judicial orders, we would be at a loss to describe the situation. We would be in the presence of a *lusus naturae* worth thinking about only because it sharpens our awareness of what is often too obvious to be noticed.

There are therefore two minimum conditions necessary and sufficient for the existence of a legal system. On the one hand, those rules of behaviour which are valid according to the system's ultimate criteria of validity must be generally obeyed, and, on the other hand, its rules of recognition specifying the criteria of legal validity and its rules of change and adjudication must be effectively accepted as common public standards of official behaviour by its officials. The first condition is the only one which private citizens *need* satisfy: they may obey each "for his part only" and from any motive whatever; though in a healthy society they will in fact often accept these rules as common standards of behaviour and acknowledge obligation to obey them, or even trace this obligation to a more general obligation to respect the constitution. The second condition must also be satisfied by the officials of the system. They must regard these as common standards of official behaviour and appraise critically their own and each other's deviations as lapses. Of course it is also true that besides these there will be many primary rules which apply to officials in their merely personal capacity which they need only obey.

The assertion that a legal system exists is therefore a Janus-faced statement looking both towards obedience by ordinary citizens and to the acceptance by officials of secondary rules as critical common standards of official behaviour. We need not be surprised at this duality. It is merely the reflection of the composite character of a legal system as compared with a simpler decentralized pre-legal form of social structure which consists only of primary rules. In the simpler structure, since there are no officials, the rules must be widely accepted as setting critical standards for the behaviour of the group. If, there, the internal point of view is not widely disseminated there could not logically be any rules. But where there is a union of primary and secondary rules, which is, as we have argued, the most fruitful way of regarding a legal system, the acceptance of the rules as common standards for the group may be split off from the relatively passive matter of the ordinary individual acquiescing in the rules by obeying them for his part alone. In an extreme case the internal point of view with its characteristic normative use of legal language ("This is a valid rule") might be confined to the official world. In this more complex system, only officials might accept and use the system's criteria of legal validity. The society in which this was so might be deplorably sheeplike; the sheep might end in the slaughter-house. But there is little reason for thinking that it could not exist or for denying it the title of a legal system....

◆ ◆ ◆ ◆ ◆

STUDY QUESTIONS

1. Does Hart offer persuasive criticisms of Austin's 'command theory' of legal obligation?

2. How is Hart's explanation of the 'minimum natural law content' of a legal system compatible with his thesis that there is no necessary connection between law and morality?

3. Does Hart's characterization of legal standards as a special type of rule capture adequately all types of legal standard?

4. How persuasive are Hart's criticisms of Austin's idea of the 'sovereign'? Can Austin's idea be modified to save it from Hart's criticism?

5. What is the rule of recognition for your country? What difficulties will any investigator encounter when trying to specify a rule of recognition for any given social situation?

◆ ◆ ◆ ◆ ◆

FURTHER READINGS

Michael Bayles, *Hart's Legal Philosophy: An Examination*. Dordrecht: Kluwer Academic Publishers, 1992.

Tom Campbell, *Prescriptive Legal Positivism: Law, Rights and Democracy*, London: UCL Press, 2004.

Jules Coleman, *The Practice of Principle*. Oxford: Clarendon Press, 2001.

Jules Coleman, ed. *Hart's Postscript: Essays on the Postscript to The Concept of Law*. Oxford: Oxford University Press, 2001.

Julie Dickson, *Evaluation and Legal Theory*. Portland, OR: Hart Publishing, 2001.

Ruth Gavison, ed. *Issues in Contemporary Legal Philosophy: The Influence of H.L.A. Hart*. Oxford: Clarendon Press, 1987.

Robert P. George, ed. *The Autonomy of Law: Essays in Legal Positivism*. Oxford: Clarendon Press, 1996.

Nicola Lacey, *H.L.A. Hart; A Life*. Oxford: Oxford University Press, 2004.

W.L. Morison, *John Austin*. Stanford: Stanford University Press, 1982.

Brian Tamanaha, *A General Jurisprudence of Law and Society*. Oxford: Oxford University Press, 2001.

Wilfrid Waluchow, *Inclusive Legal Positivism*. Oxford: Clarendon Press, 1994.

CHAPTER 3

Integrity

INTRODUCTION

Professor Ronald Dworkin is the most famous of contemporary legal philosophers, both in Britain where he was Hart's successor as Professor of Jurisprudence at Oxford University, and in the United States, where he teaches at the New York University School of Law. Within legal philosophy, he is famous for his criticism of Hart's positivism and his development of a new theory of law. Outside of legal philosophy, he is known for his vigorous participation in American debates over such troubling issues as abortion and the best interpretation of the American Constitution. Two pieces of Dworkin's work are included in this volume: his 1967 article "The Model of Rules I," and an excerpt from his 1986 book *Law's Empire*. In "The Model of Rules I" Dworkin criticizes several views defended by Hart in *The Concept of Law*, and in *Law's Empire* Dworkin offers his own view of "law as integrity." This introduction does not attempt to provide a comprehensive overview of these works, concentrating instead on some central themes and terms crucial to understanding Dworkin's arguments.

1. "The Model of Rules I"

In this article, Dworkin provides a wide-ranging critical analysis of legal positivism and legal realism (whose adherents he calls "nominalists"). Dworkin's own theory of law uses certain ideas developed in this article, but for the most part this article is devoted to demonstrating why legal positivism ought not to be accepted as the best theory of law. Many criticisms of positivism are offered; however, one criticism in particular has been widely recognized as especially important, even by Hart himself. Dworkin argues that there is a serious hole in Hart's explanation of what judges do when they apply the law: in his effort to explain how judges in fact interpret legal rules, Hart forgets the role of *principles* in judges' reasoning when they decide cases.

As Dworkin sketches Hart's view, Hart endorses a "pedigree" theory of the validity of legal rules. (If you have already read the chapter on Hart's work, you will be familiar with his "rule of recognition" by which valid rules of a legal system may be identified.) According to this theory, judges identify and distinguish valid legal rules from other rules (e.g., rules of etiquette or morality, or lawyers' mistaken arguments about legal rules) by looking at where the rules come from. Valid legal rules have the right pedigree—they are derived from accepted sources in statute, custom, case law, and so forth.

In what might be called "easy" cases, judges reach a decision by applying a clearly understood legal rule with an appropriate pedigree to the facts of the case. However, complications can arise which make the process of reaching a decision much more difficult. The law may be written in ambiguous terms, or the most clearly applicable legal rule may not exactly fit the set of facts to which it is to be applied. In cases of this sort, judges cannot simply appeal to the core meaning of a legal rule; instead they must venture out into the surrounding penumbra of the rule's meaning, and apply a more controversial and less settled understanding of the rule to the facts of the case at hand. In some cases, the judges' task will be even more difficult: the facts of a certain case may extend *beyond* the scope of the legal rule. In such "hard" cases, judges are said by Hart to use *discretion* and *make* law. To the extent that judges make a new legal rule where none previously existed, discretionary decisions appear to step outside the law and thus deserve to be called "extra-legal." But this does not mean that they are simply wild decisions guided by nothing more than judges' personal tastes. Hart explains, "We can say laws are incurably incomplete and we must decide the penumbral cases rationally by reference to social aims."[1] In other words, judges assess the purpose or social aim of a legal rule, and in their decisions they advance the spirit of the law even when the letter of the law does not clearly apply.

This account of hard cases does not go far enough, according to Dworkin. He believes it is possible to be more specific about the factors weighing in judges' reasoning, and in being more specific we uncover a rather different and better picture of law. Dworkin argues that in hard cases judges do not reach outside the law to non- or extra-legal standards in order to arrive at decisions. Rather, where legal rules fail to provide adequate guidance, judges use "legal principles" as a basis for decisions. "Principles" are "considerations of justice or fairness," and according to Dworkin, these principles may be found throughout the law. Dworkin makes this point in his discussion of two American cases, *Henningsen v. Bloomfield Motors, Inc.* and *Riggs v. Palmer*. In both cases, Dworkin claims, the courts rely on principles found in the law rather than legal rules to reach a decision. For the purposes of this introduction, the identity of the principles at play in these cases is not important. What *is* important is the *difference* between rules and principles, and Dworkin's reasons for thinking that Hart has committed a serious error

in failing to note the place of legal principles alongside legal rules.

Rules and principles are both standards which guide judges' reasoning when judges try to reach decisions in cases. Rules and principles differ in the *type* of guidance they offer. Dworkin thinks rules and principles may be logically distinguished by the way in which they operate in judges' reasoning. Rules, according to Dworkin, are standards which apply in an "all or nothing fashion"—either a rule does apply, or it does not. Principles, on the other hand, *contribute* to judges' reasoning toward a decision, but do not require any specific decision. Dworkin draws a series of contrasts to clarify the *logical* difference between rules and principles.

First, rules can have exceptions, while principles do not. If a rule does not quite capture a rule-maker's purpose, the rule-maker may add an exception to the rule, e.g., "Always return club equipment to the storage shed *except* those items which are too large to fit in the shed." Principles are unaffected by exceptions and there is no need to take them into account when phrasing the principle. Dworkin points to the legal principle that no man may profit from his own wrong. Even if it is possible to find in the law certain counter-examples to this principle, these counter-examples do not disprove the claim that the principle exists. Principles embody a more general claim that, for the most part, a certain standard exists, and in matters where the standard is relevant, it ought to weigh in reasoning about those matters.

Second, while rules contain conditions which ordinarily make clear when the rule has or has not been followed, principles do not have any such conditions to be met. Principles simply give a reason to make a decision in a particular way, but do not specify what that decision must be. For example, we might be at our club and find that a member has left a medium-sized piece of quite expensive equipment outside the equipment shed, and in our deliberations over whether we ought to fine the offender for an infraction of club rules, we may be uncertain whether

---

1   See in Chapter 2, Hart, "Positivism and the Separation of Law and Morals," § III.

the equipment really counts as "large equipment" within the meaning of the club rule regarding storage of equipment. Our deliberations may be swayed one way or another by a member noting that "it's a principle of our club to behave responsibly with club equipment, and surely leaving our best equipment unsecured is irresponsible." The rule itself is no clearer, but we *are* given a *reason* to decide in one way (in favour of fining the offender) rather than another.

Third, principles have "weight" in judges' reasoning while rules do not. We noted above that Dworkin supposes that rules operate in an on/off fashion: a rule either applies to the facts at hand and requires a particular decision, or it does not. Principles, however, only add weight to the argument in favour of deciding a case in one way rather than another. Returning to the example sketched above, when we consider whether we ought to fine the club member who left a medium-sized piece of equipment outside the equipment shed, we might be swayed in favour of charging a fine by the principle that members ought to behave responsibly, and we might say that we are less concerned with the precise details of what counts as "large equipment" and more concerned to enforce the principle that members ought to behave responsibly with expensive equipment. We might then say that the lack of clarity in the club rule is no excuse. The principle of responsibility is sufficient reason for members to take further steps to ensure the safety of club equipment when unsure about the meaning of the club rule, and this principle gives us sufficient reason to extend the "penumbral" meaning of the rule regarding large equipment to cover medium-sized equipment as well, thus justifying our assessing the offending club member with a fine. In this case, the principle cited has weight in our reasoning, not requiring that we decide to fine the offender, but providing us with a reason to interpret the club rule in one way (to include medium-sized equipment) rather than another (accepting the literal meaning

of the rule as excluding the possibility of fining a member for leaving medium-sized equipment outside). It is important to note also that in a given case principles may compete against one another. In our example, we might weigh *against* the principle of responsibility another principle, that no one should be punished arbitrarily for breaking rules which did not clearly exist prior to the time of the alleged offence. Principles compete against one another, and judges must in their deliberations consider which principles have the most weight in a particular case, and rely on those principles accordingly. Judges, according to Dworkin, must use their discretion in a very specific way: to choose amongst legal principles already at play in the body of the law.

What are we to make of Hart's views in light of this criticism? If Dworkin is right, and Hart has simply missed a large element of judicial reasoning, at the very least Hart must revise his theory to meet these objections. At worst, if Dworkin is correct about the importance of legal principles *and* Hart can find no way to fit these morally charged principles into his view of law, Dworkin has found a serious problem with legal positivism. If judges do in fact rely on moral principles in their deliberations, then Hart cannot be correct in his claim that law can be identified without reference to its moral merit. The separation thesis must then be abandoned, and the other insights of legal positivism into law are also thrown into doubt.

2. *Law's Empire*

In *Law's Empire* Dworkin advances his view of "law as integrity." The excerpt included here is taken from the chapter entitled "Integrity in Law," in which many important features of Dworkin's view are discussed. In contrast to Hart's aim to provide a general, descriptive account of law, Dworkin focuses on the activities of courts.

"Law as integrity" is presented as an alternative to what Dworkin calls "conventionalism" (a set of views very near legal positivism) and "pragmatism" (a set of views very near legal realism). According to law as integrity, judges neither find nor make law. Instead, they *interpret* law. Dworkin employs a carefully explained, technical sense of "interpretation" as an attitude or approach to the thing being interpreted, and not just a series of techniques to be mechanically applied to law by judges. This explanation of interpretation as part of law as integrity appears to be part description and part prescription. This view of law is plausibly viewed as standing midway between legal positivism and natural law theory.

Interpretation, on Dworkin's view, involves explaining something with the aim of understanding its purpose, and trying to understand that purpose in its best light. Dworkin sometimes calls this "constructive interpretation." (This sense of interpretation is familiar to lawyers and judges, who use what are called "rules of construction" to guide interpretation of law.) When interpreting law to make it the best that it can be, judges are not simply left to their own devices, according to Dworkin. Rather, judicial interpretation has two dimensions: fit and justification. Judges try to interpret laws in a way which is consistent with and fits with past decisions and the body of laws as a whole. The dimension of "fit" is thus backward-looking as judges interpret laws in a way which integrates them into past decisions (usually in a fairly narrow area of law). Judges also try to interpret laws in a way which best justifies them and the entire body of laws according to the best available standards of political morality. The dimension of justification is thus forward-looking as judges interpret laws in a way which leaves the body of laws *as a whole* best justified according to the best available principles of political morality. Judges interpret the law in this way, according to Dworkin, because they aim to live in a "community of principle"—a community striving for justice.

Dworkin adds two further explanations of the actions of judges committed to law as integrity. The first is the chain novel analogy. Dworkin compares judges' interpretation of law to a novel written by many authors. The law, Dworkin suggests, is very much like a novel or perhaps a soap-opera screenplay when written by many writers. Even if different writers have different personal views as to the best way to develop the plot and theme of the novel or soap-opera, they are constrained by the plot and theme established by previous writers, and must from time to time compromise their own personal views in order to write in a way which leaves the novel most coherent and internally consistent. The law is like this insofar as many different judges over several hundred years have given decisions which have added to the case law contributing to the identity of the law and the principles in it, and judges have recognized the principles of political morality as justified constraints on their interpretation of law.

The second constraint Dworkin explains might be called the "single author" constraint. The law, viewed as something like a chain novel written to be the best it can be, is also similar to the chain novel insofar as the multiple authors of the chain novel try to write as though they were one. Judges attempt to decide cases in a way which makes the law coherent and integrated in the way it might be if a single author had decided all cases ever brought before the courts.

Law as integrity does not promise that adjudication of this sort will always be easy. On the contrary, because reasonable persons may disagree about the best way to interpret law with respect to fit *and* justification there may frequently be considerable dispute over the best interpretation of the law in a particular instance. There may be further dispute over the best course for law to take as it develops in response to new social situations. Which principles ought to be advanced in which areas of law? Which reading of the law best preserves the consistency of the preceding body of law? In their decisions in specific cases, individual judges each advance a specific conception of law, each interpreting the law with special emphasis on a particular understanding of legal principles which the individual judge thinks leaves the body of laws best justified as a whole. The law may appear to develop in contradictory directions, as judges at varying levels of the court system issue contradictory judgments, and the identity of that area of the law becomes clear only over time as judgments are overruled by higher courts or replaced by legislation. Judges committed to law as integrity do not automatically produce a coherent, consistent, and perfectly justified body of law, according to Dworkin; but this is a minor point compared to the more important point that these judges *try* to produce such a body of law.

3. Where Has the Hart/Dworkin Debate Gone?

If you have read all of the material included here from the writings of H.L.A. Hart and Ronald Dworkin, you have seen much of the course of an important debate over the nature of law. Is law, as Hart says, identifiable without reference to its moral merit? Or must law always be identified with one eye on consistency with what has gone before, and the other eye on ideals of justice? If, after reflection on the debate, you still find yourself unable to pick a winner, you are in good company. Many legal theorists are now convinced that the conflict between Hart and Dworkin was more complex than either realized. It is plausible to view Dworkin in *Law's Empire* as being concerned mainly with adjudication, rather than the general conditions under which law is properly said to exist. Hart, by contrast, is plausibly viewed as being concerned mainly with a general description of what it is for law to be said to exist, and only secondarily concerned with an account of judges' role in law. If the debate is viewed in this way, it becomes all the more plain that there is more to the Hart/Dworkin debate than a dispute about the meaning of the word "law" or the role of judges in a body of law. Each writer writes with a significantly different set of concerns,

and consequently produces a significantly different view of law.

The likely future for Hart's and Dworkin's views of law is perhaps a little surprising. Since Hart's death in 1992, Dworkin has for the most part stepped back from the debate and its ideas, taking his skill and efforts to political theory instead. Dworkin's "law as integrity" remains a topic of discussion, yet there are very few legal theorists writing today who identify themselves as sharing or defending Dworkin's view. Hart's philosophy of law is treated much differently. Many analytical legal theorists continue to regard Hart's views as their point of departure, developing various responses to criticisms of legal positivism. These responses often seem to be contributing to a substantially renovated kind of positivism, focusing on issues raised by the Hart-Dworkin debate yet not treated within it—in particular, questions about the *purpose* of legal theory and the conditions under which a theory of law can be said to be useful or successful. In encountering those questions, legal positivists seem to have given up some ground to Dworkin, accepting at least that the relation of morality to law and adjudication is more complex than Hart's version of the "separation thesis" allows. So while the Hart-Dworkin debate is now a matter of history, it is far from forgotten, and far from irrelevant to understanding philosophy of law today.

◆ ◆ ◆ ◆ ◆

RONALD DWORKIN

"The Model of Rules I," from *Taking Rights Seriously*

1. Embarrassing Questions

Lawyers lean heavily on the connected concepts of legal right and legal obligation. We say that someone has a legal right or duty, and we take that statement as a sound basis for making claims and demands, and for criticizing the acts of public officials. But our understanding of these concepts is remarkably fragile, and we fall into trouble when we try to say what legal rights and obligations are. We say glibly that whether someone has a legal obligation is determined by applying "the law" to the particular facts of his case, but this is not a helpful answer, because we have the same difficulties with the concept of law.

We are used to summing up our troubles in the classic questions of jurisprudence: What is "the law"? When two sides disagree, as often happens, about a proposition "of law," what are they disagreeing about, and how shall we decide which side is right? Why do we call what "the law" says a matter of legal "obligation"? Is "obligation" here just a term of art, meaning only what the law says? Or does legal obligation have something to do with moral obligation? Can we say that we have, in principle at least, the same reasons for meeting our legal obligations that we have for meeting our moral obligations?

These are not puzzles for the cupboard, to be taken down on rainy days for fun. They are sources of continuing embarrassment, and they nag at our attention. They embarrass us in dealing with particular problems that we must solve, one way or another. Suppose a novel right-of-privacy case comes to court, and there is no statute or precedent claimed by the plaintiff. What role in the court's decision should be played by the fact that most people in the community think that private individuals are "morally" entitled to that particular privacy? Supposing the Supreme Court orders some prisoner freed because the police used procedures that the Court now says are constitutionally forbidden, although the Court's earlier decisions upheld these procedures. Must the Court, to be consistent, free all other prisoners previously convicted through these same procedures?[1] Conceptual puzzles about "the law" and "legal obligation" become acute when a court is confronted with a problem like this.

These eruptions signal a chronic disease. Day in and day out we send people to jail, or take money away from them, or make them do things they do not want to do, under coercion of force, and we justify all of this by speaking of such persons as having broken the law or having failed to meet their legal obligations, or having interfered with other people's legal rights. Even in clear cases (a bank robber or a wilful breach of contract), when we are confident that someone had a legal obligation and broke it, we are not able to give a satisfactory account of what that means, or why that entitles the state to punish or coerce him. We may feel confident that what we are doing is proper, but until we can identify the principles we are following we cannot be sure that they are sufficient, or whether we are applying them consistently. In less clear cases, when the issue of whether an obligation has been broken is for some reason controversial, the pitch of these nagging questions rises, and our responsibility to find answers deepens.

Certain lawyers (we may call them "nominalists") urge that we solve these problems by ignoring them. In their view the concepts of "legal obligation" and "the law" are myths, invented and sustained by lawyers for a dismal mix of conscious and subconscious motives. The puzzles we find in these concepts are merely symptoms that they are myths. They are unsolvable because unreal, and our concern with them

---

1 See *Linkletter v. Walker*, 381 U.S. 618 (1965).

is just one feature of our enslavement. We would do better to flush away the puzzles and the concepts altogether, and pursue our important social objectives without this excess baggage.

This is a tempting suggestion, but it has fatal drawbacks. Before we can decide that our concepts of law and of legal obligation are myths, we must decide what they are. We must be able to state, at least roughly, what it is we all believe that is wrong. But the nerve of our problem is that we have great difficulty in doing just that. Indeed, when we ask what law is and what legal obligations are, we are asking for a theory of how we use those concepts and of the conceptual commitments our use entails. We cannot conclude, before we have such a general theory, that our practices are stupid or superstitious.

Of course, the nominalists think they know how the rest of us use these concepts. They think that when we speak of "the law" we mean a set of timeless rules stocked in some conceptual warehouse awaiting discovery by judges, and that when we speak of legal obligation we mean the invisible chains these mysterious rules somehow drape around us. The theory that there are such rules and chains they call "mechanical jurisprudence," and they are right in ridiculing its practitioners. Their difficulty, however, lies in finding practitioners to ridicule. So far they have had little luck in caging and exhibiting mechanical jurisprudents (all specimens captured—even Blackstone and Joseph Beale—have had to be released after careful reading of their texts).

In any event, it is clear that most lawyers have nothing like this in mind when they speak of the law and of legal obligation. A superficial examination of our practices is enough to show this for we speak of laws changing and evolving, and of legal obligation sometimes being problematical. In these and other ways we show that we are not addicted to mechanical jurisprudence.

Nevertheless, we do use the concepts of law and legal obligation, and we do suppose that society's warrant to punish and coerce is written in that currency. It may be that when the details of this practice are laid bare, the concepts we do use will be shown to be as silly and as thick with illusion as those the nominalists invented. If so, then we shall have to find other ways to describe what we do, and either provide other justifications or change our practices. But until we have discovered this and made these adjustments, we cannot accept the nominalists' premature invitation to turn our backs on the problems our present concepts provide.

Of course the suggestion that we stop talking about "the law" and "legal obligation" is mostly bluff. These concepts are too deeply cemented into the structure of our political practices—they cannot be given up like cigarettes or hats. Some of the nominalists have half-admitted this and said that the myths they condemn should be thought of as Platonic myths and retained to seduce the masses into order. This is perhaps not so cynical a suggestion as it seems; perhaps it is a covert hedging of a dubious bet.

If we boil away the bluff, the nominalist attack reduces to an attack on mechanical jurisprudence. Through the lines of the attack, and in spite of the heroic calls for the death of law, the nominalists themselves have offered an analysis of how the terms "law" and "legal obligation" should be used which is not very different from that of more classical philosophers. Nominalists present their analysis as a model of how legal institutions (particularly courts) "really operate." But their model differs mainly in emphasis from the theory first made popular by the nineteenth century philosopher John Austin, and now accepted in one form or another by most working and academic lawyers who hold views on jurisprudence. I shall call this theory, with some historical looseness, "legal positivism." I want to examine the soundness of legal positivism, particularly in the powerful form that Professor H.L.A. Hart has given to it. I choose to focus on his position, not only because of its clarity and elegance, but because here, as almost everywhere else in legal philosophy, constructive thought must start with a consideration of his views.

2. Positivism

Positivism has a few central and organizing propositions as its skeleton, and though not every philosopher who is called a positivist would subscribe to these in the way I present them, they do define the general position I want to examine. These key tenets may be stated as follows:

(a) The law of a community is a set of special rules used by the community directly or indirectly for the purpose of determining which behavior will be punished or coerced by the public power. These special rules can be identified and distinguished by specific criteria, by tests having to do not with their content but with their *pedigree* or the manner in which they were adopted or developed. These tests of pedigree can be used to distinguish valid legal rules from spurious legal rules (rules which lawyers and litigants wrongly argue are rules of law) and also from other sorts of social rules (generally lumped together as "moral rules") that the community follows but does not enforce through public power.

(b) The set of these valid legal rules is exhaustive of "the law," so that if someone's case is not clearly covered by such a rule (because there is none that seems appropriate, or those that seem appropriate are vague, or for some other reason) then that case cannot be decided by "applying the law." It must be decided by some official, like a judge, "exercising his discretion," which means reaching beyond the law for some other sort of standard to guide him in manufacturing a fresh legal rule or supplementing an old one.

(c) To say that someone has a "legal obligation" is to say that his case falls under a valid legal rule that requires him to do or to forbear from doing something. (To say he has a legal right, or has a legal power of some sort, or a legal privilege or immunity, is to assert, in a shorthand way, that others have actual or hypothetical legal obligations to act or not to act in certain ways touching him.) In the absence of such a valid legal rule there is no legal obligation;

it follows that when the judge decides an issue by exercising his discretion, he is not enforcing a legal right as to that issue.

This is only the skeleton of positivism. The flesh is arranged differently by different positivists, and some even tinker with the bones. Different versions differ chiefly in their description of the fundamental test of pedigree a rule must meet to count as a rule of law.

Austin, for example, framed his version of the fundamental test as a series of interlocking definitions and distinctions.[2] He defined having an obligation as lying under a rule, a rule as a general command, and a command as an expression of desire that others behave in a particular way, backed by the power and will to enforce that expression in the event of disobedience. He distinguished classes of rules (legal, moral or religious) according to which person or group is the author of the general command the rule represents. In each political community, he thought, one will find a sovereign—a person or a determinate group whom the rest obey habitually, but who is not in the habit of obeying anyone else. The legal rules of a community are the general commands its sovereign has deployed. Austin's definition of legal obligation followed from this definition of law. One has a legal obligation, he thought, if one is among the addressees of some general order of the sovereign, and is in danger of suffering a sanction unless he obeys that order.

Of course, the sovereign cannot provide for all contingencies through any scheme of orders, and some of his orders will inevitably be vague or have furry edges. Therefore (according to Austin) the sovereign grants those who enforce the law (judges) discretion to make fresh orders when novel or troublesome cases are presented. The judges then make new rules or adapt old rules, and the sovereign either overturns their creations or tacitly confirms them by failing to do so.

---

2   J. Austin, *The Province of Jurisprudence Determined* (1832).

Austin's model is quite beautiful in its simplicity. It asserts the first tenet of positivism, that the law is a set of rules specially selected to govern public order, and offers a simple factual test—what has the sovereign commanded?—as the sole criterion for identifying those special rules. In time, however, those who studied and tried to apply Austin's model found it too simple. Many objections were raised, among which were two that seemed fundamental. First, Austin's key assumption that in each community a determinate group or institution can be found, which is in ultimate control of all other groups, seemed not to hold in a complex society. Political control in a modern nation is pluralistic and shifting, a matter of more or less, of compromise and cooperation and alliance, so that it is often impossible to say that any person or group has that dramatic control necessary to qualify as an Austinian sovereign. One wants to say, in the United States for example, that the "people" are sovereign. But this means almost nothing, and in itself provides no test for determining what the "people" have commanded, or distinguishing their legal from their social or moral commands.

Second, critics began to realize that Austin's analysis fails entirely to account for, even to recognize, certain striking facts about the attitudes we take toward "the law." We make an important distinction between law and even the general orders of a gangster. We feel that the law's strictures—and its sanctions—are different in that they are obligatory in a way that the outlaw's commands are not. Austin's analysis has no place for any such distinction, because it defines an obligation as subjection to the threat of force, and so founds the authority of law entirely on the sovereign's ability and will to harm those who disobey. Perhaps the distinction we make is illusory—perhaps our feelings of some special authority attaching to the law is based on religious hangover or another sort of mass self-deception. But Austin does not demonstrate this, and we are entitled to insist that an analysis of our concept of law either acknowledge and explain our attitudes, or show why they are mistaken.

H.L.A. Hart's version of positivism is more complex than Austin's, in two ways. First, he recognizes, as Austin did not, that rules are of different logical kinds. (Hart distinguishes two kinds, which he calls "primary" and "secondary" rules.) Second, he rejects Austin's theory that a rule is a kind of command, and substitutes a more elaborate general analysis of what rules are. We must pause over each of these points, and then note how they merge in Hart's concept of law.

Hart's distinction between primary and secondary rules is of great importance.[3] Primary rules are those that grant rights or impose obligations upon members of the community. The rules of the criminal law that forbid us to rob, murder or drive too fast are good examples of primary rules. Secondary rules are those that stipulate how, and by whom, such primary rules may be formed, recognized, modified or extinguished. The rules that stipulate how Congress is composed, and how it enacts legislation, are examples of secondary rules. Rules about forming contracts and executing wills are also secondary rules because they stipulate how very particular rules governing particular legal obligations (i.e., the terms of a contract or the provisions of a will) come into existence and are changed.

His general analysis of rules is also of great importance.[4] Austin had said that every rule is a general command, and that a person is obligated under a rule if he is liable to be hurt should he disobey it. Hart points out that this obliterates the distinction between being *obliged* to do some thing and being *obligated* to do it. If one is bound by a rule he is obligated, not merely obliged, to do what it provides, and therefore being bound by a rule must be different from being subject to an injury if one disobeys an order. A rule differs from an order,

---

3   See H.L.A. Hart, *The Concept of Law*, 89–96 (1961).
4   *Id.* at 79–88.

among other ways, by being *normative*, by setting a standard of behavior that has a call on its subject beyond the threat that may enforce it. A rule can never be binding just because some person with physical power wants it to be so. He must have authority to issue the rule or it is no rule, and such *authority* can only come from another rule which is already binding on those to whom he speaks. That is the difference between a valid law and the orders of a gunman.

So Hart offers a general theory of rules that does not make their authority depend upon the physical power of their authors. If we examine the way different rules come into being, he tells us, and attend to the distinction between primary and secondary rules, we see that there are two possible sources of a rule's authority:[5]

(a) A rule may become binding upon a group of people because that group through its practices *accepts* the rule as a standard for its conduct. It is not enough that the group simply conforms to a pattern of behavior: even though most Englishmen may go to the movies on Saturday evening, they have not accepted a rule requiring that they do so. A practice constitutes the acceptance of a rule only when those who follow the practice regard the rule as binding, and recognize the rule as a reason or justification for their own behavior and as a reason for criticizing the behavior of others who do not obey it.

(b) A rule may also become binding in quite a different way, namely by being enacted in conformity with some *secondary* rule that stipulates that rules so enacted shall be binding. If the constitution of a club stipulates, for example, that by-laws may be adopted by a majority of the members, then particular by-laws so voted are binding upon all the members, not because of any practice of acceptance of these particular by-laws, but because the constitution says so. We use the concept of *validity* in this connection: rules binding because they have been created in a manner stipulated by some secondary rule are called "valid" rules.

Thus we can record Hart's fundamental distinction this way: a rule may be binding (a) because it is accepted or (b) because it is valid.

Hart's concept of law is a construction of these various distinctions.[6] Primitive communities have only primary rules, and these are binding entirely because of practices of acceptance. Such communities cannot be said to have "law," because there is no way to distinguish a set of legal rules from amongst other social rules, as the first tenet of positivism requires. But when a particular community has developed a fundamental secondary rule that stipulates how legal rules are to be identified, the idea of a distinct set of legal rules, and thus of law, is born.

Hart calls such a fundamental secondary rule a "rule of recognition." The rule of recognition of a given community may be relatively simple ("What the king enacts is law") or it may be very complex (the United States Constitution, with all its difficulties of interpretation, may be considered a single rule of recognition). The demonstration that a particular rule is valid may therefore require tracing a complicated chain of validity back from that particular rule ultimately to the fundamental rule. Thus a parking ordinance of the city of New Haven is valid because it is adopted by a city council, pursuant to the procedures and within the competence specified by the municipal law adopted by the state of Connecticut, in conformity with the procedures and within the competence specified by the constitution of the state of Connecticut, which was in turn adopted consistently with the requirements of the United States Constitution.

Of course, a rule of recognition cannot itself be valid, because by hypothesis it is ultimate, and so cannot meet tests stipulated by a more fundamental rule. The rule of recognition is the sole rule in a legal system whose binding force depends upon its

---

5   *Id.* at 97–107.

6   *Id. passim*, particularly ch. 6.

acceptance. If we wish to know what rule of recognition a particular community has adopted or follows, we must observe how its citizens, and particularly its officials, behave. We must observe what ultimate arguments they accept as showing the validity of a particular rule, and what ultimate arguments they use to criticize other officials or institutions. We can apply no mechanical test, but there is no danger of our confusing the rule of recognition of a community with its rules of morality. The rule of recognition is identified by the fact that its province is the operation of the governmental apparatus of legislatures, courts, agencies, policemen, and the rest.

In this way Hart rescues the fundamentals of positivism from Austin's mistakes. Hart agrees with Austin that valid rules of law may be created through the acts of officials and public institutions. But Austin thought that the authority of these institutions lay only in their monopoly of power. Hart finds their authority in the background of constitutional standards against which they act, constitutional standards that have been accepted, in the form of a fundamental rule of recognition, by the community which they govern. This background legitimates the decisions of government and gives them the cast and call of obligation that the naked commands of Austin's sovereign lacked. Hart's theory differs from Austin's also, in recognizing that different communities use different ultimate tests of law, and that some allow other means of creating law than the deliberate act of a legislative institution. Hart mentions "long customary practice" and "the relation [of a rule] to judicial decisions" as other criteria that are often used, though generally along with and subordinate to the test of legislation.

So Hart's version of positivism is more complex than Austin's, and his test for valid rules of law is more sophisticated. In one respect, however, the two models are very similar. Hart, like Austin, recognizes that legal rules have furry edges (he speaks of them as having "open texture") and, again like Austin, he accounts for troublesome cases by say-ing that judges have and exercise discretion to decide these cases by fresh legislation.[7] (I shall later try to show why one who thinks of law as a special set of rules is almost inevitably drawn to account for difficult cases in terms of someone's exercise of discretion.)

3. Rules, Principles, and Policies

I want to make a general attack on positivism, and I shall use H.L.A. Hart's version as a target, when a particular target is needed. My strategy will be organized around the fact that when lawyers reason or dispute about legal rights and obligations, particularly in those hard cases when our problems with these concepts seem most acute, they make use of standards that do not function as rules, but operate differently as principles, policies, and other sorts of standards. Positivism, I shall argue, is a model of and for a system of rules, and its central notion of a single fundamental test for law forces us to miss the important roles of these standards that are not rules.

I just spoke of "principles, policies, and other sorts of standards." Most often I shall use the term "principle" generically, to refer to the whole set of these standards other than rules; occasionally, however, I shall be more precise, and distinguish between principles and policies. Although nothing in the present argument will turn on the distinction, I should state how I draw it. I call a "policy" that kind of standard that sets out a goal to be reached, generally an improvement in some economic, political, or social feature of the community (though some goals are negative, in that they stipulate that some present feature is to be protected from adverse change). I call a "principle" a standard that is to be observed, not because it will advance or secure an economic, political, or social situation deemed desirable, but because it is a requirement of justice or fairness or

---

7   *Id.* ch. 7.

some other dimension of morality. Thus the standard that automobile accidents are to be decreased is a policy, and the standard that no man may profit by his own wrong a principle. The distinction can be collapsed by construing a principle as stating a social goal (i.e., the goal of a society in which no man profits by his own wrong), or by construing a policy as stating a principle (i.e., the principle that the goal the policy embraces is a worthy one) or by adopting the utilitarian thesis that principles of justice are disguised statements of goals (securing the greatest happiness of the greatest number). In some contexts the distinction has uses which are lost if it is thus collapsed.[8]

My immediate purpose, however, is to distinguish principles in the generic sense from rules, and I shall start by collecting some examples of the former. The examples I offer are chosen haphazardly; almost any case in a law school casebook would provide examples that would serve as well. In 1889 a New York court, in the famous case of *Riggs v. Palmer*[9] had to decide whether an heir named in the will of his grandfather could inherit under that will, even though he had murdered his grandfather to do so. The court began its reasoning with this admission: "It is quite true that statutes regulating the making, proof and effect of wills, and the devolution of property, if literally construed, and if their force and effect can in no way and under no circumstances be controlled or modified, give this property to the murderer."[10] But the court continued to note that "all laws as well as all contracts may be controlled in their operation and effect by general, fundamental maxims of the common law. No one shall be permitted to profit by his own fraud, or to take advantage of his own wrong, or to found any claim upon his own iniquity, or to

acquire property by his own crime."[11] The murderer did not receive his inheritance.

In 1960, a New Jersey court was faced, in *Henningsen v. Bloomfield Motors, Inc.*[12] with the important question of whether (or how much) an automobile manufacturer may limit his liability in case the automobile is defective. Henningsen had bought a car, and signed a contract which said that the manufacturer's liability for defects was limited to "making good" defective parts—"this warranty being expressly in lieu of all other warranties, obligations or liabilities." Henningsen argued that, at least in the circumstances of his case, the manufacturer ought not to be protected by this limitation, and ought to be liable for the medical and other expenses of persons injured in a crash. He was not able to point to any statute, or to any established rule of law, that prevented the manufacturer from standing on the contract. The court nevertheless agreed with Henningsen. At various points in the court's argument the following appeals to standards are made: (a) "[We] must keep in mind the general principle that, in the absence of fraud, one who does not choose to read a contract before signing it cannot later relieve himself of its burdens."[13] (b) "In applying that principle, the basic tenet of freedom of competent parties to contract is a factor of importance."[14] (c) "Freedom of contract is not such an immutable doctrine as to admit of no qualification in the area in which we are concerned."[15] (d) "In a society such as ours, where the automobile is a common and necessary adjunct of daily life, and where its use is so fraught with danger to the driver, passengers and the public, the manufacturer is under a special obligation in connection with the construction, promotion and sale of his cars. Consequently, the courts must examine purchase agreements closely to see if

---

8   See Chapter 4. See also Dworkin, "Wasserstrom: The Judicial Decision," 75 *Ethics* 47 (1964), reprinted as "Does Law Have a Function?" 74 *Yale Law Journal* 640 (1965).
9   115 N.Y. 506, 22 N.E. 188 (1889).
10 *Id.* at 509, 22 N.E. at 189.

11 *Id.* at 511, 22 N.E. at 190.
12 32 N.J. 358, 161 A.2d 69 (1960).
13 *Id.* at 386, 161 A.2d at 84.
14 *Id.*
15 *Id.* at 388, 161 A.2d at 86.

consumer and public interests are treated fairly."[16] (e) "'[I]s there any principle which is more familiar or more firmly embedded in the history of Anglo-American law than the basic doctrine that the courts will not permit themselves to be used as instruments of inequity and injustice?'"[17] (f) "'More specifically the courts generally refuse to lend themselves to the enforcement of a "bargain" in which one party has unjustly taken advantage of the economic necessities of other....'"[18]

The standards set out in these quotations are not the sort we think of as legal rules. They seem very different from propositions like "The maximum legal speed on the turnpike is sixty miles an hour" or "A will is invalid unless signed by three witnesses." They are different because they are legal principles rather than legal rules.

The difference between legal principles and legal rules is a logical distinction. Both sets of standards point to particular decisions about legal obligation in particular circumstances, but they differ in the character of the direction they give. Rules are applicable in an all-or-nothing fashion. If the facts a rule stipulates are given, then either the rule is valid, in which case the answer it supplies must be accepted, or it is not, in which case it contributes nothing to the decision.

This all-or-nothing approach is seen most plainly if we look at the way rules operate, not in law, but in some enterprise they dominate—a game, for example. In baseball a rule provides that if the batter has had three strikes, he is out. An official cannot consistently acknowledge that this is an accurate statement of a baseball rule, and decide that a batter who has had three strikes is not out. Of course, a rule may have exceptions (the batter who has taken three strikes is not out if the catcher drops the third

strike). However, an accurate statement of the rule would take this exception into account, and any that did not would be incomplete. If the list of exceptions is very large, it would be too clumsy to repeat them each time the rule is cited; there is, however, no reason in theory why they could not all be added on, and the more that are, the more accurate is the statement of the rule.

If we take baseball rules as a model, we find that rules of law, like the rule that a will is invalid unless signed by three witnesses, fit the model well. If the requirement of three witnesses is a valid legal rule, then it cannot be that a will has been signed by only two witnesses and is valid. The rule might have exceptions, but if it does then it is inaccurate and incomplete to state the rule so simply, without enumerating the exceptions. In theory, at least, the exceptions could all be listed, and the more of them that are, the more complete is the statement of the rule.

But this is not the way the sample principles in the quotations operate. Even those which look most like rules do not set out legal consequences that follow automatically when the conditions provided are met. We say that our law respects the principle that no man may profit from his own wrong, but we do not mean that the law never permits a man to profit from wrongs he commits. In fact, people often profit, perfectly legally, from their legal wrongs. The most notorious case is adverse possession—if I trespass on your land long enough, some day I will gain a right to cross your land whenever I please. There are many less dramatic examples. If a man leaves one job, breaking a contract, to take a much higher paying job, he may have to pay damages to his first employer, but he is usually entitled to keep his new salary. If a man jumps bail and crosses state lines to make a brilliant investment in another state, he may be sent back to jail, but he will keep his profits.

We do not treat these—and countless other counter-instances that can easily be imagined—as showing that the principle about profiting from

16 *Id.* at 387, 161 A.2d at 85.

17 *Id.* at 389, 161 A.2d at 86 (quoting Frankfurter, J., in *United States v. Bethlehem Steel*, 315 U.S. 289, 326 [1942]).

18 *Id.*

one's wrongs is not a principle of our legal system, or that it is incomplete and needs qualifying exceptions. We do not treat counter-instances as exceptions (at least not exceptions in the way in which a catcher's dropping the third strike is an exception) because we could not hope to capture these counter-instances simply by a more extended statement of the principle. They are not, even in theory, subject to enumeration, because we would have to include not only these cases (like adverse possession) in which some institution has already provided that profit can be gained through a wrong, but also those numberless imaginary cases in which we know in advance that the principle would not hold. Listing some of these might sharpen our sense of the principle's weight (I shall mention that dimension in a moment), but it would not make for a more accurate or complete statement of the principle.

A principle like "No man may profit from his own wrong" does not even purport to set out conditions that make its application necessary. Rather, it states a reason that argues in one direction, but does not necessitate a particular decision. If a man has or is about to receive something, as a direct result of something illegal he did to get it, then that is a reason which the law will take into account in deciding whether he should keep it. There may be other principles or policies arguing in the other direction—a policy of securing title, for example, or a principle limiting punishment to what the legislature has stipulated. If so, our principle may not prevail, but that does not mean that it is not a principle of our legal system, because in the next case, when these contravening considerations are absent or less weighty, the principle may be decisive. All that is meant, when we say that a particular principle is a principle of our law, is that the principle is one which officials must take into account, if it is relevant, as a consideration inclining in one direction or another.

The logical distinction between rules and principles appears more clearly when we consider principles that do not even look like rules. Consider the prop-osition, set out under "(d)" in the excerpts from the *Henningsen* opinion, that "the manufacturer is under a special obligation in connection with the construction, promotion and sale of his cars." This does not even purport to define the specific duties such a special obligation entails, or to tell us what rights automobile consumers acquire as a result. It merely states—and this is an essential link in the *Henningsen* argument—that automobile manufacturers must be held to higher standards than other manufacturers, and are less entitled to rely on the competing principle of freedom of contract. It does not mean that they may never rely on that principle, or that courts may rewrite automobile purchase contracts at will; it means only that if a particular clause seems unfair or burdensome, courts have less reason to enforce the clause than if it were for the purchase of neckties. The "special obligation" counts in favor, but does not in itself necessitate, a decision refusing to enforce the terms of an automobile purchase contract.

This first difference between rules and principles entails another. Principles have a dimension that rules do not—the dimension of weight or importance. When principles intersect (the policy of protecting automobile consumers intersecting with principles of freedom of contract, for example), one who must resolve the conflict has to take into account the relative weight of each. This cannot be, of course, an exact measurement, and the judgment that a particular principle or policy is more important than another will often be a controversial one. Nevertheless, it is an integral part of the concept of a principle that it has this dimension, that it makes sense to ask how important or how weighty it is.

Rules do not have this dimension. We can speak of rules as being *functionally* important or unimportant (the baseball rule that three strikes are out is more important than the rule that runners may advance on a balk, because the game would be much more changed with the first rule altered than the second). In this sense, one legal rule may be more important than another because it has a greater or more important role in regulating behavior. But we cannot say that one rule is more important than another within the system of rules, so that when two rules conflict one supersedes the other by virtue of its greater weight.

If two rules conflict, one of them cannot be a valid rule. The decision as to which is valid, and which must be abandoned or recast, must be made by appealing to considerations beyond the rules themselves. A legal system might regulate such conflicts by other rules, which prefer the rule enacted by the higher authority, or the rule enacted later, or the more specific rule, or something of that sort. A legal system may also prefer the rule supported by the more important principles. (Our own legal system uses both of these techniques.)

It is not always clear from the form of a standard whether it is a rule or a principle. "A will is invalid unless signed by three witnesses" is not very different in form from "A man may not profit from his own wrong," but one who knows something of American law knows that he must take the first as stating a rule and the second as stating a principle. In many cases the distinction is difficult to make—it may not have been settled how the standard should operate, and this issue may itself be a focus of controversy. The first amendment to the United States Constitution contains the provision that Congress shall not abridge freedom of speech. Is this a rule, so that if a particular law does abridge freedom of speech, it follows that it is unconstitutional? Those who claim that the first amendment is "an absolute" say that it must be taken in this way, that is, as a rule. Or does it merely state a principle, so that when an abridgement of speech is discovered, it is unconstitutional unless the context presents some other policy or principle which in the circumstances is weighty enough to permit the abridgement? That is the position of those who argue for what is called the "clear and present danger" test or some other form of "balancing."

Sometimes a rule and a principle can play much the same role, and the difference between them is al-

most a matter of form alone. The first section of the Sherman Act states that every contract in restraint of trade shall be void. The Supreme Court had to make the decision whether this provision should be treated as a rule in its own terms (striking down every contract "which restrains trade," which almost any contract does) or as a principle, providing a reason for striking down a contract in the absence of effective contrary policies. The Court construed the provision as a rule, but treated that rule as containing the word "unreasonable," and as prohibiting only "unreasonable" restraints of trade.[19] This allowed the provision to function logically as a rule (whenever a court finds that the restraint is "unreasonable" it is bound to hold the contract invalid) and substantially as a principle (a court must take into account a variety of other principles and policies in determining whether a particular restraint in particular economic circumstances is "unreasonable").

Words like "reasonable," "negligent," "unjust," and "significant" often perform just this function. Each of these terms makes the application of the rule which contains it depend to some extent upon principles or policies lying beyond the rule, and in this way makes that rule itself more like a principle. But they do not quite turn the rule into a principle, because even the least confining of these terms restricts the *kind* of other principles and policies on which the rule depends. If we are bound by a rule that says that "unreasonable" contracts are void, or that grossly "unfair" contracts will not be enforced, much more judgment is required than if the quoted terms were omitted. But suppose a case in which some consideration of policy or principle suggests that a contract should be enforced even though its restraint is not reasonable, or even though it is grossly unfair. Enforcing these contracts would be forbidden by our rules, and thus permitted only if

---

19 *Standard Oil v. United States*, 221 U.S. 1, 60 (1911); *United States v. American Tobacco Co.*, 221 U.S. 106, 180 (1911).

these rules were abandoned or modified. If we were dealing, however, not with a rule but with a policy against enforcing unreasonable contracts, or a principle that unfair contracts ought not to be enforced, the contracts could be enforced without alteration of the law.

4. Principles and the Concept of Law

Once we identify legal principles as separate sorts of standards, different from legal rules, we are suddenly aware of them all around us. Law teachers teach them, lawbooks cite them, legal historians celebrate them. But they seem most energetically at work, carrying most weight, in difficult lawsuits like *Riggs* and *Henningsen*. In cases like these, principles play an essential part in arguments supporting judgments about particular legal rights and obligations. After the case is decided, we may say that the case stands for a particular rule (e.g., the rule that one who murders is not eligible to take under the will of his victim). But the rule does not exist before the case is decided; the court cites principles as its justification for adopting and applying a new rule. In *Riggs*, the court cited the principle that no man may profit from his own wrong as a background standard against which to read the statute of wills and in this way justified a new interpretation of that statute. In *Henningsen*, the court cited a variety of intersecting principles and policies as authority for a new rule respecting manufacturers' liability for automobile defects.

An analysis of the concept of legal obligation must therefore account for the important role of principles in reaching particular decisions of law. There are two very different tacks we might take:

(a) We might treat legal principles the way we treat legal rules and say that some principles are binding as law and must be taken into account by judges and lawyers who make decisions of legal obligation. If we took this tack, we should say that in the United States, at least, the "law" includes principles as well as rules.

(b) We might, on the other hand, deny that principles can be binding the way some rules are. We would say, instead, that in cases like *Riggs* or *Henningsen* the judge reaches beyond the rules that he is bound to apply (reaches, that is, beyond the "law") for extra-legal principles he is free to follow if he wishes.

One might think that there is not much difference between these two lines of attack, that it is only a verbal question of how one wants to use the word "law." But that is a mistake, because the choice between these two accounts has the greatest consequences for an analysis of legal obligation. It is a choice between two *concepts* of a legal principle, a choice we can clarify by comparing it to a choice we might make between two concepts of a legal rule. We sometimes say of someone that he "makes it a rule" to do something, when we mean that he has chosen to follow a certain practice. We might say that someone has made it a rule, for example, to run a mile before breakfast because he wants to be healthy and believes in a regimen. We do not mean, when we say this, that he is *bound* by the rule that he must run a mile before breakfast, or even that he regards it as binding upon him. Accepting a rule as binding is something different from making it a rule to do something. If we use Hart's example again, there is a difference between saying that Englishmen make it a rule to see a movie once a week, and saying that the English have a rule that one must see a movie once a week. The second implies that if an Englishman does not follow the rule, he is subject to criticism or censure, but the first does not. The first does not exclude the possibility of a *sort* of criticism—we can say that one who does not see movies is neglecting his education—but we do not suggest that he is doing something wrong *just* in not following the rule.[20]

---

20 The distinction is in substance the same as that made by Rawls, "Two Concepts of Rules," 64 *Philosophical Review* 3 (1955).

If we think of the judges of a community as a group, we could describe the rules of law they follow in these two different ways. We could say, for instance, that in a certain state the judges make it a rule not to enforce wills unless there are three witnesses. This would not imply that the rare judge who enforces such a will is doing anything wrong just for that reason. On the other hand we can say that in that state a rule of law requires judges not to enforce such wills; this does imply that a judge who enforces them is doing something wrong. Hart, Austin and other positivists, of course, would insist on this latter account of legal rules; they would not at all be satisfied with the "make it a rule" account. It is not a verbal question of which account is right. It is a question of which describes the social situation more accurately. Other important issues turn on which description we accept. If judges simply "make it a rule" not to enforce certain contracts, for example, then we cannot say, before the decision, that anyone is "entitled" to that result, and that proposition cannot enter into any justification we might offer for the decision.

The two lines of attack on principles parallel these two accounts of rules. The first tack treats principles as binding upon judges, so that they are wrong not to apply the principles when they are pertinent. The second tack treats principles as summaries of what most judges "make it a principle" to do when forced to go beyond the standards that bind them. The choice between these approaches will affect, perhaps even determine, the answer we can give to the question whether the judge in a hard case like *Riggs* or *Henningsen* is attempting to enforce pre-existing legal rights and obligations. If we take the first tack, we are still free to argue that because such judges are applying binding legal standards they are enforcing legal rights and obligations. But if we take the second, we are out of court on that issue, and we must acknowledge that the murderer's family in *Riggs* and the manufacturer in *Henningsen* were deprived of their property by an act of judicial discretion applied *ex post facto*. This may not shock many readers—the notion of judicial discretion has percolated through the legal community—but it does illustrate one of the most nettlesome of the puzzles that drive philosophers to worry about legal obligation. If taking property away in cases like these cannot be justified by appealing to an established obligation, another justification must be found, and nothing satisfactory has yet been supplied.

In my skeleton diagram of positivism, previously set out, I listed the doctrine of judicial discretion as the second tenet. Positivists hold that when a case is not covered by a clear rule, a judge must exercise his discretion to decide that case by what amounts to a fresh piece of legislation. There may be an important connection between this doctrine and the question of which of the two approaches to legal principles we must take. We shall therefore want to ask whether the doctrine is correct, and whether it implies the second approach, as it seems on its face to do. En route to these issues, however, we shall have to polish our understanding of the concept of discretion. I shall try to show how certain confusions about that concept and in particular a failure to discriminate different senses in which it is used, account for the popularity of the doctrine of discretion. I shall argue that in the sense in which the doctrine does have a bearing on our treatment of principles, it is entirely unsupported by the arguments the positivists use to defend it.

5. Discretion

The concept of discretion was lifted by the positivists from ordinary language, and to understand it we must put it back in *habitat* for a moment. What does it mean, in ordinary life, to say that someone "has discretion"? The first thing to notice is that the concept is out of place in all but very special contexts. For example, you would not say that I either do or do not have discretion to choose a house for my family. It is not true that I have "no discretion" in making that choice, and yet it would be almost equally misleading to say that I do have discretion. The concept of discretion is at home in only one sort of context; when someone is in general charged with making decisions subject to standards set by a particular authority. It makes sense to speak of the discretion of a sergeant who is subject to orders of superiors, or the discretion of a sports official or contest judge who is governed by a rule book or the terms of the contest. Discretion, like the hole in a doughnut, does not exist except as an area left open by a surrounding belt of restriction. It is therefore a relative concept. It always makes sense to ask, "Discretion under which standards?" or "Discretion as to which authority?" Generally the context will make the answer to this plain, but in some cases the official may have discretion from one standpoint though not from another.

Like almost all terms, the precise meaning of "discretion" is affected by features of the context. The term is always colored by the background of understood information against which it is used. Although the shadings are many, it will be helpful for us to recognize some gross distinctions.

Sometimes we use "discretion" in a weak sense, simply to say that for some reason the standards an official must apply cannot be applied mechanically but demand the use of judgment. We use this weak sense when the context does not already make that clear, when the background our audience assumes does not contain that piece of information. Thus we might say, "The sergeant's orders left him a great deal of discretion," to those who do not know what the sergeant's orders were or who do not know something that made those orders vague or hard to carry out. It would make perfect sense to add, by way of amplification, that the lieutenant had ordered the sergeant to take his five most experienced men on patrol but that it was hard to determine which were the most experienced.

Sometimes we use the term in a different weak sense, to say only that some official has final authority to make a decision and cannot be reviewed and reversed by any other official. We speak this way when the official is part of a hierarchy of officials structured so that some have higher authority but in which the patterns of authority are different for different classes of decision. Thus we might say that in baseball certain decisions, like the decision whether the ball or the runner reached second base first, are left to the discretion of the second base umpire, if we mean that on this issue the head umpire has no power to substitute his own judgment if he disagrees.

I call both of these senses weak to distinguish them from a stronger sense. We use "discretion" sometimes not merely to say that an official must use judgment in applying the standards set him by authority, or that no one will review that exercise of judgment, but to say that on some issue he is simply not bound by standards set by the authority in question. In this sense we say that a sergeant has discretion who has been told to pick any five men for patrol he chooses or that a judge in a dog show has discretion to judge airedales before boxers if the rules do not stipulate an order of events. We use this sense not to comment on the vagueness or difficulty of the standards, or on who has the final word in applying them, but on their range and the decisions they purport to control. If the sergeant is told to take the five most experienced men, he does not have discretion in this strong sense because that order purports to govern his decision. The boxing referee who must decide which fighter has been the more aggressive does not have discretion, in the strong sense, for the same reason.[21]

---

21 I have not spoken of that jurisprudential favorite, "limited" discretion, because that concept presents no special difficulties if we remember the relativity of discretion. Suppose the sergeant is told to choose from "amongst" experienced men, or to "take experience into account." We might say either that he has (limited) discretion in picking his patrol, or (full) discretion to either pick amongst experienced men or decide what else to take into account.

If anyone said that the sergeant or the referee had discretion in these cases, we should have to understand him, if the context permitted, as using the term in one of the weak senses. Suppose, for example, the lieutenant ordered the sergeant to select the five men he deemed most experienced, and then added that the sergeant had discretion to choose them. Or the rules provided that the referee should award the round to the more aggressive fighter, with discretion in selecting him. We should have to understand these statements in the second weak sense, as speaking to the question of review of the decision. The first weak sense—that the decisions take judgment—would be otiose, and the third, strong sense is excluded by the statements themselves.

We must avoid one tempting confusion. The strong sense of discretion is not tantamount to license, and does not exclude criticism. Almost any situation in which a person acts (including those in which there is no question of decision under special authority, and so no question of discretion) makes relevant certain standards of rationality, fairness, and effectiveness. We criticize each other's acts in terms of these standards, and there is no reason not to do so when the acts are within the center rather than beyond the perimeter of the doughnut of special authority. So we can say that the sergeant who was given discretion (in the strong sense) to pick a patrol did so stupidly or maliciously or carelessly, or that the judge who had discretion in the order of viewing dogs made a mistake because he took boxers first although there were only three airedales and many more boxers. An official's discretion means not that he is free to decide without recourse to standards of sense and fairness, but only that his decision is not controlled by a standard furnished by the particular authority we have in mind when we raise the question of discretion. Of course this latter sort of freedom is important; that is why we have the strong sense of discretion. Someone who has discretion in this third sense can be criticized, but not for being disobedient, as in the case of the soldier. He can be

said to have made a mistake, but not to have deprived a participant of a decision to which he was entitled, as in the case of a sports official or contest judge.

We may now return, with these observations in hand, to the positivists' doctrine of judicial discretion. That doctrine argues that if a case is not controlled by an established rule, the judge must decide it by exercising discretion. We want to examine this doctrine and to test its bearing on our treatment of principles; but first we must ask in which sense of discretion we are to understand it.

Some nominalists argue that judges always have discretion, even when a clear rule is in point, because judges are ultimately the final arbiters of the law. This doctrine of discretion uses the second weak sense of that term, because it makes the point that no higher authority reviews the decisions of the highest court. It therefore has no bearing on the issue of how we account for principles, any more than it bears on how we account for rules.

The positivists do not mean their doctrine this way, because they say that a judge has no discretion when a clear and established rule is available. If we attend to the positivists' arguments for the doctrine we may suspect that they use discretion in the first weak sense to mean only that judges must sometimes exercise judgment in applying legal standards. Their arguments call attention to the fact that some rules of law are vague (Professor Hart, for example, says that all rules of law have "open texture"), and that some cases arise (like *Henningsen*) in which no established rule seems to be suitable. They emphasize that judges must sometimes agonize over points of law, and that two equally trained and intelligent judges will often disagree.

These points are easily made; they are commonplace to anyone who has any familiarity with law. Indeed, that is the difficulty with assuming that positivists mean to use "discretion" in this weak sense. The proposition that when no clear rule is available discretion in the sense of judgment must be used is a tautology. It has no bearing, moreover, on the problem of how to account for legal principles. It is perfectly consistent to say that the judge in *Riggs*, for example, had to use judgment, and that he was bound to follow the principle that no man may profit from his own wrong. The positivists speak as if their doctrine of judicial discretion is an insight rather than a tautology, and as if it does have a bearing on the treatment of principles. Hart, for example, says that when the judge's discretion is in play, we can no longer speak of his being bound by standards, but must speak rather of what standards he "characteristically uses."[22] Hart thinks that when judges have discretion, the principles they cite must be treated on our second approach, as what courts "make it a principle" to do.

It therefore seems that positivists, at least sometimes, take their doctrine in the third, strong sense of discretion. In that sense it does bear on the treatment of principles; indeed, in that sense it is nothing less than a restatement of our second approach. It is the same thing to say that when a judge runs out of rules he has discretion, in the sense that he is not bound by any standards from the authority of law, as to say that the legal standards judges cite other than rules are not binding on them.

So we must examine the doctrine of judicial discretion in the strong sense. (I shall henceforth use the term "discretion" in that sense.) Do the principles judges cited in cases like *Riggs* or *Henningsen* control their decisions, as the sergeant's orders to take the most experienced men or the referee's duty to choose the more aggressive fighter control the decisions of these officials? What arguments could a positivist supply to show that they do not?

(1) A positivist might argue that principles cannot be binding or obligatory. That would be a mistake. It is always a question, of course, whether any particular principle is *in fact* binding upon some legal official. But there is nothing in the logical char-

acter of a principle that renders it incapable of binding him. Suppose that the judge in *Henningsen* had failed to take any account of the principle that automobile manufacturers have a special obligation to their consumers, or the principle that the courts seek to protect those whose bargaining position is weak, but had simply decided for the defendant by citing the principle of freedom of contract without more. His critics would not have been content to point out that he had not taken account of considerations that other judges have been attending to for some time. Most would have said that it was his duty to take the measure of these principles and that the plaintiff was entitled to have him do so. We mean no more, when we say that a *rule* is binding upon a judge, than that he must follow it if it applies, and that if he does not he will on that account have made a mistake.

It will not do to say that in a case like *Henningsen* the court is only obligated to take particular principles into account, or that it is "institutionally" obligated, or obligated as a matter of judicial "craft," or something of that sort. The question will still remain why this type of obligation (whatever we call it) is different from the obligation that rules impose upon judges, and why it entitles us to say that principles and policies are not part of the law but are merely extra-legal standards "courts characteristically use."

(2) A positivist might argue that even though some principles are binding, in the sense that the judge must take them into account, they cannot determine a particular result. This is a harder argument to assess because it is not clear what it means for a standard to "determine" a result. Perhaps it means that the standard *dictates* the result whenever it applies so that nothing else counts. If so, then it is certainly true that the individual principles do not determine results, but that is only another way of saying that principles are not rules. Only rules dictate results, come what may. When a contrary result has been reached, the rule has been abandoned or changed. Principles do not work that way; they in-

---

22 H.L.A. Hart, *The Concept of Law*, 144 (1961).

cline a decision one way, though not conclusively, and they survive intact when they do not prevail. This seems no reason for concluding that judges who must reckon with principles have discretion because a set of principles *can* dictate a result. If a judge believes that principles he is bound to recognize point in one direction and that principles pointing in the other direction, if any, are not of equal weight, then he must decide accordingly, just as he must follow what he believes to be a binding rule. He may, of course, be wrong in his assessment of the principles, but he may also be wrong in his judgment that the rule is binding. The sergeant and the referee, we might add, are often in the same boat. No one factor dictates which soldiers are the most experienced or which fighter the more aggressive. These officials must make judgments of the relative weights of these various factors; they do not on that account have discretion.

(3) A positivist might argue that principles cannot count as law because their authority, and even more so their weight, are congenitally *controversial*. It is true that generally we cannot *demonstrate* the authority or weight of a particular principle as we can sometimes demonstrate the validity of a rule by locating it in an act of Congress or in the opinion of an authoritative court. Instead, we make a case for a principle, and for its weight, by appealing to an amalgam of practice and other principles in which the implications of legislative and judicial history figure along with appeals to community practices and understandings. There is no litmus paper for testing the soundness of such a case—it is a matter of judgment, and reasonable men may disagree. But again this does not distinguish the judge from other officials who do not have discretion. The sergeant has no litmus paper for experience, the referee none for aggressiveness. Neither of these has discretion, because he is bound to reach an understanding, controversial or not, of what his orders or the rules require, and to act on that understanding. That is the judge's duty as well.

Of course, if the positivists are right in another of their doctrines—the theory that in each legal system there is an ultimate *test* for binding law like Professor Hart's rule of recognition—it follows that principles are not binding law. But the incompatibility of principles with the positivists' theory can hardly be taken as an argument that principles must be treated any particular way. That begs the question; we are interested in the status of principles because we want to evaluate the positivists' model. The positivist cannot defend his theory of a rule of recognition by fiat; if principles are not amenable to a test he must show some other reason why they cannot count as law. Since principles seem to play a role in arguments about legal obligation (witness, again, *Riggs* and *Henningsen*), a model that provides for that role has some initial advantage over one that excludes it, and the latter cannot properly be inveighed in its own support.

These are the most obvious of the arguments a positivist might use for the doctrine of discretion in the strong sense, and for the second approach to principles. I shall mention one strong counterargument against that doctrine and in favor of the first approach. Unless at least some principles are acknowledged to be binding upon judges, requiring them as a set to reach particular decisions, then no rules, or very few rules, can be said to be binding upon them either.

In most American jurisdictions, and now in England also, the higher courts not infrequently reject established rules. Common law rules—those developed by earlier court decisions—are sometimes overruled directly, and sometimes radically altered by further development. Statutory rules are subjected to interpretation and reinterpretation, sometimes even when the result is not to carry out what is called the "legislative intent."[23] If courts had discretion to

---

23 See Wellington and Albert, "Statutory Interpretation and the Political Process: A Comment on Sinclair v. Atkinson," 72 *Yale L. J.* 1547 (1963).

change established rules, then these rules would of course not be binding upon them, and so would not be law on the positivists' model. The positivist must therefore argue that there are standards, themselves binding upon judges, that determine when a judge may overrule or alter an established rule, and when he may not.

When, then, is a judge permitted to change an existing rule of law? Principles figure in the answer in two ways. First, it is necessary, though not sufficient, that the judge find that the change would advance some principle, which principle thus justifies the change. In *Riggs* the change (a new interpretation of the statute of wills) was justified by the principle that no man should profit from his own wrong; in *Henningsen* the previously recognized rules about automobile manufacturers' liability were altered on the basis of the principles I quoted from the opinion of the court.

But not any principle will do to justify a change, or no rule would ever be safe. There must be some principles that count and others that do not, and there must be some principles that count for more than others. It could not depend on the judge's own preferences amongst a sea of respectable extra-legal standards, any one in principle eligible, because if that were the case we could not say that any rules were binding. We could always imagine a judge whose preferences amongst extra-legal standards were such as would justify a shift or radical reinterpretation of even the most entrenched rule.

Second, any judge who proposes to change existing doctrine must take account of some important standards that argue against departures from established doctrine, and these standards are also for the most part principles. They include the doctrine of "legislative supremacy," a set of principles that require the courts to pay a qualified deference to the acts of the legislature. They also include the doctrine of precedent, another set of principles reflecting the equities and efficiencies of consistency. The doctrines of legislative supremacy and precedent incline to-

ward the *status quo*, each within its sphere, but they do not command it. Judges are not free, however, to pick and choose amongst the principles and policies that make up these doctrines—if they were, again, no rule could be said to be binding.

Consider, therefore, what someone implies who says that a particular rule is binding. He may imply that the rule is affirmatively supported by principles the court is not free to disregard, and which are collectively more weighty than other principles that argue for a change. If not, he implies that any change would be condemned by a combination of conservative principles of legislative supremacy and precedent that the court is not free to ignore. Very often, he will imply both, for the conservative principles, being principles and not rules, are usually not powerful enough to save a common law rule or an aging statute that is entirely unsupported by substantive principles the court is bound to respect. Either of these implications, of course, treats a body of principles and policies as law in the sense that rules are; it treats them as standards binding upon the officials of a community, controlling their decisions of legal right and obligation.

We are left with this issue. If the positivists' theory of judicial discretion is either trivial because it uses "discretion" in a weak sense, or unsupported because the various arguments we can supply in its defense fall short, why have so many careful and intelligent lawyers embraced it? We can have no confidence in our treatment of that theory unless we can deal with that question. It is not enough to note (although perhaps it contributes to the explanation) that "discretion" has different senses that may be confused. We do not confuse these senses when we are not thinking about law.

Part of the explanation, at least, lies in a lawyer's natural tendency to associate laws and rules, and to think of "the law" as a collection or system of rules. Roscoe Pound, who diagnosed this tendency long ago, thought that English speaking lawyers were tricked into it by the fact that English uses the same word, changing only the article, for "a law" and "the law."[24] (Other languages, on the contrary, use two words: "loi" and "droit," for example, and "Gesetz" and "Recht.") This may have had its effect, with the English speaking positivists, because the expression "a law" certainly does suggest a rule. But the principal reason for associating law with rules runs deeper, and lies, I think, in the fact that legal education has for a long time consisted of teaching and examining those established rules that form the cutting edge of law.

In any event, if a lawyer thinks of law as a system of rules, and yet recognizes, as he must, that judges change old rules and introduce new ones, he will come naturally to the theory of judicial discretion in the strong sense. In those other systems of rules with which he has experience (like games), the rules are the only special authority that govern official decisions, so that if an umpire could change a rule, he would have discretion as to the subject matter of that rule. Any principles umpires might mention when changing the rules would represent only their "characteristic" preferences. Positivists treat law like baseball revised in this way.

There is another, more subtle consequence of this initial assumption that law is a system of rules. When the positivists do attend to principles and policies, they treat them as rules *manquées*. They assume that *if* they are standards of law they must be rules, and so they read them as standards that are trying to be rules. When a positivist hears someone argue that legal principles are part of the law, he understands this to be an argument for what he calls the "higher law" theory, that these principles are the rules of a law about the law.[25] He refutes this theory by pointing out that these "rules" are sometimes followed and sometimes not, that for every "rule" like "no man shall profit from his own wrong" there

is another competing "rule" like "the law favors security of title," and that there is no way to test the validity of "rules" like these. He concludes that these principles and policies are not valid rules of a law above the law, which is true, because they are not rules at all. He also concludes that they are extralegal standards which each judge selects according to his own lights in the exercise of his discretion, which is false. It is as if a zoologist had proved that fish are not mammals, and then concluded that they are really only plants.

6. The Rule of Recognition

This discussion was provoked by our two competing accounts of legal principles. We have been exploring the second account, which the positivists seem to adopt through their doctrine of judicial discretion, and we have discovered grave difficulties. It is time to return to the fork in the road. What if we adopt the first approach? What would the consequences of this be for the skeletal structure of positivism? Of course we should have to drop the second tenet, the doctrine of judicial discretion (or, in the alternative, to make plain that the doctrine is to be read merely to say that judges must often exercise judgment). Would we also have to abandon or modify the first tenet, the proposition that law is distinguished by tests of the sort that can be set out in a master rule like Professor Hart's rule of recognition? If principles of the *Riggs* and *Henningsen* sort are to count as law, and we are nevertheless to preserve the notion of a master rule for law, then we must be able to deploy some test that all (and only) the principles that do count as law meet. Let us begin with the test Hart suggests for identifying valid *rules* of law, to see whether these can be made to work for principles as well.

Most rules of law, according to Hart, are valid because some competent institution enacted them. Some were created by a legislature, in the form of statutory enactments. Others were created by judges

---

24 R. Pound, *An Introduction to the Philosophy of Law* 56 (rev. ed. 1954).

25 See, e.g., Dickinson, "The Law Behind Law (pts. 1 & 2)," 29, *Columbia Law Review* 112, 254 (1929).

who formulated them to decide particular cases, and thus established them as precedents for the future. But this test of pedigree will not work for the *Riggs* and *Henningsen* principles. The origin of these as legal principles lies not in a particular decision of some legislature or court, but in a sense of appropriateness developed in the profession and the public over time. Their continued power depends upon this sense of appropriateness being sustained. If it no longer seemed unfair to allow people to profit by their wrongs, or fair to place special burdens upon oligopolies that manufacture potentially dangerous machines, these principles would no longer play much of a role in new cases, even if they had never been overruled or repealed. (Indeed, it hardly makes sense to speak of principles like these as being "overruled" or "repealed." When they decline they are eroded, not torpedoed.)

True, if we were challenged to back up our claim that some principle is a principle of law, we would mention any prior cases in which that principle was cited, or figured in the argument. We would also mention any statute that seemed to exemplify that principle (even better if the principle was cited in the preamble of the statute, or in the committee reports or other legislative documents that accompanied it). Unless we could find some such institutional support, we would probably fail to make out our case, and the more support we found, the more weight we could claim for the principle.

Yet we could not devise any formula for testing how much and what kind of institutional support is necessary to make a principle a legal principle, still less to fix its weight at a particular order of magnitude. We argue for a particular principle by grappling with a whole set of shifting, developing and interacting standards (themselves principles rather than rules) about institutional responsibility, statutory interpretation, the persuasive force of various sorts of precedent, the relation of all these to contemporary moral practices, and hosts of other such standards. We could not bolt all of these together

into a single "rule," even a complex one, and if we could the result would bear little relation to Hart's picture of a rule of recognition, which is the picture of a fairly stable master rule specifying "some feature or features possession of which by a suggested rule is taken as a conclusive affirmative indication that it is a rule ..."[26]

Moreover, the techniques we apply in arguing for another principle do not stand (as Hart's rule of recognition is designed to) on an entirely different level from the principles they support. Hart's sharp distinction between acceptance and validity does not hold. If we are arguing for the principle that a man should not profit from his own wrong, we could cite the acts of courts and legislatures that exemplify it, but this speaks as much to the principle's acceptance as its validity. (It seems odd to speak of a principle as being valid at all, perhaps because validity is an all-or-nothing concept, appropriate for rules, but inconsistent with a principle's dimension of weight.) If we are asked (as we might well be) to defend the particular doctrine of precedent, or the particular technique of statutory interpretation, that we used in this argument, we should certainly cite the practice of others in using that doctrine or technique. But we should also cite other general principles that we believe support that practice, and this introduces a note of validity into the chord of acceptance. We might argue, for example, that the use we make of earlier cases and statutes is supported by a particular analysis of the point of the practice of legislation or the doctrine of precedent, or by the principles of democratic theory, or by a particular position on the proper division of authority between national and local institutions, or something else of that sort. Nor is this path of support a one-way street leading to some ultimate principle resting on acceptance alone. Our principles of legislation, precedent, democracy, or federalism might be challenged too; and if they were we should argue for them, not only in terms of

---

26 H.L.A. Hart, *The Concept of Law* 92 (1961).

practice, but in terms of each other and in terms of the implications of trends of judicial and legislative decisions, even though this last would involve appealing to those same doctrines of interpretation we justified through the principles we are now trying to support. At this level of abstraction, in other words, principles rather hang together than link together.

So even though principles draw support from the official acts of legal institutions, they do not have a simple or direct enough connection with these acts to frame that connection in terms of criteria specified by some ultimate master rule of recognition. Is there any other route by which principles might be brought under such a rule?

Hart does say that a master rule might designate as law not only rules enacted by particular legal institutions, but rules established by *custom* as well. He has in mind a problem that bothered other positivists, including Austin. Many of our most ancient legal rules were never explicitly created by a legislature or a court. When they made their first appearance in legal opinions and texts, they were treated as already being part of the law because they represented the customary practice of the community, or some specialized part of it, like the business community. (The examples ordinarily given are rules of mercantile practice, like the rules governing what rights arise under a standard form of commercial paper.)[27] Since Austin thought that all law was the command of a determinate sovereign, he held that these customary practices were not law until the courts (as agents of the sovereign) recognized them, and that the courts were indulging in a fiction in pretending otherwise. But that seemed arbitrary. If everyone thought

custom might in itself be law, the fact that Austin's theory said otherwise was not persuasive.

Hart reversed Austin on this point. The master rule, he says, might stipulate that some custom counts as law even before the courts recognize it. But he does not face the difficulty this raises for his general theory because he does not attempt to set out the criteria a master rule might use for this purpose. It cannot use, as its only criterion, the provision that the community regard the practice as *morally* binding, for this would not distinguish legal customary rules from moral customary rules, and of course not all of the community's long-standing customary moral obligations are enforced at law. If, on the other hand, the test is whether the community regards the customary practice as *legally* binding, the whole point of the master rule is undercut, at least for this class of legal rules. The master rule, says Hart, marks the transformation from a primitive society to one with law, because it provides a test for determining social rules of law other than by measuring their acceptance. But if the master rule says merely that whatever other rules the community accepts as legally binding are legally binding, then it provides no such test at all, beyond the test we should use were there no master rule. The master rule becomes (for these cases) a non-rule of recognition; we might as well say that every primitive society has a secondary rule of recognition, namely the rule that whatever is accepted as binding is binding. Hart himself, in discussing international law, ridicules the idea that such a rule could be a rule of recognition, by describing the proposed rule as "an empty repetition of the mere fact that the society concerned ... observes certain standards of conduct as obligatory rules."[28]

---

27 See Note, "Custom and Trade Usage: Its Application to Commercial Dealings and the Common Law," 55 *Columbia Law Review* 1192 (1955), and materials cited therein at 1193 n.l. As that note makes plain, the actual practices of courts in recognizing trade customs follow the pattern of applying a set of general principles and policies rather than a test that could be captured as part of a rule of recognition.

28 H.L.A. Hart, *The Concept of Law* 230 (1961). A master rule might specify some particular feature of a custom that is independent of the community's attitude; it might provide, for example, that all customs of very great age, or all customs having to do with negotiable instruments count as law. I can think of no such features that in fact distinguish the customs that have been recognized as law

Hart's treatment of custom amounts, indeed, to a confession that there are at least some rules of law that are not binding because they are valid under standards laid down by a master rule but are binding—like the master rule—because they are accepted as binding by the community. This chips at the neat pyramidal architecture we admired in Hart's theory: we can no longer say that only the master rule is binding because of its acceptance, all other rules being valid under its terms.

This is perhaps only a chip, because the customary rules Hart has in mind are no longer a very significant part of the law. But it does suggest that Hart would be reluctant to widen the damage by bringing under the head of "custom" all those crucial principles and policies we have been discussing. If he were to call these part of the law and yet admit that the only test of their force lies in the degree to which they are accepted as law by the community or some part thereof, he would very sharply reduce that area of the law over which his master rule held any dominion. It is not just that all the principles and policies would escape its sway, though that would be bad enough. Once these principles and policies are accepted as law, and thus as standards judges must follow in determining legal obligations, it would follow that *rules* like those announced for the first time in *Riggs* and *Henningsen* owe their force at least in part to the authority of principles and policies, and so not entirely to the master rule of recognition.

So we cannot adapt Hart's version of positivism by modifying his rule of recognition to embrace

principles. No tests of pedigree, relating principles to acts of legislation, can be formulated, nor can his concept of customary law, itself an exception to the first tenet of positivism, be made to serve without abandoning that tenet altogether. One more possibility must be considered, however. If no rule of recognition can provide a test for identifying principles, why not say that principles are ultimate, and *form* the rule of recognition of our law? The answer to the general question "What is valid law in an American jurisdiction?" would then require us to state all the principles (as well as ultimate constitutional rules) in force in that jurisdiction at the time, together with appropriate assignments of weight. A positivist might then regard the complete set of these standards as the rule of recognition of the jurisdiction. This solution has the attraction of paradox, but of course it is an unconditional surrender. If we simply designate our rule of recognition by the phrase "the complete set of principles in force," we achieve only the tautology that law is law. If, instead, we tried actually to list all the principles in force we would fail. They are controversial, their weight is all important, they are numberless, and they shift and change so fast that the start of our list would be obsolete before we reached the middle. Even if we succeeded, we would not have a key for law because there would be nothing left for our key to unlock.

I conclude that if we treat principles as law we must reject the positivists' first tenet, that the law of a community is distinguished from other social standards by some test in the form of a master rule. We have already decided that we must then abandon the second tenet—the doctrine of judicial discretion—or clarify it into triviality. What of the third tenet, the positivists' theory of legal obligation?

This theory holds that a legal obligation exists when (and only when) an established rule of law imposes such an obligation. It follows from this that in a hard case—when no such established rule can be found—there is no legal obligation until the judge creates a new rule for the future. The judge may

in England or America, however. Some customs that are not legally enforceable are older than some that are, some practices relating to commercial paper are enforced and others not, and so forth. In any event, even if a distinguishing feature were found that identified all rules of law established by custom, it would remain unlikely that such a feature could be found for principles which vary widely in their subject matter and pedigree and some of which are of very recent origin.

apply that new rule to the parties in the case, but this is *ex post facto* legislation, not the enforcement of an existing obligation.

The positivists' doctrine of discretion (in the strong sense) required this view of legal obligation, because if a judge has discretion there can be no legal right or obligation—no entitlement—that he must enforce. Once we abandon that doctrine, however, and treat principles as law, we raise the possibility that a legal obligation might be imposed by a constellation of principles as well as by an established rule. We might want to say that a legal obligation exists whenever the case supporting such an obligation, in terms of binding legal principles of different sorts, is stronger than the case against it.

Of course, many questions would have to be answered before we could accept that view of legal obligation. If there is no rule of recognition, no test for law in that sense, how do we decide which principles are to count, and how much, in making such a case? How do we decide whether one case is better than another? If legal obligation rests on an undemonstrable judgment of that sort, how can it provide a justification for a judicial decision that one party had a legal obligation? Does this view of obligation square with the way lawyers, judges and laymen speak, and is it consistent with our attitudes about moral obligation? Does this analysis help us to deal with the classical jurisprudential puzzles about the nature of law?

These questions must be faced, but even the questions promise more than positivism provides. Positivism, on its own thesis, stops short of just those puzzling, hard cases that send us to look for theories of law. When we read these cases, the positivist remits us to a doctrine of discretion that leads nowhere and tells nothing. His picture of law as a system of rules has exercised a tenacious hold on our imagination, perhaps through its very simplicity. If we shake ourselves loose from this model of rules, we may be able to build a model truer to the complexity and sophistication of our own practices.

♦ ♦ ♦ ♦ ♦

RONALD DWORKIN

"Integrity in Law," *Law's Empire*

A Large View

In this chapter we construct the third conception of law I introduced in Chapter 3. Law as integrity denies that statements of law are either the backward-looking factual reports of conventionalism or the forward-looking instrumental programs of legal pragmatism. It insists that legal claims are interpretive judgments and therefore combine backward- and forward-looking elements; they interpret contemporary legal practice seen as an unfolding political narrative. So law as integrity rejects as unhelpful the ancient question whether judges find or invent law; we understand legal reasoning, it suggests, only by seeing the sense in which they do both and neither.

Integrity and Interpretation

The adjudicative principle of integrity instructs judges to identify legal rights and duties, so far as possible, on the assumption that they were all created by a single author—the community personified—expressing a coherent conception of justice and fairness. We form our third conception of law, our third view of what rights and duties flow from past political decisions, by restating this instruction as a thesis about the grounds of law. According to law as integrity, propositions of law are true if they figure in or follow from the principles of justice, fairness, and procedural due process that provide the best constructive interpretation of the community's legal practice. Deciding whether the law grants Mrs.

McLoughlin* compensation for her injury, for example, means deciding whether legal practice is seen in a better light if we assume the community has accepted the principle that people in her position are entitled to compensation.

Law as integrity is therefore more relentlessly interpretive than either conventionalism or pragmatism. These latter theories offer themselves *as* interpretations. They are conceptions of law that claim to show our legal practices in the best light these can bear, and they recommend, in their postinterpretive conclusions, distinct styles or programs for adjudication. But the programs they recommend are not themselves programs *of* interpretation: they do not ask judges deciding hard cases to carry out

---

*   *Ed. note:* Here Dworkin refers to an English case he discusses in Chapter 1 of *Law's Empire*, *McLoughlin v. O'Brian* [1983] 1 A.C. 410, reversing [1981] Q.B. 599. Dworkin's sketch of the case (at p. 24) is as follows:

Mrs. McLoughlin's husband and four children were injured in an automobile accident in England at about 4 p.m. on October 19, 1973. She heard about the accident at home from a neighbor at about 6 p.m. and went immediately to the hospital, where she learned that her daughter was dead and saw the serious condition of her husband and other children. She suffered nervous shock and later sued the defendant driver, whose negligence had caused the accident, as well as other parties who were in different ways involved, for compensation for her emotional injuries. Her lawyer pointed to several earlier decisions of English courts awarding compensation to people who had suffered emotional injury on seeing serious injury to a close relative. But in all these cases the plaintiff had either been at the scene of the accident or had arrived within minutes. In a 1972 case, for example, a wife recovered—won compensation—for emotional injury; she had come upon the body of her husband immediately after his fatal accident [*Marshall v. Lionel Enterprises Inc.* [1972] O.R. 177]. In 1967 a man who was not related to any of the victims of a train crash worked for hours trying to rescue victims and suffered nervous shock from the experience. He was allowed to recover [*Chadwick v. British Transport* [1967] 1 W.L.R. 912]. Mrs. McLoughlin's lawyer relied on these cases as precedents, decisions which had made it part of the law that people in her position are entitled to compensation.

any further, essentially interpretive study of legal doctrine. Conventionalism requires judges to study law reports and parliamentary records to discover what decisions have been made by institutions conventionally recognized to have legislative power. No doubt interpretive issues will arise in that process: for example, it may be necessary to interpret a text to decide what statutes our legal conventions construct from it. But once a judge has accepted conventionalism as his guide, he has no further occasion for interpreting the legal record as a whole in deciding particular cases. Pragmatism requires judges to think instrumentally about the best rules for the future. That exercise may require interpretation of something beyond legal material: a utilitarian pragmatist may need to worry about the best way to understand the idea of community welfare, for example. But once again, a judge who accepts pragmatism is then done with interpreting legal practice as a whole.

Law as integrity is different: it is both the product of and the inspiration for comprehensive interpretation of legal practice. The program it holds out to judges deciding hard cases is essentially, not just contingently, interpretive; law as integrity asks them to continue interpreting the same material that it claims to have successfully interpreted itself. It offers itself as continuous with—the initial part of—the more detailed interpretations it recommends. We must therefore now return to the general study of interpretation we began in Chapter 2. We must continue the account given there of what interpretation is and when it is done well, but in more detail and directed more to the special interpretive challenge put to judges and others who must say what the law is.

Integrity and History

History matters in law as integrity: very much but only in a certain way. Integrity does not require consistency in principle over all historical stages of a community's law; it does not require that judges try to understand the law they enforce as continuous in principle with the abandoned law of a previous century or even a previous generation. It commands a horizontal rather than vertical consistency of principle across the range of the legal standards the community now enforces. It insists that the law—the rights and duties that flow from past collective decisions and for that reason license or require coercion—contains not only the narrow explicit content of these decisions but also, more broadly, the scheme of principles necessary to justify them. History matters because that scheme of principle must justify the standing as well as the content of these past decisions. Our justification for treating the Endangered Species Act as law, unless and until it is repealed, crucially includes the fact that Congress enacted it, and any justification we supply for treating that fact as crucial must itself accommodate the way we treat other events in our political past.

Law as integrity, then, begins in the present and pursues the past only so far as and in the way its contemporary focus dictates. It does not aim to recapture, even for present law, the ideals or practical purposes of the politicians who first created it. It aims rather to justify what they did (sometimes including, as we shall see, what they said) in an overall story worth telling now, a story with a complex claim: that present practice can be organized by and justified in principles sufficiently attractive to provide an honorable future. Law as integrity deplores the mechanism of the older "law is law" view as well as the cynicism of the newer "realism." It sees both views as rooted in the same false dichotomy of finding and inventing law. When a judge declares that a particular principle is instinct in law, he reports not a simple-minded claim about the motives of past statesmen, a claim a wise cynic can easily refute, but an interpretive proposal: that the principle both fits and justifies some complex part of legal practice, that it provides an attractive way to see, in the structure of that practice, the consistency of principle integrity requires. Law's optimism is in that way conceptual; claims of law are endemically constructive, just in virtue of the kind of claims they are. This optimism may be misplaced: legal practice may in the end yield to nothing but a deeply skeptical interpretation. But that is not inevitable just because a community's history is one of great change and conflict. An imaginative interpretation can be constructed on morally complicated, even ambiguous terrain.

The Chain of Law
The Chain Novel

I argued in Chapter 2 that creative interpretation takes its formal structure from the idea of intention, not (at least not necessarily) because it aims to discover the purposes of any particular historical person or group but because it aims to impose purpose over the text or data or tradition being interpreted. Since all creative interpretation shares this feature, and therefore has a normative aspect or component, we profit from comparing law with other forms or occasions of interpretation. We can usefully compare the judge deciding what the law is on some issue not only with the citizens of courtesy deciding what that tradition requires, but with the literary critic teasing out the various dimensions of value in a complex play or poem.

Judges, however, are authors as well as critics. A judge deciding *McLoughlin* or *Brown** adds to the

---

* *Ed. note:* Here Dworkin refers to a famous American case he discusses in Chapter I of *Law's Empire, Brown v. Board of Education* 347 U.S. 483 (1954). Dworkin's sketch of the case (at pp. 29–30) is as follows:

After the American Civil War the victorious North amended the Constitution to end slavery and many of its incidents and consequences. One of these amendments, the Fourteenth, declared that no state might deny any person the "equal protection of the laws." After Reconstruction the southern states, once more in control of their own politics, segregated many public facilities by race. Blacks had to ride in the back of the bus and were allowed to attend only segregated schools with other blacks. In the famous case of *Plessy v. Ferguson* [163 U.S. 537 (1896)]. the defendant argued, ultimately before

tradition he interprets; future judges confront a new

the Supreme Court, that these practices of segregation automatically violated the equal protection clause. The Court rejected their claim; it said that the demands of that clause were satisfied if the states provide separate but equal facilities and that the fact of segregation alone did not make facilities automatically unequal.

In 1954 a group of black schoolchildren in Topeka, Kansas, raised the question again. A great deal had happened to the United States in the meantime—a great many blacks had died for that country in a recent war, for example—and segregation seemed more deeply wrong to more people than it had when *Plessy* was decided. Nevertheless, the states that practiced segregation resisted integration fiercely, particularly in the schools. Their lawyers argued that since *Plessy* was a decision by the Supreme Court, that precedent had to be respected. This time the Supreme Court decided for the black plaintiffs. Its decision was unexpectedly unanimous, though the unanimity was purchased by an opinion, written by Chief Justice Earl Warren, that was in many ways a compromise. He did not reject the "separate but equal" formula outright; instead he relied on controversial sociological evidence to show that racially segregated schools could not be equal, for that reason alone. Nor did he say flatly that *if* the present decision was inconsistent with *Plessy*, then that earlier decision was being overruled. The most important compromise, for practical purposes, was in the design of the remedy the opinion awarded the plaintiffs. It did not order the schools of the southern states to be desegregated immediately, but only, in a phrase that became an emblem of hypocrisy and delay, "with all deliberate speed."

The decision was very controversial, the process of integration that followed was slow, and significant progress required many more legal, political, and even physical battles. Critics said that segregation, however deplorable as a matter of political morality, is not unconstitutional. They pointed out that the phrase "equal protection" does not in itself decide whether segregation is forbidden or not, that the particular congressmen and state officials who drafted, enacted, and ratified the Fourteenth Amendment were well aware of segregated education and apparently thought their amendment left it perfectly legal, and that the Court's decision in *Plessy* was an important precedent of almost ancient lineage and ought not lightly be overturned. These were arguments about the proper grounds of constitutional law, not arguments of morality or repair: many who made them agreed that segregation

tradition that includes what he has done. Of course literary criticism contributes to the traditions of art in which authors work; the character and importance of that contribution are themselves issues in critical theory. But the contribution of judges is more direct, and the distinction between author and interpreter more a matter of different aspects of the same process. We can find an even more fruitful comparison between literature and law, therefore, by constructing an artificial genre of literature that we might call the chain novel.

In this enterprise a group of novelists writes a novel *seriatim*; each novelist in the chain interprets the chapters he has been given in order to write a new chapter, which is then added to what the next novelist receives, and so on. Each has the job of writing his chapter so as to make the novel being constructed the best it can be, and the complexity of this task models the complexity of deciding a hard case under law as integrity. The imaginary literary enterprise is fantastic but not unrecognizable. Some novels have actually been written in this way, though mainly for a debunking purpose, and certain parlor games for rainy weekends in English country houses have something of the same structure. Television soap operas span decades with the same characters and some minimal continuity of personality and plot, though they are written by different teams of authors even in different weeks. In our example, however, the novelists are expected to take their responsibilities of continuity more seriously; they aim

---

was immoral and that the Constitution would be a better document if it had forbidden it. Nor were the arguments of those who agreed with the Court arguments of morality or repair. If the Constitution did not as a matter of law prohibit official racial segregation, then the decision in *Brown* was an illicit constitutional amendment, and few who supported the decision thought they were supporting that. This case, like our other sample cases, was fought over the question of law. Or so it seems from the opinion, and so it seemed to those who fought it.

jointly to create, so far as they can, a single unified novel that is the best it can be.[1]

Each novelist aims to make a single novel of the material he has been given, what he adds to it, and (so far as he can control this) what his successors will want or be able to add. He must try to make this the best novel it can be construed as the work of a single author rather than, as is the fact, the product of many different hands. That calls for an overall judgment on his part, or a series of overall judgments as he writes and rewrites. He must take up some view about the novel in progress, some working theory about its characters, plot, genre, theme, and point, in order to decide what counts as continuing it and not as beginning anew. If he is a good critic, his view of these matters will be complicated and multifaceted, because the value of a decent novel cannot be captured from a single perspective. He will aim to find layers and currents of meaning rather than a single, exhaustive theme. We can, however, in our now familiar way give some structure to any interpretation he adopts, by distinguishing two dimensions on which it must be tested. The first is what we have been calling the dimension of fit. He cannot adopt any interpretation, however complex, if he believes that no single author who set out to write a novel with the various readings of character, plot, theme, and point that interpretation describes could have written substantially the text he has been given. That does not mean his interpretation must fit every bit of the text. It is not disqualified simply because

he claims that some lines or tropes are accidental, or even that some events of plot are mistakes because they work against the literary ambitions the interpretation states. But the interpretation he takes up must nevertheless flow throughout the text; it must have general explanatory power, and it is flawed if it leaves unexplained some major structural aspect of the text, a subplot treated as having great dramatic importance or a dominant and repeated metaphor. If no interpretation can be found that is not flawed in that way, then the chain novelist will not be able fully to meet his assignment; he will have to settle for an interpretation that captures most of the text, conceding that it is not wholly successful. Perhaps even that partial success is unavailable; perhaps every interpretation he considers is inconsistent with the bulk of the material supplied to him. In that case he must abandon the enterprise, for the consequence of taking the interpretive attitude toward the text in question is then a piece of internal skepticism; that nothing can count as continuing the novel rather than beginning anew.

He may find, not that no single interpretation fits the bulk of the text, but that more than one does. The second dimension of interpretation then requires him to judge which of these eligible readings makes the work in progress best, all things considered. At this point his more substantive aesthetic judgments, about the importance or insight or realism or beauty of different ideas the novel might be taken to express, come into play. But the formal and structural considerations that dominate on the first dimension figure on the second as well, for even when neither of two interpretations is disqualified out of hand as explaining too little, one may show the text in a better light because it fits more of the text or provides a more interesting integration of style and content. So the distinction between the two dimensions is less crucial or profound than it might seem. It is a useful analytical device that helps us give structure to any interpreter's working theory or style. He will form a sense of when an interpretation fits so poorly

1 Perhaps this is an impossible assignment; perhaps the project is doomed to produce not just an impossibly bad novel but no novel at all, because the best theory of art requires a single creator or, if more than one, that each must have some control over the whole. (But what about legends and jokes? What about the Old Testament, or, on some theories, the *Iliad*?) I need not push that question further, because I am interested only in the fact that the assignment makes sense, that each of the novelists in the chain can have some grasp of what he is asked to do, whatever misgivings he might have about the value or character of what will then be produced.

that it is unnecessary to consider its substantive appeal, because he knows that this cannot outweigh its embarrassments of fit in deciding whether it makes the novel better, everything taken into account, than its rivals. This sense will define the first dimension for him. But he need not reduce his intuitive sense to any precise formula; he would rarely need to decide whether some interpretation barely survives or barely fails, because a bare survivor, no matter how ambitious or interesting it claimed the text to be, would almost certainly fail in the overall comparison with other interpretations whose fit was evident.

We can now appreciate the range of different kinds of judgments that are blended in this overall comparison. Judgments about textual coherence and integrity, reflecting different formal literary values, are interwoven with more substantive aesthetic judgments that themselves assume different literary aims. Yet these various kinds of judgments, of each general kind, remain distinct enough to check one another in an overall assessment, and it is that possibility of contest, particularly between textual and substantive judgments, that distinguishes a chain novelist's assignment from more independent creative writing. Nor can we draw any flat distinction between the stage at which a chain novelist interprets the text he has been given and the stage at which he adds his own chapter, guided by the interpretation he has settled on. When he begins to write he might discover in what he has written a different, perhaps radically different, interpretation. Or he might find it impossible to write in the tone or theme he first took up, and that will lead him to reconsider other interpretations he first rejected. In either case he returns to the text to reconsider the lines it makes eligible.

Scrooge

We can expand this abstract description of the chain novelist's judgment through an example. Suppose you are a novelist well down the chain. Suppose Dickens never wrote *A Christmas Carol*, and the text

you are furnished, though written by several people, happens to be the first part of that short novel. You consider these two interpretations of the central character: Scrooge is inherently and irredeemably evil, an embodiment of the untarnished wickedness of human nature freed from the disguises of convention he rejects; or Scrooge is inherently good but progressively corrupted by the false values and perverse demands of high capitalist society. Obviously it will make an enormous difference to the way you continue the story which of these interpretations you adopt. If you have been given almost all of *A Christmas Carol* with only the very end to be written—Scrooge has already had his dreams, repented, and sent his turkey—it is too late for you to make him irredeemably wicked, assuming you think, as most interpreters would, that the text will not bear that interpretation without too much strain. I do not mean that no interpreter could possibly think Scrooge inherently evil after his supposed redemption. Someone might take that putative redemption to be a final act of hypocrisy, though only at the cost of taking much else in the text not at face value. This would be a poor interpretation, not because no one could think it a good one, but because it is in fact, on all the criteria so far described, a poor one.[2]

But now suppose you have been given only the first few sections of *A Christmas Carol*. You find that neither of the two interpretations you are considering is decisively ruled out by anything in the text so far; perhaps one would better explain some minor incidents of plot that must be left unconnected on the other, but each interpretation can be seen generally to flow through the abbreviated text as a whole. A competent novelist who set out to write a novel along either of the lines suggested could well have written what you find on the pages. In that case you have a further decision to make. Your assignment is to make of the text the best it can be, and you will therefore choose the interpretation you believe

---

2   See the debate cited in Chapter 2, n. 16.

makes the work more significant or otherwise better. That decision will probably (though not inevitably) depend on whether you think that real people somewhat like Scrooge are born bad or are corrupted by capitalism. But it will depend on much else as well, because your aesthetic convictions are not so simple as to make only this aspect of a novel relevant to its overall success. Suppose you think that one interpretation integrates not only plot but image and setting as well; the social interpretation accounts, for example, for the sharp contrast between the individualistic fittings and partitions of Scrooge's countinghouse and the communitarian formlessness of Bob Cratchit's household. Now your aesthetic judgment—about which reading makes the continuing novel better as a novel—is itself more complex because it must identify and trade off different dimensions of value in a novel. Suppose you believe that the original sin reading is much the more accurate depiction of human nature, but that the sociorealist reading provides a deeper and more interesting formal structure for the novel. You must then ask yourself which interpretation makes the work of art better on the whole. You may never have reflected on that sort of question before—perhaps the tradition of criticism in which you have been trained takes it for granted that one or the other of these dimensions is the more important—but that is no reason why you may not do so now. Once you make up your mind you will believe that the correct interpretation of Scrooge's character is the interpretation that makes the novel better on the whole, so judged.

This contrived example is complex enough to provoke the following apparently important question. Is your judgment about the best way to interpret and continue the sections you have been given of *A Christmas Carol* a free or a constrained judgment? Are you free to give effect to your own assumptions and attitudes about what novels should be like? Or are you bound to ignore these because you are enslaved by a text you cannot alter? The answer is plain enough: neither of these two crude de-

scriptions—of total creative freedom or mechanical textual constraint—captures your situation, because each must in some way be qualified by the other. You will sense creative freedom when you compare your task with some relatively more mechanical one, like direct translation of a text into a foreign language. But you will sense constraint when you compare it with some relatively less guided one, like beginning a new novel of your own.

It is important not only to notice this contrast between elements of artistic freedom and textual constraint but also not to misunderstand its character. It is *not* a contrast between those aspects of interpretation that are dependent on and those that are independent of the interpreter's aesthetic convictions. And it is not a contrast between those aspects that may be and those that cannot be controversial. For the constraints that you sense as limits to your freedom to read *A Christmas Carol* so as to make Scrooge irredeemably evil are as much matters of judgment and conviction, about which different chain novelists might disagree, as the convictions and attitudes you call on in deciding whether the novel would have been better if he had been irredeemably evil. If the latter convictions are "subjective" (I use the language of external skepticism, reluctantly, because some readers will find it helpful here) then so are the former. Both major types of convictions any interpreter has—about which readings fit the text better or worse and about which of two readings makes the novel substantively better—are internal to his overall scheme of beliefs and attitudes; neither type is independent of that scheme in some way that the other is not.

That observation invites the following objection. "If an interpreter must in the end rely on what seems right to him, as much in deciding whether some interpretation fits as in deciding whether it makes the novel more attractive, then he is actually subject to no genuine constraint at all, because no one's judgment can be constrained except by external, hard facts that everyone must agree about." The objection is misconceived because it rests on a piece of dogmatism. It is a familiar part of our cognitive experience that some of our beliefs and convictions operate as checks in deciding how far we can or should accept or give effect to others, and the check is effective even when the constraining beliefs and attitudes are controversial. If one scientist accepts stricter standards for research procedure than another, he will believe less of what he would like to believe. If one politician has scruples that another politician in good faith rejects, the first will be constrained when the second is not. There is no harm, once again, in using the language of subjectivity the external skeptic favors. We might say that in these examples the constraint is "internal" or "subjective." It is nevertheless phenomenologically genuine, and that is what is important here. We are trying to see what interpretation is like from the point of view of the interpreter, and from that point of view the constraint he feels is as genuine as if it were uncontroversial, as if everyone else felt it as powerfully as he does. Suppose someone then insists that from an "objective" point of view there is no real constraint at all, that the constraint is *merely* subjective. If we treat this further charge as the external skeptic's regular complaint, then it is pointless and misleading in the way we noticed in Chapter 2. It gives a chain novelist no reason to doubt or abandon the conclusions he reaches, about which interpretations fit the text well enough to count, for example, or so poorly that they must be rejected if other interpretations, otherwise less attractive, are available.

The skeptical objection can be made more interesting, however, if we weaken it in the following way. It now insists that a felt constraint may sometimes be illusory not for the external skeptic's dogmatic reason, that a genuine constraint must be uncontroversial and independent of other beliefs and attitudes, but because it may not be sufficiently disjoint, within the system of the interpreter's more substantive artistic convictions, ever actually to check or impede these, even from his point of

view.[3] That is a lively possibility, and we must be on guard against it when we criticize our own or other people's interpretive arguments. I made certain assumptions about the structure of your aesthetic opinions when I imagined your likely overall judgment about *A Christmas Carol*. I assumed that the different types of discrete judgments you combine in your overall opinion are sufficiently independent of one another, within the system of your ideas, to allow some to constrain others. You reject reading Scrooge's supposed redemption as hypocritical for "formal" reasons about coherence and integration of plot and diction and figure. A decent novel (you think) would not make a hypocritical redemption the upshot of so dramatic and shattering an event as Scrooge's horrifying night. These formal convictions are independent of your more substantive opinions about the competing value of different literary aims: even if you think a novel of original sin would be more exciting, that does not transform your formal conviction into one more amenable to the original sin interpretation. But suppose I am wrong in these assumptions about your mental life. Suppose we discover in the process of argument that your formal convictions are actually soldered to and driven by more substantive ones. Whenever you prefer a reading of some text on substantive grounds, your formal convictions automatically adjust to endorse it as a decent reading of that text. You might, of course, only be pretending that this is so, in which case you are acting in bad faith. But the adjustment may be unconscious, in which case you think you are constrained but, in the sense that matters, you actually are not. Whether any interpreter's convictions actually check one another, as they must if he is genuinely interpreting at all, depends on the complexity and structure of his pertinent opinions as a whole.

Our chain-novel example has so far been distorted by the unrealistic assumption that the text you were

---

3 See *A Matter of Principle*, chap. 7.

furnished miraculously had the unity of something written by a single author. Even if each of the previous novelists in the chain took his responsibilities very seriously indeed, the text you were given would show the marks of its history, and you would have to tailor your style of interpretation to that circumstance. You might not find any interpretation that flows through the text, that fits everything the material you have been given treats as important. You must lower your sights (as conscientious writers who join the team of an interminable soap opera might do) by trying to construct an interpretation that fits the bulk of what you take to be artistically most fundamental in the text. More than one interpretation may survive this more relaxed test. To choose among these, you must turn to your background aesthetic convictions, including those you will regard as formal. Possibly no interpretation will survive even the relaxed test. That is the skeptical possibility I mentioned earlier: you will then end by abandoning the project, rejecting your assignment as impossible. But you cannot know in advance that you will reach that skeptical result. You must try first. The chain-novel fantasy will be useful in the later argument in various ways, but that is the most important lesson it teaches. The wise-sounding judgment that no one interpretation could be best must be earned and defended like any other interpretive claim.

A Misleading Objection

A chain novelist, then, has many difficult decisions to make, and different chain novelists can be expected to make these differently. But his decisions do not include, nor are they properly summarized as, the decision whether and how far he should depart from the novel-in-progress he has been furnished. For he has nothing he *can* depart from or cleave to until he has constructed a novel-in-process from the text, and the various decisions we have canvassed are all decisions he must make just to do this. Suppose you have decided that a sociorealist interpretation of the opening sections of *A Christmas Carol* makes that text, on balance, the best novel-so-far it can be, and so you continue the novel as an exploration of the uniformly degrading master-servant relation under capitalism rather than as a study of original sin. Now suppose someone accuses you of rewriting the "real" novel to produce a different one that you like better. If he means that the "real" novel can be discovered in some way other than by a process of interpretation of the sort you conducted, then he has misunderstood not only the chain-novel enterprise but the nature of literature and criticism. Of course, he may mean only that he disagrees with the particular interpretive and aesthetic convictions on which you relied. In that case your disagreement is not that he thinks you should respect the text, while you think you are free to ignore it. Your disagreement is more interesting: you disagree about what respecting this text means.

Law: The Question of Emotional Damages

Law as integrity asks a judge deciding a common-law case like *McLoughlin* to think of himself as an author in the chain of common law. He knows that other judges have decided cases that, although not exactly like his case, deal with related problems; he must think of their decisions as part of a long story he must interpret and then continue, according to his own judgment of how to make the developing story as good as it can be. (Of course the best story for him means best from the standpoint of political morality, not aesthetics.) We can make a rough distinction once again between two main dimensions of this interpretive judgment. The judge's decision—his postinterpretive conclusions—must be drawn from an interpretation that both fits and justifies what has gone before, so far as that is possible. But in law as in literature the interplay between fit and justification is complex. Just as interpretation within a chain novel is for each interpreter a delicate balance among different types of literary and artistic attitudes, so in law it is a delicate balance among political convictions of different sorts; in law as in literature these must be sufficiently related yet disjoint to allow an overall judgment that trades off an interpretation's success on one type of standard against its failure on another. I must try to exhibit that complex structure of legal interpretation, and I shall use for that purpose an imaginary judge of superhuman intellectual power and patience who accepts law as integrity.

Call him Hercules.[4] In this and the next several chapters we follow his career by noticing the types of judgments he must make and tensions he must resolve in deciding a variety of cases. But I offer this caution in advance. We must not suppose that his answers to the various questions he encounters *define* law as integrity as a general conception of law. They are the answers I now think best. But law as integrity consists in an approach, in questions rather than answers, and other lawyers and judges who accept it would give different answers from his to the questions it asks. You might think other answers would be better. (So might I, after further thought.) You might, for example, reject Hercules' views about how far people's legal rights depend on the reasons past judges offered for their decisions enforcing these rights, or you might not share his respect for what I shall call "local priority" in common-law decisions. If you reject these discrete views because you think them poor constructive interpretations of legal practice, however, you have not rejected law as integrity but rather have joined its enterprise.

Six Interpretations

Hercules must decide *McLoughlin*. Both sides in that case cited precedents; each argued that a decision in its favor would count as going on as before, as continuing the story begun by the judges who decided those precedent cases. Hercules must form his own

view about that issue. Just as a chain novelist must find, if he can, some coherent view of character and theme such that a hypothetical single author with that view could have written at least the bulk of the novel so far, Hercules must find, if he can, some coherent theory about legal rights to compensation for emotional injury such that a single political official with that theory could have reached most of the results the precedents report.

He is a careful judge, a judge of method. He begins by setting out various candidates for the best interpretation of the precedent cases even before he reads them. Suppose he makes the following short list: (1) No one has a moral right to compensation except for physical injury. (2) People have a moral right to compensation for emotional injury suffered at the scene of an accident against anyone whose carelessness caused the accident but have no right to compensation for emotional injury suffered later. (3) People should recover compensation for emotional injury when a practice of requiring compensation in their circumstances would diminish the overall costs of accidents or otherwise make the community richer in the long run. (4) People have a moral right to compensation for any injury, emotional or physical, that is the direct consequence of careless conduct, no matter how unlikely or unforeseeable it is that that conduct would result in that injury. (5) People have a moral right to compensation for emotional or physical injury that is the consequence of careless conduct, but only if that injury was reasonably foreseeable by the person who acted carelessly. (6) People have a moral right to compensation for reasonably foreseeable injury but not in circumstances when recognizing such a right would impose massive and destructive financial burdens on people who have been careless out of proportion to their moral fault.

These are all relatively concrete statements about rights and, allowing for a complexity in (3) we explore just below, they contradict one another. No more than one can figure in a single interpreta-

---

4   Hercules played an important part in *Taking Rights Seriously*, chap. 4.

tion of the emotional injury cases. (I postpone the more complex case in which Hercules constructs an interpretation from competitive rather than contradictory principles, that is, from principles that can live together in an overall moral or political theory though they sometimes pull in different directions.)[5] Even so, this is only a partial list of the contradictory interpretations someone might wish to consider; Hercules chooses it as his initial short list because he knows that the principles captured in these interpretations have actually been discussed in the legal literature. It will obviously make a great difference which of these principles he believes provides the best interpretation of the precedents and so the nerve of his postinterpretive judgment. If he settles on (1) or (2), he must decide for Mr. O'Brian; if on (4), for Mrs. McLoughlin. Each of the others requires further thought, but the line of reasoning each suggests is different. (3) invites an economic calculation. Would it reduce the cost of accidents to extend liability to emotional injury away from the scene? Or is there some reason to think that the most efficient line is drawn just between emotional injuries at and those away from the scene? (5) requires a judgment about foreseeability of injury, which seems to be very different, and (6) a judgment both about foreseeability and the cumulative risk of financial responsibility if certain injuries away from the scene are included.

Hercules begins testing each interpretation on his short list by asking whether a single political official could have given the verdicts of the precedent cases if that official were consciously and coherently enforcing the principles that form the interpretation. He will therefore dismiss interpretation (1) at once. No one who believed that people never have rights to compensation for emotional injury could have reached the results of those past decisions cited in *McLoughlin* that allowed compensation. Hercules

will also dismiss interpretation (2), though for a different reason. Unlike (1), (2) fits the past decisions; someone who accepted (2) as a standard would have reached these decisions, because they all allowed recovery for emotional injury at the scene and none allowed recovery for injury away from it. But (2) fails as an interpretation of the required kind because it does not state a principle of justice at all. It draws a line that it leaves arbitrary and unconnected to any more general moral or political consideration.

What about (3)? It might fit the past decisions, but only in the following way. Hercules might discover through economic analysis that someone who accepted the economic theory expressed by (3) and who wished to reduce the community's accident costs would have made just those decisions. But it is far from obvious that (3) states any principle of justice or fairness. Remember the distinction between principles and policies we discussed toward the end of the last chapter. (3) supposes that it is desirable to reduce accident costs overall. Why? Two explanations are possible. The first insists that people have a right to compensation whenever a rule awarding compensation would produce more wealth for the community overall than a rule denying it. This has the form, at least, of a principle because it describes a general right everyone is supposed to have. I shall not ask Hercules to consider (3) understood in that way now, because he will study it very carefully in Chapter 8. The second, quite different, explanation suggests that it is sometimes or even always in the community's general interest to promote overall wealth in this way, but it does not suppose that anyone has any right that social wealth always be increased. It therefore sets out a policy that government might or might not decide to pursue in particular circumstances. It does not state a principle of justice, and so it cannot figure in an interpretation of the sort Hercules now seeks.[6]

---

5   See the discussion of critical legal studies later in this chapter.

6   The disagreement between Lords Edmund Davies and Scarman in *McLoughlin*, described in Chapter 1, was per-

Law as integrity asks judges to assume, so far as this is possible, that the law is structured by a coherent set of principles about justice and fairness and procedural due process, and it asks them to enforce these in the fresh cases that come before them, so that each person's situation is fair and just according to the same standards. That style of adjudication respects the ambition integrity assumes, the ambition to be a community of principle. But as we saw at the end of Chapter 6, integrity does not recommend what would be perverse, that we should all be governed by the same goals and strategies of policy on every occasion. It does not insist that a legislature that enacts one set of rules about compensation today, in order to make the community richer on the whole, is in any way committed to serve that same goal of policy tomorrow. For it might then have other goals to seek, not necessarily in place of wealth but beside it, and integrity does not frown on this diversity. Our account of interpretation, and our consequent elimination of interpretation (3) read as a naked appeal to policy, reflects a discrimination already latent in the ideal of integrity itself.

We reach the same conclusion in the context of *McLoughlin* through a different route, by further reflection on what we have learned about interpretation. An interpretation aims to show what is interpreted in the best light possible, and an interpretation of any part of our law must therefore attend not only to the substance of the decisions made by earlier officials but also to how—by which officials in which circumstances—these decisions were made. A legislature does not need reasons of principle to justify the rules it enacts about driving, including rules about compensation for accidents, even though these rules will create rights and duties for the future that will then be enforced by coercive

threat. A legislature may justify its decision to create new rights for the future by showing how these will contribute, as a matter of sound policy, to the overall good of the community as a whole. There are limits to this kind of justification, as we noticed in Chapter 6. The general good may not be used to justify the death penalty for careless driving. But the legislature need not show that citizens already have a moral right to compensation for injury under particular circumstances in order to justify a statute awarding damages in those circumstances.

Law as integrity assumes, however, that judges are in a very different position from legislators. It does not fit the character of a community of principle that a judge should have authority to hold people liable in damages for acting in a way he concedes they had no legal duty not to act. So when judges construct rules of liability not recognized before, they are not free in the way I just said legislators are. Judges must make their common-law decisions on grounds of principle, not policy: they must deploy arguments why the parties actually had the "novel" legal rights and duties they enforce at the time the parties acted or at some other pertinent time in the past.[7] A legal pragmatist would reject that claim. But Hercules rejects pragmatism. He follows law as integrity and therefore wants an interpretation of what judges did in the earlier emotional damage cases that shows them acting in the way he approves, not in the way he thinks judges must decline to act. It does not follow that he must dismiss interpretation (3) read in the first way I described, as supposing that past judges acted to protect a general legal right to compensation when this would make the community richer. For if people actually have such a right, others have a corresponding duty, and judges do not act unjustly in ordering the police to enforce it. The argument disqualifies interpretation (3) only when this is read to deny any such general duty and to rest on grounds of policy alone.

---

haps over just this claim. Edmund Davies's suggestions, about the arguments that might justify a distinction between compensable and non-compensable emotional injury, seemed to appeal to arguments of policy Scarman refused to acknowledge as appropriate.

---

7 See *Taking Rights Seriously*, chap. 4.

Expanding the Range

Interpretations (4), (5), and (6) do, however, seem to pass these initial tests. The principles of each fit the past emotional injury decisions, at least on first glance, if only because none of these precedents presented facts that would discriminate among them. Hercules must now ask, as the next stage of his investigation, whether any one of the three must be ruled out because it is incompatible with the bulk of legal practice more generally. He must test each interpretation against other past judicial decisions, beyond those involving emotional injury, that might be thought to engage them. Suppose he discovers, for example, that past decisions provide compensation for physical injury caused by careless driving only if the injury was reasonably foreseeable. That would rule out interpretation (4) unless he can find some principled distinction between physical and emotional injury that explains why the conditions for compensation should be more restrictive for the former than the latter, which seems extremely unlikely.

Law as integrity, then, requires a judge to test his interpretation of any part of the great network of political structures and decisions of his community by asking whether it could form part of a coherent theory justifying the network as a whole. No actual judge could compose anything approaching a full interpretation of all of his community's law at once. That is why we are imagining a Herculean judge of superhuman talents and endless time. But an actual judge can imitate Hercules in a limited way. He can allow the scope of his interpretation to fan out from the cases immediately in point to cases in the same general area or department of law, and then still farther, so far as this seems promising. In practice even this limited process will be largely unconscious: an experienced judge will have a sufficient sense of the terrain surrounding his immediate problem to know instinctively which interpretation of a small set of cases would survive if the range it must fit were

expanded. But sometimes the expansion will be deliberate and controversial. Lawyers celebrate dozens of decisions of that character, including several on which the modern law of negligence was built.[8] Scholarship offers other important examples.[9]

Suppose a modest expansion of Hercules' range of inquiry does show that plaintiffs are denied compensation if their physical injury was not reasonably foreseeable at the time the careless defendant acted, thus ruling out interpretation (4). But this does not eliminate either (5) or (6). He must expand his survey further. He must look also to cases involving economic rather than physical or emotional injury, where damages are potentially very great: for example, he must look to cases in which professional advisers like surveyors or accountants are sued for losses others suffer through their negligence. Interpretation (5) suggests that such liability might be unlimited in amount, no matter how ruinous in total, provided that the damage is foreseeable, and (6) suggests, on the contrary, that liability is limited just because of the frightening sums it might otherwise reach. If one interpretation is uniformly contradicted by cases of that sort and finds no support in any other area of doctrine Hercules might later inspect, and the other is confirmed by the expansion, he will regard the former as ineligible, and the latter alone will have survived. But suppose he finds, when he expands his study in this way, a mixed pattern. Past decisions permit extended liability for members of some professions but not for those of others, and this mixed pattern holds for other areas of doctrine that Hercules, in the exercise of his imaginative skill, finds pertinent.

The contradiction he has discovered, though genuine, is not in itself so deep or pervasive as to justify a skeptical interpretation of legal practice as a

---

8   See *Thomas v. Winchester*, 6 N.Y. 397, and *MacPherson v. Buick Motor Co.*, 217 N.Y. 382, 111 N.E. 1050.

9   C. Haar and D. Fessler, *The Wrong Side of the Tracks* (New York, 1986), is a recent example of integrity working on a large canvas.

whole, for the problem of unlimited damages, while important, is not so fundamental that contradiction within it destroys the integrity of the larger system. So Hercules turns to the second main dimension, but here, as in the chain-novel example, questions of fit surface again, because an interpretation is *pro tanto* more satisfactory if it shows less damage to integrity than its rival. He will therefore consider whether interpretation (5) fits the expanded legal record better than (6). But this cannot be a merely mechanical decision; he cannot simply count the number of past decisions that must be conceded to be "mistakes" on each interpretation. For these numbers may reflect only accidents like the number of cases that happen to have come to court and not been settled before verdict. He must take into account not only the numbers of decisions counting for each interpretation, but whether the decisions expressing one principle seem more important or fundamental or wide-ranging than the decisions expressing the other. Suppose interpretation (6) fits only those past judicial decisions involving charges of negligence against one particular profession— say, lawyers—and interpretation (5) justifies all other cases, involving all other professions, and also fits other kinds of economic damage cases as well. Interpretation (5) then fits the legal record better on the whole, even if the number of cases involving lawyers is for some reason numerically greater, unless the argument shifts again, as it well might, when the field of study expands even more.

Now suppose a different possibility: that though liability has in many and varied cases actually been limited to an amount less than interpretation (5) would allow, the opinions attached to these cases made no mention of the principle of interpretation (6), which has in fact never before been recognized in official judicial rhetoric. Does that show that interpretation (5) fits the legal record much better, or that interpretation (6) is ineligible after all? Judges in fact divide about this issue of fit. Some would not seriously consider interpretation (6)

if no past judicial opinion or legislative statement had ever explicitly mentioned its principle. Others reject this constraint and accept that the best interpretation of some line of cases may lie in a principle that has never been recognized explicitly but that nevertheless offers a brilliant account of the actual decisions, showing them in a better light than ever before.[10] Hercules will confront this issue as a special question of political morality. The political history of the community is *pro tanto* a better history, he thinks, if it shows judges making plain to their public, through their opinions, the path that later judges guided by integrity will follow and if it shows judges making decisions that give voice as well as effect to convictions about morality that are widespread through the community. Judicial opinions formally announced in law reports, moreover, are themselves acts of the community personified that, particularly if recent, must be taken into the embrace of integrity.[11] These are among his reasons for somewhat preferring an interpretation that is not too novel, not too far divorced from what past judges and other officials said as well as did. But he must set these reasons against his more substantive political convictions about the relative moral value of the two interpretations, and if he believes that interpretation (6) is much superior from that perspective, he will think he makes the legal record better overall by selecting it even at the cost of the more procedural values. Fitting what judges did is more important than fitting what they said.

Now suppose an even more unpatterned record. Hercules finds that unlimited liability has been enforced against a number of professions but has not been enforced against a roughly equal number of others, that no principle can explain the distinction,

---

10 See, for example, Benjamin Cardozo's decision in *Hynes v. New York Central R.R. Co.*, 231 N.Y. 229.

11 These various arguments why a successful interpretation must achieve some fit with past judicial opinions as well as with the decisions themselves are discussed in Chapter 9 in the context of past legislative statements.

that judicial rhetoric is as split as the actual decisions, and that this split extends into other kinds of actions for economic damage. He might expand his field of survey still further, and the picture might change if he does. But let us suppose he is satisfied that it will not. He will then decide that the question of fit can play no more useful role in his deliberations even on the second dimension. He must now emphasize the more plainly substantive aspects of that dimension: he must decide which interpretation shows the legal record to be the best it can be from the standpoint of substantive political morality. He will compose and compare two stories. The first supposes that the community personified has adopted and is enforcing the principle of foreseeability as its test of moral responsibility for damage caused by negligence, that the various decisions it has reached are intended to give effect to that principle, though it has often lapsed and reached decisions that foreseeability would condemn. The second supposes, instead, that the community has adopted and is enforcing the principle of foreseeability limited by some overall ceiling on liability, though it has often lapsed from that principle. Which story shows the community in a better light, all things considered, from the standpoint of political morality?

Hercules' answer will depend on his convictions about the two constituent virtues of political morality we have considered: justice and fairness.[12] It will depend, that is, not only on his beliefs about which of these principles is superior as a matter of abstract justice but also about which should be followed, as a matter of political fairness, in a community whose members have the moral convictions his fellow citizens have. In some cases the two kinds of judgment—the judgment of justice and that of fairness—will come together. If Hercules and the public at large share the view that people are entitled to be compensated fully whenever they are injured by others' carelessness, without regard to how harsh this requirement might turn out to be, then he will think that interpretation (5) is plainly the better of the two in play. But the two judgments will sometimes pull in different directions. He may think that interpretation (6) is better on grounds of abstract justice, but know that this is a radical view not shared by any substantial portion of the public and unknown in the political and moral rhetoric of the times. He might then decide that the story in which the state insists on the view he thinks right, but against the wishes of the people as a whole, is a poorer story, on balance. He would be preferring fairness to justice in these circumstances, and that preference would reflect a higher-order level of his own political convictions, namely his convictions about how a decent government committed to both fairness and justice should adjudicate between the two in this sort of case.

Judges will have different ideas of fairness, about the role each citizen's opinion should ideally play in the state's decision about which principles of justice to enforce through its central police power. They will have different higher-level opinions about the best resolution of conflicts between these two political ideals. No judge is likely to hold the simplistic theory that fairness is automatically to be preferred to justice or vice versa. Most judges will think that the balance between the opinions of the community and the demands of abstract justice must be struck differently in different kinds of cases. Perhaps in ordinary commercial or private law cases, like *McLoughlin*, an interpretation supported in popular morality will be deemed superior to one that is not, provided it is not thought very much inferior as a matter of abstract justice. But many judges will think the interpretive force of popular morality very much weaker in constitutional cases like *Brown*, because they will think the point of the Constitution is in part to protect individuals from what the majority thinks right.[13]

---

12 I have in mind the distinction and the special sense of fairness described in Chapter 6.

13 But see the discussion of "passivism" as a theory of constitutional adjudication in Chapter 10.

• • •

A Provisional Summary

… Judges who accept the interpretive ideal of integrity decide hard cases by trying to find, in some coherent set of principles about people's rights and duties, the best constructive interpretation of the political structure and legal doctrine of their community. They try to make that complex structure and record the best these can be. It is analytically useful to distinguish different dimensions or aspects of any working theory. It will include convictions about both fit and justification. Convictions about fit will provide a rough threshold requirement that an interpretation of some part of the law must meet if it is to be eligible at all. Any plausible working theory would disqualify an interpretation of our own law that denied legislative competence or supremacy outright or that claimed a general principle of private law requiring the rich to share their wealth with the poor. That threshold will eliminate interpretations that some judges would otherwise prefer, so the brute facts of legal history will in this way limit the role any judge's personal convictions of justice can play in his decisions. Different judges will set this threshold differently. But anyone who accepts law as integrity must accept that the actual political history of his community will sometimes check his other political convictions in his overall interpretive judgment. If he does not—if his threshold of fit is wholly derivative from and adjustable to his convictions of justice, so that the latter automatically provide an eligible interpretation—then he cannot claim in good faith to be interpreting his legal practice at all. Like the chain novelist whose judgments of fit automatically adjusted to his substantive literary opinions, he is acting from bad faith or self-deception.

Hard cases arise, for any judge, when his threshold test does not discriminate between two or more interpretations of some statute or line of cases. Then he must choose between eligible interpretations by asking which shows the community's structure of institutions and decisions—its public standards as a whole—in a better light from the standpoint of political morality. His own moral and political convictions are now directly engaged. But the political judgment he must make is itself complex and will sometimes set one department of his political morality against another: his decision will reflect not only his opinions about justice and fairness but his higher-order convictions about how these ideals should be compromised when they compete. Questions of fit arise at this stage of interpretation as well, because even when an interpretation survives the threshold requirement, any infelicities of fit will count against it, in the ways we noticed, in the general balance of political virtues. Different judges will disagree about each of these issues and will accordingly take different views of what the law of their community, properly understood, really is.

Any judge will develop, in the course of his training and experience, a fairly individualized working conception of law on which he will rely, perhaps unthinkingly, in making these various judgments and decisions, and the judgments will then be, for him, a matter of feel or instinct rather than analysis. Even so, we as critics can impose structure on his working theory by teasing out its rules of thumb about fit—about the relative importance of consistency with past rhetoric and popular opinion, for example—and its more substantive opinions or leanings about justice and fairness. Most judges will be like other people in their community, and fairness and justice will therefore not often compete for them. But judges whose political opinions are more eccentric or radical will find that the two ideals conflict in particular cases, and they will have to decide which resolution of that conflict would show the community's record in the best light. Their working conceptions will accordingly include higher-order principles that have proved necessary to that further decision. A particular judge may think or assume, for example, that political decisions should mainly respect majority opinion, and yet believe that this requirement relaxes and even disappears when serious constitutional rights are in question.

We should now recall two general observations we made in constructing the chain-novel model, because they apply here as well. First, the different aspects or dimensions of a judge's working approach—the dimensions of fit and substance, and of different aspects of substance—are in the last analysis all responsive to his political judgment. His convictions about fit, as these appear either in his working threshold requirement or analytically later in competition with substance, are political not mechanical. They express his commitment to integrity: he believes that an interpretation that falls below his threshold of fit shows the record of the community in an irredeemably bad light, because proposing that interpretation suggests that the community has characteristically dishonored its own principles. When an interpretation meets the threshold, remaining defects of fit may be compensated, in his overall judgment, if the principles of that interpretation are particularly attractive, because then he sets off the community's infrequent lapses in respecting these principles against its virtue in generally observing them. The constraint fit imposes on substance, in any working theory, is therefore the constraint of one type of political conviction on another in the overall judgment which interpretation makes a political record the best it can be overall, everything taken into account. Second, the mode of this constraint is the mode we identified in the chain novel. It is not the constraint of external hard fact or of interpersonal consensus. But rather the structural constraint of different kinds of principle within a system of principle, and it is none the less genuine for that.

No mortal judge can or should try to articulate his instinctive working theory so far, or make that theory so concrete and detailed, that no further thought will be necessary case by case. He must treat any general principles or rules of thumb he has followed in the past as provisional and stand ready to abandon these in favor of more sophisticated and searching analysis when the occasion demands. These will be moments of special difficulty for any judge, calling for fresh political judgments that may be hard to make. It would be absurd to suppose that he will always have at hand the necessary background convictions of political morality for such occasions. Very hard cases will force him to develop his conception of law and his political morality together in a mutually supporting way. But it is nevertheless possible for any judge to confront fresh and challenging issues as a matter of principle, and this is what law as integrity demands of him. He must accept that in finally choosing one interpretation over another of a much contested line of precedents, perhaps after demanding thought and shifting conviction, he is developing his working conception of law in one rather than another direction. This must seem to him the right direction as a matter of political principle, not just appealing for the moment because it recommends an attractive decision in the immediate case. There is, in this counsel, much room for deception, including self-deception. But on most occasions it will be possible for judges to recognize when they have submitted an issue to the discipline it describes. And also to recognize when some other judge has not.

♦ ♦ ♦ ♦ ♦

Riggs v. *Palmer* (Court of Appeals of New York, 1889)

Earl, J. On the 13th day of August, 1880, Francis B. Palmer made his last will and testament, in which he gave small legacies to his two daughters, Mrs. Riggs and Mrs. Preston, the plaintiffs in this action, and the remainder of his estate to his grandson, the defendant Elmer E. Palmer, subject to the support of Susan Palmer, his mother, with a gift over to the two daughters, subject to the support of Mrs. Palmer in case Elmer should survive him and die under age, unmarried, and without any issue. The testator at the date of his will, owned a farm, and considerable personal property. He was a widower, and thereafter, in March, 1882, he was married to Mrs. Bresee, with whom, before his marriage, he entered into an antenuptial contract, in which it was agreed that in lieu of dower and all other claims upon his estate in case she survived him she should have her support upon his farm during her life, and such support was expressly charged upon the farm. At the date of the will, and subsequently to the death of the testator, Elmer lived with him as a member of his family, and at his death was 16 years old. He knew of the provisions made in his favor in the will, and, that he might prevent his grandfather from revoking such provisions, which he had manifested some intention to do, and to obtain the speedy enjoyment and immediate possession of his property, he willfully murdered him by poisoning him. He now claims the property, and the sole question for our determination is, can he have it?

The defendants say that the testator is dead; that his will was made in due form, and has been admitted to probate; and that therefore it must have effect according to the letter of the law. It is quite true that statutes regulating the making, proof, and effect of wills and the devolution of property, if literally construed, and if their force and effect can in no way and under no circumstances be controlled or modified, give this property to the murderer. The purpose of those statutes was to enable testators to dispose of their estates to the objects of their bounty at death, and to carry into effect their final wishes legally expressed; and in considering and giving effect to them this purpose must be kept in view. It was the intention of the law-makers that the donees in a will should have the property given to them. But it never could have been their intention that a

donee who murdered the testator to make the will operative should have any benefit under it. If such a case had been present to their minds, and it had been supposed necessary to make some provision of law to meet it, it cannot be doubted that they would have provided for it. It is a familiar canon of construction that a thing which is within the intention of the makers of a statute is as much within the statute as if it were within the letter; and a thing which is within the letter of the statute is not within the statute unless it be within the intention of the makers. The writers of laws do not always express their intention perfectly, but either exceed it or fall short of it, so that judges are to collect it from probable or rational conjectures only, and this is called "rational interpretation;" and Rutherford, in his *Institutes*, (page 420) says:

> Where we make use of rational interpretation, sometimes we restrain the meaning of the writer so as to take in less, and sometimes we extend or enlarge his meaning so as to take in more, than his words express.

Such a construction ought to be put upon a statute as will best answer the intention which the makers had in view, for *qui haeret in liera, haeret in cortice*. In Bac. Abr. "Statutes," 1, 5; Puff. Law Nat. bk. 5, c. 12; Ruth. Inst. 422, 427, and in Smith's Commentaries, 814, many cases are mentioned where it was held that matters embraced in the general words of statutes nevertheless were not within the statutes, because it could not have been the intention of the law-makers that they should be included. They were taken out of the statutes by an equitable construction; and it is said in Bacon:

> By an equitable construction a case not within the letter of a statute is some-times holden to be within the meaning, because it is within the mischief for which a remedy is provided. The reason for such construction is that the law-makers could not set

down every case in express terms. In order to form a right judgment whether a case be within the equity of a statute, it is a good way to suppose the law-maker present, and that you have asked him this question: Did you intend to comprehend this case? Then you must give yourself such answer as you imagine he, being an upright and reasonable man, would have given. If this be that he did mean to comprehend it, you may safely hold the case to be within the equity of the statute; for while you do no more than he would have done, you do not act contrary to the statute, but in conformity thereto.

9 Bac. Abr. 248. In some cases the letter of a legislative act is restrained by an equitable construction; in others, it is enlarged; in others, the construction is contrary to the letter. The equitable construction which restrains the letter of a statute is defined by Aristotle as frequently quoted in this manner: *Aequitas est correctio legis generaliter latae qua parte deficit.* If the law-makers could, as to this case, be consulted, would they say that they intended by their general language that the property of a testator or of an ancestor should pass to one who had taken his life for the express purpose of getting his property? In 1 Bl. Comm. 91, the learned author, speaking of the construction of statutes, says:

if there arise out of them collaterally any absurd consequences manifestly contradictory to common reason, they are with regard to those collateral consequences void. * * * Where some collateral matter arises out of the general words, and happens to be unreasonable, there the judges are in decency to conclude that this consequence was not foreseen by the parliament, and therefore they are at liberty to expound the statute by equity, and only *quo ad hoc* disregard it;

and he gives as an illustration, if an act of parliament gives a man power to try all causes that arise within his manor of Dale, yet, if a cause should arise in which he himself is party, the act is construed not to extend to that, because it is unreasonable that any man should determine his own quarrel. There was a statute in Bologna that whoever drew blood in the streets should be severely punished, and yet it was held not to apply to the case of a barber who opened a vein in the street. It is commanded in the decalogue that no work shall be done upon the Sabbath, and yet giving the command a rational interpretation founded upon its design the Infallible Judge held it that it did not prohibit works of necessity, charity, or benevolence on that day.

What could be more unreasonable than to suppose that it was the legislative intention in the general laws passed for the orderly, peaceable, and just devolution of property that they should have operation in favor of one who murdered his ancestor that he might speedily come into the possession of his estate? Such an intention is inconceivable. We need not, therefore, be much troubled by the general language contained in the laws. Besides, all laws, as well as all contracts, may be controlled in their operation and effect by general, fundamental maxims of the common law. No one shall be permitted to profit by his own fraud, or to take advantage of his own wrong, or to found any claim upon his own iniquity, or to acquire property by his own crime. These maxims are dictated by public policy, have their foundation in universal law administered in all civilized countries, and have nowhere been superseded by statutes. They were applied in the decision of the case of *Insurance Co. v. Armstrong*, 117 U.S. 599, 6 Sup. Ct. Rep. 877. There it was held that the person who procured a policy upon the life of another, payable at his death, and then murdered the assured to make the policy payable, could not recover thereon. Mr. Justice Field, writing the opinion, said:

Independently of any proof of the motives of Hunter in obtaining the policy, and even assuming that they were just and proper, he forfeited all rights under it when, to secure its immediate payment, he murdered the assured. It would be a reproach to the jurisprudence of the country if one could recover insurance money payable on the death of a party whose life he had feloniously taken. As well might he recover insurance money upon a building that he had willfully fired.

These maxims, without any statute giving them force or operation, frequently control the effect and nullify the language of wills. A will procured by fraud and deception, like any other instrument, may be decreed void, and set aside; and so a particular portion of a will may be excluded from probate, or held inoperative, if induced by the fraud or undue influence of the person in whose favor it is. *Allen v. McPherson*, 1 H.L. Cas. 191; *Harrison's Appeal*, 48 Conn. 202. So a will may contain provisions which are immoral, irreligious, or against public policy, and they will be held void.

Here there was no certainty that this murderer would survive the testator, or that the testator would not change his will, and there was no certainty that he would get this property if nature was allowed to take its course. He therefore murdered the testator expressly to vest himself with an estate. Under such circumstances, what law, human or divine, will allow him to take the estate and enjoy the fruits of his crime? The will spoke and became operative at the death of the testator. He caused that death, and thus by his crime made it speak and have operation. Shall it speak and operate in his favor? If he had met the testator, and taken his property by force, he would have had no title to it. Shall he acquire title by murdering him? If he had gone to the testator's house and by force compelled him, or by fraud or undue influence had induced him, to will him his property

the law would not allow him to hold it. But can he give effect and operation to a will by murder, and yet take the property? To answer these questions in the affirmative it seems to me would be a reproach to the jurisprudence of our state, and an offense against public policy. Under the civil law, evolved from the general principles of natural law and justice by many generations of jurisconsults, philosophers, and statesmen, one cannot take property by inheritance or will from an ancestor or benefactor whom he has murdered. Dom. Civil Law, pt. 2, bk. 1, tit. 1, §. 3; Code Nap. § 727; Mack. Rom. Law, 530, 550. In the Civil Code of Lower Canada the provisions on the subject in the Code Napoleon have been substantially copied. But, so far as I can find, in no country where the common law prevails has it been deemed important to enact a law to provide for such a case. Our revisers and law-makers were familiar with the civil law, and they did not deem it important to incorporate into our statutes its provisions upon this subject. This is not a *casus omissus*. It was evidently supposed that the maxims of the common law were sufficient to regulate such a case, and that a specific enactment for that purpose was not needed. For the same reasons the defendant Palmer cannot take any of this property as heir. Just before the murder he was not an heir, and it was not certain that he ever would be. He might have died before his grandfather, or might have been disinherited by him. He made himself an heir by the murder, and he seeks to take property as the fruit of his crime. What has before been said as to him as legatee applies to him with equal force as an heir. He cannot vest himself with title by crime. My view of this case does not inflict upon Elmer any greater or other punishment for his crime than the law specifies. It takes from him no property, but simply holds that he shall not acquire property by his crime, and thus be rewarded for its commission.

Our attention is called to *Owens v. Owens*, 100 N.C. 240, 6 S.E. Rep. 794, as a case quite like this. There a wife had been convicted of being an accessory before the fact to the murder of her husband, and it was held that she was nevertheless entitled to dower. I am unwilling to assent to the doctrine of that case. The statutes provide dower for a wife who has the misfortune to survive her husband, and thus lose his support and protection. It is clear beyond their purpose to make provision for a wife who by her own crime makes herself a widow, and willfully and intentionally deprives herself of the support and protection of her husband. As she might have died before him, and thus never have been his widow, she cannot by her crime vest herself with an estate. The principle which lies at the bottom of the maxim *volenti non fit injuria* should be applied to such a case, and a widow should not, for the purpose of acquiring, as such, property rights, be permitted to allege a widowhood which she has wickedly and intentionally created.

The facts found entitled the plaintiffs to the relief they seek. The error of the referee was in his conclusion of law. Instead of granting a new trial, therefore, I think the proper judgment upon the facts found should be ordered here. The facts have been passed upon twice with the same result,—first upon the trial of Palmer for murder, and then by the referee in this action. We are therefore of opinion that the ends of justice do not require that they should again come in question. The judgment of the general term and that entered upon the report of the referee should therefore be reversed, and judgment should be entered as follows: That Elmer E. Palmer and the administrator be enjoined from using any of the personalty or real estate left by the testator for Elmer's benefit; that the devise and bequest in the will to Elmer be declared ineffective to pass the title to him; that by reason of the crime of murder committed upon the grandfather he is deprived of any interest in the estate left by him; that the plaintiffs are the true owners of the real and personal estate left by the testator, subject to the charge in favor of Elmer's mother and the widow of the testator, under the antenuptial agreement, and that the plaintiffs

have costs in all the courts against Elmer. All concur, except *Gray, J.*, who reads dissenting opinion, and *Danforth, J.*, concurs.

Gray, J., (dissenting.) This appeal presents an extraordinary state of facts, and the case, in respect of them, I believe, is without precedent in this state. The respondent, a lad of 16 years of age, being aware of the provisions in his grandfather's will, which constituted him the residuary legatee of the testator's estate, caused his death by poison, in 1882. For this crime he was tried, and was convicted of murder in the second degree, and at the time of the commencement of this action he was serving out his sentence in the state reformatory. This action was brought by two of the children of the testator for the purpose of having those provisions of the will in the favor canceled and annulled. The appellants' argument for a reversal of the judgment, which dismissed their complaint, is that the respondent unlawfully prevented a revocation of the existing will, or a new will from being made, by his crime; and that he terminated the enjoyment by the testator of his property, and effected his own succession to it, by the same crime. They say that to permit the respondent to take the property willed to him would be to permit him to take advantage of his own wrong. To sustain their position the appellants' counsel has submitted an able and elaborate brief, and, if I believed that the decision of the question could be effected by considerations of an equitable nature, I should not hesitate to assent to views which commend themselves to the conscience. But the matter does not lie within the domain of conscience. We are bound by the rigid rules of law, which have been established by the legislature, and within the limits of which the determination of this question is confined. The question we are dealing with is whether a testamentary disposition can be altered, or a will revoked, after the testator's death, through an appeal to the courts, when the legislature has by its enactments prescribed exactly when and how wills may be made, altered, and revoked, and apparently, as it seems to me, when they have been fully complied with, has left no room for the exercise of an equitable jurisdiction by courts over such matters. Modern jurisprudence, in recognizing the right of the individual, under more or less restrictions, to dispose of his property after his death, subjects it to legislative control, both as to extent and as to mode of exercise. Complete freedom of testamentary disposition of one's property has not been and is not the universal rule, as we see from the provisions of the Napoleonic Code, from the systems of jurisprudence in countries which are modeled upon the Roman law, and from the statutes of many of our states. To the statutory restraints which are imposed upon the disposition of one's property by will are added strict and systematic statutory rules for the execution, alteration, and revocation of the will, which must be, at least substantially, if not exactly, followed to insure validity and performance. The reason for the establishment of such rules, we may naturally assume, consists in the purpose to create those safeguards about these grave and important acts which experience has demonstrated to be the wisest and surest. That freedom which is permitted to be exercised in the testamentary disposition of one's estate by the laws of the state is subject to its being exercised in conformity with the regulations of the statutes. The capacity and the power of the individual to dispose of his property after death, and the mode by which that power can be exercised, are matters of which the legislature has assumed the entire control, and has undertaken to regulate with comprehensive particularity.

The appellants' argument is not helped by reference to those rules of the civil law, or to those laws of other governments, by which the heir, or legatee is excluded from benefit under the testament if he has been convicted of killing, or attempting to kill the testator. In the absence of such legislation here, the courts are not empowered to institute such a system of remedial justice. The deprivation of the heir of his testamentary succession by the Roman law, when guilty of such a crime, plainly was intended to be in the nature of a punishment imposed upon him. The succession, in such a case of guilt, escheated to the exchequer. See Dom. Civil Law, pt. 2, bk. 1, tit. 1, § 3. I concede that rules of law which annul testamentary provisions made for the benefit of those who have become unworthy of them may be based on principles of equity and of natural justice. It is quite reasonable to suppose that a testator would revoke or alter his will, where his mind has been so angered and changed as to make him unwilling to have his will executed as it stood. But these principles only suggest sufficient reasons for the enactment of laws to meet such cases.

The statutes of this state have prescribed various ways in which a will may be altered or revoked; but the very provision defining the modes of alteration and revocation implies a prohibition of alteration or revocation in any other way. The words of the section of the statute are:

> No will in writing, except in the cases hereinafter mentioned, nor any part thereof, shall be revoked or altered otherwise,

etc. Where, therefore, none of the cases mentioned are met by the facts, and the revocation is not in the way described in the section, the will of the testator is unalterable. I think that a valid will must continue as a will always, unless revoked in the manner provided by the statutes. Mere intention to revoke a will does not have the effect of revocation. The intention to revoke is necessary to constitute the effective revocation of a will, but it must be demonstrated by one of the acts contemplated by the statute. As *Woodworth, J.*, said in *Dan v. Brown*, 4 Cow. 490: "Revocation is an act of the mind, which must be demonstrated by some outward and visible sign of revocation." The same learned judge said in that case:

> The rule is that if the testator lets the will stand until he dies, it is his will; if he does not suffer it to do so, it is not his will.

And see *Goodright v. Glazier*, 4 Burrows, 2512, 2514; *Pemberton v. Pemberton*, 13 Ves. 290. The finding of fact of the referee that presumably the testator would have altered his will had he known of his grandson's murderous intent cannot affect the question. We may concede it to the fullest extent; but still the cardinal objection is undisposed of,—that the making and the revocation of a will are purely matters of statutory regulation, by which the court is bound in the determination of questions relating to these acts.

Two cases,—in this state and in Kentucky, at an early day, seem to me to be much in point. *Gains v. Gains*, 2 A.K. Marsh. 190, was decided by the Kentucky court of appeals in 1820. It was there urged that the testator intended to have destroyed his will, and that he was forcibly prevented from doing so by the defendant in error or devisee; and it was insisted that the will, though not expressly, was thereby virtually, revoked. The court held, as the act concerning wills prescribed the manner in which a will might be revoked, that, as none of the acts evidencing revocation were done, the intention could not be substituted for the act. In that case the will was snatched away, and forcibly retained. In 1854, Surrogate Bradford, whose opinions are entitled to the highest consideration, decided the case of *Leaycraft v. Simmons*, 3 Bradf. Sur. 35. In that case the testator, a man of 89 years of age, desired to make a codicil to his will, in order to enlarge the provisions for his daughter. His son, having the custody of the instrument, and the one to be prejudiced by the change, refused to produce the will at testator's request, for the purpose of alteration. The learned surrogate refers to the provisions of the civil law for such and other cases of unworthy conduct in the heir or legatee, and says:

> Our statute has undertaken to prescribe the mode in which wills can be revoked [citing the statutory provision]. This is the law by which I am governed in passing upon questions touching the revocation of wills.

The whole of this subject is now regulated by statute; and a mere intention to revoke, how ever well authenticated, or however defeated, is not sufficient.

And he held that the will must be admitted to probate. I may refer also to a case in the Pennsylvania courts. In that state the statute prescribed the mode for repealing or altering a will, and in *Clingan v. Micheltree*, 31 Pa. St. 25, the supreme court of the state held, where a will was kept from destruction by the fraud and misrepresentation of the devisee, that to declare it canceled as against the fraudulent party would be to enlarge the statute.

I cannot find any support for the argument that the respondent's succession to the property should be avoided because of his criminal act, when the laws are silent. Public policy does not demand it; for the demands of public policy are satisfied by the proper execution of the laws and the punishment of the crime. There has been no convention between the testator and his legatee; nor is there any such contractual element, in such a disposition of property by a testator, as to impose or imply conditions in the legatee. The appellants' argument practically amounts to this: that, as the legatee has been guilty of a crime, by the commission of which he is placed in a position to sooner receive the benefits of the testamentary provision, his rights to the property should be forfeited, and he should be divested of his estate. To allow their argument to prevail would involve the diversion by the court of the testator's estate into the hands of persons whom, possibly enough, for all we know, the testator might not have chosen or desired as its recipients. Practically the court is asked to make another will for the testator. The laws do not warrant this judicial action, and mere presumption would not be strong enough to sustain it. But, more than this, to concede the appellants' views would involve the imposition of an additional punishment or penalty upon the respondent. What power or warrant have the courts to add to the respondent's penalties by depriving him of property? The law has punished him for his crime, and we may not say that it was an insufficient punishment. In the trial and punishment of the respondent the law has vindicated itself for the outrage which he committed, and further judicial utterance upon the subject of punishment or deprivation of rights is barred. We may not, in the language of the court in *People v. Thornton*, 25 Hun., 456,

> enhance the pains, penalties, and forfeitures provided by law for the punishment of crime.

The judgment should be affirmed, with costs.

Danforth, J. concurs.

◆ ◆ ◆ ◆ ◆

STUDY QUESTIONS

1. Are Dworkin's criticisms of Hart's idea of "social rules" persuasive criticisms?

2. Does Dworkin's account of judicial discretion explain successfully how judges need not venture outside the law in making decisions in unclear areas of law?

3. How successful are Dworkin's two central metaphors in his argument for law as integrity? Can these metaphors apply to any legal system?

4. Does law as integrity enable us to evaluate whether what is called international law really has the characteristics of law? Does the success of law as integrity as a theory of law depend on its ability to provide an account of the legal quality of international law?

◆ ◆ ◆ ◆ ◆

FURTHER READINGS

Marshall Cohen, ed. *Ronald Dworkin and Contemporary Jurisprudence*. Totowa, NJ: Rowman and Allanheld, 1983.

Ronald Dworkin, "Thirty Years On" 115 *Harvard Law Review* (2003), 1655.

Ronald Dworkin, "Hart's Postscript and the Character of Political Philosophy" 24 *Oxford Journal of Legal Studies*, no. 1 (2004), 1.

Stephen Guest, *Ronald Dworkin*. Edinburgh: Edinburgh University Press, 1997.

Brian Leiter "Beyond the Hart/Dworkin Debate: The Methodology Problem in Jurisprudence," 48 *American Journal of Jurisprudence* (2003), 17.

Alan Hunt, ed. *Reading Dworkin Critically*. New York: Berg, 1992.

Scott Hershovitz, ed. *Exploring Law's Empire: The Jurisprudence of Ronald Dworkin*. Oxford: Oxford University Press, 2006.

CHAPTER 4

Legal Realism

INTRODUCTION

"Legal Realism" is the name given to the views of a group of American jurists whose writing dominated American legal thought in the early to mid-twentieth century.[1] Legal Realists, as they are called, are best known for their opposition to the "classical" or "formalist" view that law consists of a body of definite, logically related rules applied in a logical and impersonal fashion by impartial judges. According to Legal Realists, the actual facts about the nature of law and legal systems are a great deal more complex than this simple, optimistic picture allows. Much of what is called "Legal Realism" is devoted to showing the classical view to be composed largely of what the Legal Realist writer Jerome Frank called "myths." The Legal Realists were not, however, entirely agreed in their assessments of precisely why the classical theory of law ought to be abandoned, and they ought not to be thought of as a "school" of thinkers devoted as a group to supporting certain views. Their association was much more loose. Nonetheless, as we shall see, it is still possible to identify some general views shared by Legal Realists. More precise characterizations of the varieties of Legal Realism are discussed by Jerome Frank in a passage excerpted in this chapter.

The classical view that the Legal Realists opposed was developed in the late nineteenth and early twentieth centuries by judges and lawyers who tried to demonstrate that law could be a "science," complete with methods allowing a knowledgeable practitioner to answer with scientific certainty the question "What is the law in this instance?" According to the classical approach, this question always has a definite, certain answer, and that answer can always be found with nothing more than knowledge of the customs, conventions, court decisions, and legislation which constitute the law. There need never be any appeal to any standards or information found outside the law.

On the classical theory of law, the determination of what the law is in a given case is never a matter of individual judgment or interpretation. Rather, it is simply a matter of discovering or clarifying what the law already says, and applying it to the facts of the case at hand. Judges who discover and apply the law in this way are properly said to be impartial: they are simply applying mechanically and logically the principles and rules of interpretation of law to determine the correct result in individual cases. There is no danger that two persons who commit the same act yet appear before different judges will be treated any differently, because the judges never have any opportunity to inject their own personal beliefs regarding, for example, morality or economics into the judgment. Justice is in this sense "blind," because judges simply determine the facts in a given case and apply pre-existing rules which exist whether judges like those rules or not.

There can be no doubt that this picture of the courts and the law has attractive aspects. It captures

1   "Legal Realism" is sometimes used to refer also to Scandanavian Legal Realism, advanced in the writings of, e.g., Karl Olivecrona, Alf Ross, and others. Here we shall be concerned with American Legal Realism only.

the common hope that judges impose the law and not simply their own personal convictions; and it expresses the hope that laws are standards with a definite range of meanings which do not change from moment to moment. Yet according to the Legal Realists, this picture of law is fundamentally flawed, and a new understanding of law is needed. Here we shall explore three of the Legal Realists' major criticisms of orthodox legal theory, and examine their attempts to introduce reforms to resolve the problems they saw.

1. Skepticism About the Objectivity of Judges' Reasoning

One hallmark of Legal Realists is their concern with the courts' role in shaping the law. The Legal Realists claimed that judges are *not* impartial discoverers of pre-existing rules. Such rules, say the Legal Realists, far from being discovered and applied in a logical fashion, are flexible and open to interpretation, and that interpretation frequently depends on judges' personal and political biases or philosophies of law and interpretation. The realist writer Oliver Wendell Holmes expresses succinctly the Legal Realists' concern that courts do not operate in a neutral, impartial way.

> The life of the law has not been logic: it has been experience. The felt necessities of the time, the prevalent moral and political theories, intuitions of public policy, avowed or unconscious, even the prejudices which judges share with their fellow-men, have had a good deal more to do than the syllogism in determining the rules by which men should be governed. The law embodies the story of a nation's development through many centuries, and it cannot be dealt with as if it contained only the axioms and corollaries of a book of mathematics....[2]

2   Oliver Wendell Holmes, *The Common Law* (Boston: Little, Brown, 1881), p. 1.

Holmes provides here a useful list of some of the influences which play a role in judges' reasoning. First, judges may in their decisions reflect contemporary public values. The law may be ambiguous and judges may choose to read it in a way which advances community standards or other values already broadly accepted in a particular society. Second, judges may interpret the law in light of what judges believe to be the best moral theories available. Judges may, for example, attempt to apportion civil damages in a way which seems to be morally justified according to a currently accepted moral theory, even when no part of the law instructs that judges must impose morally justified judgments. Third, judges may knowingly or subconsciously interpret the law in a way which advances what judges believe is the public interest. (Judges' understanding of the public interest may, of course, be at odds with what the public interest actually is, or what a legislature or other law-making body conceives to be the public interest.) Fourth, judges, as any other persons, are prone to prejudices which may sway them away from what the text of the law requires. With this observation we see most clearly the truth contained in Holmes' assertion that the life of law has been experience rather than logic. Judges are humans formed by their experience of the world, and it seems that judges are not always able to detach themselves from their experiences in order to reason in a purely logical way.

2. Skepticism Regarding Logical Reasoning About the Law

The Legal Realists were quick to realize the implications of their observations of the variability of judges' reasoning. If judges are not impartial interpreters who rely on logic alone as they find what the law is, it is not plausible to claim that there are certain, definite answers to the question "What is the law in this instance?" The answer to that question may be determined in part by examining the relevant statutes, cases, and so forth; but the character and leanings of the judge must always be taken into account also. According to the Legal Realists, legal rules are not settled, definite standards. It is perhaps reasonable to claim that legal rules do have a definite *range* of meanings, but the limits of that range are determined as much by psychological facts as by logic.

At the same time as the Legal Realists recorded these shrewd observations of the actual operations of courts, the new discipline of psychology and the established discipline of philosophy made discoveries which seemed to confirm the Legal Realists' views. At the turn of the century and throughout the period when Legal Realists were most active, psychology appeared to be on the verge of explaining nearly all human attitudes and behaviour. The Legal Realists were particularly interested in the idea that persons' actions and views might be more the product of their environment than of their own reasoning, and the idea that there could be a "subconscious" which influences conscious persons' reasoning without their knowledge. Various Legal Realists attempted to show that judges' reasoning reflected not a mechanical application of logic to the rules of law, but rather the views of a particular social and economic class, or judges' personal peculiarities. Developments in philosophy provided further evidence that judges were likely not operating as the classical view supposed they were. Many philosophers of logic and philosophers of language came to believe that the language of law is much more flexible or "open-textured" than previously believed. There are terms and phrases in ordinary language (and the language used in the law) which have not a single, set meaning, but rather a range of meanings, and so legal rules using those terms might reasonably be interpreted in different ways in different situations, all without going plainly against the ordinary meaning of the language of the legal rules.

3. Skepticism About Law as Consisting of "Pre-existing" or "Settled" Rules

It is unsurprising, given the emergence of evidence casting doubt on the classical view of judges' determination of legal rules, that Legal Realists thought that the meaning of the text of the law is in principle uncertain. This uncertainty opens (at least) two problems. First, if the law is uncertain, can ordinary citizens be justifiably confident that the law will protect them? Will a contract made today mean the same thing tomorrow? Second, if the law is in principle unsettled and may be interpreted in various ways by different judges, can ordinary citizens rest assured that they will be held to reasonable standards and treated fairly in any court, regardless of the identity of the judge? To the first question the Legal Realists answered that legal certainty of the sort desired by the classical legal theorists is a myth. Instead, many Legal Realists claimed, the law cannot be known prior to its interpretation by the courts. To say what the law is in a given case, according to the Legal Realists, is nothing more and nothing less than to make a prediction of what the courts will do. This is the nearest approximation of certainty in determining what the law is in given case. (Jerome Frank illustrates this view very clearly with his discussion of the course of a hypothetical case through a court system.) In considering the Legal Realists' solution to the second problem we turn from their scepticism regarding the classical theory of law to their attempts to fix the problems they found in the classical theory.

4. Legal Realists' Program of Reform

The Legal Realists' solution to the second problem was typical of their attempts to reform the law: they tried to turn the apparent weaknesses of law and judges into virtues. According to the Legal Realists, if the law is phrased in terms whose meaning appears different in different contexts, then judges ought in those different contexts to try honestly and without pretense to advance the public interest. And if it is impossible for judges to apply the law impartially and mechanically, the Legal Realists thought, then the next best thing is to rely on the wisdom of judges and require explicitly that they use their understanding of the changing needs and values of society to apply the law in a way which best serves those needs and promotes those values. Here one of the main problems with Legal Realism appears. Although the Legal Realists were anxious to reveal law and its operations for what they were, the Legal Realists' attempts to reform the law were not so well argued as their criticisms of the law. In particular, there seems to be a tension between their advocacy of an active role for judges in using the law as a tool to promote the public interest, and their contrasting belief that law exists and can be identified as law even if it does not serve the public interest or is plainly immoral.

Most Legal Realists accepted, with Legal Positivists, that the existence of law is independent of its justification. Even poorly phrased, badly devised, or clearly immoral laws may still be laws which courts have a duty to uphold. The Legal Realists had both social scientific and political reasons to accept this view. First, the Legal Realists accepted the insight of sociology that laws change to meet changing values in the societies they govern, and so were committed to what H.L.A. Hart later called the "separation thesis" of legal positivism. Second, the Legal Realists were Americans working within the accepted framework of American constitutional democracy, and so were committed to accepting that the law is made by authority of the majority of the people, and judges have a duty to apply the law as the expression of the will of the people. This may require judges to apply laws which they personally think unjustified, but in a democracy, it is necessary that judges defer to the wishes of the people. The problem emerging here is not difficult to see. On the one hand, Legal Real-

ists wanted judges to turn the uncertainty of legal rules into an asset, by requiring judges to interpret legal rules in the way which best advanced the public interest. Yet on the other hand, the Legal Realists recognized and accepted that in a democracy the voters and not the judges ought to determine what is in the public interest. Many critics of Legal Realism think that the Legal Realists did not provide solutions to the problems they saw in the classical view of law, and instead only drew renewed attention to the difficulty of writing legal rules sufficiently clearly to ensure that in applying those laws judges advance the wishes of the public as understood not by judges but by the voting public.

These tensions in the Legal Realists' position should not be taken as detracting from the value of the assault on classical jurisprudence. We have as a lasting legacy of the Legal Realists the sense amongst lawyers, judges, legislators, and some portion of the public in common law systems that the law is not a set, unchangeable tool. Rather, as the Legal Realists' criticisms have shown, the law is a flexible instrument which can be changed and used to advance the public interest. Much of the effect Legal Realists have had on contemporary thinking about the law is a result of their tremendous influence on legal education in the United States of America in the interwar years, roughly 1920–40. During this time Legal Realists held conferences for discussion of reform of law and changed the way law was taught in law schools by bringing sociologists, economists, and others into the law schools. Some Legal Realists reached prominent positions as judges and government administrators.

5. Oliver Wendell Holmes and Jerome Frank

The authors included here are two of the foremost representatives of Legal Realism. Oliver Wendell Holmes predates the main period of Legal Realism, yet it is in his writing that some of the clearest exposition of the central themes of Legal Realism may be found. Holmes was famous in his day as a justice in the state of Massachusetts, and later as a United States Supreme Court Justice. His essay "The Path of the Law," excerpted here, was originally given as a speech at the dedication of a new law school hall at Boston University. In it may be found several of the themes discussed above, expressed in a way designed to convince the law students, lawyers, and judges who sat in the audience.

Following the selection from Holmes are two brief selections from Jerome Frank's 1930 book *Law and the Modern Mind*. The first selection is somewhat unusual. It contains the remarks Frank made in 1948 for a preface to the sixth edition of *Law and the Modern Mind*, long after the first publication of the book, after his appointment as a judge, and with the benefit of eighteen years of observation of the running debates amongst Legal Realists. This selection provides an extremely useful and interesting series of insights. Frank comments on the central doctrines of Legal Realism, the issues Legal Realists debated amongst themselves, and captures the heated nature of the debates. The second selection, "Legal Realism," provides in no uncertain terms the Legal Realist view of "the law" as a prediction of what the courts will do. This well-known selection uses a hypothetical case to illustrate the uncertainty of the law prior to its consideration by the courts.

These selections from two authors are not meant to provide a complete representation of Legal Realism. Holmes and Frank do, however, provide a good sense of the central concerns of Legal Realists, and they provide good examples of the strong, forthright style in which the Legal Realists wrote. The Legal Realists were deeply committed to reform of a system in which they all felt they had a personal stake, as judges, scholars, lawyers, and private citizens, and this commitment is reflected in the urgency of their prose.

The final selection in this chapter is taken from *Lochner v. New York* (1905). In this case Oliver Wendell Holmes delivers a famous dissenting opinion, making plain his worry that judges who claim to "find" the meaning of the law according to legal principles may in fact do something quite different. Judges often *add* to the law in various ways as they interpret it in light of their own or commonly held beliefs. In Holmes's worries and his remarks on the proper limits to judicial reasoning we can see the beginning of the Legal Realists' conviction that judges' interpretation of law is not simply a neutral practice of finding what the law means.

◆ ◆ ◆ ◆ ◆

OLIVER WENDELL HOLMES

"The Path of the Law," [1] from *The Common Law*

When we study law we are not studying a mystery but a well known profession. We are studying what we shall want in order to appear before judges, or to advise people in such a way as to keep them out of court. The reason why it is a profession, why people will pay lawyers to argue for them or to advise them, is that in societies like ours the command of the public force is intrusted to the judges in certain cases, and the whole power of the state will be put forth, if necessary, to carry out their judgments and decrees. People want to know under what circumstances and how far they will run the risk of coming against what is so much stronger than themselves, and hence it becomes a business to find out when

---

1   An Address delivered by Mr Justice Holmes, of the Supreme Judicial Court of Massachusetts, at the dedication of the new hall of the Boston University School of Law, on January 8, 1897, Copyrighted by O.W. Holmes, 1897.

this danger is to be feared. The object of our study, then, is prediction, the prediction of the incidence of the public force through the instrumentality of the court.

The means of the study are a body of reports, of treatises, and of statutes, in this country and in England, extending back for six hundred years, and now increasing annually by hundreds. In these sibylline leaves are gathered the scattered prophecies of the past upon the cases in which the axe will fall. These are what properly have been called the oracles of the law. Far the most important and pretty nearly the whole meaning of every new effort of legal thought is to make these prophecies more precise, and to generalize them into a thoroughly connected system. The process is one, from a lawyer's statement of a case, eliminating as it does all the dramatic elements with which his client's story has clothed it, and retaining only the facts of legal import, up to the final analyses and abstract universals of theoretic jurisprudence. The reason why a lawyer does not mention that his client wore a white hat when he made a contract, while Mrs. Quickly would be sure to dwell upon it along with the parcel gilt goblet and the sea-coal fire, is that he forsees that the public force will act in the same way whatever his client had upon his head. It is to make the prophecies easier to be remembered and to be understood that the teachings of the decisions of the past are put into general propositions and gathered into textbooks, or that statutes are passed in a general form. The primary rights and duties with which jurisprudence busies itself again are nothing but prophecies. One of the many evil effects of the confusion between legal and moral ideas, about which I shall have something to say in a moment, is that theory is apt to get the cart before the horse, and to consider the right or the duty as something existing apart from and independent of the consequences of its breach, to which certain sanctions are added afterward. [But, as I shall try to show, a legal duty so called is nothing but a prediction that if a man does or omits certain things he will be made to suffer in this or that way by judgment of the court;—and so of a legal right.]

• • •

The first thing for a businesslike understanding of the matter is to understand its limits, and therefore I think it desirable at once to point out and dispel a confusion between morality and law, which sometimes rises to the height of conscious theory, and more often and indeed constantly is making trouble in detail without reaching the point of consciousness. You can see very plainly that a bad man has as much reason as a good one for wishing to avoid an encounter with the public force, and therefore you can see the practical importance of the distinction between morality and law. A man who cares nothing for an ethical rule which is believed and practised by his neighbors is likely nevertheless to care a good deal to avoid being made to pay money, and will want to keep out of jail if he can.

I take it for granted that no hearer of mine will misinterpret what I have to say as the language of cynicism. The law is the witness and external deposit of our moral life. Its history is the history of the moral development of the race. The practice of it, in spite of popular jests, tends to make good citizens and good men. When I emphasize the difference between law and morals I do so with reference to a single end, that of learning and understanding the law. For that purpose you must definitely master its specific marks, and it is for that that I ask you for the moment to imagine yourselves indifferent to other and greater things.

I do not say that there is not a wider point of view from which the distinction between law and morals becomes of secondary or no importance, as all mathematical distinctions vanish in presence of the infinite. But I do say that that distinction is of the first importance for the object which we are here to consider,—a right study and mastery of the law as a business with well understood limits, a body of dogma enclosed within definite lines. I have just shown the practical reason for saying so. If you want to know the law and nothing else, you must look at it as a bad man, who cares only for the material consequences which such knowledge enables him to predict, not as a good one, who finds his reasons for conduct, whether inside the law or outside of it, in the vaguer sanctions of conscience. The theoretical importance of the distinction is no less, if you would reason on your subject aright. The law is full of phraseology drawn from morals, and by the mere force of language continually invites us to pass from one domain to the other without perceiving it, as we are sure to do unless we have the boundary constantly before our minds. The law talks about rights, and duties, and malice, and intent, and negligence, and so forth, and nothing is easier, or, I may say, more common in legal reasoning, than to take these words in their moral sense, at some stage of the argument, and so to drop into fallacy. For instance, when we speak of the rights of man in a moral sense, we mean to mark the limits of interference with individual freedom which we think are prescribed by conscience, or by our ideal, however reached. Yet it is certain that many laws have been enforced in the past, and it is likely that some are enforced now, which are condemned by the most enlightened opinion of the time, or which at all events pass the limit of interference as many consciences would draw it. Manifestly, therefore, nothing but confusion of thought can result from assuming that the rights of man in a moral sense are equally rights in the sense of the Constitution and the law. No doubt simple and extreme cases can be put of imaginable laws which the statute-making power would not dare to enact, even in the absence of written constitutional prohibitions, because the community would rise in rebellion and fight; and this gives some plausibility to the proposition that the law, if not a part of morality, is limited by it. But this limit of power is not coextensive with any system of morals. For the most part it falls far within the lines of any such system; and in some cases may

extend beyond them, for reasons drawn from the habits of a particular people at a particular time. I once heard the late Professor Agassiz say that a German population would rise if you added two cents to the price of a glass of beer. A statute in such a case would be empty words, not because it was wrong, but because it could not be enforced. No one will deny that wrong statutes can be and are enforced, and we should not all agree as to which were the wrong ones.

The confusion with which I am dealing besets confessedly legal conceptions. Take the fundamental question, What constitutes the law? You will find some text writers telling you that it is something different from what is decided by the courts of Massachusetts or England, that it is a system of reason, that it is a deduction from principles of ethics or admitted axioms or what not, which may or may not coincide with the decisions. But if we take the view of our friend the bad man we shall find that he does not care two straws for the axioms or deductions, but that he does want to know what the Massachusetts or English courts are likely to do in fact. I am much of his mind. The prophecies of what the courts will do in fact, and nothing more pretentious, are what I mean by the law.

Take again a notion which as popularly understood is the widest conception which the law contains;—the notion of legal duty, to which already I have referred. We fill the word with all the content which we draw from morals. But what does it mean to a bad man? Mainly, and in the first place, a prophecy that if he does certain things he will be subjected to disagreeable consequences by way of imprisonment or compensatory payment of money.

• • •

I mentioned, as other examples of the use by the law of words drawn from morals, malice, intent, and negligence. It is enough to take malice as it is used in the law of civil liability for wrongs,—what we lawyers call the law of torts,—to show you that it means something different in law from what it means in morals, and also to show how the difference has been obscured by giving to principles which have little or nothing to do with each other the same name. Three hundred years ago a parson preached a sermon and told a story out of Fox's Book of Martyrs of a man who had assisted at the torture of one of the saints, and afterward died, suffering compensatory inward torment. It happened that Fox was wrong. The man was alive and chanced to hear the sermon, and thereupon he sued the parson. Chief Justice Wray instructed the jury that the defendant was not liable, because the story was told innocently, without malice. He took malice in the moral sense, as importing a malevolent motive. But nowadays no one doubts that a man may be liable, without any malevolent motive at all, for false statements manifestly calculated to inflict temporal damage. In stating the case in pleading, we still should call the defendant's conduct malicious; but, in my opinion at least, the word means nothing about motives, or even about the defendant's attitude toward the future, but only signifies that the tendency of his conduct under the known circumstances was very mainly to cause the plaintiff temporal harm.[2]

* * *

So much for the limits of the law. The next thing which I wish to consider is what are the forces which determine its content and its growth. You may assume, with Hobbes and Bentham and Austin, that all law emanates from the sovereign, even when the first human beings to enunciate it are the judges, or you may think that law is the voice of the Zeitgeist, or what you like. It is all one to my present purpose. Even if every decision required the sanction of an emperor with despotic power and a whimsical turn of mind, we should be interested none the less, still with a view to prediction, in discovering some order,

some rational explanation, and some principle of growth for the rules which he laid down. In every system there are such explanations and principles to be found. It is with regard to them that a second fallacy comes in, which I think it important to expose.

The fallacy to which I refer is the notion that the only force at work in the development of the law is logical. In the broadest sense, indeed, that notion would be true. The postulate on which we think about the universe is that there is a fixed quantitative relation between every phenomenon and its antecedents and consequents. If there is such a thing as a phenomenon without these fixed quantitative relations, it is a miracle. It is outside the law of cause and effect, and as such transcends our power of thought, or at least is something to or from which we cannot reason. The condition of our thinking about the universe is that it is capable of being thought about rationally, or, in other words, that every part of it is effect and cause in the same sense in which those parts are with which we are most familiar. So in the broadest sense it is true that the law is a logical development, like everything else. The danger of which I speak is not the admission that the principles governing other phenomena also govern the law, but the notion that a given system, ours, for instance, can be worked out like mathematics from some general axioms of conduct. This is the natural error of the schools, but it is not confined to them. I once heard a very eminent judge say that he never let a decision go until he was absolutely sure that it was right. So judicial dissent often is blamed, as if it meant simply that one side or the other were not doing their sums right, and, if they would take more trouble, agreement inevitably would come.

This mode of thinking is entirely natural. The training of lawyers is a training in logic. The processes of analogy, discrimination, and deduction are those in which they are most at home. The language of judicial decision is mainly the language of logic. And the logical method and form flatter that longing for certainty and for repose which is in every

2   See Hanson *v* Globe Newspaper Co., 159 Mass. 293, 302.

human mind. But certainty generally is illusion, and repose is not the destiny of man. Behind the logical form lies a judgment as to the relative worth and importance of competing legislative grounds, often an inarticulate and unconscious judgment, it is true, and yet the very root and nerve of the whole proceeding. You can give any conclusion a logical form. You always can imply a condition in a contract. But why do you imply it? It is because of some belief as to the practice of the community or of a class, or because of some opinion as to policy, or, in short, because of some attitude of yours upon a matter not capable of exact quantitative measurement, and therefore not capable of founding exact logical conclusions. Such matters really are battle grounds where the means do not exist for determinations that shall be good for all time, and where the decision can do no more than embody the preference of a given body in a given time and place. We do not realize how large a part of our law is open to reconsideration upon a slight change in the habit of the public mind. No concrete proposition is self-evident, no matter how ready we may be to accept it, not even Mr. Herbert Spencer's. Every man has a right to do what he wills, provided he interferes not with a like right on the part of his neighbors.

Why is a false and injurious statement privileged, if it is made honestly in giving information about a servant? It is because it has been thought more important that information should be given freely, than that a man should be protected from what under other circumstances would be an actionable wrong. Why is a man at liberty to set up a business which he knows will ruin his neighbor? It is because the public good is supposed to be best subserved by free competition. Obviously such judgments of relative importance may vary in different times and places. Why does a judge instruct a jury that an employer is not liable to an employee for an injury received in the course of his employment unless he is negligent, and why do the jury generally find for the plaintiff if the case is allowed to go to them? It is because the traditional policy of our law is to confine liability to cases where a prudent man might have foreseen the injury, or at least the danger, while the inclination of a very large part of the community is to make certain classes of persons insure the safety of those with whom they deal. Since the last words were written, I have seen the requirement of such insurance put forth as part of the programme of one of the best known labor organizations. There is a concealed, half conscious battle on the question of legislative policy, and if any one thinks that it can be settled deductively, or once for all, I only can say that I think he is theoretically wrong, and that I am certain that his conclusion will not be accepted in practice *semper ubique et ab omnibus*.

• • •

At present, in very many cases, if we want to know why a rule of law has taken its particular shape, and more or less if we want to know why it exists at all, we go to tradition. We follow it into the Year Books, and perhaps beyond them to the customs of the Salian Franks, and somewhere in the past, in the German forests, in the needs of Norman kings, in the assumptions of a dominant class, in the absence of generalized ideas, we find out the practical motive for what now best is justified by the mere fact of its acceptance and that men are accustomed to it. The rational study of law is still to a large extent the study of history. History must be a part of the study, because without it we cannot know the precise scope of rules which it is our business to know. It is a part of the rational study, because it is the first step toward an enlightened scepticism, that is, toward a deliberate reconsideration of the worth of those rules. When you get the dragon out of his cave on to the plain and in the daylight, you can count his teeth and claws, and see just what is his strength. But to get him out is only the first step. The next is either to kill him, or tame him and make him a useful animal. For the rational study of the law the black-letter man may be the man of the present, but the man of the future is the man of statistics and the master of economics. It is revolting to have no better reason for a rule of law than that so it was laid down in the time of Henry IV. It is still more revolting if the grounds upon which it was laid down have vanished long since, and the rule simply persists from blind imitation of the past ...

• • •

I trust that no one will understand me to be speaking with disrespect of the law, because I criticise it so freely. I venerate the law, and especially our system of law, as one of the vastest products of the human mind. No one knows better than I do the countless number of great intellects that have spent themselves in making some addition or improvement, the greatest of which is trifling when compared with the mighty whole. It has the final title to respect that it exists, that it is not a Hegelian dream, but a part of the lives of men. But one may criticise even what one reveres. Law is the business to which my life is devoted, and I should show less than devotion if I did not do what in me lies to improve it, and, when I perceive what seems to me the ideal of its future, if I hesitated to point it out and to press toward it with all my heart.

♦ ♦ ♦ ♦ ♦

JEROME FRANK

"Preface to Sixth Printing," *Law and the Modern Mind*

Said Bernard Shaw in his 1913 preface to his book, "The Quintessence of Ibsenism," originally published in 1891: "In the pages which follow I have made no attempt to tamper with the work of the bygone man of thirty-five who wrote them. I have never admitted the right of an elderly author to alter the work of a young author, even when the young author happens to be himself." I am no Shaw, but, in penning this preface to a new printing of a book I published in 1930, I echo his sentiments.

I confess, however, that I would not today write that book precisely as I wrote it eighteen years ago. For one thing, I seriously blundered when I offered my own definition of the word Law. Since that word drips with ambiguity, there were already at least a dozen defensible definitions. To add one more was vanity. Worse, I found myself promptly assailed by other Law-definers who, in turn, differed with one another. A more futile, time-consuming contest is scarcely imaginable. Accordingly, I promptly backed out of that silly word battle. In 1931, I published an article in which I said that, in any future writing on the subject-matter of this book, I would, when possible, shun the use of the word Law; instead I would state directly—without an intervening definition of that term—what I was writing about, namely (1) specific court decisions, (2) how little they are predictable and uniform, (3) the process by which they are made, and (4) how far, in the interest of justice to citizens, that process can and should be improved. I wish I had followed that procedure in this book. I trust that the reader, whenever he comes upon "Law," will understand that (as I said at the end of Chapter V in Part One) I meant merely to talk of actual past decisions, or guesses about future decisions, of specific lawsuits.

I made another blunder, leading to misunderstandings, when I employed the phrase "legal realism" to label the position, concerning the work of the courts, which I took in this book. That phrase I had enthusiastically borrowed from my friend Karl Llewellyn. He had used it to designate the views of a number of American lawyers who, each in his own way, during the first two decades of this century had in their writings expressed doubts about one or another of the traditional notions of matters legal. But, in 1931, less than a year after this book appeared, I published an article stating regrets at the use of this label, because, among other things, "realism," in philosophic discourse, has an accepted meaning wholly unrelated to the views of the so-called "legal realists." I then suggested that the legal realists be called "constructive skeptics," and their attitude, "constructive skepticism."[1]

There was a more cogent reason for regretting the use of "realists" as a method of ticketing these legal skeptics. The label enabled some of their critics to bracket the realists as a homogeneous "school," in virtual accord with one another on all or most subjects. This misconception—not certainly the result of any careful reading of their works—led to the specious charge that the "realistic school" embraced fantastically inconsistent ideas. Actually no such "school" existed. In the article mentioned above, I referred to one critic's use of this lumping-together method as follows: "It may be roughly described thus: (1) Jones disagrees with Smith about the tariff. (2) Robinson disagrees with Smith about the virtues of sauerkraut juice. (3) Since both Jones and Robinson disagree with Smith about something, it follows that (a) each disagrees with Smith about everything, and that (b) Jones and Robinson agree with one another about the tariff, the virtues of sauerkraut juice, the League of Nations, the quantity theory of money, vitalism, Bernard Shaw, Proust, Lucky Strikes, Communism, Will Rogers—and everything else. Llewellyn, Green, Cook, Yntema, Oliphant, Hutcheson, Bingham, and Frank in their several ways have expressed disagreement with conventional legal theory. Dickinson therefore assumes (a) that they disagree with that theory for identical reasons; and (b) that they agree with one another on their proposed substitutes for that theory. It is as if he were to assume that all men leaving Chicago at a given instant were going north and were bound for the same town. Dickinson has produced a composite photograph of the writers he is discussing. One sees, so to speak, the hair of Green, the eyebrows of Yntema, the teeth of Cook, the neck of Oliphant, the lips of Llewellyn.... The picture is the image of an unreal imaginary creature, of a strange, misshapen, infertile, hybrid."

Actually, these so-called realists have but one common bond, a negative characteristic already noted: skepticism as to some of the conventional legal theories, a skepticism stimulated by a zeal to reform, in the interest of justice, some court-house ways. Despite the lack of any homogeneity in their positive views, these "constructive skeptics," roughly speaking, do divide into two groups; however, there are marked differences, ignored by the critics, between the two groups.

The first group, of whom Llewellyn is perhaps the outstanding representative, I would call "rule skeptics." They aim at greater legal certainty. That is, they consider it socially desirable that lawyers should be able to predict to their clients the decisions in most lawsuits not yet commenced. They feel that, in too many instances, the layman cannot act with assurance as to how, if his acts become involved in a suit, the court will decide. As these skeptics see it, the trouble is that the formal legal rules enunciated in courts' opinions—sometimes called "paper rules"—too often prove unreliable as guides in the prediction of decisions. They believe that they can discover, behind the "paper rules," some "real rules" descriptive of uniformities or regularities in actual judicial behavior, and that those "real rules" will serve as more reliable prediction—instruments, yielding a large measure of workable predictability of the outcome of future suits. In this undertaking, the rule skeptics concentrate almost exclusively on upper-court opinions. They do not ask themselves whether their own or any other prediction-device will render it possible for a lawyer or layman to prophesy, before an ordinary suit is instituted or comes to trial in a trial court, how it will be decided. In other words, these rule skeptics seek means for making accurate guesses, not about decisions of trial courts, but about

---

1   In an article published in 1933, I suggested that the "realists" might be named "experimentalists."

decisions of upper courts when trial-court decisions are appealed. These skeptics cold-shoulder the trial courts. Yet, in most instances, these skeptics do not inform their readers that they are writing chiefly of upper courts.

The second group I would call "fact skeptics." They, too, engaging in "rule skepticism," peer behind the "paper rules." Together with the rule skeptics, they have stimulated interest in factors, influencing upper-court decisions, of which, often, the opinions of those courts give no hint. But the fact skeptics go much further. Their primary interest is in the trial courts. No matter how precise or definite may be the formal legal rules, say these fact skeptics, no matter what the discoverable uniformities behind these formal rules, nevertheless it is impossible, and will always be impossible, because of the elusiveness of the facts on which decisions turn, to predict future decisions in most (not all) lawsuits, not yet begun or not yet tried. The fact skeptics, thinking that therefore the pursuit of greatly increased legal certainty is, for the most part, futile—and that its pursuit, indeed, may well work injustice—aim rather at increased judicial justice. This group of fact skeptics includes, among others, Dean Leon Green, Max Radin, Thurman Arnold, William O. Douglas (now Mr. Justice Douglas), and perhaps E.M. Morgan.

Within each of these groups there is diversity of opinion as to many ideas. But I think it can be said that, generally, most of the rule skeptics, restricting themselves to the upper-court level, live in an artificial two-dimensional legal world, while the legal world of the fact skeptics is three-dimensional. Obviously, many events occurring in the fact skeptics' three-dimensional cosmos are out of sight, and therefore out of mind, in the rule skeptics' cosmos.

The critical anti-skeptics also live in the artificial upper-court world. Naturally, they have found less fault with the rule skeptics than with the fact skeptics. The critics, for instance, said that Llewellyn was a bit wild, yet not wholly unsound, but that men like Dean Green grossly exaggerated the extent of legal

uncertainty (i.e., the unpredictability of decisions). To my mind, the critics shoe the wrong foot: Both the rule skeptics and the critics grossly exaggerate the extent of legal certainty, because their own writings deal only with the prediction of upper-court decisions. The rule skeptics are, indeed, but the left-wing adherents of a tradition. It is from the tradition itself that the fact skeptics revolted.

As a reading of this book will disclose, I am one of the fact skeptics ... The point there made may be summarized thus: If one accepts as correct the conventional description of how courts reach their decisions, then a decision of any lawsuit results from the application of a legal rule or rules to the facts of the suit. That sounds rather simple, and apparently renders it fairly easy to prophesy the decision, even of a case not yet commenced or tried, especially when, as often happens, the applicable rule is definite and precise (for instance, the rule about driving on the right side of the road). But, particularly when pivotal testimony at the trial is oral and conflicting, as it is in most lawsuits, the trial court's "finding" of the facts involves a multitude of elusive factors: First, the trial judge in a nonjury trial or the jury in a jury trial must learn about the facts from the witnesses; and witnesses, being humanly fallible, frequently make mistakes in observation of what they saw and heard, or in their recollections of what they observed, or in their court-room reports of those recollections. Second, the trial judges or juries, also human, may have prejudices—often unconscious, unknown even to themselves—for or against some of the witnesses, or the parties to the suit, or the lawyers.

Those prejudices, when they are racial, religious, political, or economic, may sometimes be surmised by others. But there are some hidden, unconscious biases of trial judges or jurors—such as, for example, plus or minus reactions to women, or unmarried women, or red-haired women, or brunettes, or men with deep voices or high-pitched voices, or fidgety men, or men who wear thick eye-glasses, or those who have pronounced gestures or nervous tics—

biases of which no one can be aware. Concealed and highly idiosyncratic, such biases—peculiar to each individual judge or juror—cannot be formulated as uniformities or squeezed into regularized "behavior patterns." In that respect, neither judges nor jurors are standardized.

The chief obstacle to prophesying a trial-court decision is, then, the inability, thanks to these inscrutable factors, to foresee what a particular trial judge or jury will believe to be the facts. Consider, particularly, the perplexity of a lawyer asked to guess the outcome of a suit not yet commenced: He must guess whether some of the witnesses will persuasively lie, or will honestly but persuasively give inaccurate testimony; as, usually, he does not even know the trial judge or jury who will try the case, he must also guess the reactions—to the witnesses, the parties and the lawyers—of an unknown trial judge or jury.

These difficulties have been overlooked by most of those (the rule skeptics included) who write on the subject of legal certainty or the prediction of decisions. They often call their writings "jurisprudence"; but, as they almost never consider juries and jury trials, one might chide them for forgetting "juriesprudence."

◆ ◆ ◆ ◆ ◆

JEROME FRANK

"Legal Realism," from *Law and the Modern Mind*

We have talked much of the law. But what is "the law"? A complete definition would be impossible and even a working definition would exhaust the patience of the reader. But it may not be amiss to inquire what, in a rough sense, the law means to the average man of our times when he consults his lawyer.

The Jones family owned the Blue & Gray Taxi Company, a corporation incorporated in Kentucky. That company made a contract with the A. & B. Railroad Company, also a Kentucky corporation, by which it was agreed that the Blue & Gray Taxi Company was to have the exclusive privilege of soliciting taxi-cab business on and adjacent to the railroad company's depot.

A rival taxi-cab company, owned by the Williams family, the Purple Taxi Company, began to ignore this contract; it solicited business and parked its taxi-cabs in places assigned by the railroad company to the Blue & Gray Company and sought in other ways to deprive the Blue & Gray Company of the benefits conferred on it by the agreement with the railroad.

The Jones family were angered; their profits derived from the Blue & Gray stock, which they owned, were threatened. They consulted their lawyer, a Louisville practitioner, and this, we may conjecture, is about what he told them: "I'm afraid your contract is not legally valid. I've examined several decisions of the highest court of Kentucky and they pretty clearly indicate that you can't get away with that kind of an agreement in this state. The Kentucky court holds such a contract to be bad as creating an unlawful monopoly. But I'll think the matter over. You come back tomorrow and I'll try meanwhile to find some way out."

So, next day, the Joneses returned. And this time their lawyer said he thought he had discovered how to get the contract sustained: "You see, it's this way. In most courts, except those of Kentucky and of a few other states, an agreement like this is perfectly good. But, unfortunately, as things now stand, you'll have to go into the Kentucky courts.

"If we can manage to get our case tried in the Federal court, there's a fair chance that we'll get a different result, because I think the Federal court will follow the majority rule and not the Kentucky rule. I'm not sure of that, but it's worth trying.

"So this is what we'll do. We'll form a new Blue & Gray Company in Tennessee. And your Kentucky Blue & Gray Company will transfer all its assets to the new Tennessee Blue & Gray Company. Then we'll have the railroad company execute a new contract with the new Tennessee Blue & Gray Company, and at the same time cancel the old contract and, soon after, dissolve the old Kentucky Blue & Gray Company."

"But," interrupted one of the Joneses, "what good will all that monkey-business do?"

The lawyer smiled broadly. "Just this," he replied with pride in his cleverness. "The A.& B. Railroad Company is organized in Kentucky. So is the Purple Taxi which we want to get at. The Federal court will treat these companies as if they were citizens of Kentucky. Now a corporation which is a citizen of Kentucky can't bring this kind of suit in the Federal court against other corporations which are also citizens of Kentucky. But if your company becomes a Tennessee corporation, it will be considered as if it were a citizen of Tennessee. Then your new Tennessee company can sue the other two in the Federal court, because the suit will be held to be one between citizens of different states. And that kind of suit, based on what we lawyers call "diversity of citizenship," can be brought in the Federal court by a corporation which organized in Tennessee against corporations which are citizens of another State, Kentucky. And the Federal court, as I said, ought to sustain your contract."

"That sounds pretty slick," said one of the Joneses admiringly. "Are you sure it will work?"

"No," answered the lawyer. "You can't ever be absolutely sure about such a plan. I can't find any case completely holding our way on all these facts. But I'm satisfied that's the law and that that's the way the Federal court ought to decide. I won't guarantee success. But I recommend trying out my suggestion."

His advice was followed. Shortly after the new Tennessee Blue & Gray Company was organized and had entered into the new contract, suit was brought by the Joneses' new Blue & Gray Corporation of Tennessee in the Federal District Court against the competing Purple Company and the railroad company. In this suit, the Blue & Gray Taxi Company of Tennessee asked the court to prevent interference with the carrying out of its railroad contract.

As the Joneses' lawyer had hoped, the Federal court held, against the protest of the Purple Company's lawyer, first that such a suit could be brought in the Federal court and, second, that the contract was valid. Accordingly the court enjoined the Purple Company from interfering with the depot business of the Joneses' Blue & Gray Company. The Joneses were elated, for now their profits seemed once more assured.

But not for long. The other side appealed the case to the Federal Circuit Court of Appeals. And the Joneses' lawyer was somewhat worried that that court might reverse the lower Federal court. But it didn't and the Joneses again were happy.[1]

Still the Purple Company persisted. It took the case to the Supreme Court of the United States. That Court consists of nine judges. And the Joneses' lawyer couldn't be certain just how those judges would line up on all the questions involved. "Some new men on the bench, and you never can tell about Holmes and Brandeis. They're very erratic," was his comment.

When the United States Supreme Court gave its decision, it was found that six of the nine judges agreed with counsel for the Joneses. Three justices (Holmes, Brandeis, and Stone) were of the contrary opinion. But the majority governs in the United States Supreme Court, and the Joneses' prosperity was at last firmly established.

Now what was "the law" for the Joneses, who owned the Blue & Gray Company, and the William-

---

1   The case discussed in the text and especially the conversations there quoted are suppositions. But the questions involved are very nearly those involved in *Black & White Taxi & T. Co.* v. *Brown & Yellow Taxi & T. Co.*, 276 U.S. 518.

ses, who owned the Purple Company? The answer will depend on the date of the question. If asked before the new Tennessee company acquired the contract, it might have been said that it was almost surely "the law" that the Joneses would lose; for any suit involving the validity of that contract could then have been brought only in the Kentucky state court and the prior decisions of that court seemed adverse to such an agreement.

After the suggestion of the Joneses' lawyer was carried out and the new Tennessee corporation owned the contract, "the law" was more doubtful. Many lawyers would have agreed with the Joneses' lawyer that there was a good chance that the Jones family would be victorious if suit were brought in the Federal courts. But probably an equal number would have disagreed: they would have said that the formation of the new Tennessee company was a trick used to get out of the Kentucky courts and into the Federal court, a trick of which the Federal court would not approve. Or that, regardless of that question, the Federal court would follow the well-settled Kentucky rule as to the invalidity of such contracts as creating unlawful monopolies (especially because the use of Kentucky real estate was involved) and that therefore the Federal court would decide against the Joneses.[2] "The law," at any time before the decision of the United States Supreme Court, was indeed unsettled.[3] No one could know what the court would decide. Would it follow the Kentucky cases? If so, the law was that no "rights" were conferred by the contract. Would it refuse to follow the Kentucky cases? If so, rights were conferred by the contract. To speak of settled law governing that controversy, or of the fixed legal rights of those parties, as antedating

the decision of the Supreme Court, is mere verbiage. If two more judges on that bench had agreed with Justices Holmes, Brandeis and Stone, the law and the rights of the parties would have been of a directly opposite kind.

After the decision, "the law" was fixed. There were no other courts to which an appeal could be directed. The judgment of the United States Supreme Court could not be disturbed and the legal "rights" of the Joneses and the Williamses were everlastingly established.

We may now venture a rough definition of law from the point of view of the average man: For any particular lay person, the law, with respect to any particular set of facts, is a decision of a court with respect to those facts so far as that decision affects that particular person. Until a court has passed on those facts no law on that subject is yet in existence. Prior to such a decision, the only law available is the opinion of lawyers as to the law relating to that person and to those facts. Such opinion is not actually law but only a guess as to what a court will decide.[4]

Law, then, as to any given situation is either (a) actual law, i.e., a specific past decision, as to that situation,[5] or (b) probable law, i.e., a guess as to a specific future decision.

Usually when a client consults his lawyer about "the law," his purpose is to ascertain not what courts have actually decided in the past but what the courts will probably decide in the future. He asks, "Have I a right, as a stockholder of the American Taffy Company of Indiana, to look at the corporate books?" Or, "Do I have to pay an inheritance tax to the State

---

2 This was what three of the justices of the United States Supreme Court (Holmes, Brandeis and Stone) did hold to be the law.

3 That is, it was unsettled whether the Williamses had the energy, patience and money to push an appeal. If not, then the decision of the lower Federal court was the actual settled law for the Jones and Williams families.

4 The United States Supreme Court has wittily been called the "court of ultimate conjecture."

5 That is, a past decision in a case which has arisen between the specific persons in question as to the specific facts in question. Even a past decision fixes the rights of the parties to the suit only to a limited extent. In other words, what a court has actually decided as between the parties may in part still be open to question by other courts and therefore may continue to be the subject of guesses.

of New York on bonds left me by my deceased wife, if our residence was in Ohio, but the bonds, at the time of her death, were in a safety deposit box in New York?" Or, "Is there a right of "peaceful" picketing in a strike in the State of California?" Or, "If Jones sells me his Chicago shoe business and agrees not to compete for ten years, will the agreement be binding?" The answers (although they may run "There is such a right," "The law is that the property is not taxable," "Such picketing is unlawful," "The agreement is not legally binding") are in fact prophecies or predictions of judicial action.[6] It is from this point of view that the practice of law has been aptly termed an art of prediction.

Actual specific past *decisions*, and guesses as to actual specific future *decisions*. Is that how lawyers customarily define the law? Not at all.

◆ ◆ ◆ ◆ ◆

6   The emphasis in this book on the conduct of judges is admittedly artificial. Lawyers and their clients are vitally concerned with the ways of all governmental officials and with the reactions of non-official persons to the ways of judges and other officials. There is a crying need in the training of lawyers for clear and unashamed recognition and study of all these phenomena as part of the legitimate business of lawyers.

But one job at a time. Inasmuch as the major portion of a lawyer's time is today devoted to predicting or bringing about decisions of judges, the law considered in this book is "court law." "Actual law" and "probable law" here discussed mean "actual or probable court law." This limitation, while artificial, is perhaps the more excusable because it roughly corresponds to the notion of the contemporary layman when consulting his lawyer.

Of course, anyone can define "law" as he pleases. The word "law" is ambiguous and it might be well if we could abolish it. But until a substitute is invented, it seems not improper to apply it to that which is central in the work of the practising lawyer. *This book is primarily concerned with "law" as it affects the work of the practising lawyer and the needs of the clients who retain him.*

From that point of view, court law may roughly be defined as *specific past or future judicial decisions which are enforced or complied with.*

Lochner v. New York (1905)

Mr. Justice Peckham:

... The indictment, it will be seen, charges that the plaintiff in error violated the 110th section of article 8, chapter 415, of the Laws of 1897, known as the labor law of the state of New York, in that he wrongfully and unlawfully required and permitted an employee working for him to work more than sixty hours in one week. There is nothing in any of the opinions delivered in this case, either in the supreme court or the court of appeals of the state, which construes the section, in using the word "required," as referring to any physical force being used to obtain the labor of an employee. It is assumed that the word means nothing more than the requirement arising from voluntary contract for such labor in excess of the number of hours specified in the statute. There is no pretense in any of the opinions that the statute was intended to meet a case of involuntary labor in any form. All the opinions assume that there is no real distinction, so far as this question is concerned, between the words "required" and "permitted." The mandate of the statute, that "no employee shall be required or permitted to work," is the substantial equivalent of an enactment that "no employee shall contract or agree to work," more than ten hours per day; and, as there is no provision for special emergencies, the statute is mandatory in all cases. It is not an act merely fixing the number of hours which shall constitute a legal day's work, but an absolute prohibition upon the employer permitting, under any circumstances, more than ten hours' work to be done in his establishment. The employee may desire to earn the extra money which would arise from his working more than the prescribed time, but this statute forbids the employer from permitting the employee to earn it.

The statute necessarily interferes with the right of contract between the employer and employees, concerning the number of hours in which the latter may labor in the bakery of the employer. The general right to make a contract in relation to his business is part of the liberty of the individual protected by the 14th Amendment of the Federal Constitution. *Allgeyer v. Louisiana*, 165 U.S. 578, 41 L. ed. 832, 17 Sup. Ct. Rep. 427. Under that provision no state can deprive any person of life, liberty, or property without due process of law. The right to purchase or to sell labor is part of the liberty protected by this amendment, unless there are circumstances which exclude the right. There are, however, certain powers, existing in the sovereignty of each state in the Union, somewhat vaguely termed police powers, the exact description and limitation of which have not been attempted by the courts. Those powers, broadly stated, and without, at present, any attempt at a more specific limitation, relate to the safety, health, morals, and general welfare of the public. Both property and liberty are held on such reasonable conditions as may be imposed by the governing power of the state in the exercise of those powers, and with such conditions the 14th Amendment was not designed to interfere. *Mugler v. Kansas*, 123 U.S. 623, 31 L. ed. 205, 8 Sup. Ct. Rep. 273; *Re Kemmler*, 136 U.S. 436, 34 L. ed. 519, 10 Sup. Ct. Rep. 930; *Crowley v. Christensen*, 137 U.S. 86, 34 L. ed. 620, 11 Sup. Ct. Rep. 13; *Re Converse*, 137 U.S. 624, 34 L. ed. 796, 11 Sup. Ct. Rep. 191.

The state, therefore, has power to prevent the individual from making certain kinds of contracts, and in regard to them the Federal Constitution offers no protection. If the contract be one which the state, in the legitimate exercise of its police power, has the right to prohibit, it is not prevented from prohibiting it by the 14th Amendment. Contracts in violation of a statute, either of the Federal or state government, or a contract to let one's property for immoral purposes, or to do any other unlawful act, could obtain no protection from the Federal Constitution, as coming under the liberty of person or of free contract. Therefore, when the state, by its

legislature, in the assumed exercise of its police powers, has passed an act which seriously limits the right to labor or the right of contract in regard to their means of livelihood between persons who are *sui juris* (both employer and employee), it becomes of great importance to determine which shall prevail,—the right of the individual to labor for such time as he may choose, or the right of the state to prevent the individual from laboring, or from entering into any contract to labor, beyond a certain time prescribed by the state....

Mr. Justice Holmes dissenting:

I regret sincerely that I am unable to agree with the judgment in this case, and that I think it my duty to express my dissent.

This case is decided upon an economic theory which a large part of the country does not entertain. If it were a question whether I agreed with that theory, I should desire to study it further and long before making up my mind. But I do not conceive that to be my duty, because I strongly believe that my agreement or disagreement has nothing to do with the right of a majority to embody their opinions in law. It is settled by various decisions of this court that state constitutions and state laws may regulate life in many ways which we as legislators might think as injudicious, or if you like as tyrannical, as this, and which, equally with this, interfere with the liberty to contract. Sunday laws and usury laws are ancient examples. A more modern one is the prohibition of lotteries. The liberty of the citizen to do as he likes so long as he does not interfere with the liberty of others to do the same, which has been a shibboleth for some well-known writers, is interfered with by school laws, by the Postoffice, by every state or municipal institution which takes his money for purposes thought desirable, whether he likes it or not. The 14th Amendment does not enact Mr. Herbert Spencer's Social Statics. The other day we sustained the Massachusetts vaccination law. *Jacobson v. Massachusetts*, 197 U.S. 11, 25 Sup. Ct.

Rep. 358, 49 L. ed.—United States and state statutes and decisions cutting down the liberty to contract by way of combination are familiar to this court. *Northern Securities Co. v. United States*, 193 U.S. 197, 48 L. ed. 679, 24 Sup. Ct. Rep. 436. Two years ago we upheld the prohibition of sales of stock on margins, or for future delivery, in the Constitution of California. *Otis v. Parker*, 187 U.S. 608, 47 L. ed. 323, 23 Sup. Ct. Rep. 168. The decision sustaining an eight-hour law for miners is still recent. *Holden v. Hardy*, 169 U.S. 366, 42 L. ed. 780, 18 Sup. Ct. Rep. 383. Some of these laws embody convictions or prejudices which judges are likely to share. Some may not. But a Constitution is not intended to embody a particular economic theory, whether of paternalism and the organic relation of the citizen to the state or of *laissez faire*. It is made for people of fundamentally differing views, and the accident of our finding certain opinions natural and familiar, or novel, and even shocking, ought not to conclude our judgment upon the question whether statutes embodying them conflict with the Constitution of the United States. General propositions do not decide concrete cases. The decision will depend on a judgment or intuition more subtle than any articulate major premise. But I think that the proposition just stated, if it is accepted, will carry us far toward the end. Every opinion tends to become a law. I think that the word "liberty," in the 14th Amendment, is perverted when it is held to prevent the natural outcome of a dominant opinion, unless it can be said that a rational and fair man necessarily would admit that the statute proposed would infringe fundamental principles as they have been understood by the traditions of our people and our law. It does not need research to show that no such sweeping condemnation can be passed upon the statute before us. A reasonable man might think it a proper measure on the score of health. Men whom I certainly could not pronounce unreasonable would uphold it as a first instalment of a general regulation of the hours of work. Whether in the latter aspect it would be open to the charge of inequality I think it unnecessary to discuss.

• • • • • •

STUDY QUESTIONS

1. Why does Holmes suppose the view of the "bad man" provides an answer to the question "What is law?"

2. Is Frank's refusal to offer a *definition* of law justifiable? Why or why not?

3. Is Frank's answer to the question "What is law?" *complete*? If not, what elements must be added?

4. What, if anything, is wrongly omitted from a realist picture of law which focuses on the operations of courts, as Holmes and Frank do?

• • • • • •

FURTHER READINGS

Benjamin N. Cardozo, *The Nature of the Judicial Process*. New Haven: Yale University Press, 1921.

Neil Duxbury, *Patterns of American Jurisprudence*. Oxford: Clarendon Press, 1995.

William W. Fisher, Morton J. Horwitz and Thomas A. Reed, eds. *American Legal Realism*. Oxford: Oxford University Press, 1993.

John Chipman Gray, *The Nature and Sources of the Law*. New York: Columbia University Press, 1909.

Brian Leiter, "American Legal Realism" in Martin Golding and William Edmundson, eds. *The Blackwell Guide to the Philosophy of Law and Legal Theory*. Oxford: Blackwell, 2004.

Karl Llewellyn, *Bramble Bush: On our Law and its Study*. Oxford: Oceana Publications, 1960.

CHAPTER 5

Recent Developments: Feminist Jurisprudence and Critical Race Theory

INTRODUCTION

This chapter contains work from the feminist jurisprudence movement, and the Critical Race Theory movement. These movements share certain features, so while we shall discuss each movement independently, it may be helpful to begin with a short list of similarities.

First, both movements are relatively new. Feminist jurisprudence is rooted in the feminist movement which first flourished in the 1960s. Critical Race Theory or "CRT" gained its name in 1989, drawing on the Critical Legal Studies or "CLS" movement which emerged from a conference held in Madison, Wisconsin in the summer of 1977. The conference brought together a group of lawyers, law professors, sociologists and anthropologists who shared generally socialist leanings and great dissatisfaction with prevailing views of law and legal practice—particularly views which apparently ignore the extent to which law is an embodiment of the interests of the most powerful persons in a given society. The Critical Legal Studies movement is nearly exclusively American, yet its main criticisms of law in American society could in principle be advanced against any of the other common law societies. Since the initial conference in 1977, in journals and in subsequent conferences the CLS writers have developed a vast literature criticizing and advocating reform in nearly

all areas of law, from legal education to the courts, to revision of criminal and civil law. In recent years, however, the CLS movement seems to have lost its sense of urgency and unity, perhaps because writers sympathetic to CLS have not been concerned with developing a CLS theory of law in general. They have focused instead on application of CLS insights across a wide range of specific areas of jurisprudence. You can see an example of this tendency in the work of Martti Koskenniemi on international law, included in Section IV of this book.

Second, both feminist jurisprudence and CRT movements are composed largely of "outsiders on the inside" of law schools and universities, united in their concern to understand the gap between the ideals taught in law schools, and the actual consequences of life under law. These movements began from the "outsider" observation that important aspects of lived experience are ignored by academic treatment of law, and insist that individuals' experience of law in the world must be better accounted for by law and legal theory.

Third, both movements are skeptical of "conceptual" jurisprudence of the sort done by positivists and natural lawyers. Taking a position reminiscent of the American Legal Realists, many feminist and CRT scholars are skeptical of the possibility of "objective" or "neutral" analysis of legal concepts such as legal norms, legal duties, legal rights, property, and harm. According to feminists, the law and legal concepts reflect a distinctively male or "patriarchal" view of the world. According to Critical Legal Studies scholars the law and legal concepts reflect a certain narrow group of political values—an insight they derive from Marxist thought. Critical Race Theory accepts this insight, then turns it on its head, asking us to examine not just the way class or group interests influence law, but the way law affects the specific lived experience of individual members of a particular group, such as minorities of color. We then find, CRT scholars argue, that apparently neutral legal concepts are often interpreted and applied in ways which reinforce the interests of elites. Some CRT writers go so far as to argue that key legal concepts are indeterminate, lacking fixed edges to their meaning and application. They point to various examples of indeterminate legal concepts whose application in practice shows little about any possible determinate "core" meaning of the term, and much more about the interests of those with power to apply the concept in practice. The idea of legal equality, for example, is sometimes interpreted in a "color-blind" or "difference-blind" fashion as though that will ensure that minorities of color are not singled out for discrimination. Yet this "blindness" is in fact discriminatory in its own way, as it ignores the fact that African-American women differ from African-American men in their needs, experiences and opportunities, and the needs and experience of African-Americans may differ from the needs and experience of Hispanic-Americans and other minorities of color. Legal concepts such as equality must be interpreted and applied much differently if they are to be more than tools of elite interests.

Fourth, feminist jurisprudence and CRT writers agree that race and gender have been mistakenly viewed as topics at the edge of jurisprudence, worth considering only once core tasks in conceptual jurisprudence are complete. Feminist and CRT writers hold the opposite view: race and gender should be at the center of jurisprudence, since race and gender are at the center of the assumptions of the elites who control the structure and practice of law in ways which distort and undervalue the experience and needs of women and minorities of color. This insight is the key to another, closely associated insight. The centrality of race and gender to elite conceptions of law means that racist and male-serving legal structures and practices are not occasional mis-steps in the life of legal systems. Instead, feminists and CRT writers argue, racist and male-centered social structures and law are the norm—a state of affairs which needs to change, but until that time of change, stands as the ordinary, normal social situation.

Fifth, each movement holds that the political and legal spheres of public life are not separable. The orthodox view holds that politics ends once legislation is enacted. After that point, the will of the legislative body is captured in a legal rule with determinate content and meaning, applied by politically neutral judges who merely enforce the will of the legislative body. Yet according to feminist jurisprudence and Critical Race Theory scholars, the making of law and the application of law are never distinct. In fact, judges' application of law frequently reflects the fact that judges come from the same social class or gender or race as legislators and share legislators' views about the values which ought to be supported by the courts. Feminist jurisprudence shares with American Legal Realism the conviction that more attention must be paid to the people and institutions which apply laws, and more attention must be paid to the impossibility of achieving politically neutral interpretation and application of legal norms.

Sixth, both feminists and CLS scholars look to history and social science for evidence that law, legal concepts, and legal institutions contain biases against certain groups or interests. Evidence from disciplines such as sociology and criminology show that gender, class and ethnic differences between rulers and ruled are large, even in common law societies whose laws and democratic systems promote equality of opportunity and do not explicitly give any one group privileges not equally available to any other group.

Seventh, and linked to the sixth similarity, feminists and Critical Race Theory writers are concerned with the *substantive* effect of law more than its *formal* appearance. This is a crucial point. Where orthodox legal theory often proceeds on the assumption that the institutions and language of the law are very closely related to what in fact happens in the world, feminists and Critical Race Theory scholars argue that there is often a great difference between the formal language and apparatus of the law and the actual practical, or substantive, effect of law. Both movements point to equality rights to illustrate this point: despite the introduction of equality rights in common law systems, women and minorities have not in fact achieved effective, substantive equality with men in daily life. At best, only partial progress has been made toward the state of equality required by law. Reflection on the reasons behind the failure of "color-blind" and "gender-blind" attempts to achieve equality may even cause us to doubt the value of the ideal of equality as the best means to justice for all. Perhaps we need something quite different, possibly a kind of *pluralism* recognising the diversity of experiences and human situations governed by law, adjusted to meet their diverse characteristics and needs. Whatever we do, feminists and Critical Race Theory scholars are agreed that reform is needed. Precisely what ought to be done, and how, remains a matter of controversy.

1. Feminist Jurisprudence

Feminist jurisprudence spans a large spectrum of views about the differences between characteristically male and female reasoning and experience of the world, and political views about what changes ought to be made in law to reflect those differences. Feminist jurisprudence is likely best characterized in terms of two central features agreed upon by nearly all feminists. Feminists agree that male-dominated institutions and ways of thinking must be rejected, and nearly all feminists advocate rapid, effective reform promoted through changes in present laws and in the ways lawmakers think about making laws. Massive debate surrounds both aspects of feminist jurisprudence. To what *extent* are male-dominated perspectives flawed and in need of repair? What *sort* of repair is appropriate? Is law as traditionally conceived *worth repairing* and revising to meet women's needs? Feminist thought is so diverse that it is impossible to isolate "the feminist position" on one of these issues without unfairly ignoring another plausible and clearly feminist position. The article by Professor Patricia Smith (Professor of Philosophy at the City University of New York) included here treats the diversity of feminist thought in closer detail, so we shall leave this topic to her. Here we shall suggest that feminist jurisprudence, at least at present, is primarily *critical*, and its criticism forms part of a demand for a complete revision of the way legal and social norms are understood. We shall begin with the type of criticism characteristic of feminism.

1.1 Criticism of Laws Advancing Patriarchal Views

The roots of feminist thought, in the western world and beyond, lie in dissatisfaction with *patriarchy*—literally, "father-rule." Early feminist writers lived in a social environment controlled by men and directed largely to serving the interests of men. Consciously or not, male holders of power tended (and likely still tend) to exclude women from power, and when making laws these power-holders usually excluded female perspectives and experience. It is unsurprising, then, that much early feminist writing about law focused on the law's treatment of women as less than equal, and argued that such treatment was based on an arbitrary, ill-considered distinction between men and women. Many feminist writers came to believe that patriarchal domination of society is much more deeply entrenched than initially expected, and a great effort has been made to understand the *extent* to which male-dominated modes of thinking have been embedded so deeply in social practices that they are taken as the "obvious" or "natural" perspective. While conducting this investigation into male nature and male bias in law and other social practices, many feminists have tried to develop a contrasting view of female nature and typically female characteristics, to better understand which aspects of law are most dominated by masculine modes of thought. This has revealed a huge number of problems, as women vary in religion, culture, level of education, and so forth. So even when feminist writers are convinced that some aspect of social life is dominated by patriarchy, it is often very difficult to uncover the identity of any distinctively and essentially female perspective, both because it is obscured by so many generations of patriarchal domination and because women's perspectives are so diverse. Debate continues regarding the possibility of feminist "essentialism," the view that some parts of female experience are universal and so form the essential or necessary core of a feminist account of some topic. Some of the most successful attempts to determine the existence of a distinctly female perspective on law and social norms have come in work on areas of law relevant to all women: rape, pornography, abortion and reproductive rights, marriage, and traditionally unpaid domestic labour. Historically women have had the least control over these aspects of their lives, and the law in these areas has typically been designed by men without consultation with women. Feminist writers' work in these areas have contributed a great deal to the legal literature and to reform of law.

1.2 Criticism of the Patriarchal Mode of Thinking

From what has been said above, it may seem that feminist jurisprudence has been more critical than constructive and directed only toward reform of law in ways directly relevant to women. Seen in this light, feminist jurisprudence appears to fall short of being a theory of law or of forming a basis for a larger theory of law in the future. Yet this would be a serious misunderstanding of the possibilities opened by feminist jurisprudence. Feminists' attempts to reform laws which harm women are motivated in part by the obvious need to stop the harmful effects of bad law sooner rather than later; but many feminists are also motivated by the need to show plain, indisputable examples of the way patriarchy and patriarchal thinking have become embedded in law. Such examples are evidence for feminists' larger concern that typically male ways of thinking about law must be replaced.

In an article included in this volume, University of Michigan law professor Catharine MacKinnon suggests that it is difficult to even conceive of what a feminist jurisprudence might look like. Why is this so difficult? According to feminist thought, patriarchal modes of thinking dominate the way we evaluate claims to knowledge and claims about the existence of certain features of social life (e.g., the existence of oppression). MacKinnon and many other feminist writers believe that it is difficult to uncover female perspectives and female ideas for reform of law because women are so completely immersed in a male-dominated and frequently hostile society. An analogy will help to clarify the situation: it is as if feminists find themselves in a society which assumes that everyone is right-handed, yet feminists are left-handed and are forced to use the available right-handed tools until something better can be devised. And of course, in a situation where a right-handed tool has accomplished the task in an apparently adequate manner for a long time, there would be a great deal of debate about the design of the new tool for left-handers. Should it be an exact copy of the right-handed tool but converted to the left-handed way of doing things, or should it be a different tool altogether? Many feminists claim that the law should be revised entirely, to escape what they perceive to be the negative consequences of patriarchal *epistemology* (theory of knowledge) and *ontology* (theory of what it is for something to exist). A new jurisprudence must reflect women's experience and women's perceptions of social relations, acknowledge the existence of unfair and oppressive social norms which must be eliminated, and acknowledge the value of women's knowledge gained from their position as the oppressed. So, although there can be no doubting the importance of feminist criticism of laws relating specifically to women, the more far-reaching feminist challenge is epistemological and ontological—a challenge to re-examine and revise the foundations of legal thought.

2. *Critical Race Theory*

Critical Race Theory includes a wide range of views, so this introduction necessarily offers only a sketch of themes and points of departure shared by CRT writers. As you explore Critical Race Theory, it is also worth remembering that it is always dangerous to try to identify central themes of movements which are new and still finding their identity. This danger may be especially evident in thinking about Critical Race Theory, a movement which emphasizes experiences of race which might not be fully understood by writers who have not had those experiences themselves. It is up to you to consider this possibility, and to use these introductory remarks on CRT themes as just that: an introduction to be supplemented with your own reading and thinking.

We have seen above that CRT shares some views with the feminist movement, and owes some of its insights to the Critical Legal Studies movement. In fact, the link to the Critical Legal Studies movement is more than just a similarity of views: as Professor Richard Nunan has remarked, the first Critical Race Theory Workshop in 1989 was "underwritten by a grant provided by David Trubek, who had also been instrumental in the organization of the CLS

conference more than a decade earlier."[1] Yet CRT scholars have gone beyond these related movements in important ways related to the particular history and challenges faced by minorities of color in the United States.

The article provided here was written by one of the founders of the Critical Race Theory movement, Professor Richard Delgado, University Distinguished Professor of Law & Derrick Bell Fellow at the University of Pittsburgh Law School. Delgado's article expresses what this introduction identifies as some defining themes of Critical Race Theory, and shows us what those themes do to advance our understanding of race and law in both American society and others. Some of the conclusions of Delgado's argument may also be very useful, for example, to the understanding of societies such as South Africa in which race has long played a central role in conceptions of society, law, and justice.

2.1 Narratives

Critical Race Theory writers have often tried to break out of usual or expected ways of expressing experiences relevant to understanding the actual effects of law on minorities of color. One especially controversial approach is the use of narratives, dramatic representation of particular situations. Professor Delgado is famous for his *Rodrigo Chronicles* which use a narrative approach. Something of the flavor of that style can be found in the article included here. He begins his discussion with a dialogue between a lawyer and St. Peter as the lawyer asks to be let into heaven. Some critics of this approach say that it loses the message in the mechanism of the dramatic dialogue, or worse, that the narrative approach just is not capable of providing the sort of careful, rigorous marshalling of evidence and argument needed to support CRT's insights. Others respond that

---

1   Richard Nunan, "Critical Race Theory: An Overview," *APA Newsletter on Philosophy, Law, and the Black Experience* Vol. 98, No. 2, 1999.

dramatic characterizations of ideas have long been known to be effective as ways of putting a certain kind of argument forward. Plato, for example, conducted dialogues in which a particular approach to questioning ideas is shown in action as well as discussed in more formal terms.

Critical Race Theorists have used narrative approaches in various ways, all united in expressing specific experiences that resist easy classification under an essentialist account of what it is like to be a member of a minority of color. Some narratives are used to provide a context for an account of an experience which might otherwise be easily misinterpreted. Other narratives try to express vividly and forcefully an experience whose nature and importance might not be completely captured by ordinary methods of description. Still other narratives show how events might be viewed differently by someone with a different set of assumptions and priorities. In the article provided here Delgado's lawyer is quite surprised that his having followed the rules might not be enough to get him into heaven. His point of view led him to assume that following the rules was the same thing as doing justice and being the kind of person worthy of admission to heaven. This narrative approach offers a striking and memorable way to raise the question of the limits of a particular point of view to life under law, leaving the reader ready to hear more about what might be missing from particular ways of understanding law.

2.2 Specific Experiences Under Specific Laws

At the core of the Critical Legal Studies movement there is wide agreement that law and legal systems very often fall short of delivering justice. Instead, law and legal systems tend to be the tools of elites who intentionally or unthinkingly use law to support their own elite interests. As we saw in discussion of the similarities between the feminist jurisprudence movement and Critical Race Theory, CRT writers have often agreed with the general claim that law is a tool used by elites to manipulate others. Where CLS does not go far enough, according to many CRT writers, is in its understanding of the specific and diverse ways in which minorities of color can experience the way elites use law to support their interests.

Professor Delgado's article is an excellent example of the way many CRT writers have used close analysis of a specific situation to simultaneously draw attention to the issues in that particular situation, and to make a larger point. Professor Delgado uses the interaction between the apparently compatible civil liberty of freedom of speech[2] and the civil right to equality[3] to show that they are in tension or competition in various ways. Minorities of color have suffered the consequences of some of these tensions, particularly when free speech rights serve to protect hate speech that aims to undermine equality. At the same time he develops the more general argument that this particular conflict between a civil right and a civil liberty is just one instance of the way conflicts between civil rights and civil liberties are more generally resolved so that the dominance of elites over minorities of color is reinforced.

---

2   This is the civil right protected in the United States Constitution's first amendment, which reads: "Congress shall make no law respecting an establishment of religion, or prohibiting the free exercise thereof; or abridging the freedom of speech, or of the press; or the right of the people peaceably to assemble, and to petition the Government for a redress of grievances."

3   This is the civil right protected in the United States Constitution's fourteenth amendment, which reads in part: "All persons born or naturalized in the United States, and subject to the jurisdiction thereof, are citizens of the United States and of the State wherein they reside. No State shall make or enforce any law which shall abridge the privileges or immunities of citizens of the United States; nor shall any State deprive any person of life, liberty, or property, without due process of law; nor deny to any person within its jurisdiction the equal protection of the laws."

Immediately following his narrative regarding the lawyer and St. Peter, Delgado's article asks a question which builds from the narrative's contrast of rule-following with actual justice, asking us to now consider in greater detail the actual effects and interactions of ideals and laws. He asks: "What is the relationship between the group of largely formal rules known as civil liberties and the set of substantive values known as racial justice or civil rights?" Professor Delgado begins his answer to the question by examining the way freedom of speech (a civil liberty) really does sometimes support civil rights (such as equality), together with an explanation of the justifications often given when exercise of freedom of speech seems to endanger justice, often by conflicting with civil rights. Analysis of the value of freedom of speech does not, however, stop there.

In what might be regarded as the core of his argument, Delgado explains the elements of a Critical Race Theory analysis of freedom of speech. Tracing a chain of court decisions as well as arguments from Critical Race Theory writers, Delgado shows how legal theorists and practitioners have come to recognize that the practice of free speech is more complicated than its supporters let on. Professor Delgado identifies three aspects of the complex interaction between free speech (a positive "freedom to" speak) and the social and legal context in which speech is made, a context including a civil right to equality (a negative "freedom from" certain forms of discrimination).

The first interaction is the "conceptual" or theoretical conflict between speech and equality, closely related to what Delgado views as a conflict between the capitalist or free market economic model, and the needs of democracy. The civil liberty of free speech is typically exercised by individuals, yet its effects can be felt by both individuals and groups. In an extreme instance of legally protected speech, hate speech by an individual can damage an entire group and its attempts to assert its members' civil right to a quality of citizenship equal to that enjoyed by other citizens.

Similarly, a system of property-holding which serves free-market goals tends to be a system in which a few persons control a great deal of private property and the majority have relatively little. Hate speech can make a powerful contribution to this imbalance, as the denial of equality can limit access to employment and property, leaving poorer citizens focussing on survival rather than democratic participation. If liberties can routinely be interpreted in ways which impair equality rights, originally designed to carry force equal to that of the liberties, what is the real value of the equality rights? This conceptual tension shows that further attention is needed, Delgado suggests, to the way we understand the balance between the important interests expressed in both civil liberties and civil rights.

The second interaction is "historical," drawing attention to the way the balance between specific civil liberties and specific civil rights has varied over time. When the United States has focused on its core ideals as it has sought to define itself in the face of international competition and opposition, civil rights have been strongly emphasized. Yet when the United States has suffered a sense of insecurity, civil rights have sometimes been curbed as part of efforts to regain a sense of security. Civil rights, then, are perhaps not the bedrock of American society, always guaranteeing a basic minimum kind of citizenship for all.

Identification of an "ideological and constitutional" tension between free speech and justice completes Delgado's discussion. Professor Delgado argues that it is a mistake to think that America's great successes as a society can be attributed to its support of civil liberties such as free speech rights. While there are great American successes in terms of national wealth and power, freedom of speech has received too much credit for its contribution. Freedom of speech is also closely tied to the less happy results of America's constitution and political ideals. Professor Delgado points to the way free speech rights have protected media stereotypes which leave real people bearing the weight of false claims about the threat or burden posed by persons fitting within a stereotype. The continued strength of American democracy and justice requires a different approach to interpreting the proper balance between civil liberties and civil rights, perhaps permitting slightly weaker civil liberties in some circumstances, to allow civil rights their proper effect and to foster a just American society and legal system. It may be helpful to thorough understanding of Delgado's argument on this topic to spend some time investigating the recent history of hate speech in the United States, Canada, the United Kingdom, and elsewhere. You might, for example, look at Alabama of the early 1960s, where Governor George Wallace famously said in his 1963 inaugural speech that he would support "segregation today, segregation tomorrow, segregation forever."

2.3 A Pragmatic Attitude Toward Rights

Many CLS writers have been quite forceful in their insistence that the problems with existing legal orders can only be fixed by quite radical reforms. Professor Delgado's arguments are one instance of the much more pragmatic tendencies of many Critical Race Theorists. As Delgado's article makes clear, there is no shortage of evidence that civil liberties have sometimes been harmful or of little use to minorities of color, yet civil liberties have also been of undeniable benefit to minorities of color. Professor Delgado's conclusion faces the double-edged nature of civil liberties and their relation to civil rights. He suggests that there is an ongoing tension between two "equally valid" views of the world driving the sometimes opposed positions of those who emphasize the individual-focussed aspects of civil rights, and those who support the group- or community-focussed aspects of civil rights. Both emphases are part of a viable overall system of justice under law, Delgado seems to suggest. Changes are certainly needed, according to his form of Critical Race Theory, but these changes

can be identified while using some of the tools available in the system undergoing change.

It is up to you to consider the value of the pragmatic approach of many Critical Race Theorists, and to evaluate the CRT contribution to the understanding of law, legal concepts, and the relation between legal practice and legal ideals. As you consider the strengths and weaknesses of Delgado's argument, you can find more resources for your thinking in the references listed in the *Further Readings* for this chapter.

◆ ◆ ◆ ◆ ◆

PATRICIA SMITH

"Feminist Jurisprudence and the Nature of Law," from *Feminist Jurisprudence*

What is feminist jurisprudence? One prominent feminist scholar, Catharine MacKinnon, explained that feminist jurisprudence is the analysis of law from the perspective of all women. This provides us with a good point of departure, as it captures the central focus of feminism, which is to attempt to represent women's side of things. Feminist theory recognizes that throughout history and even today, public discourse has been almost exclusively conducted by men from (quite naturally) the perspective of men. That is, the nature of women has been formulated by men, and the interests of women have been determined by men. Historically, women have never been allowed to represent themselves. They have always been represented by men, but this representation has hardly been accurate or fair. Even though it claims to represent all human beings, the fact is that public discourse has left out, silenced, misrepresented, disadvantaged, and subordinated women throughout all of history, relegating them to a single role and reserving the rest of life for men. MacKinnon's explanation underscores this point.

Using her explanation as a definition, however, might create the impression that there is a single perspective of all women, which is certainly false. Not even all feminists hold a single perspective, and not all women, of course, are feminists. But all feminism does begin with one presumption, namely, that a patriarchal world is not good for women. Virtually everyone agrees that the world is, in fact, patriarchal; that is, human societies have always been organized in a hierarchical structure that subordinates women to men. This is simply the observation of a social fact. Until recently it was virtually impossible to imagine the world any other way, and even now a great many men and women think that patriarchy is good, natural, or inevitable. Feminists think that patriarchy (the subjugation of women) is not good, not ordained by nature, and not inevitable.

The rejection of patriarchy is the one point on which all feminists agree. It is also apparently a distinguishing feature of feminism as a school of thought, as no other school of thought focuses on the critique of institutions and attitudes as patriarchal. Only feminism analyzes the patriarchal origin, nature, and effects of human attitudes, concepts, relations, and institutions and criticizes them on that ground. So we might take as a reasonable working definition that feminist jurisprudence is the analysis and critique of law as a patriarchal institution.

This analysis and critique manifests itself in a variety of ways, owing partly to the range of issues it covers and partly to divergence among feminists on virtually all points other than the rejection of patriarchy. Feminists tend to concentrate on issues of particular concern to women, such as equal protection law; discrimination in education, hiring, promotion, and pay; protection of reproductive freedom and other freedoms; protection from rape, sexual harassment, and spouse abuse; regulation of sexual and reproductive services such as surrogate mother contracts, prostitution, and pornography; and patriarchal bias in law and adjudication. But feminist analysis is appropriate to any area, concepts, relations, and institutions of law, and many legal theorists offer feminist critiques of standard legal categories such as contracts, property, and tort law. Clearly, the issues covered by feminist jurisprudence are as wide ranging as the areas covered by law. To appreciate the diversity of feminist jurisprudence, consider the differences among feminist theories.

Feminist Theories

The earliest explicit feminist writing is associated with the liberal tradition, as exemplified by Mary Walstonecraft's [sic] eighteenth-century book *A Vindication of the Rights of Women*, by John Stuart Mill's nineteenth-century *Subjection of Women*, and by Betty Friedan's twentieth-century *Feminine Mystique*. The general view is that the subordination of women is caused by the legal and social barriers that block or preclude their access to the public sphere of economic and political life. Liberal feminists demand that liberals follow their own principles of universal human rights. If all human beings are moral equals, as liberals have claimed since at least the seventeenth century, then men and women should be treated equally, which means that no one should be excluded from participating in political, educational, or economic life. Because they followed the classical liberal tradition, the early liberal feminists tended to be very individualistic, arguing for equal rights and equal freedom. They felt that the law should be gender blind, that there should be no special restrictions or special assistance on the basis of sex. Most of the gains made for women's equal rights and freedom in the 1960s and 1970s were made using liberal feminist arguments. The solution to the oppression of women, in this view, is to remove all formal barriers to their equal participation in social, political, and economic life, thus providing equal opportunity for all.

In the 1970s and 1980s some liberal feminists (including Friedan) began to rethink their position, as simply removing formal or legal restrictions did not seem to provide equal opportunity after all. Women still faced a great deal of informal discrimination and an uphill battle against old stereotypes that portrayed them as emotional, incompetent, and passive. Furthermore, even women who did manage to break into the male world of politics, economics, or academic life found themselves faced with a choice of eliminating any personal life whatsoever or working a double day, a choice that men did not have to face. Women found themselves responsible for home and family whether or not they also had a career, and this meant that most women could not compete on an equal footing with men who did not have this responsibility, precisely because it had been delegated to women. In response to this situation, many liberal feminists began to focus more on the socialization of children, the removal of stereotypes, the reorganization of family life, and the restructuring of state institutions to be more supportive of family needs. This change in focus mirrors the difference between classical liberal and modern welfare liberal views, but it is not a real change of position. The view of liberal feminists, whether classical or modern, is still that the solution to the oppression of women is to provide equal opportunity for all. The difference between the two views is in what constitutes equal opportunity.

Radical feminists believe that neither the classical nor the modern liberal view adequately explains women's oppression or provides effective solutions to it. Changing economic structures, eliminating political and educational barriers, and even socializing children will not abolish the subjugation of women so long as society is organized in a patriarchal system. Patriarchy is so pervasive that it structures our thoughts and attitudes, our assumptions and basic institutions, including the family and church. The only way to change the position of women is to change the way we think about gender itself, to

reexamine our assumptions about our nature and relations to others. Although radical feminist views vary widely, most do focus on some aspect of the effect that biology has on women's psychology, their lives and their status, to recognize good effects as valuable and to overcome negative ones.

Some radical feminists (such as Adrienne Rich or Mary O'Brien) have concentrated on the significance of women as mothers (as child bearers and rearers), arguing either that women must be relieved of having the sole responsibility for these things or that because women are responsible for them, they must also be in control of them. Others (such as Shulamith Firestone or Kate Millett) look at the ways that gender and sexuality oppress women, for example, through sexual harassment, spouse abuse, rape, pornography, and the use of women as sex objects. Most radical feminists insist that male power or male dominance is the basis of the construction of gender and that this construction pervades all other institutions and ensures the perpetuation of patriarchy and thus the subordination of women. Some have suggested the promotion of androgyny (the appropriation of the full range of traits to both men and women) as a solution to the problem of patriarchy. Others contend that androgyny is not liberating for women and that the goal is, rather, to revalue those characteristics associated with the feminine role, such as nurturing and gentleness. Still others believe that because the feminine role and character have been constructed by patriarchy, women must reconstruct them for themselves—must find their true nature. Overall, in the most general terms, the focus of radical feminism is on the domination of women by men through the social construction of gender within patriarchy. For them the solution to the oppression of women is to reverse the institutional structures of domination and to reconstruct gender, thereby eliminating patriarchy.

Marxist and socialist feminists, however, believe that the construction of gender is not the primary issue. They think that equality for women is not possible in a class-based society established on the basic principles of private property and exploitation of the powerless. According to the Marxists, the oppression of women originated, or at least solidified, when the introduction of capitalism and private property sharply divided the world into private and public spheres of life, relegated women to the non-economic private sphere, and devalued that sphere, that is, made it worthless in market terms. To relieve the oppression of women, the capitalist system must be replaced with a socialist system in which no class will be economically dependent or exploited by any other. The solution to the oppression of women is to change the economic system so that women will not be economically dependent, marginal, and exploited.

Many modern socialist feminists have nonetheless become dissatisfied with the traditional Marxist approach, as it fails to account adequately for the oppression of women as women rather than as workers, fails to explain the domination of women in the private as well as the public sphere, and fails to provide an analysis of gender and patriarchy. Some feminists have tried to combine economic (Marxist or socialist) theories with radical theories or psychoanalytical theories that attempt to deal with gender and patriarchy as such. In fact, many modern feminists think that no single theory can account for all aspects of the domination and oppression of women.

Furthermore, some feminists deny altogether the usefulness of general theories in their traditional form. This skepticism or denial of the utility of theory, at least "Grand Theory," is commonly associated with a loose collection of views often called *postmodern* or *French feminism*. The term *French feminism* originated from the fact that most of the early contributors were French (e.g., Helene Cixous and Luce Irigaray) and that most follow the work of French thinkers associated with the postmodern movement, such as Jacques Derrida, Jacques Lacan, and Jean-Francois Lyotard. In law and jurisprudence, this approach is associated with a movement called *critical legal studies*, with which many postmodern feminists are closely associated. Like most postmodern thinkers, these feminists deny that categorical, abstract theories derived through reason and assumptions about the essence of human nature can serve as the foundation of knowledge. They call such ambitious theorizing *phallologocentric*, meaning that it is centered on an absolute word (*logos*) that reflects a male perspective (*phallus*). They claim that it is a male approach to believe that a single answer or a single truth can be found that will organize all issues and lead to a single reformative strategy. Above all, postmodern feminism is critical. Often following Derrida, many postmodern feminists use techniques of *deconstruction* to expose the internal contradictions of apparently coherent systems of thought. This has been a useful method of debunking patriarchal structures of thought and social organization, including law. Other postmodern feminists, following Lacan, are interested in reinterpreting traditional Freudian psychoanalysis, with all its implications for biological determinism and the subordination of women.

In addition, many postmodern feminists display attachments to existentialism in terms of their focus on the "Other." Existentialists have always portrayed the Other as a negative status. To be the Other is to be objectified, determined, and marginalized. Simone de Beauvoir considered the fundamental question of feminism to be "why is woman the Other?" She considered the oppression of women to be an expression of their status as the Other, as the sex objectified by men. Postmodern feminists, however, celebrate Otherness. Because they are criticizing the mainstream of thought and society, the "Law of the Fathers" or the "Symbolic Order," there is a positive side to Otherness, as it disassociates itself from the mainstream accepted structures of reality, knowledge, and society: To be Other to patriarchy is not necessarily a bad thing.

In general, postmodern feminists do not offer a single solution to the oppression of women, first, because they do not think that there can be single solutions to anything. Second, to propose a single solution to *the* oppression of women suggests that all women's experiences are alike, that women's oppression is a unitary thing. But real human problems cannot be solved by abstract rules and generalizations. Rather, attacking the oppression of women requires contextual judgments that recognize and accommodate the particularity of human experience. As Deborah Rhode put it, "Such an approach demands that feminists shift self-consciously among needs to acknowledge both distinctiveness and commonality between sexes and unity and diversity among their members." For postmodern feminists there is no single solution and no single oppression of women, but only solutions tailored to the concrete experience of actual people.

One problem with postmodern views, particularly those associated with deconstruction, is that they tend to be better at destroying theories than at building them, which may generate a debilitating skepticism that is not useful to the feminist cause in the long run. One response to this skepticism has been a revitalization of pragmatism within feminism. Pragmatism also subscribes to a postmodern antiessentialist theory of human nature and knowledge. In law it is associated with legal realist theory, which views law as a dynamic process of conflict resolution and focuses on the function of courts to analyze law and legal reasoning. Feminists are drawn to the practical, personal, contextual approach of pragmatism, which coincides with feminist rejection of traditional abstract categories, dichotomies, and the conceptual pretensions of the logical analysis of law.

Finally, a trend sometimes called *relational feminism* in some ways reverses the focus of some earlier theories, especially liberal theories that call for equal rights for women on the ground that men and women are fundamentally similar. Many recent relational feminist writers have been greatly influenced by the work of Harvard educational psychologist Carol Gilligan. In her book *In a Different Voice*, Gilligan hypothesizes that men and women are not fundamentally similar; rather, men and women typically undergo a different moral development. The predominant moral attitude of men she calls the *ethic of justice*, which concentrates on abstract rules, principles, and rights. The predominant moral attitude of women Gilligan calls the *ethic of care*, which focuses on concrete relationships, concern for others, and responsibility. The important thing for Gilligan is to recognize the value of both, and especially not to devalue the ethic of care.

Following Gilligan, many relational feminists have argued that the important task for feminists today is not to fit women into a man's world, not to assimilate women into patriarchy, and not to prove that women can function like men and meet male norms, but to change institutions to reflect and accommodate the value that should properly be accorded to characteristics and virtues traditionally associated with women, nurturing virtues such as love, sympathy, patience, and concern. It is not that women should change to meet existing institutions but that institutions should be changed to accommodate women (or at least the best virtues associated with women). Of course, when put in these terms, most feminists would agree. No feminist thinks that women should be turned into clones of men, and there is increasing concern over what might be lost in the unthinking assimilation of women into male institutions.

The difference between liberal feminists on the one hand and relational feminists on the other represents a split among feminists and others as to whether men and women are fundamentally similar or fundamentally different, particularly in psychological and/or moral terms. This split is actually an old one that was prominent in the early twentieth century in debates about women's rights. The question is whether women, being basically similar to men, require equal treatment or, being significantly different from men, require special treatment. This question is reflected in many jurisprudential and legal debates today, and each side has its hazards. The deficiency of the liberal view is that treating men and women as exactly alike ignores genuine physical and social differences that tend to disadvantage the vast majority of women. But the deficiency of the relational view is that it can easily be transformed into the old, traditional stereotype of women as biologically domestic and dependent, which perpetuate bias, discrimination, and domination instead of counteracting it. Many feminists now think that this old debate needs to be ended or transcended, but exactly how to do this is not clear. It is clear, however, that the sameness/difference debate is a snag that has often divided feminists and hindered social progress.

There are (at least) three points that provide some ground for optimism that the old sameness/difference debate may, this time, be overcome. First, for postmodern theorists, the sameness/difference problem is a nonstarter in the first place, because dichotomies like sameness and difference are illusions caused by the flawed structural frameworks that generate them. That is, they rely on a faulty essentialist view of human nature. Insofar as postmodern thinking dominates intellectual life (which it may, at least among feminists, as the antiessentialist view is shared by pragmatists, existentialists, and many Marxists, socialists, and liberals), the sameness/difference problem has already been resolved by an overall critical view that does not recognize an essential human nature.

Second, unlike feminist theories of an earlier era, virtually every feminist theory today challenges male norms. This, for example, is the intended objective of relational feminism, even though it is highly susceptible to abuse or misinterpretation. So the following question has been raised: Even if men and women are different, why should the standard of measure be male? The simple (and accurate) answer, that historically it has always been male, is one explanation, but it is obviously not a justification. Because historical standards relied on historical discrimination, some ground other than history must

be found for retaining them. But no other supportable ground has been forthcoming.

Finally, the fact that many feminists see the sameness/difference debate as a misformulation of the problem provides more possibilities for progress beyond it. To see how easy it is to fall into the patriarchal trap, look back to the statement that the question is whether women, being basically similar to men, require equal treatment, or being significantly different from men, require special treatment. What may not be obvious is that this essentially means, Heads I win, tails you lose. That is, it assumes the outcome in advance, for to agree that if women are "different" (i.e., different from men) they will require "special treatment" is to assume a male or patriarchal standard of what normal treatment is. Feminists today reject such a formulation of the problem, and so this question is no longer viewed as the crucial question that must be answered before further steps can be taken. In fact, many feminists now think that it is not even an answerable, or perhaps even a meaningful, question, and some have proposed alternative views. For example, some feminists suggest that it is not difference but disadvantage that should be the goal of legal and social reform; some argue that the focus should be directly on eliminating domination; and some seek common standards of human flourishing and/or pragmatic approaches that can contextualize the problem instead of presuming abstract or essentialist models of human nature or the structure of gender.

We do not need a final unified vision of society and gender, however, to argue against oppression, disadvantage, domination, and discrimination. We do not need to know beforehand the nature of the good society or the ideal person so long as we know what prevents a society from being minimally good or prevents an individual from realizing the basic potentials of personhood. We do not need an ultimate vision when we have not yet met threshold conditions for a minimally just society. Many visions are possible, and many theories are useful. The commitment to foster open dialogue that allows the expression of diverse views and gives particular attention to eliciting views not usually heard is a unifying thread among feminists that attempts to represent the commonality of fundamental values without misrepresenting the plurality of experience.

Some Basic Objections

The acceptance of diversity within feminism has led some critics (and even some feminists) to contend that there is therefore no common feminist perspective. There is no point of view of all women. Feminism can be reduced to those theories that inform its many facets. Liberal feminism is reducible to liberalism; postmodern feminism is reducible to postmodernism; and so on. Thus, it is claimed, feminism provides no new idea, no new theory. It is simply the application of old theories to the particular problem of women's oppression.

This objection is mistaken, however, for several reasons. First, even if it were true of some views (such as liberal feminism or Marxist feminism), it cannot be true of radical feminism, because the centerpiece of radical feminism is the structure of gender or sexual identity itself. Radical feminism starts with the idea of sexism as gender, the idea that gender is socially constructed within a hierarchy that embodies male domination and female subordination. Everything else flows from that. One may agree or disagree with this idea, but it cannot be reduced to another theory.

Furthermore, this core insight now informs all other feminist theories, whose differences are largely differences of emphasis. Nearly all feminists are too eclectic to fit neatly into any one category, and so it is misleading to set up categories or theories as though they worked in that limiting sort of way for feminists. Creating distinct or rigid categories within which to fit particular accounts or limit dialogue is a decidedly antifeminist way of proceeding, as feminists generally oppose this sort of abstract concep-

tualization without attention to context and detail. Instead, the way to use the general descriptions of the various feminist theories, such as those in the previous section, is simply to note and trace their influences, interactions, and manifestations in the particular views that people offer on specific issues. The function of general descriptions of theories in feminism is clarification and simplification, not limitation or reduction.

Finally, the one thing that unites all feminist theories and distinguishes them from all other theories is that their primary goal is the rejection of patriarchy. No matter what differences there are among these divergent views, and there certainly are many, this one point of reference is always shared. It is an irreducible point, and it distinguishes feminism from all the other ones.

Nonetheless, one can argue that if the entire project of feminist jurisprudence is to show that law is patriarchal, it is not intellectually very interesting. How can an entire jurisprudence be supported by the single ground of rejecting patriarchy? But this is a political position, one may contend, not a philosophical one.

The problem with this objection is that it assumes that the recognition and rejection of patriarchy is a small point, when in fact it is a revolutionary one. Likewise, noting that the world is not flat but round is a small point in the sense that it can be stated in a brief and simple sentence, and it is not philosophical in the sense that it is the observation of an empirical fact. But in another sense, it changes everything. Its implications are profound, and exploring some of those implications is of great philosophical interest, and so it is with the rejection of patriarchy.

Thus, the one new thing about feminism (or feminist jurisprudence) is the very fact that it is feminism, that it constitutes a critique of patriarchal institutions from the perspective of women. To put it more generally, it constitutes, at least potentially, a genuine critique of patriarchal institutions, structures, and assumptions from the perspective of a group that is outside those patriarchal structures, institutions, and assumptions, at least in the sense (among other things) that it did not participate in their formulation. This is the first time in the history of civilization that anything like that has been possible at a level that can be taken seriously.

Intellectually, this provides a new basis for an external critique of social structures. In *The Structure of Scientific Revolutions*, Thomas Kuhn explains such external critiques as paradigm shifts that represent revolutionary changes in thinking. Internal critique refines thinking within a framework. External critique rejects the old framework altogether and proposes a new paradigm in its place. External critique is not everything, but it can be extremely useful, especially for spotting assumptions that otherwise go unexamined because they are unnoticed. Internal critique tends to develop and refine details and spot inconsistencies within a structure or framework. External critique can challenge the entire framework, and thus, external critique is also the most threatening and the hardest to understand or accept. It is like Martin Luther saying to the pope, "Why, as a Christian, do I need to be Catholic at all?" Luther's critique is external to Catholicism but still internal to Christianity and, of course, to religion. When Nietzsche declared that "God is dead," his critique was external to the idea of religion. Needless to say, both critiques were viewed with hostility and disbelief by those who were defending the status quo. Similarly, feminist jurisprudence challenges basic legal categories and concepts rather than analyzing them as given. Feminist jurisprudence asks what is implied in traditional categories, distinctions, or concepts and rejects them if they imply the subordination of women. In this sense, feminist jurisprudence is normative and claims that traditional jurisprudence and law are implicitly normative as well.

Because of this, feminist jurisprudence has the potential to offer some of the most intellectually stimulating critiques of legal structures today, and this would be much more readily recognized if it were not so politically and socially frightening. That is the problem with revolutionary critique: It is revolutionary. This means, first, that it is hard to understand or else to take seriously. Revolutionary external critique may sound strange, heretical, irrational, or silly because it starts from a different set of basic assumptions. The most difficult thing in the world for two people (let alone a group of people) to discuss reasonably are differing basic assumptions. They need some common ground to begin the discussion. So the first problem is just to understand the critique or to be able to take it seriously. The elimination of patriarchy would constitute a cultural revolution at least as profound as the Copernican revolution, the Protestant revolution, or the Industrial Revolution. Could anyone living before these revolutions imagine what life or human thought would be like after them? The first response to early feminism was ridicule. People could not imagine the status or role of women being different from what it always had been.

Second, if the critique is understood and taken seriously, it often scares people to death. Why? Why was the pope upset with Luther? Revolutionary critiques are frightening just because they are revolutionary. If they succeed, life will never be the same again. The end of patriarchy will be the end of social life as we know it. And so the critique of patriarchy tends to generate hostility, misunderstanding, ridicule, and fear almost as soon as it is mentioned. Like religion, it is one of the most difficult topics to discuss with, for example, nonbelievers. Accordingly, most feminists discuss the critique of patriarchy primarily with one another, and for good reason. Anyone who speaks of it too much "in public" is considered an extremist (and generally tiresome and ill tempered as well). For these reasons (and some others) many women disassociate themselves from feminism, and most men do not want to hear about it. It is dubbed a women's issue and ignored. And when some feminist takes the critique directly to the patriarchs, so to speak, it tends to be hostilely delivered or hostilely received, or both.

Feminists tend, therefore, to concentrate on more specific issues rather than on the general critique, and there are many good reasons for doing that, in addition to the difficulty of the more general topic. Nevertheless, the critique of patriarchy is the general rationale behind feminism itself and behind all those discussions of more specific topics, such as pregnancy leave, rape, pornography, or child care. That means that all those issues also proceed from different basic assumptions, which in turn can lead to the same problems just mentioned: hostility, ridicule, disregard, and resistance. And this also expresses the progress of so-called women's issues.

All that is understandable, but it is not excusable, nor is it wise. Hostility is misplaced when directed against cultural revolutions, which is what we are talking about here. Cultural revolutions are profound but not violent. Cultural revolution is the discovery (usually after the fact) that everyone or almost everyone has joined a new order (usually without realizing it). It is internally developed rather than externally imposed. When women and men no longer think of women first and foremost as mothers, and secondarily as anything else, then the world will have changed. When women are thought of and think of themselves as primarily self-supporting and not as dependent, the world will have changed. In sum, when women and men actually think of themselves as equals, the world will have changed. In a cultural revolution, what changes is what people think, their basic assumptions about what is normal. So, cultural revolutions are inevitable because they follow from a change of worldview.

Thus, cultural revolutions should not be confused with political revolutions, which are not necessarily internal and not inevitable. Hostility to political revolutions makes sense. Hostility to cultural revolutions is understandable but relatively useless. To return to my analogy, it really did not do the Catholic church any good at all to reject Martin Luther when

the rest of the world was ready for him. At a certain point in time, certain ideas become part of history, and they cannot be reversed. They can be affected, sometimes revised or modestly changed, possibly guided or directed, but not reversed or erased.

This is now the status of the women's movement and feminist thought. It cannot be reversed or erased. The bridges have been burned. This can easily be seen by comparing the lives of women today with those of one hundred years ago. Some of the biggest steps in the revolution have already been taken, as is illustrated by the legal changes in the status of women, which recognize them as independent individuals and equal citizens. Whether the legal system fashions the future from cooperative endeavor or hammers it out of the adversarial system, it will respond to the requirements of social change. To think, therefore, that the rejection of patriarchy is philosophically or intellectually uninteresting is to underestimate the extent or profundity of the change entailed in rejecting it. For philosophers and social analysts to ignore the feminist revolution today, thinking their work is outside it, is like philosophers and social analysts some centuries ago who ignored the Industrial Revolution, thinking that their work was outside it. Basic revolutions such as this touch everything and change assumptions about human nature and human life. Nothing could be more philosophically interesting.

The Pervasiveness of Patriarchy

Obviously, some thinkers reject the idea that the feminist critique is as fundamental or as revolutionary as I am suggesting. Accordingly, the following chapters [of *Feminist Jurisprudence*] are intended to represent the breadth of feminist jurisprudence, which in turn illustrates the pervasiveness of patriarchy and the enormity of the change that follows from its rejection. Several important areas are, however, not represented, owing to limitations of space. Of particular note here is the feminist work on reproductive rights, the nature of self-defense, child custody and family law, divorce and property settlement, and the nature and function of rights.

This book is intended to illuminate the extent and subtlety of patriarchy, particularly in regard to an interesting recent phenomenon. Historically, the challenge was to prove that women were entitled to be treated equally with men. That battle is still not completely over, but many people today are convinced that women are entitled to equal treatment. The interesting twist is that although many people do believe that men and women are entitled to equal treatment, they also believe that this goal has already been accomplished in law. Because formal barriers (at least the most obvious ones) have, for the most part, been removed—women can vote, hold office, attend college, participate in business, own property, execute contracts, and so forth—many people think that legal equality has been achieved. So, discrepancies in accomplishments—the wage gap, for example—must be explained by differences in abilities or by social factors that are beyond the purview of law. But the chapters in this volume show that this view is premature. Law is affected by patriarchy in many subtle ways that have not yet been eradicated by the simple change of some obvious sexist barriers like the prohibition of women from voting or owning property. Patriarchy is an all-encompassing worldview, and as an institution of patriarchy, law reflects that worldview as well. But because of its distinctive features as law—its reliance on precedent, which perpetuates the status quo—law is not like an ordinary mirror that instantly reflects the reality before it. Rather, it is like a magic mirror that always reflects a vision that is slightly in the past; that is, it can reflect reality only if reality moves slowly. Transient changes are therefore not reflected. Big changes or fast changes are reflected only after a period of transition. Because law is a somewhat selective, delayed-action mirror, feminist jurisprudence is concerned with correcting the current lag.

◆ ◆ ◆ ◆ ◆

CATHARINE A. MacKINNON

"Toward Feminist Jurisprudence," from *Toward a Feminist Theory of the State*

Happy above all Countries is our Country where that equality is found, without destroying the necessary subordination.
—Thomas Lee Shippen (1788)

If I fight, some day some woman will win.
—Michelle Vinson (1987)

A jurisprudence is a theory of the relation between life and law. In life, "woman" and "man" are widely experienced as features of being, not constructs of perception, cultural interventions, or forced identities. Gender, in other words, is lived as ontology, not as epistemology. Law actively participates in this transformation of perspective into being. In liberal regimes, law is a particularly potent source and badge of legitimacy, and site and cloak of force. The force underpins the legitimacy as the legitimacy conceals the force. When life becomes law in such a system, the transformation is both formal and substantive. It reenters life marked by power.

In male supremacist societies, the male standpoint dominates civil society in the form of the objective standard—that standpoint which, because it dominates in the world, does not appear to function as a standpoint at all. Under its aegis, men dominate women and children, three-quarters of the world. Family and kinship rules and sexual mores guarantee reproductive ownership and sexual access and control to men as a group. Hierarchies among men are ordered on the basis of race and class, stratifying women as well. The state incorporates these facts of social power in and as law. Two things happen: Law becomes legitimate, and social dominance becomes invisible. Liberal legalism is thus a medium for making male dominance both invisible and legitimate by adopting the male point of view in law at the same time as it enforces that view on society.

Through legal mediation, male dominance is made to seem a feature of life, not a one-sided construct imposed by force for the advantage of a dominant group. To the degree it succeeds ontologically, male dominance does not look epistemological: Control over being produces control over consciousness, fusing material conditions with consciousness in a way that is inextricable short of social change. Dominance reified becomes difference. Coercion legitimated becomes consent. Reality objectified becomes ideas; ideas objectified become reality. Politics neutralized and naturalized becomes morality. Discrimination in society becomes nondiscrimination in law. Law is a real moment in the social construction of these mirror-imaged inversions as truth. Law, in societies ruled and penetrated by the liberal form, turns angle of vision and construct of social meaning into dominant institution. In the liberal state, the rule of law—neutral, abstract, elevated, pervasive—both institutionalizes the power of men over women and institutionalizes power in its male form.

From a feminist perspective, male supremacist jurisprudence erects qualities valued from the male point of view as standards for the proper and actual relation between life and law. Examples include standards for scope of judicial review, norms of judicial restraint, reliance on precedent, separation of powers, and the division between public and private law. Substantive doctrines like standing, justiciability, and state action adopt the same stance. Those with power in civil society, not women, design its norms and institutions, which become the status quo. Those with power, not usually women, write constitutions, which become law's highest standards. Those with power in political systems that women did not design and from which women have been excluded write legislation, which sets ruling values. Then, jurisprudentially, judicial review is said to go beyond its proper scope—to delegitimate courts and the rule of law itself—when legal questions are not confined to assessing the formal correspondence between legislation and the constitution, or legislation and social reality, but scrutinize the underlying substance. Lines of precedent fully developed before women were permitted to vote, continued while women were not allowed to learn to read and write, sustained under a reign of sexual terror and abasement and silence and misrepresentation continuing to the present day are considered valid bases for defeating "unprecedented" interpretations or initiatives from women's point of view. Doctrines of standing suggest that because women's deepest injuries are shared in some way by most or all women, no individual woman is differentially injured enough to be able to sue for women's deepest injuries.

Structurally, only when the state has acted can constitutional equality guarantees be invoked.[1] But no law gives men the right to rape women. This has not been necessary, since no rape law has ever seriously undermined the terms of men's entitlement to sexual access to women. No government is, yet, in the pornography business. This has not been necessary, since no man who wants pornography encounters serious trouble getting it, regardless of obscenity laws. No law gives fathers the right to abuse their daughters sexually. This has not been necessary, since no state has ever systematically intervened in their social possession of and access to them. No law gives husbands the right to batter their wives. This has not been necessary, since there is nothing to stop them. No law silences women. This has not been necessary,

---

1   In the United States, the "state action" requirement restricts review under the Fourteenth Amendment. See Lawrence Tribe, *American Constitutional Law* (Mineola, N.Y.: Foundation Press, 1978), pp. 1688-1720, for summary. In Canada, under the Canadian Charter of Rights and Freedoms, Section 32 restricts charter review to acts of government.

for women are previously silenced in society—by sexual abuse, by not being heard, by not being believed, by poverty, by illiteracy, by a language that provides only unspeakable vocabulary for their most formative traumas, by a publishing industry that virtually guarantees that if they ever find a voice it leaves no trace in the world. No law takes away women's privacy. Most women do not have any to take, and no law gives them what they do not already have. No law guarantees that women will forever remain the social unequals of men. This is not necessary, because the law guaranteeing sex equality requires, in an unequal society, that before one can be equal legally, one must be equal socially. So long as power enforced by law reflects and corresponds—in form and in substance—to power enforced by men over women in society, law is objective, appears principled, becomes just the way things are. So long as men dominate women effectively enough in society without the support of positive law, nothing constitutional can be done about it.

Law from the male point of view combines coercion with authority, policing society where its edges are exposed: at points of social resistance, conflict, and breakdown. Since there is no place outside this system from a feminist standpoint, if its solipsistic lock could be broken, such moments could provide points of confrontation, perhaps even openings for change. The point of view of a total system emerges as particular only when confronted, in a way it cannot ignore, by a demand from another point of view. This is why epistemology must be controlled for ontological dominance to succeed and why consciousness raising is subversive. It is also why, when law sides with the powerless, as it occasionally has,[2] it is said to engage in something other than law—politics or policy or personal opinion—and

to delegitimate itself.[3] When seemingly ontological conditions are challenged from the collective standpoint of a dissident reality, they become visible as epistemological. Dominance suddenly appears no longer inevitable. When it loses its ground, it loosens its grip.

Thus when the Supreme Court held that racial segregation did not violate equality rights, it said that those who felt that to be segregated on the basis of race implied inferiority merely chose to place that construction upon it. The harm of forced separation was a matter of point of view.[4] When the Supreme Court later held that racial segregation violated equality rights, it said that segregation generated a feeling of inferiority in the hearts and minds of black children which was unlikely ever to be undone. Both Courts observed the same reality: the feelings of inferiority generated by apartheid. *Plessy* saw it from the standpoint of white supremacy; *Brown* saw it from the standpoint of the black challenge to white supremacy, envisioning a social equality that did not yet exist. Inequality is difficult to see when everything tells the unequal that the status quo is equality—for them. To the Supreme Court, the way black people saw their own condition went from being sneered at as a point of view within their own control, a self-inflicted epistemological harm, to being a constitutional measure of the harm a real social condition imposed upon them. Consciousness raising shifts the episteme in a similar way, exposing the political behind the personal, the dominance behind the submission, participating in altering the balance of power subtly but totally. The question is, What can extend this method to the level of the state for women?

To begin with, Why law? Marx saw the modern state as "the official expression of antagonism

2   Brown v. Board of Education, 347 U.S. 483 (1954): Swann v. Charlotte-Mecklenburg Board of Education, 402 U.S. 2 (1971): Griggs v. Duke Power, 401 U.S. 424 (1971).

3   Herbert Wechsler, "Toward Neutral Principles of Constitutional Law," 73 *Harvard Law Review* 1 (1959).

4   Plessy v. Ferguson. 163 U.S. 537, 551 (1896): Wechsler, "Toward Neutral Principles," p. 33.

in civil society."[5] Because political power in such a state could emancipate the individual only within the framework of the existing social order, law could emancipate women to be equal only within "the slavery of civil society."[6] By analogy, women would not be freed from forced sex, but freed to engage in it and initiate it. They would not be freed from reproductive tyranny and exploitation, but freed to exercise it. They would not be liberated from the dialectic of economic and sexual dominance and submission, but freed to dominate. Depending upon the substantive analysis of civil dominance, either women would dominate men, or some women (with all or some men) would dominate other women. In other words, the liberal vision of sex equality would be achieved. Feminism unmodified, methodologically post-Marxist feminism, aspires to better.

From the feminist point of view, the question of women's collective reality and how to change it merges with the question of women's point of view and how to know it. What do women live, hence know, that can confront male dominance? What female ontology can confront male epistemology; that is, what female epistemology can confront male ontology? What point of view can question the code of civil society? The answer is simple, concrete, specific, and real: women's social inequality with men on the basis of sex, hence the point of view of women's subordination to men. Women are not permitted fully to know what sex equality would look like, because they have never lived it. It is idealist, hence elitist, to hold that they do. But they do not need to. They know inequality because they have lived it, so they know what removing barriers to equality would be. Many of these barriers are legal; many of them are

social; most of them exist at an interface between law and society.

Inequality on the basis of sex, women share. It is women's collective condition. The first task of a movement for social change is to face one's situation and name it. The failure to face and criticize the reality of women's condition, a failure of idealism and denial, is a failure of feminism in its liberal forms. The failure to move beyond criticism, a failure of determinism and radical paralysis, is a failure of feminism in its left forms. Feminism on its own terms has begun to give voice to and describe the collective condition of women as such, so largely composed as it is of all women's particularities. It has begun to uncover the laws of motion of a system that keeps women in a condition of imposed inferiority. It has located the dynamic of the social definition of gender in the sexuality of dominance and subordination, the sexuality of inequality: sex as inequality and inequality as sex. As sexual inequality is gendered as man and women, gender inequity is sexualized as dominance and subordination. The social power of men over women extends through laws that purport to protect women as part of the community, like the rape law; laws that ignore women's survival stake in the issue, like the obscenity law, or obscure it, like the abortion law; and laws that announce their intent to remedy that inequality but do not, like the sex equality law. This law derives its authority from reproducing women's social inequality to men in legal inequality, in a seamless web of life and law.

Feminist method adopts the point of view of women's inequality to men. Grasping women's reality from the inside, developing its specificities, facing the intractability and pervasiveness of male power, relentlessly criticizing women's condition as it identifies with all women, it has created strategies for change, beginning with consciousness raising. On the level of the state, legal guarantees of equality in liberal regimes provide an opening. Sex inequality is the true name for women's social condition. It is also, in words anyway, illegal sometimes. In some

5   Karl Marx, *The Poverty of Philosophy* (New York: International Publishers, 1963), p. 174.

6   Karl Marx and Friedrich Engels, *The Holy Family*, trans. R. Dixon (Moscow: Progress, 1956), p. 157. See generally M. Cain and A. Hunt, *Marx and Engels on Law* (London: Academic Press, 1979).

liberal states, the belief that women already essentially have sex equality extends to the level of law. From a perspective that understands that women do not have sex equality, this law means that once equality is meaningfully defined, the law cannot be applied without changing society. To make sex equality meaningful in law requires identifying the real issues, and establishing that sex inequality, once established, matters.

Sex equality in law has not been meaningfully defined for women but has been defined and limited from the male point of view to correspond to the existing social reality of sex inequality. An alternative approach to this mainstream view threads through existing law. It is the reason sex equality law exists at all. In this approach, inequality is a matter not of sameness and difference, but of dominance and subordination. Inequality is about power, its definition, and its maldistribution. Inequality at root is grasped as a question of hierarchy, which—as power succeeds in constructing social perception and social reality—derivatively becomes categorical distinctions, differences. Where mainstream equality law is abstract, this approach is concrete; where mainstream equality law is falsely universal, this approach remains specific.[7] The goal is not to make legal categories that trace and trap the status quo, but to confront by law the inequalities in women's condition in order to change them.

This alternative approach centers on the most sex-differential abuses of women as a gender, abuses

that sex equality law in its sameness/difference obsession cannot confront. It is based on the reality that feminism, beginning with consciousness raising, has most distinctively uncovered, a reality about which little systematic was known before 1970: the reality of sexual abuse. It combines women's sex-based destitution and enforced dependency and permanent relegation to disrespected and starvation-level work—the lived meaning of class for women—with the massive amount of sexual abuse of girls apparently endemic to the patriarchal family, the pervasive rape and attempted rape about which nothing is done, the systematic battery of women in homes, and prostitution—the fundamental condition of women—of which the pornography industry is an arm. Keeping the reality of gender in view makes it impossible to see gender as a difference, unless this subordinated condition of women is that difference. This reality has called for a new conception of the problem of sex inequality, hence a new legal conception of it, both doctrinally and jurisprudentially.

Experiences of sexual abuse have been virtually excluded from the mainstream doctrine of sex equality because they happen almost exclusively to women and because they are experienced as sex. Sexual abuse has not been seen to raise sex equality issues because these events happen specifically and almost exclusively to women as women. Sexuality is socially organized to require sex inequality for excitement and satisfaction. The least extreme expression of gender inequality, and the prerequisite for all of it, is dehumanization and objectification. The most extreme is violence. Because sexual objectification and sexual violence are almost uniquely done to women, they have been systematically treated as the sex difference when they represent the socially situated subjection of women to men. The whole point of women's social relegation to inferiority as a gender is that this is not generally done to men. The systematic relegation of an entire people to a condition of inferiority is attributed to them, made a feature of theirs, and read out of equality demands and equal-

---

7   Examples are Loving v. Virginia, 388 U.S. 1(1967); Brown v. Board of Education, 347 U.S. 483(1954); some examples of the law against sexual harassment (e.g., Barnes v. Costle, 561 F.2d 983 [D.C. Cir. 1977]; Vinson v. Taylor, 753 F.2d 141 [D.C. Cir. 1985], aff'd. 477 U.S. 57 [1986]; Priest v. Rotary, 98 F.R.D. 755 [D.Cal. 1983]), some athletics cases (e.g.. Clark v. Arizona Interscholastic Assn., 695 F.2d 1126 [9th Cir. 1986]), some affirmative action cases (e.g., Johnson v. Transportation Agency, Santa Clara County, 480 U.S. 616 [1987]), and California Federal Savings and Loan Association v. Guerra, 492 U.S. 272 (1987).

ity law when it is termed a *difference*. This condition is ignored entirely, with all the women who are determined by it, when only features women share with the privileged group are allowed to substantiate equality claims.

It follows that seeing sex equality questions as matters of reasonable or unreasonable classification of relevant social characteristics expresses male dominance in law. If the shift in perspective from gender as difference to gender as dominance is followed, gender changes from a distinction that is ontological and presumptively valid to a detriment that is epistemological and presumptively suspect. The given becomes the contingent. In this light, liberalism, purporting to discover gender, has discovered male and female in the mirror of nature; the left has discovered masculine and feminine in the mirror of society. The approach from the standpoint of the subordination of women to men, by contrast, criticizes and claims the specific situation of women's enforced inferiority and devaluation, pointing a way out of the infinity of reflections in law-and-society's hall of mirrors where sex equality law remains otherwise trapped.

Equality understood substantively rather than abstractly, defined on women's own terms and in terms of women's concrete experience, is what women in society most need and most do not have. Equality is also what society holds that women have already and therefore guarantees women by positive law. The law of equality, statutory and constitutional, therefore provides a peculiar jurisprudential opportunity, a crack in the wall between law and society. Law does not usually guarantee rights to things that do not exist. This may be why equality issues have occasioned so many jurisprudential disputes about what law is and what it can and should do. Every demand from women's point of view looks substantive, just as every demand from women's point of view requires change. Can women, demanding actual equality through law, be part of changing the state's relation to women and women's relation to men?

The first step is to claim women's concrete reality. Women's inequality occurs in a context of unequal pay, allocation to disrespected work, demeaned physical characteristics, targeting for rape, domestic battery, sexual abuse as children, and systematic sexual harassment. Women are daily dehumanized, used in denigrating entertainment, denied reproductive control, and forced by the conditions of their lives into prostitution. These abuses occur in a legal context historically characterized by disenfranchisement, preclusion from property ownership, exclusion from public life, and lack of recognition of sex specific injuries.[8] Sex inequality is thus a social and political institution.

The next step is to recognize that male forms of power over women are affirmatively embodied as individual rights in law. When men lose power, they feel they lose rights. Often they are not wrong. Examples include the defense of mistaken belief in consent in the rape law, which legally determines whether or not a rape occurred from the rapist's perspective; freedom of speech, which gives pimps rights to torture, exploit, use, and sell women to men through pictures and words and gives consumers rights to buy them; the law of privacy, which defines the home and sex as presumptively consensual and protects the use of pornography in the home; the law of child custody, which purports gender neutrality while applying a standard of adequacy of parenting based on male-controlled resources and male-defined norms, sometimes taking children away from women but more generally controlling women through the threat and fear of loss of their children. Real sex equality under

---

8   This context was argued as the appropriate approach to equality in an intervention by the Women's Legal Education and Action Fund (LEAF) in Law Society of British Columbia v. Andrews (May 22, 1987) before the Supreme Court of Canada. This approach to equality in general, giving priority to concrete disadvantage and rejecting the "similarly situated" test, was adopted by the Supreme Court of Canada in that case (1989)—D.L.R. (3d)—.

law would qualify or eliminate these powers of men, hence men's current "rights" to use, access, possess, and traffic women and children.

In this context, many issues appear as sex equality issues for the first time—sexual assault, for example. Rape is a sex-specific violation. Not only are the victims of rape overwhelmingly women, perpetrators overwhelmingly men, but also the rape of women by men is integral to the way inequality between the sexes occurs in life. Intimate violation with impunity is an ultimate index of social power. Rape both evidences and practices women's low status relative to men. Rape equates female with violable and female sexuality with forcible intrusion in a way that defines and stigmatizes the female sex as a gender. Threat of sexual assault is threat of punishment for being female. The state has laws against sexual assault, but it does not enforce them. Like lynching at one time, rape is socially permitted, though formally illegal. Victims of sex crimes, mostly women and girls, are thus disadvantaged relative to perpetrators of sex crimes, largely men.

A systemic inequality between the sexes therefore exists in the social practice of sexual violence, subjection to which defines women's status, and victims of which are largely women, and in the operation of the state, which *de jure* outlaws sexual violence but de facto permits men to engage in it on a wide scale. Making sexual assault laws gender neutral does nothing to address this, nothing to alter the social equation of female with rapeable, and may obscure the sex specificity of the problem. Rape should be defined as sex by compulsion, of which physical force is one form. Lack of consent is redundant and should not be a separate element of the crime.[9] Ex-

panding this analysis would support as sex equality initiatives laws keeping women's sexual histories out of rape trials[10] and publication bans on victims' names and identities.[11] The defense of mistaken belief in consent—which measures whether a rape occurred from the standpoint of the (male) perpetrator—would violate women's sex equality rights by law because it takes the male point of view on sexual violence against women.[12] Similarly, the systematic failure of the state to enforce the rape law effectively or at all excludes women from equal access to justice, permitting women to be savaged on a mass scale, depriving them of equal protection and equal benefit of the laws.

Reproductive control, formerly an issue of privacy, liberty, or personal security, would also become a sex equality issue. The frame for analyzing reproductive issues would expand from focus on the individual at the moment of the abortion decision to women as a group at all reproductive moments. The social context of gender inequality denies women control over the reproductive uses of their bodies and places that control in the hands of men. In a context of inadequate and unsafe contraceptive technology, women are socially disadvantaged in controlling sexual access to their bodies through social learning, lack of information, social pressure, custom, poverty and enforced economic dependence, sexual force, and ineffective enforcement of laws against sexual

---

9   See Ill. Rev. Stat. 1985, ch. 38, par. 12-14; People v. Haywood, 515 N.E.2d 45 (Ill. App. 1987) (prosecution not required to prove nonconsent, since sexual penetration by force implicitly shows nonconsent); but cf. People v. Coleman, 520 N.E.2d 55 (Ill. App. 1987) (state must prove victim's lack of consent beyond reasonable doubt).

10   This is argued by LEAF in its intervention application with several groups in Seaboyer v. The Queen (July 12, 1988) and Gayme v. The Queen (November 18, 1988), both on appeal before the Supreme Court of Canada. The rulings below are The Queen v. Seaboyer and Gayme (1986) 50 C.R. (3d) 395 (Ont. C.A.).

11   LEAF and a coalition of rape crisis centers, groups opposing sexual assault of women and children, and feminist media made this argument in an intervention in The Queen v. Canadian Newspapers Co., Ltd. The Canadian statute was upheld by a unanimous court. (1988)—D.L.R. (3d)—.

12   This is argued by LEAF intervening in The Queen v. Gayme.

assault. As a result, they often do not control the conditions under which they become pregnant. If intercourse cannot be presumed to be controlled by women, neither can pregnancy. Women have also been allocated primary responsibility for intimate care of children yet do not control the conditions under which they rear them, hence the impact of these conditions on their own lives.

In this context, access to abortion is necessary for women to survive unequal social circumstances. It provides a form of relief, however punishing, in a life otherwise led in conditions that preclude choice in ways most women have not been permitted to control. This approach also recognizes that whatever is done to the fetus is done to a woman. Whoever controls the destiny of a fetus controls the destiny of a woman. Whatever the conditions of conception, if reproductive control of a fetus is exercised by any-one but the woman, reproductive control is taken only from women, as women. Preventing a woman from exercising the only choice an unequal society leaves her is an enforcement of sex inequality. Giving women control over sexual access to their bodies and adequate support of pregnancies and care of children extends sex equality. In other words, forced maternity is a practice of sex inequality.[13] Because motherhood without choice is a sex equality issue, legal abortion should be a sex equality right. Reproductive technology, sterilization abuse, and surrogate motherhood, as well as abortion funding, would be transformed if seen in this light.

Pornography, the technologically sophisticated traffic in women that expropriates, exploits, uses, and abuses women, also becomes a sex equality issue. The mass production of pornography univer-salizes the violation of the women in it, spreading it to all women, who are then exploited, used, abused, and reduced as a result of men's consumption of it.

In societies pervaded by pornography, all women are defined by it: This is what a woman wants; this is what a woman is. Pornography sets the public stan-dard for the treatment of women in private and the limits of tolerance for what can be permitted in pub-lic, such as in rape trials. It sexualizes the definition of male as dominant and female as subordinate. It equates violence against women with sex and pro-vides an experience of that fusion. It engenders rape, sexual abuse of children, battery, forced prostitution, and sexual murder.

In liberal legalism, pornography is said to be a form of freedom of speech. It seems that women's inequality is something pornographers want to say, and saying it is protected even if it requires doing it. Being the medium for men's speech supersedes any rights women have. Women become men's speech in this system. Women's speech is silenced by por-nography and the abuse that is integral to it. From women's point of view, obscenity law's misrepre-sentation of the problem as moral and ideational is replaced with the understanding that the problem of pornography is political and practical. Obscenity law is based on the point of view of male dominance. Once this is exposed, the urgent issue of freedom of speech for women is not primarily the avoidance of state intervention as such, but getting equal access to speech for those to whom it has been denied. First the abuse must be stopped.[14] The endless moral debates between good and evil, conservative and liberal, artists and philistines, the forces of darkness and repression and suppression and the forces of light and liberation and tolerance would be super-seded by the political debate, the abolitionist debate: Are women human beings or not? Apparently, the answer provided by legal mandates of sex equality requires repeating.

---

13 This argument was advanced by LEAF in an intervention in Borowski v. Attorney General of Canada (October 7, 1987).

14 The Anti-Pornography Civil Rights Ordinance aims to do this. See Andrea Dworkin and Catharine A. MacKinnon, *Pornography and Civil Rights: A New Day for Women's Equality* (Minneapolis: Organizing Against Pornography, 1988).

The changes that a sex equality perspective provides as an interpretive lens include the law of sex equality itself. The intent requirement would be eliminated. The state action requirement would weaken. No distinction would be made between nondiscrimination and affirmative action. Burdens of proof would presuppose inequality rather than equality as a factual backdrop and would be more substantively sensitive to the particularities of sex inequality. Comparable worth would be required. Statistical proofs of disparity would be conclusive. The main question would be, Does a practice participate in the subordination of women to men, or is it no part of it? Whether statutes are sex specific or gender neutral would not be as important as whether they work to end or reinforce male supremacy, whether they are concretely grounded in women's experience of subordination or not. Discrimination law would not be confined to employment, education, and accommodation. Civil remedies in women's hands would be emphasized. Gay and lesbian rights would be recognized as sex equality rights. Since sexuality largely defines gender, discrimination based on sexuality is discrimination based on gender. Other forms of social discrimination and exploitation by men against women, such as prostitution and surrogate motherhood, would become actionable.

The relation between life and law would also change. Law, in liberal jurisprudence, objectifies social life. The legal process reflects itself in its own image, makes be there what it puts there, while presenting itself as passive and neutral in the process. To undo this, it will be necessary to grasp the dignity of women without blinking at the indignity of women's condition, to envision the possibility of equality without minimizing the grip of inequality, to reject the fear that has become so much of women's sexuality and the corresponding denial that has become so much of women's politics, and to demand civil parity without pretending that the demand is neutral or that civil equality already exists. In this attempt, the idealism of liberalism and the materialism of the left have come to much the same for women. Liberal jurisprudence that the law should reflect nature or society and left jurisprudence that all law does or can do is reflect existing social relations are two guises of objectivist epistemology. If objectivity is the epistemological stance of which women's sexual objectification is the social process, its imposition the paradigm of power in the male form, then the state appears most relentless in imposing the male point of view when it comes closest to achieving its highest formal criterion of distanced aperspectivity. When it is most ruthlessly neutral, it is most male; when it is most sex blind, it is most blind to the sex of the standard being applied. When it most closely conforms to precedent, to "facts," to legislative intent, it most closely enforces socially male norms and most thoroughly precludes questioning their content as having a point of view at all.

Abstract rights authorize the male experience of the world. Substantive rights for women would not. Their authority would be the currently unthinkable: nondominant authority, the authority of excluded truth, the voice of silence. It would stand against both the liberal and left views of law. The liberal view that law is society's text, its rational mind, expresses the male view in the normative mode; the traditional left view that the state, and with it the law, is superstructural or ephiphenomenal expresses it in the empirical mode. A feminist jurisprudence, stigmatized as particularized and protectionist in male eyes of both traditions, is accountable to women's concrete conditions and to changing them. Both the liberal and the left views rationalize male power by presuming that it does not exist, that equality between the sexes (room for marginal corrections conceded) is society's basic norm and fundamental description. Only feminist jurisprudence sees that male power does exist and sex equality does not, because only feminism grasps the extent to which antifeminism is misogyny and both are as normative as they are empirical. Masculinity then appears as a specific position, not just the way things are, its judgments and partialities revealed in process and procedure, adjudication and legislation.

Equality will require change, not reflection—a new jurisprudence, a new relation between life and law. Law that does not dominate life is as difficult to envision as a society in which men do not dominate women, and for the same reasons. To the extent feminist law embodies women's point of view, it will be said that its law is not neutral. But existing law is not neutral. It will be said that it undermines the legitimacy of the legal system. But the legitimacy of existing law is based on force at women's expense. Women have never consented to its rule—suggesting that the system's legitimacy needs repair that women are in a position to provide. It will be said that feminist law is special pleading for a particular group and one cannot start that or where will it end. But existing law is already special pleading for a particular group, where it has ended. The question is not where it will stop but whether it will start for any group but the dominant one. It will be said that feminist law cannot win and will not work. But this is premature. Its possibilities cannot be assessed in the abstract but must engage the world. A feminist theory of the state has barely been imagined; systematically, it has never been tried.

◆ ◆ ◆ ◆ ◆

RICHARD DELGADO

"About Your Masthead: A Preliminary Inquiry into the Compatibility of Civil Rights and Civil Liberties," from *Harvard Civil Rights— Civil Liberties Law Review*

Introduction: Formal Rules and Substantive Justice

> *One day, a lawyer dies and goes to Heaven, where he is met by St. Peter outside the Pearly Gates.*
>
> *"What do we have here?" St. Peter asks.*
>
> *"A lawyer," he replies.*
>
> *"Another one. We've sure been getting a lot of those lately. Well, what do you have to say for yourself?"*
>
> *"I followed all the rules," the lawyer replies, modestly, but with quiet pride. "I never broke any of the canons of professional responsibility, and I got all my briefs in on time. Except one, when my wife had a baby. But the judge gave me an extension."*
>
> *"Not bad. Did you represent plaintiffs or defendants?"*
>
> *"Both, in equal numbers. And I was respectful to everyone—my adversary, witnesses, and, of course, the judge."*
>
> *"Let's see," says St. Peter, picking up a thick book marked LEGALITY. After thumbing through a few pages, he says "Here you are. Right there on page three. Not bad. It seems you colored between the lines at all times. You cited case law accurately, so far as we can tell, given the indeterminacy thesis.[1] And you*

---

1   On the indeterminacy thesis, see Robert L. Hayman, Jr., Nancy Levit & Richard Delgado, *Jurisprudence Classical*

never coached a witness or engaged in a conflict of interest."

"So, do I get in?" the lawyer asks, eagerly.

"There's just one more thing," St. Peter replies, picking up a second book labeled JUSTICE. "Hmmm. I don't see you on page three in this one." He leafs through several more pages, then looks up. "We'll have to look into this a little further. Please take a seat over there for a minute." Clapping his hands: "Research assistant!"[2]

The point of this story, of course, is that formal rules do not necessarily guarantee justice; indeed some of history's most ignoble chapters—slavery, Indian relocation, World War II internment, the Holocaust, Operation Wetback—seem to have been completely legal at the time.[3] This quandary suggests a second one that is the subject of this Essay: What is the relationship between the group of largely formal rules known as civil liberties and the set of substantive values known as racial justice or civil rights?

The editors of *CR-CL* [*Harvard Civil Rights-Civil Liberties Law Review*] have invited me to offer my thoughts on the relationship between civil rights and civil liberties. Both are emblazoned on their masthead. A few years ago, one of my favorite authors,

historian Robin Kelley, wrote a prize-winning book about white media, black culture, and the huge gulf between them, entitled *Yo' Mama's Disfunktional.*[4] Does a similar gap exist between civil rights and civil liberties? Is the masthead dysfunctional, committing *CR-CL* by its terms to an inherently self-contradictory agenda, like a law review that billed itself as "The Global Development and Environmental Protection Journal" or "The Review of Religion and Atheism"?

Are civil liberties and civil rights in tension, pulling in different directions? Is it possible for a society to have both, in full measure and without limitation? If not, should *CR-CL* split up into two separate journals? Part I of this Essay examines a few instances in which civil rights and civil liberties may be entirely compatible. Then, Part II shows how our system of civil rights and civil liberties can exhibit tensions and strains, as exemplified in the area of hate speech. Part III explains the source of these tensions, while Part IV offers some thoughts on how to live with them. I hope that what follows will prove helpful not just in this one area but will also enable us to understand better the relations between civil rights and civil liberties in general. As you may recall, the poor lawyer who spent his life maximizing one variable is still sitting anxiously on that chair outside the Pearly Gates, waiting for the overall verdict on whether his life served justice in the law.

I. Some Initial Instances in Which Civil Rights and Civil Liberties May Be Compatible

In one sense, civil liberties and civil rights are certainly compatible in that they are both aspects of the good life. One would not want to live in a society

---

and Contemporary: From Natural Law to Postmodernism 402–09, 431 (2002).

2   This story occurred to me when I learned that a liberal legal advocacy organization declined to send a speaker to a Harvard Law School program on the ground that civil rights and civil liberties are exactly the same and cannot conflict. Telephone conversation with Joi Chaney, Editor, *CR-CL* (Apr. 2, 2003).

3   *See, e.g.*, Dred Scott v. Sandford, 60 U.S. (19 How.) 393 (1856) (declaring that slaves and their descendants are not U.S. citizens entitled to the privileges and immunities of citizenship); Korematsu v. United States, 323 U.S. 214 (1944) (upholding internment of Japanese Americans). *See also* Juan Perea et al., *Race and Races: Cases and Resources for a Diverse America* 190, 317, 320 (2000) (discussing Indian relocation and Operation Wetback, a Congressionally approved program in which at least 1.3 million Latinos, many of them U.S. citizens, were deported in 1954).

4   Robin D. G. Kelley, *Yo' Mama's Disfunktional: Fighting the Culture Wars in Urban America* (1997) (showing how establishment writers and social scientists depict black "ghetto" society according to frames of reference radically different from those of the residents of inner-city neighborhoods).

that scrupulously protected the interests of minority groups and did not tolerate violations of their civil rights but denied its citizens the rights of free speech, privacy, worship and assembly. By the same token, one would not want to live in a society that safeguarded those rights but treated minorities harshly outside those spheres.

This, however, is not to say very much about their fundamental compatibility. Civil rights and civil liberties may both be desirable, though not simultaneously. When one legal interest is realized, it may interfere with another.[5] One might occupy a higher place in our echelon of values, so that we hesitate to advance the other at its expense.[6] Civil rights and civil liberties might not always be coextensive, so that one could maximize one value in certain settings without interfering with the other. In other settings, the two might conflict.[7] They may be only trivially compatible because of an unimportant element they have in common[8] or by means of a bogus monetization.[9]

One can insist that another person's favorite interest, *properly understood*, is really an aspect of one's own,[10] or imagine civil rights and civil liberties only during good times, when society is faced with little scarcity and people are on their best behavior.[11] One can also frame the issue as pitting a grand, systemic value against an individualized, particularized one held unreasonably by the other side.[12] For example, adherents of free speech absolutism sometimes assert the worth of the generalized value society derives from our system of freedom of expression in light of the momentary annoyance of a Latino or black who is the target of a single, isolated racial epithet. How can the temporary offense of mere wounded feelings stack up against the tremendous gains, including inventions, libraries, presidential debates, and PBS, that spring from our system of free expression?[13]

---

5   For example, national security may conflict with the right of privacy.

6   One might argue that environmental protection trumps the right to drive a large, gas-guzzling car.

7   National security (again) may or may not affect the right to travel—by car to the grocery store versus by private plane above a military base or to a theater of conflict.

8   For example, the Iraqi and U.S. scrap metal associations might both agree that the war in Iraq was a bonanza.

9   Recall how the Bush administration, in March 2003, called for a study to explore assigning monetary values to each of our civil liberties. The idea is that, in times of war, the Executive branch would like to feel free to engage in surveillance of private citizens, read their mail and credit card records, and see what books and videos they check out from libraries. To prevent its doing so too cavalierly, the Office of Management and Budget proposed to find out how much value citizens assign these rights; the government would then weigh that against the value it placed on national security objectives. According to press accounts, the ACLU thought this was a good idea. *See* Edmund L. Andrews, "Threats and Responses: Liberty and Security," *N.Y. Times*, Mar. 11, 2003, at A13.

10   For example, some pro-development forces insist that environmental interests, properly understood, are really part of national energy policy.

11   In an idyllic society, in which few speakers use hate speech to threaten equality and human dignity, why would one need hate speech controls? Racist speech would carry little sting, while protection against the rare case could chill legitimate expression.

12   In the free-speech-versus-hate-speech setting, see Samuel Walker, *Hate Speech: The History of an American Controversy* 20–21, 165–67 (1994); Nadine Strossen, "Regulating Racist Speech on Campus," in *Speaking of Race, Speaking of Sex: Hate Speech, Civil Rights and Civil Liberties* 212 (Henry Louis Gates et al. eds., 1994) [hereinafter, Strossen, "Regulating Racist Speech"]; Nadine Strossen, "A Feminist Critique of 'The' Feminist Critique of Pornography," 79 *Va. L. Rev.* 1099, 1170–71 (1993) [hereinafter, Strossen, "A Feminist Critique"].

13   Of course, advocates for minority causes are sometimes guilty of asking the same sort of loaded question. They may ask how anyone could sacrifice *their* favorite value—equality—for the mere momentary relief some Nazi or skinhead derives from hurling invective or burning a cross in the front yard of an African American family. *See* Richard Delgado, "Campus Antiracism Rules: Constitutional Narratives in Collision," 85 *Nw. U. L. Rev.* 343 (1991) [hereinafter Delgado, "Narratives in Collision"] (calling attention to this and similar strate-

These efforts at reconciliation are unsuccessful because they dodge hard cases, minimize conflicts that are real, or define the area of disagreement in a manner that allows only one answer.[14] Using the example of hate speech, I will demonstrate that the alleged tension between civil liberties and civil rights is real, and examine what drives it and how we should think about and learn to live with it.

II. Hate Speech and the Debate Surrounding Civil Rights and Civil Liberties

Free speech absolutists and critical race theorists have taken opposing positions regarding hate speech. Absolutists, including the ACLU [ed. note: American Civil Liberties Union], maintain that a certain amount of vigorous criticism, even hate speech, is inherent in a democracy such as ours. A vital liberty and a cornerstone of democracy, speech must never be suppressed. In contrast, the Critical Race Theory position holds that hate speech silences its victims, contributes to a climate of disrespect for women and minorities, and undermines the very democracy that free speech is said to undergird. Each side marshals case law and policy justifications in support of its position.

A. The Absolutist Position

The national organization of the ACLU represents the absolutist position, that all speech should receive blanket protection under the First Amendment.[15] Except for speech used in the furtherance of crime, few restraints on its exercise are acceptable. If campus authorities wish to confront a tide of racist slurs, graffiti, and e-mails disparaging students of color, a speech code is not an appropriate remedy. Instead, it is argued that minority students should learn to speak back or ignore the offenders.[16] Authorities can condemn racist remarks, declaring them tawdry and in poor taste.[17] Moreover, if hate speech is delivered in a way that inspires fear, authorities can charge assault; if the speech defaces university property, they can charge trespass or similar offenses.[18] Civil rights and minority interests are thus worthy of protection but only insofar as they do not limit speech.

The absolutist scholars believe that both constitutional bedrock and current case law support their position. Doctrines such as the prohibition of

---

gies on the part of the minority Left). Both approaches juxtapose an emaciated, individualized, slice-of-life version of the competing interest against a robust, grand picture of their own; guess which one prevails? See Richard Delgado & Jean Stefancic, *Understanding Words that Wound* (forthcoming 2004) [hereinafter Delgado & Stefancic, *Understanding Words that Wound*] (discussing this strategy).

14 For instance, one might argue that equality is a matter of giving everyone enough rights, and so civil rights collapses into—and is "nothing more than"—civil liberties distributed widely and impartially. See Peter Weston, "The Empty Idea of Equality," 95 *Harv. L. Rev.* 537 (1982) (making a version of this argument). If this were the case, however, the problem with which this essay is concerned would emerge in another form, since one very large component of rights (free speech) would be at odds with another (freedom from hate speech). Similarly, the counterposing of a large, generalized value dressed up in dramatic language against the opponent's value depicted in emaciated, unattractive terms is a transparent debater's device—the way one asks the question implies that only one answer is possible. See supra note 13.

---

15 See, e.g., Nat Hentoff, *Free Speech for Me—But Not for Thee* (1992); Aryeh Neier, *Defending My Enemy* (1979); Walker, *supra* note 12; Strossen, "Regulating Racist Speech," *supra* note 12.

16 See, e.g., Hentoff, *supra* note 15, at 100–02, 111, 159, 167 (forcefully advocating the talk-back solution).

17 See Charles Calleros, "Paternalism, Counterspeech, and Campus Hate Speech," 27 *Ariz. St. L.J.* 1249 (1995); Nadine Strossen, "Regulating Hate Speech on Campus: A Modest Proposal?," 1990 *Duke L.J.* 484, 562 (1990) [hereinafter Strossen, "Hate Speech on Campus"].

18 Nadine Strossen made this comment during a debate with this author at Cornell University in the fall of 1995.

content and viewpoint discrimination,[19] Supreme Court decisions such as *R.A.V. v. St. Paul*,[20] *Texas v. Johnson*,[21] and *New York Times v. Sullivan*,[22] and a trio of lower court cases invalidating university speech codes at Wisconsin,[23] Michigan,[24] and Stanford,[25] all suggest that campus hate speech rules are unlikely to withstand judicial scrutiny.[26]

Still, a few cases can be read to uphold speech codes,[27] and the belated development of First Amendment legal realism[28] has been engendering doubt in some of the faithful absolutist scholars. In response, they have sought to fortify their position with policy arguments. One, the "best friend" argument, holds that free speech is minorities' most reliable ally. If those clamoring for hate speech regulation knew the history of minorities in this country, the argument goes, they would realize the vital part that speech, marching, and protests have played in the struggle for civil rights; consequently, they would hesitate to impose limitations on such a precious instrument.[29] A second, "pressure valve" argument holds that permitting racists to unburden themselves of vituperative language allows them to discharge anger that might otherwise explode in more damaging forms, such as physical attacks. If outsider groups realized this, they would stop demanding hate speech rules that only place them in greater jeopardy.[30] A third argument asserts that hate speech rules will end up hurting minorities because authorities will inevitably apply the new rules against them when they speak out against their oppressors. Lastly, another absolutist argument holds that more speech is always the preferred response to bad speech. Hate speech rules preempt private responses, so that minorities never learn how to defend themselves. Talking back to the aggressor is empowering, while running to the authorities whenever one hears a hurtful word increases one's sense of helplessness and victimization.[31] Free speech absolutists deploy such policy arguments to reason that even if free speech law were to some extent malleable, decision makers should exercise discretion in favor of the cherished freedom of expression.

B. The Critical Race Theory Position

Twenty years ago, *CR-CL* published the first piece of legal scholarship specifically addressing hate speech. Entitled "Words That Wound: A Tort Action for Racial Insults, Epithets, and Name-Calling,"[32] the

---

19   *See* Laurence Tribe, *American Constitutional Law* 790 (2nd ed. 1988).

20   505 U.S. 377 (1992) (striking down an ordinance prohibiting hate speech and conduct).

21   491 U.S. 397 (1989) (striking down a flag-burning statute).

22   376 U.S. 254 (1964) (increasing protection for disfavored libelous speech).

23   UWM Post, Inc. v. Bd. of Regents of Univ. of Wis. Sys., 774 F. Supp. 1163 (E.D. Wis. 1991).

24   Doe v. Univ. of Mich., 721 F. Supp. 852 (E.D. Mich. 1989).

25   Corry v. Stanford Univ., No. 1-94-CV-740309 (Cal. Super. Ct. Feb. 27, 1995).

26   For a review of the ACLU position, see Strossen, "Hate Speech on Campus," *supra* note 17. *See also* Marjorie Heins, "Banning Words: A Comment on Words that Wound," 18 *Harv. C.R.-C.L. L. Rev.* 585 (1983) (reviewing these First Amendment doctrines).

27   *See, e.g.*, Beauharnais v. Illinois, 343 U.S. 250 (1952) (upholding criminal libel statute in face of First Amendment challenge).

28   *See* J.M. Balkin, "Some Realism about Pluralism: Legal Realist Approaches to the First Amendment," 1990 *Duke L.J.* 375 (1990); Richard Delgado, "First Amendment Formalism is Giving Way to First Amendment Legal Realism," 29 *Harv. C.R.-C.L. L. Rev.* 169 (1994) [hereinafter Delgado, "Giving Way"]; Stanley Ingber, "The Marketplace of Ideas: A Legitimizing Myth," 1984 *Duke L.J.* 1 (1984).

29   *See* Richard Delgado & David Yun, "Pressure Valves and Bloodied Chickens: An Analysis of Paternalistic Objections to Hate-Speech Regulation," 82 *Cal. L. Rev.* 871, 881–82 (1994) [hereinafter Delgado & Yun, "Bloodied Chickens"].

30   *Id.* at 876–80.

31   *Id.* at 883–85.

32   Richard Delgado, "Words That Wound: A Tort Action for Racial Insults, Epithets, and Name-Calling," 17

article reviewed a number of harms associated with hate speech and name-calling. Urging recognition of a new, freestanding tort, I pointed out that courts were already affording relief under such rubrics as defamation, intentional infliction of emotional distress, assault, and statutory discrimination. A number of United States courts and a landmark Canadian Supreme Court decision followed suit.[33]

A few years later, critical race theorist Mari Matsuda, in a much-cited article, urged that protection against hate speech should be expanded to include public law remedies, such as criminal prosecutions.[34] Then, in the course of a colloquy with ACLU president and law professor Nadine Strossen, Charles Lawrence argued that *Brown v. Board of Education* was a hate speech case, specifically addressing the problem of campus antiracism rules. When the Court reversed long-standing precedent and held that separate schooling sent a socially pernicious message to black schoolchildren, Lawrence argued that it was tacitly holding that certain messages of hate and inferiority should not be spoken. *Brown*, then, would stand as a precedent justifying campus rules aimed at curtailing racist hate speech.[35]

These three articles, and a book growing out of them,[36] could be said to constitute the first wave of hate speech writing and activism. The next major development saw diverging lines of case authority and the advent of a legal theory aimed at interpreting

them. In the early 1990s, two federal courts endorsed the absolutist position in striking down campus hate speech rules at leading universities,[37] while the Canadian Supreme Court, citing American critical race theorists, weighed in with a free speech case asserting more or less the direct opposite.[38] At the same time, federal and state courts were affirming causes of action for minority and female plaintiffs targeted by hate speech in other settings, such as K–12 schools and at work.[39]

Many people then questioned what was happening in the civil rights and civil liberties arena. A second article in the pages of *CR-CL* posited that the judiciary was belatedly beginning to apply the lessons of legal realism to the First Amendment.[40] Rejecting mechanistic tests, shopworn maxims, and per se rules, courts were beginning to consider a host of factors, including setting, power disparities, history, communication theory, and social science, on the way to a decision.[41] Scholars addressed each of the paternalistic objections to hate speech regulation put forth by liberals[42] and another "toughlove" set favored by the neoconservative right.[43] These authors also examined First Amendment romanticism and the idea that only by protecting "the speech we hate" can we safeguard the speech we love.[44]

Further scholarship built upon narrative theory and cognitive psychology to address why more

---

Harv. C.R.-C.L. L. Rev. 133 (1982) [hereinafter Delgado, "Words That Wound: A Tort Action"].

33 *See* Delgado & Stefancic, *Understanding Words that Wound*, *supra* note 13 (discussing this subsequent history).

34 Mari J. Matsuda, "Public Response to Racist Speech: Considering the Victim's Story," 87 *Mich. L. Rev.* 2320 (1989).

35 *See* Charles R. Lawrence III, "If He Hollers Let Him Go: Regulating Racist Speech on Campus," 1990 *Duke L.J.* 431 (1990).

36 Richard Delgado et al., *Words that Wound: Critical Race Theory, Assaultive Speech, and the First Amendment* (1993).

37 UWM Post, 774 F. Supp. 1163; Doe v. Univ. of Mich., 721 F. Supp. 852.

38 The Queen v. Keegstra, [1990] 3 S.C.R. 697.

39 *See* Delgado & Stefancic, *Understanding Words that Wound*, *supra* note 13.

40 Delgado, "Giving Way," *supra* note 28.

41 *Id.* at 174.

42 *See* Delgado & Yun, "Bloodied Chickens," *supra* note 29.

43 *See* Richard Delgado & David Yun, "The Neoconservative Case Against Hate-Speech Regulation—Lively, D'Souza, Gates, Carter, and the Toughlove Crowd," 47 *Vand. L. Rev.* 1807 (1994).

44 Richard Delgado & David Yun, "'The Speech We Hate': First Amendment Totalism, the ACLU, and the Principle of Dialogic Politics," 27 *Ariz. St. L.J.* 1281 (1995).

speech—an accurate, countervailing message—cannot always counter the evil of hate speech and why judges find it so difficult to balance free speech and extrinsic interests.[45] Authors examined the experience of other Western democracies that prize freedom of expression, but that nevertheless punish hate speech;[46] they demonstrated that a climate of hate propaganda often precedes and accompanies atrocities like Indian extermination or the Holocaust.[47] The debate over hate speech, then, has become more nuanced, while showing no sign of diminished intensity.

III. *The Source of the Tension*

If the hate speech debate highlights a tension between civil liberties and civil rights generally, what is the source of that tension conceptually, historically, and ideologically?

A. Conceptually

Speech and equality are, as mentioned earlier, aspects of the good life. But they correspond to somewhat different facets. Like most civil liberties, speech exhibits an individual dimension; it is an element of self-expression. Unlike equality and civil rights, which are inherently social in nature, liberty interests are ones we are capable of exercising by ourselves. "Leave me alone; I've got my rights." "Stay off that property; it's mine." "I'll say what I please, this is a free country." As our Critical Legal Studies forebears pointed out, rights of this type correspond to our individual natures. They separate us, emphasizing our individualistic, rights-guarding, solitary tendencies.[48]

Although that characterization might seem needlessly dire, with hate speech at least it may contain a grain of truth. Race may be a social construction, requiring a tacit agreement to endow certain minor human differences with great significance. But how do racial categories receive their content, if not from a system of images, messages, media roles and coverage, narratives, scripts, jokes, and code words such as "those people," "inner city resident," and "unassimilable hordes"—in short, hate speech?[49] Defenders of hate speech emphasize its liberty aspect; detractors focus on its impact on social values and justice. The tension arises from what each group chooses to highlight in its own and then minimize in the other's position.

A second dichotomy, between capitalism and democratic ideals, built into our system of law and politics takes on special force in connection with

---

45   Richard Delgado & Jean Stefancic, "Images of the Outsider in American Law and Culture: Can Free Expression Remedy Systemic Social Ills?," 77 *Cornell L. Rev.* 1258 (1992); Richard Delgado & Jean Stefancic, "Norms and Narratives: Can Judges Avoid Serious Moral Error?," 69 *Tex. L. Rev.* 1929 (1991). *See also* Richard Delgado & Jean Stefancic, "Hateful Speech, Loving Communities: Why Our Notion of 'A Just Balance' Changes So Slowly," 82 *Cal. L. Rev.* 851 (1994) [hereinafter Delgado & Stefancic, "Hateful Speech"].

46   *See, e.g.*, Kevin Boyle, "Hate Speech—The United States Versus the Rest of the World," 53 *Me. L. Rev.* 487, 489 (2001). *See also* Lee Bollinger, *The Tolerant Society* 38 (1986).

47   See generally Alexander Tsesis, *Destructive Messages: How Hate Speech Paves the Way for Harmful Social Movements* (2002).

48   *See, e.g.*, Richard Delgado, "Critical Legal Studies and the Realities of Race—Does the Fundamental Contradiction Have a Corollary?," 23 *Harv. C.R.-C.L. L. Rev.* 407 (1988) (considering the Critical Legal Studies view of rights in relation to minorities' situation); Richard Delgado, "The Ethereal Scholar: Does Critical Legal Studies Have What Minorities Want?," 22 Harv. *C.R.-C.L. L. Rev.* 301 (1987); Peter Gabel, "The Phenomenology of Rights-Consciousness and the Pact of the Withdrawn Selves," 62 *Tex. L. Rev.* 1563 (1984). Civil liberties may hold special appeal to those whose experience has taught them that solo activity is the road to happiness and success; civil rights and broad social justice may attract those whose lives have taught them the need for cooperation and community.

49   *See* Delgado & Stefancic, "Images of the Outsider," *supra* note 45.

hate speech.[50] Our public law, as everyone knows, is committed to radical democracy. All men and women are equal; one person, one vote, and so on. By the same token, our system of tripartite government features a system of checks and balances, with each branch of government playing its own role and limiting the discretion of the others.[51] Our private law, however, is based on libertarian principles and, in the marketplace, capitalism.[52]

This disjunction between a public law full of lofty democratic precepts and aspirations, and a system of moneymaking essentially governed by the acquisitive impulse and protection of settled interests, rarely attracts notice, at least when the two spheres are operating smoothly.[53] Hate speech is a civil liberty that, much like most manifestations of racial discrimination, distorts the marketplace so that private preferences operate irrationally and are impervious to change. It also disserves the dominant values of the public sphere, endangering democratic decisionmaking and full inclusion.[54] Regardless of the public or private terms with which one seeks to justify hate speech, one finds little to commend in it. A strange form of liberty, it wars with other liberties at the same time that it erodes the system of mutual respect on which our society aspires to build a just state.

B. Historically

If civil rights and civil liberties correspond to different impulses and conceptions of national life, they also contract and expand in response to different forces. Many free speech advocates seem to assume a romantic dynamic in which both civil rights and civil liberties expand in response to advancing morality. They believe that when we are good, virtuous, generous, and mindful of our better natures, we expand both our freedoms and the inclusiveness of our institutions.

Derrick Bell and other historians have shown that the interaction of civil rights and civil liberties is more complicated than this idealistic view.[55] Civil rights expand most during wartime or periods of international competition, such as the Cold War, when African Americans registered impressive gains.[56] Those times, of course, are when civil liberties are most in danger of contraction.[57] Conversely, during times of *internal* competition and scarcity, for example when jobs are scarce, the nation experiences an upsurge in racism and a decrease in generosity towards the perceived outcast.[58] But domestic socioeconomic competition seems to have little effect on our regime of civil liberties. Thus, the material forces that drive civil rights and civil liberties differ. One could, of course, still maintain that the two are aspects of the same broader system of social goods or ideal governance. But one would need to concede, I think, that they flourish and contract at different times, in response to different forces.

---

50 *See* Richard Delgado, "Where Is My Body? Stanley Fish's Long Goodbye to Law," 99 *Mich. L. Rev.* 1370, 1384–89 (2001).

51 *Id.* at 1380–89.

52 *Id.* at 1385–89.

53 *Id.* at 1386.

54 *See* Richard Delgado, "Rodrigo's Second Chronicle: The Economics and Politics of Race," 91 *Mich. L. Rev.* 1183, 1189–98 (1993).

55 *See, e.g.*, Derrick Bell, "*Brown v. Board of Education* and the Interest-Convergence Dilemma," 93 *Harv. L. Rev.* 518 (1980).

56 *See* Mary Dudziak, *Cold War Civil Rights: Race and the Image of American Democracy* 79–114, 249–54 (2000). *See also* Richard Delgado, "Explaining the Rise and Fall of African American Fortunes—Interest Convergence and Civil Rights Gains," 37 *Harv. C.R.-C.L. L. Rev.* 369 (2002) (book review) (discussing Cold War tensions as contributing to *Brown v. Board of Education* and the Civil Rights Act of 1964).

57 *See* Richard Delgado, *Justice at War: Civil Liberties and Civil Rights During Times of Crisis* 56–91 (2003).

58 This socioeconomic competition theory of racism and discrimination was probably first explained by Gordon Allport. *See generally* Gordon W. Allport, *The Nature of Prejudice* (1979).

C. Ideologically and Constitutionally

The original Constitution protected the property and political interests of white males, while providing for the continuation of the institution of slavery in no fewer than six clauses.[59] When the Bill of Rights added protection of speech, the Framers almost certainly had in mind the speech, music, literature, arts, and scientific discourse of elite, educated white males, rather than that of women writers, poets, anarchists, immigrants, or black slaves.[60] The document was, in short, stronger on liberty than equality. The protection of the latter came much later, after a bloody civil war and three constitutional amendments.

One could argue that the Fourteenth Amendment gives the First Amendment an equality-protecting gloss, since a common legal maxim holds that a later writing supersedes a previous one on the same subject.[61] But courts and the ACLU have not endorsed this argument. In the meantime, the two sets of constitutional values—protecting equality and safeguarding liberty—operate side by side. They enable us to say, at times of crisis, "We may be sacrificing X—temporarily and slightly—but we are still the Y-est country in the world." Embracing contradictory values enhances legitimacy; when the need arises, one can limit one value and point out how the other remains in full force.

Occasionally, one hears that it is the First Amendment that makes America the most prosperous, freest, most generous country in the world, with the highest standard of living and the greatest degree of personal freedom. However, it may be that the exceptions to the system of free expression, rather than the system itself, make America the country it is. The United States today stands unquestionably atop the world in two dominant respects—military might and economic power.[62] But if our system of free speech plays any part in those achievements, it is because of the protection we afford official and commercial secrets, inventions and creative works.[63] And, of course, everyone knows that the speech of soldiers and government workers is much less free than that of the citizenry at large.

Apart from economic and military power, the United States does not stand at the top of the world.[64] A great income gap separates the richest and poorest sectors, and the country also exhibits high rates of misery in minority communities, including suicide, alcoholism, divorce, incarceration, and early death.[65] Hate speech and media stereotypes, which undoubtedly contribute to the discrimination that engenders this misery, are free under current law. Free speech law, then, may contribute to the flaws of the United States, while the exceptions are responsible for much of its military-industrial prowess. Our reigning free speech ideology pays scant attention to this, just as it screens from view the compromises between liberty and equality reflected in the original Constitution. Thus, many people would wrongly conclude that speech is equally good for everyone and responsible for much of this country's wealth and well-being, when matters are more complicated than that and close to being the other way around.

IV. Is Your Masthead Dysfunctional? How To Live with Competing Paradigms While on the Law Review or Anywhere Else

We want and need both liberty and equality. Yet those two values often are at odds. Hate speech may

---

59   See Derrick Bell, *Race, Racism, and American Law* 45–48 (3rd ed. 2000).

60   See Delgado & Stefancic, "Hateful Speech," *supra* note 45, at 862.

61   See Richard Delgado, "Toward a Legal Realist View of the First Amendment," 113 *Harv. L. Rev.* 778, 800 (2000).

62   *Id.* at 794–95.

63   *Id.*

64   *Id.*

65   *Id.*

bring this conflict into bold relief, but I suspect that examining other areas would reveal similar strains and tensions between what we consider civil rights and civil liberties.

In part because we bring different histories to such controversies, we tend to act as though one half of the problem is insignificant or should be solved by the other side's coming around to our position. For instance, when some people learn that a university is considering a hate speech code, they will frame the issue as a First Amendment problem. This position then shifts the burden to the adversary to show that the interest in protecting members of the minority community from insults and name-calling is compelling enough to overcome the usual presumption that speech should be free.[66] Moreover, the university must show that no less restrictive means are available to advance its objective of protecting outsider groups from disparagement. It must also contend with a host of legal rules, such as the prohibition on content or viewpoint regulation,[67] and maxims such as "the best cure for bad speech is more speech."[68] Furthermore, what of the decisionmaker who will adjudicate claims under the new rules? Might he or she not turn into an overbearing tyrant, imposing his or her own notions of political correctness on an environment that flourishes best when speech is free? For the one whose sympathies run to free speech, certain slopes will look slippery and hard to draw. Couldn't practically everything be considered hate speech, even *Hamlet*?

Others, however, will frame the problem in terms of a different value, equality.[69] Hate speech targets vulnerable minority groups by silencing, marginalizing, and causing some to underperform or drop out. It teaches all who hear or learn about it that equality and civil rights are of no great value, and demoralizes those who would wish to live in a more respectful society. This group will see nothing problematic with granting campuses the power to enact reasonable rules protecting vulnerable members of their communities in order to safeguard core values and institutional concerns emanating from the Thirteenth and Fourteenth amendments.[70]

If one characterizes the issue in this light, a similar set of doctrines and discursive strategies comes into play, but from a different direction. The side championing the right of the hate speaker now needs to show that protecting that form of speech is compelling enough to overcome the legal system's usual presumption in favor of equality and civil rights. It will need to show that the interest of the supremacist in hurling abuse is discharged in the way least damaging to equality. This group, too, will harbor concerns about the adjudicator of such controversies, but from the opposite standpoint. Will he or she have a sufficient background in minority history, code words, and vulnerabilities to know what to look for? A different set of slopes will look slippery, different lines hard to draw.[71]

It is not just that the two sides begin with different constitutional paradigms. Each hears and is attuned to different stories. One side will see the issue as an extension of society's struggle against superstition and ignorance.[72] Its heroes will be Hollywood figures who stood up to the House Un-American Activities Committee, martyrs like Socrates, Gali-

---

66   Delgado, "Narratives in Collision," *supra* note 13, at 345–46.

67   *See supra* text accompanying note 19. *See also* Rodney A. Smolla, "Information as Contraband: The First Amendment and Liability for Trafficking in Speech," 96 *Nw. U. L. Rev.* 1099, 1122 (2002).

68   *See supra* text accompanying note 16. *See also* Felicity Barringer, "Campus Battle Pits Freedom of Speech against Racial Slurs," *N.Y. Times*, Apr. 25, 1989, at A1; Garry Wills, "In Praise of Censure," *Time*, July 31, 1989, at 71.

69   *See* Delgado, "Narratives in Collision," *supra* note 13, at 345–46 (commenting on how the adversaries' slopes always look slipperier than one's own).

70   *Id.* at 346.

71   *Id.* at 345–46.

72   *Id.*

leo, and Peter Zenger, and theorists like Hobbes, Voltaire, and Hume who defended the value of free expression. They will evoke struggles against state-sponsored censorship, Hollywood blacklists, official religion, and book burning.[73] Juxtaposed with stories like these, the interest of a minority group in guarding against an occasional wounded feeling will not loom large.

The other side, however, will tell a story of its own.[74] That story includes World War II resistance fighters who stood up for Jews and members of the underground railroad who risked their lives to help slaves reach freedom. It includes Martin Luther King, college students who put their lives on the line during the Civil Rights movement, and Mexican farm-workers who picketed California grape producers to protest inhumane working conditions. Compared to that stirring, centuries-long struggle for equality and human decency, the interest of an ignoramus or white supremacist in cussing out a fellow student of color will look pretty attenuated.[75]

My view, and here is where your masthead comes in, is that both views are equally valid but not because they are complementary or coexist easily side by side. They are no more compatible than a private system of competitive free market economics that coexists with a public law system based on radical democracy and equal participation.[76]

Nor can judges easily and comfortably balance the two sets of values. Any new proposal (such as hate speech rules) runs counter to a host of entrenched narratives. The judge, a member of an interpretive community, will be asked to strike the balance in a way that changes the contours of that community,[77] treating groups who are currently

outsiders with greater respect than that which they now receive. Judges are not simply balancing two discrete interests, like one neighbor's desire to have a fence and another's wish to receive unblocked sunlight in her living room. Rather they are deciding between two versions of speech/equality, two interpretive communities in which we might live.[78] It is easy to overlook that a vigorous system of free speech requires a respectful audience, while equality, at least in an instrumental sense, requires speech, remonstrance, the right to petition and protest unfair conditions. Thus, speech and equality both presuppose and endanger each other by mechanisms so subtle and linked that shifting the balance in either direction from that to which we are accustomed is a formidable task.[79] The group asking for change can easily be seen as impossible, petty, humorless, or dangerous fanatics prepared to sacrifice precious rights and liberties.

Still, one can reason around the edges. For example, concerted speech, as hate speech is apt to be since it often targets the same victim time and again, stands on a different footing from the isolated kind. Equality means something more when a black undergraduate is told to go back to Africa than it does when a shopper knocks some groceries off a shelf and is reproved for being a clumsy oaf.[80] We can expand analysis, as the legal realists urge, to include considerations of power, communication science and social theory in examining speech in different settings. We can, occasionally, move each other marginally in a different direction, by force of argument or an apt example.

Changing the way we look at core values, especially in relation to others with which they hold a

---

73 *Id.* at 347 (citing Zechariah Chafee, *Free Speech in the United States* 497–501 (1941)).

74 *Id.*

75 *Id.*

76 *See supra* text accompanying notes 50–54.

77 Delgado & Stefancic, "Hateful Speech," *supra* note 45, at 854–59.

78 *Id.* This, in turn, would seem to require a pre-political normative reckoning—perhaps because relatively few cases call for this sort of analysis.

79 *Id.* at 854–59, 868–69.

80 *See* Delgado, "Words That Wound: A Tort Action," *supra* note 32, at 136 (arguing that racist slurs are more damaging than most other kinds).

close association, is a challenging, sometimes uncomfortable task. Recall the lawyer we left nervously waiting to find out his standing in that second book, the one that evaluated him from the unfamiliar reference point of justice. I do not believe such predicaments are forms of cultural schizophrenia. Instead, I think the willingness to confront social reality in all its guises is an indication of courage and good health. *CR-CL*, in my opinion, should keep its masthead exactly the same—but continue to consider, struggle, and reckon with the tension it bespeaks.

◆ ◆ ◆ ◆ ◆

STUDY QUESTIONS

1. Can feminist criticisms of law be met by ensuring that women are treated as moral equals under the law?

2. What problems does Professor MacKinnon find with male-centred conceptions of sex equality?

3. What, according to CRT theorists such as Professor Delgado, is wrong with seeking justice for all by treating all citizens in exactly the same way?

4. Does a 'Critical Race Theory of Law' emerge from the combination of a narrative approach, focus on particular experiences of law, and a pragmatic attitude to civil rights and liberties? Does justice for minorities of color need such an independent theory?

◆ ◆ ◆ ◆ ◆

FURTHER READINGS

Carol A. Aylward, *Canadian Critical Race Theory: Racism and the Law*. Black Point, NS: Fernwood Publishing, 1999.

Judith A. Baer, *Our Lives Before the Law: Constructing a Feminist Jurisprudence*. Princeton: Princeton University Press, 1999.

Derrick A. Bell, *Race, Racism and American Law*, 4th ed. Boston: Little Brown & Co., 2000.

Brown v. Board of Education of Topeka, 347 U.S. 483 (1954).

Kimberlé Crenshaw, N. Gotanda, G. Peller, and K. Thomas, eds. *Critical Race Theory: The Key Writings That Formed the Movement*. New York: The New Press, 1995.

Richard Delgado and Jean Stefancic, *Critical Race Theory: An Introduction*. New York: New York University Press, 2001.

Mark Kelman, *A Guide to Critical Legal Studies*. Cambridge, MA: Harvard University Press, 1987.

Nicola Lacey, *Unspeakable Subjects*. Oxford: Hart Publications, 1998.

Catharine MacKinnon, *Women's Lives, Men's Laws*. Cambridge, MA: Harvard University Press, 2005.

Matsuda, Mari J., *Words That Wound: Critical Race Theory, Assaultive Speech, and the First Amendment, New Perspectives on Law, Culture, and Society*. Boulder, CO: Westview Press, 1993.

R v. Butler, [1992] 1 S. C. R. 452.

Patricia Williams, *The Alchemy of Race and Rights*. Cambridge, MA: Harvard University Press, 1991.

SECTION II

Law and Limits on Individual Liberty

LAW AND LIMITS ON INDIVIDUAL LIBERTY

INTRODUCTION

The articles in this section examine legal limits on individual freedoms. We often hear in films or on television that "It's a free country so I'll do what I want," and we may desire a great deal of individual freedom. Yet even a very little experience soon shows that we cannot have both unlimited individual freedom and the benefits of social life. Some freedoms must be limited for the sake of group coordination in the use of some shared resource, as occurs when we all accept the rule that in North America cars are to be driven on the right side of the road. In other situations it appears that certain limits on individual freedoms are necessary to preserve the good of the group against the few who will not "play fairly" according to the rules of the group, as we see in rules against riding public transportation without paying. And in still other situations, it seems that an individual's freedom must be limited for the sake of the individual, as when, for example, we refuse to return to our drunk and suicidal friend the elephant gun he left with us for safekeeping. We are familiar with a wide range of limits on individual freedoms, and the justification for many of these limits is plain to see. But how are we certain that we have arrived at the right balance between individual freedom and social good? And who is to say when we are justified in limiting a person's freedom "for her own good"? The authors of the selections in this section offer arguments about the minimum freedoms necessary for a free individual and a good society, and ways to justify limiting individuals' freedoms for their own or their society's good.

1. Mill's *On Liberty*

This section begins with an excerpt from John Stuart Mill's *On Liberty*. John Stuart Mill (1806–1873) lived at the height of the power of the British Empire, and participated vigorously in the intellectual life of the day. He was educated rigorously at home by his famous father, James Mill, who was known for his own writings and his association with Jeremy Bentham, the social philosopher and advocate of the moral theory called Utilitarianism. John Stuart Mill grew up in an atmosphere of boisterous debate over contemporary politics and ways to improve society, and he soon became a leading intellectual voice as he entered his adult career of writing, working for the British East India Company, and serving as a Member of Parliament. By the time Mill's *On Liberty* was published in 1859 he was well-established as one of the keenest minds of the day.

The excerpt from *On Liberty* included here focuses on the freedom or liberty of the individual, and the appropriate limits on laws which interfere with liberty. Here we will focus on three elements of that discussion: autonomy, what has been called the "harm principle," and the idea of paternalism. This introduction will not examine the specific freedoms Mill thinks essential to autonomous persons. Those freedoms are so widespread in the law and culture of the Western world that Mill's arguments are likely to seem very familiar.

The term "autonomy" is derived from two Ancient Greek words, *auto*, which means "self," and *nomos*, which means "law" or "rule." For a person to be autonomous is to be self-ruling, and your autonomy as a person is your ability to make choices and to carry out those choices in practice. For Mill, preservation of individuals' autonomy is fundamentally important to the best society, in which all or nearly all persons can find happiness through making and carrying out their own life-plans. We need individual freedom, according to Mill, because we find happiness in various ways, and we are not good judges of what will make one another happiest. Nor are we generally good guardians of other persons' best interests. As Mill argues, the individual person "is the person most interested in his well-being: the interest which any other person, except in cases of strong personal attachment, can have in it, is trifling, compared with that which he himself has."[1] Finally, it seems that there is something valuable about the freedom to choose how we wish, as individuals, to live. Simply having the freedom to choose is an important aspect of being an independent human being with a unique personal identity and a unique life-plan—including those plans for new ways of living which run contrary to currently accepted ways of living.

If we recognize the desirability of a society in which all or nearly all persons can find happiness, Mill suggests, we must protect as strongly as possible the freedom of individuals to make and carry out their own life-plans. The only acceptable legal limit on freedom is the requirement that our actions do not harm others—and in this requirement we find the harm principle. Mill supposes that "the only freedom worth the name, is that of pursuing our own good in our own way, so long as we do not attempt to deprive others of theirs, or impede their efforts to obtain it."[2] We are only justified, then, in interfering with others' liberties in order to protect ourselves from their impeding our exercise of our liberties. Mill famously asserts that "The sole end for

which mankind are warranted, individually or collectively, in interfering with the liberty of action of any of their number, is self-protection."[3] Whatever else an individual chooses to do is the private concern of that person. We may still criticize persons' private practices, but we may not interfere except when those private practices harm others and in that way are no longer merely private.

When we deny that others know what is really good for them and make decisions on their behalf for their own good we act in a paternal manner. "Paternalism" is derived from the Latin *pater*, meaning "father," and can be intuitively understood as an excess of the sort of concern parents have for their children. For reasons including the assertion that no one knows better than the individual person what will make that person happy, Mill supposes that paternalistic limits on individual freedom are not justified. We are only justified in limiting freedoms when their use harms others. As you will see in the articles by Gerald Dworkin and H.L.A. Hart, Mill's opposition to paternalism may be too strongly stated, and in need of modification.

The harm principle is very controversial, so it is worth returning to it for a moment to discuss a few of the problems you will see as you progress through the articles in this section. Many critics have suggested that it is not possible to distinguish, as Mill does, between an individual's "self-regarding" actions, whose consequences affect only the individual, and "other-regarding" actions, whose consequences affect others beyond the individual. It is not possible, the critics claim, to simply separate all actions into one of these two categories. An action which initially appears to be self-regarding may in the longer term have other-regarding consequences, as a person who abuses alcohol may come to depend on the goodwill and resources of others. Other problems arise from the difficulty of explaining precisely what counts as "harm." Clearly, there are harms beyond the obvious

---

1   *On Liberty*, Chapter IV.
2   *On Liberty*, Chapter I.

3   *On Liberty*, Chapter I.

physical harms we may suffer at the hands of others. False statements about a person's competence or trustworthiness may harm that person's reputation and ability to make a living. Or, conduct may harm valuable institutions which are not persons, yet may nonetheless be damaged. Finally, and perhaps most controversially, persons exposed to certain false or distorted views may come to believe and act on those false views, with harmful consequences to themselves and others. Yet somewhere amongst these setbacks to persons and institutions there must be room for what is offensive or distasteful, but not harmful and not reasonably limited by law. Certain art or politicians' speeches may be in stunningly bad taste, yet still part of the ordinary rough-and-tumble of competing ideas in a free society which values diversity and new ideas for improvements in living. Even these few examples show that the idea of "harm" is far more complex than our daily use of the term might reveal.

2. Gerald Dworkin, "Paternalism"

Professor Gerald Dworkin (of the University of California, Davis, and not the same person as Professor Ronald Dworkin) explores the idea of paternalism. Dworkin asks whether paternalism is ever justified, and in what circumstances. Dworkin suggests that Mill's apparently simple explanation of when we are justified in restricting others' freedoms is actually rather more complex than Mill allows. Further careful investigation is required to reach a clear understanding of the conditions under which freedoms are justifiably limited.

Professor Dworkin defines paternalism as "the interference with a person's liberty of action justified by reasons referring exclusively to the welfare, good, happiness, needs, interests, or values of the person being coerced."[4] Dworkin offers a list of

examples of paternalism, and suggests that it is difficult to find "pure" paternalism which does not accidentally limit the freedom of other persons beyond those specific persons the paternalistic policy is intended to benefit. Often there is a sort of "splash-over" effect in which some persons suffer a limitation of their freedom, yet do not gain any benefit from that limitation. A "pure" act of paternalism limits a person's freedom for that person's own good, and the only apparent drawback is the fact that the person is denied the freedom to make his or her own choice. "Impure" paternalism occurs when the only way to protect the interests of some persons involves restricting the freedom of other persons. For example, we might ban the sale of alcohol in our village during our annual Pole Vault Festival to avoid the problems which have arisen in the past when a few yahoos have become drunk and have injured themselves by vaulting wildly onto their heads rather than onto the protective mats. Yet the remainder of the participants in the festival also suffer from the restriction against the sale of alcohol, despite their having the good sense to vault first and drink later. This sort of impure paternalism is common, and is ordinarily thought to be justified because it does not pose an excessive threat to the freedom of the persons who are able to distinguish safely between vaulting time and drinking time. Justification of impure paternalism becomes rather more difficult when persons might genuinely wish to carry out what is commonly thought to be an ill-advised course of action, particularly when they are certain that the course of action is in fact valuable for them. Laws against recreational use of so-called soft drugs such as marijuana may fall into this category of impure paternalism. It is commonly believed that laws prohibiting marijuana are required to save persons from becoming addicted to a drug which may cause long-term memory loss or perhaps a slide to harder drugs. Yet other persons dispute what they view as exaggerations regarding the negative effects of marijuana, and genuinely and ration-

---

4 "Paternalism," §I.

ally wish to enjoy whatever benefits marijuana use may have. If the negative effects of marijuana use can be shown to be self-regarding, it is difficult to see how our respect for the importance of freedom can be reconciled with the urge to paternalistically limit access to a substance whose use is harmless to others. The bulk of Dworkin's essay examines the conditions under which impure paternalism might create so much good that it could outweigh the harm it does to the freedom of persons who do not clearly benefit from it. Dworkin offers a variety of observations about Mill's understanding of freedom and autonomy, and powerful arguments designed to show that "[p]aternalism is justified only to preserve a wider range of freedom for the individual in question."[5]

3. H.L.A. Hart and Lord Devlin on Legal Moralism

If you have read the chapters on the nature of law, you will be aware that the relation between law and morality is a matter of enduring controversy and confusion. One area of controversy is the question of "legal moralism." Roughly, legal moralism concerns whether the law does in fact or ought to enforce moral standards—the conclusions of moral philosophy. The famous Hart-Devlin debate involves questions about the nature and purpose of law, and the nature and role of morality in law.

In Section I, Chapter 2, a brief sketch of H.L.A. Hart is offered, so we will proceed directly to Lord Devlin. Patrick Devlin was a senior judge in England, well known also for his writing in jurisprudence. The debate between Hart and Devlin rose out of Devlin's arguments in a lecture later published as *The Enforcement of Morals*, from which our selection is taken. In his lecture in 1959, Devlin disputed the conclusion of the Wolfenden Report of 1957, which contained the results of a commit-

tee investigation into homosexuality and prostitution. The writers of that report recommended to the United Kingdom Parliament that the English law prohibiting homosexual behaviour between consenting adults in private should be repealed.[6] According to the writers of the report, such private conduct is not the proper concern of the criminal law. The proper concern of the criminal law is to protect individual citizens. Devlin criticized the findings of the report, and argued for a much different conclusion: the proper concern of the criminal law is to protect society, and that concern may require prohibition of immoral acts, even those carried out in private and with no outward other-regarding effects. Let us examine more closely some important parts of the reasoning behind Devlin's view, before turning to Hart's response.

3.1 Morality in the Criminal Law

According to Devlin, moral purposes may be found in a large number of criminal laws, and this fact is simply a mirror of the further fact that a society requires a shared morality in order to survive. More importantly, the moral purpose of the criminal law is not limited to laws aimed at protecting individuals from other individuals' conduct. Rather, the criminal law serves to protect certain accepted social values which make up the moral fabric of an enduring society. To illustrate his claim, Devlin points to the fact that no one can consent to being murdered. At first glance, it seems to be a very good thing that a murderer cannot defend herself in court by claiming that the victim consented. On the other hand, however, it seems that this rejection of the possibility of consenting to murder does not exist simply to protect

---

5 "Paternalism," §V.

6 This debate over homosexuality may seem to be merely a part of ancient history. It is worth considering, however, that significant political groups in the USA, Canada and the UK vigorously deny the right to freedom from discrimination on the basis of sexual orientation. It may be useful for you to look into the ongoing debate over the issue of "gay marriage."

prospective murder victims. In fact, the legal rejection of possibility of consenting to murder makes it impossible for terminally ill persons who need help in committing suicide to receive help. The person who helps will likely be charged and found guilty of murder, regardless of the fact that the "victim" consented to her murder. The law, in rejecting the "consent" defence, refuses to permit assisted suicide, despite the fact that assisted suicide is self-regarding and may be carried out privately without offense or harm to others. The law, Devlin claims, plainly has the purpose of advancing the moral principle of respect for human life, and will not tolerate immoral lack of respect for human life, even in private, self-regarding conduct.

3.2 Morality and Preservation of Society

Devlin argues that a society requires agreement on moral values. As Devlin puts it, "... society means a community of ideas; without shared ideas on politics, morals, and ethics, no society can exist." If a society comes to lack shared acceptance of a group of ideas, that society will not survive. Devlin explains, "If men and women try to create a society in which there is no fundamental agreement about good and evil they will fail; if, having based it on common agreement, the agreement goes, the society will disintegrate."[7] Unfortunately, Devlin does not point to any examples of a society disintegrating under the weight of disagreement about what is good and evil, but the general thread of his argument can still be understood: societies need morality if they are to avoid chaos. Yet, as you will see in Hart's criticisms, Devlin's argument appears to be incomplete. He does not specify clearly just what a society is. Nor does he explain how a change in public morality can be tolerated by a system which requires agreement in order to survive.

3.3 What Morality Should the Criminal Law Enforce?

Devlin offers an account of morality which diverges significantly from what you may have learned in a course in moral philosophy. According to Devlin, the public morality of England is composed of its Christian heritage, and the standard of the "reasonable man" or "right minded man" as developed by the courts. What is morally right or morally wrong, for the purposes of the courts, is what the reasonable man, in England, views as morally right or morally wrong.

Devlin accepts without question the historical role of the established church in the formation of English morality. By "established church" Devlin means the Church of England, also called the Anglican Church, tied constitutionally to the government of England. This situation is unfamiliar to the context of Canadian and American law where separation of church and state is more clearly drawn. Yet Devlin's view need not be rejected in Canada and the USA simply because the church does not play the same role in public life. Devlin simply points to the church as a source of moral values, and Christian moral views are very often used in the same way in Canada and the USA, as standards for criticism and evaluation. Given this understanding of the historical and contemporary importance of Christian values in Canada and the USA, Devlin's assertion that the law needs the church may be understood as the claim that the law needs some set of accepted moral values as its underpinning. Devlin argues that "... the law must base itself on Christian morals and to the limit of its ability enforce them, not simply because they are the morals which are taught by the established Church—on these points the law recognizes the right to dissent—but for the compelling reason that without the help of Christian teaching the law will fail."[8]

---

7   "Morals and the Criminal Law."

8   "Morals and the Criminal Law."

We may now assemble the full train of Devlin's argument against repeal of the law prohibiting homosexual activities conducted in private between consenting adults. The criminal law is and has long been concerned to enforce the moral standards which must be maintained if English society is to survive. For better or for worse, English society and the historical interpretation of Christian values has resulted in a public morality which feels repugnance toward the very idea of homosexual activities—even those activities conducted in private between consenting adults. Even an atheist who rejects the existence of the Christian God may recognize that this view is in fact held in England, and the atheist may also recognize that this view is part of the moral fabric which binds English society. Homosexual activities are therefore justifiably made illegal, according to Devlin, because they are a threat to the public morality which preserves English society, and they are the sort of activities which are properly controlled by law.

4. Hart's Response

Let us turn now to Hart's criticism of Devlin. In *Law, Liberty and Morality*, the short book from which our excerpt is taken, Hart challenges the arguments of Lord Devlin and a famous judge and writer of the Victorian era, James Fitzjames Stephen. This introduction and our excerpt will not be concerned with Stephen's arguments, since the core of the debate is between Hart and Devlin.

4.1 Moral Criticism of Social Institutions

Hart's main dispute with Devlin concerns Devlin's claim that a society is justified in taking whatever measures are required for its continued existence. Yet, Hart argues, it is surely still possible to argue that certain societies pursue such horrible goals that it is better for that society to collapse. It seems, then, that the activity in which Devlin participates as he offers his argument is an activity at two levels: an argument about the measures the society of England ought to take to preserve itself, and an argument that preservation of a society is a worthwhile goal. Devlin has begun a legitimate critical activity which Hart may join on the same basis: on the assumption that it is possible to reason about the nature and limits of the steps societies ought to take to govern themselves.

The nature of this critical activity can be explained further by Hart's distinction between "positive" morality, "the morality actually accepted and shared by a given social group," and "critical" morality, the "general moral principles used in the criticism of actual social institutions including positive morality." In our common activity of critical discussion of social institutions such as law, we readily understand the difference between the social norms of some group and what on reflection we suppose are the standards by which that group's norms may be evaluated. We understand, for example, that North American social standards or "positive morality" regarding premarital sex have changed dramatically between 1950 and now. We use standards of critical morality when we discuss whether these changes reflect a general worsening of moral character amongst North Americans, or perhaps instead a badly needed loosening of misguided restrictions.

4.2 Justifying Legal Moralism

What does reasoning according to the standards of critical morality have to do with legal enforcement of morality? According to Hart, the legal moralism Devlin proposes needs to be carefully justified, because it proposes to punish certain conduct with a variety of significant punishments, and because it limits freedom of choice and the happiness which freedom of choices has the potential to produce. As Hart explains, "This is of particular importance in the case of laws enforcing a sexual morality. They may create misery of a quite special degree... [since] suppression of sexual impulses generally is something which affects the development or balances of the individual's emotional life, happiness, and personality."[9] If Devlin proposes such miserable penalties against immoral behaviour, Devlin must show that this behaviour really is so seriously wrong as to justify the harshness of the proposed punishments.

4.3 Moral Purposes in the Criminal Law

Devlin argues that it is justifiable to prohibit and punish even private, self-regarding immorality, on the grounds that it threatens the fabric of society. And he asserts that the law already contains measures whose only purpose is to enforce a moral principle. An important part of Hart's argument disputes this assertion. It is an error, Hart supposes, to think that laws such as those prohibiting the possibility of consenting to one's own murder can only be understood as enforcing a moral principle (perhaps the principle of respect for life). It is more plausible to understand such laws as instances of paternalism, where individuals are protected against themselves and their weaknesses as human beings. Regardless of whether such paternalism is good or bad, paternalism itself is quite different from enforcement of a particular principle of morality. Devlin's assertion that the criminal law serves only to enforce moral principles seems to be an exaggeration, since many laws which appear to involve enforcement of moral principles are in fact instances of paternalism or legal advancement of other goals.

4.4 Shared Morality and Society

Finally, let us consider Hart's criticism of Devlin's idea that a society requires a shared morality for survival, and is justified in prohibiting even private conduct which weakens that shared morality. Hart observes that Devlin provides little evidence that a society tends to be worse off when private, self-regarding conduct strays from that society's positive morality. In particular, Hart claims, tolerance of

---

9 *Law, Liberty, and Morality.*

homosexual activity conducted in private between consenting adults does not seem to have led to a moral breakdown in those European societies which tolerate it. Further, Hart claims, there are problems with Devlin's understanding of the idea of "society" as meaning "a group whose members hold in common a shared morality." If a society is simply a shared morality, Devlin cannot explain shifts in a society's morality without also admitting that the original society has changed and has been replaced by a new society corresponding to the changed morality. Yet this view runs contrary to our ordinary observation that a society may remain the same society despite changes in its positive morality.

Let us sum up Hart's argument. Devlin has failed to distinguish between positive and critical morality, and has left open the possibility that a society might be justified in following standards of morality which are terribly immoral according to the standards of critical morality. Such a society might inflict painful punishment on persons whose actions are seen to be immoral yet are plainly self-regarding. Contrary to Devlin's assertion that English criminal law enforces moral principles of this sort in order to preserve English society, such criminal laws seem to serve other purposes, such as paternalistic intervention to protect persons from themselves. Finally, tolerance of activities Devlin construes as immoral does not seem to lead to moral chaos of the sort Devlin predicts.

What is the end of this debate? It is not easy to see whether Hart or Devlin won. Devlin's argument has likely not survived Hart's criticisms without a scratch. Nor, however, has Hart offered a complete defence of Mill's distinction between other-regarding action which is justifiably limited by law, and self-regarding action which is properly the private business of individual persons and no one else. The problems Hart and Devlin engage are sufficiently complex that it is very difficult to determine what an acceptable final solution might consist of. Yet these problems *require* that we at least attempt to provide answers if we are to avoid mistaken toleration or unjustified punishment of persons for what they really ought to be free to do.

◆ ◆ ◆ ◆ ◆

JOHN STUART MILL

from *On Liberty*

The object of this Essay is to assert one very simple principle, as entitled to govern absolutely the dealings of society with the individual in the way of compulsion and control, whether the means used be physical force in the form of legal penalties, or the moral coercion of public opinion. That principle is, that the sole end for which mankind are warranted, individually or collectively, in interfering with the liberty of action of any of their number, is self-protection. That the only purpose for which power can be rightfully exercised over any member of a civilized community, against his will, is to prevent harm to others. His own good, either physical or moral, is not a sufficient warrant. He cannot rightfully be compelled to do or forbear because it will be better for him to do so, because it will make him happier, because, in the opinions of others, to do so would be wise, or even right. These are good reasons for remonstrating with him, or reasoning with him, or persuading him, or entreating him, but not for compelling him, or visiting him with any evil in case he do otherwise. To justify that, the conduct from which it is desired to deter him, must be calculated to produce evil to some one else. The only part of the conduct of any one, for which he is amenable to society, is that which concerns others. In the part which merely concerns himself, his independence is, of right, absolute. Over himself, over his own body and mind, the individual is sovereign.

It is, perhaps, hardly necessary to say that this doctrine is meant to apply only to human beings in the maturity of their faculties. We are not speaking of children, or of young persons below the age which the law may fix as that of manhood or womanhood. Those who are still in a state to require being taken care of by others, must be protected against their own actions as well as against external injury. For the same reason, we may leave out of consideration those backward states of society in which the race itself may be considered as in its nonage. The early difficulties in the way of spontaneous progress are so great, that there is seldom any choice of means for overcoming them; and a ruler full of the spirit of improvement is warranted in the use of any expedients that will attain an end, perhaps otherwise unattainable. Despotism is a legitimate mode of government in dealing with barbarians, provided the end be their improvement, and the means justified by actually effecting that end. Liberty, as a principle, has no application to any state of things anterior to the time when mankind have become capable of being improved by free and equal discussion. Until then, there is nothing for them but implicit obedience to an Akbar or a Charlemagne, if they are so fortunate as to find one. But as soon as mankind have attained the capacity of being guided to their own improvement by conviction or persuasion (a period long since reached in all nations with whom we need here concern ourselves), compulsion, either in the direct form or in that of pains and penalties for non-compliance, is no longer admissible as a means to their own good, and justifiable only for the security of others.

It is proper to state that I forgo any advantage which could be derived to my argument from the idea of abstract right, as a thing independent of utility. I regard utility as the ultimate appeal on all ethical questions; but it must be utility in the largest sense, grounded on the permanent interests of man as a progressive being. Those interests, I contend, authorize the subjection of individual spontaneity to external control, only in respect to those actions of each, which concern the interest of other people. If any one does an act hurtful to others, there is a prima facie case for punishing him, by law, or, where legal penalties are not safely applicable, by general disapprobation. There are also many positive acts for the benefit of others, which he may rightfully be compelled to perform; such as, to give evidence in a court of justice; to bear his fair share in the common defence, or in any other joint work necessary to the interest of the society of which he enjoys the protection; and to perform certain acts of individual beneficence, such as saving a fellow creature's life or interposing to protect the defenceless against ill-usage, things which whenever it is obviously a man's duty to do, he may rightfully be made responsible to society for not doing. A person may cause evil to others not only by his actions but by his inaction, and in either case he is justly accountable to them for the injury. The latter case, it is true, requires a much more cautious exercise of compulsion than the former. To make any one answerable for doing evil to others, is the rule; to make him answerable for not preventing evil, is, comparatively speaking, the exception. Yet there are many cases clear enough and grave enough to justify that exception. In all things which regard the external relations of the individual, he is *de jure* amenable to those whose interests are concerned, and if need be, to society as their protector. There are often good reasons for not holding him to the responsibility; but these reasons must arise from the special expediencies of the case: either because it is a kind of case in which he is on the whole likely to act better, when left to his own discretion, than when controlled in any way in which society have it in their power to control him; or because the attempt to exercise control would produce other evils, greater than those which it would prevent. When such reasons as these preclude the enforcement of responsibility, the conscience of the agent himself should step into the vacant judgement-seat, and protect those interests of others which have no external protection; judging himself all the more rigidly, because the case does not admit of his being made accountable to the judgement of his fellow creatures.

But there is a sphere of action in which society, as distinguished from the individual, has, if any, only an indirect interest; comprehending all that portion of a person's life and conduct which affects only himself, or if it also affects others, only with their free, voluntary, and undeceived consent and participation. When I say only himself, I mean directly, and in the first instance: for whatever affects himself, may affect others through himself; and the objection which may be grounded on this contingency will receive consideration in the sequel. This, then, is the appropriate region of human liberty. It comprises, first, the inward domain of consciousness; demanding liberty of conscience, in the most comprehensive sense; liberty of thought and feeling; absolute freedom of opinion and sentiment on all subjects, practical or speculative, scientific, moral, or theological. The liberty of expressing and publishing opinions may seem to fall under a different principle, since it belongs to that part of the conduct of an individual which concerns other people; but, being almost of as much importance as the liberty of thought itself, and resting in great part on the same reasons, is practically inseparable from it. Secondly, the principle requires liberty of tastes and pursuits; of framing the plan of our life to suit our own character; of doing as we like, subject to such consequences as may follow: without impediment from our fellow creatures, so long as what we do does not harm them, even though they should think our conduct foolish, perverse, or wrong. Thirdly, from this liberty of each individual, follows the liberty, within the same limits, of combination among individuals; freedom to unite, for any purpose not involving harm to others: the persons combining being supposed to be of full age, and not forced or deceived.

No society in which these liberties are not, on the whole, respected, is free, whatever may be its form of government and none is completely free in which they do not exist absolute and unqualified. The only freedom which deserves the name, is that of pursuing our own good in our own way, so long as we do not attempt to deprive others of theirs, or impede their efforts to obtain it. Each is the proper guardian of his own health, whether bodily, or mental and spiritual. Mankind are greater gainers by suffering each other to live as seems good to themselves, than by compelling each to live as seems good to the rest.

• • •

Of the Limits to the Authority of Society Over the Individual

What, then, is the rightful limit to the sovereignty of the individual over himself? Where does the authority of society begin? How much of human life should be assigned to individuality, and how much to society?

Each will receive its proper share, if each has that which more particularly concerns it. To individuality should belong the part of life in which it is chiefly the individual that is interested; to society, the part which chiefly interests society.

Though society is not founded on a contract, and though no good purpose is answered by inventing a contract in order to deduce social obligations from it, every one who receives the protection of society owes a return for the benefit, and the fact of living in society renders it indispensable that each should be bound to observe a certain line of conduct towards the rest. This conduct consists, first, in not injuring the interests of one another; or rather certain interests, which, either by express legal provision or by tacit understanding, ought to be considered as rights; and secondly, in each person's bearing his share (to be fixed on some equitable principle) of the labours and sacrifices incurred for defending the society or its members from injury and molestation. These conditions society is justified in enforcing at all costs to those who endeavour to withhold fulfilment. Nor is this all that society may do. The acts of an individual may be hurtful to others, or wanting in due consideration for their welfare, without go-

ing the length of violating any of their constituted rights. The offender may then be justly punished by opinion, though not by law. As soon as any part of a person's conduct affects prejudicially the interests of others, society has jurisdiction over it, and the question whether the general welfare will or will not be promoted by interfering with it, becomes open to discussion. But there is no room for entertaining any such question when a person's conduct affects the interests of no persons besides himself, or needs not affect them unless they like (all the persons concerned being of full age, and the ordinary amount of understanding). In all such cases there should be perfect freedom, legal and social, to do the action and stand the consequences.

It would be a great misunderstanding of this doctrine to suppose that it is one of selfish indifference, which pretends that human beings have no business with each other's conduct in life, and that they should not concern themselves about the well-doing or well-being of one another, unless their own interest is involved. Instead of any diminution, there is need of a great increase of disinterested exertion to promote the good of others. But disinterested benevolence can find other instruments to persuade people to their good, than whips and scourges, either of the literal or the metaphorical sort. I am the last person to undervalue the self-regarding virtues; they are only second in importance, if even second, to the social. It is equally the business of education to cultivate both. But even education works by conviction and persuasion as well as by compulsion, and it is by the former only that, when the period of education is past, the self-regarding virtues should be inculcated. Human beings owe to each other help to distinguish the better from the worse, and encouragement to choose the former and avoid the latter. They should be for ever stimulating each other to increased exercise of their higher faculties, and increased direction of their feelings and aims towards wise instead of foolish, elevating instead of degrading, objects and contemplations. But neither one person, nor any number of persons, is warranted in saying to another human creature of ripe years, that he shall not do with his life for his own benefit what he chooses to do with it. He is the person most interested in his own well-being: the interest which any other person, except in cases of strong personal attachment, can have in it, is trifling, compared with that which he himself has; the interest which society has in him individually (except as to his conduct to others) is fractional, and altogether indirect: while, with respect to his own feelings and circumstances, the most ordinary man or woman has means of knowledge immeasurably surpassing those that can be possessed by any one else. The interference of society to overrule his judgement and purposes in what only regards himself, must be grounded on general presumptions; which may be altogether wrong, and even if right, are as likely as not to be misapplied to individual cases, by persons no better acquainted with the circumstances of such cases than those are who look at them merely from without. In this department, therefore, of human affairs, individuality has its proper field of action. In the conduct of human beings towards one another, it is necessary that general rules should for the most part be observed, in order that people may know what they have to expect; but in each person's own concerns, his individual spontaneity is entitled to free exercise. Considerations to aid his judgement, exhortations to strengthen his will, may be offered to him, even obtruded on him, by others but he himself is the final judge. All errors which he is likely to commit against advice and warning, are far outweighed by the evil of allowing others to constrain him to what they deem his good.

I do not mean that the feelings with which a person is regarded by others, ought not to be in any way affected by his self-regarding qualities or deficiencies. This is neither possible nor desirable. If he is eminent in any of the qualities which conduce to his own good he is, so far, a proper object of admiration. He is much the nearer to the ideal perfection of human nature. If he is grossly deficient in those qualities a sentiment the opposite of admiration will follow. There is a degree of folly, and a degree of what may be called (though the phrase is not unobjectionable) lowness or depravation of taste, which, though it cannot justify doing harm to the person who manifests it, renders him necessarily and properly a subject of distaste, or, in extreme cases, even of contempt: a person could not have the opposite qualities in due strength without entertaining these feelings. Though doing no wrong to any one, a person may so act as to compel us to judge him, and feel to him, as a fool, or as a being of an inferior order: and since this judgement and feeling are a fact which he would prefer to avoid, it is doing him a service to warn him of it beforehand, as of any other disagreeable consequence to which he exposes himself. It would be well, indeed, if this good office were much more freely rendered than the common notions of politeness at present permit, and if one person could honestly point out to another that he thinks him in fault, without being considered unmannerly or presuming. We have a right, also, in various ways, to act upon our unfavourable opinion of any one, not to the oppression of his individuality, but in the exercise of ours. We are not bound, for example, to seek his society; we have a right to avoid it (though not to parade the avoidance), for we have a right to choose the society most acceptable to us. We have a right, and it may be our duty, to caution others against him, if we think his example or conversation likely to have a pernicious effect on those with whom he associates. We may give others a preference over him in optional good offices, except those which tend to his improvement. In these various modes a person may suffer very severe penalties at the hands of others, for faults which directly concern only himself; but he suffers these penalties only in so far as they are the natural, and, as it were, the spontaneous consequences of the faults themselves, not because they are purposely inflicted on him for the sake of punishment. A person who shows rashness, obstinacy, self-conceit—who cannot live within moderate means—who cannot restrain himself from hurtful indulgences—who pursues animal pleasures at the expense of those of feeling and intellect—must expect to be lowered in the opinion of others, and to have a less share of their favourable sentiments; but of this he has no right to complain, unless he has merited their favour by special excellence in his social relations, and has thus established a title to their good offices, which is not affected by his demerits towards himself.

What I contend for is, that the inconveniences which are strictly inseparable from the unfavourable judgement of others, are the only ones to which a person should ever be subjected for that portion of his conduct and character which concerns his own good, but which does not affect the interests of others in their relations with him. Acts injurious to others require a totally different treatment. Encroachment on their rights; infliction on them of any loss or damage not justified by his own rights; falsehood or duplicity in dealing with them; unfair or ungenerous use of advantages over them; even selfish abstinence from defending them against injury—these are fit objects of moral reprobation, and, in grave cases, of moral retribution and punishment. And not only these acts, but the dispositions which lead to them, are properly immoral, and fit subjects of disapprobation which may rise to abhorrence. Cruelty of disposition; malice and ill nature; that most anti-social and odious of all passions, envy; dissimulation and insincerity; irascibility on insufficient cause, and resentment disproportioned to the provocation; the love of domineering over others; the desire to engross more than one's share of advantages (the *pleonexia* of the Greeks); the pride which derives gratification from the abasement of others; the egotism which thinks self and its concerns more important than everything else, and decides all doubtful questions in its own favour; these are moral vices, and constitute a bad and odious moral character: unlike the self-regarding faults previously mentioned, which are not

properly immoralities, and to whatever pitch they may be carried do not constitute wickedness. They may be proofs of any amount of folly, or want of personal dignity and self-respect; but they are only a subject of moral reprobation when they involve a breach of duty to others, for whose sake the individual is bound to have care for himself. What are called duties to ourselves are not socially obligatory, unless circumstances render them at the same time duties to others. The term duty to oneself, when it means any thing more than prudence, means self-respect or self-development; and for none of these is any one accountable to his fellow creatures, because for none of them is it for the good of mankind that he be held accountable to them.

The distinction between the loss of consideration which a person may rightly incur by defect of prudence or of personal dignity, and the reprobation which is due to him for an offence against the rights of others, is not a merely nominal distinction. It makes a vast difference both in our feelings and in our conduct towards him, whether he displeases us in things in which we think we have a right to control him, or in things in which we know that we have not. If he displeases us, we may express our distaste, and we may stand aloof from a person as well as from a thing that displeases us; but we shall not therefore feel called on to make his life uncomfortable. We shall reflect that he already bears, or will bear, the whole penalty of his error; if he spoils his life by mismanagement, we shall not, for that reason, desire to spoil it still further: instead of wishing to punish him, we shall rather endeavour to alleviate his punishment, by showing him how he may avoid or cure the evils his conduct tends to bring upon him. He may be to us an object of pity, perhaps of dislike, but not of anger or resentment; we shall not treat him like an enemy of society: the worst we shall think ourselves justified in doing is leaving him to himself, if we do not interfere benevolently by showing interest or concern for him. It is far otherwise if he has infringed the rules necessary for the protection of his fellow creatures, individually or collectively. The evil consequences of his acts do not then fall on himself, but on others; and society, as the protector of all its members, must retaliate on him; must inflict pain on him for the express purpose of punishment, and must take care that it be sufficiently severe. In the one case, he is an offender at our bar, and we are called on not only to sit in judgement on him, but, in one shape or another, to execute our own sentence; in the other case, it is not our part to inflict any suffering on him, except what may incidentally follow from our using the same liberty in the regulation of our own affairs, which we allow to him in his.

The distinction here pointed out between the part of a person's life which concerns only himself, and that which concerns others, many persons will refuse to admit. How (it may be asked) can any part of the conduct of a member of society be a matter of indifference to the other members? No person is an entirely isolated being; it is impossible for a person to do anything seriously or permanently hurtful to himself, without mischief reaching at least to his near connexions, and often far beyond them. If he injures his property, he does harm to those who directly or indirectly derived support from it, and usually diminishes, by a greater or less amount, the general resources of the community. If he deteriorates his bodily or mental faculties, he not only brings evil upon all who depended on him for any portion of their happiness, but disqualifies himself for rendering the services which he owes to his fellow creatures generally; perhaps becomes a burden on their affection or benevolence; and if such conduct were very frequent, hardly any offence that is committed would detract more from the general sum of good. Finally, if by his vices or follies a person does no direct harm to others, he is nevertheless (it may be said) injurious by his example; and ought to be compelled to control himself, for the sake of those whom the sight or knowledge of his conduct might corrupt or mislead.

And even (it will be added) if the consequences of misconduct could be confined to the vicious or thoughtless individual, ought society to abandon to their own guidance those who are manifestly unfit for it? If protection against themselves is confessedly due to children and persons under age, is not society equally bound to afford it to persons of mature years who are equally incapable of self-government? If gambling, or drunkenness, or incontinence, or idleness, or uncleanliness, are as injurious to happiness, and as great a hindrance to improvement, as many or most of the acts prohibited by law, why (it may be asked) should not law, so far as is consistent with practicability and social convenience, endeavour to repress these also? And as a supplement to the unavoidable imperfections of law, ought not opinion at least to organize a powerful police against those vices, and visit rigidly with social penalties those who are known to practise them? There is no question here (it may be said) about restricting individuality, or impeding the trial of new and original experiments in living. The only things it is sought to prevent are things which have been tried and condemned from the beginning of the world until now; things which experience has shown not to be useful or suitable to any person's individuality. There must be some length of time and amount of experience, after which a moral or prudential truth may be regarded as established: and it is merely desired to prevent generation after generation from falling over the same precipice which has been fatal to their predecessors.

I fully admit that the mischief which a person does to himself may seriously affect, both through their sympathies and their interests, those nearly connected with him, and in a minor degree, society at large. When, by conduct of this sort, a person is led to violate a distinct and assignable obligation to any other person or persons, the case is taken out of the self-regarding class, and becomes amenable to moral disapprobation in the proven sense of the term. If, for example, a man, through intemperance or extravagance, becomes unable to pay his debts, or, having undertaken the moral responsibility of a family, becomes from the same cause incapable of supporting or educating them, he is deservedly reprobated, and might be justly punished; but it is for the breach of duty to his family or creditors, not for the extravagance. If the resources which ought to have been devoted to them had been diverted from them for the most prudent investment, the moral culpability would have been the same. George Barnwell murdered his uncle to get money for his mistress, but if he had done it to set himself up in business, he would equally have been hanged. Again, in the frequent case of a man who causes grief to his family by addiction to bad habits, he deserves reproach for his unkindness or ingratitude; but so he may for cultivating habits not in themselves vicious, if they are painful to those with whom he passes his life, or who from personal ties are dependent on him for their comfort. Whoever fails in the consideration generally due to the interests and feelings of others, not being compelled by some more imperative duty, or justified by allowable self-preference, is a subject of moral disapprobation for that failure, but not for the cause of it, nor for the errors, merely personal to himself, which may have remotely led to it. In like manner, when a person disables himself, by conduct purely self-regarding, from the performance of some definite duty incumbent on him to the public, he is guilty of a social offence. No person ought to be punished simply for being drunk; but a soldier or a policeman should be punished for being drunk on duty. Whenever, in short, there is a definite damage, or a definite risk of damage, either to an individual or to the public, the case is taken out of the province of liberty, and placed in that of morality or law.

But with regard to the merely contingent, or, as it may be called, constructive, injury which a person causes to society, by conduct which neither violates any specific duty to the public, nor occasions perceptible hurt to any assignable individual except himself; the inconvenience is one which society can afford to bear, for the sake of the greater good of human freedom. If grown persons are to be punished for not taking proper care of themselves, I would rather it were for their own sake, than under pretence of preventing them from impairing their capacity of rendering to society benefits which society does not pretend it has a right to exact. But I cannot consent to argue the point as if society had no means of bringing its weaker members up to its ordinary standard of rational conduct, except waiting till they do something irrational, and then punishing them, legally or morally, for it. Society has had absolute power over them during all the early portion of their existence: it has had the whole period of childhood and nonage in which to try whether it could make them capable of rational conduct in life. The existing generation is master both of the training and the entire circumstances of the generation to come; it cannot indeed make them perfectly wise and good, because it is itself so lamentably deficient in goodness and wisdom; and its best efforts are not always, in individual cases, its most successful ones; but it is perfectly well able to make the rising generation, as a whole, as good as, and a little better than, itself. If society lets any considerable number of its members grow up mere children, incapable of being acted on by rational consideration of distant motives, society has itself to blame for the consequences. Armed not only with all the powers of education, but with the ascendancy which the authority of a received opinion always exercises over the minds who are least fitted to judge for themselves; and aided by the *natural* penalties which cannot be prevented from falling on those who incur the distaste or the contempt of those who know them; let not society pretend that it needs, besides all this, the power to issue commands and enforce obedience in the personal concerns of individuals, in which, on all principles of justice and policy, the decision ought to rest with those who are to abide the consequences. Nor is there anything which tends more to discredit and frustrate the better means of influencing conduct, than a resort to the worse. If there be among those whom it is attempted to coerce into prudence or temperance, any of the material of which vigorous and independent characters are made, they will infallibly rebel against the yoke. No such person will ever feel that others have a right to control him in his concerns, such as they have to prevent him from injuring them in theirs; and it easily comes to be considered a mark of spirit and courage to fly in the face of such usurped authority, and do with ostentation the exact opposite of what it enjoins; as in the fashion of grossness which succeeded, in the time of Charles II, to the fanatical moral intolerance of the Puritans. With respect to what is said of the necessity of protecting society from the bad example set to others by the vicious or the self-indulgent; it is true that bad example may have a pernicious effect, especially the example of doing wrong to others with impunity to the wrong-doer. But we are now speaking of conduct which, while it does no wrong to others, is supposed to do great harm to the agent himself: and I do not see how those who believe this, can think otherwise than that the example, on the whole, must be more salutary than hurtful, since, if it displays the misconduct, it displays also the painful or degrading consequences which, if the conduct is justly censured, must be supposed to be in all or most cases attendant on it.

But the strongest of all the arguments against the interference of the public with purely personal conduct, is that when it does interfere, the odds are that it interferes wrongly, and in the wrong place. On questions of social morality, of duty to others, the opinion of the public, that is, of an overruling majority, though often wrong, is likely to be still oftener right; because on such questions they are only required to judge of their own interests; of the manner in which some mode of conduct, if allowed to be practised, would affect themselves. But the opinion of a similar majority, imposed as a law on the minority, on questions of self-regarding conduct, is quite as likely to be wrong as right; for in these cases public opinion means, at the best, some people's opinion of what is good or bad for

other people while very often it does not even mean that; the public, with the most perfect indifference, passing over the pleasure or convenience of those whose conduct they censure, and considering only their own preference. There are many who consider as an injury to themselves any conduct which they have a distaste for, and resent it as an outrage to their feelings; as a religious bigot, when charged with disregarding the religious feelings of others, has been known to retort that they disregard his feelings, by persisting in their abominable worship or creed. But there is no parity between the feeling of a person for his own opinion, and the feeling of another who is offended at his holding it; no more than between the desire of a thief to take a purse, and the desire of the right owner to keep it. And a person's taste is as much his own peculiar concern as his opinion or his purse. It is easy for any one to imagine an ideal public, which leaves the freedom and choice of individuals in all uncertain matters undisturbed, and only requires them to abstain from modes of conduct which universal experience has condemned. But where has there been seen a public which set any such limit to its censorship? Or when does the public trouble itself about universal experience? In its interferences with personal conduct it is seldom thinking of anything but the enormity of acting or feeling differently from itself; and this standard of judgement, thinly disguised, is held up to mankind as the dictate of religion and philosophy, by ninetenths of all moralists and speculative writers. These teach that things are right because they are right; because we feel them to be so. They tell us to search in our own minds and hearts for laws of conduct binding on ourselves and on all others. What can the poor public do but apply these instructions, and make their own personal feelings of good and evil, if they are tolerably unanimous in them, obligatory on all the world?

The evil hero pointed out is not one which exists only in theory; and it may perhaps be expected that I should specify the instances in which the public of this age and country improperly invests its own preferences with the character of moral laws. I am not writing an essay on the aberrations of existing moral feeling. That is too weighty a subject to be discussed parenthetically, and by way of illustration. Yet examples are necessary, to show that the principle I maintain is of serious and practical moment, and that I am not endeavouring to erect a barrier against imaginary evils. And it is not difficult to show, by abundant instances, that to extend the bounds of what may be called moral police, until it encroaches on the most unquestionably legitimate liberty of the individual, is one of the most universal of all human propensities.

As a first instance, consider the antipathies which men cherish on no better grounds than that persons whose religious opinions are different from theirs, do not practise their religious observances, especially their religious abstinences. To cite a rather trivial example, nothing in the creed or practice of Christians does more to envenom the hatred of Mohammedans against them, than the fact of their eating pork. There are few acts which Christians and Europeans regard with more unaffected disgust, than Mussulmans regard this particular mode of satisfying hunger. It is, in the first place, an offence against their religion; but this circumstance by no means explains either the degree or the kind of their repugnance; for wine also is forbidden by their religion, and to partake of it is by all Mussulmans accounted wrong, but not disgusting. Their aversion to the flesh of the "unclean beast" is, on the contrary, of that peculiar character, resembling an instinctive antipathy, which the idea of uncleanliness, when once it thoroughly sinks into the feelings, seems always to excite even in those whose personal habits are anything but scrupulously cleanly, and of which the sentiment of religious impurity, so intense in the Hindoos, is a remarkable example. Suppose now that in a people, of whom the majority were Mussulmans, that majority should insist upon not permitting pork to be eaten within the limits of the country. This would be nothing new in Mohammedan countries.[1] Would it be a legitimate exercise of the moral authority of public opinion? And if not, why not? The practise is really revolting to such a public. They also sincerely think that it is forbidden and abhorred by the Deity. Neither could the prohibition be censured as religious persecution. It might be religious in its origin, but it would not be persecution for religion, since nobody's religion makes it a duty to eat pork. The only tenable ground of condemnation would be, that with the personal tastes and self-regarding concerns of individuals the public has no business to interfere.

To come somewhat nearer home: the majority of Spaniards consider it a gross impiety, offensive in the highest degree to the Supreme Being, to worship him in any other manner than the Roman Catholic; and no other public worship is lawful on Spanish soil. The people of all Southern Europe look upon a married clergy as not only irreligious but unchaste, indecent, gross, disgusting. What do Protestants think of these perfectly sincere feelings, and of the attempt to enforce them against non-Catholics? Yet, if mankind are justified in interfering with each other's liberty in things which do not concern the interests of others, on what principle is it possible consistently to exclude these cases? Or who can blame people for desiring to suppress what they regard as a scandal in the sight of God and man? No

---

1 The case of the Bombay Parsees is a curious instance in point. When this industrious and enterprising tribe, the descendants of the Persian fire-worshippers, flying from their native country before the Caliphs, arrived in Western India, they were admitted to toleration by the Hindoo sovereigns, on condition of not eating beef. When those regions afterwards fell under the dominion of Mohammedan conquerors, the Parsees obtained from them a continuance of indulgence, on condition of refraining from pork. What was at first obedience to authority became a second nature, and the Parsees to this day abstain both from beef and pork. Though not required by their religion, the double abstinence has had time to grow into a custom of their tribe; and custom, in the East, is a religion.

stronger case can be shown for prohibiting anything which is regarded as a personal immorality, than is made out for suppressing these practices in the eyes of those who regard them as impieties; and unless we are willing to adopt the logic of persecutors, and to say that we may persecute others because we are right, and that they must not persecute us because they are wrong, we must beware of admitting a principle of which we should resent as a gross injustice the application to ourselves.

The preceding instances may be objected to, although unreasonably, as drawn from contingencies impossible among us: opinion, in this country, not being likely to enforce abstinence from meats, or to interfere with people for worshipping, and for either marrying or not marrying, according to their creed or inclination. The next example, however, shall be taken from an interference with liberty which we have by no means passed all danger of. Wherever the Puritans have been sufficiently powerful, as in New England, and in Great Britain at the time of the Commonwealth, they have endeavoured, with considerable success, to put down all public, and nearly all private, amusements: especially music, dancing, public games, or other assemblages for purposes of diversion, and the theatre. There are still in this country large bodies of persons by whose notions of morality and religion these recreations are condemned; and those persons belonging chiefly to the middle class, who are the ascendant power in the present social and political condition of the kingdom, it is by no means impossible that persons of these sentiments may at some time or other command a majority in Parliament. How will the remaining portion of the community like to have the amusements that shall be permitted to them regulated by the religious and moral sentiments of the stricter Calvinists and Methodists? Would they not, with considerable peremptoriness, desire these intrusively pious members of society to mind their own business? This is precisely what should be said to every government and every public, who have the

pretension that no person shall enjoy any pleasure which they think wrong. But if the principle of the pretension be admitted, no one can reasonably object to its being acted on in the sense of the majority, or other preponderating power in the country; and all persons must be ready to conform to the idea of a Christian commonwealth, as understood by the early settlers in New England, if a religious profession similar to theirs should ever succeed in regaining its lost ground, as religions supposed to be declining have so often been known to do.

To imagine another contingency, perhaps more likely to be realized than the one last mentioned. There is confessedly a strong tendency in the modern world towards a democratic constitution of society, accompanied or not by popular political institutions. It is affirmed that in the country where this tendency is most completely realized—where both society and the government are most democratic—the United States—the feeling of the majority, to whom any appearance of a more showy or costly style of living than they can hope to rival is disagreeable, operates as a tolerably effectual sumptuary law, and that in many parts of the Union it is really difficult for a person possessing a very large income, to find any mode of spending it, which will not incur popular disapprobation. Though such statements as these are doubtless much exaggerated as a representation of existing facts, the state of things they describe is not only a conceivable and possible, but a probable result of democratic feeling, combined with the notion that the public has a right to a veto on the manner in which individuals shall spend their incomes. We have only further to suppose a considerable diffusion of Socialist opinions, and it may become infamous in the eyes of the majority to possess more property than some very small amount, or any income not earned by manual labour. Opinions similar in principle to these, already prevail widely among the artisan class, and weigh oppressively on those who are amenable to the opinion chiefly of that class, namely, its own members. It is known that the bad workmen who form the majority of the operatives in many branches of industry, are decidedly of opinion that bad workmen ought to receive the same wages as good, and that no one ought to be allowed, through piecework or otherwise, to earn by superior skill or industry more than others can without it. And they employ a moral police, which occasionally becomes a physical one, to deter skillful workmen from receiving, and employers from giving, a larger remuneration for a more useful service. If the public have any jurisdiction over private concerns, I cannot see that these people are in fault, or that any individual's particular public can be blamed for asserting the same authority over his individual conduct, which the general public asserts over people in general.

But, without dwelling upon supposititious cases, there are, in our own day, gross usurpations upon the liberty of private life actually practised, and still greater ones threatened with some expectation of success, and opinions propounded which assert an unlimited right in the public not only to prohibit by law everything which it thinks wrong, but in order to get at what it thinks wrong, to prohibit any number of things which it admits to be innocent.

Under the name of preventing intemperance, the people of one English colony, and of nearly half the United States, have been interdicted by law from making any use whatever of fermented drinks, except for medical purposes: for prohibition of the sale is in fact, as it is intended to be, prohibition of their use. And though the impracticability of executing the law has caused its repeal in several of the States which had adopted it, including the one from which it derives its name, an attempt has notwithstanding been commenced, and is prosecuted with considerable zeal by many of the professed philanthropists, to agitate for a similar law in this country. The association, or "Alliance" as it terms itself, which has been formed for this purpose has acquired some notoriety through the publicity given to a correspondence between its Secretary and one of the very few English public men who hold that a politician's opinions ought to be founded on principles. Lord Stanley's share in this correspondence is calculated to strengthen the hopes already built on him, by those who know how rare such qualities as are manifested in some of his public appearances, unhappily are among those who figure in political life. The organ of the Alliance, who would "deeply deplore the recognition of any principle which could be wrested to justify bigotry and persecution," undertakes to point out the "broad and impassable barrier" which divides such principles from those of the association. "All matters relating to thought, opinion, conscience, appear to me," he says, "to be without the sphere of legislation; all pertaining to social act, habit, relation, subject only to a discretionary power vested in the State itself, and not in the individual, to be within it." No mention is made of a third class, different from either of these, viz. acts and habits which are not social, but individual; although it is to this class, surely, that the act of drinking fermented liquors belongs. Selling fermented liquors, however, is trading, and trading is a social act. But the infringement complained of is not on the liberty of the seller, but on that of the buyer and consumer; since the State might just as well forbid him to drink wine, as purposely make it impossible for him to obtain it. The Secretary, however, says, "I claim, as a citizen, a right to legislate whenever my social rights are invaded by the social act of another." And now for the definition of these "social rights." "If anything invades my social rights, certainly the traffic in strong drink does. It destroys my primary right of security, by constantly creating and stimulating social disorder. It invades any right of equality, by deriving a profit from the creation of a misery I am taxed to support. It impedes my right to free moral and intellectual development by surrounding my path with dangers, and by weakening and demoralizing society, from which I have a right to claim mutual aid and intercourse." A theory of "social rights," the like of which probably never before found its way into distinct language: being nothing short of this—that it is the absolute social right of every individual, that every other individual shall act in every respect exactly as he ought; that whosoever fails thereof in the smallest particular, violates my social right, and entitles me to demand from the legislature the removal of the grievance. So monstrous a principle is far more dangerous than any single interference with liberty; there is no violation of liberty which it would not justify; it acknowledges no right to any freedom whatever, except perhaps to that of holding opinions in secret, without ever disclosing them: for, the moment an opinion which I consider noxious passes any one's lips, it invades all the "social rights" attributed to me by the Alliance. The doctrine ascribes to all mankind a vested interest in each other's moral, intellectual, and even physical perfection, to be defined by each claimant according to his own standard.

Another important example of illegitimate interference with the rightful liberty of the individual, not simply threatened, but long since carried into triumphant effect, is Sabbatarian legislation. Without doubt, abstinence on one day in the week, so far as the exigencies of life permit, from the usual daily occupation, though in no respect religiously binding on any except Jews, is a highly beneficial custom. And inasmuch as this custom cannot be observed without a general consent to that effect among the industrious classes, therefore, in so far as some persons by working may impose the same necessity on others, it may be allowable and right that the law should guarantee to each the observance by others of the custom, by suspending the greater operations of industry on a particular day. But this justification, grounded on the direct interest which others have in each individual's observance of the practice, does not apply to the self-chosen occupations in which a person may think fit to employ his leisure; nor does it hold good, in the smallest degree, for legal restrictions on amusements. It is true that the amusement of some is the day's work of others; but the pleasure, not to say the useful recreation, or many, is worth

the labour of a few, provided the occupation is freely chosen, and can be freely resigned. The operatives are perfectly right in thinking that if all worked on Sunday, seven days' work would have to be given for six days' wages: but so long as the great mass of employments are suspended, the small number who for the enjoyment of others must still work, obtain a proportional increase of earnings; and they are not obliged to follow those occupations, if they prefer leisure to emolument. If a further remedy is sought, it might be found in the establishment by custom of a holiday on some other day of the week for those particular classes of persons. The only ground, therefore, on which restrictions on Sunday amusements can be defended, must be that they are religiously wrong; a motive of legislation which never can be too earnestly protested against. "Deorum injuriae Diis curae." It remains to be proved that society or any of its officers holds a commission from on high to avenge any supposed offence to Omnipotence, which is not also a wrong to our fellow creatures. The notion that it is one man's duty that another should be religious, was the foundation of all the religious persecutions ever perpetrated, and if admitted, would fully justify them. Though the feeling which breaks out in the repeated attempts to stop railway travelling on Sunday, in the resistance to the opening of Museums, and the like, has not the cruelty of the old persecutors, the state of mind indicated by it is fundamentally the same. It is a determination not to tolerate others in doing what is permitted by their religion, because it is not permitted by the persecutor's religion. It is a belief that God not only abominates the act of the misbeliever, but will not hold us guiltless if we leave him unmolested.

I cannot refrain from adding to these examples of the little account commonly made of human liberty, the language of downright persecution which breaks out from the press of this country, whenever it feels called on to notice the remarkable phenomenon of Mormonism. Much might be said on the unexpected and instructive fact, that an alleged new revelation, and a religion founded on it, the product of palpable imposture, not even supported by the *prestige* of extraordinary qualities in its founder, is believed by hundreds of thousands, and has been made the foundation of a society, in the age of newspapers, railways, and the electric telegraph. What here concerns us is, that this religion, like other and better religions, has its martyrs; that its prophet and founder was, for his teaching, put to death by a mob; that others of its adherents lost their lives by the same lawless violence; that they were forcibly expelled, in a body, from the country in which they first grew up; while, now that they have been chased into a solitary recess in the midst of a desert, many in this country openly declare that it would be right (only that it is not convenient) to send an expedition against them, and compel them by force to conform to the opinions of other people. The article of the Mormonite doctrine which is the chief provocative to the antipathy which thus breaks through the ordinary restraints of religious tolerance, is its sanction of polygamy; which, though permitted to Mohammedans, and Hindoos, and Chinese, seems to excite unquenchable animosity when practised by persons who speak English, and profess to be a kind of Christians. No one has a deeper disapprobation than I have of this Mormon institution; both for other reasons, and because, far from being in any way countenanced by the principle of liberty, it is a direct infraction of that principle, being a mere riveting of the chains of one-half of the community, and an emancipation of the other from reciprocity of obligation towards them. Still, it must be remembered that this relation is as much voluntary on the part of the women concerned in it, and who may be deemed the sufferers by it, as is the case with any other form of the marriage institution; and however surprising this fact may appear, it has its explanation in the common ideas and customs of the world, which teaching women to think marriage the one thing needful, make it intelligible that many a woman should prefer being one of several wives, to not being a wife at all. Other countries are not asked to recognize such unions, or release any portion of their inhabitants from their own laws on the score of Mormonite opinions. But when the dissentients have conceded to the hostile sentiments of others, far more than could justly be demanded; when they have left the countries to which their doctrines were unacceptable, and established themselves in a remote corner of the earth, which they have been the first to render habitable to human beings; it is difficult to see on what principles but those of tyranny they can be prevented from living there under what laws they please, provided they commit no aggression on other nations, and allow perfect freedom of departure to those who are dissatisfied with their ways. A recent writer, in some respects of considerable merit, proposes (to use his own words) not a crusade, but a *civilizade*, against this polygamous community, to put an end to what seems to him a retrograde step in civilization. It also appears so to me, but I am not aware that any community has a right to force another to be civilized. So long as the sufferers by the bad law do not invoke assistance from other communities, I cannot admit that persons entirely unconnected with them ought to step in and require that a condition of things with which all who are directly interested appear to be satisfied, should be put an end to because it is a scandal to persons some thousands of miles distant, who have no part or concern in it. Let them send missionaries, if they please, to preach against it; and let them, by any fair means (of which silencing the teachers is not one), oppose the progress of similar doctrines among their own people. If civilization has got the better of barbarism when barbarism had the world to itself, it is too much to profess to be afraid lest barbarism, after having been fairly got under, should revive and conquer civilization. A civilization that can thus succumb to its vanquished enemy, must first have become so degenerate, that neither its appointed priests and teachers, nor anybody else, has the capacity, or will take the trouble, to stand up for it. If this be so, the sooner such a civilization receives notice to quit, the better. It can only go on from bad to worse, until destroyed and regenerated (like the Western Empire) by energetic barbarians.

◆ ◆ ◆ ◆ ◆

GERALD DWORKIN

"Paternalism," from *Morality, Harm and the Law*

> Neither one person, nor any number of persons, is warranted in saying to another human creature of ripe years, that he shall not do with his life for his own benefit what he chooses to do with it. [Mill]

> I do not want to go along with a volunteer basis. I think a fellow should be compelled to become better and not let him use his discretion whether he wants to get smarter, more healthy or more honest. [General Hershey]

I take as my starting point the "one very simple principle" proclaimed by Mill in *On Liberty* ... "That principle is, that the sole end for which mankind are warranted, individually or collectively, in interfering with the liberty of action of any of their number, is self-protection. That the only purpose for which power can be rightfully exercised over any member of a civilized community, against his will, is to prevent harm to others. He cannot rightfully be compelled to do or forbear because it will be better for him to do so, because it will make him happier, because, in the opinion of others, to do so would be wise, or even right."

This principle is neither "one" nor "very simple." It is at least two principles; one asserting that self-protection or the prevention of harm to others is sometimes a sufficient warrant and the other claim-ing that the individual's own good is *never* a sufficient warrant for the exercise of compulsion either by the society as a whole or by its individual members. I assume that no one, with the possible exception of extreme pacifists or anarchists, questions the correctness of the first half of the principle. This essay is an examination of the negative claim embodied in Mill's principle—the objection to paternalistic interferences with a man's liberty.

I

By paternalism I shall understand roughly the interference with a person's liberty of action justified by reasons referring exclusively to the welfare, good, happiness, needs, interests or values of the person being coerced. One is always well-advised to illustrate one's definitions by examples but it is not easy to find "pure" examples of paternalistic interferences. For almost any piece of legislation is justified by several different kinds of reasons and even if historically a piece of legislation can be shown to have been introduced for purely paternalistic motives, it may be that advocates of the legislation with an anti-paternalistic outlook can find sufficient reasons justifying the legislation without appealing to the reasons which were originally adduced to support it. Thus, for example, it may be that the original legislation requiring motorcyclists to wear safety helmets was introduced for purely paternalistic reasons. But the Rhode Island Supreme Court recently upheld such legislation on the grounds that it was "not persuaded that the legislature is power-less to prohibit individuals from pursuing a course of conduct which could conceivably result in their becoming public charges," thus clearly introducing reasons of a quite different kind. Now I regard this decision as being based on reasoning of a very dubi-ous nature but it illustrates the kind of problem one has in finding examples. The following is a list of the kinds of interferences I have in mind as being paternalistic.

II

1. Laws requiring motorcyclists to wear safety helmets when operating their machines.

2. Laws forbidding persons from swimming at a public beach when lifeguards are not on duty.

3. Laws making suicide a criminal offense.

4. Laws making it illegal for women and children to work at certain types of jobs.

5. Laws regulating certain kinds of sexual conduct, e.g., homosexuality among consenting adults in private.

6. Laws regulating the use of certain drugs which may have harmful consequences to the user but do not lead to anti-social conduct.

7. Laws requiring a license to engage in certain professions with those not receiving a license subject to fine or jail sentence if they do engage in the practice.

8. Laws compelling people to spend a specified fraction of their income on the purchase of retirement annuities (Social Security).

9. Laws forbidding various forms of gambling (often justified on the grounds that the poor are more likely to throw away their money on such activities than the rich who can afford to).

10. Laws regulating the maximum rates of interest for loans.

11. Laws against duelling.

In addition to laws which attach criminal or civil penalties to certain kinds of action there are laws, rules, regulations, decrees which make it either difficult or impossible for people to carry out their plans and which are also justified on paternalistic grounds.

Examples of this are:

1. Laws regulating the types of contracts which will be upheld as valid by the courts, e.g., (an example of Mill's to which I shall return) no man may make a valid contract for perpetual involuntary servitude.

2. Not allowing assumption of risk as a defense to an action based on the violation of a safety statute.

3. Not allowing as a defense to a charge of murder or assault the consent of the victim.

4. Requiring members of certain religious sects to have compulsory blood transfusions. This is made possible by not allowing the patient to have recourse to civil suits for assault and battery and by means of injunctions.

5. Civil commitment procedures when these are specifically justified on the basis of preventing the person being committed from harming himself. The D.C. Hospitalization of the Mentally Ill Act provides for involuntary hospitalization of a person who "is mentally ill, and because of that illness, is likely to injure himself or others if allowed to remain at liberty." The term injure in this context applies to unintentional as well as intentional injuries.

All of my examples are of existing restrictions on the liberty of individuals. Obviously one can think of interferences which have not yet been imposed. Thus one might ban the sale of cigarettes, or require that people wear safety-belts in automobiles (as opposed to merely having them installed), enforcing this by not allowing motorists to sue for injuries even when caused by other drivers if the motorist was not wearing a seat-belt at the time of the accident.

I shall not be concerned with activities which though defended on paternalistic grounds are not interferences with the liberty of persons, e.g., the giving of subsidies in kind rather than in cash on the grounds that the recipients would not spend the money on the goods which they really need, or not including a $1,000 deductible provision in a basic protection automobile insurance plan on the ground that the people who would elect it could least afford it. Nor shall I be concerned with measures such as "truth-in-advertising" acts and Pure Food and Drug legislation which are often attacked as paternalistic but which should not be considered so. In these cases all that is provided—it is true by the use of compulsion—is information which it is presumed that rational persons are interested in having in order to make wise decisions. There is no interference with the liberty of the consumer unless one wants to stretch a point beyond good sense and say that his liberty to apply for a loan without knowing the true rate of interest is diminished. It is true that sometimes there is sentiment for going further than providing information, for example when laws against usurious interest are passed preventing those who might wish to contract loans at high rates of interest from doing so, and these measures may correctly be considered paternalistic.

III

Bearing these examples in mind, let me return to a characterization of paternalism. I said earlier that I meant by the term, roughly, interference with a person's liberty for his own good. But, as some of the examples show, the class of persons whose good is involved is not always identical with the class of persons whose freedom is restricted. Thus, in the case of professional licensing it is the practitioner who is directly interfered with but it is the would-be patient whose interests are presumably being served. Not allowing the consent of the victim to be a defense to certain types of crime primarily affects the would-be aggressor but it is the interests of the willing victim that we are trying to protect. Sometimes a person may fall into both classes as would be the case if we banned the manufacture and sale of cigarettes and a given manufacturer happened to be a smoker as well.

Thus we may first divide paternalistic interferences into "pure" and "impure" cases. In "pure" paternalism the class of persons whose freedom is restricted is identical with the class of persons whose benefit is intended to be promoted by such restrictions. Examples: the making of suicide a crime, re-

quiring passengers in automobiles to wear seat-belts, requiring a Christian Scientist to receive a blood transfusion. In the case of "impure" paternalism in trying to protect the welfare of a class of persons we find that the only way to do so will involve restricting the freedom of other persons besides those who are benefitted. Now it might be thought that there are no cases of "impure" paternalism since any such case could always be justified on nonpaternalistic grounds, i.e., in terms of preventing harm to others. Thus we might ban cigarette manufacturers from continuing to manufacture their product on the grounds that we are preventing them from causing illness to others in the same way that we prevent other manufacturers from releasing pollutants into the atmosphere, thereby causing danger to the members of the community. The difference is, however, that in the former but not the latter case the harm is of such a nature that it could be avoided by those individuals affected if they so chose. The incurring of the harm requires, so to speak, the active cooperation of the victim. It would be mistaken theoretically and hypocritical in practice to assert that our interference in such cases is just like our interference in standard cases of protecting others from harm. At the very least someone interfered with in this way can reply that no one is complaining about his activities. It may be that impure paternalism requires arguments or reasons of a stronger kind in order to be justified, since there are persons who are losing a portion of their liberty and they do not even have the solace of having it be done "in their own interest." Of course in some sense, if paternalistic justifications are ever correct, then we are protecting others, we are preventing some from injuring others, but it is important to see the differences between this and the standard case.

Paternalism then will always involve limitations on the liberty of some individuals in their own interest but it may also extend to interferences with the liberty of parties whose interests are not in question.

IV

Finally, by way of some more preliminary analysis, I want to distinguish paternalistic interference with liberty from a related type with which it is often confused. Consider, for example, legislation which forbids employees to work more than, say, 40 hours per week. It is sometimes argued that such legislation is paternalistic for if employees desired such a restriction on their hours of work they could agree among themselves to impose it voluntarily. But because they do not the society imposes its own conception of their best interests upon them by the use of coercion. Hence this is paternalism.

Now it may be that some legislation of this nature is, in fact, paternalistically motivated. I am not denying that. All I want to point out is that there is another possible way of justifying such measures which is not paternalistic in nature. It is not paternalistic because, as Mill puts it in a similar context, such measures are "required not to overrule the judgment of individuals respecting their own interest, but to give effect to that judgment: they being unable to give effect to it except by concert, which concert again cannot be effectual unless it receives validity and sanction from the law." (*Principles of Political Economy*).

The line of reasoning here is a familiar one first found in Hobbes and developed with great sophistication by contemporary economists in the last decade or so. There are restrictions which are in the interests of a class of persons taken collectively but are such that the immediate interest of each individual is furthered by his violating the rule when others adhere to it. In such cases the individuals involved may need the use of compulsion to give effect to their collective judgment of their own interest by guaranteeing each individual compliance by the others. In these cases compulsion is not used to achieve some benefit which is not recognized to be a benefit by those concerned, but rather because it is the only feasible means of achieving some benefit

which is recognized as such by all concerned. This way of viewing matters provides us with another characterization of paternalism in general. Paternalism might be thought of as the use of coercion to achieve a good which is not recognized as such by those persons for whom the good is intended. Again while this formulation captures the heart of the matter—it is surely what Mill is objecting to in *On Liberty*—the matter is not always quite like that. For example, when we force motorcyclists to wear helmets we are trying to promote a good—the protection of the person from injury—which is surely recognized by most of the individuals concerned. It is not that a cyclist doesn't value his bodily integrity; rather, as a supporter of such legislation would put it, he either places, perhaps irrationally, another value or good (freedom from wearing a helmet) above that of physical well-being or, perhaps, while recognizing the danger in the abstract, he either does not fully appreciate it or he underestimates the likelihood of its occurring. But now we are approaching the question of possible justifications of paternalistic measures and the rest of this essay will be devoted to that question.

V

I shall begin for dialectical purposes by discussing Mill's objections to paternalism and then go on to discuss more positive proposals.

An initial feature that strikes one is the absolute nature of Mill's prohibitions against paternalism. It is so unlike the carefully qualified admonitions of Mill and his fellow Utilitarians on other moral issues. He speaks of self-protection as the sole end warranting coercion, of the individual's own goals as never being a sufficient warrant. Contrast this with his discussion of the prohibition against lying in Utilitarianism:

> Yet that even this rule, sacred as it is, admits
> of possible exception, is acknowledged by

all moralists, the chief of which is where the with-holding of some fact ... would save an individual ... from great and unmerited evil.

The same tentativeness is present when he deals with justice:

It is confessedly unjust to break faith with any one: to violate an engagement, either express or implied, or disappoint expectations raised by our own conduct, at least if we have raised these expectations knowingly and voluntarily. Like all the other obligations of justice already spoken of, this one is not regarded as absolute, but as capable of being overruled by a stronger obligation of justice on the other side.

This anomaly calls for some explanation. The structure of Mill's argument is as follows:

1. Since restraint is an evil the burden of proof is on those who propose such restraint.

2. Since the conduct which is being considered is purely self-regarding, the normal appeal to the protection of the interests of others is not available.

3. Therefore we have to consider whether reasons involving reference to the individual's own good, happiness, welfare, or interests are sufficient to overcome the burden of justification.

4. We either cannot advance the interests of the individual by compulsion, or the attempt to do so involves evils which outweigh the good done.

5. Hence the promotion of the individual's own interests does not provide a sufficient warrant for the use of compulsion.

Clearly the operative premise here is (4), and it is bolstered by claims about the status of the individual as judge and appraiser of his welfare, interests, needs, etc.:

With respect to his own feelings and circumstances, the most ordinary man or woman has means of knowledge immeasurably surpassing those that can be possessed by any one else.

He is the man most interested in his own well-being: the interest which any other person, except in cases of strong personal attachment, can have in it is trifling, compared to that which he himself has.

These claims are used to support the following generalizations concerning the utility of compulsion for paternalistic purposes.

The interferences of society to overrule his judgment and purposes in what only regards himself must be grounded on general presumptions; which may be altogether wrong, and even if right, are as likely as not to be misapplied to individual cases.

But the strongest of all the arguments against the interference of the public with purely personal conduct is that when it does interfere, the odds are that it interferes wrongly and in the wrong place.

All errors which the individual is likely to commit against advice and warning are far outweighed by the evil of allowing others to constrain him to what they deem his good.

Performing the utilitarian calculation by balancing the advantages and disadvantages we find that: "Mankind are greater gainers by suffering each other to live as seems good to themselves, than by compelling each other to live as seems good to the rest." Ergo, (4).

This classical case of a utilitarian argument with all the premises spelled out is not the only line of reasoning present in Mill's discussion. There are asides, and more than asides, which look quite different and I shall deal with them later. But this is clearly the main channel of Mill's thought and it is one which has been subjected to vigorous attack from the moment it appeared—most often by fellow Utilitarians. The link that they have usually seized on is, as Fitzjames Stephen put it in *Liberty, Equality, Fraternity*, the absence of proof that the "mass of adults are so well acquainted with their own interests and so much disposed to pursue them that no compulsion or restraint put upon them by any others for the purpose of promoting their interest can really promote them." Even so sympathetic a critic as H.L.A. Hart is forced to the conclusion that:

> In Chapter 5 of his essay [*On Liberty*] Mill carried his protests against paternalism to lengths that may now appear to us as fantastic ... No doubt if we no longer sympathise with this criticism this is due, in part, to a general decline in the belief that individuals know their own interest best.
>
> Mill endows the average individual with "too much of the psychology of a middle-aged man whose desires are relatively fixed, not liable to be artificially stimulated by external influences; who knows what he wants and what gives him satisfaction or happiness; and who pursues these things when he can."

Now it is interesting to note that Mill himself was aware of some of the limitations on the doctrine that the individual is the best judge of his own interests. In his discussion of government intervention in general (even where the intervention does not interfere with liberty but provides alternative institutions to those of the market) after making claims which are parallel to those just discussed, e.g., "People understand their own business and their own interests better, and care for them more, than the government does, or can be expected to do." He goes on to an intelligent discussion of the "very large and conspicuous exceptions" to the maxim that:

> Most persons take a juster and more intelligent view of their own interest, and of the means of promoting it than can either be prescribed to them by a general enactment of the legislature, or pointed out in the particular case by a public functionary.

Thus there are things

> of which the utility does not consist in ministering to inclinations, nor in serving the daily uses of life, and the want of which is least felt where the need is greatest. This is peculiarly true of those things which are chiefly useful as tending to raise the character of human beings. The uncultivated cannot be competent judges of cultivation. Those who most need to be made wiser and better, usually desire it least, and, if they desired it, would be incapable of finding the way to it by their own lights.
>
> ... A second exception to the doctrine that individuals are the best judges of their own interest, is when an individual attempts to decide irrevocably now what will be best for his interest at some future and distant time. The presumption in favor of individual judgment is only legitimate, where the judgment is grounded on actual, and especially on present, personal experience; not where it is formed antecedently to experience, and not suffered to be reversed even after experience has condemned it.

The upshot of these exceptions is that Mill does not declare that there should never be government interference with the economy but rather that

> ... in every instance, the burden of making out a strong case should be thrown not on those who resist but on those who recommend government interference. Letting alone, in short, should be the general practice: every departure from it, unless required by some great good, is a certain evil.

In short, we get a presumption, not an absolute prohibition. The question is why doesn't the argument against paternalism go the same way?

I suggest that the answer lies in seeing that in addition to a purely utilitarian argument Mill uses another as well. As a Utilitarian, Mill has to show, in Fitzjames Stephen's words, that: "Self-protection apart, no good object can be attained by any compulsion which is not in itself a greater evil than the absence of the object which the compulsion obtains." To show this is impossible; one reason being that it isn't true. Preventing a man from selling himself into slavery (a paternalistic measure which Mill himself accepts as legitimate), or from taking heroin, or from driving a car without wearing seat-belts may constitute a lesser evil than allowing him to do any of these things. A consistent Utilitarian can only argue against paternalism on the grounds that it (as a matter of fact) does not maximize the good. It is always a contingent question that may be refuted by the evidence. But there is also a non-contingent argument which runs through *On Liberty*. When Mill states that "there is a part of the life of every person who has come to years of discretion, within which the individuality of that person ought to reign uncontrolled either by any other person or by the public collectively," he is saying something about what it means to be a person, an autonomous agent. It is because coercing a person for his own good denies this status as an independent entity that Mill objects to it so strongly and in such absolute terms. To be able to choose is a good that is independent of the wisdom of what is chosen. A man's "mode of laying out his existence is the best, not because it is the best in itself, but because it is his own mode." It is the privilege and proper condition of a human being, arrived at the maturity of his faculties, to use and interpret experience in his own way.

As further evidence of this line of reasoning in Mill, consider the one exception to his prohibition against paternalism.

> In this and most civilised countries, for example, an engagement by which a person should sell himself, or allow himself to be sold, as a slave, would be null and void; neither enforced by law nor by opinion. The ground for thus limiting his power of voluntarily disposing of his own lot in life, is apparent, and is very clearly seen in this extreme case. The reason for not interfering, unless for the sake of others, with a person's voluntary acts, is consideration for his liberty. His voluntary choice is evidence that what he so chooses is desirable, or at least endurable, to him, and his good is on the whole best provided for by allowing him to take his own means of pursuing it. But by selling himself for a slave, he abdicates his liberty; he foregoes any future use of it beyond that single act. He therefore defeats, in his own case, the very purpose which is the justification of allowing him to dispose of himself. He is no longer free; but is thenceforth in a position which has no longer the presumption in its favour, that would be afforded by his voluntarily remaining in it. The principle of freedom cannot require that he should be free not to be free. It is not freedom to be allowed to alienate his freedom.

Now leaving aside the fudging on the meaning of freedom in the last line it is clear that part of this argument is incorrect. While it is true that *future* choices of the slave are not reasons for thinking that what he chooses then is desirable for him, what is at issue is limiting his immediate choice; and since this choice is made freely, the individual may be correct in thinking that his interests are best provided for by entering such a contract. But the main consideration for not allowing such a contract is the need to preserve the liberty of the person to make future choices. This gives us a principle—a very narrow one—by which to justify some paternalistic interferences. Paternalism is justified only to preserve a wider range of freedom for the individual in question. How far this principle could be extended, whether it can justify all the cases in which we are inclined upon reflection to think paternalistic measures justified, remains to be discussed. What I have tried to show so far is that there are two strains of argument in Mill—one a straight-forward Utilitarian mode of reasoning and one which relies not on the goods which free choice leads to but on the absolute value of the choice itself. The first cannot establish any absolute prohibition but at most a presumption and indeed a fairly weak one given some fairly plausible assumptions about human psychology; the second, while a stronger line of argument, seems to me to allow on its own grounds a wider range of paternalism than might be suspected. I turn now to a consideration of these matters.

VI

We might begin looking for principles governing the acceptable use of paternalistic power in cases where it is generally agreed that it is legitimate. Even Mill intends his principles to be applicable only to mature individuals, not those in what he calls "nonage." What is it that justifies us in interfering with children? The fact that they lack some of the emotional and cognitive capacities required in order to make fully rational decisions. It is an empirical question to just what extent children have an adequate conception of their own present and future interests but there is not much doubt that there are many deficiencies. For example, it is very difficult for a child to defer gratification for any considerable period of time. Given these deficiencies and given the very real and permanent dangers that may befall the child it becomes not only permissible but even a duty of the parent to restrict the child's freedom in various ways. There is however an important moral limitation on the exercise of such parental power which is provided by the notion of the child eventually coming to see the correctness of his parent's interventions. Parental paternalism may be thought of as a wager by the parent on the child's subsequent recognition of the wisdom of the restrictions. There is an emphasis on what could be called future-oriented consent—on what the child will come to welcome, rather than on what he does welcome.

The essence of this idea has been incorporated by idealist philosophers into various types of "real-will" theory as applied to fully adult persons. Extensions of paternalism are argued for by claiming that in various respects, chronologically mature individuals share the same deficiencies in knowledge, capacity to think rationally, and the ability to carry out decisions that children possess. Hence in interfering with such people we are in effect doing what they would do if they were fully rational. Hence we are not really opposing their will, hence we are not really interfering with their freedom. The dangers of this move have been sufficiently exposed by Berlin in his *Two Concepts of Freedom*. I see no gain in theoretical clarity nor in practical advantage in trying to pass over the real nature of the interferences with liberty that we impose on others. Still the basic notion of consent is important and seems to me the only acceptable way of trying to delimit an area of justified paternalism.

Let me start by considering a case where the consent is not hypothetical in nature. Under certain conditions it is rational for an individual to agree that others should force him to act in ways which, at the time of action, the individual may not see as desirable. If, for example, a man knows that he is subject to breaking his resolves when temptation is present, he may ask a friend to refuse to entertain his requests at some later stage.

A classical example is given in the Odyssey when Odysseus commands his men to tie him to the mast and refuse all future orders to be set free, because he knows the power of the Sirens to enchant men with their songs. Here we are on relatively sound ground in later refusing Odysseus' request to be set free. He may even claim to have changed his mind but since it is *just* such changes that he wished to guard against we are entitled to ignore them.

A process analogous to this may take place on a social rather than individual basis. An electorate may mandate its representatives to pass legislation which when it comes time to "pay the price" may be unpalatable. I may believe that a tax increase is necessary to halt inflation though I may resent the lower pay check each month. However in both this case and that of Odysseus the measure to be enforced is specifically requested by the party involved and at some point in time there is genuine consent and agreement on the part of those persons whose liberty is infringed. Such is not the case for the paternalistic measures we have been speaking about. What must be involved here is not consent to specific measures but rather consent to a system of government, run by elected representatives, with an understanding that they may act to safeguard our interests in certain limited ways.

I suggest that since we are all aware of our irrational propensities, deficiencies in cognitive and emotional capacities, and avoidable and unavoidable ignorance it is rational and prudent for us to in effect take out "social insurance policies." We may argue for and against proposed paternalistic measures in terms of what fully rational individuals would accept as forms of protection. Now clearly, since the initial agreement is not about specific measures we are dealing with a more-or-less blank check and therefore there have to be carefully defined limits. What I am looking for are certain kinds of conditions which make it plausible to suppose that rational men could reach agreement to limit their liberty even when other men's interests are not affected.

Of course as in any kind of agreement schema there are great difficulties in deciding what rational individuals would or would not accept. Particularly in sensitive areas of personal liberty, there is always a danger of the dispute over agreement and rationality being a disguised version of evaluative and normative disagreement.

Let me suggest types of situations in which it seems plausible to suppose that fully rational individuals would agree to having paternalistic restrictions imposed upon them. It is reasonable to suppose that there are "goods" such as health which any person would want to have in order to pursue his own good—no matter how that good is conceived. This is an argument used in connection with compulsory education for children but it seems to me that it can be extended to other goods which have this character. Then one could agree that the attainment of such goods should be promoted even when not recognized to be such, at the moment, by the individuals concerned.

An immediate difficulty arises from the fact that men are always faced with competing goods and that there may be reasons why even a value such as health—or indeed life—may be overridden by competing values. Thus the problem with the Christian Scientist and blood transfusions. It may be more important for him to reject "impure substances" than to go on living. The difficult problem that must be faced is whether one can give sense to the notion of a person irrationally attaching weights to competing values.

Consider a person who knows the statistical data on the probability of being injured when not wearing seat-belts in an automobile and knows the types and gravity of the various injuries. He also insists that the inconvenience attached to fastening the belt every time he gets in and out of the car outweighs for him the possible risks to himself. I am inclined in this case to think that such a weighing is irrational. Given his life-plans, which we are assuming are those of the average person, his interests and commitments already undertaken, I think it is safe to predict that we can find inconsistencies in his calculations at some point. I am assuming that this is not a man who for some conscious or unconscious reasons is trying to injure himself nor is he a man who just likes to "live dangerously." I am assuming that he is like us in all the relevant respects but just puts an enormously high negative value on inconvenience—one which does not seem comprehensible or reasonable.

It is always possible, of course, to assimilate this person to creatures like myself. I, also, neglect to fasten my seat-belt and I concede such behavior is not rational but not because I weigh the inconvenience differently from those who fasten the belts. It is just that having made (roughly) the same calculation as everybody else I ignore it in my actions. [Note: a much better case of weakness of the will than those usually given in ethics texts.] A plausible explanation for this deplorable habit is that although I know in some intellectual sense what the probabilities and risks are I do not fully appreciate them in an emotionally genuine manner.

We have two distinct types of situation in which a man acts in a nonrational fashion. In one case he attaches incorrect weights to some of his values; in the other he neglects to act in accordance with his actual preferences and desires. Clearly there is a stronger and more persuasive argument for paternalism in the latter situation. Here we are really not—by assumption—imposing a good on another person. But why may we not extend our interference to what we might call evaluative delusions? After all, in the case of cognitive delusions we are prepared, often, to act against the expressed will of the person involved. If a man believes that when he jumps out the window he will float upwards—Robert Nozick's example—would not we detain him, forcibly if necessary? The reply will be that this man doesn't wish to be injured and if we could convince him that he is mistaken as to the consequences of his action he would not wish to perform the action. But part of what is involved in claiming that the man who doesn't fasten his seat-belts is attaching an incorrect weight to the inconvenience of fastening them is that if he were to be involved in an accident and severely injured he would look back and admit that the inconvenience wasn't as bad as all that. So there is a sense in which if I could convince him of the consequences of his action he also would not wish to continue his present course of action. Now the notion of consequences being used here is covering a lot of ground. In one

case it's being used to indicate what will or can happen as a result of a course of action and in the other it's making a prediction about the future evaluation of the consequences—in the first sense—of a course of action. And whatever the difference between facts and values—whether it be hard and fast or soft and slow—we are genuinely more reluctant to consent to interferences where evaluative differences are the issue. Let me now consider another factor which comes into play in some of these situations which may make an important difference in our willingness to consent to paternalistic restrictions.

Some of the decisions we make are of such a character that they produce changes which are in one or another way irreversible. Situations are created in which it is difficult or impossible to return to anything like the initial stage at which the decision was made. In particular, some of these changes will make it impossible to continue to make reasoned choices in the future. I am thinking specifically of decisions which involve taking drugs that are physically or psychologically addictive and those which are destructive of one's mental and physical capacities.

I suggest we think of the imposition of paternalistic interferences in situations of this kind as being a kind of insurance policy which we take out against making decisions which are far-reaching, potentially dangerous and irreversible. Each of these factors is important. Clearly there are many decisions we make that are relatively irreversible. In deciding to learn to play chess I could predict in view of my general interest in games that some portion of my free time was going to be preempted and that it would not be easy to give up the game once I acquired a certain competence. But my whole life-style was not going to be jeopardized in an extreme manner. Further it might be argued that even with addictive drugs such as heroin one's normal life plans would not be seriously interfered with if an inexpensive and adequate supply were readily available. So this type of argument might have a much narrower scope than appears to be the case at first.

A second class of cases concerns decisions which are made under extreme psychological and sociological pressures. I am not thinking here of the making of the decision as being something one is pressured into—e.g., a good reason for making duelling illegal is that unless this is done many people might have to manifest their courage and integrity in ways in which they would rather not do so—but rather of decisions, such as that to commit suicide, which are usually made at a point where the individual is not thinking clearly and calmly about the nature of his decision. In addition, of course, this comes under the previous heading of all-too-irrevocable decisions. Now there are practical steps which a society could take if it wanted to decrease the possibility of suicide—for example not paying social security benefits to the survivors or, as religious institutions do, not allowing persons to be buried with the same status as natural deaths. I think we may count these as interferences with the liberty of persons to attempt suicide and the question is whether they are justifiable.

Using my argument schema the question is whether rational individuals would consent to such limitations. I see no reason for them to consent to an absolute prohibition but I do think it is reasonable for them to agree to some kind of enforced waiting period. Since we are all aware of the possibility of temporary states, such as great fear or depression, that are inimical to the making of well-informed and rational decisions, it would be prudent for all of us if there were some kind of institutional arrangement whereby we were restrained from making a decision which is so irreversible. What this would be like in practice is difficult to envisage and it may be that if no practical arrangements were feasible we would have to conclude that there should be no restriction at all on this kind of action. But we might have a "cooling off" period, in much the same way that we now require couples who file for divorce to go through a waiting period. Or, more far-fetched, we might imagine a Suicide Board composed of a psychologist and another member picked by the applicant. The Board would be required to meet and talk with the person proposing to take his life, though its approval would not be required.

A third class of decisions—these classes are not supposed to be disjoint—involves dangers which are either not sufficiently understood or appreciated correctly by the persons involved. Let me illustrate, using the example of cigarette smoking, a number of possible cases.

1. A man may not know the facts—e.g., smoking between 1 and 2 packs a day shortens life expectancy 6.2 years, the costs and pain of the illness caused by smoking, etc.

2. A man may know the facts, wish to stop smoking, but not have the requisite will-power.

3. A man may know the facts but not have them play the correct role in his calculation because, say, he discounts the danger psychologically since it is remote in time and/or inflates the attractiveness of other consequences of his decision which he regards as beneficial.

In case 1 what is called for is education, the posting of warnings, etc. In case 2 there is no theoretical problem. We are not imposing a good on someone who rejects it. We are simply using coercion to enable people to carry out their own goals. (Note: There obviously is a difficulty in that only a subclass of the individuals affected wish to be prevented from doing what they are doing.) In case 3 there is a sense in which we are imposing a good on someone in that given his current appraisal of the facts he doesn't wish to be restricted. But in another sense we are not imposing a good since what is being claimed—and what must be shown or at least argued for—is that an accurate accounting on his part would lead him to reject his current course of action. Now we all know that such cases exist, that we are prone to disregarding dangers that are only possibilities, that immediate pleasures are often magnified and distorted.

If in addition the dangers are severe and far-reaching, we could agree to allow the state a certain degree of power to intervene in such situations. The difficulty is in specifying in advance, even vaguely, the class of cases in which intervention will be legitimate.

A related difficulty is that of drawing a line so that it is not the case that all ultra-hazardous activities are ruled out, e.g., mountain-climbing, bull-fighting, sports-car racing, etc. There are some risks—even very great ones—which a person is entitled to take with his life.

A good deal depends on the nature of the deprivation—e.g., does it prevent the person from engaging in the activity completely or merely limit his participation—and how important to the nature of the activity is the absence of restriction when this is weighed against the role that the activity plays in the life of the person. In the case of automobile seat-belts, for example, the restriction is trivial in nature, interferes not at all with the use or enjoyment of the activity, and does, I am assuming, considerably reduce a high risk of serious injury. Whereas, for example, making mountain-climbing illegal completely prevents a person from engaging in an activity which may play an important role in his life and his conception of the person he is.

In general, the easiest cases to handle are those which can be argued about in the terms which Mill thought to be so important—a concern not just for the happiness or welfare, in some broad sense, of the individual but rather a concern for the autonomy and freedom of the person. I suggest that we would be most likely to consent to paternalism in those instances in which it preserves and enhances for the individual his ability to rationally consider and carry out his own decisions.

I have suggested in this essay a number of types of situations in which it seems plausible that rational men would agree to granting the legislative powers of a society the right to impose restrictions on what Mill calls "self-regarding" conduct. However, rational men knowing something about the resources of ignorance, ill-will and stupidity available to the law-makers of a society—a good case in point is the history of drug legislation in the United States—will be concerned to limit such intervention to a minimum. I suggest in closing two principles designed to achieve this end.

In all cases of paternalistic legislation there must be a heavy and clear burden of proof placed on the authorities to demonstrate the exact nature of the harmful effects (or beneficial consequences) to be avoided (or achieved) and the probability of their occurrence. The burden of proof here is two-fold—what lawyers distinguish as the burden of going forward and the burden of persuasion. That the authorities have the burden of going forward means that it is up to them to raise the question and bring forward evidence of the evils to be avoided. Unlike the case of new drugs where the manufacturer must produce some evidence that the drug has been tested and found not harmful, no citizen has to show with respect to self-regarding conduct that it is not harmful or promotes his best interests. In addition the nature and cogency of the evidence for the harmfulness of the course of action must be set at a high level. To paraphrase a formulation of the burden of proof for criminal proceedings—better 10 men ruin themselves than one man be unjustly deprived of liberty.

Finally, I suggest a principle of the least restrictive alternative. If there is an alternative way of accomplishing the desired end without restricting liberty although it may involve great expense, inconvenience, etc., the society must adopt it.

◆ ◆ ◆ ◆ ◆

PATRICK DEVLIN

"Morals and the Criminal Law,"* from *The Enforcement of Morals*

The Report of the Committee on Homosexual Offences and Prostitution, generally known as the Wolfenden Report, is recognized to be an excellent study of two very difficult legal and social problems. But it has also a particular claim to the respect of those interested in jurisprudence; it does what law reformers so rarely do; it sets out clearly and carefully what in relation to its subjects it considers the function of the law to be.[1] Statutory additions to the criminal law are too often made on the simple principle that "there ought to be a law against it." The greater part of the law relating to sexual offences is the creation of statute and it is difficult to ascertain any logical relationship between it and the moral ideas which most of us uphold. Adultery, fornication, and prostitution are not, as the Report[2] points out, criminal offences: homosexuality between males is a criminal offence, but between females it is not. Incest was not an offence until it was declared so by statute only fifty years ago. Does the legislature select these offences haphazardly or are there some principles which can be used to determine what part of the moral law should be embodied in the criminal? There is, for example, being now considered a proposal to make A.I.D., that is, the practice of artificial insemination of a woman with the seed of a man who is not her husband, a criminal offence; if, as is usually the case, the woman is married, this is in substance, if not in form, adultery. Ought it to be made punishable when adultery is not? This sort of question is of practical importance, for a law that appears to be arbitrary and illogical, in the end and after the wave of moral indignation that has put it on the statute book subsides, forfeits respect. As a practical question it arises more frequently in the field of sexual morals than in any other, but there is no special answer to be found in that field. The inquiry must be general and fundamental. What is the connexion between crime and sin and to what extent, if at all, should the criminal law of England concern itself with the enforcement of morals and punish sin or immorality as such?

The statements of principle in the Wolfenden Report provide an admirable and modern starting-point for such an inquiry. In the course of my examination of them I shall find matter for criticism. If my criticisms are sound, it must not be imagined that they point to any shortcomings in the Report. Its authors were not, as I am trying to do, composing a paper on the jurisprudence of morality; they were evolving a working formula to use for reaching a number of practical conclusions. I do not intend to express any opinion one way or the other about these; that would be outside the scope of a lecture on jurisprudence. I am concerned only with general principles; the statement of these in the Report illuminates the entry into the subject and I hope that its authors will forgive me if I carry the lamp with me into places where it was not intended to go.

Early in the Report[3] the Committee put forward:

---

* Maccabaean Lecture in Jurisprudence read at the British Academy on 18 March 1959 and printed in the *Proceedings of the British Academy*, vol xlv, under the title "The Enforcement of Morals."

---

1 The Committee's "statement of juristic philosophy" (to quote Lord Pakenham) was considered by him in a debate in the House of Lords on 4 December 1957, reported in *Hansard Lords Debates*, vol. ccvi at 738; and also in the same debate by the Archbishop of Canterbury at 753 and Lord Denning at 806. The subject has also been considered by Mr. J.E. Hall Williams in the *Law Quarterly Review*, January 1958, vol. lxxiv, p.76.

2 Para. 14.

---

3 Para. 13.

Our own formulation of the function of the criminal law so far as it concerns the subjects of this enquiry. In this field, its function, as we see it, is to preserve public order and decency, to protect the citizen from what is offensive or injurious, and to provide sufficient safeguards against exploitation and corruption of others, particularly those who are specially vulnerable because they are young, weak in body or mind, inexperienced, or in a state of special physical, official or economic dependence.

It is not, in our view, the function of the law to intervene in the private lives of citizens, or to seek to enforce any particular pattern of behaviour, further than is necessary to carry out the purposes we have outlined.

The Committee preface their most important recommendation[4]

that homosexual behaviour between consenting adults in private should no longer be a criminal offence, [by stating the argument[5]] which we believe to be decisive, namely, the importance which society and the law ought to give to individual freedom of choice and action in matters of private morality. Unless a deliberate attempt is to be made by society, acting through the agency of the law, to equate the sphere of · crime with that of sin, there must remain a realm of private morality and immorality which is, in brief and crude terms, not the law's business. To say this is not to condone or encourage private immorality.

Similar statements of principle are set out in the chapters of the Report which deal with prostitution. No case can be sustained, the Report says,

for attempting to make prostitution itself illegal.[6] The Committee refer to the general reasons already given and add: "We are agreed that private immorality should not be the concern of the criminal law except in the special circumstances therein mentioned." They quote[7] with approval the report of the Street Offences Committee,[8] which says: "As a general proposition it will be universally accepted that the law is not concerned with private morals or with ethical sanctions." It will be observed that the emphasis is on *private* immorality. By this is meant immorality which is not offensive or injurious to the public in the ways defined or described in the first passage which I quoted. In other words, no act of immorality should be made a criminal offence unless it is accompanied by some other feature such as indecency, corruption, or exploitation. This is clearly brought out in relation to prostitution: "It is not the duty of the law to concern itself with immorality as such ... it should confine itself to those activities which offend against public order and decency or expose the ordinary citizen to what is offensive or injurious."[9]

These statements of principle are naturally restricted to the subject-matter of the Report. But they are made in general terms and there seems to be no reason why, if they are valid, they should not be applied to the criminal law in general. They separate very decisively crime from sin, the divine law from the secular, and the moral from the criminal. They do not signify any lack of support for the law, moral or criminal, and they do not represent an attitude that can be called either religious or irreligious. There are many schools of thought among those who may think that morals are not the law's business. There is first of all the agnostic or free-thinker. He does not of course disbelieve in morals, nor in sin if it be given the wider of the two meanings assigned to it

---

4   Para. 62.
5   Para. 61.
6   Para. 224.
7   Para. 227.
8   Cmd. 3231 (1928).
9   Para. 257.

in the *Oxford English Dictionary* where it is defined as "transgression against divine law or the principles of morality." He cannot accept the divine law; that does not mean that he might not view with suspicion any departure from moral principles that have for generations been accepted by the society in which he lives; but in the end he judges for himself. Then there is the deeply religious person who feels that the criminal law is sometimes more of a hindrance than a help in the sphere of morality, and that the reform of the sinner—at any rate when he injures only himself—should be a spiritual rather than a temporal work. Then there is the man who without any strong feeling cannot see why, where there is freedom in religious belief, there should not logically be freedom in morality as well. All these are powerfully allied against the equating of crime with sin.

I must disclose at the outset that I have as a judge an interest in the result of the inquiry which I am seeking to make as a jurisprudent. As a judge who administers the criminal law and who has often to pass sentence in a criminal court, I should feel handicapped in my task if I thought that I was addressing an audience which had no sense of sin or which thought of crime as something quite different. Ought one, for example, in passing sentence upon a female abortionist to treat her simply as if she were an unlicensed midwife? If not, why not? But if so, is all the panoply of the law erected over a set of social regulations? I must admit that I begin with a feeling that a complete separation of crime from sin (I use the term throughout this lecture in the wider meaning) would not be good for the moral law and might be disastrous for the criminal. But can this sort of feeling be justified as a matter of jurisprudence? And if it be a right feeling, how should the relationship between the criminal and the moral law be stated? Is there a good theoretical basis for it, or is it just a practical working alliance, or is it a bit of both? That is the problem which I want to examine, and I shall begin by considering the standpoint of the strict logician. It can be supported by cogent arguments, some of which I believe to be unanswerable and which I put as follows.

Morals and religion are inextricably joined—the moral standards generally accepted in Western civilization being those belonging to Christianity. Outside Christendom other standards derive from other religions. None of these moral codes can claim any validity except by virtue of the religion on which it is based. Old Testament morals differ in some respects from New Testament morals. Even within Christianity there are differences. Some hold that contraception is an immoral practice and that a man who has carnal knowledge of another woman while his wife is alive is in all circumstances a fornicator; others, including most of the English-speaking world, deny both these propositions. Between the great religions of the world, of which Christianity is only one, there are much wider differences. It may or may not be right for the State to adopt one of these religions as the truth, to found itself upon its doctrines, and to deny to any of its citizens the liberty to practise any other. If it does, it is logical that it should use the secular law wherever it thinks it necessary to enforce the divine. If it does not, it is illogical that it should concern itself with morals as such. But if it leaves matters of religion to private judgement, it should logically leave matters of morals also. A State which refuses to enforce Christian beliefs has lost the right to enforce Christian morals.

If this view is sound, it means that the criminal law cannot justify any of its provisions by reference to the moral law. It cannot say, for example, that murder and theft are prohibited because they are immoral or sinful. The State must justify in some other way the punishments which it imposes on wrongdoers and a function for the criminal law independent of morals must be found. This is not difficult to do. The smooth functioning of society and the preservation of order require that a number of activities should be regulated. The rules that are made for that purpose and are enforced by the criminal law are often designed simply to achieve uniformity and convenience and rarely involve any choice between good and evil. Rules that impose a speed limit or prevent obstruction on the highway have nothing to do with morals. Since so much of the criminal law is composed of rules of this sort, why bring morals into it at all? Why not define the function of the criminal law in simple terms as the preservation of order and decency and the protection of the lives and property of citizens, and elaborate those terms in relation to any particular subject in the way in which it is done in the Wolfenden Report? The criminal law in carrying out these objects will undoubtedly overlap the moral law. Crimes of violence are morally wrong and they are also offences against good order; therefore they offend against both laws. But this is simply because the two laws in pursuit of different objectives happen to cover the same area. Such is the argument.

Is the argument consistent or inconsistent with the fundamental principles of English criminal law as it exists today? That is the first way of testing it, though by no means a conclusive one. In the field of jurisprudence one is at liberty to overturn even fundamental conceptions if they are theoretically unsound. But to see how the argument fares under the existing law is a good starting-point.

It is true that for many centuries the criminal law was much concerned with keeping the peace and little, if at all, with sexual morals. But it would be wrong to infer from that that it had no moral content or that it would ever have tolerated the idea of a man being left to judge for himself in matters of morals. The criminal law of England has from the very first concerned itself with moral principles. A simple way of testing this point is to consider the attitude which the criminal law adopts towards consent.

Subject to certain exceptions inherent in the nature of particular crimes, the criminal law has never permitted consent of the victim to be used as a defence. In rape, for example, consent negatives an essential element. But consent of the victim is no defence to a charge of murder. It is not a defence to any form of assault that the victim thought his punishment well deserved and submitted to it; to make a good defence the accused must prove that the law gave him the right to chastise and that he exercised it reasonably. Likewise, the victim may not forgive the aggressor and require the prosecution to desist; the right to enter a *nolle prosequi* belongs to the Attorney-General alone.

Now, if the law existed for the protection of the individual, there would be no reason why he should avail himself of it if he did not want it. The reason why a man may not consent to the commission of an offence against himself beforehand or forgive it afterwards is because it is an offence against society. It is not that society is physically injured; that would be impossible. Nor need any individual be shocked, corrupted, or exploited; everything may be done in private. Nor can it be explained on the practical ground that a violent man is a potential danger to others in the community who have therefore a direct interest in his apprehension and punishment as being necessary to their own protection. That would be true of a man whom the victim is prepared to forgive but not of one who gets his consent first; a murderer who acts only upon the consent, and maybe the request, of his victim is no menace to others, but he does threaten one of the great moral principles upon which society is based, that is, the sanctity of human life. There is only one explanation of what has hitherto been accepted as the basis of the criminal law and that is that there are certain standards of behaviour or moral principles which society requires to be observed; and the breach of them is an offence not merely against the person who is injured but against society as a whole.

Thus, if the criminal law were to be reformed so as to eliminate from it everything that was not designed to preserve order and decency or to protect citizens (including the protection of youth from corruption), it would overturn a fundamental principle. It would also end a number of specific crimes. Euthanasia or the killing of another at his own request, suicide, attempted suicide and suicide pacts, duelling, abortion, incest between brother and sister, are all acts which can be done in private and without offence to others and need not involve the corruption or exploitation of others. Many people think that the law on some of these subjects is in need of reform, but no one hitherto has gone so far as to suggest that they should all be left outside the criminal law as matters of private morality. They can be brought within it only as a matter of moral principle. It must be remembered also that although there is much immorality that is not punished by the law, there is none that is condoned by the law. The law will not allow its processes to be used by those engaged in immorality of any sort. For example, a house may not be let for immoral purposes; the lease is invalid and would not be enforced. But if what goes on inside there is a matter of private morality and not the law's business, why does the law inquire into it at all?

I think it is clear that the criminal law as we know it is based upon moral principle. In a number of crimes its function is simply to enforce a moral principle and nothing else. The law, both criminal and civil, claims to be able to speak about morality and immorality generally. Where does it get its authority to do this and how does it settle the moral principles which it enforces? Undoubtedly, as a matter of history, it derived both from Christian teaching. But I think that the strict logician is right when he says that the law can no longer rely on doctrines in which citizens are entitled to disbelieve. It is necessary therefore to look for some other source.

In jurisprudence, as I have said, everything is thrown open to discussion and, in the belief that they cover the whole field, I have framed three interrogatories addressed to myself to answer:

1. Has society the right to pass judgement at all on matters of morals? Ought there, in other words, to be a public morality, or are morals always a matter for private judgement?

2. If society has the right to pass judgement, has it also the right to use the weapon of the law to enforce it?

3. If so, ought it to use that weapon in all cases or only in some; and if only in some, on what principles should it distinguish?

I shall begin with the first interrogatory and consider what is meant by the right of society to pass a moral judgement, that is, a judgement about what is good and what is evil. The fact that a majority of people may disapprove of a practice does not of itself make it a matter for society as a whole. Nine men out of ten may disapprove of what the tenth man is doing and still say that it is not their business. There is a case for a collective judgement (as distinct from a large number of individual opinions which sensible people may even refrain from pronouncing at all if it is upon somebody else's private affairs) only if society is affected. Without a collective judgement there can be no case at all for intervention. Let me take as an illustration the Englishman's attitude to religion as it is now and as it has been in the past. His attitude now is that a man's religion is his private affair; he may think of another man's religion that it is right or wrong, true or untrue, but not that it is good or bad. In earlier times that was not so; a man was denied the right to practise what was thought of as heresy, and heresy was thought of as destructive of society.

The language used in the passages I have quoted from the Wolfenden Report suggests the view that there ought not to be a collective judgement about immorality *per se.* Is this what is meant by "private morality" and "individual freedom of choice and action"? Some people sincerely believe that homosexuality is neither immoral nor unnatural. Is the "freedom of choice and action" that is offered to the individual, freedom to decide for himself what is moral or immoral, society remaining neutral; or is it freedom to be immoral if he wants to be? The language of the Report may be open to question, but the conclusions at which the Committee arrive answer this question unambiguously. If society is not prepared to say that homosexuality is morally wrong, there would be no basis for a law protecting youth from "corruption" or punishing a man for living on the "immoral" earnings of a homosexual prostitute, as the Report recommends.[10] This attitude the Committee make even clearer when they come to deal with prostitution. In truth, the Report takes it for granted that there is in existence a public morality which condemns homosexuality and prostitution. What the Report seems to mean by private morality might perhaps be better described as private behaviour in matters of morals.

This view—that there is such a thing as public morality—can also be justified by *a priori* argument. What makes a society of any sort is community of ideas, not only political ideas but also ideas about the way its members should behave and govern their lives; these latter ideas are its morals. Every society has a moral structure as well as a political one: or rather, since that might suggest two independent systems, I should say that the structure of every society is made up both of politics and morals. Take, for example, the institution of marriage. Whether a man should be allowed to take more than one wife is something about which every society has to make up its mind one way or the other. In England we believe in the Christian idea of marriage and therefore adopt monogamy as a moral principle. Consequently the Christian institution of marriage has become the basis of family life and so part of the structure of our society. It is there not because it is Christian. It has got there because it is Christian, but it remains there because it is built into the house in which we live and could not be removed without bringing it down. The great majority of those who live in this country accept it because it is the Christian idea of marriage and for them the only true one. But a non-Christian is bound by it, not because it is part of Christianity but because, rightly or wrongly, it has been adopted

by the society in which he lives. It would be useless for him to stage a debate designed to prove that polygamy was theologically more correct and socially preferable; if he wants to live in the house, he must accept it as built in the way in which it is.

We see this more clearly if we think of ideas or institutions that are purely political. Society cannot tolerate rebellion; it will not allow argument about the rightness of the cause. Historians a century later may say that the rebels were right and the Government was wrong and a percipient and conscientious subject of the State may think so at the time. But it is not a matter which can be left to individual judgement.

The institution of marriage is a good example for my purpose because it bridges the division, if there is one, between politics and morals. Marriage is part of the structure of our society and it is also the basis of a moral code which condemns fornication and adultery. The institution of marriage would be gravely threatened if individual judgements were permitted about the morality of adultery; on these points there must be a public morality. But public morality is not to be confined to those moral principles which support institutions such as marriage. People do not think of monogamy as something which has to be supported because our society has chosen to organize itself upon it; they think of it as something that is good in itself and offering a good way of life and that it is for that reason that our society has adopted it. I return to the statement that I have already made, that society means a community of ideas; without shared ideas on politics, morals, and ethics no society can exist. Each one of us has ideas about what is good and what is evil; they cannot be kept private from the society in which we live. If men and women try to create a society in which there is no fundamental agreement about good and evil they will fail; if, having based it on common agreement, the agreement goes, the society will disintegrate. For society is not something that is kept together physically; it is held by the invisible bonds of common thought. If the bonds were too far relaxed the members would drift

10 Para. 76.

apart. A common morality is part of the bondage. The bondage is part of the price of society; and mankind, which needs society, must pay its price.

Common lawyers used to say that Christianity was part of the law of the land. That was never more than a piece of rhetoric as Lord Sumner said in *Bowman v. The Secular Society.*[11] What lay behind it was the notion which I have been seeking to expound, namely that morals—and up till a century or so ago no one thought it worth distinguishing between religion and morals—were necessary to the temporal order. In 1675 Chief Justice Hale said: "To say that religion is a cheat is to dissolve all those obligations whereby civil society is preserved."[12] In 1797 Mr. Justice Ashurst said of blasphemy that it was "not only an offence against God but against all law and government from its tendency to dissolve all the bonds and obligations of civil society."[13] By 1908 Mr. Justice Phillimore was able to say: "A man is free to think, to speak and to teach what he pleases as to religious matters, but not as to morals."[14]

You may think that I have taken far too long in contending that there is such a thing as public morality, a proposition which most people would readily accept, and may have left myself too little time to discuss the next question which to many minds may cause greater difficulty: to what extent should society use the law to enforce its moral judgements? But I believe that the answer to the first question determines the way in which the second should be approached and may indeed very nearly dictate the answer to the second question. If society has no right to make judgements on morals, the law must find some special justification for entering the field of morality: if homosexuality and prostitution are not in themselves wrong, then the onus is very clearly on the lawgiver who wants to frame a law against certain aspects of them to justify the exceptional treatment.

But if society has the right to make a judgement and has it on the basis that a recognized morality is as necessary to society as, say, a recognized government, then society may use the law to preserve morality in the same way as it uses it to safeguard anything else that is essential to its existence. If therefore the first proposition is securely established with all its implications, society has a prima facie right to legislate against immorality as such.

The Wolfenden Report, notwithstanding that it seems to admit the right of society to condemn homosexuality and prostitution as immoral, requires special circumstances to be shown to justify the intervention of the law. I think that this is wrong in principle and that any attempt to approach my second interrogatory on these lines is bound to break down. I think that the attempt by the Committee does break down and that this is shown by the fact that it has to define or describe its special circumstances so widely that they can be supported only if it is accepted that the law *is* concerned with immorality as such.

The widest of the special circumstances are described as the provision of "sufficient" safeguards against exploitation and corruption of others, particularly those who are specially vulnerable because they are young, weak in body or mind, inexperienced, or in a state of special physical, official or economic dependence."[15] The corruption of youth is a well-recognized ground for intervention by the State and for the purpose of any legislation the young can easily be defined. But if similar protection were to be extended to every other citizen, there would be no limit to the reach of the law. The "corruption and exploitation of others" is so wide that it could be used to cover any sort of immorality which involves, as most do, the co-operation of another person. Even if the phrase is taken as limited to the categories that are particularized as "specially vulnerable," it is so elastic as to be practically no restriction. This is not

---

11 (1917), A.C. 406, at 457.

12 *Taylor's Case,* 1 Vent. 293.

13 *R. v. Williams,* 26 St. Tr. 653, at 715.

14 *R. v. Boulter,* 72 J.P. 188.

15 Para. 13.

merely a matter of words. For if the words used are stretched almost beyond breaking-point, they still are not wide enough to cover the recommendations which the Committee make about prostitution.

Prostitution is not in itself illegal and the Committee do not think that it ought to be made so.[16] If prostitution is private immorality and not the law's business, what concern has the law with the ponce or the brothel-keeper or the householder who permits habitual prostitution? The Report recommends that the laws which make these activities criminal offences should be maintained or strengthened and brings them (so far as it goes into principle; with regard to brothels it says simply that the law rightly frowns on them) under the head of exploitation.[17] There may be cases of exploitation in this trade, as there are or used to be in many others, but in general a ponce exploits a prostitute no more than an impresario exploits an actress. The Report finds that "the great majority of prostitutes are women whose psychological makeup is such that they choose this life because they find in it a style of living which is to them easier, freer and more profitable than would be provided by any other occupation.... In the main the association between prostitute and ponce is voluntary and operates to mutual advantage."[18] The Committee would agree that this could not be called exploitation in the ordinary sense. They say: "It is in our view an over-simplification to think that those who live on the earnings of prostitution are exploiting the prostitute as such. What they are really exploiting is the whole complex of the relationship between prostitute and customer; they are, in effect, exploiting the human weaknesses which cause the customer to seek the prostitute and the prostitute to meet the demand."[19]

All sexual immorality involves the exploitation of human weaknesses. The prostitute exploits the lust of her customers and the customer the moral weakness of the prostitute. If the exploitation of human weaknesses is considered to create a special circumstance, there is virtually no field of morality which can be defined in such a way as to exclude the law.

I think, therefore, that it is not possible to set theoretical limits to the power of the State to legislate against immorality. It is not possible to settle in advance exceptions to the general rule or to define inflexibly areas of morality into which the law is in no circumstances to be allowed to enter. Society is entitled by means of its laws to protect itself from dangers, whether from within or without. Here again I think that the political parallel is legitimate. The law of treason is directed against aiding the king's enemies and against sedition from within. The justification for this is that established government is necessary for the existence of society and therefore its safety against violent overthrow must be secured. But an established morality is as necessary as good government to the welfare of society. Societies disintegrate from within more frequently than they are broken up by external pressures. There is disintegration when no common morality is observed and history shows that the loosening of moral bonds is often the first stage of disintegration, so that society is justified in taking the same steps to preserve its moral code as it does to preserve its government and other essential institutions.[20] The

---

16 Paras. 224, 285, and 318.
17 Paras. 302 and 320.
18 Para. 223.
19 Para. 306.

20 It is somewhere about this point in the argument that Professor Hart in *Law, Liberty and Morality* discerns a proposition which he describes as central to my thought. He states the proposition and his objection to it as follows (p. 51). "He appears to move from the acceptable proposition that *some* shared morality is essential to the existence of any society [this I take to be the proposition on p. 12] to the unacceptable proposition that a society is identical with its morality as that is at any given moment of its history, so that a change in its morality is tantamount to the destruction of a society. The former proposition might be even accepted as a necessary rather than an empirical truth depending on a quite plausible

suppression of vice is as much the law's business as

definition of society as a body of men who hold certain moral views in common. But the latter proposition is absurd. Taken strictly, it would prevent us saying that the morality of a given society had changed, and would compel us instead to say that one society had disappeared and another one taken its place. But it is only on this absurd criterion of what it is for the same society to continue to exist that it could be asserted without evidence that any deviation from a society's shared morality threatens its existence." In conclusion (p.82) Professor Hart condemns the whole thesis in the lecture as based on "a confused definition of what a society is."

I do not assert that *any* deviation from a society's shared morality threatens its existence any more than I assert that *any* subversive activity threatens its existence. I assert that they are both activities which are capable in their nature of threatening the existence of society so that neither can be put beyond the law.

For the rest, the objection appears to me to be all a matter of words. I would venture to assert, for example, that you cannot have a game without rules and that if there were no rules there would be no game. If I am asked whether that means that the game is "identical" with the rules, I would be willing for the question to be answered either way in the belief that the answer would lead to nowhere. If I am asked whether a change in the rules means that one game has disappeared and another has taken its place, I would reply probably not, but that it would depend on the extent of the change.

Likewise I should venture to assert that there cannot be a contract without terms. Does this mean that an "amended" contract is a "new" contract in the eyes of the law? I once listened to an argument by an ingenious counsel that a contract, because of the substitution of one clause for another, had "ceased to have effect" within the meaning of a statutory provision. The judge did not accept the argument; but if most of the fundamental terms had been changed, I dare say he would have done.

The proposition that I make in the text is that if (as I understand Professor Hart to agree, at any rate for the purposes of the argument) you cannot have a society without "morality," the law can be used to enforce morality as something that is essential to a society. I cannot see why this proposition (whether it is right or wrong) should mean that morality can never be changed without the destruction of society. If morality is changed, the law can be changed. Professor Hart refers (p.72) to the proposition as "the use of legal punishment to freeze into

the suppression of subversive activities; it is no more possible to define a sphere of private morality than it is to define one of private subversive activity. It is wrong to talk of private morality or of the law not being concerned with immorality as such or to try to set rigid bounds to the part which the law may play in the suppression of vice. There are no theoretical limits to the power of the State to legislate against treason and sedition, and likewise I think there can be no theoretical limits to legislation against immorality. You may argue that if a man's sins affect only himself it cannot be the concern of society. If he chooses to get drunk every night in the privacy of his own home, is any one except himself the worse for it? But suppose a quarter or a half of the population got drunk every night, what sort of society would it be? You cannot set a theoretical limit to the number of people who can get drunk before society is entitled to legislate against drunkenness. The same may be said of gambling. The Royal Commission on Betting, Lotteries, and Gaming took as their test the character of the citizen as a member of society. They said: "Our concern with the ethical significance of gambling is confined to the effect which it may have on the character of the gambler as a member of society. If we were convinced that whatever the degree of gambling this effect must be harmful we should be inclined to think that it was the duty of the state to restrict gambling to the greatest extent practicable."[21]

In what circumstances the State should exercise its power is the third of the interrogatories I have framed. But before I get to it I must raise a point which might have been brought up in any one of

---

immobility the morality dominant at a particular time in a society's existence." One might as well say that the inclusion of a penal section into a statute prohibiting certain acts freezes the whole statute into immobility and prevents the prohibitions from ever being modified.

These points are elaborated in the sixth lecture at pp. 115–16.

21 (1951) Cmd. 8190, para. 159.

the three. How are the moral judgements of society to be ascertained? By leaving it until now, I can ask it in the more limited form that is now sufficient for my purpose. How is the law-maker to ascertain the moral judgements of society? It is surely not enough that they should be reached by the opinion of the majority; it would be too much to require the individual assent of every citizen. English law has evolved and regularly uses a standard which does not depend on the counting of heads. It is that of the reasonable man. He is not to be confused with the rational man. He is not expected to reason about anything and his judgement may be largely a matter of feeling. It is the viewpoint of the man in the street—or to use an archaism familiar to all lawyers—the man in the Clapham omnibus. He might also be called the right-minded man. For my purpose I should like to call him the man in the jury box, for the moral judgement of society must be something about which any twelve men or women drawn at random might after discussion be expected to be unanimous. This was the standard the judges applied in the days before Parliament was as active as it is now and when they laid down rules of public policy. They did not think of themselves as making law but simply as stating principles which every right-minded person would accept as valid. It is what Pollock called "practical morality," which is based not on theological or philosophical foundations but "in the mass of continuous experience half-consciously or unconsciously accumulated and embodied in the morality of common sense." He called it also "a certain way of thinking on questions of morality which we expect to find in a reasonable civilized man or a reasonable Englishman, taken at random."[22]

Immorality then for the purpose of the law, is what every right-minded person presumed to consider to be immoral. Any immorality is capable of affecting society injuriously and in effect to a greater

or lesser extent it usually does; this is what gives the law its *locus standi.* It cannot be shut out. But—and this brings me to the third question—the individual has a *locus standi* too; he cannot be expected to surrender to the judgement of society the whole conduct of his life. It is the old and familiar question of striking a balance between the rights and interests of society and those of the individual. This is something which the law is constantly doing in matters large and small. To take a very down-to-earth example, let me consider the right of the individual whose house adjoins the highway to have access to it; that means in these days the right to have vehicles stationary in the highway, sometimes for a considerable time if there is a lot of loading or unloading. There are many cases in which the courts have had to balance the private right of access against the public right to use the highway without obstruction. It cannot be done by carving up the highway into public and private areas. It is done by recognizing that each have rights over the whole; that if each were to exercise their rights to the full, they would come into conflict; and therefore that the rights of each must be curtailed so as to ensure as far as possible that the essential needs of each are safeguarded.

I do not think that one can talk sensibly of a public and private morality any more than one can of a public or private highway. Morality is a sphere in which there is a public interest and a private interest, often in conflict, and the problem is to reconcile the two. This does not mean that it is impossible to put forward any general statements about how in our society the balance ought to be struck. Such statements cannot of their nature be rigid or precise; they would not be designed to circumscribe the operation of the lawmaking power but to guide those who have to apply it. While every decision which a court of law makes when it balances the public against the private interest is an *ad hoc* decision, the cases contain statements of principle to which the court should have regard when it reaches its decision. In the same way it is possible to make general statements of prin-

---

22   *Essays in Jurisprudence and Ethics* (1882), Macmillan, pp. 278 and 353.

ciple which it may be thought the legislature should bear in mind when it is considering the enactment of laws enforcing morals.

I believe that most people would agree upon the chief of these elastic principles. There must be toleration of the maximum individual freedom that is consistent with the integrity of society. It cannot be said that this is a principle that runs all through the criminal law. Much of the criminal law that is regulatory in character—the part of it that deals with *malum prohibitum* rather than *malum in se*—is based upon the opposite principle, that is, that the choice of the individual must give way to the convenience of the many. But in all matters of conscience the principle I have stated is generally held to prevail. It is not confined to thought and speech; it extends to action, as is shown by the recognition of the right to conscientious objection in war-time; this example shows also that conscience will be respected even in times of national danger. The principle appears to me to be peculiarly appropriate to all questions of morals. Nothing should be punished by the law that does not lie beyond the limits of tolerance. It is not nearly enough to say that a majority dislike a practice; there must be a real feeling of reprobation. Those who are dissatisfied with the present law on homosexuality often say that the opponents of reform are swayed simply by disgust. If that were so it would be wrong, but I do not think one can ignore disgust if it is deeply felt and not manufactured. Its presence is a good indication that the bounds of toleration are being reached. Not everything is to be tolerated. No society can do without intolerance, indignation, and disgust;[23] they are the forces behind the moral law, and indeed it can be argued that if they or something like them are not present, the feelings of society cannot be weighty enough to deprive the individual of freedom of choice. I suppose that there is hardly anyone nowadays who would not be disgusted by

the thought of deliberate cruelty to animals. No one proposes to relegate that or any other form of sadism to the realm of private morality or to allow it to be practised in public or in private. It would be possible no doubt to point out that until a comparatively short while ago nobody thought very much of cruelty to animals and also that pity and kindliness and the unwillingness to inflict pain are virtues more generally esteemed now than they have ever been in the past. But matters of this sort are not determined by rational argument. Every moral judgement, unless it claims a divine source, is simply a feeling that no right-minded man could behave in any other way without admitting that he was doing wrong. It is the power of a common sense and not the power of reason that is behind the judgements of society. But before a society can put a practice beyond the limits of tolerance there must be a deliberate judgement that the practice is injurious to society. There is, for example, a general abhorrence of homosexuality. We should ask ourselves in the first instance whether, looking at it calmly and dispassionately, we regard it as a vice so abominable that its mere presence is an offence. If that is the genuine feeling of the society in which we live, I do not see how society can be denied the right to eradicate it. Our feeling may not be so intense as that. We may feel about it that, if confined, it is tolerable, but that if it spread it might be gravely injurious; it is in this way that most societies look upon fornication, seeing it as a natural weakness which must be kept within bounds but which cannot be rooted out. It becomes then a question of balance, the danger to society in one scale and the extent of the restriction in the other. On this sort of point the value of an investigation by such a body as the Wolfenden Committee and of its conclusions is manifest.

The limits of tolerance shift. This is supplementary to what I have been saying but of sufficient importance in itself to deserve statement as a separate principle which law-makers have to bear in mind. I suppose that moral standards do not shift; so far as

---

23 These words which have been much criticized, are considered again in the Preface at p. viii.

they come from divine revelation they do not, and I am willing to assume that the moral judgements made by a society always remain good for that society. But the extent to which society will tolerate—I mean tolerate, not approve—departures from moral standards varies from generation to generation. It may be that over-all tolerance is always increasing. The pressure of the human mind, always seeking greater freedom of thought, is outwards against the bonds of society forcing their gradual relaxation. It may be that history is a tale of contraction and expansion and that all developed societies are on their way to dissolution. I must not speak of things I do not know; and anyway as a practical matter no society is willing to make provision for its own decay. I return therefore to the simple and observable fact that in matters of morals the limits of tolerance shift. Laws, especially those which are based on morals, are less easily moved. It follows as another good working principle that in any new matter of morals the law should be slow to act. By the next generation the swell of indignation may have abated and the law be left without the strong backing which it needs. But it is then difficult to alter the law without giving the impression that moral judgement is being weakened. This is now one of the factors that is strongly militating against any alteration to the law on homosexuality.

A third elastic principle must be advanced more tentatively. It is that as far as possible privacy should be respected. This is not an idea that has ever been made explicit in the criminal law. Acts or words done or said in public or in private are all brought within its scope without distinction in principle. But there goes with this a strong reluctance on the part of judges and legislators to sanction invasions of privacy in the detection of crime. The police have no more right to trespass than the ordinary citizen has; there is no general right of search; to this extent an Englishman's home is still his castle. The Government is extremely careful in the exercise even of those powers which it claims to be undisputed.

Telephone tapping and interference with the mails afford a good illustration of this. A Committee of three Privy Councillors who recently inquired[24] into these activities found that the Home Secretary and his predecessors had already formulated strict rules governing the exercise of these powers and the Committee were able to recommend that they should be continued to be exercised substantially on the same terms. But they reported that the power was "regarded with general disfavour."

This indicates a general sentiment that the right to privacy is something to be put in the balance against the enforcement of the law. Ought the same sort of consideration to play any part in the formation of the law? Clearly only in a very limited number of cases. When the help of the law is invoked by an injured citizen, privacy must be irrelevant; the individual cannot ask that his right to privacy should be measured against injury criminally done to another. But when all who are involved in the deed are consenting parties and the injury is done to morals, the public interest in the moral order can be balanced against the claims of privacy. The restriction on police powers of investigation goes further than the affording of a parallel; it means that the detection of crime committed in private and when there is no complaint is bound to be rather haphazard and this is an additional reason for moderation. These considerations do not justify the exclusion of all private immorality from the scope of the law. I think that, as I have already suggested, the test of "private behaviour" should be substituted for "private morality" and the influence of the factor should be reduced from that of a definite limitation to that of a matter to be taken into account. Since the gravity of the crime is also a proper consideration, a distinction might well be made in the case of homosexuality between the lesser acts of indecency and the full offence, which on the principles of the Wolfenden Report it would be illogical to do.

---

24 (1957) Cmd. 283.

The last and the biggest thing to be remembered is that the law is concerned with the minimum and not with the maximum; there is much in the Sermon on the Mount that would be out of place in the Ten Commandments. We all recognize the gap between the moral law and the law of the land. No man is worth much who regulates his conduct with the sole object of escaping punishment, and every worthy society sets for its members standards which are above those of the law. We recognize the existence of such higher standards when we use expressions such as "moral obligation" and "morally bound." The distinction was well put in the judgement of African elders in a family dispute: "We have power to make you divide the crops, for this is our law, and we will see this is done. But we have not power to make you behave like an upright man."[25]

It can only be because this point is so obvious that it is so frequently ignored. Discussion among law-makers, both professional and amateur, is too often limited to what is right or wrong and good or bad for society. There is a failure to keep separate the two questions I have earlier posed—the question of society's right to pass a moral judgement and the question of whether the arm of the law should be used to enforce the judgement. The criminal law is not a statement of how people ought to behave; it is a statement of what will happen to them if they do not behave; good citizens are not expected to come within reach of it or to set their sights by it, and every enactment should be framed accordingly.

The arm of the law is an instrument to be used by society, and the decision about what particular cases it should be used in is essentially a practical one. Since it is an instrument, it is wise before deciding to use it to have regard to the tools with which it can be fitted and to the machinery which operates it. Its tools are fines, imprisonment, or lesser forms of supervision (such as Borstal and probation) and—not to be ignored—the degradation that often follows upon the publication of the crime. Are any of these suited to the job of dealing with sexual immorality? The fact that there is so much immorality which has never been brought within the law shows that there can be no general rule. It is a matter for decision in each case; but in the case of homosexuality the Wolfenden Report rightly has regard to the views of those who are experienced in dealing with this sort of crime and to those of the clergy who are the natural guardians of public morals.

The machinery which sets the criminal law in motion ends with the verdict and the sentence; and a verdict is given either by magistrates or by a jury. As a general rule, whenever a crime is sufficiently serious to justify a maximum punishment of more than three months, the accused has the right to the verdict of a jury. The result is that magistrates administer mostly what I have called the regulatory part of the law. They deal extensively with drunkenness, gambling, and prostitution, which are matters of morals or close to them, but not with any of the graver moral offences. They are more responsive than juries to the ideas of the legislature; it may not be accidental that the Wolfenden Report, in recommending increased penalties for solicitation, did not go above the limit of three months. Juries tend to dilute the decrees of Parliament with their own ideas of what should be punishable. Their province of course is fact and not law, and I do not mean that they often deliberately disregard the law. But if they think it is too stringent, they sometimes take a very merciful view of the facts. Let me take one example out of many that could be given. It is an offence to have carnal knowledge of a girl under the age of sixteen years. Consent on her part is no defence; if she did not consent, it would of course amount to rape. The law makes special provision for the situation when a boy and girl are near in age. If a man under twenty-four can prove that he had reasonable cause to believe that the girl was over the age of sixteen

25 A case in the Saa-Katengo Kuta at Lialiu, August 1942, quoted in *The Judicial Process among the Barotse of Northern Rhodesia* by Max Gluckman, Manchester University Press, 1955, p. 172.

years, he has a good defence. The law regards the offence as sufficiently serious to make it one that is triable only by a judge at assizes. "Reasonable cause" means not merely that the boy honestly believed that the girl was over sixteen but also that he must have had reasonable grounds for his belief. In theory it ought not to be an easy defence to make out but in fact it is extremely rare for anyone who advances it to be convicted. The fact is that the girl is often as much to blame as the boy. The object of the law, as judges repeatedly tell juries, is to protect young girls against themselves; but juries are not impressed.

The part that the jury plays in the enforcement of the criminal law, the fact that no grave offence against morals is punishable without their verdict, these are of great importance in relation to the statements of principle that I have been making. They turn what might otherwise be pure exhortation to the legislature into something like rules that the lawmakers cannot safely ignore. The man in the jury box is not just an expression; he is an active reality. It will not in the long run work to make laws about morality that are not acceptable to him.

This then is how I believe my third interrogatory should be answered—not by the formulation of hard and fast rules, but by a judgement in each case taking into account the sort of factors I have been mentioning. The line that divides the criminal law from the moral is not determinable by the application of any clear-cut principle. It is like a line that divides land and sea, a coastline of irregularities and indentations. There are gaps and promontories, such as adultery and fornication, which the law has for centuries left substantially untouched. Adultery of the sort that breaks up marriage seems to me to be just as harmful to the social fabric as homosexuality or bigamy. The only ground for putting it outside the criminal law is that a law which made it a crime would be too difficult to enforce; it is too generally regarded as a human weakness not suitably punished by imprisonment. All that the law can do with fornication is to act against its

worst manifestations; there is a general abhorrence of the commercialization of vice, and that sentiment gives strength to the law against brothels and immoral earnings. There is no logic to be found in this. The boundary between the criminal law and the moral law is fixed by balancing in the case of each particular crime the pros and cons of legal enforcement in accordance with the sort of considerations I have been outlining. The fact that adultery, fornication, and lesbianism are untouched by the criminal law does not prove that homosexuality ought not to be touched. The error of jurisprudence in the Wolfenden Report is caused by the search for some single principle to explain the division between crime and sin. The Report finds it in the principle that the criminal law exists for the protection of individuals; on this principle fornication in private between consenting adults is outside the law and thus it becomes logically indefensible to bring homosexuality between consenting adults in private within it. But the true principle is that the law exists for the protection of society. It does not discharge its function by protecting the individual from injury, annoyance, corruption, and exploitation; the law must protect also the institutions and the community of ideas, political and moral, without which people cannot live together. Society cannot ignore the morality of the individual any more than it can his loyalty; it flourishes on both and without either it dies.

I have said that the morals which underly the law must be derived from the sense of right and wrong which resides in the community as a whole; it does not matter whence the community of thought comes, whether from one body of doctrine or another or from the knowledge of good and evil which no man is without. If the reasonable man believes that a practice is immoral and believes also—no matter whether the belief is right or wrong, so be it that it is honest and dispassionate—that no right-minded member of his society could think otherwise, then for the purpose of the law it is immoral. This, you may say, makes immorality a question of fact—what the law would consider as self-evident fact no doubt, but still with no higher authority than any other doctrine of public policy. I think that that is so, and indeed the law does not distinguish between an act that is immoral and one that is contrary to public policy. But the law has never yet had occasion to inquire into the differences between Christian morals and those which every right-minded member of society is expected to hold. The inquiry would, I believe, be academic. Moralists would find differences; indeed they would find them between different branches of the Christian faith on subjects such as divorce and birth-control. But for the purpose of the limited entry which the law makes into the field of morals, there is no practical difference. It seems to me therefore that the free-thinker and the non-Christian can accept, without offence to his convictions, the fact that Christian morals are the basis of the criminal law and that he can recognize, also without taking offence, that without the support of the churches the moral order, which has its origin in and takes its strength from Christian beliefs, would collapse.

This brings me back in the end to a question I posed at the beginning. What is the relationship between crime and sin, between the Church and the Law? I do not think that you can equate crime with sin. The divine law and the secular have been disunited, but they are brought together again by the need which each has for the other. It is not my function to emphasize the Church's need of the secular law; it can be put tersely by saying that you cannot have a ceiling without a floor. I am very clear about the law's need for the Church. I have spoken of the criminal law as dealing with the minimum standards of human conduct and the moral law with the maximum. The instrument of the criminal law is punishment; those of the moral law are teaching, training, and exhortation. If the whole dead weight of sin were ever to be allowed to fall upon the law, it could not take the strain. If at any point there is

a lack of clear and convincing moral teaching, the administration of the law suffers. Let me take as an illustration of this the law on abortion. I believe that a great many people nowadays do not understand why abortion is wrong. If it is right to prevent conception, at what point does it become sinful to prevent birth and why? I doubt if anyone who has not had a theological training would give a satisfactory answer to that question. Many people regard abortion as the next step when by accident birth-control has failed; and many more people are deterred from abortion not because they think it sinful or illegal but because of the difficulty which illegality puts in the way of obtaining it. The law is powerless to deal with abortion *per se*; unless a tragedy occurs or a "professional" abortionist is involved—the parallel between the "professional" in abortions and the "professional" in fornication is quite close—it has to leave it alone. Without one or other of these features the crime is rarely detected; and when detected, the plea *ad misericordiam* is often too strong. The "professional" abortionist is usually the unskilled person who for a small reward helps girls in trouble; the man and the girl involved are essential witnesses for the prosecution and therefore go free; the paid abortionist generally receives a very severe sentence, much more severe than that usually given to the paid assistant in immorality, such as the ponce or the brothel-keeper. The reason is because unskilled abortion endangers life. In a case in 1949,[26] Lord Chief Justice Goddard said: "It is because the unskilful attentions of ignorant people in cases of this kind often result in death that attempts to produce abortion are regarded by the law as very serious offences." This gives the law a twist which disassociates it from morality and, I think, to some extent from sound sense. The act is being punished because it is dangerous, and it is dangerous largely because it is illegal and therefore performed only by the unskilled.

---

26 *R. v. Tate, The Times*, 22 June 1949.

The object of what I have said is not to criticize theology or law in relation to abortion. That is a large subject and beyond my present scope. It is to show what happens to the law in matters of morality about which the community as a whole is not deeply imbued with a sense of sin; the law sags under a weight which it is not constructed to bear and may become permanently warped.

I return now to the main thread of my argument and summarize it. Society cannot live without morals. Its morals are those standards of conduct which the reasonable man approves. A rational man, who is also a good man, may have other standards. If he has no standards at all he is not a good man and need not be further considered. If he has standards, they may be very different; he may, for example, not disapprove of homosexuality or abortion. In that case he will not share in the common morality; but that should not make him deny that it is a social necessity. A rebel may be rational in thinking that he is right but he is irrational if he thinks that society can leave him free to rebel.

A man who concedes that morality is necessary to society must support the use of those instruments without which morality cannot be maintained. The two instruments are those of teaching, which is doctrine, and of enforcement, which is the law. If morals could be taught simply on the basis that they are necessary to society, there would be no social need for religion; it could be left as a purely personal affair. But morality cannot be taught in that way. Loyalty is not taught in that way either. No society has yet solved the problem of how to teach morality without religion. So the law must base itself on Christian morals and to the limit of its ability enforce them, not simply because they are the morals of most of us, nor simply because they are the morals which are taught by the established Church—on these points the law recognizes the right to dissent—but for the compelling reason that without the help of Christian teaching the law will fail.

◆ ◆ ◆ ◆ ◆

H.L.A. HART

from *Law, Liberty and Morality*

... Much dissatisfaction has for long been felt in England with the criminal law relating to both prostitution and homosexuality, and in 1954 the committee well known as the Wolfenden Committee was appointed to consider the state of the law. This committee reported[1] in September 1957 and recommended certain changes in the law on both topics. As to homosexuality they recommended by a majority of 12 to 1 that homosexual practices between consenting adults in private should no longer be a crime; as to prostitution they unanimously recommended that, though it should not itself be made illegal, legislation should be passed "to drive it off the streets" on the ground that public soliciting was an offensive nuisance to ordinary citizens. The government eventually introduced legislation[2] to give effect to the Committee's recommendations concerning prostitution but not to that concerning homosexuality, and attempts by private members to introduce legislation modifying the law on this subject have so far failed.

What concerns us here is less the fate of the Wolfenden Committee's recommendations than the principles by which these were supported. These are strikingly similar to those expounded by Mill in his essay *On Liberty*. Thus section 13 of the Committee's Report reads:

> [The] function [of the criminal law], as we see it, is to preserve public order and

---

1   Report of the Committee on Homosexual Offences and Prostitution (CMD 247) 1957.
2   The Street Offences Act 1959.

decency, to protect the citizen from what is offensive or injurious and to provide sufficient safeguards against exploitation or corruption of others, particularly those who are specially vulnerable because they are young, weak in body or mind or inexperienced ...

This conception of the positive functions of the criminal law was the Committee's main ground for its recommendation concerning prostitution that legislation should be passed to suppress the offensive public manifestations of prostitution, but not to make prostitution itself illegal. Its recommendation that the law against homosexual practices between consenting adults in private should be relaxed was based on the principle stated simply in section 61 of the Report as follows: "There must remain a realm of private morality and immorality which is, in brief and crude terms, not the law's business."

It is of some interest that these developments in England have had near counterparts in America. In 1955 the American Law Institute published with its draft Model Penal Code a recommendation that all consensual relations between adults in private should be excluded from the scope of the criminal law. Its grounds were (*inter alia*) that "no harm to the secular interests of the community is involved in atypical sex practice in private between consenting adult partners";[3] and "there is the fundamental question of the protection to which every individual is entitled against state interference in his personal affairs when he is not hurting others."[4] This recommendation had been approved by the Advisory Committee of the Institute but rejected by a majority vote of its Council. The issue was therefore referred to the annual meeting of the Institute at Washington in May 1955, and the recommendation, supported by an eloquent speech of the late Justice Learned Hand,

was, after a hot debate, accepted by a majority of 35 to 24.[5]

It is perhaps clear from the foregoing that Mill's principles are still very much alive in the criticism of law, whatever their theoretical deficiencies may be. But twice in one hundred years they have been challenged by two masters of the Common Law. The first of these was the great Victorian judge and historian of the Criminal Law, James Fitzjames Stephen. His criticism of Mill is to be found in the sombre and impressive book *Liberty, Equality, Fraternity,*[6] which he wrote as a direct reply to Mill's essay On Liberty. It is evident from the tone of this book that Stephen thought he had found crushing arguments against Mill and had demonstrated that the law might justifiably enforce morality as such or, as he said, that the law should be "a persecution of the grosser forms of vice."[7] Nearly a century later, on the publication of the Wolfenden Committee's report, Lord Devlin, now a member of the House of Lords and a most distinguished writer on the criminal law, in his essay on *The Enforcement of Morals*[8] took as his target the Report's contention "that there must be a realm of morality and immorality which is not the law's business" and argued in opposition to it that "the suppression of vice is as much the law's business as the suppression of subversive activities."

Though a century divides these two legal writers, the similarity in the general tone and sometimes in the detail of their arguments is very great. I shall devote the remainder of these lectures to an examination of them. I do this because, though their arguments are at points confused, they certainly still deserve the compliment of rational opposition. They are not only admirably stocked with concrete examples, but they express the considered views of skilled, sophisticated lawyers experienced in the ad-

---

3 American Law Institute Model Penal Code, Tentative Draft No. 4, p. 277.

4 *Ibid.*, p. 278.

5 An account of the debate is given in *Time*, May 30, 1955, p. 13.

6 2nd edition, London, 1874.

7 *Ibid.*, p. 162.

8 Oxford University Press, 1959.

ministration of the criminal law. Views such as theirs are still quite widely held especially by lawyers both in England and in this country; it may indeed be that they are more popular, in both countries, than Mill's doctrine of Liberty.

Positive and Critical Morality

Before we consider the detail of these arguments, it is, I think, necessary to appreciate three different but connected features of the question with which we are concerned.

[*Ed. note:* Earlier in his lecture Hart states that his goal is to consider a question which "...concerns the legal enforcement of morality and has been formulated in many different ways: Is the fact that certain conduct is by common standards immoral sufficient to justify making that conduct punishable by law? Is it morally permissible to enforce morality as such? Ought immorality as such be a crime?"]

In all the three formulations given ... it is plain that the question is one *about* morality, but it is important to observe that it is also itself a question of morality. It is the question whether the enforcement *of* morality is morally justified; so morality enters into the question in two ways. The importance of this feature of the question is that it would plainly be no sufficient answer to show that in fact in some society—our own or others—it was widely regarded as morally quite right and proper to enforce, by legal punishment, compliance with the accepted morality. No one who seriously debates this question would regard Mill as refuted by the simple demonstration that there are some societies in which the generally shared morality endorses its own enforcement by law, and does so even in those cases where the immorality was thought harmless to others. The existence of societies which condemn association between white and coloured persons as immoral and punish it by law still leaves our question to be argued. It is true that Mill's critics have often made much of the fact that English law does in several instances, appar-

ently with the support of popular morality, punish immorality as such, especially in sexual matters; but they have usually admitted that this is where the argument begins, not where it ends. I shall indeed later claim that the play made by some legal writers with what they treat as examples of the legal enforcement of morality "as such" is sometimes confused. But they do not, at any rate, put forward their case as simply proved by pointing to these social facts. Instead they attempt to base their own conclusion that it is morally justifiable to use the criminal law in this way on principles which they believe to be universally applicable, and which they think are either quite obviously rational or will be seen to be so after discussion.

Thus Lord Devlin bases his affirmative answer to the question on the quite general principle that it is permissible for any society to take the steps needed to preserve its own existence as an organized society,[9] and he thinks that immorality—even private sexual immorality—may, like treason, be something which jeopardizes a society's existence. Of course many of us may doubt this general principle, and not merely the suggested analogy with treason. We might wish to argue that whether or not a society is justified in taking steps to preserve itself must depend both on what sort of society it is and what the steps to be taken are. If a society were mainly devoted to the cruel persecution of a racial or religious minority, or if the steps to be taken included hideous tortures, it is arguable that what Lord Devlin terms the "disintegration"[10] of such a society would be morally better than its continued existence, and steps ought not to be taken to preserve it. Nonetheless Lord Devlin's principle that a society may take the steps required to preserve its organized existence is not itself tendered as an item of English popular morality, deriving its cogency from its status as part of our institutions. He puts it forward as a principle,

---

9 *The Enforcement of Morals*, pp. 13–14.
10 *Ibid.* pp. 14–15.

rationally acceptable, to be used in the evaluation or criticism of social institutions generally. And it is surely clear that anyone who holds the question whether a society has the "right" to enforce morality, or whether it is morally permissible for any society to enforce its morality by law, to be discussable at all, must be prepared to deploy some such general principles of critical morality.[11] In asking the question, we are assuming the legitimacy of a standpoint which permits criticism of the institutions of any society, in the light of general principles and knowledge of the facts.

To make this point clear, I would revive the terminology much favoured by the Utilitarians of the last century, which distinguished "positive morality," the morality actually accepted and shared by a given social group, from the general moral principles used in the criticism of actual social institutions including positive morality. We may call such general principles "critical morality" and say that our question is one of critical morality about the legal enforcement of positive morality.

A second feature of our question worth attention is simply that it is a question of *justification*. In asking it we are committed at least to the general critical principle that the use of legal coercion by any society calls for justification as something *prima facie* objectionable to be tolerated only for the sake of some countervailing good. For where there is no *prima facie* objection, wrong, or evil, men do not ask for or give justifications of social practices, though they may ask for and give *explanations* of these practices or may attempt to demonstrate their value.

---

11 Lord Devlin has been criticised for asking the question whether society has a *right* to enforce its judgment in matters of morality on the ground that to talk of "right" in such a context is meaningless. See Graham Hughes, "Morals and the Criminal Law," 71 *Yale L.J.* (1962) at 672. This criticism is mistaken, just because Lord Devlin invokes some general critical principle in support of his affirmative answer to the question.

It is salutary to inquire precisely what it is that is *prima facie* objectionable in the legal enforcement of morality; for the idea of legal enforcement is in fact less simple than is often assumed. It has two different but related aspects. One is the actual punishment of the offender. This characteristically involves depriving him of liberty of movement or of property or of association with family or friends, or the infliction upon him of physical pain or even death. All these are things which are assumed to be wrong to inflict on others without special justification, and in fact they are so regarded by the law and morality of all developed societies. To put it as a lawyer would, these are things which, if they are not justified as sanctions, are delicts or wrongs.

The second aspect of legal enforcement bears on those who may never offend against the law, but are coerced into obedience by the threat of legal punishment. This rather than physical restrictions is what is normally meant in the discussion of political arrangements by restrictions on liberty. Such restrictions, it is to be noted, may be thought of as calling for justification for several quite distinct reasons. The unimpeded exercise by individuals of free choice may be held a value in itself with which it is *prima facie* wrong to interfere; or it may be thought valuable because it enables individuals to experiment—even with living—and to discover things valuable both to themselves and to others. But interference with individual liberty may be thought an evil requiring justification for simpler, utilitarian reasons; for it is itself the infliction of a special form of suffering—often very acute—on those whose desires are frustrated by the fear of punishment. This is of particular importance in the case of laws enforcing a sexual morality. They may create misery of a quite special degree. For both the difficulties involved in the repression of sexual impulses and the consequences of repression are quite different from those involved in the abstention from "ordinary" crime. Unlike sexual impulses, the impulse to steal or to wound or even kill is not, except in a minority of mentally abnormal cases, a recurrent and insistent part of daily life. Resistance to the temptation to commit these crimes is not often, as the suppression of sexual impulses generally is, something which affects the development or balance of the individual's emotional life, happiness, and personality.

Thirdly, the distinction already made, between positive morality and principles of critical morality, may serve to dissipate a certain misunderstanding of the question and to clarify its central point. It is sometimes said that the question is not whether it is morally justifiable to enforce morality as such, but only *which* morality may be enforced. Is it only a utilitarian morality condemning activities which are harmful to others? Or is it a morality which also condemns certain activities whether they are harmful or not? This way of regarding the question misrepresents the character of, at any rate, modern controversy. A utilitarian who insists that the law should only punish activities which are harmful adopts this as a critical principle, and, in so doing, he is quite unconcerned with the question whether a utilitarian morality is or is not already accepted as the positive morality of the society to which he applies his critical principles. If it is so accepted, that is not, in his view, the reason why it should be enforced. It is true that if he is successful in preaching his message to a given society, members of it will then be compelled to behave as utilitarians in certain ways, but these facts do not mean that the vital difference between him and his opponent is only as to the content of the morality to be enforced. For as may be seen from the main criticisms of Mill, the Utilitarian's opponent, who insists that it is morally permissible to enforce morality as such, believes that the mere fact that certain rules or standards of behaviour enjoy the status of a society's positive morality is the reason—or at least part of the reason—which justifies their enforcement by law. No doubt in older controversies the opposed positions were different: the question may have been whether the state could punish only activities causing secular harm or also acts of disobedience to what were believed to be divine commands or prescriptions of Natural Law. But what is crucial to the dispute in its modern form is the significance to be attached to the historical fact that certain conduct, no matter what, is prohibited by a positive morality. The utilitarian denies that this has any significance sufficient to justify its enforcement; his opponent asserts that it has. These are divergent critical principles which do not differ merely over the content of the morality to be enforced, but over a more fundamental and, surely, more interesting issue.

The Use and Abuse of Examples

Both in England and in America the criminal law still contains rules which can only be explained as attempts to enforce morality as such: to suppress practices condemned as immoral by positive morality though they involve nothing that would ordinarily be thought of as harm to other persons. Most of the examples come from the sphere of sexual morals, and in England they include laws against various forms of homosexual behaviour between males, sodomy between persons of different sex even if married, bestiality, incest, living on the earnings of prostitution, keeping a house for prostitution, and also, since the decision in Shaw's case, a conspiracy to corrupt public morals, interpreted to mean, in substance, leading others (in the opinion of a jury) "morally astray." To this list some would add further cases: the laws against abortion, against those forms of bigamy or polygamy which do not involve deception, against suicide and the practice of euthanasia. But, as I shall later argue, the treatment of some of these latter as attempts to enforce morality as such, is a mistake due to the neglect of certain important distinctions....

Paternalism and the Enforcement of Morality

I shall start with an example stressed by Lord Devlin. He points out that,[12] subject to certain exceptions such as rape, the criminal law has never admitted the consent of the victim as a defence. It is not a defence to a charge of murder or a deliberate assault, and this is why euthanasia or mercy killing terminating a man's life at his own request is still murder. This is a rule of criminal law which many now would wish to retain, though they would also wish to object to the legal punishment of offences against positive morality which harm no one. Lord Devlin thinks that these attitudes are inconsistent, for he asserts of the rule under discussion, "There is only one explanation," and this is that "there are certain standards of behaviour or moral principles which society requires to be observed."[13] Among these are the sanctity of human life and presumably (since the rule applies to assaults) the physical integrity of the person. So in the case of this rule and a number of others Lord Devlin claims that the "function" of the criminal law is "to enforce a moral principle and nothing else."[14]

But this argument is not really cogent, for Lord Devlin's statement that "there is only one explanation" is simply not true. The rules excluding the victim's consent as a defence to charges of murder or assault may perfectly well be explained as a piece of paternalism, designed to protect individuals against themselves. Mill no doubt might have protested against a paternalistic policy of using the law to protect even a consenting victim from bodily harm nearly as much as he protested against laws used merely to enforce positive morality; but this does not mean that these two policies are identical. Indeed, Mill himself was very well aware of the difference between them: for in condemning interference with individual liberty except to prevent harm to others he mentions *separate* types of inadequate ground which have been proffered for the use of compulsion. He distinguishes "because it will be better for him" and "because it will make him happier" from "because in the opinion of others it would be right."[15]

Lord Devlin says of the attitude of the criminal law to the victim's consent that if the law existed for the protection of the individual there would be no reason why he should avail himself of it if he did not want it.[16] But paternalism—the protection of people against themselves—is a perfectly coherent policy. Indeed, it seems very strange in mid-twentieth century to insist upon this, for the wane of laissez faire since Mill's day is one of the commonplaces of social history, and instances of paternalism now abound in our law, criminal and civil. The supply of drugs or narcotics, even to adults, except under medical prescription is punishable by the criminal law, and it would seem very dogmatic to say of the law creating this offence that "there is only one explanation," namely, that the law was concerned not with the protection of the would-be purchasers against themselves, but only with the punishment of the seller for his immorality. If, as seems obvious, paternalism is a possible explanation of such laws, it is also possible in the case of the rule excluding the consent of the victim as a defence to a charge of assault. In neither case are we forced to conclude with Lord Devlin that the law's "function is to enforce a moral principle and nothing else."[17]

In Chapter 5 of his essay Mill carried his protests against paternalism to lengths that may now appear to us fantastic. He cites the example of restrictions of the sale of drugs, and criticises them as interferences with the liberty of the would-be purchaser rather than with that of the seller. No doubt if we no longer sympathise with this criticism this is due,

---

12 *The Enforcement of Morals*, p. 8.
13 *Ibid.*
14 *Ibid.*, p. 9.

15 *On Liberty*, Chapter I.
16 *The Enforcement of Morals*, p. 8.
17 See, for other possible explanations of these rules, Hughes, "Morals and the Criminal Law," p. 670.

in part, to a general decline in the belief that individuals know their own interests best, and to an increased awareness of a great range of factors which diminish the significance to be attached to an apparently free choice or to consent. Choices may be made or consent given without adequate reflection or appreciation of the consequences; or in pursuit of merely transitory desires; or in various predicaments when the judgment is likely to be clouded; or under inner psychological compulsion; or under pressure by others of a kind too subtle to be susceptible of proof in a law court. Underlying Mill's extreme fear of paternalism there perhaps is a conception of what a normal human being is like which now seems not to correspond to the facts. Mill, in fact, endows him with too much of the psychology of a middle-aged man whose desires are relatively fixed, not liable to be artificially stimulated by external influences; who knows what he wants and what gives him satisfaction or happiness; and who pursues these things when he can.

Certainly a modification in Mill's principles is required, if they are to accommodate the rule of criminal law under discussion or other instances of paternalism. But the modified principles would not abandon the objection to the use of the criminal law merely to enforce positive morality. They would only have to provide that harming others is something we may still seek to prevent by use of the criminal law, even when the victims consent to or assist in the acts which are harmful to them. The neglect of the distinction between paternalism and what I have termed legal moralism is important as a form of a more general error. It is too often assumed that if a law is not designed to protect one man from another its only rationale can be that it is designed to punish moral wickedness or, in Lord Devlin's words, "to enforce a moral principle." Thus it is often urged that statutes punishing cruelty to animals can only be explained in that way. But it is certainly intelligible, both as an account of the original motives inspiring such legislation and as the specification of an aim

widely held to be worth pursuing, to say that the law is here concerned with the *suffering*, albeit only of animals, rather than with the immorality of torturing them.[18] Certainly no one who supports this use of the criminal law is thereby bound in consistency to admit that the law may punish forms of immorality which involve no suffering to any sentient being....

The Moderate and the Extreme Thesis

When we turn from these examples which are certainly disputable to the positive grounds held to justify the legal enforcement of morality it is important to distinguish a moderate and an extreme thesis, though critics of Mill have sometimes moved from one to the other without marking the transition. Lord Devlin seems to me to maintain, for most of his essay, the moderate thesis and Stephen the extreme one.

According to the moderate thesis, a shared morality is the cement of society; without it there would be aggregates of individuals but no society. "A recognized morality" is, in Lord Devlin's words, "as necessary to society's existence as a recognized government,"[19] and though a particular act of immorality may not harm or endanger or corrupt others nor, when done in private, either shock or give offence to others, this does not conclude the matter. For we must not view conduct in isolation from its effect on the moral code: if we remember this, we can see that one who is "no menace to others" nonetheless may by his immoral conduct "threaten one of the great moral principles on which society is based."[20] In this sense the breach of moral principle is an offence "against society as a whole,"[21] and society may use the

---

18 Lord Devlin seems quite unaccountably to ignore this point in his brief reference to cruelty to animals, *The Enforcement of Morals*, p. 17.

19 *The Enforcement of Morals*, p. 13.

20 *Ibid.*, p. 8.

21 *Ibid.*

law to preserve its morality as it uses it to safeguard anything else essential to its existence. This is why "the suppression of vice is as much the law's business as the suppression of subversive activities."[22]

By contrast, the extreme thesis does not look upon a shared morality as of merely instrumental value analogous to ordered government, and it does not justify the punishment of immorality as a step taken, like the punishment of treason, to preserve society from dissolution or collapse. Instead, the enforcement of morality is regarded as a thing of value, even if immoral acts harm no one directly, or indirectly by weakening the moral cement of society. I do not say that it is possible to allot to one or other of these two theses every argument used, but they do, I think, characterise the main critical positions at the root of most arguments, and they incidentally exhibit an ambiguity in the expression "enforcing morality as such." Perhaps the clearest way of distinguishing the two theses is to see that there are always two levels at which we may ask whether some breach of positive morality is harmful. We may ask first, Does this act harm anyone independently of its repercussion on the shared morality of society? And secondly we may ask, Does this act affect the shared morality and thereby weaken society? The moderate thesis requires, if the punishment of the act is to be justified, an affirmative answer at least at the second level. The extreme thesis does not require an affirmative answer at either level.

Lord Devlin appears to defend the moderate thesis. I say "appears" because, though he says that society has the right to enforce a morality as such on the ground that a shared morality is essential to society's existence, it is not at all clear that for him the statement that immorality jeopardizes or weakens society is a statement of empirical fact. It seems sometimes to be an *a priori* assumption, and sometimes a necessary truth and a very odd one. The most important indication that this is so is that,

apart from one vague reference to "history" showing that "the loosening of moral bonds is often the first stage of disintegration,"[23] no evidence is produced to show that deviation from accepted sexual morality, even by adults in private, is something which, like treason, threatens the existence of society. No reputable historian has maintained this thesis, and there is indeed much evidence against it. As a proposition of fact it is entitled to no more respect than the Emperor Justinian's statement that homosexuality was the cause of earthquakes.[24] Lord Devlin's belief in it, and his apparent indifference to the question of evidence, are at points traceable to an undiscussed assumption. This is that all morality—sexual morality together with the morality that forbids acts injurious to others such as killing, stealing, and dishonesty—forms a single seamless web, so that those who deviate from any part are likely or perhaps bound to deviate from the whole. It is of course clear (and one of the oldest insights of political theory) that society could not exist without a morality which mirrored and supplemented the law's proscription of conduct injurious to others. But there is again no evidence to support, and much to refute, the theory that those who deviate from conventional sexual morality are in other ways hostile to society.

There seems, however, to be central to Lord Devlin's thought something more interesting, though no more convincing, than the conception of social morality as a seamless web. For he appears to move from the acceptable proposition that *some* shared morality is essential to the existence of any society to the unacceptable proposition that a society is identical[25] with its morality as that is at any given moment of its history, so that a change in its morality is tantamount to the destruction of a society. The former proposition might be even accepted as a necessary

22 *Ibid.*, p. 15.

23 *The Enforcement of Morals*, pp. 14-15.

24 *Novels*, 77 Cap. 1 and 141.

25 See, for this important point, Richard Wollheim, "Crime, Sin, and Mr. Justice Devlin," *Encounter*, November 1959, p. 34.

rather than an empirical truth depending on a quite plausible definition of society as a body of men who hold certain moral views in common. But the latter proposition is absurd. Taken strictly, it would prevent us saying that the morality of a given society had changed, and would compel us instead to say that one society had disappeared and another one taken its place. But it is only on this absurd criterion of what it is for the same society to continue to exist that it could be asserted without evidence that any deviation from a society's shared morality threatens its existence.

It is clear that only this tacit identification of a society with its shared morality supports Lord Devlin's denial that there could be such a thing as private immorality and his comparison of sexual immorality, even when it takes place "in private," with treason. No doubt it is true that if deviations from conventional sexual morality are tolerated by the law and come to be known, the conventional morality might change in a permissive direction, though this does not seem to be the case with homosexuality in those European countries where it is not punishable by law. But even if the conventional morality did so change, the society in question would not have been destroyed or "subverted." We should compare such a development not to the violent overthrow of government but to a peaceful constitutional change in its form, consistent not only with the preservation of a society but with its advance.

Conclusion

I have from the beginning assumed that anyone who raises, or is willing to debate, the question whether it is justifiable to enforce morality, accepts the view that the actual institutions of any society, including its positive morality, are open to criticism. Hence the proposition that it is justifiable to enforce morality is, like its negation, a thesis of critical morality requiring for its support some general critical principle. It cannot be established or refuted simply by pointing to the actual practices or morality of a particular society or societies. Lord Devlin, whose thesis I termed the moderate thesis, seems to accept this position, but I have argued that the general critical principle which he deploys, namely, that a society has the right to take any step necessary for its preservation, is inadequate for his purpose. There is no evidence that the preservation of a society requires the enforcement of its morality "as such." His position only appears to escape this criticism by a confused definition of what a society is.

I have also assumed from the beginning that anyone who regards this question as open to discussion necessarily accepts the critical principle, central to all morality, that human misery and the restriction of freedom are evils; for that is why the legal enforcement of morality calls for justification. I then endeavoured to extricate, and to free from ambiguity of statement, the general principles underlying several varieties of the more extreme thesis that the enforcement of morality or its preservation from change were valuable apart from their beneficial consequences in preserving society. These principles in fact invite us to consider as values, for the sake of which we should restrict human freedom and inflict the misery of punishment on human beings, things which seem to belong to the prehistory of morality and to be quite hostile to its general spirit. They include mere outward conformity to moral rules induced simply by fear; the gratification of feelings of hatred for the wrongdoer or his "retributory" punishment, even where there has been no victim to be avenged or to call for justice; the infliction of punishment as a symbol or expression of moral condemnation: the mere insulation from change of any social morality however repressive or barbarous. No doubt I have not *proved* these things not to be values worth their price in human suffering and loss of freedom; it may be enough to have shown what it is that is offered for the price.

◆ ◆ ◆ ◆ ◆

STUDY QUESTIONS

1. Can Mill's distinction between self- and other-regarding actions be maintained in contemporary Western society?

2. What dangerous consequences might arise from distinguishing between harmful conduct which may justifiably be legally limited, and merely offensive conduct which does not cause harm and for that reason may not justifiably be legally limited?

3. Even when we know what is in our interests, we often make mistakes as we choose courses of action intended to support those interests. Is our fallibility a good reason for the law to be paternalistic?

4. Is Devlin's argument that a society has the right to legislate against disgusting conduct a good argument? Why or why not?

5. Is Hart's criticism of Devlin's conception of society plausible? What might a society under law be besides a community of shared ideals?

♦ ♦ ♦ ♦ ♦

FURTHER READINGS

Gerald Dworkin, ed. *Morality, Harm, and the Law*. Boulder, CO: Westview Press, 1994.

Joel Feinberg, *The Moral Limits of the Criminal Law: Harm to Others*. Oxford: Oxford University Press, 1984.

——, *Harm to Self*. Oxford: Oxford University Press, 1986.

——, *Offense to Others*. Oxford: Oxford University Press, 1986.

——, *Harmless Wrongdoing*. Oxford: Oxford University Press, 1988.

James FitzJames Stephens, *Liberty, Equality Fraternity*. Chicago: University of Chicago Press, 1991.

Rolf Sartorius, ed. *Paternalism*. Minneapolis: University of Minnesota Press, 1983.

Wayne Sumner, *The Hateful and the Obscene: Studies in the Limits of Free Expression*. Toronto: University of Toronto Press, 2003.

SECTION III

Responsibility

RESPONSIBILITY

INTRODUCTION

In this section we will examine a series of readings which each contribute to an understanding of what it is to be responsible for some state of affairs. Specifically, this section focuses on understanding *criminal* responsibility for voluntary, intentional criminal wrongdoing which is typically punished by substantial restrictions on personal liberty. This focus will lead us to what are sometimes called "analytical problems" about criminal responsibility: tricky questions about how to understand and label wrongdoers' intentions and actions. We will leave analysis and justification of appropriate punishment to other writers in other books as far as possible.

This section contains excerpts from works by Professor H.L.A. Hart and Professor R. Antony Duff and from a recent English criminal case. The first excerpt is taken from Hart's article "Postscript: Responsibility and Retribution." Hart discusses the idea of responsibility and marks the special character of "liability-responsibility," or responsibility in the sense of being accountable for some situation in a way which merits punishment. The second excerpt in this section turns from a general discussion of responsibility to the context of criminal responsibility for voluntary, intentional conduct—conduct the actor "meant to do." In his book *Criminal Attempts*, from which our excerpt is taken, Duff examines the difficult question of how far intention, or what someone "meant to do," must be put into action before a crime occurs. This section concludes with the English criminal case *R v Shivpuri*, which demonstrates how important, yet difficult, it can be to state precisely when intention and conduct amount to criminal wrongdoing. The remainder of this

introduction discusses some of the main ideas found in these readings.

1. Hart on Four Senses of "Responsibility"

In "Postscript: Responsibility and Retribution," Hart explores four senses in which we speak of someone or thing being responsible for some state of affairs in legal or moral life. (1) "Role responsibility" refers to particular responsibilities held in the context of occupying a special position, as a sergeant has responsibilities which a corporal does not. We speak differently of (2) "causal responsibility," Hart argues, as we isolate the cause of some occurrence, whether it be a person or some other force. (3) "Liability-responsibility" applies when we hold someone to be blameworthy or reasonably "made to pay" for certain consequences, whether she caused them or not. Liability-responsibility can be very complicated, since it is often difficult to say precisely how and why someone is connected to wrongdoing in a way worth punishing, especially if that person did not plainly and directly cause a wrong to occur. Hart isolates mental, causal, and relationship-based criteria for liability-responsibility. Findings of liability-responsibility for serious wrongdoing typically take account of the *mental* state of the wrongdoer, her actual *causal* relation to the wrongdoing, and any personal *relationships* which bear on our understanding of the wrongdoing, as might occur in, e.g., a conspiracy which leads to one member's committing a criminal offence. Finally, (4) Hart discusses "capacity responsibility," which refers to a person's ability to reason through the consequences of her actions. It is important to note that this analysis of the senses of responsibility for a particular state of affairs applies equally to legal and moral responsibility. Hart discusses extensively the relation between the two types of responsibility, and the way in which these senses of responsibility may apply singly or in a group to a particular situation.

We will leave for your investigation the precise details of the distinctions Hart draws. It is enough here to note the importance of Hart's demonstration that there can be more than meets the eye in a situation where some terribly harmful consequence has occurred and a number of well-meaning people point to one person and shout "He's responsible!" There are different senses in which someone may be responsible for some situation, and liability-responsibility is a special sort of responsibility. Someone may be responsible in a sense which does not deserve punishment, or may lack the capacity to be properly said to be responsible in anything more than the sense of someone accidentally caught up in a chain of events. Even in situations when we are certain someone bears liability-responsibility for wrongdoing and therefore ought to be punished, our analysis is not done. We ordinarily suppose that conduct which someone voluntarily and intentionally carried out is the most blameworthy and deserves the most serious punishment. It is most plainly really the wrongdoer's *own wrongdoing* and not accident or carelessness, since it is deliberate and "owned" by the wrongdoer in a way which even serious wrongdoing found in recklessness and negligence is not.

2. *Intentions and Actions*

Our next selection is taken from the arguments of Professor R. Antony Duff, who teaches at the University of Stirling in Scotland. He is well known for his work on responsibility and punishment. In our selection Duff is concerned with how we may best characterize this most serious type of voluntary,

intentional criminal wrongdoing in a way which captures those who are genuinely guilty, and guards against wrongful conviction of those who ought not to bear liability-responsibility for some situation, or ought to bear a lesser degree of liability-responsibility. Here we will explore that type of crime, and how some of the main ideas of Duff's discussion are illustrated by *R v Shivpuri*, the case which concludes this section.

2.1 *Mens Rea* and *Actus Reus*

A large number of serious crimes are understood in terms of two elements: intention and conduct. A crime of this type consists of the *intention* to commit an action which is prohibited by criminal law, and completion of the prohibited *conduct*. Two Latin terms are commonly used to capture these two ideas. The idea of intention or "guilty mind" is contained in the term *mens rea* and the idea of conduct is contained in the term *actus reus*. So, for example, the crime of murder requires both the intention to kill and the completed conduct in which a person is actually killed. This apparently simple way of analyzing and categorizing the components of the crime of murder is in fact part of a very complex understanding of voluntary, intentional criminal wrongdoing. More must be added to this picture if it is to provide useful analysis of less straightforward situations where, e.g., it is uncertain just what the killer intended or the killer's gun jammed and so the intended victim was not killed. Much of Duff's discussion is concerned with these difficult problems in less straightforward situations such as criminal attempts in which the *actus reus* is incomplete. When we talk of crimes composed of *mens rea* and *actus reus*, we know that we are concerned with crimes where the accused "meant to do it," but *what* did he have to mean or intend in order for us to hold him liable, and *how much* of "it" must he do? Is the *actus reus* simply *evidence* of a defect of character which the criminal law properly aims to identify and punish? Or does the *actus reus* in fact *constitute* or *make up* the wrong done in a crime? We must find a way to state precisely how intentions mix with actions in an "inculpatory" or "guilt-producing" way and how other information might be "exculpatory" or "guilt-excusing."

2.2 Subjectivism and Objectivism

The subjectivist approach claims that the wrong done in a crime is found in intention, or what a wrong-doer "meant to do." Supporters of the subjectivist position often point out that this view matches our sense that what is wrong about a crime is the *willingness* to commit some action prohibited by criminal law. We can see this in our reluctance to excuse from liability a person who intends to commit a crime, yet fails to do so out of bad luck. We are not keen, for example, to excuse the would-be poisoner Bob who slips lethal poison into Aunt Ethel's tea, yet fails in his plan because Fluffy the greedy poodle slurps her owner's tea and saves Aunt Ethel. Bob *meant* to kill his Aunt Ethel, and were it not for the greedy and unthinking intervention of Fluffy, Bob would have succeeded. Bob ought to bear liability for his attempt, we might think, in the same way that murderers who do not suffer bad luck bear liability for murder. Bob's bad luck does not change the fact that he meant to kill his Aunt Ethel.

Supporters of the objectivist approach reject subjectivism on various grounds. Objectivists argue that although intentions matter, the actual consequences of intended actions must *also* be taken into account when holding someone liable for wrongdoing. Objectivists complain that while the subjectivists' goal of excluding the role of luck from understanding wrongdoing is laudable, there are insurmountable practical difficulties in understanding criminal wrongdoing as occurring "in the head" or in intentions only, regardless of how the intended plan works out in practice. How, objectivists ask, can subjectivists determine reliably what someone intended, when we cannot simply peer into heads to see what thoughts are in them? How can subjectivists show

that Bob really intended to poison his aunt and did not, as he claims, merely mistake poison for sugar in Aunt Ethel's badly organized kitchen cupboard? And if a crime consists in intention regardless of completion of the plan, at what point are intentions so plainly criminal that we can be confident that the would-be criminal is beyond turning back? These practical problems of assessing action cannot be overcome, objectivists charge. The only fair way to match crime to punishment is to hold people liable for what actually followed from their intentions.

In our excerpt, Duff explores two ways subjectivists have tried to solve the problems objectivists have raised, while preserving the subjectivist goal of excluding luck from determinations of liability-responsibility for criminal wrongdoing.

2.3 The "Choice" Version of Subjectivism

The choice version of subjectivism understands persons as essentially free-willed, rational individuals whose freedom allows them to make decisions and to change those decisions. Even while in the midst of carrying out a particular plan of action, a free-willed person might decide at the last moment to withhold from completing that action. If we are to have proper respect for a person's freedom to stop short of criminal wrongdoing, we must avoid judging an action as even an attempted crime until it is quite plain from the context that the actor really *chose* to carry out that particular action. On the choice version of subjectivism, criminal wrongdoing consists in a seamless flow of intention into action, to a point at which there can be no denying an actor's choice to carry out a course of action which happens to be prohibited by criminal law.

As Duff observes, this does not explain fully the relationship between intention, action, and wrongdoing. The practical need for a usable understanding of this sort of wrongdoing requires that we be able to specify how far Christine the would-be kidnapper must progress in her preparatory actions before we are justified in ascribing to her the choice to kidnap Mike. Perhaps we are not justified in arresting Christine for attempted kidnapping on the evidence of the friend from whom Christine borrowed a getaway van, with the explanation that she was off to kidnap Mike. This might be merely an expression of an intention, or a joke in poor taste. But must we wait until the last possible moment before Christine has forcibly taken Mike to the van and has pressed the accelerator to complete her escape plan, leaving Christine every possible opportunity to re-think and call off her plan (a *locus poenitentiae*, in the commonly used Latin phrase)? When does an intention become more than just an idea, and become evidence of a choice made by the wrongdoer? If the choice version of subjectivism is to be a plausible explanation of criminal wrongdoing, it must offer an answer to these questions. In our selection Duff examines some of the answers.

2.4 The "Character" Version of Subjectivism

The character version of subjectivism understands persons as having settled character traits or dispositions which are revealed in action. An intention to commit a crime is an expression of a particular character trait, and the action following from the intention is merely evidence of the undesirable character trait the criminal law aims to discourage. The character version of subjectivism solves the problem the choice theorist encounters when trying to decide whether a person's actions have gone beyond the possibility of a change of mind and withholding from completion of the crime. The character theorist understands action as evidence of a disposition to disobey the law, so whether the action is completed is immaterial to a finding of at least some degree of criminal liability. Both a criminal attempt and a completed crime reveal the character trait the criminal law seeks to limit.

As attractive as the character version of subjectivism may be, it, too, comes with certain problems. Supporters of the character argument must explain *what* action shows that a person has a *specific* character trait, and we must be given an account of how to regard persons who have undesirable character traits but do not act on those traits. Should criminal law aim to punish *defects of character*, even those that do not in fact result in criminal wrongdoing? Or should these weaknesses be regarded as nothing more than the cause of *actions* which, *if* committed, deserve punishment? Duff argues that both choice and character versions of subjectivism contain problems which cannot be overcome. In the remainder of his book, beyond the selection included here, Duff argues that we ought to understand the sort of crimes people meant to do in terms of subjective intentions *and* objective effects of wrongdoing. As a matter of fact, however, the *mens rea* component of this sort of crime continues to be regarded by most courts as a *subjective* matter, as you will see in *Regina v Shivpuri*. It is for you to decide whether one of these versions of subjectivism is adequate, or whether Duff's further alternative might need to be pursued if the criminal law is to be rational and fair.

3. *Regina v Shivpuri*

Regina v *Shivpuri* [1986] illustrates some of the difficulties in devising a coherent, consistent understanding of how intentions and actions can add up to liability-responsibility for criminal wrongdoing.

3.1 The Case

Mr. Shivpuri agreed to participate in importation of what he confessed to police was legally prohibited heroin or cannabis. He was caught, and charged with *attempting* to (1) "deal with" and (2) "harbour" a controlled drug. Yet when the powder Shivpuri carried was analyzed, it was "found not to be a controlled drug but snuff or some similar harmless vegetable matter." At trial Shivpuri was convicted as charged, on the grounds that it did not matter whether he knew with certainty that the powder he possessed really was a prohibited drug, so long as he intended to possess a prohibited drug.

Shivpuri appealed his conviction for reasons including the claim that he had not committed an attempt, which in English criminal law consists of "an act which is more than merely preparatory to the commission of the offence." Shivpuri clearly *did* fulfill the *mens rea* portion of the criminal attempts with which he was charged as he intended to import what he thought were illegal drugs. Yet the facts of the situation made it "factually impossible" for him to act in a more than merely preparatory way to fulfill the *actus reus* of the crime, since he did not in fact possess the drugs which are a necessary part of "dealing with" and "harbouring" a controlled drug.

Mr. Shivpuri's appeal was eventually heard by the House of Lords (commonly referred to in legal writing as "the House"), the highest court of appeal for criminal matters in the United Kingdom. Mr. Shivpuri's appeal was dismissed, and so his conviction was upheld. The judgement of the House in *Shivpuri* is interesting both for its reasoning regarding Mr. Shivpuri's intentions and actions, and for the fact that this judgement overrules the House's then-recent ruling in *Anderton v Ryan* [1985] in which Ms. Ryan was acquitted of criminal wrongdoing in circumstances very similar to those of *Shivpuri*. Although the House of Lords has since 1966 overruled its own prior decisions, it has done so very rarely in the interest of maintaining the stability of the law. In the excerpt included here from the ruling in *Shivpuri*, the House reflects on its reasoning in *Anderton v Ryan* and explains why the reasoning in that case must be rejected. The House considers and rejects the possibility that *Anderton v Ryan* and *Shivpuri* might be regarded as quite different cases and so "distinguished" from one another and not judged according to the same standard. The House decided that an error was made in acquitting Ms. Ryan in *Anderton v Ryan*, and *Shivpuri* must be con-

victed despite the fact that this means two quite different understandings of criminal wrongdoing were embraced by the House over a very short period of time.

3.2 Objective Innocence

Let us explore the reasons for the court's changed understanding of criminal wrongdoing. In *Anderton v Ryan*, Ms. Ryan was charged with attempting to handle stolen goods. As Lord Bridge writes in *Shivpuri*, "She bought a video recorder believing it to be stolen. On the facts as they were to be assumed it was not stolen. By a majority the House decided that she was entitled to be acquitted" on the grounds that what she intended to be an illegal act was as a matter of fact "objectively innocent." The court accepted that it is impossible to be guilty of attempting to handle stolen goods if the goods are in fact not stolen. This view has the ring of common sense, as it construes a crime as an intention to commit the legally prohibited act and conduct which is in fact illegal. Ms. Ryan's intentions alone are not enough for her to be found guilty of criminal wrongdoing, because in this factual context her intentions simply couldn't culminate in the sort of conduct the law aims to limit. Yet in *Shivpuri* the court rejects this commonsensical view of crime. Why?

Lord Bridge admits in *Shivpuri* that he is no longer convinced that it is possible to state clearly and unambiguously what is to count as "objectively innocent" conduct. As he explains, "any attempt to commit an offence which involves "an act which is more than merely preparatory to the commission of the offence" but which for any reason fails, so that in the event no offence is committed, must ex hypothesi, from the point of view of the criminal law, be "objectively innocent."" Lord Bridge seems to indicate here that the criminal wrongdoing of a criminal attempt cannot be found in the conduct or *actus reus*, since it is part of the nature of criminal attempt that its conduct is incomplete. If the criminal wrongdoing of a criminal attempt is found in the conduct part of the attempt, then no criminal attempt can ever be wrong, since no attempt ever actually completes the substance of the wrongful conduct the criminal law prohibits. Yet this conclusion runs very strongly against our sense that even crimes where conduct is incomplete involve wrongdoing.

3.3 Choice

What, then, does criminal wrongdoing consist in, if the "objective innocence" of conduct cannot serve as an excuse? Lord Bridge examines and rejects something very like a "choice" solution to understanding attempted criminal wrongdoing. We might, Bridge suggests, distinguish a defendant's "dominant intention" from his "incidental intention." Ms. Ryan might be saved from legal liability by the fact that her choice to buy a VCR was part of a dominant intention to get a cheap VCR, and she only incidentally intended that it be stolen. What she really wanted and *chose* to do was to buy a cheap VCR. If this distinction works, Ms. Ryan can be acquitted, and Mr. Shivpuri convicted since it *was* part of his dominant intention that the goods he smuggled should be illegal drugs. Yet Lord Bridge rejects this understanding of criminal wrongdoing on both practical and theoretical grounds, and concludes, as we have mentioned, that there is no way of distinguishing the cases of Ms. Ryan and Mr. Shivpuri. We will leave you to discover in our excerpt Lord Bridge's precise reasons for rejecting this version of the choice theory, and we will now proceed instead to examine what he supposes is the right way to understand both Ms. Ryan's and Mr. Shivpuri's intentions and actions.

3.4 Character

After rejecting both his reasoning in *Anderton v Ryan* and a version of the "choice" theory, Lord Bridge now argues in *Shivpuri* that "What turns what would otherwise, from the point of view of the criminal law, be an innocent act into a crime is the intent of the actor to commit an offence ... A puts his hand into B's pocket. Whether or not there is anything in the pocket capable of being stolen, if A intends to steal, his act is a criminal attempt; if he does not so intend his act is innocent." Lord Bridge and the House have now adopted something very near the character view that criminal wrongdoing consists in the intention to act, regardless of whether the facts of the situation permit the intended action or choice to be carried out. By taking this route Lord Bridge avoids the problem of determining precisely when Mr. Shivpuri's intentions flowed far enough into conduct to be called a criminal choice. If criminal wrongdoing is understood as consisting in the intention to act, action is merely evidence of the intention which expresses Mr. Shivpuri's disposition of character to commit the illegal act, and Mr. Shivpuri's powder is evidence enough of this disposition.

Over only two cases the House swings between three distinct ways of holding an accused person responsible for criminal wrongdoing. In *Anderton v Ryan* the House understood criminal wrongdoing *objectively*, and in *Shivpuri* the House weighs both *choice* and *character* versions of subjectivism before settling on something like the latter. Has the House of Lords made the right decision at last in *Shivpuri*? The importance of a sound understanding of criminal liability requires very little explanation: if we value personal freedom, we must take care to restrict liberty only on well-justified grounds. The stakes are high, so it is well worth the effort to evaluate and accept or reject the reasoning in *Shivpuri*.

♦ ♦ ♦ ♦ ♦

H.L.A. HART

"Postcript: Responsibility and Retribution," from *Punishment and Responsibility*

The essays in this volume are all concerned with the legal doctrine which requires, as a normal condition of liability to punishment, that the person to be punished should, at the time of his offence, have had a certain knowledge or intention, or possessed certain powers of understanding and control. This doctrine prescribing the psychological criteria of responsibility takes different forms in different legal systems, but in all its forms it has presented both problems of analysis and problems of policy and moral justification. It is no easy matter to determine precisely what English law actually requires when it is said to require, or to treat as sufficient for liability, a certain "intention" or an "act of will" or "recklessness" or "negligence;" hence some of the preceding essays are concerned in part with such problems of analysis. But most of them are also concerned with problems of justification: with the credentials of principles or "theories of punishment" which require liability to punishment to be restricted by reference to such psychological conditions, and with the claims of newer theories that would eliminate these restrictions either completely or in part. A central theme of these essays is that it is not only within the framework of a retributive theory of punishment that insistence on the importance of these restrictions makes sense; there are important reasons, both moral and prudential, for adhering to these restrictions which are perfectly consistent with a general utilitarian conception of the aim of punishment.

In most of these essays I have attempted to confront these issues without any full-scale discussion of the notions of Responsibility and Retribution, though I turned aside to distinguish, in the first of these essays, two meanings of "retribution" and, in the last essay, two meanings of "responsibility." The distinctions I made there have drawn fire from some critics, and it is plain from the criticism that some more comprehensive account of the complexities and ambiguities of these notions is required. The purpose of this postscript is to supply it.

1. Responsibility

A wide range of different, though connected, ideas is covered by the expressions "responsibility," "responsible," and "responsible for," as these are standardly used in and out of the law. Though connexions exist between these different ideas, they are often very indirect, and it seems appropriate to speak of different *senses* of these expressions. The following simple story of a drunken sea captain who lost his ship at sea can be told in the terminology of responsibility to illustrate, with stylistically horrible clarity, these differences of sense.

> As captain of the ship, X was responsible for the safety of his passengers and crew. But on his last voyage he got drunk every night and was responsible for the loss of the ship with all aboard. It was rumoured that he was insane, but the doctors considered that he was responsible for his actions.
>
> Throughout the voyage he behaved quite irresponsibly, and various incidents in his career showed that he was not a responsible person. He always maintained that the exceptional winter storms were responsible for the loss of the ship, but in the legal proceedings brought against him he was found criminally responsible for his negligent conduct, and in separate civil proceedings he was held legally responsible for the loss of life and property. He is still alive and

he is morally responsible for the deaths of many women and children.

This welter of distinguishable senses of the word "responsibility" and its grammatical cognates can, I think, be profitably reduced by division and classification. I shall distinguish four heads of classification to which I shall assign the following names:

(a) Role-Responsibility
(b) Causal-Responsibility
(c) Liability-Responsibility
(d) Capacity-Responsibility

I hope that in drawing these dividing lines, and in the exposition which follows, I have avoided the arbitrary pedantries of classificatory systematics, and that my divisions pick out and clarify the main, though not all, varieties of responsibility to which reference is constantly made, explicitly or implicitly, by moralists, lawyers, historians, and ordinary men. I relegate to the notes[1] discussion of what unifies these varieties and explains the extension of the terminology of responsibility.

2. Role-Responsibility

A sea captain is responsible for the safety of his ship, and that is his responsibility, or one of his responsibilities. A husband is responsible for the maintenance of his wife; parents for the upbringing of their children; a sentry for alerting the guard at the enemy's approach; a clerk for keeping the accounts of his firm. These examples of a person's responsibilities suggest the generalization that, whenever a person occupies a distinctive place or office in a social organization, to which specific duties are attached to provide for the welfare of others or to advance in some specific way the aims or purposes of the organization, he is properly said to be responsible for the performance of these duties, or for doing what is necessary to fulfil them. Such duties are a person's

responsibilities. As a guide to this sense of responsibility this generalization is, I think, adequate, but the idea of a distinct role or place or office is, of course, a vague one, and I cannot undertake to make it very precise. Doubts about its extension to marginal cases will always arise. If two friends, out on a mountaineering expedition, agree that the one shall look after the food and the other the maps, then the one is correctly said to be responsible for the food, and the other for the maps, and I would classify this as a case of role-responsibility. Yet such fugitive or temporary assignments with specific duties would not usually be considered by sociologists, who mainly use the word, as an example of a "role." So "role" in my classification is extended to include a task assigned to any person by agreement or otherwise. But it is also important to notice that not all the duties which a man has in virtue of occupying what in a quite strict sense of role is a distinct role, are thought or spoken of as "responsibilities." A private soldier has a duty to obey his superior officer and, if commanded by him to form fours or present arms on a given occasion, has a duty to do so. But to form fours or present arms would scarcely be said to be the private's responsibility; nor would he be said to be responsible for doing it. If on the other hand a soldier was ordered to deliver a message to H.Q. or to conduct prisoners to a base camp, he might well be said to be responsible for doing these things, and these things to be his responsibility. I think, though I confess to not being sure, that what distinguishes those duties of a role which are singled out as responsibilities is that they are duties of a relatively complex or extensive kind, defining a "sphere of responsibility" requiring care and attention over a protracted period of time, while short-lived duties of a very simple kind, to do or not do some specific act on a particular occasion, are not termed responsibilities. Thus a soldier detailed off to keep the camp clean and tidy for the general's visit of inspection has this as his sphere of responsibility and is responsible for it. But if merely

---

1   *infra.* pp. 264–65.

told to remove a piece of paper from the approaching general's path, this would be at most his duty.

A "responsible person," "behaving responsibly" (not "irresponsibly"), require for their elucidation a reference to role-responsibility. A responsible person is one who is disposed to take his duties seriously; to think about them, and to make serious efforts to fulfil them. To behave responsibly is to behave as a man would who took his duties in this serious way. Responsibilities in this sense may be either legal or moral, or fall outside this dichotomy. Thus a man may be morally as well as legally responsible for the maintenance of his wife and children, but a host's responsibility for the comfort of his guests, and a referee's responsibility for the control of the players is neither legal nor moral, unless the word "moral" is unilluminatingly used simply to exclude legal responsibility.

3. *Causal Responsibility*

"The long drought was responsible for the famine in India." In many contexts, as in this one, it is possible to substitute for the expression "was responsible for" the words "caused" or "produced" or some other causal expression in referring to consequences, results, or outcomes. The converse, however, is not always true. Examples of this causal sense of responsibility are legion. "His neglect was responsible for her distress." "The Prime Minister's speech was responsible for the panic." "Disraeli was responsible for the defeat of the Government." "The icy condition of the road was responsible for the accident." The past tense of the verb used in this causal sense of the expression "responsible for" should be noticed. If it is said of a living person, who has in fact caused some disaster, that he is responsible for it, this is not, or not merely, an example of causal responsibility, but of what I term "liability-responsibility;" it asserts his liability on account of the disaster, even though it is also true that he is responsible in that sense *because* he caused the disaster, and that he caused the disaster

may be expressed by saying that he was responsible for it. On the other hand, if it is said of a person no longer living that he was responsible for some disaster, this may be either a simple causal statement or a statement of liability-responsibility, or both.

From the above examples it is clear that in this causal sense not only human beings but also their actions or omissions, and things, conditions, and events, may be said to be responsible for outcomes. It is perhaps true that only where an outcome is thought unfortunate or felicitous is its cause commonly spoken of as responsible for it. But this may not reflect any aspect of the meaning of the expression "responsible for;" it may only reflect the fact that, except in such cases, it may be pointless and hence rare to pick out the causes of events. It is sometimes suggested that, though we may speak of a human being's action as responsible for some outcome in a purely causal sense, we do not speak of a person, as distinct from his actions, as responsible for an outcome, unless he is felt to deserve censure or praise. This is, I think, a mistake. History books are full of examples to the contrary. "Disraeli was responsible for the defeat of the Government" need not carry even an implication that he was deserving of censure or praise; it may be purely a statement concerned with the contribution made by one human being to an outcome of importance, and be entirely neutral as to its moral or other merits. The contrary view depends, I think, on the failure to appreciate sufficiently the ambiguity of statements of the form "X *was* responsible for Y" as distinct from "X *is* responsible for Y" to which I have drawn attention above. The former expression in the case of a person no longer living may be (though it *need* not be) a statement of liability-responsibility.

4. *Legal Liability-Responsibility*

Though it was noted that role-responsibility might take either legal or moral form, it was not found necessary to treat these separately. But in the case of the present topic of liability-responsibility, separate treatment seems advisable. For responsibility seems to have a wider extension in relation to the law than it does in relation to morals, and it is a question to be considered whether this is due merely to the general differences between law and morality, or to some differences in the sense of responsibility involved.

When legal rules require men to act or abstain from action, one who breaks the law is usually liable, according to other legal rules, to punishment for his misdeeds, or to make compensation to persons injured thereby, and very often he is liable to both punishment and enforced compensation. He is thus liable to be "made to pay" for what he has done in either or both of the senses which the expression "He'll pay for it" may bear in ordinary usage. But most legal systems go much further than this. A man may be legally punished on account of what his servant has done, even if he in no way caused or instigated or even knew of the servant's action, or knew of the likelihood of his servant so acting. Liability in such circumstances is rare in modern systems of criminal law; but it is common in all systems of civil law for men to be made to pay compensation for injuries caused by others, generally their servants or employees. The law of most countries goes further still. A man may be liable to pay compensation for harm suffered by others, though neither he nor his servants have caused it. This is so, for example, in Anglo-American law when the harm is caused by dangerous things which escape from a man's possession, even if their escape is not due to any act or omission of his or his servants, or if harm is caused to a man's employees by defective machinery whose defective condition he could not have discovered.

It will be observed that the facts referred to in the last paragraph are expressed in terms of "liability" and not "responsibility." In the preceding essay in this volume I ventured the general statement that to say that someone is legally responsible for something often means that under legal rules he is liable to be made either to suffer or to pay compensation in cer-

tain eventualities. But I now think that this simple account of liability-responsibility is in need of some considerable modification. Undoubtedly, expressions of the form "he is legally responsible for Y" (where Y is some action or harm) and "he is legally liable to be punished or to be made to pay compensation for Y" are very closely connected, and sometimes they are used as if they were identical in meaning. Thus, where one legal writer speaks of "strict responsibility" and "vicarious responsibility," another speaks of "strict liability" and "vicarious liability;" and even in the work of a single writer the expressions "vicarious responsibility" and "vicarious liability" are to be found used without any apparent difference in meaning, implication, or emphasis. Hence, in arguing that it was for the law to determine the mental conditions of responsibility, Fitzjames Stephen claimed that this must be so because "the meaning of responsibility is liability to punishment."[2]

But though the abstract expressions "responsibility" and "liability" are virtually equivalent in many contexts, the statement that a man is responsible for his actions, or for some act or some harm, is usually not identical in meaning with the statement that he is liable to be punished or to be made to pay compensation for the act or the harm, but is directed to a narrower and more specific issue. It is in this respect that my previous account of liability-responsibility needs qualification.

The question whether a man is or is not legally liable to be punished for some action that he has done opens up the quite general issue whether all of the various requirements for criminal liability have been satisfied, and so will include the question whether the kind of action done, whatever mental element accompanied it, was ever punishable by law. But the question whether he is or is not legally responsible for some action or some harm is usually not concerned with this general issue, but with the narrower issue whether any of a certain range of conditions (mainly,

---

2   *A History of The Criminal Law*, Vol.II, p. 183.

but not exclusively, psychological) are satisfied, it being assumed that all other conditions are satisfied. Because of this difference in scope between questions of liability to punishment and questions of responsibility, it would be somewhat misleading, though not unintelligible, to say of a man who had refused to rescue a baby drowning in a foot of water, that he was not, according to English law, legally responsible for leaving the baby to drown or for the baby's death, if all that is meant is that he was not liable to punishment because refusing aid to those in danger is not generally a crime in English law. Similarly, a book or article entitled "Criminal Responsibility" would not be expected to contain the whole of the substantive criminal law determining the conditions of liability, but only to be concerned with a specialized range of topics such as mental abnormality, immaturity, *mens rea*, strict and vicarious liability, proximate cause, or other general forms of connexion between acts and harm sufficient for liability. These are the specialized topics which are, in general, thought and spoken of as "criteria" of responsibility. They may be divided into three classes: (i) mental or psychological conditions; (ii) causal or other forms of connexion between act and harm; (iii) personal relationships rendering one man liable to be punished or to pay for the acts of another. Each of these three classes requires some separate discussion.

(i) *Mental or psychological criteria of responsibility.* In the criminal law the most frequent issue raised by questions of responsibility, as distinct from the wider question of liability, is whether or not an accused person satisfied some mental or psychological condition required for liability, or whether liability was strict or absolute, so that the usual mental or psychological conditions were not required. It is, however, important to notice that these psychological conditions are of two sorts, of which the first is far more closely associated with the use of the word responsibility than the second. On the one hand, the law of most countries requires that the person liable to be punished should at the time of his crime have had the capacity to understand what he is required by law to do or not to do, to deliberate and to decide what to do, and to control his conduct in the light of such decisions. Normal adults are generally assumed to have these capacities, but they may be lacking where there is mental disorder or immaturity, and the possession of these normal capacities is very often signified by the expression "responsible for his actions." This is the fourth sense of responsibility which I discuss below under the heading of "Capacity-Responsibility." On the other hand, except where responsibility is strict, the law may excuse from punishment persons of normal capacity if, on particular occasions where their outward conduct fits the definition of the crime, some element of intention or knowledge, or some other of the familiar constituents of *mens rea*, was absent, so that the particular action done was defective, though the agent had the normal capacity of understanding and control. Continental codes usually make a firm distinction between these two main types of psychological conditions: questions concerning general capacity are described as matters of responsibility or "imputability," whereas questions concerning the presence or absence of knowledge or intention on particular occasions are not described as matters of "imputability," but are referred to the topic of "fault" (*schuld, faute, dolo,* &c.).

English law and English legal writers do not mark quite so firmly this contrast between general capacity and the knowledge or intention accompanying a particular action; for the expression *mens rea* is now often used to cover all the variety of psychological conditions required for liability by the law, so that both the person who is excused from punishment because of lack of intention or some ordinary accident or mistake on a particular occasion and the person held not to be criminally responsible on account of immaturity or insanity are said not to have the requisite *mens rea*. Yet the distinction thus blurred by the extensive use of the expression *mens rea* between a persistent incapacity and a particular defective action is indirectly marked in terms of responsibility in most Anglo-American legal writing, in the following way. When a person is said to be not responsible for a particular act or crime, or when (as in the formulation of the M'Naghten Rules and s.2 of the Homicide Act, 1957) he is said not to be responsible for his "acts and omissions in doing" some action on a particular occasion, the reason for saying this is usually some mental abnormality or disorder. I have not succeeded in finding cases where a normal person, merely lacking some ordinary element of knowledge or intention on a particular occasion, is said for that reason not to be responsible for that particular action, even though he is for that reason not liable to punishment. But though there is this tendency in statements of liability-responsibility to confine the use of the expression "responsible" and "not responsible" to questions of mental abnormality or general incapacity, yet all the psychological conditions of liability are to be found discussed by legal writers under such headings as "Criminal Responsibility" or "Principles of Criminal Responsibility." Accordingly I classify them here as criteria of responsibility. I do so with a clear conscience, since little is to be gained in clarity by a rigid division which the contemporary use of the expression *mens rea* often ignores.

The situation is, however, complicated by a further feature of English legal and non-legal usage. The phrase "responsible for his actions" is, as I have observed, frequently used to refer to the capacity-responsibility of the normal person, and, so used, refers to one of the major criteria of liability-responsibility. It is so used in s.2 of the Homicide Act 1957, which speaks of a person's mental "responsibility" for his actions being *impaired*, and in the rubric to the section, which speaks of persons "suffering from diminished responsibility." In this sense the expression is the name or description of a psychological condition. But the expression is also used to signify liability-responsibility itself, that is, liability to punishment so far as such liability depends on psychological conditions, and is so used when the

law is said to "relieve insane persons of responsibility for their actions." It was probably also so used in the form of verdict returned in cases of successful pleas of insanity under English law until this was altered by the Insanity Act 1964: the verdict was "guilty but insane so as not to be responsible according to law for his actions."

(ii) *Causal or other forms of connexion with harm.* Questions of legal liability-responsibility are not limited in their scope to psychological conditions of either of the two sorts distinguished above. Such questions are also (though more frequently in the law of tort than in the criminal law) concerned with the issue whether some form of connexion between a person's act and some harmful outcome is sufficient according to law to make him liable; so if a person is accused of murder the question whether he was or was not legally responsible for the death may be intended to raise the issue whether the death was too remote a consequence of his acts for them to count as its cause. If the law, as frequently in tort, is not that the defendant's action should have caused the harm, but that there be some other form of connexion or relationship between the defendant and the harm, e.g., that it should have been caused by some dangerous thing escaping from the defendant's land, this connexion or relationship is a condition of civil responsibility for harm, and, where it holds, the defendant is said to be legally responsible for the harm. No doubt such questions of connexion with harm are also frequently phrased in terms of liability.

(iii) *Relationship with the agent.* Normally in criminal law the minimum condition required for liability for punishment is that the person to be punished should himself have done what the law forbids, at least so far as outward conduct is concerned; even if liability is "strict," it is not enough to render him liable for punishment that someone else should have done it. This is often expressed in the terminology of responsibility (though here, too, "liability" is frequently used instead of "responsibility") by saying that, generally, vicarious responsibility is not known to the criminal law. But there are exceptional cases; an innkeeper is liable to punishment if his servants, without his knowledge and against his orders, sell liquor on his premises after hours. In this case he is vicariously responsible for the sale, and of course, in the civil law of tort there are many situations in which a master or employer is liable to pay compensation for the torts of his servant or employee, and is said to be vicariously responsible.

It appears, therefore, that there are diverse types of criteria of legal liability-responsibility: the most prominent consist of certain mental elements, but there are also causal or other connexions between a person and harm, or the presence of some relationship, such as that of master and servant, between different persons. It is natural to ask why these very diverse conditions are singled out as criteria of responsibility, and so are within the scope of questions about responsibility, as distinct from the wider question concerning liability for punishment. I think that the following somewhat Cartesian figure may explain this fact. If we conceive of a person as an embodied mind and will, we may draw a distinction between two questions concerning the conditions of liability and punishment. The first question is what general types of outer conduct (*actus reus*) or what sorts of harm are required for liability? The second question is how closely connected with such conduct or such harm must the embodied mind or will of an individual person be to render him liable to punishment? Or, as some would put it, to what extent must the embodied mind or will be the author of the conduct or the harm in order to render him liable? Is it enough that the person made the appropriate bodily movements? Or is it required that he did so when possessed of a certain capacity of control and with a certain knowledge or intention? Or that he caused the harm or stood in some other relationship to it, or to the actual doer of the deed? The legal rules, or parts of legal rules, that answer these various questions define the various forms of connexion

which are adequate for liability, and these constitute conditions of legal responsibility which form only a part of the total conditions of liability for punishment, which also include the definitions of the *actus reus* of the various crimes.

We may therefore summarize this long discussion of legal liability-responsibility by saying that, though in certain general contexts legal responsibility and legal liability have the same meaning, to say that a man is legally responsible for some act or harm is to state that his connexion with the act or harm is sufficient according to law for liability. Because responsibility and liability are distinguishable in this way, it will make sense to say that because a person is legally responsible for some action he is liable to be punished for it.

5. *Legal Liability Responsibility and Moral Blame*

My previous account of legal liability-responsibility, in which I claimed that in one important sense to say that a person is legally responsible meant that he was legally liable for punishment or could be made to pay compensation, has been criticized on two scores. Since these criticisms apply equally to the above amended version of my original account, in which I distinguish the general issue of liability from the narrower issue of responsibility, I shall consider these criticisms here. The first criticism, made by Mr. A.W.B. Simpson,[3] insists on the strong connexion between statements of legal responsibility and moral judgment, and claims that even lawyers tend to confine statements that a person is legally responsible for something to cases where he is considered morally blameworthy, and, where this is not so, tend to use the expression "liability" rather than "responsibility." But, though moral blame and legal responsibility may be connected in some

---

3 In a review of "Changing Conceptions of Responsibility," Chap. VIII, *supra*, in *Crim.L.R.* (1966) 124.

ways, it is surely not in this simple way. Against any such view not only is there the frequent use already mentioned of the expressions "strict responsibility" and "vicarious responsibility," which are obviously independent of moral blameworthiness, but there is the more important fact that we can, and frequently do, intelligibly debate the question whether a mentally disordered or very young person who has been held legally responsible for a crime is morally blameworthy. The coincidence of legal responsibility with moral blameworthiness may be a laudable ideal, but it is not a necessary truth nor even an accomplished fact.

The suggestion that the statement that a man is responsible generally means that he is blameworthy and not that he is liable to punishment is said to be supported by the fact that it is possible to cite, without redundancy, the fact that a person is responsible as a ground or reason for saying that he is liable to punishment. But, if the various kinds or senses of responsibility are distinguished, it is plain that there are many explanations of this last mentioned fact, which are quite independent of any essential connexion between legal responsibility and moral blameworthiness. Thus cases where the statement that the man is responsible constitutes a reason for saying that he is liable to punishment may be cases of role-responsibility (the master is legally responsible for the safety of his ship, therefore he is liable to punishment if he loses it) or capacity-responsibility (he was responsible for his actions therefore he is liable to punishment for his crimes); or they may even be statements of liability-responsibility, since such statements refer to part only of the conditions of liability and may therefore be given, without redundancy, as a reason for liability to punishment. In any case this criticism may be turned against the suggestion that responsibility is to be equated with moral blameworthiness; for plainly the statement that someone is responsible may be given as part of the reason for saying that he is morally blameworthy.

6. Liability Responsibility For Particular Actions

An independent objection is the following, made by Mr. George Pitcher.[4] The wide extension I have claimed for the notion of liability-responsibility permits us to say not only that a man is legally responsible in this sense for the consequences of his action, but also for his action or actions. According to Mr. Pitcher "this is an improper way of talking,: though common amongst philosophers. Mr. Pitcher is concerned primarily with moral, not legal, responsibility, but even in a moral context it is plain that there is a very well established use of the expression "responsible for his actions" to refer to capacity-responsibility for which Mr. Pitcher makes no allowance. As far as the law is concerned, many examples may be cited from both sides of the Atlantic where a person may be said to be responsible for his actions, or for his act, or for his crime, or for his conduct. Mr. Pitcher gives, as a reason for saying that it is improper to speak of a man being responsible for his own actions, the fact that a man does not produce or cause his own actions. But this argument would prove far too much. It would rule out as improper not only the expression "responsible for his actions," but also our saying that a man was responsible vicariously or otherwise for harmful outcomes which he had not caused, which is a perfectly well established legal usage.

None the less, there are elements of truth in Mr Pitcher's objection. First, it seems to be the case that even where a man is said to be legally responsible for what he has done, it is rare to find this expressed by a phrase conjoining the verb of action with the expression "responsible for." Hence, "he is legally responsible for killing her" is not usually found, whereas "he is legally responsible for her death" is common, as are the expressions "legally responsible for his act

---

4   In "Hart on Action and Responsibility," *The Philosophical Review* (1960), p. 266.

(in killing her);" "legally responsible for his crime;" or, as in the official formulation of the M'Naghten Rules, "responsible for his actions or omissions in doing or being a party to the killing." These common expressions in which a noun, not a verb, follows the phrase "responsible for" are grammatically similar to statements of causal responsibility, and the tendency to use the same form no doubt shows how strongly the overtones of causal responsibility influence the terminology ordinarily used to make statements of liability-responsibility. There is, however, also in support of Mr. Pitcher's view, the point already cited that, even in legal writing, where a person is said to be responsible for his act or his conduct, the relevant mental element is usually the question of insanity or immaturity, so that the ground in such cases for the assertion that the person is responsible or is not responsible for his act is the presence of absence of "responsibility for actions" in the sense of capacity-responsibility, and not merely the presence or absence of knowledge or intention in relation to the particular act.

7. Moral Liability-Responsibility

How far can the account given above of legal liability-responsibility be applied *mutatis mutandis* to moral responsibility? The *mutanda* seem to be the following: "deserving blame" or "blameworthy" will have to be substituted for "liable to punishment," and "morally bound to make amends or pay compensation" for "liable to be made to pay compensation." Then the moral counterpart to the account given of legal liability-responsibility would be the following: to say that a person is morally responsible for something he has done or for some harmful outcome of his own or others' conduct, is to say that he is morally blameworthy, or morally obliged to make amends for the harm, so far as this depends on certain conditions: these conditions relate to the character or extent of a man's control over his own conduct, or to the causal or other connexion between his action and harmful

occurrences, or to his relationship with the person who actually did the harm.

In general, such an account of the meaning of "morally responsible" seems correct, and the striking differences between legal and moral responsibility are due to substantive differences between the content of legal and moral rules and principles rather than to any variation in meaning of responsibility when conjoined with the word "moral" rather than "legal." Thus, both in the legal and the moral case, the criteria of responsibility seem to be restricted to the psychological elements involved in the control of conduct, to causal or other connexions between acts and harm, and to the relationships with the actual doer of misdeeds. The interesting differences between legal and moral responsibility arise from the differences in the particular criteria falling under these general heads. Thus a system of criminal law may make responsibility strict, or even absolute, not even exempting very young children or the grossly insane from punishment; or it may vicariously punish one man for what another has done, even though the former had no control of the latter; or it may punish an individual or make him compensate another for harm which he neither intended nor could have foreseen as likely to arise from his conduct. We may condemn such a legal system which extends strict or vicarious responsibility in these ways as barbarous or unjust, but there are no conceptual barriers to be overcome in speaking of such a system as a legal system, though it is certainly arguable that we should not speak of "punishment" where liability is vicarious or strict. In the moral case, however, greater conceptual barriers exist: the hypothesis that we might hold individuals morally blameworthy for doing things which they could not have avoided doing, or for things done by others over whom they had no control, conflicts with too many of the central features of the idea of morality to be treated merely as speculation about a rare or inferior kind of moral system. It may be an exaggeration to say that there could not logically be such a morality or that blame administered according to principles of strict or vicarious responsibility, even in a minority of cases, could not logically be moral blame; none the less, admission of such a system as a morality would require a profound modification in our present concept of morality, and there is no similar requirement in the case of law.

Some of the most familiar contexts in which the expression "responsibility" appears confirm these general parallels between legal and moral liability-responsibility. Thus in the famous question "Is moral responsibility compatible with determinism?" the expression "moral responsibility" is apt just because the bogey raised by determinism specifically relates to the usual criteria of responsibility; for it opens the question whether, if "determinism" were true, the capacities of human beings to control their conduct would still exist or could be regarded as adequate to justify moral blame.

In less abstract or philosophical contexts, where there is a present question of blaming someone for some particular act, the assertion or denial that a person is morally responsible for his actions is common. But this expression is as ambiguous in the moral as in the legal case: it is most frequently used to refer to what I have termed "capacity-responsibility," which is the most important criterion of moral liability-responsibility; but in some contexts it may also refer to moral liability-responsibility itself. Perhaps the most frequent use in moral contexts of the expression "responsible for" is in cases where persons are said to be morally responsible for the outcomes or results of morally wrong conduct, although Mr. Pitcher's claim that men are never said in ordinary usage to be responsible for their actions is, as I have attempted to demonstrate above with counter-examples, an exaggerated claim.

8. Capacity-Responsibility

In most contexts, as I have already stressed, the expression "he is responsible for his actions" is used to assert that a person has certain normal capacities. These constitute the most important criteria of moral liability-responsibility, though it is characteristic of most legal systems that they have given only a partial or tardy recognition to all these capacities as general criteria of legal responsibility. The capacities in question are those of understanding, reasoning, and control of conduct: the ability to understand what conduct legal rules or morality require, to deliberate and reach decisions concerning these requirements, and to conform to decisions when made. Because "responsible for his actions" in this sense refers not to a legal status but to certain complex psychological characteristics of persons, a person's responsibility for his actions may intelligibly be said to be "diminished" or "impaired" as well as altogether absent, and persons may be said to be "suffering from diminished responsibility" much as a wounded man may be said to be suffering from a diminished capacity to control the movements of his limbs.

No doubt the most frequent occasions for asserting or denying that a person is "responsible for his actions" are cases where questions of blame or punishment for particular actions are in issue. But, as with other expressions used to denote criteria of responsibility, this one also may be used where no particular question of blame or punishment is in issue, and it is then used simply to describe a person's psychological condition. Hence it may be said purely by way of description of some harmless inmate of a mental institution, even though there is no present question of his misconduct, that he is a person who is not responsible for his actions. No doubt if there were no social practice of blaming and punishing people for their misdeeds, and excusing them from punishment because they lack the normal capacities of understanding and control, we should lack this shorthand description for describing their condition which we now derive from these social practices. In that case we should have to describe the condition of the inmate directly, by saying that he could not understand what people told him to do, or could not reason about it, or come to, or adhere to any decisions about his conduct.

Legal systems left to themselves may be very niggardly in their admission of the relevance of liability to legal punishment of the several capacities, possession of which are necessary to render a man morally responsible for his actions. So much is evident from the history sketched in the preceding chapter of the painfully slow emancipation of English criminal law from the narrow, cognitive criteria of responsibility formulated in the M'Naghten Rules. Though some continental legal systems have been willing to confront squarely the question whether the accused "lacked the ability to recognize the wrongness of his conduct and to act in accordance with that recognition,"[5] such an issue, if taken seriously, raises formidable difficulties of proof, especially before juries. For this reason I think that, instead of a close determination of such questions of capacity, the apparently coarser-grained technique of exempting persons from liability to punishment if they fall into certain recognized categories of mental disorder is likely to be increasingly used. Such exemption by general category is a technique long known to English law; for in the case of very young children it has made no attempt to determine, as a condition of liability, the question whether on account of their immaturity they could have understood what the law required and could have conformed to its requirements, or whether their responsibility on account of their immaturity was "substantially impaired," but exempts them from liability for punishment if under a specified age. It seems likely that exemption by medical category rather than by individualized findings of absent or diminished capacity will be found more likely to lead in practice to satisfactory results, in spite of the difficulties pointed out in the last essay in the discussion of s.60 of the Mental Health Act, 1959.

Though a legal system may fail to incorporate in its rules any psychological criteria of responsibility, and so may apply its sanction to those who are not morally blameworthy, it is none the less dependent for its efficacy on the possession by a sufficient number of those whose conduct it seeks to control of the capacities of understanding and control of conduct which constitute capacity-responsibility. For if a large proportion of those concerned could not understand what the law required them to do or could not form and keep a decision to obey, no legal system could come into existence or continue to exist. The general possession of such capacities is therefore a condition of the *efficacy* of law, even though it is not made a condition of liability to legal sanctions. The same condition of efficacy attaches to all attempts to regulate or control human conduct by forms of *communication*: such as orders, commands, the invocation of moral or other rules or principles, argument, and advice.

"The notion of prevention through the medium of the mind assumes mental ability adequate to restraint." This was clearly seen by Bentham and by Austin, who perhaps influenced the seventh report of the Criminal Law Commissioners of 1833 containing this sentence. But they overstressed the point; for they wrongly assumed that this condition of efficacy must also be incorporated in legal rules as a condition of liability. This mistaken assumption is to be found not only in the explanation of the doctrine of *mens rea* given in Bentham's and Austin's works, but is explicit in the Commissioners' statement preceding the sentence quoted above that "the object of penal law being the prevention of wrong, the principle does not extend to mere involuntary acts or even to harmful consequences the result of inevitable accident." The case of morality is however different in precisely this respect: the possession by those to whom its injunctions are addressed of "mental ability adequate to restraint" (capacity-responsibility) has there a double status and importance. It is not only a condition of the efficacy of morality; but a

---

5 German Criminal Code, Art. 51.

system or practice which did not regard the possession of these capacities as a necessary condition of liability, and so treated blame as appropriate even in the case of those who lacked them, would not, as morality is at present understood, be a morality....

• • • • •

R.A. DUFF

"Choice, Character, and Action," from *Criminal Attempts**

... Disagreements between subjectivists and objectivists can best be understood as concerning the proper criteria for action-ascriptions. Both sides agree that a person should be held criminally liable for, and only for, what can properly be ascribed to her as an agent—for what can properly be described as *hers*; she is justly convicted, and punished, only in so far as an action matching the law's definition of an offence can properly be ascribed to her. Subjectivists then argue that the criteria of action-ascription must be "subjective:" actions which are to be ascribed to the agent must be described in "subjective" terms. Objectivists, by contrast, argue that what is mine as an agent cannot be identified in purely "subjective" terms; it must be described in partly "objective" terms. What we then need is some account of what such "subjective" or "objective" terms are; and different versions of subjectivism and of objectivism are distinguished in part by the different accounts which they offer. We will also, of course, need some

account of *why* these are the appropriate terms in which to identify the actions that can be ascribed to an agent.

• • •

Subjectivism I: Culpability and Choice

Any subjectivist account of criminal liability must explain what the "subjective," on which criminal liability is to depend, consists in. In its broadest sense, the "subjective" consists in the person's psychological states and attributes. However, not *every* aspect of a person's psychology will be relevant to her criminal liability: we need an account of just which aspects of the "subjective" are relevant.

Two forms of subjectivism have dominated recent discussion: one focuses on the idea of "choice," the other on that of "character."[1] I begin with the former.

6.1 Choice, Intention, and Belief

Criminal liability, on this subjectivist account, should be determined by *choice*. The actions which can properly be ascribed to me, for which I should be held liable, are those that I choose to do.

Choice, Control, and Chance

Why is choice so important? One answer is that a system of criminal law which makes liability depend on choice respects individual freedom, and maximizes citizens' control over their own lives. If we know that we will be liable to criminal sanctions only if we choose to break the law, we have the power to determine for ourselves whether or not we will be subject to those sanctions.[2] Another answer, which reveals the Kantian inspiration of this

---

* *Ed. note:* In his argument Duff frequently refers to parts of his book which are not included in this excerpt; however, these references and Duff's numbering of sections have been left in the excerpted text in the interest of its completeness as a resource for further exploration of the full text of *Criminal Attempts*.

---

1 See below, ch. 7, at n. 1.
2 See Hart, *Punishment and Responsibility*, 21–24, 44–47, 181–83, 227–30.

form of subjectivism,[3] is that I should be criminally liable only for that for which I can properly be held responsible and culpable; that I am responsible and culpable only for that which I control; and that I control only that which I choose to do or to bring about, my actions *qua* chosen.[4]

This line of argument is often buttressed by a contrast between "choice" and "chance." I control my choices, my actions *qua* chosen: but what happens independently of my choices, and so outside my control, is a matter of chance or luck; and such matters should not affect my criminal liability, since they cannot affect my culpability. Thus a "fully subjective principle" of criminal liability "draws a straight line through the vicissitudes of life and the vagaries of fortune, minimising the influence of chance and keeping as close as possible to the defendant's choice and to what lay within her control."[5] If, on the other hand, we assign liability "according to how things turned out," we improperly "attribute significance to chance rather than choice."[6]

What is choice? A minimal notion of choice can be defined in terms of intention and belief. I choose to bring about those results which I intend to bring about, or believe that I will bring about; I choose to take a risk of bringing about those results that I believe my action might bring about.[7] This gives us two "basic principles of criminal liability:" the "intent principle," that agents ought to be "held liable for what they intended to do, and not according to what actually did or did not occur;" and the "belief principle," that we must judge them "on the basis of what they believed they were doing, not on the basis of actual facts and circumstances which were not known to them at the time."[8]

This is not to say that agents are to be held liable *merely* for their intentions and beliefs. We are liable for what we *do*, not for our bare intentions or beliefs. The point is rather that a properly subjective description of my actions *qua* chosen, of the actions that can properly be ascribed to me, must describe those actions in terms of the intentions and beliefs with which they are done.

Exculpation and Inculpation

The intent and belief principles are meant, at least, to specify *necessary* conditions of criminal liability. As such, they often play an *exculpatory* role, to exempt from liability those who might otherwise be held liable. So someone who does not realize that her action might damage another's property should not be convicted of criminal damage, even if it "in fact creates an obvious risk" of such damage: she has not chosen to damage or risk damaging another's property.[9] A man who honestly but mistakenly believes that the woman with whom he has intercourse consents to it should not be convicted of rape, even if that belief is quite unreasonable: for he has not chosen to have, or to take a risk of having, intercourse without her consent.[10]

Even in this role, these principles are of course controversial. They preclude liability for negligence, since a negligent agent does not choose to take or create the risk as to which he is negligent.[11] They also require us to define recklessness, as an appropriate type of criminal fault, in terms of *conscious* risk-tak-

---

3   See further below, ch. 12.

4   See esp Ashworth, "Sharpening the Subjective Element in Criminal Liability" (hereafter, "Sharpening"), "Belief, Intent and Criminal Liability" (hereafter, "Belief"); Moore, "Choice, Character and Excuse," 29.

5   *Ashworth Attempts*, 742.

6   Ashworth, "Sharpening," 82; see further at nn. 14–22, below.

7   See J C. Smith, "Some Problems of the Reform of the Law of Offences Against the Person," 19.

8   Ashworth, "Belief," 7: for the "belief principle," see Cross, "Centenary Reflections on Prince's Case," 540.

9   Contrast, notoriously, *Caldwell* [1982] AC 341; *Elliott v C* [1983] 1 WLR 939.

10 See *Morgan* [1976] AC 182, *Cogan* [1976] QB 217.

11 Some "choice" theorists accept this implication (see e.g., Moore, *op. cit.* n. 4, above, 56–58): but see Hart, "Negligence, Mens Rea and Criminal Responsibility," on how the theory could be adapted to portray negligence as a genuine, if lesser, species of fault.

ing: but some would argue that an agent's criminal recklessness can be displayed in his very failure to notice the risk that he is taking or creating.[12]

Our present concern, however, is with the more ambitious role that these principles may be given as *inculpatory* principles, specifying *sufficient* conditions of criminal liability. This is the role which they play in subjectivist accounts of criminal attempts: they render criminally liable some who might be otherwise not liable at all, or liable only to a lesser degree. An otherwise innocent action may be transformed into a criminal attempt by the fact that it was done "with intent to commit an offence:" that it actualized a choice to commit an offence. The fact of failure in a criminal attempt does not by itself entitle the defendant to any lighter sentence than she would have received had it succeeded: for in making the attempt she chose to commit an offence; it is that choice, rather than the attempt's success or failure, which should determine her liability.

Why should choice play this more ambitious, inculpatory role? A concern to maximize citizens' control over their own lives requires only an exculpatory principle of choice:[13] that they should *not* find themselves criminally liable for what they did not choose to do. The answer seems to be that we must give choice this inculpatory role if we are to take seriously the relation of choice to culpability, the importance of "minimising the influence of chance" on criminal liability,[14] and the demand of justice that we "treat like cases alike." If two people each actualize a choice to commit murder, by trying to kill another person, they are equally culpable, equally deserving of punishment; the fact that one fails, or even that her attempt is inevitably doomed to failure by some kind of impossibility, cannot be allowed to reduce or negate her criminal liability. There is "no relevant moral difference" as far as their respective

culpability is concerned between the would-be killer who succeeds and one who fails:[15] since the former is properly held liable as having chosen to murder, so also must the latter.[16]

Can "Choice" Be Sufficient for Liability?

The belief and intent principles do not, as they stand, specify sufficient conditions of liability: for those who act under exculpatory kinds of duress, or as a result of exculpatory mental disorder, might, in the minimal sense defined by those principles, "choose" to act as they do. Nor indeed do they really "minimis[e] the influence of chance" on criminal liability.[17] They make "outcome-luck," "luck in the way our actions and projects turn out,"[18] irrelevant: if I am liable for all and only what I intend to do or believe myself to be doing, my liability will be unaffected by the success or failure of my actions, or by the truth or falsity of my beliefs about the results that they will or might bring about. However, there are other kinds of luck that bear on our actions.[19] It is a matter of "constitutive" luck that I have become the kind of person who would choose to commit a crime; it is a matter of "situational" luck that I find myself in a situation in which I am tempted or have the opportunity to commit a crime, or am not prevented from attempting to commit it. These are matters of "luck," in so far as they depend on factors outside my control, factors which can be said to make the difference between me and someone who does not attempt to commit a crime.

To solve these difficulties we need either a richer account of "choice" or an account of the precondi-

---

12 See my *Intention, Agency and Criminal Liability*, ch. 7.
13 See at n. 2, above.
14 See at n. 5, above.

15 See Ashworth, "Belief," 16–20.
16 Other subjectivists may be more concerned about the agent's dangerousness as manifested in her conduct, but such a concern bears more on a "character" conception of criminal liability; see below, ch. 7.
17 See at n. 5, above.
18 Nagel, "Moral Luck," 28; see Ashworth, "Taking the Consequences;" and above, ch. 4, at nn. 53–55.
19 See Nagel, *op cit.*; Feinberg, "Problematic Responsibility in Law and Morals."

tions of responsible choice. Such an account must enable us to say either that the person acting under exculpatory duress or mental disorder does not in the relevant sense "choose" to act as he does, or that in his case some essential precondition of responsible choice is absent. It must also allow us to insist that, whatever role might be played by "constitutive" and "situational" luck, it is still up to the agent (if those preconditions are satisfied) to choose how she will act in the situations in which she finds herself. It will thus need to be an account of "free will," as consisting in the capacity for choice; and of choice as a rational capacity which manifests our freedom as responsible agents.

I will not discuss here the form that this account might take,[20] save to note that its development might require us to attend to the ways in which an agent's "choices" are connected to broader aspects of her character.[21] However, given some such account, a subjectivist can then argue that whilst "outcome-luck" should indeed be irrelevant to criminal liability, we need not in the same way try to discount the influences of other types of luck: for once those types of luck have played their part, the agent still must and (if she has the capacity for rational choice which defines responsible agency) can choose how she will act, and can therefore be properly held responsible for her choice. Outcome-luck, however, helps to determine the actual results of our choices; and that is why it must still be discounted.[22]

• • •

6.4 The Conduct Element in Attempts

To see what kind of conduct element subjectivists might specify for attempts, we must ask why they

should require any such element, and what significance it has for them.

The Significance of Conduct

Fletcher thinks that on "the subjective theory" the conduct element serves a purely evidential function. For the core of liability is "the intention to violate a legally protected interest;" and "any act whatever" that justifies an inference to such a (firm) intention will then suffice for liability. Such a theory, he objects, subverts the principle of legality, which requires that liability be founded on an act which "violate[s some] preannounced standard," and "objectively conforms to criteria specified in advance."[23]

Some subjectivists do give the act-requirement such an evidential function:[24] not only those who take the basis of criminal liability to be an agent's dangerous disposition as revealed in his conduct,[25] but also some who take it to be the firm *intention* to commit an offence, whether such an intention is seen as constitutive of culpability or as indicative of future dangerousness.[26]

Intention is of course logically related to action: to intend to do X is to be disposed to do X unless something intervenes.[27] Sometimes, indeed, intentions have no existence independent of action: action flows directly from the agent's perception of her situation, without any intervening process of intention-formation.[28] However, there is often a

---

20 But see Pillsbury, "The Meaning of Deserved Punishment;" Moore, *op cit.* n. 4, above.

21 See below, ch. 7, at nn. 3–14.

22 See Lewis, "The Punishment that Leaves Something to Chance," 55–56.

23 *Fletcher*, esp 118–20, 157–59: for criticism, see Schulhofer's Review of *Fletcher*, Weinreb, "Manifest Criminality, Criminal Intent, and the 'Metamorphosis of Larceny;'" Galloway, "Patterns of Trying;" see further below, ch. 8.2.

24 See above, ch. 2, at n. 233.

25 See below, ch. 7, at n. 54.

26 See eg. G. Williams, "Police Control of Intending Criminals;" *Gordon*, 181 ("what is punished in attempts is basically the intention"); Husak, *Philosophy of Criminal Law*, 103–05 (see below, ch. 9, at nn. 23, 29–30).

27 See Malcolm, "The Conceivability of Mechanism."

28 See my *Intention, Agency, and Criminal Liability*, ch 3.2, ch. 6.

gap between intention and action: an agent might intend to do X, but find no opportunity to do it, or be prevented from doing it. Someone can thus have a firm criminal intention which he has not yet put into action; he is criminally culpable, but the law should not convict him until he takes some active steps to carry that intention out. For only action provides reliable public evidence of his intention (evidence that he would have committed the crime if he could); and not to require such evidence would encourage intrusively oppressive policing and unreliable convictions.[29]

This rationale for the act-requirement grounds it in considerations *external* to the agent's criminal culpability. A person who has the kind of firm criminal intention which constitutes criminal culpability escapes liability if she has, for whatever reason, not (yet) actualized it. She avoids liability, not because she is not someone whom the law should ideally aim to convict (she has the kind of culpability which concerns the law), but because for other reasons (to protect citizens against oppressive policing and unreliable convictions) the law should be so formulated that she avoids liability.

The "choice" version of subjectivism, however, is more plausibly read as making the conduct element *constitutive* of criminal culpability—of the particular kind of culpability which properly concerns the criminal law. What makes an agent criminally culpable, what constitutes him as a criminal, is not a bare criminal intention, but the *choice* to put that intention into effect; and choice is necessarily actualized in action. Someone who has formed a bare future intention to commit a crime has not yet, in this sense, "chosen" to commit the crime, since he must still choose to put (and could still choose not to put) that intention into effect; only in taking that further step does he define himself as a criminal. The conduct which constitutes the conduct element of an attempt is, therefore, not merely evidence of

some underlying criminal culpability that does not itself necessarily involve action: it partly constitutes *criminal* culpability.[30] On this view the act requirement is *internal* to the basic conception of criminal culpability.

Why, though, should we take this view, since someone who forms a bare criminal intention is surely already culpable? Part of the answer is that to take choice seriously as the basis of criminal liability is to take seriously our status as responsible autonomous agents: this requires the law to respect, and as far as possible to allow us to exercise, our capacity to determine our own actions; to leave us to decide for ourselves to abandon (or, therefore, to persist in) even our intended criminal enterprises.[31] Another part of the answer is that the culpability of someone who puts her criminal intention into action differs categorically from that of one who has yet to do so. The former has committed herself to the crime in a way that the latter has not; she has spurned one significant *locus poenitentiae*, in moving from (mere or bare) intention to action; she has embarked on doing harm.[32]

This version of subjectivism, we should notice, accords with the "principle of legality," in that agents will be criminally liable only for actions which violate a "preannounced standard."[33] It does not, admittedly, require some action which "objectively conforms to criteria specified in advance,"[34] if that means an action which can be recognized as potentially criminal independently of knowledge of the agent's intentions or beliefs: for it may be only her intentions and beliefs which render her apparently

---

29 See above, ch 2, at nn. 19, 78–89, 134–40, 150–51.

30 Cf. Morris, "Punishment for Thoughts," 9–15, on "firm resolve." "[T]he intent is the essence of the crime" (*Whybrow* [1951] 35 Cr. App. R. 141, 147); but that "intent" must be an *intention in action*.

31 See at n. 2, above; ch. 2, at nn. 20–21.

32 For a Kantian version of this argument see Chapman, "Agency and Contingency;" see below, ch. 8, at n. 35.

33 See at nn. 58–59, 94, above.

34 See at n. 94, above.

innocent action criminal, as an attempt. However, it is not clear why we should take *this* to be a requirement of the principle of legality.

What Kind of Conduct?

We still need to know what *kind* of conduct a criminal attempt should require on this account: how far should the intending criminal have progressed in actualizing his intention if he is to be criminally liable for an attempt?

The "fully subjective principle," Ashworth thinks, requires only "a minimal *actus reus*;" "the doing of any overt act with the necessary intention." Any more stringent act-requirement must be justified by other considerations which outweigh that principle: in particular, considerations of "individual rights and freedom from interference," and of leaving intending criminals a *locus poenitentiae*.[35]

Now the subjective principle is indeed *consistent* with a "first act" test for attempts, since an agent makes himself culpable, in a way that can properly concern the criminal law, as soon as he begins to put a criminal intention into action. However, it does not *require* us to adopt that test. There is a real difference in criminal culpability between one who has only just embarked on a criminal enterprise, and one who has come close to completing it. Someone who is still in the early stages of a criminal enterprise is less culpable (culpably responsible for less) than someone who has completed her criminal attempt: for she has not yet chosen to progress beyond the stage of mere preparation; she has not to the same extent actualized a criminal intention; nor has she, therefore, to the same degree actualized her potential criminal culpability. Since the subjectivist principle presumably does not require us to criminalize anyone who is, *to any degree*, culpable in a way which could concern the criminal law, some narrower specification of the conduct element in attempts would thus not compromise a subjectivist's "basic principles of

culpability and of equality of treatment:"[36] for it would distinguish more culpable from less culpable conduct.

Furthermore, a desire to leave the agent a *locus poenitentiae* is *internal* to the subjective principle, not a consideration which must be weighed against that principle: it is an implication of taking choice seriously.[37] This might seem to favour a "last act" test for attempts: for only then has the agent fully actualized his criminal choice, and spurned every *locus poenitentiae*.[38] Subjectivists can deal with this, however, by distinguishing complete, "last act," attempts from incomplete attempts, at least at the sentencing stage, and perhaps also at the stage of conviction.[39] They can still criminalize incomplete attempts, as marking at least a partial actualization of a criminal choice which makes the agent criminally culpable.

Of course, this does not tell us just where we should draw the line between "mere preparation" and incomplete attempt. Nor can the "choice" principle answer that question: subjectivists could favour, with equal consistency, either a "substantial step" test[40] or the "more than merely preparatory act" test.[41] Ashworth is therefore right to argue that we must appeal to considerations other than "the fully subjective principle" to decide just how narrowly, or broadly, the conduct element should be defined. However, this is not a matter of weighing the subjective principle *against* such other considerations: it is rather a matter of deciding, in the light of those other considerations, just how that principle should be applied.

No matter how the conduct element in attempts is specified, subjectivists must of course insist that that specification be applied to the agent's conduct as *she* conceived it: to her actions as described in

---

35 *Ashworth Attempts*, 750–51.

36 *Ashworth Attempts*, 757.
37 See at nn. 102–03, above.
38 See above, at nn. 30–31; and ch. 2, at n. 22.
39 See above, at nn. 33–37.
40 See *Ashworth Attempts*, 753.
41 See *Law Com 102*, para 2.49; above, ch. 2, at n. 186.

terms of her own intentions and beliefs. An action of "handling non-stolen goods," or of "administering an innoxious substance," is in fact neither "proximate" to nor "a substantial step" towards the offence of handling stolen goods or of administering a noxious thing.[42] However, an action of "handling stolen goods," or of "administering a noxious thing," clearly satisfies such tests; and if that is what the agent believed she was doing, that is how we must describe her action when we ask whether it constituted a criminal attempt.[43]

However, this is not to say that whether she is guilty of an attempt depends on whether she believed that her conduct satisfied whatever test the law specifies for the conduct element in attempts (that it was, for instance, "more than merely preparatory"). For even if the question of whether her conduct satisfied that test is a question of "fact" for the jury, rather than one of "law" for the judge,[44] that "fact" is not included in the "facts as she believed them to be" on which she is to be judged. The specification and application of any test for the conduct element in attempts involve an essentially normative judgment: about how far an agent must have progressed in a criminal enterprise to be properly convicted of an attempt.[45] That judgement might fail to be made by the legislature, the judge, or the jury—but not by the defendant herself.[46]

• • •

Subjectivism II: Character and Action

The previous chapter focused on that form of subjectivism which takes "choice" to be the key determinant of criminal liability. I am responsible, and should therefore be criminally liable, for and only for what I choose to do, since it is through my choices that I actualize myself as a free and responsible agent; thus the "subjective," on which criminal liability should depend, consists in choice, which can itself be minimally defined in terms of intention and belief.

We must now turn to a different form of subjectivism which bases criminal liability on "character," rather than on "choice."[47] This is still a subjectivist theory: it founds liability on what is "subjective" to the agent, rather than on the actual, "objective" nature or results of her conduct.[48] However, it offers a different account of those "subjective" grounds of liability: to explicate that account, we can begin by looking again at a problem faced by the "choice" theorist.

7.1 From "Choice" to "Character"

The problem for the "choice" theorist was that the "belief" and "intent" principles, which give more precise content to the doctrine that criminal liability should be determined by choice, do not specify *suf-*

---

42 See eg. *Haughton* v *Smith* 119751 AC 476, 499–500 (Lord Reid); and above, ch. 3, at nn. 189–90.

43 As both the 1981 Act and the *Model Penal Code* make clear; see above, at n. 80, and ch. 3, n. 249.

44 See Criminal Attempts Act 1981, s 4(3); above, ch. 2, at nn. 186–88.

45 See above, ch. 2, at nn. 212–20.

46 Similarly, a subjectivist judgement on whether an agent was reckless involves asking whether the risk which he believed he was taking *was* "reasonable," not whether he *believed* it was reasonable: the "facts as he believed then to be," on which he is judged, do not include the "fact" of the risk's (un)reasonableness.

47 See eg. Bayles, "Character, Purpose, and Criminal Responsibility;" Lacey, *State Punishment*; Pincoffs, "Legal Responsibility and Moral Character;" Brandt, "A Motivational Theory of Excuses in the Criminal Law;" Vuoso, "Background, Responsibility and Excuse." For criticisms, see Pillsbury, "The Meaning of Deserved Punishment;" Moore, "Choice, Character, and Excuse;" Dressler, "Reflections on Excusing Wrongdoers." (I will refer to these hereafter by italicized author's name.) For subtle discussions of the issues see Arenella, "Character, Choice and Moral Agency;" "Convicting the Morally Blameless." See also *Fletcher*, ch. 10.3; and my "Choice, Character and Criminal Liability."

48 But see at nn. 42–47, below for qualification.

ficient conditions of liability, since someone could in that sense "choose" to commit a crime but still not be criminally liable.[49] To meet that problem, the theorist must provide a richer account, either of "choice" or of the preconditions of free, responsible choice. That account must allow us to say of one who acts under exculpatory duress or mental disorder either that he does not in the appropriate sense "choose" to act as he does; or that an essential precondition of responsible choice is lacking. This is one route into something like a "character-based" conception of liability, since a plausible account of how or why such conditions as duress and mental disorder should exculpate will have to refer to the ways in which the agent's immediate "choice" is connected to, or disconnected from, the deeper structures of attitudes and concerns that constitute his character.[50]

Duress as an Excuse

We can sketch this argument by considering duress as an excuse.[51] Someone commits perjury because she is threatened with serious physical injury if she refuses to do so.[52] That duress might not be such as to *justify* her action. Nor is her action *involuntary*: she knows that she is giving false evidence, and "chooses" to do so, to avoid the threatened injury. None the less, she can be excused if her "will" was "overborne" by the threat;[53] or if "a person of reasonable firmness in [her] situation would have been unable to resist" it.[54] If we now ask what it means for someone to be "unable" to resist a threat, we might notice that other accounts of duress do not use that term. They

say instead that duress can excuse only if the threat was such that "a sober person of reasonable firmness sharing the characteristics of the defendant" would have acted as she did:[55] the threat must be "one which in all the circumstances (including any of (her) personal circumstances that affect its gravity) [s]he cannot reasonably be expected to resist,"[56] or which "human nature could not be expected to resist."[57]

These accounts imply that the notion of being "able" or "unable" to resist a threat is a normative one. In asking whether a defendant could "reasonably be expected" to resist this threat, we are asking about a normative, not a factual, expectation: that is, the question is not whether we could reasonably *predict* that she would resist the threat, but whether we can reasonably *demand* that she resist it; and the answer to that question is to be found by asking whether someone of "reasonable firmness" would have resisted it. The imagined person of "reasonable firmness" (the "reasonable person," we might say more simply) thus plays a *criterial*, not an *evidential*, role: that such a person would have resisted that threat is not merely (weak) evidence that this defendant was in fact "able" to resist it; it proves that this defendant was at fault in not resisting that threat.

A "sober person of reasonable firmness" is someone with a reasonable or proper regard for the law and the values it protects, and a reasonable or proper degree of courage: what is "reasonable" here is what we can reasonably expect or demand of citizens. To say that such a person would have resisted a particular threat is thus to say that anyone with the kind of regard for the law and its values, and the degree of courage that can properly be demanded of any citizen, would have resisted it. From this it follows that someone who gives in to that threat lacks either that reasonable regard for the law and its values, or that reasonable degree of courage, and is thus justly

---

49 See above, ch. 6, at nn. 17–21.

50 For more detailed discussion see my *op cit.* n. 1, above, 350–61.

51 See *1989 Draft Code*, cl 42; *Model Penal Code*, s.2.09; *Smith & Hogan*, 232–42; *LaFave & Scott*, 432–41.

52 See *Hudson and Taylor* [1971] 2 QB 202.

53 Ibid., 206.

54 *Model Penal Code*, s2.09(1). See also Aristotle, *Nicomachean Ethics*, III.1, 1110a23–6, on actions done "under pressure which overstrains human nature and which no one could withstand."

---

55 *Graham* [1982] 74 Cr App. R. 235, 241.

56 *1989 Draft Code*, cl 42(3)(b).

57 *Stratton* (1779) 1 Doug KB 239.

condemned. On the other hand, to say that such a person would have given in is to say that (even) someone with a proper regard for the law and its values, and with a proper degree of courage, would have given in: in which case this defendant's giving in did not display a lack or failing for which she can properly be condemned.[58]

Of course, it remains to be asked whether a reasonable person *sharing the characteristics of the defendant*" would have withstood that threat, and we must thus determine which of this defendant's characteristics to ascribe to the "reasonable person." None the less, we can at least now see how to tackle that task: we should ascribe to the reasonable person any of the defendant's actual characteristics that affected her response to the threat, *other than* characteristics which involve either some lack of reasonable regard for the law and its values, or a lack of reasonable courage. So we ascribe to the reasonable person, for instance, this defendant's pathological fear of spiders, but not her unusual (non-pathological) lack of concern for the property rights of others.

From "Choice" to "Character"

This account of the defence of duress suggests that criminal liability does depend partly on "character," and not purely on "choice." We must look behind the defendant's immediate choice to give in to the threat, to those attitudes or concerns (a disregard for the law and its values; an excess concern for one's own safety; cowardice) which her choice did or did not manifest: but these are aspects of her character.[59]

I think that similar conclusions would emerge from an account of other defences, such as mental disorder or provocation. The agent is to be excused because, although his criminal action was intention-

al, indeed "chosen," it did not manifest that kind of disregard for, or indifference to, the interests and rights of others, or the law and its values, for which agents are properly condemned. We must, therefore, attend not merely to his actions or choices themselves, but to their connection with, or disconnection from, that deeper set of attitudes and concerns which partly constitute his character.

This argument is one aspect of a wider critique of the "choice" conception of criminal liability: that it offers no adequate account of what it is to be a responsible agent, or of what makes an action mine as its responsible agent. What matters is not simply whether an action is "chosen," but how that choice is related to the agent's attitudes and concerns, her conceptions of value and of reasons for action; and these are aspects of her character. This reflects a more general critique of the (roughly) Kantian conception of moral agency and moral worth as residing in "the will," which sometimes inspires "choice" theorists.[60] The moral character of a person's actions, the critic argues, and her moral standing as the agent of those actions, depend not solely or primarily upon what she "chooses" to do, but on those structures of attitudes, motives, and values from which action and choice flow—on the character which her actions manifest.

What kind of account of criminal liability could emerge from such anti-Kantian thoughts about moral agency and worth? We must question more closely what a "character" theorist takes to be the proper ground of criminal liability.

7.2 Character and Criminal Liability

The criminal process should properly focus, the "character" theorist argues, not on the particular ac-

---

58 The normative character of such judgments of what a person "could" or "could not" resist appears in Aristotle's remark that "some acts, perhaps, we cannot be forced to do, but ought rather to face death after the most fearful sufferings" (*Nicomachean Ethics*, 1110a26–8).

59 See Kadish, "Excusing Crime," 94–95.

60 See *Moore*, and his *Act and Crime*, 46–53. For versions of this critique see Murdoch, *The Sovereignty of Good*; B. Williams, *Problems of the Self*, and *Moral Luck*; Blum, *Friendship, Altruism, and Morality*, and *Moral Perception and Particularity*; Winch, "Moral Integrity;" Hudson, *Human Character and Morality*.

tion for which the defendant is formally convicted, but on some character trait which that criminal action revealed. He is properly convicted if and because his action warranted an inference to some undesirable character trait. If he is acquitted because he lacked the requisite fault element, or had some further defence, this is because the inference from criminal action to undesirable character trait was blocked.

D breaks *V*'s window and is charged with criminal damage. If he broke the window intentionally or recklessly, without lawful excuse, he merits conviction:[61] we can infer from his conduct an undesirable character trait that merits condemnation and punishment. That trait might be described as "the absence of an adequate aversion" to infringing the property rights of others;[62] or as a "practical attitude" of "hostility or indifference towards, or rejection of, either that particular norm [prohibiting criminal damage] or the standards of the criminal law in general."[63]

If, however, he acted without the requisite fault element or has some suitable defence, then he merits acquittal: for no inference to any undesirable character trait is warranted. If he reasonably did not realize that what he was doing might damage another's property, we cannot infer any undesirable character trait from his action. If he broke the window intentionally but under duress (a threat of serious injury if he refused to do so), we can infer something about his character: that he values his own physical safety more than property; or that he lacks the courage to resist such a threat. However, if we think that a person of "reasonable firmness" would have given in to that threat, we cannot infer a *defective* character trait: we cannot infer that he had less regard for the property rights of others or for the law's norms, or less courage in relation to those rights and norms, than we can reasonably expect any citizen to have.

This sketch raises various questions. Most immediately, what are character traits? What kinds of character trait should make a person criminally liable? Why should the law focus on "character?"

Character Traits

Character traits are relatively stable patterns of thought, emotion, and action. They are analysed dispositionally: as dispositions to act in certain ways, to be motivated or affected by certain kinds of consideration, to think in certain ways. Thus the character trait of generosity involves a disposition to give (either money or other goods, such as time), especially to those in need, and even when the giving involves real deprivation. It also involves a disposition to be motivated to give by the other's need—rather than, for instance, by a desire for reward—and to be moved to sympathy by another's need.[64] Generosity also involves a disposition to notice and attend to others' needs as reasons for action to help them. Meanness, by contrast, involves the absence of such dispositions (for some character traits must be understood in such essentially negative terms): a mean person is not disposed to be motivated to act, or to be moved to sympathy, by the needs of others; nor is he disposed even to notice their needs or to see them as a source of reasons for action. His meanness might also involve more positive dispositions: his thoughts, his attention, his deliberations and motivations are structured by an excessive concern to preserve his own money or other goods.

A person's character traits embody her settled values, concerns, and attitudes. We can thus see several reasons why the criminal law should be concerned with character, in particular with those aspects of character which constitute virtues or vices. First, what the law demands of us is not simply a set of discrete acts, but certain dispositions: of obedience to its rules, and of respect for the values it protects. This demands particular character traits: *dispositions*

---

61 See Criminal Damage Act 1971, 5 1(1).
62 See *Brandt*, 174.
63 *Lacey*, 76.

64 See Blum, *Friendship, Altruism and Morality*, 146–49.

of thought, attitude, and motivation which enable us to respond appropriately to the law.[65] Secondly, in so far as punishment has any corrective aim, what justifies punishment must be something about the offender that requires correction: this cannot be the particular past action or choice for which he was convicted; it must be an underlying, continuing character trait, revealed by his action.[66] Thirdly, what makes my actions "mine," as their responsible agent, is their relationship to my character: they are mine to the extent that they flow from my character: the relationship between action and character is thus crucial if I am to be justly condemned and punished for what I do.[67]

Identifying Criminal Character Traits

The suggestion that the criminal law should focus on "character" is likely to provoke familiar liberal anxieties. The deep structures of thought and motivation which constitute our *moral* characters are certainly proper objects of moral appraisal; and a concern with each other's moral character is proper in close personal relationships, between friends and within families. However, it is surely not the proper task of the criminal law to detect and punish moral vice, or to take such interest in citizens' moral characters. Its proper task is to declare and enforce the fairly minimal standards of conduct which are necessary for any social life: most obviously, to forbid and to prevent those kinds of conduct which harm or might harm the central interests which the law should protect. The law can properly demand that

we conform our conduct to its requirements, and punish us if we wilfully fail to do so. But it should not seek to pry into the inner reaches of our characters; for the primary goal of punishment should be rational deterrence, and/or the censure of wrongful conduct, not moral correction or reform.[68]

A "character" conception of criminal liability can certainly be related to a more communitarian account of the proper nature and purposes of the criminal law: one which portrays the law, being the law of a moral community, as having a proper interest in the moral character of its citizens.[69] "Character" theorists, though, more usually meet such liberal worries by limiting the extent of the law's interest in character. It is not properly interested in every aspect of citizens' moral characters, but only in those character traits that are defective or undesirable because they are liable to lead to familiar types of criminal conduct: types of conduct which, liberals would agree, should be criminal because they are likely to infringe rights or injure interests which the law should protect. The law is not a general moral inquisitor; it is concerned only with dangerous character traits which are liable to produce obviously harmful conduct.

There are, however, psychological attributes which might result in conduct that harms the legally protected interests of others, but which we would not count as "defective character traits" warranting criminal liability. For example, the conduct of one who "systematically, characteristically makes unreasonable mistakes, causing danger to the interests of others" *might* reveal "a genuine practical indifference to the interests protected by the criminal

---

65 See *Pincoffs*.

66 Hence the *Model Penal Code*'s focus on "dangerous agents:" see above, ch. 2, at n. 146; ch. 4, at nn. 2–3; and below, at nn. 42–47.

67 Must we then ask whether I am responsible for my character (see Aristotle *Nicomachean Ethics* 111.5; *Pincoffs*, 919–23; Arenella, "Character, Choice and Moral Agency")? "Character" theorists might rather argue what we *are* our characters, and are therefore responsible for the actions which flow from them: see *Lacey*, 67–68; *Vuoso*, 1679–81; *Moore*, 44–46.

68 Von Hirsch, *Censure and Sanctions* is a good example of such a liberal concern to limit the scope and ambitions of the criminal law.

69 See my *op cit.* n. 1, above, 380–83; and my "Penal Communications," 45–57. *Lacey's* character-based account of criminal liability is related to a qualifiedly communitarian perspective.

law"[70] which is criminally culpable. On the other hand, it might reflect a purely cognitive deficiency in intelligence, which is surely not criminally culpable. Someone who is seriously mentally disordered might have dispositions of thought and motivation that are dangerous because they are liable to lead to criminal conduct: but should he be criminally liable?

Bayles argues that mentally disordered criminals *should* be convicted: for their conduct is "good evidence of an undesirable character trait justifying a social response" (although that "social response" need not be punishment, since other responses "may be more effective and appropriate").[71] However, this is to abandon any attempt to justify a "character" theory of *criminal liability*: it destroys the distinction, vital to any system of law and punishment, between condemning and punishing responsible wrong-doers for their crimes, and diagnosing and treating those who are dangerous to themselves or to others. "Character" theorists who want to rationalize something like our existing structures of criminal law and punishment must be able to rationalize this central distinction.[72]

They can do this by reminding us first that defects of *character* are defects of attitude or motivation. Lack of intelligence is thus not a defective character trait warranting liability, so long as it involves, not a lack of appropriate motivation, but a cognitive deficiency inhibiting the actualization of that respect for the rights and interests of others which a well-meaning but stupid person does have. They can argue, secondly, that mental disorder does not involve a kind of "defective character trait" which merits criminal liability. For character, as an object of moral or legal criticism, consists in a person's *rational* dispositions of thought, feeling, and motivation—those which reflect an intelligible conception of reality and value. It is, though, a defining feature of mental disorder that it involves *non*-rational, or rationally unintelligible, patterns of thought, feeling, and motivation. This means that we cannot engage with the mentally disordered person in a critical discussion of his conduct or of what motivated it. We cannot then hold him morally responsible or criminally liable, since moral criticism and criminal condemnation are (or should be) modes of communication with a rational agent about her intelligible attitudes and actions.[73]

We now have a clearer idea of the kinds of character trait which are, on this account, the proper concern of the criminal law. We do not yet know enough about the relationship between such character traits and the particular kinds of action which are the immediate focus of the criminal process: about why, if criminal liability is founded on defective character traits, it should formally depend on whether the defendant committed a specified type of action. Before tackling that central question, we can ask what implications the "character" conception of liability might have for the law of attempts....

• • •

7.4 Character, Action, and Liability

"Character" theorists who see the purpose of punishing attempts as being to neutralize dangerous individuals," or to apply "corrective sanctions" to a defendant's "anti-social disposition"[74] should favour a broad specification of the conduct element in attempts. For their concern is not with whether the defendant's particular actions were themselves

---

70 *Lacey*, 66.

71 *Bayles*, 17–18.

72 I will not try here to justify the claim that we *should* look for an account of criminal liability, rather than merely for an account of the kinds of dangerous condition which warrant a "social response" but see my *Trials and Punishments*.

73 See my "Mental Disorder and Criminal Responsibility;" *Lacey*, 76.

74 *Model Penal Code*, Commentary to s5.01, 323 (see 321–33 generally), and to s.5.05, 490 (see at n. 30, above): see above, ch. 2, at nn. 146–56.

"dangerously proximate" to the completed crime,[75] or whether she had spurned some significant *locus poenitentiae*:[76] it is with whether she had provided adequate evidence of her dangerousness or "anti-social disposition;" and, the *Model Penal Code* argues, that concern is satisfied if her actions constituted "a substantial step" towards the commission of the crime, or were "strongly corroborative of [her] criminal purpose."[77]

Why, though, should action be required at all: why should the law not convict and punish anyone who can be shown to have the relevant type of "anti-social disposition," whether or not it has yet been actualized in a criminal enterprise? Or, if action should be required, why require more than a "first act," since "any act done for the purpose of committing a crime is an act that demonstrates dangerousness?"[78]

Justifying the "Act Requirement"

One obvious rationale for a substantial act requirement is that only conduct going beyond a "first act" provides sufficient *evidence* of the defendant's "anti-social disposition," especially if his disposition must involve some "firmness of criminal purpose:" evidence, that is, which is reasonably reliable, and obtainable by reasonably non-oppressive and non-intrusive means. To subject people to punishment without such evidence would invite oppressively intrusive modes of police investigation, and risk convicting too many innocents.[79]

---

75 See above, ch2, at nn. 99–101.

76 See above, ch2, at n. 22; ch. 6, at nn. 30–31, 108–10.

77 S 5.01 (1)(c)–(2); see above, ch. 2, at nn. 30–31, 108–10.

78 Commentary to s 5.01, 326; see above, ch. 2, at nn. 15–16.

79 See *Model Penal Code*, Commentary to s5.01, 326–31. See also *Bayles*, 19; *Brandt*, 189. The force of such an argument depends, of course, on large empirical claims about the likely costs and benefits of a law which did not include an "act requirement"—claims which it is not easy to assess (see above, ch. 4, at nn. 38–44; ch. 6, at n. 129).

This justification of the act requirement for attempts (and for criminal liability generally) grounds it in considerations *external* to the agent's criminality: a person might have an "anti-social disposition" which requires "corrective sanction," but escape liability because a law which allowed for her conviction would also have other unacceptable implications.[80] It thus portrays the connection between antisocial disposition or undesirable character trait and criminal conduct as *contingent*: it could be true that someone has a dangerous character trait, or a criminally antisocial disposition, though she has never yet exhibited it in criminal conduct.

Now some theorists argue that the relationship between character and action is generally contingent: someone could *be* courageous, although she has never *acted* courageously, if she has never faced a situation calling for courage.[81] As a *general* claim about the relationship between character and action, I think this is mistaken: a courageous person is not merely someone who *would* behave courageously, but someone who *does* behave courageously; if someone has never yet faced a situation calling for courage, the point is not that we might not know whether she is courageous, but that there is as yet no fact of the matter to be known.[82] However, it might be more plausible as a claim about the relationship between *criminal* character and *criminal* conduct.

First, it could surely be true (and knowable) that someone has a criminal trait (a trait such that he would, in certain likely circumstances, attempt to commit a crime), although he has as yet done nothing criminal: the kind of dishonesty which would motivate theft or fraud, for instance, could be clearly manifested in non-criminal types of dishonest behaviour. Secondly, if (for the reasons indicated above) anything more than a "first act" is specified as the conduct element in attempts, an intending

---

80 See above, ch. 6, at nn. 95–101.

81 For instance, Brandt, "Traits of Character: A Conceptual Analysis," 26; *Moore*, 41.

82 See Dummett, *Truth and Other Enigmas*, 14–16.

criminal could have begun to manifest his criminal disposition in conduct which is not yet criminal, because it does not yet constitute a "substantial step" towards the crime. Thus, even if the general connection between character traits and action is logical or constitutive, rather than contingent, that between *criminal* character traits (those that should attract criminal liability) and *criminal* action (conduct that the law defines as criminal) is contingent; and the reasons for having an act requirement at all, or for requiring more than a "first act," are indeed external to the underlying conception of criminal liability.

The force of the first of these arguments depends partly on whether there is any substantive, pre-legal difference between what the law defines as criminal and what it defines as non-criminal. Is the manifested disposition to engage in non-criminal kinds of dishonest conduct already a disposition to engage in *criminally* dishonest conduct; or could we argue that, given the substantial moral difference between criminal and non-criminal types of dishonesty, one who manifests a disposition to non-criminal kinds of dishonesty does not yet or thereby manifest a *criminally* dishonest disposition? It also depends on what significance we should attach to a disposition to break the law as such, as distinct from a disposition to engage in conduct which the law in fact prohibits.[83] However, the second argument seems to be strong enough by itself to establish the desired conclusion: that the connection between criminal conduct and criminal character trait is indeed contingent and evidential. Nor should this seem startling: for many legal rules, substantive as well as procedural, aim not so much to define criminality as to protect citizens against mistaken convictions and oppressive policing; and such rules will typically allow some who are indeed criminal to escape liability.

"Choice" theorists, and others, might still be unhappy with this account of the act requirement, since it still implies that offenders are punished essentially for what they *are*—whereas a system of law which is to respect its citizens as responsible agents should surely punish them only for what they *do*.[84] There is, though, another question for the "character" theorist to answer: why should one criminal action be *sufficient*, as well as *necessary*, for criminal liability?

How Can One Criminal Action Be Sufficient?

If what makes a person criminally liable is a settled or lasting disposition (for that is what requires correction), and if the relationship between criminal disposition and criminal action is contingent: how can one criminal action alone suffice to establish the existence of a criminal disposition? For on this account, someone could surely commit one criminal action without having a settled criminal disposition: before convicting and punishing a defendant who was proved to have committed a criminal action (with the usually appropriate fault element), courts should therefore have to determine whether that one action really did manifest an undesirably dangerous disposition, and exempt her from criminal liability if it did not.

It is not enough simply to say that, while the "attitudes" which constitute the various orthodox types of criminal fault might indeed be "fleeting," the law operates with "a general presumption that the combination of behaviour and attitude indicates an undesirable character trait:"[85] we need to know what justifies that presumption. Nor is it enough to say that this admittedly artificial presumption protects the defendant "against a free-ranging inquiry of the state into his moral worth."[86] The purpose of such an inquiry would be to determine whether the inference to an undesirable character trait (for which the defendant's criminal conduct provided strong grounds) could be rebutted, thus exempting him

---

83 On both these points see above, ch. 6, at nn. 65–72.

84 Compare *Vuoso*, 1673: "[a] person is good or bad directly because of what he is, and not directly because of what he *does*." See further below, at n. 78.

85 *Bayles*, 10.

86 *Fletcher*, 801.

from liability; and any defendant who objected to this (possibly exculpating) inquiry could avoid it by pleading guilty.

Lacey argues that courts should indeed often "look more broadly at the defendant's attitudes as manifested in other relevant areas of behaviour" to establish "the inference from action to disposition;" and implies that defendants should not be held criminally liable for "out of character" actions in which their "settled dispositions" are not "centrally expressed."[87] "Choice" theorists might reply that the mere fact that a crime was "out of character" for a defendant surely should not exempt her from conviction and punishment; if the "character" theory would exempt her, that theory is unacceptable.[88]

To clarify this issue, however, we must ask more carefully just what it is for a crime to be "out of character."

A trusted employee steals a large sum from his employer; this is his first and only act of criminal dishonesty. What might lead us to count this action as "out of character?" Would it also incline us to acquit him of theft?

The mere fact that he had not previously stolen does not render his action out of character. Perhaps this was the first opportunity he had to steal without (he thought) being detected: even if he was not actually waiting for such an opportunity, in taking it he showed himself to be criminally dishonest—disposed to steal if an opportunity arose.

Perhaps his action was weak-willed, rather than whole-heartedly larcenous: on this one occasion he gave in to the temptation to do what he knew was wrong, and now bitterly repents it. Lacey implies that such weak-willed actions are "out of character." Actions should attract liability (i.e., are "in character") only when they are "genuinely expressive of the agent's relevant disposition;" only if they are actions

"with which the agent truly identifies, and can call her own:"[89] but my weak-willed actions flow from motives or dispositions which I *disown* (that is what makes them *weak-willed*). None the less, we surely are morally, and must be criminally, liable for weak-willed actions, and they do reflect relevant character traits: a lack of commitment to the values they infringe; weakness in the face of temptation.[90]

Perhaps the theft was motivated by some change in his situation which provoked a change in his attitudes. A sudden need of money, or the discovery that his employer had been exploiting him, led him to think (as he had not previously thought) that such theft was morally permissible, or induced a new willingness to steal. Whether this change of attitude is lasting or temporary however, he must surely still be criminally liable (unless those circumstances *justified* his action); and his action was still "in character," as reflecting attitudes and values which intelligibly developed his existing character.

We might, though, give a different account: of the devastating effect on an honest man of suddenly desperate need (for money to get treatment for his seriously ill child), or of perceived injustice (being made redundant, for no good reason that he could see, from a job to which he had devoted himself for twenty years). We might now ascribe his theft not to vice (greed, a lack of respect for others' rights), nor to weakness of will (failing to resist temptation that an honest person would resist), but to emotional disturbance: his anxiety, his rage, was such that it impaired his capacity to guide his actions by the values to which he was truly committed. His action still reveals something about him: that he is a person who breaks down in this way in such a situation. However, if we think that he should be excused (and this thought is more plausible in this case), we might say that his action was "out of character:" it did not

---

87 *Lacey*, 75, 68 ("it is unfair to hold people responsible" for "out of character" actions).

88 See *Moore*, 51–54; *Dressler*, 697.

89 *Lacey*, 77; contrast *Moore*, 42–43 on "narrow" and "broad" views of character.

90 See Aristotle, *Nicomachean Ethics* 113, II–III, VI–VII.

show him to be really dishonest, or manifest a culpably dishonest character.[91]

I think that some such account must be given if we are to portray his theft as "out of character" in any way which could plausibly bear on his criminal liability. One thing that this suggests is that the controversy between "choice" and "character" theorists over "out of character" actions is spurious. For the "choice" theorist should surely say that in this case the thief did not "freely choose" to do wrong, since his capacity for free, responsible choice (to guide his actions by a rational conception of the good) was impaired. Then, however, it could never be the case that an agent "freely chooses to do wrong" (i.e., he has the capacity and a fair opportunity not to so choose), and yet the action is "out of character" for that agent:[92] criminal actions which a "character" theorist could plausibly excuse as being "out of character" are precisely those that "choice" theorists would excuse as being not "freely chosen."

Criminal Action as Constitutive of Criminal Character

The preceding discussion also suggests that we should see criminal actions as *constitutive* of, and not merely as evidence for, the kinds of "character trait" or "disposition" which should concern the criminal law. A single act of theft, committed by someone who is not mentally disordered or acting under an exculpating kind of pressure, is *logically sufficient* for criminal liability: that is, it is sufficient not because it provides empirically adequate evidence for a settled disposition which is likely to issue in further thefts (for it suffices to convict a weak-willed thief who we are sure will not steal again), but because it defines the agent as a dishonest thief. We do not make a contingent *inference* from this dishonest action to a distinct character trait or disposition that

caused it: the action itself is constitutive of the thief's criminal dishonesty, since it manifests his dishonest willingness to steal—to *act* thus is to *be* dishonest. By contrast, what makes a person's action "out of character," in the relevant sense, is not just its inconsistency with the settled dispositions he has displayed in other contexts, but that it does not reveal "character" at all: it not display the valuational and motivational structure of attitudes and practical reasoning in which "character," as an object of moral appraisal, consists.

Of course the attitudes, the structures of value and motivation, that we can see displayed in the thief's action, and cannot see displayed in "out of character" action, are not merely fleeting aspects of a person's psychology. This is the element of truth in the "character" theory: that the actions for which a person is convicted and punished must be "hers;" they must be suitably related to attitudes or motives which are aspects of her continuing identity as a person. This is not to say that she is convicted and punished *for* those character traits, *rather than* for the actions in which they are manifested: for what properly concerns the criminal law, I am arguing, are the agent's practical attitudes *as manifested in and constituted by* her criminal actions.

But if one (non-disordered, non-excused) criminal action is thus logically or constitutively, rather than merely evidentially, sufficient for criminal liability, we might also say that criminal action should be constitutively, rather than merely evidentially, necessary for criminal liability.[93] That is, the "act" requirement is not just an evidential requirement grounded in considerations external to the basic conception of criminal liability: rather, it is only by criminal action that an agent constitutes herself as criminally culpable. We might know of someone who has not yet committed theft that she is *potentially* a thief: given the dispositions or character traits that she has already manifested, we can predict confidently that in

---

91 We might add that any reasonable person would or might have reacted as he did in that situation: see at nn. 5–13 above, on duress.

92 *Moore*, 51.

93 See at nn. 53–59, above.

certain likely circumstances she will or would commit theft. She is, however, not yet a thief; nor does she yet, on this account, *actually* have a criminally dishonest character: only by committing theft does she constitute herself as a thief, and her character as criminally dishonest.[94]

Why should we accept such an account of the notion of a criminal character trait or disposition (a character trait or disposition of a kind warranting criminal liability), instead of the simpler view that it is a trait or disposition which will predictably result in criminal conduct, but need not logically yet have done so?

One answer is that if the law is to treat its citizens as rational and responsible agents (as it should), it must be an "enterprise of subjecting human conduct to the governance of rules,"[95] not just of controlling their conduct by whatever means might be economically effective. That is, it should seek to guide their conduct by giving them good reasons to obey its legitimate requirements, thus treating them as rational agents who are susceptible to rational persuasion—who can recognize and act in accordance with the reasons for action that it provides. However, this also requires that it should subject them to criminal sanctions only if or when they have definitively refused to recognize or to act in accordance with those reasons: for if they were to be made liable to sanctions because of what they *would* do or *might* do, rather than because of what they have actually done, they would no longer be treated as rational agents who can, and should therefore be allowed to, determine their own conduct. We may be certain that someone *will* break the law, that he will not be dissuaded from doing so by the reasons which the law offers him: but we must still treat him as someone who could be rationally persuaded to obey, even at the last moment.[96]

If we take criminal conduct to be merely evidence of a kind of disposition which should attract criminal liability, and if dispositions should attract liability because they are likely to result in criminally harmful conduct (and so require correction),[97] then people are being held criminally liable and punished because of what they will or might do, and are therefore not being treated as responsible agents. By contrast, this alternative account respects the citizens' capacities for rational and responsible agency: it holds them criminally liable only when they actually engage in criminal conduct, not because only then do we have appropriate evidence of their dangerous disposition, but because only then do they constitute, or actualize, themselves as having a criminal character.[98]

"Choice" v. "Character:" A False Dichotomy?

It might seem that I am trying to import central elements of the "choice" conception into the "character" conception: although I have not talked explicitly about leaving citizens free to "choose" for themselves whether to break the law, the argument sketched above obviously has close affinities with the kinds of argument that could be offered by a "choice" theorist for a restrictive specification of the conduct element in attempts.[99] The account suggested here, which makes criminal action both necessary and sufficient for criminal liability because it is constitutive of criminality, is certainly at odds with the perspective of many "character" theorists, whose concern is precisely with the agent's "dangerousness" as evidenced

---

94 See above, ch. 6, at nn. 95–101, for an analogous argument in relation to the "choice" conception.

95 Fuller, *The Morality of Law,* 122.

96 See my *Trials and Punishments,* esp chs. 3, 6.3–4.

97 See above, at nn. 23, 47.

98 So this account provides *a* reason for a "last act" test for attempt: only then has the agent fully actualized her criminal character. While it does require the conduct element to be fairly restrictively defined, however, it does not *require* a "last act" test, since someone who is engaged in, but has not yet completed, a criminal attempt has done *something* to constitute herself as a criminal: see above, ch. 6, at nn. 106–10, and below ch. 13, at nn. 184–87.

99 See above, ch. 6, at nn. 101–02, 106–10.

but not constituted by her conduct. It also differs from the "choice" conception, however, in that it takes action, and the practical attitudes which actions manifest, rather than "choice," to be the proper foundation of liability.

Indeed, an account which takes "action," rather than "character" or "choice," as the proper basis of criminal liability can claim to dissolve the conflict between "choice" and "character" conceptions of liability, by arguing that each of those two conceptions captures but also distorts part of the truth.

A "character" conception expresses a significant truth about *who* can be held criminally liable: that only moral agents, whose actions exhibit the structures of thought, attitude, and motivation that constitute "character," should be held liable. For only such agents are responsible for, as the authors of, their actions; so only they can be called to answer for their wrongful actions through the criminal process of trial and punishment, to accept those actions as theirs, and to repent them.[100] It also reminds us that actions can be criminally wrongful not merely because they reflect some wrongful *choice*, but because of the *attitudes* that they manifest: an attitude of disrespect for, or indifference to, the rights and interests of others, for instance. However, it distorts these truths by portraying the connection between action and character as contingent and inferential, and by suggesting that offenders are liable for (because of) their attitudes or dispositions, *rather than* for their actions. We should say instead that offenders are liable for their actions *as manifesting* the kinds of practical attitude which properly concern the criminal law; that those attitudes are constituted, not merely evidenced, by the actions which display them.

The "choice" conception expresses a significant truth about *that for which* agents can properly be held liable: they should be called to answer, and be convicted and punished, for their actions, not for what they "are" in so far as that is distinct from what they "do." It distorts that truth, though, by defining "action" in terms of "choice:" it fails to allow for the ways in which "choices" can be understood as responsible or culpable only in virtue of their relation to "character;"[101] and it wrongly supposes that *only* choice can ground criminal liability.[102]

The "character" theorist might say that we are criminally liable for what we *are*, rather than for what we *do*; "choice" theorists will respond that we should be liable for what we (choose to) *do*, rather than for what we *are*.[103] This is a spurious contrast: in the eyes of the criminal law what a person "is" consists in what she "does;" her criminal character is constituted by the character of her actions alone. The law is indeed interested in "character," and not merely in "choice:" but what it is interested in is the character of our actions, not in "character" as distinct from action.

These points can be briefly illustrated by looking at recklessness as a species of criminal fault. "Choice" theorists insist that recklessness must be defined in terms of *conscious* risk-taking: I choose to take or to create only those risks which I realize that I am taking or creating.[104] A critic might respond that recklessness should rather be understood as a species of culpable indifference to the rights and interests of others: an indifference which might be displayed in an agent's very failure to notice the obvious risk that her action creates; and a "character" theorist might argue that that indifference is an undesirable or dangerous character trait which we can empirically infer from her conduct. But that would be a mistake: the kind of "indifference" which properly concerns the criminal law is *practical* indifference, an indifference *in action* (not in feeling as distinct from action); and

---

100 For the communicative conception of the criminal process that underpins these remarks see my *Trials and Punishments*.

101 See at nn. 3–14, above.
102 See above, at ch. 6, at nn. 11–12.
103 See at n. 59, above.
104 See above, ch. 6, at nn. 7–10.

such indifference is displayed only in actively taking or creating an unreasonable risk of causing harm.[105]

I will say more later about *why* we should take action to be the proper basis of criminal liability.[106] We must turn now to a further question about the concept of "action" as it should figure in this context.

Both "choice" and "character" conceptions of criminal liability are subjectivist: they hold that liability should be determined, not by the "objective" aspects of the agent's action (its actual impact on the world), but by its "subjective" dimension—by the intentions and beliefs with which he acted, or by the attitudes or dispositions which his action revealed. The actions which we ascribe to an agent, in assigning criminal liability, should therefore be identified and described in subjective terms: their objective aspects, their actual circumstances and consequences, are irrelevant. By contrast, "objectivist" theories of liability argue that the actions which are to be ascribed to agents, for which they are to be criminally liable, cannot be identified in such purely subjective terms: that "action," in this as in other contexts, must be understood (in part) objectively. We must now see what such an objectivist claim involves ...

Works Cited in Notes

American Law Institute, *Model Penal Code* (text and commentaries; Philadelphia: American Law Institute, 1985).

Arenella, P., "Character, Choice and Moral Agency," *Social Philosophy and Policy* 7 (1990), 59–83.

——. "Convicting the Morally Blameless: Reassessing the Relationship between Legal and Moral Accountability," *UCLA LR* 39 (1992), 1511–622.

Aristotle, *Nicomachean Ethics* (trans. Ross; Oxford: OUP, 1980).

Ashworth, A.J., "Sharpening the Subjective Element in Criminal Liability," in R.A. Duff and N.E. Simmonds (eds.), *Philosophy and the Criminal Law* (Wiesbaden: Franz Steiner, 1984), 79–89.

——. "Belief, Intent and Criminal Liability," in J. Eekelaar and J. Bell (eds.), *Oxford Essays in Jurisprudence*, 3rd Series (Oxford: OUP, 1987), 1–31.

——. "Taking the Consequences," in S. Shute, J. Gardener, J. Horder (eds.), *Action and Value in Criminal Law* (Oxford: OUP, 1993), 107–24.

——. *Principles of Criminal Law* (2nd ed.; Oxford: OUP, 1995).

Bayles, A.C., "Character, Purpose and Criminal Responsibility," *Law and Philosophy* 1 (1982), 5–20.

Blum, L., *Friendship, Altruism and Morality* (London: Routledge, 1980).

——. *Moral Perception and Particularity* (Cambridge: CUP, 1994).

Brandt, R.B., "Traits of Character: A Conceptual Analysis," *American Philosophical Quarterly* 7 (1970), 23–37.

——. "A Motivational Theory of Excuses in the Criminal Law," in J. Pennock & J. Chapman (eds.), *Criminal Justice* (New York: New York UP, 1985), 165–98.

Chapman, B., "Agency and Contingency: The Case of Criminal Attempts" (1988), 38 *University of Toronto LJ*, 355–77.

Cross, R., "Centenary Reflections on Prince's Case," *Law Quarterly Review*, 91 (1975), 540–53.

Dressler, J., *Understanding Criminal Law* (New York: Matthew Bender, 1987).

——. "Reflections on Excusing Wrongdoers: Moral Theory, New Excuses and the Moral Penal Code," *Rutgers LJ* 19 (1988), 671–716.

Duff, R.A., "Mental Disorder and Criminal Responsibility," in Duff and N.E. Simmonds (eds.), *Philosophy and the Criminal Law* (Wiesbaden: Franz Steiner, 1984), 31–48.

---

105 See my *Intention, Agency and Criminal Liability*, ch. 7, esp. 162–63.

106 See above, ch. 11.4.

——. *Trials and Punishments* (Cambridge: CUP, 1986).

——. *Intention, Agency and Criminal Liability* (Oxford: Blackwell, 1990).

——. "Choice, Character and Criminal Liability," *Law and Philosophy* 12 (1993), 345–83.

——. "Penal Communications: Recent Work in the Philosophy of Punishment," *Crime and Justice* 20 (1995), 1–97.

Dummett, M., *Truth and other Enigmas* (Cambridge, Mass.: Harvard UP, 1978).

Feinberg, J., "Problematic Responsibility in Law and Morals," in Feinberg, *Doing and Deserving* (Princeton: Princeton UP, 1970), 25–37.

Fletcher, G., *Rethinking Criminal Law* (Boston: Little Brown, 1978).

——. "Constructing a Theory of Impossible Attempts," in P. Fitzgerald (ed.), *Crime, Justice and Codification* (Toronto: Carswell, 1986), 87–113.

Fuller, L., *The Morality of Law* (2nd ed.; New Haven: Yale UP, 1969).

Galloway, D., "Patterns of Trying: A Critique of Fletcher on Criminal Attempts," *Queen's LJ* 7 (1982), 232–52.

Gordon, G.H., *The Criminal Law of Scotland* (2nd ed.; Edinburgh: W. Green, 1978).

Hart, H.L.A., *Punishment and Responsibility* (Oxford: OUP, 1968).

——. "Negligence, Mens Rea, and Criminal Responsibility," in *Punishment and Responsibility*, 136–57.

Hudson, S., *Human Character and Morality* (London: Routledge, 1986).

Husak, D., *Philosophy of Criminal Law* (Totawa: Rowman & Littlefield, 1987).

Kadish, S., "Excusing Crime," in Kadish, *Blame and Punishment* (New York: Macmillan, 1987), 81–106.

Lacey, N., *State Punishment* (London: Routledge, 1988).

——. "A Clear Concept of Intention: Elusive or Illusory?," *Modern LR* 56 (1993), 621–42.

——, Wells, C., and Meure, D., *Reconstructing Criminal Law* (London: Weindenfeld & Nicolson, 1990).

Law Commission, Working Paper No. 102, *Attempt and Impossibility in Relation to Attempt, Conspiracy and Incitement* (London: HMSO, 1985).

——. No. 177, *A Criminal Code for England and Wales*: Vol. 1, Report and Draft Criminal Code Bill; Vol. 2, Commentary (London: HMSO, 1989).

Lewis, D., "The Punishment that Leaves Something to Chance," *Philosophy and Public Affairs* 18 (1989), 53–67.

Malcolm, N., "The Conceivability of Mechanism," in G. Watson (ed.), *Free Will* (Oxford: OUP, 1982), 127–49.

Moore, M.S., "Choice. Character and Excuse," *Social Philosophy and Policy* 7 (1990), 29–58.

——. *Act and Crime* (Oxford: OUP, 1993).

Morris, H., "Punishment for Thoughts," in Morris, *Guilt and Innocence* (Berkeley: University of California Press, 1976), 1–29.

Murdoch, I., *The Sovereignty of Good* (London: Routledge, 1970).

Nagel, T., "Moral Luck," in Nagel, *Moral Questions* (Cambridge, CUP, 1979), 24–38.

Pillsbury, S.H, "The Meaning of Deserved Punishment: An Essay on Choice, Character and Responsibility," *Indiana LJ* 67 (1992), 719–52.

Pincoffs, E.L., "Legal Responsibility and Moral Character," *Wayne LR* 19 (1973), 905–23.

Schulhofer, S.J., Review of Fletcher, *Rethinking Criminal Law, California LR* 68 (1980), 181–201.

Smith, J.C., "Some Problems of the Reform of Law of Offences against the Person," *Current Legal Problems* 31 (1978), 15–29.

——, and Hogan, B., *Criminal Law* (7th edn.; London: Butterworths, 1992) (6th edn. 1988).

Von Hirsch, A., *Censure and Sanctions* (Oxford: OUP, 1993).

Vuoso, G., "Background, Responsibility and Excuse," *Yale LJ* 96 (1987), 1661–86.

Weinreb, L., "Manifest Criminality, Criminal Intent, and the 'Metamorphosis of Larceny,'" *Yale LJ* 90 (1980), 294–318.

Williams, B., *Problems of the Self* (Cambridge: CUP, 1973).

——. *Moral Luck* (Cambridge: CUP, 1981).

Williams, G., "Police Control of Intending Criminals—I," *Criminal LR* (1955), 66–75.

——. "Oblique Intention," *Cambridge LJ* 46 (1987), 417–38.

Winch, P., "Moral Integrity," in *Ethics and Action*, 171–92.

Abbreviations

The following abbreviations are used for frequently cited books, reports etc.

Ashworth Attempts

A.J. Ashworth, "Criminal Attempts and the Role of Resulting Harm under the Code, and in the Common Law."

Ashworth Principles

A.J. Ashworth, *Principles of Criminal Law* (2nd edn.).

Clarkson & Keating

C.M.V. Clarkson and H.M. Keating, *Criminal Law: Text and Materials* (3rd edn.).

Dressler

J. Dressler, *Understanding Criminal Law.*

Fletcher

G. Fletcher, *Rethinking Criminal Law.*

Gordon

G.H. Gordon, *The Criminal Law of Scotland* (2nd edn.).

LaFave & Scott

W.R. LaFave and A.W. Scott, *Criminal Law* (2nd edn.).

Smith & Hogan

J.C. Smith and B. Hogan, *Criminal Law* (7th edn.).

Williams CLGP

G. Williams, *Criminal Law: The General Part* (2nd edn.).

Williams TCL

G. Williams, *Textbook of Criminal Law* (2nd edn.).

Law Com. 102

Law Commission No.102 *Attempt, and Impossibility in Relation to Attempt, Conspiracy and Incitement* (1980).

1985 Draft Code[107]

Law Commission No.143 *Codification of the Criminal Law* (1985): Report and Draft Criminal Code Bill.

1989 Draft Code[108]

Law Commission No.177 *A Criminal Code for England and Wales* (1989): Vol.1, Report and Draft Criminal Code Bill; Vol.2, Commentary.

Model Penal Code

American Law Institute, *Model Penal Code* (text and commentaries).

Canadian Code[109]

Martin's Annual Criminal Code 1989.

◆ ◆ ◆ ◆ ◆

---

[107] Produced by a team of academic lawyers for the Law Commission.

[108] Produced by the Law Commission, after considering responses to the *1985 Draft Code.*

[109] The Current Code was enacted in 1985. Some of the cases which I discuss were decided under earlier Codes: but since only the numbering, and not the content, of the relevant sections has changed, I have translated all references into the numbering of the present Code.

R v Shivpuri
2 All ER [1986] 334

Lord Bridge:

My Lords, On 23 February 1984 the appellant was convicted at the Crown Court at Reading of two attempts to commit offences. The offences attempted were being knowingly concerned in dealing with (count 1) and in harbouring (count 2) a class A controlled drug, namely diamorphine, with intent to evade the prohibition of importation imposed by s 3(1) of the Misuse of Drugs Act 1971, contrary to s 170(1)(b) of the Customs and Excise Management Act 1979. On 5 November 1984 the Court of Appeal, Criminal Division ([1985] 1 All ER 143, [1985] QB 1029) dismissed his appeals against conviction but certified that a point of law of general public importance was involved in the decision and granted leave to appeal to your Lordships' House. The certified question granted on 13 November 1984 reads:

> Does a person commit an offence under Section I, Criminal Attempts Act, 1981, where, if the facts were as that person believed them to be, the full offence would have been committed by him, but where on the true facts the offence which that person set out to commit was in law impossible, e.g., because the substance imported and believed to be heroin was not heroin but a harmless substance?

The facts plainly to be inferred from the evidence, interpreted in the light of the jury's guilty verdicts, may be shortly summarised. The appellant, on a visit to India, was approached by a man named Desai, who offered to pay him £1,000 if, on his return to England, he would receive a suitcase which a courier would deliver to him containing packages of drugs which the appellant was then to distribute according to instructions he would receive. The suitcase was duly delivered to him in Cambridge. On 30 November 1982, acting on instructions, the appellant went to Southall station to deliver a package of drugs to a third party. Outside the station he and the man he had met by appointment were arrested. A package containing a powdered substance was found in the appellant's shoulder bag. At the appellant's flat in Cambridge, he produced to customs officers the suitcase from which the lining had been ripped out and the remaining packages of the same powdered substance. In answer to questions by customs officers and in a long written statement the appellant made what amounted to a full confession of having played his part, as described, as recipient and distributor of illegally imported drugs. The appellant believed the drugs to be either heroin or cannabis. In due course the powdered substance in the several packages was scientifically analysed and found not to be a controlled drug but snuff or some similar harmless vegetable matter.

• • •

The certified question depends on the true construction of the Criminal Attempts Act 1981. That Act marked an important new departure since, by s 6, it abolished the offence of attempt at common law and substituted a new statutory code governing attempts to criminal offences. It was considered by your Lordships' House last year in *Anderton v Ryan* [1985] 2 All ER 355, [1985] AC 560 after the decision in the Court of Appeal which is the subject of the present appeal. That might seem an appropriate starting point from which to examine the issues arising in this appeal. But your Lordships have been invited to exercise the power under the 1966 Practice Statement (*Note* [1966] 3 All ER 77, [1966] 1 WLR 1234) to depart from the reasoning in that decision if it proves necessary to do so in order to affirm the convictions appealed against in the instant case. I was not only a party to the decision in *Anderton v Ryan*, I was also the author of one of the two opinions approved by the majority which must be taken to express the House's ratio. That seems to me to afford a sound reason why, on being invited to re-examine the language of the statute in its application to the facts of this appeal, I should initially seek to put out of mind what I said in *Anderton v Ryan*. Accordingly, I propose to approach the issue in the first place as an exercise in statutory construction, applying the language of the Act to the facts of the case, as if the matter were res integra. If this leads me to the conclusion that the appellant was not guilty of any attempt to commit a relevant offence, that will be the end of the matter. But, if this initial exercise inclines me to reach a contrary conclusion, it will then be necessary to consider whether the precedent set by *Anderton v Ryan* bars that conclusion or whether it can be surmounted either on the ground that the earlier decision is distinguishable or that it would he appropriate to depart from it under the 1966 Practice Statement.

The 1981 Act provides by s 1:

(1) If, with intent to commit an offence to which this section applies, a person does an act which is more than merely preparatory to the commission of the offence, he is guilty of attempting to commit the offence.

(2) A person may be guilty of attempting to commit an offence to which this section applies even though the facts are such that the commission of the offence is impossible.

(3) In any case where—(a) apart from this subsection a person's intention would not be regarded as having amounted to an intent to commit an offence; but (b) if the facts of the case had been as he believed them to be, his intention would be so regarded, then, for the purposes of subsection (1) above, he shall be regarded as having had an intent to commit that offence.

(4) This section applies to any offence which, if it were completed, would be tri-able in England and Wales as an indictable offence, other than—(a) conspiracy (at common law or under section 1 of the Criminal Law Act 1977 or any other enactment); (b) aiding, abetting, counselling, procuring or suborning the commission of an offence; (c) offences under section 4(1) (assisting offenders) or 5(1) (accepting or agreeing to accept consideration for not disclosing information about an arrestable offence) of the Criminal Law Act 1967.

Applying this language to the facts of the case, the first question to be asked is whether the appellant intended to commit the offences of being knowingly concerned in dealing with and harbouring drugs of class A or class B with intent to evade the prohibition on their importation. Translated into more homely language the question may be rephrased without in any way altering its legal significance, in the following terms: did the appellant intend to receive and store (harbour) and in due course pass on to third parties (deal with) packages of heroin or cannabis which he knew had been smuggled into England from India? The answer is plainly Yes, he did. Next, did he, in relation to each offence, do an act which was more than merely preparatory to the commission of the offence? The act relied on in relation to harbouring was the receipt and retention of the packages found in the lining of the suitcase. The act relied on in relation to dealing was the meeting at Southall station with the intended recipient of one of the packages. In each case the act was clearly more than preparatory to the commission of the *intended* offence; it was not and could not be more than merely preparatory to the commission of the *actual* offence, because the facts were such that the commission of the actual offence was impossible. Here then is the nub of the matter. Does the "act which is more than merely preparatory to the commission of the offence" in s 1(1) of the 1981 Act (the actus reus of the statutory offence of attempt) require any more than an act which is more than merely prep-aratory to the commission of the offence which the defendant intended to commit? Section 1 (2) must surely indicate a negative answer; if it were otherwise whenever the facts were such that the commission of the actual offence was impossible it would be impos-sible to prove an act more than merely preparatory to the commission of that offence and sub-ss (1) and (2) would contradict each other.

This very simple, perhaps over-simple, analysis leads me to the provisional conclusion that the ap-pellant was rightly convicted of the two offences of attempt with which he was charged. But can this conclusion stand with *Anderton v Ryan*? The ap-pellant in that case was charged with an attempt to handle stolen goods. She bought a video recorder be-lieving it to be stolen. On the facts as they were to be assumed it was not stolen. By a majority the House decided that she was entitled to be acquitted. I have re-examined the case with care. If I could extract from the speech of Lord Roskill or from my own speech a clear and coherent principle distinguish-ing those cases of attempting the impossible which amount to offences under the statute from those which do not, I should have to consider carefully on which side of the line the instant case fell. But I have to confess that I can find no such principle.

Running through Lord Roskill's speech and my own in *Anderton v Ryan* is the concept of "object-ively innocent" acts which, in my speech certainly, are contrasted with "guilty acts." A few citations will make this clear. Lord Roskill said ([1985] 2 All ER 355 at 364, [1985] AC 560 at 580):

> My Lords, it has been strenuously and ably argued for the respondent that these provi-sions involve that a defendant is liable to conviction for an attempt even where his actions are innocent but he erroneously believes facts which, if true, would make those actions criminal, and further, that he is liable to such conviction whether or not

in the event his intended course of action is completed.

He proceeded to reject the argument. I referred to the appellant's purchase of the video recorder and said ([1985] 2 All ER 355 at 366, [1985] AC 560 at 582): "Objectively considered, therefore, her purchase of the recorder was a perfectly proper com-mercial transaction."

A further passage from my speech stated ([1985] 2 All ER 355 at 366, [1985] AC 560 at 582-583):

> The question may be stated in abstract terms as follows. Does s 1 of the 1981 Act create a new offence of attempt where a person embarks on and completes a course of con-duct, which is objectively innocent, solely on the ground that the person mistakenly believes facts which, if true, would make that course of conduct a complete crime? If the question must be answered affirma-tively it requires convictions in a number of surprising cases: the classic case, put by Bramwell B in *R v Collins* (1864) 9 Cox CC 497 at 498, of the man who takes away his own umbrella from a stand, believing it not to be his own and with intent to steal it; the case of the man who has consensual inter-course with a girl over 16 believing her to be under that age; the case of the art dealer who sells a picture which he represents to be and which is in fact a genuine Picasso, but which the dealer mistakenly believes to be a fake. The common feature of all these cases, including that under appeal, is that the mind alone is guilty, the act is innocent.

I then contrasted the case of the man who attempts to pick the empty pocket, saying ([1985] 2 All ER 355 at 367, [1985] AC 560 at 583):

> Putting the hand in the pocket is the guilty act, the intent to steal is the guilty mind,

the offence is appropriately dealt with as an attempt, and the impossibility of committing the full offence for want of anything in the pocket to steal is declared by [sub-s (2)] to be no obstacle to conviction.

If we fell into error, it is clear that our concern was to avoid convictions in situations which most people, as a matter of common sense, would not regard as involving criminality. In this connection it is to be regretted that we did not take due note of para 2.97 of the Law Commission Report, Criminal Law: Attempt and Impossibility in Relation to Attempt, Conspiracy and Incitement 1980 (Law Com no 102) which preceded the enactment of the 1981 Act, which reads:

If it is right in principle that an attempt should be chargeable even though the crime which it is sought to commit could not possibly be committed, we do not think that we should be deterred by the consideration that such a change in our law would also cover some extreme and exceptional cases in which a prosecution would be theoretically possible. An example would be where a person is offered goods at such a low price that he believes that they are stolen, when in fact they are not; if he actually purchases them, upon the principles which we have discussed he would be liable for an attempt to handle stolen goods. Another case which has been much debated is that raised in argument by Bramwell B. in *Reg. v. Collins*. If A takes his own umbrella, mistaking it for one belonging to B and intending to steal B's umbrella, is he guilty of attempted theft? Again, on the principles which we have discussed he would in theory be guilty, but in neither case would it be realistic to suppose that a complaint would be made or that a prosecution would ensue.

The prosecution in *Anderton v Ryan* itself falsified the Commission's prognosis in one of the "extreme and exceptional cases." It nevertheless probably holds good for other such cases, particularly that of the young man having sexual intercourse with a girl over 16, mistakenly believing her to be under that age, by which both Lord Roskill and I were much troubled.

However that may be, the distinction between acts which are "objectively innocent" and those which are not is an essential element in the reasoning in *Anderton v Ryan* and the decision, unless it can be supported on some other ground, must stand or fall by the validity of this distinction. I am satisfied on further consideration that the concept of "objective innocence" is incapable of sensible application in relation to the law of criminal attempts. The reason for this is that any attempt to commit an offence which involves "an act which is more than merely preparatory to the commission of the offence" but which for any reason fails, so that in the event no offence is committed, must ex hypothesi, from the point view of the criminal law, be "objectively innocent." What turns what would otherwise, from the point of view of the criminal law, be an innocent act into a crime is the intent of the actor to commit an offence. I say "from the point of view of the criminal law" because the law of tort must surely here be quite irrelevant. A puts his hand into B's pocket. Whether or not there is anything in the pocket capable of being stolen, if A intends to steal his act is a criminal attempt; if he does not so intend his act is innocent. A plunges a knife into a bolster in a bed. To avoid the complication of an offence of criminal damage, assume it to be A's bolster. If A believes the bolster to be his enemy B and intends to kill him, his act is an attempt to murder B; if he knows the bolster is only a bolster, his act is innocent. These considerations lead me to the conclusion that the distinction sought to be drawn in *Anderton v Ryan* between innocent and guilty acts considered "objectively" and independently of the state of mind of the actor cannot be sensibly maintained.

Another conceivable ground of distinction which was to some extent canvassed in argument, both in *Anderton v Ryan* and in the instant case, though no trace of it appears in the speeches in *Anderton v Ryan*, is a distinction which would make guilt or innocence of the crime of attempt in a case of mistaken belief dependent on what, for want of a better phrase, I will call the defendant's dominant intention. According to the theory necessary to sustain this distinction, the appellant's dominant intention in *Anderton v Ryan* was to buy a cheap video recorder; her belief that it was stolen was incidental. Likewise in the hypothetical case of attempted unlawful sexual intercourse, the young man's dominant intention was to have intercourse with the particular girl; his mistaken belief that she was under 16 was merely incidental. By contrast, in the instant case the appellant's dominant intention was to receive and distribute illegally imported heroin or cannabis.

While I see the superficial attraction of this suggested ground of distinction, I also see formidable practical difficulties in its application. By what test is a jury to be told that a defendant's dominant intention is to be recognised and distinguished from his incidental but mistaken belief? But there is perhaps a more formidable theoretical difficulty. If this ground of distinction is relied on to support the acquittal of the appellant in *Anderton v Ryan*, it can only do so on the basis that her mistaken belief that the video recorder was stolen played no significant part in her decision to buy it and therefore she may be acquitted of the intent to handle stolen goods. But this line of reasoning runs into head-on collision with s 1(3) of the 1981 Act. The theory produces a situation where, apart from the subsection, her intention would not be regarded as having amounted to any intent to commit an offence. Section 1 (3)(b) then requires one to ask whether, if the video recorder had in fact been stolen, her intention would have been regarded as an intent to handle stolen goods. The an-

swer must clearly be Yes, it would. If she had bought the video recorder knowing it to be stolen, when in fact it was, it would have availed her nothing to say that her dominant intention was to buy a video recorder because it was cheap and that her knowledge that it was stolen was merely incidental. This seems to me fatal to the dominant intention theory.

I am thus led to the conclusion that there is no valid ground on which *Anderton v Ryan* can be distinguished. I have made clear my own conviction, which as a party to the decision (and craving the indulgence of my noble and learned friends who agreed in it) I am the readier to express, that the decision was wrong. What then is to be done? If the case is indistinguishable, the application of the strict doctrine of precedent would require that the present appeal be allowed. Is it permissible to depart from precedent under the 1966 Practice Statement *Note* ([1966] 3 All ER 77, [1966] 1 WLR 1234) notwithstanding the especial need for certainty in the criminal law? The following considerations lead me to answer that question affirmatively. Firstly, I am undeterred by the consideration that the decision in *Anderton v Ryan* was so recent. The 1966 Practice Statement is an effective abandonment of our pretention to infallibility. If a serious error embodied in a decision of this House has distorted the law, the sooner it is corrected the better. Secondly, I cannot see how, in the very nature of the case, anyone could have acted in reliance on the law as propounded in *Anderton v Ryan* in the belief that he was acting innocently and now find that, after all, he is to be held to have committed a criminal offence. Thirdly, to hold the House bound to follow *Anderton v Ryan* because it cannot be distinguished and to allow the appeal in this case would, it seems to me, be tantamount to a declaration that the 1981 Act left the law of criminal attempts unchanged following the decision in *Haughton v Smith* [1973] 3 All ER 1109, [1975] AC 476. Finally, if, contrary to my present view, there is a valid ground on which it would be proper to distinguish cases similar to that considered in *Anderton v Ryan*, my present opinion on that point would not foreclose the option of making such a distinction in some future case.

I cannot conclude this opinion without disclosing that I have had the advantage, since the conclusion of the argument in this appeal, of reading an article by Professor Glanville Williams entitled "The Lords and Impossible Attempts, or Quis Custodiet Ipsos Custodies?" [1986] *CJL* 33. The language in which he criticises the decision in *Anderton v Ryan* is not conspicuous for its moderation, but it would be foolish, on that account, not to recognise the force of the criticism and churlish not to acknowledge the assistance I have derived from it.

I would answer the certified question in the affirmative and dismiss the appeal.

Appeal dismissed.

◆ ◆ ◆ ◆ ◆

STUDY QUESTIONS

1. Why does Hart distinguish legal from moral responsibility? Is this distinction plausible?

2. How might Lord Bridge's idea of "objective innocence" be saved from the criticisms he considers fatal to it?

3. How might a "character" subjectivist respond to the criticism that this understanding of *mens rea*

leaves too little room for a potential wrongdoer to withhold from carrying out her intentions?

4. How might a "choice" subjectivist respond to the criticism that this understanding of *mens rea* cannot distinguish adequately between acts done freely and acts which are the product of coercion?

◆ ◆ ◆ ◆ ◆

FURTHER READINGS

Andrew Ashworth, *Principles of Criminal Law*, 5th. ed. Oxford: Clarendon Press, 2006.

Jules Coleman and Allen Buchanan, eds. *In Harm's Way: Essays in Honor of Joel Feinberg*. Cambridge: Cambridge University Press, 1994.

R.A. Duff, ed. *Philosophy and the Criminal Law: Principle and Critique*. Cambridge: Cambridge University Press, 1998.

Raymond Frey and Christopher Morris, eds., *Liability and Responsibility*. Cambridge: Cambridge University Press, 1991.

Stephen Shute, John Gardner, and Jeremy Horder, eds., *Action and Value in Criminal Law*. Oxford: Clarendon Press, 1995.

Victor Tadros, *Criminal Responsibility*. Oxford: Oxford University Press, 2006.

SECTION IV

The Nature of
International Law

THE NATURE OF INTERNATIONAL LAW

INTRODUCTION

This chapter explores the idea of international law. Until quite recently, international law was not a central topic of interest for the bulk of legal philosophers. Now, as rapid advances in communications and transport technology make possible more and more interaction between people of different countries, new problems of international relations are arising, and older unresolved problems are acutely in need of solutions. Are there any basic obligations which all countries have whether they like those obligations or not? How can a country be both truly *independent* and yet a subject of *restrictions* imposed by international law? How is international law different from international politics? These and other questions are in urgent need of good answers.

This introduction surveys some facts and terms of international law, and introduces readings from four authors who examine some of the problems we have just noted. The first reading in this chapter is taken from the work of Hugo Grotius, who is regarded by many as the founder of international law theory. According to Grotius, the existence of international law is rooted in natural law requirements which hold true for all persons, regardless of time, culture, religion, and political or geographic boundaries. Other writers argue that the differences between international law and the law of individual states are so large that international law is not properly called law. H.L.A. Hart's argument in support of this view is included in this chapter. A quite different suggestion is offered in the third article of

this chapter, "The Politics of International Law," by the Finnish diplomat and law professor Martti Koskenniemi. He argues that international law has a misunderstood political dimension which must be clarified if we are to have an adequate picture of the possibilities and limits of international law. The fourth and final article of the chapter, by Scottish law professor Neil MacCormick, presents the challenge posed by the European Union's development of a balance between shared law and the independence of individual member states. Is the European Union yet another international treaty among many partners? Or is it something different, perhaps a new form of legal order?

1. The Idea of International Law

If asked to define the term "international law" many non-lawyers might respond that it refers to the laws which govern interactions between nations, as the combination of "inter" and "national" suggests. This definition is adequate for everyday purposes, but we need a more sophisticated definition for our philosophical investigation of international law. We must first distinguish "nations" from "states." The term "state" is used in international law to refer to a specific populated territory whose independent government controls activities within the state's boundaries. A nation, by contrast, consists in a people who share a culture, and often a language. Often, but not always, states embody a nation. The term "nation-state" is often used to refer to this situation. For example, the state of Japan is populated by citizens who are in the vast majority culturally Japanese and thus members of the Japanese nation. Other states such as New Zealand contain more than one nation: the Maori people, and later, mostly British immigrants.

The name for the part of international law which guides relations between independent or "sovereign" states is "public international law." Public international law ordinarily does *not* apply to the affairs of so-called "states" which are in fact part of a larger union, as are, e.g., the State of Oregon in the USA. While the terms "nation," "state," and "country" are often used in everyday talk as though they all mean the same thing, it is important for our purposes to understand that independent, sovereign *states* are the main subjects of public international law. Private international law, by contrast, is concerned with resolution of disputes which arise when some interaction between private individuals is governed by the laws of more than one state. A judge may be asked, for example, to decide what to do about a disputed contract made in one state for the purpose of having something done in another. The laws of the state where the agreement was made may conflict with the laws of the state where the agreed activity is to be carried out. The judge must decide which state's law applies, and how. This area of law is often called "conflict of laws." The writers whose work is included in this chapter are concerned mostly with public international law, even though they may refer to it simply as "international law." In this introduction, the phrase "international law" is used to mean "public international law."

We should also note the apparently unusual use of the term "municipal law" in debates about international law. This term is often used to refer to laws created by cities. Originally, however, it was used by the Romans to refer to the laws of independent, sovereign states. In this introduction, the term "municipal law" will be used in the original, Roman

sense, to refer to the laws of individual states, e.g., the law of the USA.

With these terms in hand, we may begin to examine the similarities and differences between international and municipal law. As we do so, it is worth remembering that the distinction between public and private international law is often very difficult to see in practice. In the future, it will likely be even more difficult to mark clearly the borders between public and private international law. Treaties such as the North American Free Trade Agreement are blurring the economic borders between Canada, the USA, and Mexico. Much broader agreements are at the heart of the European Union, whose member countries have established a European Parliament with far-reaching powers affecting daily life in each of the member countries. Many legal theorists suppose these arrangements are the first steps in what will become the story of law in the twenty-first century: a story of increasing integration and internationalization, and increasing interaction between international and municipal law.

2. *The Foundations of International Law*

International law first grew out of customs established by people of many nations, especially those engaged in international trade. Some of those customs were later formalized in treaties, and other entirely new treaties were made between individual nations and among groups of nations. Much more recently, the formation of the League of Nations (founded in 1920) and its successor, the United Nations (founded in 1945), has produced international bodies which pass resolutions that are often accepted by the international community of states as having binding force. International law is now taken to consist largely in customs, treaties, judicial decisions, general legal principles, and sometimes the resolutions of the United Nations. This web of international norms regulates such matters as borders, war, diplomacy, citizenship and immigration, and is for the most part accepted by nations as binding in their relations to other nations. There is, of course, a significant difference between norms being "for the most part accepted," and norms having binding force whether some individual state likes it or not. It is characteristic of municipal law that it binds citizens whether they like it or not, and where this characteristic is absent, we reasonably suspect that law is absent also. Many legal writers have observed the less than regular way in which international law is accepted as binding, and have claimed at various times that international law is not law at all. The written foundations of international law are open for all to see, but in practice the force of these written foundations is often unclear.

There are many reasons why international law is variably effective. Some of those reasons can be found in the structure and institutions of international law. For example, while resolutions passed by the United Nations certainly have great political force, international law still lacks a central, authoritative legislative body. And, while there is an International Court of Justice, it hears only a limited range of disputes. Matters heard before the International Court of Justice are submitted *voluntarily* by the disputing states. (For example, Spain and Canada brought to the International Court of Justice a dispute over fishing rights in the Atlantic Ocean.) It is not unreasonable to view the activity of the court in resolving these sorts of disputes as essentially arbitration or mediation, especially in light of the fact that there is no independent enforcement body for international law. The world community must rely on the wrongdoer to fulfil its obligations when made aware of them, or a group of states may join together to force another state to comply with the standards of international law. (For example, during the time that the Republic of South Africa violated international human rights standards by maintaining a policy of racial separation, the United Nations passed a resolution condemning South Africa, urging that member nations impose various sanctions on South Africa.) These important differences between international law and typical municipal legal systems reasonably lead us to ask whether international law really is law in the ordinary sense of "law," or whether international law is a different form of regulation of international affairs.

3. *International Law and Private Individuals*

We have marked several differences between municipal and international law, yet the largest difference has not yet been mentioned. Municipal legal systems are deeply concerned with guidance of the lives of *individual citizens*. International law, by contrast, is concerned for the most part with relations between states. Recently, however, there have been very large changes to the way international law operates, as international legal norms are applied increasingly frequently to individual persons. This change is most clearly seen in the development of international human rights law (often called international humanitarian law).

Let us examine the grounds for supposing that the operation of international law has changed fundamentally. In May, 1994 a Commission of Experts appointed by the United Nations delivered a wide-ranging report on crimes against humanity committed in the former Yugoslavia. This report formed the background for the trial of certain individuals for acts constituting the crime of genocide. Genocide involves actions "committed with intent to destroy, in whole or in part, a national, ethnical, racial or religious group, as such."[1] Investigations by United Nations officials who travelled to the former Yugoslavia revealed mass graves, and victims reported rape and murder aimed at elimination of specific religious and ethnic groups. These investigations provided

---

1   1948 Convention on the Prevention and Punishment of the Crime of Genocide, Article II.

the basis for the indictment of persons accused of genocide, crimes against humanity, and war crimes. More than one hundred and fifty persons have been tried before a UN-authorized International Criminal Tribunal for the Former Yugoslavia in The Hague, Netherlands. Shortly after the establishment of this tribunal, the United Nations also established the International Tribunal for Rwanda, to try individuals accused of crimes against humanity in the African state of Rwanda.

What makes these trials so special is not the crimes they treat. Atrocities committed against civilians are unfortunately quite common in history. Rather, these trials are unusual because they involve the application of international law in international law courts to *individuals* rather than states. With the exception of the war crimes trials at the end of World War II, the trials at The Hague were the first in which individuals are to be tried for crimes by courts not tied to a specific state. In all other recent instances of crimes against humanity, individual states have taken it upon themselves to prosecute offenders. It is also significant that the persons accused of war crimes have been captured and brought to trial without their consent. Admittedly, it has sometimes proven very difficult to capture accused war criminals, and in some places where life is still unsettled some of these persons have considerable power, consequently making local officials reluctant to make arrests. Yet despite these difficulties, many accused war criminals have been brought to trial. Both tribunals have worked for more than a decade to complete their tasks, proceeding steadily even as other world events draw public attention away from Rwanda and the former Yugoslavia. In the future, it is likely that many trials of this kind will not be held before special tribunals, which are temporary and established to address specific events. Instead, it is likely that many of the issues faced by the tribunals will be taken to the International Criminal Court, which began operations in 2002. One hundred states now accept the court's jurisdiction, so the court is an important contributor to international law. Yet some important states (such as the United States of America) have not yet agreed to accept the court. Until the court is universally accepted, its operations may be criticized as falling short of being truly international.

Concerns regarding the International Criminal Court should not distract us from the success of the tribunals we have discussed. These tribunals may even be evidence that international law is developing many of the characteristics we often associate with municipal law. But are these developments enough to show that international law really is law? Or has international law been law all along? Or is international law properly regarded as something quite different from municipal law, and justifiably so? And what should we make of the European Union? Is it a half-step toward international law, or something else? The readings included in this chapter begin to answer some of these questions, and give you resources for finding your own answers to these questions.

4. *Hugo Grotius*

The work of Dutch lawyer and diplomat Hugo Grotius (1583–1645) has had an enormous influence on thinking about international law. Grotius is admired in part because of the hard-headed practicality he brought to consideration of law. He is also admired for his attempt to gather the scattered customs, treaties, and unspoken rules of international relations into a *system* truly deserving the title of international law.

The knowledge and experience Grotius brought to his writing was earned both in university and in the very rough world of Dutch diplomacy. Grotius was a star student at the University of Leiden, where he studied law. He then served briefly as a diplomat in a mission to France, then as a historian, and later as a lawyer for the Dutch East India Company. After a trip to England to negotiate international trading rights with competing English companies, Grotius spent time in The Netherlands as a public official, but was eventually forced out of the country to live in Paris with little recognition and less money. In Paris between 1623 and 1624 Grotius wrote the book from which our excerpt is taken, *De Jure Belli ac Pacis (The Law of War and Peace)*. After further failed attempts to return to Dutch political life (opponents put a price on his head!), Grotius took up a position as Swedish Ambassador to France. He occupied this position with varying success, and was finally dismissed by the Swedish queen. After an unsuccessful appeal in Sweden for re-appointment, Grotius decided to return to Holland and died during the trip.

Grotius' legal philosophy bears the mark of his life. He was a diplomat in the midst of the Dutch struggle to reject Spain's religious and military conquest of what is now Holland, and he witnessed the death and misery which resulted from this conflict. His philosophy of law is the product of a person deeply concerned with suffering and ways to end it. Grotius' legal philosophy is often called a natural law view, but it is far more complex than this simple title indicates. Grotius flings many different types of arguments at the reader. Grotius offers arguments from a natural law position, notes on long-practiced customs, historical arguments which catalogue the views of historically important writers, and religious arguments which appeal to Christian duties. It is not unfair to characterize Grotius as having an argument ready for everyone. The effect is like a garden with so many different types of plants that it is difficult to see any one plant through the tangle of stems and leaves.

Grotius' work has achieved new prominence with the recent renewal of interest in natural law theory. This does not mean, however, that all legal theorists have come to think that Grotius' arguments are plainly true. As you will see, Grotius' view of international law has two parts which are not obviously compatible. The first is the natural law component. Grotius argues that there exist morally justified standards of conduct which apply universally, to all persons in all states. The second part is the human or conventional aspect of law, found in the customs, treaties, and other rules of international law which states have developed in different ways at different times to guide their interaction. Grotius appears to think that there is some natural unity or wholeness to be found in the shared, common features of human and natural law. Precisely what that unity is, or how we are to justify rejecting some part of human law is not clear. Nonetheless, it is remarkable that Grotius even attempts to find a truly international law which is shared between all states, and not imposed on states by the will of some small group among them. The excerpt included here is Grotius' initial statement of the basic principles underlying the long arguments of *The Law of War and Peace*. In it you will find the richness of Grotius' thought and knowledge of history, and the jumble of ideas which may ultimately be incompatible.

5. H.L.A. Hart

H.L.A. Hart is familiar from earlier chapters of this book as the author of *The Concept of Law*, perhaps the strongest defence yet of the theory of law known as legal positivism. Professor Hart's theory of social rules was explored in Section I, Chapter 2, as was his examination of the relation between law and coercion. This introduction will assume familiarity with the earlier introduction to legal positivism.

In the essay "International Law" included here, Hart argues that international law is something significantly different from what is ordinarily regarded as law. In fact, Hart argues, it may simply be wishful thinking to suppose that international law really is law. Hart discusses two problems or "sources of doubt"[2] regarding the legal status of international law. The first is a problem about the power of international law to impose binding obligations. Some

2   *The Concept of Law*, p. 210.

writers have suggested that the lack of an international enforcement power should count against the legal status of international law. Hart argues that this criticism relies on an unmentioned acceptance of the "command" or "gunman" theory of legal obligation, which Hart took great pains to disprove. To say that international law must have an enforcement body is to accept that international law would not be obeyed if it were not backed up with threats. Yet Hart has argued that where law is said to exist, it is typically accepted for reasons other than fear of threats. If the legal status of international law is to be disputed, Hart suggests, it must be for reasons other than the absence of an enforcement body.

The second source of doubt involves sovereignty. Ordinarily, "sovereign" states are those states which have complete control over their own affairs. The term "sovereign" is also used to refer to the absolute power of some body: a Parliament is said to be sovereign in the sense that no other political body can overrule it. This ordinary understanding of the power of states conflicts with what international law is supposed to do: place limits on what states do. Yet even this problem can be overcome, according to Hart. From the fact that there are limitations on a state's or even an individual's behaviour, it does not follow that we are wrong to think of the state or individual as an independent thing or person. No state or person exists in complete isolation from others. Our ordinary way of speaking about our own personal independence mirrors this: we may take on obligations or other limitations on what we can do, and yet no one thinks we are not still individual, independent persons. Similarly, a state may have limits on its power through a variety of customary or voluntary agreements with other states, and that state is still thought to be independent in a meaningful sense.

According to Hart's analysis, the trouble which international law has *not* overcome is its lack of a rule of recognition. There is no test or "master" rule generally accepted and used by legal officials of the world to identify binding international laws. There are customs, habits, and multilateral treaties, but there is no clear and accepted way of sorting true from false claims about which customs or habits and so on really are part of international law. It is worth remembering that Hart wrote this in 1961 and did not return in later years to the topic of international law. Hart was conscious of the fact that international law was changing and was careful to note that he did not deny the possibility of international law ever existing. It is for you to assess whether the world of international relations has changed enough to justify the claim that international law exists.

6. Martti Koskenniemi, "The Politics of International Law"

The third article of this chapter brings us to Martti Koskenniemi's claim that international law is essentially and unavoidably political. Let us begin by trying to understand what Koskenniemi's claim means, before proceeding to examine the reasons he offers in support of this claim.

The title of "The Politics of International Law" might seem to promise discussion of how politicians make international law. Koskenniemi's article does not do this. He is interested in a different sort of politics. By his claim that international law is political, Koskenniemi means to contrast the *settled* quality of the Rule of Law with the *unsettled* quality of politics. We often see this distinction in action in municipal legal systems when a problem occurs and a variety of solutions are offered. (Consider, for example, the question of appropriate limits on private ownership of guns.) The air soon grows thick with arguments whose strengths and weaknesses can be very difficult to assess amidst the noise of politics as one side accuses another of doctoring the facts, or as a movie star's popularity is used to lend weight to a position. It may even appear that several different solutions to the problem are each independently acceptable, or that there is no way to defeat entirely any one of the acceptable proposals. These political arguments often appear to be unending: there appears to be no principled way of proving the superiority of a single option over all others. Yet much of this turmoil comes to an end once a particular solution is made into law. This does not always mean that the best, or even a good, solution is adopted. However, so long as the making, publication, and enforcement of the law is carried out in a procedurally fair way as required by the principles of the Rule of Law, consistently applied law sets a clear and reliable standard which makes certain conduct *non-optional* and makes a previously troublesome area of life much more predictable. With this distinction in hand, we may now state Koskenniemi's main claim more precisely: what is called international law is something quite different from what we ordinarily think of as law under the principles of the Rule of Law. International law is instead a part of the continuing debates of politics. Let us turn to the reasons why Koskenniemi supposes this claim to be true.

Koskenniemi suggests that the main goal in the development of international law has been to separate international law from politics and the wishes of the powerful, and instead to give international law the clarity and stability that is characteristic of the Rule of Law in municipal legal systems. The achievement of this goal requires that states follow the requirements of international law, and treat it as making certain state conduct non-optional. Yet the entire state-system which international law tries to govern is based on the recognition of each state's right to conduct its own affairs as it wishes—according to its own self-interest, or "vital interest," as international lawyers say. Sovereign states are understandably reluctant to give up their independence to international law, which by making certain state conduct non-optional might make a state's conduct predictable to others and so leave it at a significant strategic disadvantage. We are left with a conflict between the aim to achieve the Rule of Law on an international scale, and the unwillingness of states to give up their independence to international law.

Koskenniemi provides an interesting analysis of the result of states' worries that an international Rule of Law might cramp state sovereignty. States have tended to accept as legitimate sources of obligation only those international customs or agreements which either (1) match what states were going to do anyway, or (2) are so vague or idealistic that their meaning and application in any given circumstance can nearly always be challenged and rejected by states which do not wish to comply. International law of the first type is simply pleasant words and handshakes added to what states were going to do anyway, so these standards do not impose obligations. Rather, these standards simply "apologize" for the conduct states were going to undertake (possibly even in the absence of a formal international standard). At the other extreme, Koskenniemi calls "utopian" those international standards which meet the requirements of the Rule of Law, but are unlikely to be carried out in practice by states who consider those norms to be too idealistic, too costly, too risky, or perhaps simply not in those states' self-interest. Both apologist and utopian international standards lack *normative force*: they do not function as norms treated as obligatory and non-optional whether states like those standards or not. The unfortunate result of this situation is a body of international laws which often do not contain any unequivocal guidance as to how to resolve a dispute.

Perhaps the most interesting part of Koskenniemi's argument is his insistence that there is no way to balance the Rule of Law, state sovereignty, and the need for law to be "concrete" and have normative force whether states like it or not. He sketches four attempts to demonstrate how an international Rule of Law can be established without becoming apologist or utopian, and argues that each attempt collapses. We will not discuss the four approaches here. What is important here is why Koskenniemi supposes they each collapse. He argues that each approach, no matter how strong its arguments are, can always be met with sound objections. The result, Koskenniemi suggests, is that the making and interpretation of international standards is always and necessarily a matter of politics. To establish *only* those international standards which will in fact be obeyed is to make a political choice *not* to work for better international standards which might be unpopular and for that reason inconsistently obeyed. The alternative choice also falls into politics. To establish those international standards which meet some broadly accepted goal (e.g., global justice), despite the objections of some states, is to make a political choice to ignore the sovereignty of individual states in favour of the greater value of the Rule of Law. There is no middle road, according to Koskenniemi: the making and interpreting of international law always involves political choices which cannot be successfully defended against all objections.

Koskenniemi's conclusion offers some very interesting observations on the reaction of states to the uncertainty of international law. States have responded to the uncertainty of international standards by employing both apologist and utopian types of argument when resolving a dispute, knowing that either approach on its own is always open to sound criticism. Koskenniemi suggests that states' response to this difficulty leads the international community back to where it began: making and interpreting international standards so each side in a dispute is treated *fairly* as justice requires, according to what lawyers call principles of equity. Of course, justice between states is a political idea, and so states must engage in politics as they decide disputes, offering the best understanding of what fairness requires in any particular instance. It is for you to decide whether Koskenniemi's analysis is accurate, and to assess where this leaves legal theory. Does international law resemble law as integrity, with disputing states trying to understand international law in its morally best light? Or is international law simply a matter of political argument in fancy dress, in which the latest

decision of the International Court of Justice is the best guide to what the law is on some matter?

7. Neil MacCormick, "On Sovereignty and Post-Sovereignty"

In the fourth article of this chapter we find an argument which looks into what may be the future of international law. Professor Sir Neil MacCormick sees in Europe the beginning of the end for the sovereign state, and the emergence of a new "post sovereign" legal and political order. In "Sovereignty and Post-Sovereignty" MacCormick explores the legal and political consequences of European states' integration in the European Union, or "EU" as it is usually called. We are fortunate to see that integration through the eyes of Professor MacCormick, a well-known Professor of Law in the University of Edinburgh who has also served as a Member of the European Parliament. In a time when university-based researchers are sometimes thought to be stuck in "ivory towers" far from the daily concerns of "real people," MacCormick brings both careful reflection and a practical perspective earned in the rough and tumble life of politics. According to MacCormick, Europe's integration gives us reasons to re-think the relations between sovereignty, national identity, and democracy, in turn prompting us to re-think the relation between sovereign states and international law. Is the future of international and municipal law one of overlapping boundaries eventually dissolving into a single, global legal order? What might that mean for cultures struggling to maintain their identity in a globalizing world?

It might seem surprising that Europe may be the source of a new way for states to relate to one another. After all, Europe and its politics were at the heart of the two most destructive wars of the last century, and the long stand-off of the "Cold War" divided Europe for nearly fifty years. Europe's path from conflict to union is a complex story which cannot be taken up in appropriate detail in this brief introduction. We can, however, note a few key facts which are especially relevant to understanding the lessons the European Union might offer to those of us concerned to understand the nature and future of international law.

The EU of the early twenty-first century includes twenty five member states, whose total population of more than 460 million is more than half again as large as the United States of America and its 300 million citizens. Citizens of EU member states move freely across those states' borders, living and doing business where they choose, and spending "Euros" in those member states which have adopted the common unit of currency. Citizens vote in elections of Members of the European Parliament in addition to electing governments in their home states. Member states are governed by a blend of state and European "Community law" which includes control of such key matters as human rights standards. In the near future the EU may adopt its own constitution and form its own unified defence force, taking what some think are the final steps toward state-like status. Yet however much the EU may now look like a special kind of unified state, it is worth remembering that it has arisen from a series of treaties and other agreements which at least appeared to aim at much more practical matters of economic cooperation.

The beginning of the EU is said to be found in the 1951 Treaty of Paris. This treaty established the European Coal and Steel Community, a group of six states coming together to share a market for coal and steel in the difficult circumstances facing Europe, as it re-built following World War II. These states expanded their ties in 1957 when the Treaty of Rome created the European Economic Community and the European Atomic Energy Community. In 1973 three more states joined the European Economic Community, another three joined by 1986, and by the time of the 1992 Treaty on European Union (sometimes called the "Maastricht Treaty" after the city where it was signed), there were fifteen members. In 2000 the EU adopted the "Lisbon Strategy" for an integrated, European approach to research and development, markets for products, job creation, and many other activities far beyond the Union's beginnings in coal and steel. By the time many member states adopted the Euro in 2002, ten more states were ready to join the EU, and their entrance into the EU in 2004 signalled the close of the Cold War era for Europe.

The names and dates in our sketch of the EU are important, but it is more important that we focus on a general trend visible over the life of the Union: increasing numbers of states, agreeing to increasing integration of government operations and laws. These increases have often been controversial, for reasons which deserve our attention.

European integration is often portrayed as a sort of trade-off for member states. States certainly gain a great deal by membership, but they are sometimes thought to lose their independence, or sovereignty. Some states have worried, for example, that by giving up their own currency and joining the Euro, their economies are tied to the performance of other, sometimes weaker economies. Sovereignty is also sometimes said to be lost in more important ways, as states come to share control over their internal affairs with EU institutions. Many citizens of the United Kingdom, for example, were very surprised to find that the European Court of Justice has the power to declare Community law to have priority over United Kingdom law. Beginning with a 1989 court decision known as *Factortame*, British courts themselves have recognized that where British law conflicts with Community law, Community law prevails. Some citizens now fear that their national identity and character are being sacrificed to faceless bureaucrats in Brussels, the administrative capital of the EU. Fears of this kind are not unique to Britain. Citizens across the member states of the EU are faced with the question of what it means to be European *and* a member of a particular ethnic group or nation.

Members of "internal minorities," meaning minorities within states, are particularly worried that their long struggles for recognition in their home states may be overlooked within the huge diversity of the EU, leaving small cultures struggling to survive.

The tension between sovereignty and integration has become particularly pronounced as the EU has worked toward adoption of a Constitution. After lengthy negotiations produced a constitutional document ready for approval in each individual member state, France and the Netherlands voted against adoption of the Constitution. The fate of the Constitution is now uncertain. Among the many reasons for rejection of the Constitution, it is worth emphasizing its size and complexity. At 485 pages in length in the official English version, the Constitution is not a document likely to be handed around at the pub in casual discussion of the future of Europe. Even once a reader recognizes a certain amount of repetition as minor adjustments are stated for specific states and situations, the range of activities governed by the Constitution may seem very large when compared with the relatively slim constitutions of comparable jurisdictions such as Canada and the United States. This feature of the European Constitution supports the suspicion that the EU is less a cooperative organization than a super-state standing above, and eventually replacing, the authority of member states.

While you consider what the EU's integration means for our understanding of the longstanding division between municipal and international law, it is important to continue to pay attention to the fast-changing political facts of the situation. It is increasingly difficult, for example, to support the view that the EU is something like the alien "Borg" character from the television show *Star Trek*. The Borg, you may recall, is a group of many beings functioning seamlessly as parts of a unified whole, pursuing single-mindedly an agenda of assimilation of all beings into a collective which abhors individual difference. If the EU *is* the Borg, it is doing a very poor

job, as the EU continues to operate in twenty official languages and structures constitutional debate in a way which allows individual states the freedom to adopt or reject the European Constitution as they choose. Something quite different is happening in the EU, and MacCormick's article aims to offer one explanation of this new and different way Europeans are choosing to live together.

Professor MacCormick begins with a reflection on the origin of the idea that the sovereign state is the basic way for societies to choose order over chaos, and to declare their identity and separation from other societies. This idea has gained so much support that it now seems almost natural to suppose that a society wishing to choose its own way of life in the world ought to try to ensure that it has its own state. In the 20th century we gained confidence in a further idea, that the best match between a society and a state includes a democratic political system enabling the society to guide the state's operation to suit the changing preferences of its society. A society or culture without a state seems terribly vulnerable to losing its way as it must share control of its future within other interests in the states which are willing to give at least some recognition to the culture's needs and aspirations. Against this understanding of the importance of sovereignty, MacCormick contrasts the experience of the EU and asks whether this experience shows a new way for societies or cultures to maintain a shared identity and way of life without the safeguard of sovereignty. MacCormick introduces this discussion with a provocative claim and questions leading us to consider the relation between sovereignty, democracy, and law. He writes: "Whenever we should date the emergence of the sovereign state, and wherever we may locate its first emergence, it seems that we may at last be witnessing its demise in Europe, through the development of a new and not-yet-well-theorized legal and political order in the form of the EU. If that were so, would it be a cause for concern or for satisfaction?" Notice that MacCormick does not suppose that the era of the sovereign state *has* come to a decisive end. He sees instead a *possibility* which may or may not be chosen by the states and citizens of the EU, just as they may or may not choose to govern the EU beneath the structure of a European Constitution. MacCormick does, however, make clear where he stands, using a surprisingly provocative metaphor. MacCormick asks whether we ought to think of sovereignty "like virginity, something that can be lost by one without another's gaining it—and whose loss in apt circumstances can even be a matter for celebration?" His answer to this question is provided through the remainder of his argument: "The case to be made here is one welcoming the prospect of Europe beyond sovereign statehood." The Europe imagined by MacCormick is one in which a state's loss of sovereignty is welcomed as an advancement in maturity, opening new opportunities for security and prosperity far more worthwhile than the opportunities available to a sovereign state choosing splendid isolation. As you think about this possibility, it is important to recognise that the post-sovereign era is thought to leave sovereignty behind, but it takes the idea of legal system with it. MacCormick, like Hart, supposes there may be legal orders beyond traditional sovereign states, but those orders will still be legal *systems*.

Let us go a little more deeply into the key idea of sovereignty. As you read MacCormick's analysis of the idea of sovereignty, you will see that it appears in practice in several forms. Those forms share in common one important characteristic: sovereignty, or self-control, is relative to some alternative situation, and a state can be sovereign in one sense while failing to be sovereign in another sense. We can explore this idea by considering some of the forms MacCormick discusses, beginning with the difference between internal and external sovereignty. MacCormick observes that in some states it is possible to find some body or person who is sovereign in the sense that there is no higher authority or more powerful person or body. With respect to all internal

matters of that state, the sovereign person or body answers to no one. Yet internal sovereignty does not guarantee external sovereignty. For example, Canada was once a "dominion" of the United Kingdom, which held final authority over Canada's relations with surrounding states such as the United States of America. So Canada was sovereign relative to its internal affairs, but not sovereign relative to its external affairs.

Another sense or form of sovereignty can be seen in the difference between legal and political sovereignty. Canada again serves as a useful example. The Government of Canada is now independent of the government of the United Kingdom and has legal sovereignty over its external affairs to the extent that international law allows. Yet Canada has a special relationship with the United States of America which arguably limits Canada's political sovereignty over its external affairs. If Canada were to join some international group or collaborate with some state in ways which the United States viewed as a threat to its interests, the United States would almost certainly apply considerable pressure to Canada in an effort to convince Canada to choose external relations more favourable to the interests of the United States. If the issue were sufficiently serious, such as sale of weapons technology to a state unfriendly to the United States, the government of the United States would have little difficulty in applying pressure in a number of ways. Canada relies economically on US markets for export of Canadian goods and services, and is regarded by many as depending on the much larger United States military forces to provide both Canadians and Americans with security from external threats. Closure of American borders to Canadian imports could hurt Canada very easily, as withdrawal of military cooperation could leave Canada scrambling to secure its borders. The relations between the two countries have long been a matter of deep agreement and successful collaboration, yet relations between unequal partners always involve the risk that the more powerful partner may tend to have little concern for the less powerful partner's external sovereignty. As a Canadian Prime Minister, Pierre Trudeau, once said to an audience of American journalists, "Living next to you is like sleeping with an elephant; no matter how friendly and even-tempered is the beast, one is affected by every twitch and grunt."

If MacCormick's analysis of sovereignty is acceptable, we can conclude that sovereignty is not an all or nothing matter, even within states very close to achieving the ideal of absolute sovereignty. The United States of America, for example, is externally sovereign while its internal organization means that it makes little sense to talk of a holder of internal sovereignty. There is instead what is famously called a system of "checks and balances" by which various parts of government hold authority over different parts of public life, and no one part of government holds final authority over the others. MacCormick calls this a situation of "divided" sovereignty which exists in a state which has meaningful independence from certain kinds of external interference, yet has no person or group holding internal sovereignty. Divided sovereignty is a key characteristic of the EU, according to MacCormick, as states give up both external and internal sovereignty in exchange for the economic and social benefits found in the greater partnership of the EU. Notice, however, that states are not simply transferring their sovereignty to the EU. The EU is itself an instance of divided sovereignty as the European Parliament holds certain powers, other powers are held by the European Council composed of ministers from member states, and the twenty five Commissioners of the European Commission hold another set of powers. Beyond these holders of key powers in the EU, there is a system of European Courts, and a range of councils and committees coordinating co-operation between member states. So whatever is happening to the various forms of sovereignty exercised by member states, it is not simply a surrender of powers. Instead, the EU seems to ask its member states to think differ-

ently about how the nations and cultures within states can choose democratically to live together in Europe. But what is that different kind of choice and future?

Here we arrive at the idea of subsidiarity. Talk of subsidiarity often refers to it as a "doctrine" or "principle," meaning an idea accepted as a basis for action, taken as a matter of fact to be debated only in the details of its application. As the EU "Eurojargon" webpage introduces the idea, "The "subsidiarity principle" means that EU decisions must be taken as closely as possible to the citizen. In other words, the Union does not take action (except on matters for which it alone is responsible) unless EU action is more effective than action taken at national, regional or local level."[3] Actual use of the doctrine of subsidiarity is very complex, but even this sketch shows why cultures and nations might be willing to leave sovereignty behind, choosing instead to live within a union guided by subsidiarity. If respect for the subsidiarity principle requires the EU to leave to states or regions or cultures various matters in which the Union is unlikely to be more effective, there may be a great deal of room for individual cultures and nations to democratically choose ways of living which might vary from other cultures and nations within the European Union. It may suddenly seem quite old fashioned to think that a nation needs a state in order to preserve at least the most meaningful aspects that nation's identity or way of life. If anything, the European Union might provide new ways for old nations to develop their identity within a shared legal framework. Citizens who wish to leave their national cultures behind may be more free to do so as the European Union enables them to live and work anywhere in the Union. Along the way to a different way of living together, Europeans will likely face further conflicts regarding the balance between national aspirations and European identity,

---

3   See: <http://europa.eu/abc/eurojargon/index_en.htm>. Accessed June 20, 2007.

but the peace and security Europeans enjoy within the Union will likely be a strong reason in favour of continuing to reach for compromises.

In the future you will see whether the European Union chooses to grow as it has so far, treaty by treaty, or whether it chooses instead to contain its diversity within a single constitution. You will also see whether subsidiarity operates as MacCormick argues it might, limiting the possibility of a "Euro-Borg" EU assimilating all cultures into a single, uniform set of laws and European sense of purpose and identity. However the EU in fact develops, the facts will not tell us much about the kind of legal order emerging in the European Union. That will require an understanding of the nature of municipal and international law, used as a tool to assess the facts. You will need to look back to Grotius, Hart, Koskenniemi, and other sources of argument to find tools to understand whether these facts are new paint on the same old house, or instead a genuinely new legal order in which the distinction between municipal and international law matters less and less.

◆ ◆ ◆ ◆ ◆

HUGO GROTIUS

"Prolegomena" from *De Jure Belli Ac Pacis Libri Tres* (1625) in *The Classics of International Law*

1. The municipal law of Rome and of other states has been treated by many, who have undertaken to elucidate it by means of commentaries or to reduce it to a convenient digest. That body of law, however, which is concerned with the mutual relations among states or rulers of states, whether derived from nature, or established by divine ordinances, or having its origin in custom and tacit agreement, few have touched upon. Up to the present time no one has treated it in a comprehensive and systematic manner; yet the welfare of mankind demands that this task be accomplished.

2. Cicero justly characterized as of surpassing worth a knowledge of treaties of alliance, conventions, and understandings of peoples, kings and foreign nations; a knowledge, in short, of the whole law of war and peace. And to this knowledge Euripides gives the preference over an understanding of things divine and human; for he represents Theoclymenus as being thus addressed:

> For you, who know the fate of men and
>   gods,
> What is, what shall be, shameful would it
>   be
> To know not what is just.

3. Such a work is all the more necessary because in our day, as in former times, there is no lack of men who view this branch of law with contempt as having no reality outside of an empty name. On the lips of men quite generally is the saying of Euphemus, which Thucydides quotes,[1] that in the case of a king or imperial city nothing is unjust which is expedient. Of like implication is the statement that for those whom fortune favours might makes right, and that the administration of a state cannot be carried on without injustice.

Furthermore, the controversies which arise between peoples or kings generally have Mars as their arbiter. That war is irreconcilable with all law is a view held not alone by the ignorant populace; expressions are often let slip by well-informed and

---

1 The words are in Book VI. [xxxv]. The same thought is found in Book V [V.Lxxxix], where the Athenians, who at the same time of speaking were very powerful, thus address the Melians: "According to human standards those arrangements are accounted just which are settled when the necessity on both sides is equal; as for the rest, the more powerful do all they can, the more weak endure."

thoughtful men which lend countenance to such a view. Nothing is more common than the assertion of antagonism between law and arms. Thus Ennius says:

> Not on grounds of right is battle joined,
> But rather with the sword do men
> Seek to enforce their claims.

Horace, too, describes the savage temper of Achilles in this wise:

> Laws, he declares, were not for him
> ordained;
> By dint of arms he claims all for himself.

Another poet depicts another military leader as commencing war with the words:

> Here peace and violated laws I leave
> behind.

Antigonus when advanced in years ridiculed a man who brought to him a treatise on justice when he was engaged in besieging cities that did not belong to him. Marius declared that the din of arms made it impossible for him to hear the voice of the laws.[2] Even Pompey, whose expression of countenance was so mild, dared to say: "When I am in arms, am I to think of laws?"[3]

---

2   In Plutarch Lysander displaying his sword says [*Apothegms, Lysander,* iii =190 E]: "He who is master of this is in the best position to discuss questions relating to boundaries between countries."

   In the same author Caesar declares [*Caesar,* xxxv = 725 B]: "The time for arms is not the time for laws."

   Similarly Seneca, *On Benefits,* IV. xxxviii [IV. xxxvii]: "At times, especially in time of war, kings make many grants with their eyes shut. One just man cannot satisfy so many passionate desires of men in arms; no one can at the same time act the part of a good man and good commander."

3   This view-point of Pompey in relation to the Mamertines Plutarch expresses thus [*Pompey,* x = 623 D]: "Will you not stop quoting laws to us who are girt with swords?" Curtius says in Book IX [IX. iv. 7]: "Even to such a degree does war reverse the laws of nature."

4. Among Christian writers a similar thought finds frequent expression. A single quotation from Tertullian may serve in place of many: "Deception, harshness, and injustice are the regular business of battles." They who so think will no doubt wish to confront us with this passage in Comedy:

> These things uncertain should you, by
> reason's aid,
> Try to make certain, no more would you
> gain
> Than if you tried by reason to go mad.

5. Since our discussion concerning law will have been undertaken in vain if there is no law, in order to open the way for a favourable reception of our work and at the same time to fortify it against attacks, this very serious error must be briefly refuted. In order that we may not be obliged to deal with a crowd of opponents, let us assign to them a pleader. And whom should we choose in preference to Carneades? For he had attained to so perfect a mastery of the peculiar tenet of his Academy that he was able to devote the power of his eloquence to the service of falsehood not less readily than to that of truth. [*Ed. note:* The Athenian philosopher and noted skeptic Carneades (214–129 BCE) was famous for his moral relativism.]

Carneades, then, having undertaken to hold a brief against justice, in particular against that phase of justice with which we are concerned, was able to muster no argument stronger than this, that, for reasons of expediency, men imposed upon themselves laws, which vary according to customs, and among the same peoples often undergo changes as times change; moreover that there is no law of nature, because all creatures, men as well as animals, are impelled by nature toward ends advantageous to themselves; that, consequently, there is no justice, or, if such there be, it is supreme folly, since one does violence to his own interests if he consults the advantage of others.

6. What the philosopher here says, and the poet reaffirms in verse,

> And just from unjust Nature cannot know,

must not for one moment be admitted. Man is, to be sure, an animal, but an animal of a superior kind, much farther removed from all other animals than the different kinds of animals are from one another; evidence on this point may be found in the many traits peculiar to the human species. But among the traits characteristic of man is an impelling desire for society, that is, for the social life—not of any and every sort, but peaceful, and organized according to the measure of his intelligence, with those who are of his own kind; this social trend the Stoics called "sociableness."[4] Stated as a universal truth, therefore, the assertion that every animal is impelled by nature to seek only its own good cannot be conceded.

7. Some of the other animals, in fact, do in a way restrain the appetency for that which is good for themselves alone, to the advantage, now of their offspring, now of other animals of the same species.[5]

This aspect of their behaviour has its origin, we believe, in some extrinsic intelligent principle, because with regard to other actions, which involve no more difficulty than those referred to, a like degree of intelligence is not manifest in them. The same thing must be said of children. In children, even before their training has begun, some disposition to do

---

4 Chrysostom, *On Romans*, Homily XXXI [Homily V, i, on chap. i, verse 31]: "We men have by nature a kind of fellowship with men; why not, when even wild beasts in their relation to one another have something similar?"

See also the same author, *On Ephesians*, chap. i [Homily I], where he explains that the seeds of virtue have been implanted in us by nature. The emperor Marcus Aurelius, a philosopher of parts, said [V. xvi]: "It was long ago made clear that we were born for fellowship. Is it not evident that the lower exist for the sake of the higher, and the higher for one another's sake?"

5 There is an old proverb, "Dogs do not eat the flesh of dogs." Says Juvenal [*Sat.* xv. 163, 159]:

> Tigress with ravening tigress keeps the peace;
> The wild beast spares its spotted kin."

There is a fine passage of Philo, in his commentary on the Fifth Commandment, which he who will may read in Greek. As it is somewhat long, I shall here quote it only once and in Latin [Philo, *On the Ten Commandments*, xxiii, in English as follows]:

"Men, be ye at least imitators of dumb brutes. They, trained through kindness, know how to repay in turn. Dogs defend our homes; they even suffer death for their masters, if danger has suddenly come upon them. It is said that shepherd dogs go in advance of their flocks, fighting till death, if need be, that they may protect the shepherds from hurt. Of things disgraceful is not the most disgraceful this, that in return of kindness man should be outdone by a dog, the gentlest creature by the most fierce?

"But if we fail to draw our proper lesson from the things of earth, let us pass to the realm of winged creatures that make voyage through the air, that from them we may learn our duty. Aged storks, unable to fly, stay in their nests. Their offspring fly, so to say, over lands and seas, seeking sustenance in all places for their parents; these, in consideration of their age, deservedly enjoy quiet, abundance, even comforts. And the younger storks console themselves for the irksomeness of their voyaging with the consciousness of their discharge of filial duty and the expectation of similar treatment on the part of their offspring, when they too have grown old. Thus they pay back, at the time when needed, the debt they owe, returning what they have received; for from others they cannot obtain sustenance either at the beginning of life, when they are small, or, when they have become old, at life's end. From no other teacher than nature herself have they learned to care for the aged, just as they themselves were cared for when they were young."

"Should not they who do not take care of their parents have reason to hide themselves for very shame when they hear this—they that neglect those whom alone, or above all others, they ought to help, especially when by so doing they are not really called upon to give, but merely to return what they owe? Children have as their own nothing to which their parents do not possess a prior claim; their parents have either given them what they have or have furnished to them the means of acquisition."

In regard to the extraordinary care of doves for their young, see Porphyry, *On Abstaining from Animal Food*, Book III; concerning the regard of the parrot-fish and lizard-fish for their kind, see Cassiodorus, [*Variae*] XI. xl.

good to others appears, as Plutarch sagely observed; thus sympathy for others comes out spontaneously at that age. The mature man in fact has knowledge which prompts him to similar actions under similar conditions,[6] together with an impelling desire for society, for the gratification of which he alone among animals possesses a special instrument, speech. He has also been endowed with the faculty of knowing and of acting in accordance with general principles. Whatever accords with that faculty is not common to all animals, but peculiar to the nature of man.

8. This maintenance of the social order,[7] which we have roughly sketched, and which is consonant with human intelligence, is the source of law properly so called. To this sphere of law belong the abstaining from that which is another's,[8] the restoration to another of anything of his which we may have, together with any gain which we may have received from it; the obligation to fulfil promises, the making good of a loss incurred through our fault, and the inflicting of penalties upon men according to their deserts.

9. From this signification of the word law there has flowed another and more extended meaning. Since over other animals man has the advantage of possessing not only a strong bent towards social life, of which we have spoken, but also a power of discrimination which enables him to decide what things are agreeable or harmful (as to both things present and things to come), and what can lead to either alternative: in such things it is meet for the nature of man, within the limitations of human intelligence, to follow the direction of a well-tempered judgement, being neither led astray by fear or the allurement of immediate pleasure, nor carried away by rash impulse. Whatever is clearly at variance with such judgement is understood to be contrary also to the law of nature, that is, to the nature of man.

10. To this exercise of judgement belongs moreover the rational allotment[9] to each man, or to each

---

6 Marcus Aurelius, Book IX [IX. xlii]: "Man was born to benefit others;" also [IX. ix]: "It would be easier to find a thing of earth out of relation with the earth than a human being wholly cut off from human kind." The same author in Book X [X. ii]: "That which has the use of reason necessarily also craves civic life."

Nicetas of Chonae (*On Isaac Angelus*, III. ix]: "Nature has ingrained in us, and implanted in our souls, a feeling for our kin." And what Augustine says, *On Christian Doctrine*, III. xiv.

7 Seneca, *On Benefits*, Book IV, chap. xviii: "That the warm feeling of a kindly heart is in itself desirable you may know from this, that ingratitude is something which in itself men ought to flee from, since nothing so dismembers and destroys the harmonious union of the human race as does this fault. Upon what other resource, pray tell, can we rely for safety, than mutual aid through reciprocal services? This alone it is, this interchange of kindnesses, which makes our life well equipped, and well fortified against sudden attacks.

"Imagine ourselves as isolated individuals, what are we? The prey, the victims of brute beasts—blood most cheap, and easiest to ravage; for to all other animals strength sufficient for their own protection has been given. The beasts that are born to wander and to pass segregate lives are provided with weapons; man is girt round about with weakness. Him no strength of claws or teeth makes formidable to others. To man [deity] gave two resources, reason and society; exposed as he was to danger from all other creatures, these resources rendered him the most powerful of all. Thus he who in isolation could not be the equal of any creature, is become the master of the world.

"It was society which gave to man dominion over all other living creatures; man, born for the land, society transferred to a sovereignty of a different nature, bidding him exercise dominion over the sea also. Society has checked the violence of disease, has provided succour for old age, has given comfort against sorrows. It makes us brave because it can be invoked against Fortune. Take this away and you will destroy the sense of oneness in the human race, by which life is sustained. It is, in fact, taken away, if you shall cause that an ungrateful heart is not to be avoided on its own account."

8 Porphyry, *On Abstaining from Animal Food*, Book III [III. xxiv]: "Justice consists in the abstaining from what belongs to others, and in doing no harm to those who do no harm."

9 Ambrose treats this subject in his first book *On Duties* [I xxx].

social group, of those things which are properly theirs, in such a way as to give the preference now to him who is more wise over the less wise, now to a kinsman rather than to a stranger, now to a poor man rather than to a man of means, as the conduct of each or the nature of the thing suggests. Long ago the view came to be held by many, that this discriminating allotment is a part of law, properly and strictly so called; nevertheless law, properly defined, has a far different nature, because its essence lies in leaving to another that which belongs to him, or in fulfilling our obligations to him.

11. What we have been saying would have a degree of validity even if we should concede that which cannot be conceded without the utmost wickedness, that there is no God, or that the affairs of men are of no concern to Him. The very opposite of this view has been implanted in us partly by reason, partly by unbroken tradition, and confirmed by many proofs as well as by miracles attested by all ages. Hence it follows that we must without exception render obedience to God as our Creator, to Whom we owe all that we are and have; especially since, in manifold ways, He has shown Himself supremely good and supremely powerful, so that to those who obey Him He is able to give supremely great rewards, even rewards that are eternal, since He Himself is eternal. We ought, moreover, to believe that He has willed to give rewards, and all the more should we cherish such a belief if He has so promised in plain words; that He has done this, we Christians believe, convinced by the indubitable assurance of testimonies.

12. Herein, then, is another source of law besides the source in nature, that is, the free will of God,[10] to which beyond all cavil our reason tells us we must render obedience. But the law of nature of which we have spoken, comprising alike that which relates to the social life of man and that which is so called in a larger sense, proceeding as it does from the essential

traits implanted in man, can nevertheless rightly be attributed to God,[11] because of His having willed that such traits exist in us. In this sense, too, Chrysippus and the Stoics used to say that the origin of law should be sought in no other source than Jupiter himself; and from the name Jupiter[12] the Latin word for law (ius) was probably derived.

13. There is an additional consideration in that, by means of the laws which He has given, God has made those fundamental traits more manifest, even to those who possess feebler reasoning powers; and He has forbidden us to yield to impulses drawing us in opposite directions—affecting now our own interest, now the interest of others—in an effort to control more effectively our more violent impulses and to restrain them within proper limits.

14. But sacred history, besides enjoining rules of conduct, in no slight degree reinforces man's inclination towards sociableness by teaching that all men are sprung from the same first parents. In this sense we can rightly affirm also that which Florentinus asserted from another point of view, that a blood-relationship has been established among us by nature; consequently it is wrong for a man to set a snare for a fellow-man. Among mankind generally one's parents are as it were divinities,[13] and to them is owed

---

10 Hence, in the judgement of Marcus Aurelius, Book IX [IXi]: "He who commits injustice is guilty of impiety."

11 Chrysostom, *On First Corinthians*, xi 3 [Homily XXVI, iii]: "When I say nature I mean God, for He is the creator of nature" Chrysippus in his third book *On the Gods* [Plutarch, *On the Contradictions of the Stoics*, ix = *Morals*, 1035c]: "No other beginning or origin of justice can be found than in Jupiter and common nature; from that source must the beginning be traced when men undertake to treat of good and evil."

12 Unless perhaps it would be more true to say that the Latin word for "right," *ius* is derived, by the process of cutting down, from the word for "command," *iussum*, forming *ius*, genitive *iusis*, just as the word for "bone," *os*, was shortened from *ossum*; *iusis* afterwards becoming *iuris*, as *Papirii* was formed from *Papisii*, in regard to which see Cicero, *Letters*, Book IX xxi.

13 Hierodes, in his commentary on the *Golden Verse* [rather *How parents should be treated*, quoted by Stobaeus, *Anthology*, tit lxxix. 53], calls parents "gods upon earth;"

an obedience which, if not unlimited, is nevertheless of an altogether special kind.

15. Again, since it is a rule of the law of nature to abide by pacts (for it was necessary that among men there be some method of obligating themselves one to another, and no other natural method can be imagined), out of this source the bodies of municipal law have arisen. For those who had associated themselves with some group, or had subjected themselves to a man or to men, had either expressly promised, or from the nature of the transaction must be understood impliedly to have promised, that they would conform to that which should have been determined, in the one case by the majority, in the other by those upon whom authority had been conferred.

16. What is said, therefore, in accordance with the view not only of Carneades but also of others, that

> Expediency is, as it were, the mother
> Of what is just and fair,[14]

is not true, if we wish to speak accurately. For the very nature of man, which even if we had no lack of anything would lead us into the mutual relations of society, is the mother of the law of nature. But the mother of municipal law is that obligation which arises from mutual consent; and since this obligation derives its force from the law of nature, nature may

be considered, so to say, the great-grand-mother of municipal law.

The law of nature nevertheless has the reinforcement of expediency; for the Author of nature willed that as individuals we should be weak, and should lack many things needed in order to live properly, to the end that we might be the more constrained to cultivate the social life. But expediency afforded an opportunity also for municipal law, since that kind of association of which we have spoken, and subjection to authority, have their roots in expediency. From this it follows that those who prescribe laws for others in so doing are accustomed to have, or ought to have, some advantage in view.

17. But just as the laws of each state have in view the advantage of that state, so by mutual consent it has become possible that certain laws should originate as between all states, or a great many states; and it is apparent that the laws thus originating had in view the advantage, not of particular states, but of the great society of states. And this is what is called the law of nations, whenever we distinguish that term from the law of nature.

This division of law Carneades passed over altogether. For he divided all law into the law of nature and the law of particular countries. Nevertheless if undertaking to treat of the body of law which is maintained between states—for he added a statement in regard to war and things acquired by means of war—he would surely have been obliged to make mention of this law.

18. Wrongly, moreover, does Carneades ridicule justice as folly. For since, by his own admission, the national who in his own country obeys its laws is not foolish, even though, out of regard for that law, he may be obliged to forgo certain things advantageous for himself, so that nation is not foolish which does not press its own advantage to the point of disregarding the laws common to nations. The reason in either case is the same. For just as the national, who violates the law of his country in order to obtain an

---

Philo, *On the Ten Commandments* [chap. xxiii], "visible gods, who imitate the Unbegotten God in giving life." Next after the relationship between God and man comes the relationship between parent and child; Jerome, *Letters*, xcii [cxvii. 2]. Parents are the likenesses of gods; Plato, *Laws*, Book XI [XI. 11]. Honour is due to parents as to gods; Aristotle, *Nicomachean Ethics* Book IX, chap. ii.

14 In regard to this passage Acron, or some other ancient interpreter of Horace [*Sat* I. iii. 98]: "The poet is writing in opposition to the teachings of the Stoics. He wishes to show that justice does not have its origin in nature but is born of expediency." For the opposite view see Augustine's argument, *On Christian Doctrine*, Book III, chap. xiv.

immediate advantage,[15] breaks down that by which the advantages of himself and his posterity are for all future time assured, so the state which transgresses the laws of nature and of nations cuts away also the bulwarks which safeguard its own future peace. Even if no advantage were to be contemplated from the keeping of the law, it would be a mark of wisdom, not of folly, to allow ourselves to be drawn towards that to which we feel that our nature leads.

19. Wherefore, in general, it is by no means true that

> You must confess that laws were framed
> From fear of the unjust,[16]

a thought which in Plato some one explains thus, that laws were invented from fear of receiving injury, and that men are constrained by a kind of force to cultivate justice. For that relates only to the institutions and laws which have been devised to facilitate the enforcement of right; as when many persons in themselves weak, in order that they might not be overwhelmed by the more powerful, leagued themselves together to establish tribunals and by combined force to maintain these, that as a united whole they might prevail against those with whom as individuals they could not cope.

And in this sense we may readily admit also the truth of the saying that right is that which is acceptable to the stronger; so that we may understand that law falls of its outward effect unless it has a sanction

behind it. In this way Solon accomplished very great results, as he himself used to declare,

> By joining force and law together,
> Under a like bond.

20. Nevertheless law, even though without a sanction, is not entirely void of effect. For justice brings peace of conscience, while injustice causes torments and anguish, such as Plato describes, in the breast of tyrants. Justice is approved, and injustice condemned, by the common agreement of good men. But, most important of all, in God injustice finds an enemy, justice a protector. He reserves His judgements for the life after this, yet in such a way that He often causes their effects to become manifest even in this life, as history teaches by numerous examples.

21. Many hold, in fact, that the standard of justice which they insist upon in the case of individuals within the state is inapplicable to a nation or the ruler of a nation. The reason for the error lies in this, first of all, that in respect to law they have in view nothing except the advantage which accrues from it, such advantage being apparent in the case of citizens who, taken singly, are powerless to protect themselves. But great states, since they seem to contain in themselves all things required for the adequate protection of life, seem not to have need of that virtue which looks toward the outside, and is called justice.

22. But, not to repeat what I have said, that law is not founded on expediency alone, there is no state so powerful that it may not some time need the help of others outside itself, either for purposes of trade, or even to ward off the forces of many foreign nations united against it. In consequence we see that even the most powerful peoples and sovereigns seek alliances, which are quite devoid of significance according to the point of view of those who confine law within the boundaries of states. Most true is the saying, that all things are uncertain the moment men depart from law.

23. If no association of men can be maintained without law, as Aristotle showed by his remarkable

---

15 This comparison Marcus Aurelius pertinently uses in Book IX [IX xxiii]: "Every act of thine that has no relation, direct or indirect, to the common interest, rends thy life and does not suffer it to be one; such an act is not less productive of disintegration than he is who creates a dissension among a people." The same author, Book XI [XI. viii]: "A man cut off from a single fellow man cannot but be considered as out of fellowship with the whole human race." In effect, as the same Antoninus says [VI. liv]: "What is advantageous to the swarm is advantageous to the bee."

16 As Ovid says [*Metamorphoses*, VIII 59]: "Strong is the cause when arms the cause maintain."

illustration drawn from brigands,[17] surely also that association which binds together the human race, or binds many nations together, has need of law; this was perceived by him who said that shameful deeds ought not to be committed even for the sake of one's country. Aristotle takes sharply to task[18] those who, while unwilling to allow any one to exercise authority over themselves except in accordance with law, yet are quite indifferent as to whether foreigners are treated according to law or not.

17   Chrysostom, *On Ephesians*, chap iv [Homily IX, iii]: "But how does it happen, some one will say, that brigands live on terms of peace? And when? Tell me, I pray. This happens, in fact, when they are not acting as brigands; for if, in dividing up their loot, they did not observe the precepts of justice and make an equitable apportionment, you would see them engaged in strifes and battles among themselves."

Plutarch [*Pyrrhus*, ix =388 A] quotes the saying of Pyrrhus, that he would leave his kingdom to that one of his children who should have the sharpest sword, declaring that this has the same implication as the verse of Euripides in the *Phoenician Maidens* [line 68]:

That they with gory steel the house divide.
He adds, moreover, the noble sentiment: "So inimical to the social order, and ruthless, is the determination to possess more than is one's own!"

Cicero, *Letters*, XI. xvi [*Ad Fam.* IX. xvi. 3]: "All things are uncertain when one departs from law." Polybius, Book IV [IV. xxix. 4]: "This above all other causes breaks up the private organizations of crinals and thieves, that they cease to deal fairly with one another; in fine, that good faith among them has perished."

18   Plutarch, *Agesilaus* [xxxvii = 617 D]: "In their conception of honour the Lacedaemonians assign the first place to the advantage of their country; they neither know nor learn any other kind of right than that which they think will advance the interests of Sparta."

In regard to the same Lacedaemonians the Athenians declared, in Thucydides, Book V [V. cv]: "In relations with one another and according to their conception of civil rights they are most strict in their practice of virtue. But with respect to others, though many considerations bearing upon the subject might be brought forward, he will state the fact in a word who will say that in their view what is agreeable is honourable, what is advantageous is just."

24. That same Pompey, whom I just now quoted for the opposite view, corrected the statement which a king of Sparta had made, that that state is the most fortunate whose boundaries are fixed by spear and sword; he declared that that state is truly fortunate which has justice for its boundary line. On this point he might have invoked the authority of another king of Sparta, who gave the preference to justice over bravery in war,[19] using this argument, that bravery ought to be directed by a kind of justice, but if all men were just they would have no need for bravery in war.

Bravery itself the Stoics defined as virtue fighting on behalf of equity. Themistius in his address to Valens argues with eloquence that kings who measure up to the rule of wisdom make account not only of the nation which has been committed to them, but of the whole human race, and that they are, as he himself says, not "friends of the Macedonians" alone, or "friends of the Romans"[20] but "friends of mankind," The name of Minos[21] became odious to future ages for no other reason than this, that he limited his fair-dealing to the boundaries of his realm.

25. Least of all should that be admitted which some people imagine, that in war all laws are in abeyance. On the contrary war ought not to be undertaken except for the enforcement of rights; when once undertaken, it should be carried on only

19   Hearing that the king of the Persians was called great, Agesilaus remarked: "Wherein is he greater than I, if he is not more just?" The saying is quoted by Plutarch [*Apophthegms, Agesilaus*, lxiii = *Morals*, 213 C].

20   Marcus Aurelius exceedingly well remarks [VI xliv]: "As Antoninus, my city and country are Rome; as a man, the world." Porphyry, *On Abstaining from Animal Food*, Book III [III. xxvii]:

"He who is guided by reason keeps himself blameless in relation to his fellow-citizens, likewise also in relation to strangers and men in general; the more submissive to reason, the more godlike a man is."

21   In regard to Minos there is a verse of an ancient poet:
Under the yoke of Minos all the island groaned
On this point see Cyril, *Against Julian*, Book VI.

within the bounds of law and good faith. Demosthenes well said that war is directed against those who cannot be held in check by judicial processes. For judgements are efficacious against those who feel that they are too weak to resist; against those who are equally strong, or think that they are, wars are undertaken. But in order that wars may be justified, they must be carried on with not less scrupulousness than judicial processes are wont to be.

26. Let the laws be silent, then, in the midst of arms, but only the laws of the State, those that the courts are concerned with, that are adapted only to a state of peace; not those other laws, which are of perpetual validity and suited to all times. It was exceedingly well said by Dio of Prusa, that between enemies written laws, that is, laws of particular states, are not in force, but that unwritten laws[22] are in force, that is, those which nature prescribes, or the agreement of nations has established. This, is set forth by that ancient formula of the Romans, "I think that those things ought to be sought by means of a war that is blameless and righteous."

The ancient Romans, as Varro noted, were slow in undertaking war, and permitted themselves no licence in that matter, because they held the view that a war ought not to be waged except when free from reproach. Camillus said that wars should be carried on justly no less than bravely; Scipio Africanus, that the Roman people commenced and ended wars justly. In another passage you may read: "War has its laws no less than peace." Still another writer admires Fabricius as a great man who maintained his probity in war—a thing most difficult—and believed that even in relation to an enemy there is such a thing as wrongdoing.

---

22 Thus King Alphonse, being asked whether he owed a greater debt to books or to arms, said that from books he had learned both the practice and laws of arms Plutarch [*Camillus*, x = 134 B]: "Among good men certain laws even of war are recognized, and a victory ought not to be striven for in such a way as not to spurn an advantage arising from wicked and impious actions."

27. The historians in many a passage reveal how great in war is the influence of the consciousness that one has justice on his side;[23] they often attribute victory chiefly to this cause. Hence the proverbs, that a

---

23 Pompey well says in Appian [*Civil Wars*, II viii. 51]: "We ought to trust in the gods and in the cause of a war which has been undertaken with the honourable and just purpose of defending the institutions of our country." In the same author Cassius [*Civil Wars*, IV. xii. 97]: "In wars the greatest hope lies in the justice of the cause." Josephus, *Antiquities of the Jews*, Book XV [XV. v. 3]: "God is with those who have right on their side."

   Procopius has a number of passages of similar import. One is in the speech of Belisarius, after he had started on his expedition to Africa [*Vandalic War*, I. xii. 21]: "Bravery is not going to give the victory, unless it has justice as a fellow-soldier." Another is in the speech of the same general before the battle not far from Carthage [I. xii. 19]. A third is in the address of the Lombards to the Herulians, where the following words, as corrected by me, are found [*Gothic War*, II. xiv]:

   "We call to witness God, the slightest manifestation of whose power is equal to all human strength. He, as may well be believed, making account of the causes of war, will give to each side the outcome of battle which each deserves." This saying was soon afterward confirmed by a wonderful occurrence.

   In the same author Totila thus addresses the Goths [*Gothic War*, III. viii]: "It cannot, it cannot happen, I say, that they who resort to violence and injustice can win renown in fighting; but as the life of each is, such the fortune of war that falls to his lot." Soon after the taking of Rome Totila made another speech bearing on the same point [*Gothic War*, III. xxi].

   Agathias, Book II [*Histories*, II. i]: "Injustice and forgetfulness of God are to be shunned always, and, are harmful, above all, in war and in time of battle. This statement he elsewhere proves by the notable illustrations of Darius, Xerxes, and the Athenians in Sicily [*Histories*, II. x]. See also the speech of Crispinus to the people of Aquileia, in Herodian, Book VIII [*Histories*, VIII. iii. 5, 6].

   In Thucydides, Book VII [VII. xviii], we find the Lacedaemonians reckoning the disasters which they had suffered in Pylus and elsewhere as due to themselves, because they had refused a settlement by arbitration which had been offered them. But as afterward the Athenians, having committed many wicked deeds, refused arbitra-

soldier's strength is broken or increased by his cause; that he who has taken up arms unjustly rarely comes back in safety; that hope is the comrade of a good cause; and others of the same purport.

No one ought to be disturbed, furthermore, by the successful outcome of unjust enterprises. For it is enough that the fairness of the cause exerts a certain influence, even a strong influence upon actions, although the effect of that influence, as happens in human affairs, is often nullified by the interference of other causes. Even for winning friendships, of which for many reasons nations as well as individuals have need, a reputation for having undertaken war not rashly nor unjustly, and of having waged it in a manner above reproach, is exceedingly efficacious. No one readily allies himself with those in whom he believes that there is only a slight regard for law, for the right, and for good faith.

28. Fully convinced, by the considerations which I have advanced, that there is a common law among nations, which is valid alike for war and in war, I have had many and weighty reasons for undertaking to write upon this subject. Throughout the Christian world I observed a lack of restraint in relation to war, such as even barbarous races should be ashamed of; I observed that men rush to arms for slight causes, or no cause at all, and that when arms have once been taken up there is no longer any respect for law, divine or human; it is as if, in accordance with a general decree, frenzy had openly been let loose for the committing of all crimes.

29. Confronted with such utter ruthlessness many men, who very furthest from being bad men, have come to the point of forbidding all use of arms to the Christian,[24] whose rule of conduct above everything else comprises the duty of loving all men.

To this opinion sometimes John Ferus and my fellow-countryman Erasmus seem to incline, men who have the utmost devotion to peace in both Church and State; but their purpose, as I take it, is, when things have gone in one direction, to force them in the opposite direction, as we are accustomed to do, that they may come back to a true middle ground. But the very effort of pressing too hard in the opposite direction is often so far from being helpful that it does harm, because in such arguments the detection of what is extreme is easy, and results in weakening the influence of other statements which are well within the bounds of truth. For both extremes therefore a remedy must be found, that men may not believe either that nothing is allowable, or that everything is.

30. At the same time through devotion to study in private life I have wished—as the only course now open to me, undeservedly forced out from my native land, which had been graced by so many of my labours—to contribute somewhat to the philosophy of the law, which previously, in public service, I practised with the utmost degree of probity of which I was capable. Many heretofore have purposed to give to this subject a well-ordered presentation; no one has succeeded. And in fact such a result cannot be accomplished unless—a point which until now has not been sufficiently kept in view—those elements which come from positive law are properly separated from those which arise from nature. For the principles of the law of nature, since they are always the same, can easily be brought into a systematic form; but the elements of positive law, since they often undergo change and are different in different places, are outside the domain of systematic treatment, just as other notions of particular things are.

31. If now those who have consecrated themselves to true justice should undertake to treat the parts of the natural and unchangeable philosophy of law, after having removed all that has its origin in the free will of man; if one, for example, should treat legislation, another taxation, another the ad-

---

tion, a hope of greater success in their operations revived in the Lacedaemonians.

24 Tertullian, *On the Resurrection of the Flesh* [chap xvi]: "The sword which has become bloodstained honourably in war, and thus has been employed in man-killing of a better sort."

ministration of justice, another the determination of motives, another the proving of facts, then by assembling all these parts a body of jurisprudence could be made up.

32. What procedure we think should be followed we have shown by deed rather than by words in this work, which treats by far the noblest part of jurisprudence.

• • •

40. In order to prove the existence of this law of nature, I have, furthermore, availed myself of the testimony of philosophers,[25] historians, poets, finally also of orators. Not that confidence is to be reposed in them without discrimination; for they were accustomed to serve the interests of their sect, their subject, or their cause. But when many at different times, and in different places, affirm the same thing as certain, that ought to be referred to a universal cause; and this cause, in the lines of inquiry which we are following, must be either a correct conclusion drawn from the principles of nature, or common consent. The former points to the law of nature; the latter, to the law of nations.

The distinction between these kinds of law is not to be drawn from the testimonies themselves (for writers everywhere confuse the terms law of nature and law of nations), but from the character of the matter. For whatever cannot be deduced from certain principles by a sure process of reasoning, and yet is clearly observed everywhere, must have its origin in the free will of man.

♦ ♦ ♦ ♦ ♦

---

25 Why should not one avail himself of the testimony of the philosophers, when Alexander Severus constantly read Cicero *On the Commonwealth* and *On Duties*? [Lampridius, *Alexander Severus*, xxx2.]

H.L.A. HART

"International Law," from *The Concept of Law*

1. Sources of Doubt

The idea of a union of primary and secondary rules to which so important a place has been assigned in this book may be regarded as a mean between juristic extremes. For legal theory has sought the key to the understanding of law sometimes in the simple idea of an order backed by threats and sometimes in the complex idea of morality. With both of these law has certainly many affinities and connections; yet, as we have seen, there is a perennial danger of exaggerating these and of obscuring the special features which distinguish law from other means of social control. It is a virtue of the idea which we have taken as central that it permits us to see the multiple relationships between law, coercion, and morality for what they are, and to consider afresh in what, if any, sense these are necessary.

Though the idea of the union of primary and secondary rules has these virtues, and though it would accord with usage to treat the existence of this characteristic union of rules as a sufficient condition for the application of the expression "legal system," we have not claimed that the word "law" must be defined in its terms. It is because we make no such claim to identify or regulate in this way the use of words like "law" or "legal," that this book [*The Concept of Law*] is offered as an elucidation of the *concept* of law, rather than a definition of "law" which might naturally be expected to provide a rule or rules for the use of these expressions. Consistently with this aim, we investigated ... the claim made in the German cases, that the title of valid law should be withheld from certain rules on account of their moral iniquity, even though they belonged to an existing system of primary and secondary rules. In the end we rejected this claim; but we did so, not because it conflicted with the view that rules belonging to such a system must be called "law," nor because it conflicted with the weight of usage. Instead we criticized the attempt to narrow the class of valid laws by the extrusion of what was morally iniquitous, on the ground that to do this did not advance or clarify either theoretical inquiries or moral deliberation. For these purposes, the broader concept which is consistent with so much usage and which would permit us to regard rules however morally iniquitous as law, proved on examination to be adequate.

International law presents us with the converse case. For, though it is consistent with the usage of the last 150 years to use the expression "law" here, the absence of an international legislature, courts with compulsory jurisdiction, and centrally organized sanctions have inspired misgivings, at any rate in the breasts of legal theorists. The absence of these institutions means that the rules for states resemble that simple form of social structure, consisting only of primary rules of obligation, which, when we find it among societies of individuals, we are accustomed to contrast with a developed legal system. It is indeed arguable, as we shall show, that international law not only lacks the secondary rules of change and adjudication which provide for legislature and courts, but also a unifying rule of recognition specifying "sources" of law and providing general criteria for the identification of its rules. These differences are indeed striking and the question "Is international law really law?" can hardly be put aside. But in this case also, we shall neither dismiss the doubts, which many feel, with a simple reminder of the existing usage; nor shall we simply confirm them on the footing that the existence of a union of primary and secondary rules is a necessary as well as a sufficient condition for the proper use of the expression "legal system." Instead we shall inquire into the detailed character of the doubts which have been felt, and, as in the German case, we shall ask whether the common wider usage that speaks of "international law" is likely to obstruct any practical or theoretical aim.

Though we shall devote to it only a single chapter some writers have proposed an even shorter treatment for this question concerning the character of international law. To them it has seemed that the question "Is international law really law?" has only arisen or survived, because a trivial question about the meaning of words has been mistaken for a serious question about the nature of things: since the facts which differentiate international law from municipal law are clear and well known, the only question to be settled is whether we should observe the existing convention or depart from it; and this is a matter for each person to settle for himself. But this short way with the question is surely too short. It is true that among the reasons which have led theorists to hesitate over the extension of the word "law" to international law, a too simple, and indeed absurd view, of what justifies the application of the same word to many different things has played some part. The variety of types of principle which commonly guide the extension of general classifying terms has too often been ignored in jurisprudence. None the less, the sources of doubt about international law are deeper, and more interesting than these mistaken views—about the use of words. Moreover, the two alternatives offered by this short way with the question ("Shall we observe the existing convention or shall we depart from it?") are not exhaustive; for, besides them, there is the alternative of making explicit and examining the principles that have in fact guided the existing usage.

The short way suggested would indeed be appropriate if we were dealing with a proper name. If someone were to ask whether the place called "London" is *really* London, all we could do would be to remind him of the convention and leave him to abide by it or choose another name to suit his taste. It would be absurd, in such a case, to ask on what principle London was so called and whether this principle was acceptable. This would be absurd because, whereas the allotment of proper names rests *only* on an *ad hoc* convention, the extension of the general terms of any serious discipline is never without its principle or rationale, though it may not be obvious what that is. When as, in the present case, the extension is queried by those who in effect say, "We know that it is called law, but is it really law?," what is demanded—no doubt obscurely—is that the principle be made explicit and its credentials inspected.

We shall consider two principal sources of doubt concerning the legal character of international law and, with them, the steps which theorists have taken to meet these doubts. Both forms of doubt arise from an adverse comparison of international law with municipal law, which is taken as the clear, standard example of what law is. The first has its roots deep in the conception of law as fundamentally a matter of orders backed by threats and contrasts the character of the *rules* of international law with those of municipal law. The second form of doubt springs from the obscure belief that states are fundamentally incapable of being the subjects of legal obligation, and contrasts the character of the *subjects* of international law with those of municipal law.

2. Obligations and Sanctions

The doubts which we shall consider are often expressed in the opening chapters of books on international law in the form of the question "How can international law be binding?" Yet there is something very confusing in this favourite form of question; and before we can deal with it we must face a prior question to which the answer is by no means clear. This prior question is: what is meant by saying of a whole system of law that it is "binding"? The statement that a particular rule of a system is binding on a particular person is one familiar to lawyers and tolerably clear in meaning. We may paraphrase it by the assertion that the rule in question is a valid rule, and under it the person in question has some obligation or duty.

Besides this, there are some situations in which more general statements of this form are made. We may be doubtful in certain circumstances whether one legal system or another applies to a particular person. Such doubts may arise in the conflict of laws or in public international law. We may ask, in the former case, whether French or English Law is binding on a particular person as regards a particular transaction, and in the latter case we may ask whether the inhabitants of, for example, enemy-occupied Belgium, were bound by what the exiled government claimed was Belgian law or by the ordinances of the occupying power. But in both these cases, the questions are questions of law which arise *within* some system of law (municipal or international) and are settled by reference to the rules or principles of that system. They do not call in question the general character of the rules, but only their scope or applicability in given circumstances to particular persons or transactions. Plainly the question, "Is international law binding?" and its congeners "How can international law be binding?" or "What makes international law binding?" are questions of a different order. They express a doubt not about the applicability, but about the general legal status of international law: this doubt would be more candidly expressed in the form "Can such rules as these be meaningfully and truthfully said ever to give rise to obligations?" As the discussions in the books show, one source of doubt on this point is simply the absence from the system of centrally organized sanctions. This is one point of adverse comparison with municipal law, the rules of which are taken to be unquestionably "binding" and to be paradigms of legal obligation. From this stage the further argument is simple: if for this reason the rules of international law are not "binding," it is surely indefensible to take seriously their classification as law; for however tolerant the modes of common speech may be, this is too great a difference to be overlooked. All speculation about the nature of law begins from the assumption that its existence at least makes certain conduct obligatory.

In considering this argument we shall give it the benefit of every doubt concerning the facts of the international system. We shall take it that neither Article 16 of the Covenant of the League of Nations nor Chapter VII of the United Nations Charter introduced into international law anything which can be equated with the sanctions of municipal law. In spite of the Korean war and of whatever moral may be drawn from the Suez incident, we shall suppose that, whenever their use is of importance, the law enforcement provisions of the Charter are likely to be paralysed by the veto and must be said to exist only on paper.

To argue that international law is not binding because of its lack of organized sanctions is tacitly to accept the analysis of obligation contained in the theory that law is essentially a matter of orders backed by threats. This theory, as we have seen, identifies "having an obligation" or "being bound" with "likely to suffer the sanction or punishment threatened for disobedience." Yet, as we have argued, this identification distorts the role played in all legal thought and discourse of the ideas of obligation and duty. Even in municipal law, where there are effective organized sanctions, we must distinguish, for the variety of reasons given in Chapter III [of *The Concept of Law*], the meaning of the external predictive statement "I (you) are likely to suffer for disobedience," from the internal normative statement "I (you) have an obligation to act thus" which assesses a particular person's situation from the point of view of rules accepted as guiding standards of behaviour. It is true that not all rules give rise to obligations or duties; and it is also true that the rules which do so generally call for some sacrifice of private interests, and are generally supported by serious demands for conformity and insistent criticism of deviations. Yet once we free ourselves from the predictive analysis and its parent conception of law as essentially an order backed by threats, there seems no good reason for limiting the normative idea of obligation to rules supported by organized sanctions.

We must, however, consider another form of the argument, more plausible because it is not committed to definition of obligation in terms of the likelihood of threatened sanctions. The sceptic may point out that there are in a municipal system, as we have ourselves stressed, certain provisions which are justifiably called necessary; among these are primary rules of obligation, prohibiting the free use of violence, and rules providing for the official use of force as a sanction for these and other rules. If such rules and organized sanctions supporting them are in this sense necessary for municipal law, are they not equally so for international law? That they are may be maintained without insisting that this follows from the very meaning of words like "binding" or "obligation."

The answer to the argument in this form is to be found in those elementary truths about human beings and their environment which constitute the enduring psychological and physical setting of municipal law. In societies of individuals, approximately equal in physical strength and vulnerability, physical sanctions are both necessary and possible. They are required in order that those who would voluntarily submit to the restraints of law shall not be mere victims of malefactors who would, in the absence of such sanctions, reap the advantages of respect for law on the part of others, without respecting it themselves. Among individuals living in close proximity to each other, opportunities for injuring others, by guile, if not by open attack, are so great, and the chances of escape so considerable, that no mere natural deterrents could in any but the simplest forms of society be adequate to restrain those too wicked, too stupid, or too weak to obey the law. Yet, because of the same fact of approximate equality and the patent advantages of submission to a system of restraints, no combination of malefactors is likely to exceed in strength those who would voluntarily cooperate in its maintenance. In these circumstances, which constitute the background of municipal law, sanctions may successfully be used against malefactors with relatively small risks, and the threat of them will add much to whatever natural deterrents there may be. But, just because the simple truisms which hold good for individuals do not hold good for states, and the factual background to international law is so different from that of municipal law, there is neither a similar necessity for sanctions (desirable though it may be that international law should be supported by them) nor a similar prospect of their safe and efficacious use.

This is so because aggression between states is very unlike that between individuals. The use of violence between states must be public, and though there is no international police force, there can be very little certainty that it will remain a matter between aggressor and victim, as a murder or theft, in the absence of a police force, might. To initiate a war is, even for the strongest power, to risk much for an outcome which is rarely predictable with reasonable confidence. On the other hand, because of the inequality of states, there can be no standing assurance that the combined strength of those on the side of international order is likely to preponderate over the powers tempted to aggression. Hence the organization and use of sanctions may involve fearful risks and the threat of them add little to the natural deterrents. Against this very different background of fact, international law has developed in a form different from that of municipal law. In a population of a modern state, if there were no organized repression and punishment of crime, violence and theft would be hourly expected; but for states, long years of peace have intervened between disastrous wars. These years of peace are only rationally to be expected, given the risks and stakes of war and the mutual needs of states; but they are worth regulating by rules which differ from those of municipal law in (among other things) not providing for their enforcement by any central organ. Yet what these rules require is thought and spoken of as obligatory; there is general pressure for conformity to the rules; claims and admissions are based on them and their breach is held to justify

not only insistent demands for compensation, but reprisals and counter-measures. When the rules are disregarded, it is not on the footing that they are not binding; instead efforts are made to conceal the facts. It may of course be said that such rules are efficacious only so far as they concern issues over which states are unwilling to fight. This may be so, and may reflect adversely on the importance of the system and its value to humanity. Yet that even so much may be secured shows that no simple deduction can be made from the necessity of organized sanctions to municipal law, in its setting of physical and psychological facts, to the conclusion that without them international law, in its very different setting, imposes no obligations, is not "binding," and so not worth the title of "law."

3. Obligation and the Sovereignty of States

Great Britain, Belgium, Greece, Soviet Russia have rights and obligations under international law and so are among its subjects. They are random examples of states which the layman would think of as independent and the lawyer would recognize as "sovereign." One of the most persistent sources of perplexity about the obligatory character of international law has been the difficulty felt in accepting or explaining the fact that a state which is sovereign may also be "bound" by, or have an obligation under, international law. This form of scepticism is, in a sense, more extreme than the objection that international law is not binding because it lacks sanctions. For whereas that would be met if one day international law were reinforced by a system of sanctions, the present objection is based on a radical inconsistency, said or felt to exist, in the conception of a state which is at once sovereign and subject to law.

Examination of this objection involves a scrutiny of the notion of sovereignty, applied not to a legislature or to some other element or person *within* a state, but to a state itself. Whenever the word "sovereign" appears in jurisprudence, there is a tendency to associate with it the idea of a person above the law whose word is law for his inferiors or subjects. We have seen ... how bad a guide this seductive notion is to the structure of a municipal legal system; but it has been an even more potent source of confusion in the theory of international law. It is, of course, *possible* to think of a state along such lines, as if it were a species of Superman—a Being inherently lawless but the source of law for its subjects. From the sixteenth century onwards, the symbolical identification of state and monarch ("L'état c'est moi") may have encouraged this idea which has been the dubious inspiration of much political as well as legal theory. But it is important for the understanding of international law to shake off these associations. The expression "a state" is not the name of some person or thing inherently or "by nature" outside the law; it is a way of referring to two facts: first, that a population inhabiting a territory lives under that form of ordered government provided by a legal system with its characteristic structure of legislature, courts, and primary rules; and, secondly, that the government enjoys a vaguely defined degree of independence.

The word "state" has certainly its own large area of vagueness but what has been said will suffice to display its central meaning. States such as Great Britain or Brazil, the United States or Italy, again to take random examples, possess a very large measure of independence from both legal and factual control by any authorities or persons outside their borders, and would rank as "sovereign states" in international law. On the other hand, individual states which are members of a federal union, such as the United States, are subject in many different ways to the authority and control of the federal government and constitution. Yet the independence which even these federated states retain is large if we compare it with the position, say, of an English county, of which the word "state" would not be used at all. A county may have a local council discharging, for its area, some of the functions of a legislature, but its meagre powers

are subordinate to those of Parliament and, except in certain minor respects, the area of the county is subject to the same laws and government as the rest of the country.

Between these extremes there are many different types and degrees of dependence (and so of independence) between territorial units which possess an ordered government. Colonies, protectorates, suzerainties, trust territories, confederations, present fascinating problems of classification from this point of view. In most cases the dependence of one unit on another is expressed in legal forms, so that what is law in the territory of the dependent unit will, at least on certain issues, ultimately depend on lawmaking operations in the other.

In some cases, however, the legal system of the dependent territory may not reflect its dependence. This may be so either because it is merely formally independent and the territory is in fact governed, through puppets, from outside; or it may be so because the dependent territory has a real autonomy over its internal but not its external affairs, and its dependence on another country in external affairs does not require expression as part of its domestic law. Dependence of one territorial unit on another in these various ways is not, however, the only form in which its independence may be limited. The limiting factor may be not the power or authority of another such unit, but an international authority affecting units which are alike independent of each other. It is possible to imagine many different forms of international authority and correspondingly many different limitations on the independence of states. The possibilities include, among many others, a world legislature on the model of the British Parliament, possessing legally unlimited powers to regulate the internal and external affairs of all; a federal legislature on the model of Congress, with legal competence only over specified matters or one limited by guarantees of specific rights of the constituent units; a regime in which the only form of legal control consists of rules generally accepted as applicable to all; and finally a regime in which the only form of obligation recognized is contractual or self-imposed, so that a state's independence is legally limited only by its own act.

It is salutary to consider this range of possibilities because merely to realize that there are many possible forms and degrees of dependence and independence, is a step towards answering the claim that because states are sovereign they "*cannot*" be subject to or bound by international law or "*can*" only be bound by some specific form of international law. For the word "sovereign" means here no more than "independent;" and, like the latter, is negative in force: a sovereign state is one *not* subject to certain types of control, and its sovereignty is that area of conduct in which it is autonomous. Some measure of autonomy is imported, as we have seen, by the very meaning of the word state but the contention that this "*must*" be unlimited or "*can*" only be limited by certain types of obligation is at best the assertion of a claim that states ought to be free of all other restraints, and at worst is an unreasoned dogma. For if in fact we find that there exists among states a given form of international authority, the sovereignty of states is to that extent limited, and it has just that extent which the rules allow. Hence we can only know which states are sovereign, and what the extent of their sovereignty is, when we know what the rules are; just as we can only know whether an Englishman or an American is free and the extent of his freedom when we know what English or American law is. The rules of international law are indeed vague and conflicting on many points, so that doubt about the area of independence left to states is far greater than that concerning the extent of a citizen's freedom under municipal law. None the less, these difficulties do not validate the *a priori* argument which attempts to deduce the general character of international law from an absolute sovereignty, which is assumed, without reference to international law, to belong to states.

It is worth observing that an uncritical use of the idea of sovereignty has spread similar confusion in the theory both of municipal and international law, and demands in both a similar corrective. Under its influence, we are led to believe that there *must* in every municipal legal system be a sovereign legislator subject to no legal limitations; just as we are led to believe that international law *must* be of a certain character because states are sovereign and incapable of legal limitation save by themselves. In both cases, belief in the necessary existence of the legally unlimited sovereign prejudges a question which we can only answer when we examine the actual rules. The question for municipal law is: what is the extent of the supreme legislative authority recognized in this system? For international law it is: what is the maximum area of autonomy which the rules allow to states?

Thus the simplest answer to the present objection is that it inverts the order in which questions must be considered. There is no way of knowing what sovereignty states have, till we know what the forms of international law are and whether or not they are mere empty forms. Much juristic debate has been confused because this principle has been ignored, and it is profitable to consider in its light those theories of international law which are known as "voluntarist" or theories of "autolimitation." These attempted to reconcile the (absolute) sovereignty of states with the existence of binding rules of international law, by treating all international obligations as self-imposed like the obligation which arises from a promise. Such theories are in fact the counterpart in international law of the social contract theories of political science. The latter sought to explain the facts that individuals, "naturally" free and independent, were yet bound by municipal law, by treating the obligation to obey the law as one arising from a contract which those bound had made with each other, and in some cases with their rulers. We shall not consider here the well-known objections to this theory when taken literally, nor its value when taken merely as an illuminating analogy. Instead we shall draw from its history a threefold argument against the voluntarist theories of international law.

First, these theories fail completely to explain how it is known that states "*can*" only be bound by self-imposed obligations, or why this view of their sovereignty should be accepted, in advance of any examination of the actual character of international law. Is there anything more to support it besides the fact that it has often been repeated? Secondly, there is something incoherent in the argument designed to show that states, because of their sovereignty, *can* only be subject to or bound by rules which they have imposed upon themselves. In some very extreme forms of "auto-limitation" theory, a state's agreement or treaty engagements are treated as mere declarations of its proposed future conduct, and failure to perform is not considered to be a breach of any obligation.

This, though very much at variance with the facts, has at least the merit of consistency: it is the simple theory that the absolute sovereignty of states is inconsistent with obligation of any kind, so that, like Parliament, a state cannot bind itself. The less extreme view that a state may impose obligations on itself by promise, agreement, or treaty is not, however, consistent with the theory that states are subject only to rules which they have thus imposed on themselves. For, in order that words, spoken or written, should in certain circumstances function as a promise, agreement, or treaty, and so give rise to obligations and confer rights which others may claim, *rules* must already exist providing that a state is bound to do whatever it undertakes by appropriate words to do. Such rules presupposed in the very notion of a self-imposed obligation obviously cannot derive *their* obligatory status from a self-imposed obligation to obey them.

It is true that every specific *action* which a given state was bound to do might in theory derive its obligatory character from a promise; none the less this could only be the case if the *rule* that promises, &c., create obligations is applicable to the state independently of any promise. In any society, whether composed of individuals or states, what is necessary and sufficient, in order that the words of a promise, agreement, or treaty should give rise to obligations, is that rules providing for this and specifying a procedure for these self-binding operations should be generally, though they need not be universally, acknowledged. Where they are acknowledged the individual or state who wittingly uses these procedures is bound thereby, whether he or it chooses to be bound or not. Hence, even this most voluntary form of social obligation involves some rules which are binding independently of the choice of the party bound by them, and this, in the case of states, is inconsistent with the supposition that their sovereignty demands freedom from all such rules.

Thirdly there are the facts. We must distinguish the *a priori* claim just criticized, that states *can* only be bound by self-imposed obligations, from the claim that though they could be bound in other ways under a different system, in fact no other form of obligation for states exists under the present rules of international law. It is, of course, possible that the system might be one of this wholly consensual form, and both assertions and repudiations of this view of its character are to be found in the writings of jurists, in the opinions of judges, even of international courts, and in the declarations of states. Only a dispassionate survey of the actual practice of states can show whether this view is correct or not. It is true that modern international law is very largely treaty law, and elaborate attempts have been made to show that rules which appear to be binding on states without their prior consent do in fact rest on consent, though this may have been given only "tacitly" or has to be "inferred." Though not all are fictions, some at least of these attempts to reduce to one the forms of international obligation excite the same suspicion as the notion of a "tacit command" which, as we have seen, was designed to perform a similar, though more obviously spurious, simplification of municipal law.

A detailed scrutiny of the claim that all international obligation arises from the consent of the party bound, cannot be undertaken here, but two clear and important exceptions to this doctrine must be noticed. The first is the case of a new state. It has never been doubted that when a new, independent state emerges into existence, as did Iraq in 1932, and Israel in 1948, it is bound by the general obligations of international law including, among others, the rules that give binding force to treaties. Here the attempt to rest the new state's international obligations on a "tacit" or "inferred" consent seems wholly threadbare. The second case is that of a state acquiring territory or undergoing some other change, which brings with it, for the first time, the incidence of obligations under rules which previously it had no opportunity either to observe or break, and to which it had no occasion to give or withhold consent. If a state, previously without access to the sea, acquires maritime territory, it is clear that this is enough to make it subject to all the rules of international law relating to the territorial waters and the high seas. Besides these, there are more debatable cases, mainly relating to the effect on non-parties of general or multilateral treaties; but these two important exceptions are enough to justify the suspicion that the general theory that all international obligation is self-imposed has been inspired by too much abstract dogma and too little respect for the facts.

4. International Law and Morality

In Chapter V [of *The Concept of Law*] we considered the simple form of social structure which consists of primary rules of obligation alone, and we saw that, for all but the smallest, most tightly knit and isolated societies, it suffered from grave defects. Such a regime must be static, its rules altering only by the slow processes of growth and decay; the identification of the rules must be uncertain; and the ascertainment of the fact of their violation in particular cases, and the application of social pressure to offenders must be haphazard, time-wasting, and weak. We found it illuminating to conceive the secondary rules of recognition, change, and adjudication characteristic of municipal law as different though related remedies for these different defects.

In form, international law resembles such a regime of primary rules, even though the content of its often elaborate rules are very unlike those of a primitive society, and many of its concepts, methods, and techniques are the same as those of modern municipal law. Very often jurists have thought that these formal differences between international and municipal law can best be expressed by classifying the former as "morality." Yet it seems clear that to mark the difference in this way is to invite confusion.

Sometimes insistence that the rules governing the relations between states are only moral rules, is inspired by the old dogmatism, that any form of social structure that is not reducible to orders backed by threats can only be a form of "morality." It is, of course, possible to use the word "morality" in this very comprehensive way; so used, it provides a conceptual wastepaper basket into which will go the rules of games, clubs, etiquette, the fundamental provisions of constitutional law and international law, together with rules and principles which we ordinarily think of as moral ones, such as the common prohibitions of cruelty, dishonesty, or lying. The objection to this procedure is that between what is thus classed together as "morality" there are such important differences of both form and social function, that no conceivable purpose, practical or theoretical, could be served by so crude a classification. Within the category of morality thus artificially widened, we should have to mark out afresh the old distinctions which it blurs.

In the particular case of international law there are a number of different reasons for resisting the classification of its rules as "morality." The first is that states often reproach each other for immoral conduct or praise themselves or others for living up to the standard of international morality. No doubt *one* of the virtues which states may show or fail to show is that of abiding by international law, but that does not mean that that law is morality. In fact the appraisal of states' conduct in terms of morality is recognizably different from the formulation of claims, demands, and the acknowledgements of rights and obligations under the rules of international law. In Chapter V we listed certain features which might be taken as defining characteristics of social morality: among them was the distinctive form of moral pressure by which moral rules are primarily supported. This consists not of appeals to fear or threats of retaliation or demands for compensation, but of appeals to conscience, made in the expectation that once the person addressed is reminded of the moral principle at stake, he may be led by guilt or shame to respect it and make amends.

Claims under international law are not couched in such terms though of course, as in municipal law, they may be joined with a moral appeal. What predominate in the arguments, often technical, which states address to each other over disputed matters of international law, are references to precedents, treaties, and juristic writings; often no mention is made of moral right or wrong, good or bad. Hence the claim that the Peking Government has or has not a right under international law to expel the Nationalist forces from Formosa is very different from the question whether this is fair, just, or a morally good or bad thing to do, and is backed by characteristically different arguments. No doubt in the relations between states there are half-way houses between what is clearly law and what is clearly morality, analogous to the standards of politeness and courtesy recognized in private life. Such is the sphere of international "comity" exemplified in the privilege extended to diplomatic envoys of receiving goods intended for personal use free of duty.

A more important ground of distinction is the following. The rules of international law, like those of municipal law, are often morally quite indifferent. A rule may exist because it is convenient or necessary to have some clear fixed rule about the subjects with which it is concerned, but not because any moral importance is attached to the particular rule. It may well be but one of a large number of possible rules, any one of which would have done equally well. Hence legal rules, municipal and international, commonly contain much specific detail, and draw arbitrary distinctions, which would be unintelligible as elements in moral rules or principles. It is true that we must not be dogmatic about the possible content of social morality: as we saw in Chapter V the morality of a social group may contain much by way of injunction which may appear absurd or superstitious when viewed in the light of modern knowledge. So it is possible, though difficult, to imagine that men with general beliefs very different from ours, might come to attach *moral* importance to driving on the left instead of the right of the road or could come to feel moral guilt if they broke a promise witnessed by two witnesses, but no such guilt if it was witnessed by one. Though such strange moralities are possible, it yet remains true that a morality cannot (logically) contain rules which are generally held by those who subscribe to them to be in no way preferable to alternatives and of no intrinsic importance. Law, however, though it also contains much that is of moral importance, can and does contain just such rules, and the arbitrary distinctions, formalities, and highly specific detail which would be most difficult to understand as part of morality, are consequently natural and easily comprehensible features of law. For one of the typical functions of law, unlike morality, is to introduce just these elements in order to maximize certainty and predictability and to facilitate the proof or assessments of claims. Regard for forms and detail carried to excess, has earned for law the reproaches of "formalism" and "legalism;" yet it is important to remember that these vices are exaggerations of some of the law's distinctive qualities.

It is for this reason that just as we expect a municipal legal system, but not morality, to tell us how many witnesses a validly executed will must have, so we expect international law, but not morality, to tell us such things as the number of days a belligerent vessel may stay for refuelling or repairs in a neutral port; the width of territorial waters; the methods to be used in their measurement. All these things are necessary and desirable provisions for *legal rules* to make, but so long as the sense is retained that such rules may equally well take any of several forms, or are important only as one among many possible means to specific ends, they remain distinct from rules which have the status in individual or social life characteristic of morality. Of course not all the rules of international law are of this formal, or arbitrary, or morally neutral kind. The point is only that legal rules *can* and moral rules *cannot* be of this kind.

The difference in character between international law and anything which we naturally think of as morality has another aspect. Though the effect of a law requiring or proscribing certain practices might ultimately be to bring about changes in the morality of a group, the notion of a legislature making or repealing moral rules is, as we saw in Chapter VII, an absurd one. A legislature cannot introduce a new rule and give it the status of a moral rule by its *fiat*, just as it cannot, by the same means, give a rule the status of a tradition, though the reasons why this is so may not be the same in the two cases. Accordingly morality does not merely lack or happen not to have a legislature; the very idea of change by human legislative *fiat* is repugnant to the idea of morality. This is so because we conceive of morality as the ultimate standard by which human actions (legislative or otherwise) are evaluated. The contrast with international law is clear. There is nothing in the nature or function of international law which is similarly inconsistent with the idea that the rules might be subject to legislative change; the lack of a legislature is just a lack which many think of as a defect one day to be repaired.

Finally we must notice a parallel in the theory of international law between the argument, criticized in Chapter V, that even if particular rules of municipal law may conflict with morality, none the less the system as a whole must rest on a generally diffused conviction that there is a moral obligation to obey its rules, though this may be overridden in special exceptional cases. It has often been said in the discussion of the "foundations" of international law, that in the last resort, the rules of international law *must* rest on the conviction of states that there is a moral obligation to obey them; yet, if this means more than that the obligations which they recognize are not enforceable by officially organized sanctions, there seems no reason to accept it. Of course it is possible to think of circumstances which would certainly justify our saying that a state considered some course of conduct required by international law morally obligatory, and acted for that reason. It might, for example, continue to perform the obligations of an onerous treaty because of the manifest harm to humanity that would follow if confidence in treaties was severely shaken, or because of the sense that it was only fair to shoulder the irksome burdens of a code from which it, in its turn, had profited in the past when the burden fell on others. Precisely whose motives, thoughts and feelings on such matters of moral conviction are to be attributed to the state is a question which need not detain us here.

But though there *may* be such a sense of moral obligation it is difficult to see why or in what sense it *must* exist as a condition of the existence of international law. It is clear that in the practice of states certain rules are regularly respected even at the cost of certain sacrifices; claims are formulated by reference to them; breaches of the rules expose the offender to serious criticism and are held to justify claims for compensation or retaliation. These, surely, are all the elements required to support the statement that there exist among states rules imposing obligations upon them. The proof that "binding" rules in any society exist, is simply that they are thought of, spoken of, and function as such. What more is required by way of "foundations" and why, if more is required, must it be a foundation of moral obligation? It is, of course, true that rules could not exist or function in the relations between states unless a preponderant majority accepted the rules and voluntarily cooperated in maintaining them. It is true also that the pressure exercised on those who break or threaten to break the rules is often relatively weak, and has usually been decentralized or unorganized. But as in the case of individuals, who voluntarily accept the far more strongly coercive system of municipal law, the motives for voluntarily supporting such a system may be extremely diverse. It may well be that any form of legal order is at its healthiest when there is a generally diffused sense that it is morally obligatory to conform to it. None the less, adherence to law may not be motivated by it, but by calculations of long-term interest, or by the wish to continue a tradition or by disinterested concern for others. There seems no good reason for identifying any of these as a necessary condition of the existence of law either among individuals or states.

5. Analogies of Form and Content

To the innocent eye, the formal structure of international law lacking a legislature, courts with compulsory jurisdiction and officially organized sanctions, appears very different from that of municipal law. It resembles, as we have said, in form though not at all in content, a simple regime of primary or customary law. Yet some theorists, in their anxiety to defend against the sceptic the title of international law to be called "law," have succumbed to the temptation to minimize these formal differences, and to exaggerate the analogies which can be found in international law to legislation or other desirable formal features of municipal law. Thus, it has been claimed that war, ending with a treaty whereby the defeated power cedes territory, or assumes obligations, or accepts some diminished form of independence, is essentially a legislative act; for, like legislation, it is an imposed legal change. Few would now be impressed by this analogy, or think

that it helped to show that international law had an equal title with municipal law to be called "law;" for one of the salient differences between municipal and international law is that the former usually does not, and the latter does, recognize the validity of agreements extorted by violence.

A variety of other, more respectable analogies have been stressed by those who consider the title of "law" to depend on them. The fact that in almost all cases the judgment of the International Court and its predecessor, the Permanent Court of International Justice, have been duly carried out by the parties, has often been emphasized as if this somehow offset the fact that, in contrast with municipal courts, no state can be brought before these international tribunals without its prior consent. Analogies have also been found between the use of force, legally regulated and officially administered, as a sanction in municipal law and "decentralized sanctions," i.e., the resort to war or forceful retaliation by a state which claims that its rights under international law have been violated by another. That there is some analogy is plain; but its significance must be assessed in the light of the equally plain fact that, whereas a municipal court has a compulsory jurisdiction to investigate the rights and wrongs of "self help." and to punish a wrongful resort to it, no international court has a similar jurisdiction.

Some of these dubious analogies may be considered to have been much strengthened by the obligations which states have assumed under the United Nations Charter. But, again, any assessment of their strength is worth little if it ignores the extent to which the law enforcement provisions of the Charter, admirable on paper, have been paralysed by the veto and the ideological divisions and alliances of the great powers. The reply, sometimes made, that the law-enforcement provisions of municipal law *might* also be paralysed by a general strike is scarcely convincing; for in our comparison between municipal law and international law we are concerned with what exists in fact, and here the facts are undeniably different.

There is, however, one suggested formal analogy between international and municipal law which deserves some scrutiny here. Kelsen and many modern theorists insist that, like municipal law, international law possesses and indeed must possess a "basic norm," or what we have termed a rule of recognition, by reference to which the validity of the other rules of the system is assessed, and in virtue of which the rules constitute a single system. The opposed view is that this analogy of structure is false: international law simply consists of a *set* of separate primary rules of obligation which are not united in this manner. It is, in the usual terminology of international lawyers, a set of customary rules of which the rule giving binding force to treaties is one. It is notorious that those who have embarked on the task have found very great difficulties in formulating the "basic norm" of international law. Candidates for this position include the principle *pacta sunt servanda*. This has, however, been abandoned by most theorists, since it seems incompatible with the fact that not all obligations under international law arise from "*pacta*," however widely that term is construed. So it has been replaced by something less familiar: the so-called rule that "States should behave as they customarily behave."

We shall not discuss the merits of these and other rival formulations of the basic norm of international law; instead we shall question the assumption that it must contain such an element. Here the first and perhaps the last question to ask is: why should we make this *a priori* assumption (for that is what it is) and so prejudge the actual character of the rules of international law? For it is surely conceivable (and perhaps has often been the case) that a society may live by rules imposing obligations on its members as "binding," even though they are regarded simply as a set of separate rules, not unified by or deriving their validity from any more basic rule. It is plain that the mere existence of rules does not involve the existence of such a basic rule. In most modern societies there are rules of etiquette, and, though we do not

think of them as imposing obligations, we may well talk of such rules as existing; yet we would not look for, nor could we find, a basic rule of etiquette from which the validity of the separate rules was derivable. Such rules do not form a system but a mere set, and, of course, the inconveniences of this form of social control, where matters more important than those of etiquette are at stake, are considerable. They have already been described in Chapter V. Yet if rules are in fact accepted as standards of conduct, and supported with appropriate forms of social pressure distinctive of obligatory rules, nothing more is required to show that they are binding rules, even though, in this simple form of social structure, we have not something which we do have in municipal law: namely a way of demonstrating the validity of individual rules by reference to some ultimate rule of the system.

There are of course a number of questions which we can ask about rules which constitute not a system but a simple set. We can, for example, ask questions about their historical origin, or questions concerning the causal influences that have fostered the growth of the rules. We can also ask questions about the value of the rules to those who live by them, and whether they regard themselves as morally bound to obey them or obey from some other motive. But we cannot ask in the simpler case one kind of question which we can ask concerning the rules of a system enriched, as municipal law is, by a basic norm or secondary rule of recognition. In the simpler case we cannot ask: "From what ultimate provision of the system do the separate rules derive their validity or "binding force"?" For there is no such provision and need be none. It is, therefore, a mistake to suppose that a basic rule or rule of recognition is a generally necessary condition of the existence of rules of obligation or "binding" rules. This is not a necessity, but a luxury, found in advanced social systems whose members not merely come to accept separate rules piecemeal, but are committed to the acceptance in advance of general classes of rule, marked out by general criteria of validity. In the simpler form of society we must wait and see whether a rule gets accepted as a rule or not; in a system with a basic rule of recognition we can say before a rule is actually made, that it *will* be valid *if* it conforms to the requirements of the rule of recognition.

The same point may be presented in a different form. When such a rule of recognition is added to the simple set of separate rules, it not only brings with it the advantages of system and ease of identification, but it makes possible for the first time a new form of statement. These are internal statements about the validity of the rules; for we can now ask in a new sense, "What provision of the system makes this rule binding?" or, in Kelsen's language, "What, within the system, is the reason of its validity?" The answers to these new questions are provided by the basic rule of recognition. But though, in the simpler structure, the validity of the rules cannot thus be demonstrated by reference to any more basic rule, this does not mean that there is some question about the rules or their binding force or validity which is left unexplained. It is not the case that there is some mystery as to why the rules in such a simple social structure are binding, which a basic rule, if only we could find it, would resolve. The rules of the simple structure are, like the basic rule of the more advanced systems, binding if they are accepted and function as such. These simple truths about different forms of social structure can, however, easily be obscured by the obstinate search for unity and system where these desirable elements are not in fact to be found.

There is indeed something comic in the efforts made to fashion a basic rule for the most simple forms of social structure which exist without one. It is as if we were to insist that a naked savage *must* really be dressed in some invisible variety of modern dress. Unfortunately, there is also here a standing possibility of confusion. We may be persuaded to treat as a basic rule, something which is an empty repetition of the mere fact that the society concerned (whether of individuals or states) observes certain standards of conduct as obligatory rules. This is surely the status of the strange basic norm which has been suggested for international law: "States should behave as they have customarily behaved." For it says nothing more than that those who accept certain rules must also observe a rule that the rules ought to be observed. This is a mere useless reduplication of the fact that a set of rules are accepted by states as binding rules.

Again once we emancipate ourselves from the assumption that international law *must* contain a basic rule, the question to be faced is one of fact. What is the actual character of the rules as they function in the relations between states? Different interpretations of the phenomena to be observed are of course possible; but it is submitted that there is no basic rule providing general criteria of validity for the rules of international law, and that the rules which are in fact operative constitute not a system but a set of rules, among which are the rules providing for the binding force of treaties. It is true that, on many important matters, the relations between states are regulated by multilateral treaties, and it is sometimes argued that these may bind states that are not parties. If this were generally recognized, such treaties would in fact be legislative enactments and international law would have distinct criteria of validity for its rules. A basic rule of recognition could then be formulated which would represent an actual feature of the system and would be more than an empty restatement of the fact that a set of rules are in fact observed by states. Perhaps international law is at present in a stage of transition towards acceptance of this and other forms which would bring it nearer in structure to a municipal system. If, and when, this transition is completed the formal analogies, which at present seem thin and even delusive, would acquire substance, and the sceptic's last doubts about the legal "quality" of international law may then be laid to rest. Till this stage is reached the analogies are surely those of function and content, not of form. Those of function emerge most clearly when we reflect on the ways in which international law differs from morality, some of which we examined in the last section. The analogies of content consist in the range of principles, concepts, and methods which are common to both municipal and international law, and make the lawyers' technique freely transferable from the one to the other. Bentham, the inventor of the expression "international law," defended it simply by saying that it was "sufficiently analogous"[1] to municipal law. To this, two comments are perhaps worth adding. First, that the analogy is one of content not of form: secondly, that, in this analogy of content, no other social rules are so close to municipal law as those of international law.

---

1   Principles of Morals and Legislation, XVII. 25, n. I.

◆ ◆ ◆ ◆ ◆

MARTTI KOSKENNIEMI

"The Politics of International Law"
1 *European Journal of International Law* (1990)

I. The Flight from Politics

It may be a matter of some controversy among historians as to when one should date the beginning of the modern states-system.[1] Less open to debate, however, is that somehow the idea of such a system is historically as well as conceptually linked with that of an international Rule of Law. In a system whose units are assumed to serve no higher purpose than their own interests and which assumes the perfect equality of those interests, the Rule of Law seems indeed the sole thinkable principle of organization—short of the *bellum omnium*. Since the publication of Emmerich de Vattel's *Droit des gens ou principes de loi naturelle appliqueés a la conduite et aux affaires des nations et des souverains* (1758), jurists have written about international matters by assuming that the liberal principles of the Enlightenment and their logical corollary, the Rule of Law, could be extended to apply in the organization of international society just as they had been used in the domestic one.[2]

Notwithstanding the historical difficulty with dates and origins, the connexion between the Rule of Law and the principles of the Enlightenment appear evident. Of the latter, none seems more important than that of the subjectivity of value.[3] Hobbes writes:

> For one calleth wisdom what another calleth fear and one cruelty what another justice; and prodigality what another magnanimity ... And therefrom such names can never be ground for any ratiocination.[4]

---

1   For example, A.F. von der Heydte: *Geburistunde des souveränen Staates* (1952) suggests the turn of the 14th century, 41-43, while F.H. Hinsley: *Power and the Pursuit of Peace* (1962), 153, argues that one cannot properly speak of a states-system until the 18th century.

2   The analogy is explicit in J.J. Rousseau: *The Social Contract* (trans. & introd. by Maurice Cranston) (1986) Bk.I Ch. 7 at 63; J. Locke, *Two Treatises on Government* (intr. by W.S. Carpenter) (1984) Second Treatise, sect. 183 at 211. For commentary, see, e.g., P. Vinogradoff, *Historical Types of International Law* (1920) 55-57; E.D. Dickinson, *The Equality of States in International Law* (1920) 29-31, 49-50, 97-98, 111-13. See also M. Walzer, *Just and Unjust Wars* (1980) 58-63; C.L. Beitz, *Political Theory and International Relations* (1979) 74. For useful analysis of the effect of the analogy to the conception of a state's (territorial) rights, see A. Carty, *The Decay of International Law?* (1986) 44-46, 55-56.

3   My discussion of this principle is influenced by R.M. Unger, *Knowledge and Politics* (1975) 76-81, and A. MacIntyre, *After Virtue; A Study in Moral Theory* (2nd ed.) (1985) 6-35.

4   T. Hobbes, *Leviathan* (ed. & intr. by C.B. Macpherson) (1982) Ch. 4, at 109-10.

However much later liberals may have disliked Hobbes' substantive conclusions or his political realism, the one thing which unites them with Hobbes is their criticism of relying upon natural principles to justify political authority. Appealing to principles which would preexist man and be discoverable only through faith or *recta ratio* was to appeal to abstract and unverifiable maximums which only camouflaged the subjective preferences of the speaker. It was premised on utopian ideals which were constantly used as apologies for tyranny.

From the simple denial of the existence of principles of natural justice—or at least of our capacity to know them—follow the three liberal principles of social organization: freedom, equality and the Rule of Law. If man is not born to a world of pre-existing norms, then he is born free; if there are no antecedent principles establishing the relative worths of individuals, the individuals must be assumed equal. And finally, freedom and equality are guaranteed only if social constraint is governed by public, verifiable and determining rules: "A free people obey but it does not serve; it has magistrates but not masters; it obeys nothing but the laws, and thanks to the force of laws, it does not obey men."[5]

The fight for an international Rule of Law is a fight against politics, understood as a matter of furthering subjective desires and leading into an international anarchy. Though some measure of politics is inevitable, it should be constrained by non-political rules: "... the health of the political realm is maintained by conscientious objection to the political."[6]

The diplomatic history of the 19th century is a history of such a fight. Since the Vienna Congress of 1814–15 and the defeat of Napoleon, the relations between European powers were no longer built on one power's search for primacy but on a general pursuit of the maintenance of the balance of power, guaranteed by complicated legal procedures and alliances.[7] As contemporaries increasingly saw Europe as a "system" of independent and equal political communities (instead of a *republica Christiana*) they began to assume that the governing principles needed to become neutral and objective—that is, legal.

The legal scholarship of the 19th century interpreted and systematized diplomatic practice into legal rules. It assumed that the behavior of European states was determined and explicable by reference to a body of (European) public law. The plausibility of this assumption relied on the procedural character of that law. Containing mainly rules concerning diplomatic and consular contacts, procedures for attaining statehood, territory or neutral status, it did not severely restrict the ends which European sovereigns attempted to pursue. In particular, it renounced theories of the just war: war became now one political procedure among others.[8] Though the professional lawyers of the 19th century did speak about justice in the conduct of the sovereigns' affairs, they no longer thought of justice as material principles. Woolsey put the matter adroitly:

> By justice, however, we intend not justice objective, but as it appears to the party concerned or, at least, as it is claimed to exist. From the independence of nations it results that each has a right to hold and make good its own view of right in its own affairs.[9]

Though 20th-century lawyers have not looked too kindly upon the scholarship of the preceding century, they never rejected the ideal of the Rule of

---

5   J.J. Rousseau, *Œuvres complètes*, Pléiade (Vol. III sect. 841-42) quoted by Cranston (Introduction to J.J. Rousseau, *The Social Contract, supra* note 2, at 32).

6   Wight, "Western Values in International Relations," in Butterfield, Wight, *Diplomatic Investigations: Essays in the Theory of International Politics* (1966) 122.

7   See, e.g., F.H. Hinsley, *supra* note 1, at 186-271.

8   See, e.g., H. Wheaton, *Elements of International Law* (Text of 1866 with Notes, Carnegie Endowment, Classics of International Law, No.19) (1936) 313-14.

9   T.D. Woolsey, *Introduction to the Study of International Law; Designed as an Aid in Teaching, and in Historical Studies* (5th ed.) (1879) 183.

Law. On the contrary, the reconstructive scholarship which emerged first from the catastrophe of World War I and then in the 1950s and 1960s accused the pre-war doctrines of *not going far enough* to uphold the Rule of Law. Wherever attempts by jurists to construct a solid framework of public law had faltered, it had done so not because of some defect in the liberal assumptions behind this project but because jurists had deviated from them.

The vision of a Rule of Law between states (which re-emerged most recently in United Nations General Assembly Resolution 44/23 [15 November 1989] declaring the period 1990-99 as the "United Nations Decade of International Law") is yet another reformulation of the liberal impulse to escape politics. So strong is the grip of this vision that the representative of the Soviet Union at the same session of the General Assembly explained that in his view to restructure the basis of international relations there was a need to "arrive at a comprehensive international strategy for establishing the primacy of law in relations between states."[10]

Throughout the present century, reconstructive doctrines have claimed that what merits criticism is the corruption of the Rule of Law either in the narrow chauvinism of diplomats or the speculative utopias of an academic elite. If only the Rule of Law can be fortified to exclude these contrasting distortions, then at least the jurist's part in the construction of a just world order has been adequately executed.

In this article, however, I shall extend the criticism of the liberal idea of the *Rechtstaat*, a commonplace in late modern western society,[11] into its international counterpart. I shall attempt to show

that our inherited ideal of a World Order based on the Rule of Law thinly hides from sight the fact that social conflict must still be solved by political means and that even though there may exist a common legal rhetoric among international lawyers, that rhetoric must, *for reasons internal to the ideal itself,* rely on essentially contested—political—principles to justify outcomes to international disputes.[12]

II. The Content of the Rule of Law: Concreteness and Normativity

Organizing society through legal rules is premised on the assumption that these rules are objective in some sense that political ideas, views, or preferences are not. To show that international law is objective—that is, independent from international politics—the legal mind fights a battle on two fronts. On the one hand, it aims to ensure the *concreteness* of the law by distancing it from theories of natural justice. On the other hand, it aims to guarantee the *normativity* of the law by creating distance between it and actual state behaviour, will, or interest. Law enjoys independence from politics only if both of these conditions are simultaneously present.

The requirement of concreteness results from the liberal principle of the subjectivity of value. To avoid political subjectivism and illegitimate constraint,[13] we must base law on something concrete—on the actual (verifiable) behaviour, will and interest of the members of society-states. The modern view is a *social conception of law.*[14] For it, law is not a nat-

---

10 "Memorandum: On Enhancing the Role of International Law," UN Doc.A/44/585 (2 October 1989).

11 For the ensuing text, particularly relevant are criticisms stressing the *internal* tensions of liberal theory. See generally Unger, *supra* note 3, at 63-103 and, e.g., A. Levine, *Liberal Democracy: A Critique of its Theory* (1981) 16-32; Fishkin, "Liberal Theory and the Problem of Justification," *NOMOS XXVIII* at 207-31.

12 This article is a condensed version of some of the themes in M. Koskenniemi, *From Apology to Utopia; the Structure of International Legal Argument* (1989).

13 For a typical argument stressing the political character of natural law, see, e.g., S. Sur, *L'interprétation en droit international public* (1974) 25-32 or J.H.W. Verzijl, *International Law in Historical Perspective* (Vol. I) (1968) 391-93.

14 "C'est à une conception fonctionnelle de pouvoir, à une conception sociale du droit que s'attache notre enseigne-

ural but an artificial creation, a reflexion of social circumstances.

According to the requirement of normativity, law should be applied regardless of the political preferences of legal subjects. In particular, it should be applicable even against a state which opposes its application to itself. As international lawyers have had the occasion to point out, legal rules whose content or application depends on the will of the legal subject for whom they are valid are not proper legal rules at all but apologies for the legal subject's political interest.[15]

Stated in such a fashion, I believe that the requirements of legal objectivity *vis-à-vis* political subjectivity are met. For if the law could be verified or justified only by reference to somebody's views on what the law *should* be like (i.e., theories of justice), it would coincide with their political opinions. Similarly, if we could apply the law against those states which accept it, then it would coincide with those states' political views.

This argumentative structure, however, which forces jurists to prove that their law is valid because concrete and normative in the above sense, both creates and destroys itself. For it is impossible to prove that a rule, principle or doctrine (in short, an argument) is both concrete and normative simultaneously. The two requirements *cancel each other*. An argument about concreteness is an argument about the closeness of a particular rule, principle or doctrine to state practice. But the closer to state practice an argument is, the less normative and the more political it seems. The more it seems just another apology for existing power. An argument about normativity, on the other hand, is an argument which intends to demonstrate the rule's distance from state will and practice. The more normative a rule, the more political it seems because the less it is possible

to argue it by reference to social context. It seems utopian and—like theories of natural justice—manipulable at will.

The dynamics of international legal argument are provided by the constant effort of lawyers to show that their law is either concrete or normative and their becoming thus vulnerable to the charge that such law is in fact political because apologist or utopian. Different doctrinal and practical controversies turn on transformations of this dilemma. It lies behind such dichotomies as "positivism"/ "naturalism," "consent"/"justice," "autonomy"/ "community," "process"/"rule," etc., and explains why these and other oppositions keep recurring and do not seem soluble in a permanent way. They recur because it seems possible to defend one's legal argument only by showing either its closeness to, or its distance from, state practice. They seem insoluble because both argumentative strategies are vulnerable to what appear like valid criticisms, compelled by the system itself.[16]

This provides an argumentative structure which is capable of providing a valid criticism of each substantive position but which itself cannot justify any. The fact that positions are constantly taken and solutions justified by lawyers, demonstrates that the structure does not possess the kind of distance from politics for which the Rule of Law once seemed necessary. It seems possible to adopt a position only by a political choice: a choice which must ultimately defend itself in terms of a conception of justice.

III. Doctrinal Structures

Two criticisms are often advanced against international law. One group of critics has accused international law of being too political in the sense of being too dependent on states' political power. Another group has argued that the law is too pol-

---

ment," De Visscher, "Cours général de principes de droit international public," 86 *RCDI* (1954) 451.

15   See, e.g., H. Lauterpacht, *The Function of Law in the International Community* (1933) 189 and *passim*.

16   For an alternative but similar type of exposition, see D. Kennedy, *International Legal Structure* (1987).

itical because founded on speculative utopias. The standard point about the non-existence of legislative machineries, compulsory adjudication and enforcement procedures captures both criticisms. From one perspective, this criticism highlights the infinite flexibility of international law, its character as a manipulable facade for power politics. From another perspective, the criticism stresses the moralistic character of international law, its distance from the realities of power politics. According to the former criticism, international law is too *apologetic* to be taken seriously in the construction of international order. According to the latter, it is too *utopian* to the identical effect.

International lawyers have had difficulty answering these criticisms. The more reconstructive doctrines have attempted to prove the normativity of the law, its autonomy from politics, the more they have become vulnerable to the charge of utopianism. The more they have insisted on the close connexion between international law and state behaviour, the less normative their doctrines have appeared. Let me outline the four positions which modern international lawyers have taken to prove the relevance of their norms and doctrines. These are mutually exclusive and logically exhaustive positions and account for a full explanation of the possibilities of doctrinal argument.

Many of the doctrines which emerged from the ashes of legal scholarship at the close of World War I explained the failure of pre-war international doctrines by reference to their apologist character. Particular objects of criticism were "absolutist" doctrines of sovereignty, expressed in particular in the *Selbstverpflichtunglehre*, doctrines stressing the legal significance of the balance of power or delimiting the legal functions to matters which were unrelated to questions of "honour" or "vital interest." Writings by Hersch Lauterpacht, Alfred Verdross and Hans Kelsen among others, created an extremely influential interpretation of the mistakes of prewar

doctrines.[17] By associating the failure of those doctrines with their excessive closeness to state policy and national interest and by advocating the autonomy of international legal rules, these jurists led the way to the establishment of what could be called a *rule approach* to international law, stressing the law's normativity, its capacity to oppose state policy as the key to its constraining relevance.

This approach insists on an objective, formal test of pedigree (sources) which will tell which standards qualify as legal rules and which do not. If a rule meets this test, then it is binding. Though there is disagreement between rule approach lawyers over what constitutes the proper test, there is no dispute about its importance. The distinctions between hard and soft law, rules and principles, regular norms and *jus cogens*, for instance, are suspect: these only betray political distinctions with which the lawyer should not be too concerned.[18] Two well-known criticisms have been directed against the rule approach. First, it has remained unable to exclude the influence of political considerations from its assumed tests of pedigree. To concede that rules are sometimes hard to find while their content remains, to adopt H.L.A. Hart's expression "relatively indeterminate"[19] is to undermine the autonomy which the rule approach stressed. Second, the very desire for autonomy seems suspect. A pure theory of law, the assumption of a *Völkerrechtsgemeinschaft* or the ideal of the wholeness of law—a central assumption in most rule approach

---

17 Lauterpacht, *supra* note 15; A. Verdross, *Die Verfassung der Völkerrechtsgemeinschaft* (1926); H. Kelsen, *Das Problem der Souveränität und die Theorie des Völkerrechts* (1920).

18 This approach is best illustrated in G. Schwarzenberger, *The Inductive Approach to International Law* (1965). Many of its points are forcefully made in Weil, "Towards Relative Normativity in International Law," 77 *AJIL* (1983) 413-42. For further references on this and the other approaches, see Koskenniemi, *supra* note 12, at 154-86.

19 H.L.A. Hart, *The Concept of Law* (1961) 132.

writing[20]—may only betray forms of irrelevant doctrinal utopianism. They achieve logical consistency at the cost of applicability in the real world of state practice.

The second major position in contemporary scholarship uses these criticisms to establish itself. A major continental interpretation of the mistakes of 19th-century lawyers and diplomats explains them as a result of naive utopianism: an unwarranted belief in the viability of the Congress system, with its ideas of legality and collective intervention. It failed because it had not been able to keep up with the politics of emergent nationalism and the increasing pace of social and technological change. Lawyers such as Nicolas Politis or Georges Scelle stressed the need to link international law much more closely to the social—even biological—necessities of international life.[21] Roscoe Pound's programmatic writings laid the basis for the contemporary formulation of this approach by criticizing the attempt to think of international law in terms of abstract rules. It was, rather, to be thought of "in terms of social ends."[22]

According to this approach—*the policy approach*—international law can only be relevant if it is firmly based in the social context of international policy. Rules are only trends of past decision which may or may not correspond to social necessities. "Binding force" is a juristic illusion. Standards are, in fact, more or less effective and it is their effectiveness—their capacity to further social goals—which is the relevant question, not their formal "validity."[23]

But this approach is just as vulnerable to well-founded criticisms as the rule approach. By emphasizing the law's concreteness, it will ultimately do away with its constraining force altogether. If law is only what is effective, then by definition, it becomes an apology for the interests of the powerful. If, as Myres McDougal does, this consequence is avoided by postulating some "goal values" whose legal importance is independent of considerations of effectiveness, then the (reformed) policy approach becomes vulnerable to criticisms which it originally voiced against the rule approach. In particular, it appears to assume an illegitimate naturalism which—as critics stressing the liberal principle of the subjectivity of value have noted—is in constant danger of becoming just an apology of some states' policies.[24]

The rule and the policy approaches are two contrasting ways of trying to establish the relevance of international law in the face of what appear as well-founded criticisms. The former does this by stressing the law's normativity, but fails to be convincing because it lacks concreteness. The latter builds upon the concreteness of international law, but loses the normativity, the binding force of its law. It is hardly surprising, then, that some lawyers have occupied the two remaining positions: they have either assumed that international law can neither be seen as normatively controlling nor widely applied in practice (the sceptical position), or have continued writing as if both the law's binding force as well as its correspondence with developments in international practice were a matter of course (ideal-

---

20 See, e.g., Lauterpacht, "Some Observations on the Prohibition of "Non liquet" and the Completeness of Law," *Symbolae Verzijl* (1958) 196-221, and the "realist" criticism by Stone, "Non-Liquet and the Function of Law in the International Community," XXV *BYUL* (1959) 124-61.

21 G. Scelle, *Précis de droit des gens. Principes et systématique I-II* (1932, 1936); N. Politis, *Les nouvelles tendances du droit international* (1927).

22 Pound, "Philosophical Theory and International Law," I *Bibliotheca Visseiana* (1923)1-90.

23 The contemporary formulation of this approach is perhaps clearest in McDougal, "International Law, Power

and Policy: A Contemporary Perspective," 82 *RCDI* (1953) 133-259. For useful analysis, see B. Rosenthal, *L'étude de l'œuvre de Myres Smith McDougal en matiere du droit international public* (1970).

24 For such criticisms, see, e.g., Allott, "Language, Method and the Nature of International Law," 45 *BYIL* (1971) 123-25; Boyle, "Ideals and Things: International Legal Scholarship and the Prison-House of Language," 26 *Harvard Journal Int'l Law* (1985) 349; and Fitzmaurice, "vae Victis or Woe to the Negotiators!," 65 *AJIL* (1971) 370-73.

ist position). The former ends in cynicism, the latter in contradiction.[25]

The late modern mainstream often situates itself between the rule and the policy approaches. In Richard Falk's words, the task of an adequate doctrine is to establish:

> [an] intermediate position, one that maintains the distinctiveness of the legal order while managing to be responsive to the extralegal setting of politics, history and morality.[26]

But such a movement towards pragmatic eclecticism seems self-defeating. There is no space between the four positions: rule approach, policy approach, scepticism and idealism. Middle-of-the-road doctrines may seem credible only insofar as their arguments, doctrines or norms are not contested. But as soon as disagreement emerges, such doctrines, too, must defend their positions either by showing their autonomous binding force, or by demonstrating their close relationship with what states actually do. At this point, they become vulnerable to the charge of being either utopian or apologist.

The result is a curiously incoherent doctrinal structure in which each position is *ad hoc* and therefore survives only. Mainstream doctrine retreats into general statements about the need to "combine" concreteness and normativity, realism and idealism, which bear no consequence to its normative conclusion. It then advances, emphasizing the contextuality of each solution—thus undermining its own emphasis on the general and impartial character of its system.

A doctrine's own contradictions force it into an impoverished and unreflective pragmatism. On the one hand, the "idealist" illusion is preserved that law can and does play a role in the organization of social life among states. On the other, the "realist" criticisms have been accepted and the law is seen as distinctly secondary to power and politics. Modern doctrine, as Philip Allott has shown, uses a mixture of positivistic and naturalistic, consensualistic and non-consensualistic, teleological, practical, political, logical and factual arguments in happy confusion, unaware of its internal contradictions.[27] The style survives because we recognize in it the liberal doctrine within which we have been accustomed to press our political arguments.

A final point is in order. Both of the main positions reviewed, as well as their combinations, remain distinctly modern. Each refuses to develop its concept of law in terms of some material theory of justice. Each assumes that law is an artificial, human creation which comes about through social processes and that an adequate concept of law is one which provides a reliable description of those processes. Moreover, each bases its claim to superiority *vis-à-vis* the other on that very description. The point at which they diverge is their theory on how to interpret those processes, how to understand what goes on in social life in terms of law-creation and law-application.

The difficulty in choosing between a rule and a policy approach is the difficulty of defending the set of criteria which these put forward to disentangle "law" from other aspects of state behaviour. For the rule approach lawyer, the relevant criteria are provided by his theory of sources. For the policy approach, the corresponding criteria are provided by his theory of "base-values," authority or some constellation of national or global interest and need. Because it is these criteria which claim to provide the correct description of social processes, they cannot be defended without circularity in terms of social

---

25 For references, see Koskenniemi, *supra* note 12, at 167-70, 178-86.

26 Falk, "The Interplay of Westphalia and Charter Conceptions of the International Legal Order" in R. Falk, Black (eds.), *The Future of the International Legal Order* (Vol. I) (1969) 34-35.

27 Allott, *supra* note 24, at 100-05, 113.

processes themselves.[28] To decide on the better approach, one would have to base oneself on some non-descriptive (non-social) theory about significance or about the relative justice of the types of law rendered by the two—or any alternative—matrices.[29] Such a decision would, under the social conception of law and the principle of the subjectivity of value, be one which would seem to have no claim for objective correctness at all. It would be a political decision.

IV. Substantive Structures

It is possible to depict the tension between the demands for normativity and concreteness in two contrasting methods of explaining the origin of the law's substance. From the perspective of concreteness, this substance comes about as a consequence of the fact of sovereignty of the state. One aspect of sovereignty is the liberty to "legislate" international norms which bind oneself. Wherever particular norms have not been thus established, the metaprinciple of sovereign liberty—the "Lotus principle"—remains valid.

It is equally possible to understand the law as a consequence of the functioning of normative criteria for law-emergence. From the perspective of normativity, there must be assumed criteria—"sources"—which allow us to distinguish between the fact of the existence and behaviour of certain centres of power (states) and the law. In this sense, all international legal substance is dependent on the content of those criteria. These explanations seem radically conflicting and appear to provide exhaustive but incompat-

ible methods for elucidating the origin and character of international law. Indeed, much of the dispute between "idealists" and "realists," or the rule and policy approaches, seems captured in this contrast, reflected also in the organization of the substance of standard textbooks. One style consists of preceding the law's substance with an analysis of the character of statehood and that of the international order—the "political foundations." Another starts out by listing the sources of international law and lets the law's substance follow therefrom.

Despite their initially contrasting outlook, both "methods" rely on each other. "Realist" doctrines use criteria to distinguish between law and coercion which fall short of a doctrine of sources only by not bearing that name. "Idealist" programmes look at state practice to defend the relevance of their sources and to verify the content of the law they support.[30] The fact that the available outlooks provide identical substantive systems and both remain vulnerable to well-rehearsed arguments further explains the late modern turn to doctrinal pragmatism.

In the practice of international dispute resolution the lack of a satisfactory explanation for the origin of legal rules has led lawyers to abandon seeking justification for solving interpretative controversies from any of the suggested explanations. Behind ritualistic references to well-known rules and principles of international law (the content of which remains a constant object of dispute), legal practice has increasingly resorted to solving disputes by a contextual criterion—an effort towards an equitable balance. Though this has seemed to work well, the question arises as to whether such practice can be adequately explained in terms of the Rule of Law.

A. Sovereignty

There is a body of doctrine which addresses itself to the questions: what are the character and normative

---

28 The point about conceptual matrices, scientific theories, "paradigms," interests of knowledge or prejudices, if not strictly determining what we can know of the social world at least significantly influencing our perception, is a common theme in much modern epistemology. See further Koskenniemi, *supra* note 12, at 466-71.

29 On choosing significant features for description, see, e.g., J. Finnis, *Natural Law and Natural Rights* (1980) 3, 9-18. See also MacIntyre, "The Indispensability of Political Theory," in Miller, Siedentop, *The Nature of Political Theory* (1983) 19-33.

30 Compare also Kennedy, *supra* note 16.

consequences of statehood? It deals with such themes as the acquisition and loss of statehood, the justification and extent (limits) of territorial sovereignty, the rights of states, the delimitation of competing jurisdictions, etc. The rhetorical importance of this doctrine has varied, but its urgency within the liberal doctrine remains unchallenged. In some ways, sovereignty doctrine plays a role analogous to that played by individual liberty in legitimation discourse. It explains a critical character of legal subjects and sets down basic conditions within which the relations between legal subjects must be organized.

The character and consequences of sovereign statehood might, however, be explained from different perspectives. One explanation holds sovereignty as basic in the sense that it is simply imposed upon the law by the world of facts. Sovereignty and together with it a set of territorial rights and duties are something external to the law, something the law must recognize but which it cannot control. I shall call this the "pure fact view."[31] Another explanation holds sovereignty and everything associated with it as one part of the law's substance, determined and constantly determinable within the legal system, just like any other norms. This might be called the "legal" view.[32]

Normative argument within the different realism of sovereignty doctrine uses the contrast between these explanations to constitute itself. One party argues in terms of pure facts (of effectiveness, for example) while the other makes its point by reference to a criterion external to facts (general recognition, for example). But neither position is sustainable alone. Relying on the pure fact of power is apologist.[33]

Relying on a criterion independent of effectiveness is both abstract and question-begging.[34] It is question-begging as it merely raises the further question about whose interpretation of the criterion or its application should be given precedence. A defendable argument seems compelled to make both points: it must assume that sovereign rights are somehow matters of pure fact as well as of some criterion external to those facts themselves.

The development of the positions of Norway and Denmark during the *Eastern Greenland* case (1933) illustrates this. Originally, Norway based its rights to the disputed territory on its effective occupation. Relying on the views of other states would have violated Norway's sovereign equality. Denmark based its own claim on general recognition and challenged Norwegian title on the absence of such recognition. As the title was to be valid *erga omnes*, it could not be dependent on Norway's acts. In their subsequent arguments both states replied assuming their adversary's first position: Norway argued that its occupation was sanctioned by a generally recognized rule which based title on occupation. Denmark aimed to show that Norway in fact could not have occupied the territory because it had already been effectively occupied by Denmark.[35]

Neither claim could be preferred by simply preferring the "pure fact" or the "criterion" of general recognition because both states argued both points. Consequently, the Court affirmed both argumentative tracks. To support its view that Denmark had sovereignty it argued from Danish occupation as well as general recognition and denied both in respect of Norway.[36] To reach this conclusion, the Court had

---

31 G. Jellinek, *Allgemeine Staatslehre* (3. Aufl.) (1925) 337, 364-67 and, e.g., Korowicz, "Some Present Problems of Sovereignty," 112 *RCDI* (1961) 102.

32 See, e.g., Verdross, *supra* note 17, at 35 and, e.g., Rousseau, "Principes de droit international public," 93 *RCDI* (1958) 394.

33 See, e.g., H. Lauterpacht, *International Law* (Vol. I) (1979) 341-44.

34 See, e.g., *Island of Palmas* case, II *UNRIAA* at 839, 843-46.

35 These points are belaboured at length in the written proceedings. See PCIJ, *Eastern Greenland* case, Ser.C.62 and C.63 and the parties' oral arguments, C.66. For more detailed analysis, see Koskenniemi, *supra* note 12, at 251-53.

36 PCIJ, *Eastern Greenland* case, Ser.A.53 at 45-62.

to make interpretations about the facts (effective occupation) as well as the law (the extent of general recognition) which, however, were external to the applicable facts and the law and which were difficult to justify against Norway's conflicting sovereign interpretation of them. The crucial point in the judgement was the Court's discussion of the famous "Ihlen declaration," which allowed the Court to protect Norwegian sovereignty by denying its possession in reference to the construction according to which Norway itself had already "recognized" Danish sovereignty in Eastern Greenland.[37]

The same structure can be detected in all territorial disputes. In each, the "pure fact" and "legal" approaches dissolve into each other in a way which makes it impossible for the court or tribunal to solve the case by merely choosing one over the other. There are two difficulties. First, the need to make both points loses the initial sense of both: the pure fact view was premised on the assumption that the law follows from what facts say. The legal view assumed that the sense of facts was to be determined by rules. In argument, both points claim to defer, or *overrule* each other. To assume that they could be valid (determining) simultaneously makes both meaningless. Second, that the "pure fact" and the "legal" approaches show themselves indeterminate compels the decision-maker to look closer into the relevant "facts" and the relevant "legal" criterion. Decisions turn on contextual interpretations about the facts and the law—interpretations which, by definition, can no longer be justified by reference to those facts or criteria themselves.

Late modern practice of solving sovereignty disputes pays hardly more than lip-service to the traditional bases of territorial entitlement. Deciding such questions is now thought of in terms of trying to establish the most equitable solution.[38]

The point is that the various interpretations and pragmatic considerations, as well as the final appreciation of the equity of the proposed solution, cannot be justified by reference to legal rules. On the contrary, recourse to the kind of justice involved in such appreciation can only mean, from the perspective of the Rule of Law, capitulation to arbitrariness or undermining the principle of the subjectivity of value, required in the pursuit of a Rule of Law. Let me take another example. It was often argued that the existence of states is a "matter of fact" and that "recognition" was only "declaratory" and not "constitutive" of statehood. If states were created by an external act of recognition, this would introduce for existing states a political right to decide which entities shall enjoy the status of legal subjects. This conflicts with the principles of self-determination and equality—both following from the rejection of a natural law.[39]

Yet, even such an apparently realistic and democratic view needed to assume the existence of some kind of pre-existing criteria whereby it could be ascertained whether statehood was present in some entity or not. The problem was never really that anyone would have seriously contested that the emergence of states was a factual, sociological process. The problem was—and remains—that people view the normative consequences of social process through different criteria and arrive at irreconcilable conclusions even when using the same criteria.

There is, though, a measure of common agreement on a matter as important as statehood. But it has very little to do with factual power or effectiveness. Rhodesia, Transkei and Taiwan were never regarded as states, whereas Tuvalu and Monaco were. But to explain these "anomalies"—as well as other apparently puzzling cases of statehood—simply

---

37 *Id.* at 64-74.

38 See ICJ, *Burkina Faso—Mali Frontier* case, Reports (1986) 567-68 (para. 28) and *infra* note 47.

39 The classic remains Ti-Chiang Chen, *The International Law of Recognition* (1951). See also Kato, "Recognition in International Law: Some Thoughts on Traditional Theory, Attitudes of and Practice by African States," 10 *IJIL* (1970) 299-323.

by reference to the "constitutive" view is equally unsatisfactory. The original objections against the imperialistic character of this theory remain valid. Lauterpacht's middle-of-the-road position about a *duty* to recognize when the legal criteria have been fulfilled remains question-begging:[40] if a state refuses to recognize an entity because it says that this fulfilled the relevant criteria, there is little point to insist upon the existence of the duty. The matter turns on the interpretation of either the factual circumstances or the content of the relevant norm. The real problem is that it is impossible, within liberal premises, to overrule any participant interpretation in a legitimate fashion. Under those premises norms are "auto-interpretative" and each state must be presumed to have the liberty to interpret the sense of factual events around it.[41]

These anomalies of statehood as well as the resurgence of the time-honoured practice of non-recognition after the *Namibia* Opinion (1971) suggest that the attainment of statehood territorial title—at least if the matter is of some importance—has a relationship to what is decided externally.[42] But they also show that to believe that such decision can be understood as "following a rule" requires either a rule or an imagination so flexible that neither the legal nor the pure fact view can take much credit in trying to establish itself upon it.

If the presence of the quality of sovereignty in some entity is difficult to explain in terms of pure facts or legal rules, it is even more trying to do this in respect of the consequences of sovereignty. That the boundaries of domestic jurisdiction are shifting,

and that "sovereignty" has seemed compatible with a state's hermetic isolation as well as extensive integration, indicates that whatever rights or liberties this quality may entail is, as the Permanent Court of International Justice observed, a "relative matter"—dependent on the content of the state's obligations at any given time.[43] In other words nothing determinate follows from sovereignty as a matter of "pure fact"—on the contrary, the content of sovereignty seems determinable only once we know what obligations the state has.

Lawyers adopting the "legal view" sometimes believe that the above conclusion fully vindicates their position. "Sovereignty" is not a matter outside but within the law, a convenient shorthand for the rights, liberties and competences which the law has allocated to the state—and which can be retrieved at any time.[44] To solve a sovereignty dispute it suffices only to look at the body of legal rules, and see if the state has the capacity which it claims by a legislative allocation.

The problem with such a conclusion, however, is that on most areas of state conduct no definite legislative act can be found which would establish the state's competence to act in some particular way. Moreover, and here is another paradox, the most important rules of general application seem to be precisely those rules which lay down the right of exclusive jurisdiction, self-determination, non-intervention and—sovereignty. It is not only that if sovereignty were reduced to a non-normative abstraction, then international law would appear as a huge *lacuna*, we would also lack a connected explanation, an interpretative principle to solve differences of opinion about the content or application of the few particular rules which we could then discern.

In most areas of non-treaty-related state conduct, specific obligations are, or can be, plausibly

---

40   H. Lauterpacht, *Recognition in International Law* (1948).

41   For a useful restatement of this (liberal) point, see Bin Cheng, Custom, "The Future of General State Practice in a Divided World," in Macdonald, Johnston (eds.) *The Structure and Process of International Law,* at 513, 519-23.

42   ICJ, *Namibia* case, Reports (1971) 51, 54 (paras. 112, 117, 119).

43   PCIJ, *Nationality Decrees* case, Ser.B.4. at 24.

44   Schwarzenberger, "The Forms of Sovereignty," 10 *CLP* (1957) 284; Hart, *supra* note 19, at 218.

made to seem either ambiguous or lacking. In such case, the state's sovereignty—its initial liberty—will re-emerge as a normative principle in its own right: in the absence of clear prohibitions, the state must be assumed free. This principle—the *Lotus* principle[45]—is not only a convenient rule of thumb. It encapsulates the assumption that the mere fact of statehood has a normative sense (right of self-determination) and that in the absence of unambiguous legislative prohibitions any attempt to overrule the liberty inherent in statehood can only appear as illegitimate constraint.

The difficulty with the *Lotus* principle is twofold. First, all the rules and principles are more or less indeterminate in their content. If the mere fact of the existence of differing interpretations were sufficient to trigger the presumption of liberty, then the binding force of most rules would seem an illusion. The even more important difficulty is useless if the case involves a *conflict* of liberties. But if it is assumed—as is inevitable if the idea of a material natural law is discarded—that the liberties of one state are delimited by those of another, then any dispute about the rights or obligations of two or more states can be conceptualized in terms of a conflict of their liberties and, consequently, would not seem soluble by simply preferring "liberty"—because we would not know which state's liberty to prefer.

At that point, legal practice breaks from the argumentative cycle by recourse to equity—an undifferentiated sense of justice.

Continental shelf disputes are one example. The International Court of Justice (ICJ), as is well-known, started out with the assumption that the entitlement to continental shelf was a matter of giving effect to the coastal state's *ab initio* and *ipso facto* right. It was not a matter of "abstract justice" but of (objective) fact.[46] But this view has proved unhelp-

ful. Which facts are relevant—the decisive problem—is decided by the Court *ad hoc* and it is not inscribed in some transcendental code *ex ante*. Later delimitations have even ceased paying lip-service to the *ipso facto/ab initio* theory and seen "arriving at an equitable result" as its proper task.[47] The history of the argument in continental shelf cases is the history of the Court first noting the lack, or at least the ambiguity of the relevant rule, it then making appeal to a pure fact (*ipso facto*) view; then abandoning that view (because no "fact" can be normative without an anterior criterion) in favour of a legal view (equity *infra legem*[48] as the correct rule) and the whole cycle ending in the content of that rule being dispersed into justice—a justice which can, under the principle of subjective value and the Rule of Law, only be seen as arbitrary.[49]

Transboundary pollution, to take another example, involves the juxtaposition of the freedoms of the source-state and the target-state: on the one hand, there is the former's sovereign right to exploit its natural resources in accordance with its own environmental policies; on the other hand, there is the victim's sole right to decide what acts shall take place in its territories.[50] The former's liberty to pursue economically beneficial uses of its territory is contrasted with the latter's liberty to enjoy a pure environment. The conflict is insoluble by simply preferring "liberty," or some right inscribed in the very notion of

45 PCIJ, *Lotus* case, Ser.A.10 at 30. See further Koskenniemi, *supra* note 12, at 220-23.

46 ICJ, *North Sea Continental Shelf* cases, Reports (1969) 22-23 (paras. 19-20).

47 ICJ, *Tunisia-Libya Continental Shelf* case, Reports (1982) 59 (para. 70); *Gulf of Maine* case, Reports (1984) 312 (para. 155); *Libya-Malta Continental Shelf* case, Reports (1985) 38-39 (para. 49). See further Koskenniemi, *supra* note 12, at 223-32.

48 ICJ, *North Sea Continental Shelf* cases, Reports (1969) 20-22 (paras. 15-20).

49 For this criticism, see, e.g., Gros. *diss.op.* ICJ, *Tunisia-Libya Continental Shelf* case, Reports (1982) 151-56 and *Gulf of Maine* case, Reports (1984) 378-80.

50 See Principle 21, UN Conference on the Human Environment, Stockholm 5-16 June 1972, UN Doc. A/CONF.48/14.

sovereignty. Balancing seems inevitable in order to reach a decision.[51]

A similar structure manifests itself everywhere within sovereignty doctrine. While sovereignty immunity is usually stated either in terms of the (pure fact of) sovereignty or a systematic necessity for international communication, legal practice tends to construct the foreign sovereign's exemption from local jurisdiction by balancing the two sovereigns' interests vis-à-vis each other.[52] The same seems true in cases dealing with the determination of the allowable reach of a state's extraterritorial jurisdiction.[53] The law on uses of international watercourses[54] and fishery resources,[55] as well as conflicts concerning foreign investment between the home state and the host state,[56] entails the drawing of a boundary between the two sovereigns, a determination of the extent of their sovereign liberty. In the absence of any determinate rules, and being unable to prefer one sovereign over another, legal practice has turned to equity in order to justify the delimitation of the two sovereignties vis-à-vis each other.

The substance of the law under sovereignty doctrines has dispersed into a generalized call for equitable solutions or "balancing" whenever conflicts arise. Standard academic justifications of state rights, either as a consequence of the pure fact of statehood or as laid down in legislative enactments, have no application. Nor can they have application because neither "facts" nor "rules" are self-evident in the way Enlightenment lawyers once believed. The facts which are assumed to establish title do not appear "automatically" but are the result of choosing a criterion from which facts may be invested with normative significance.[57] But rules, too, are always subject to interpretation. In order to link itself to something tangible, interpretation should refer back to some kind of facts. To establish the sense of facts, we must take the perspective of a rule; to decide interpretative controversies about the rule, we must—under the social conception—look at facts. Hence the late modern silence about theoretical justifications and the leap to *ad hoc* compromise.

B. Sources

Despite its original emphasis on actual power, the doctrine of sovereignty seemed unworkable because of the abstract and arbitrary way in which its normative content was determined. It is possible to make a fresh start and imagine that international law might just as well be described not as consequence of statehood but through a set of normative criteria—sources—for law-creation and identification.

Not surprisingly, sources doctrine is riddled with dualisms which express in different ways the conflicting pull of the demands for concreteness and normativity. The very doctrine is often understood from two perspectives: as a description of the social

---

51 See, e.g., Koskenniemi, "International Pollution in the System of International Law," 17 *Oikeustiede-Jurisprudentia* (1984) 152-64; Lammers, "Balancing the Equities: International Environmental Law," *RCDI Coll.* (1984) 153-65.

52 Crawford, "International Law and Foreign Sovereigns, Distinguishing Immune Transactions," 54 *BYIL* (1983) 114-18.

53 Meng, "Völkerrechtliche Zulässigkeit und Grenzen der wirtschaftsverwaltungsrechtlichen Hoheitsakte mit Auslandswirkung," 44 *ZaOeRV* (1984) 675-783; Lowe, "The Problem of Extraterritorial Jurisdiction: Economic Sovereignty and the Search for a Solution," 34 *ICLQ* (1985) 730.

54 Schwebel, "Third Report on the Non-Navigational Uses of International Watercourses," *YILC* (1982/II/1) 75-100.

55 *Fisheries Jurisdiction* cases, ICJ Reports (1974) 30 (paras. 69-70).

56 *The LIAMCO Award,* 20 ILM (1981) 76-77 (paras. 150-51).

57 "In the realm of law there is no fact in itself, no immediately evident fact; there are only facts ascertained by the competent authorities in a procedure determined by law." H. Kelsen, *Principles of International Law* (ed. & rev. by R.M. Tucker) (1966) 388.

processes whereby states create law (concreteness) and as a methodology for verifying the law's content independently of political opinions (normativity). By integrating both explanations, sources doctrine can maintain its apparent objectivity. On the one hand, something would not be law merely as a result of its content but as a result of a social process. On the other hand, the existence of sources as a constraining methodology creates the needed distance between it and whatever states might will at any one moment.

Though there is no major disagreement among international lawyers about the correct enumeration of sources (treaties, custom, general principles), the rhetorical force of sources ("binding force") is explained from contrasting perspectives. Their importance is sometimes linked with their capacity to reflect state will (consensualism). At other times, such binding force is linked with the relationship of sources arguments with what is "just," "reasonable," "in accordance with good faith," or some other non-consensual metaphor.

Standard disputes about the content or application of international legal norms use the contradiction between consent and justice based explanations. One party argues in terms of consent, the other in terms of what is just (reasonable, etc.). But neither argument is fully justifiable alone. A purely consensual argument cannot ultimately justify the application of a norm against non-consenting states (apologism). An argument relying only on a notion of justice violates the principle of the subjectivity of value (utopianism). Therefore, they must rely on each other. Arguments about consent must explain the relevance and content of consent in terms of what seems just. Arguments about justice must demonstrate their correctness by reference to what states have consented to. Because these movements (consent to justice; justice to consent) make the originally opposing positions look the same, no solution can be made by simply choosing one. A solution now seems possible only by either deciding what is it

that states "really" will or what the content of justice "really" is. Neither question, however, is answerable on the premises of the Rule of Law.[58]

For the modern lawyer, it is very difficult to envisage, let alone to justify, a law which would divorce itself from what states think or will to be the law. The apparent necessity of consensualism seems grounded in the very criticism of natural norms as superstition. Yet, the criticisms against full consensualism—its logical circularity, its distance from experience, its inherent apologism—are well-known.[59] Consensualism cannot justify the application of a norm against a state which opposes such application unless it creates distance between the norm and the relevant state's momentary will. It has been explained, for example, that though law emerges from consent, it does not need every state's consent all the time, that a general agreement, a *volonté générale* of a *Vereinbarung* is sufficient to apply the norm.[60]

But these explanations violate the principle of sovereign equality—they fail to explain why a state should be bound by what another state wills. This can, of course, be explained from some concept of social necessity. But in such case we have already moved away from pure consensualism and face the difficulty of explaining the legal status of the assumed necessity and why it should support one norm instead of another.

A more common strategy is to explain that the state has originally consented (by means of recognition, acquiescence, by not protesting or by "tacitly" agreeing) although it now denies it has. Such an argument is extremely important in liberal legitimation discourse. It allows defending social constraint in a consensual fashion while allowing the application of constraint against a state which denies it con-

---

58 See also Kennedy, *supra* note 16, at 11-107.
59 Koskenniemi, *supra* note 12, at 270-73.
60 For the classic, see H. Triepel, *Völkerrecht und Landesrecht* (1899) 27, 51-53.

sent.[61] But even this argument fails to be convincing because it must ultimately explain itself either in a fully consensual or fully non-consensual way and thereby become vulnerable to the objections about apologism or utopianism.

Why should a state be bound by an argument according to which it has consented, albeit "tacitly"? If the reason is stated in terms of respecting its own consent, then we have to explain why we can know better than the state itself what it has consented to. Even consensualists usually concede that such knowledge is not open to external observers. But even if it were possible to "know better," such an argument is not really defensible within the premises of the Rule of Law. It contains the unpleasant implication that we could no longer rely on the expressed will of the legal subject. It would lose the principal justification behind democratic legislation and justify the establishment of a Leviathan—the one who knows best what everyone "really" wills. It is a strategy for introducing authoritarian opinions in democratic disguise.

Tacit consent theorists usually explain that the question is not of "real" but of "presumed" will. But what then allows the application of the presumption against a state denying that it had ever consented to anything like it? At this point the tacit consent lawyer must move from consensualism to non-consensualism. Tacit consent—or the presumption of consent—binds because it is "just" or in accordance with reasonableness or good faith, or it protects legitimate expectations or the like.[62] Now the difficulty lies in defending the assumed non-consensual position. But under the principle of subjective value,

justice cannot be discussed in a non-arbitrary way.[63] Were this otherwise, the Rule of Law would be pointless if not harmful. One might, of course, say that a notion of reasonableness is justified because the state in question has itself accepted it. But this defence will re-emerge the problem of how it is possible to oppose a consensual justification against a state denying its validity. And so on, ad infinitum.

In the *Gulf of Maine* case (1984), Canada argued that the United States was bound to a certain line of delimitation as it had not protested against its *de facto* use. Relying on absence of protest reflected, Canada explained, on the one hand, U.S. consent to be bound and, on the other hand, gave expression to good faith and equity. It argued in terms of consent as well as justice. The Chamber of the Court accepted both explanations. It started out with the latter, non-consensual one. What is common to acquiescence and estoppel is that: "... both follow from the fundamental principle of good faith and equity."[64]

Had it followed this understanding, it should, because not *all* silence creates norms, have had to enter a discussion of whether or not the conditions of good faith or equity were present to bind the United States now. But there was no such discussion. This is understandable, as arguing from non-consensual justice seems so subjective. Instead, it moved to a consensual understanding of relying on absence of protest and went on to discuss whether the "Hoffmann letter" was evidence of United States acceptance of the Canadian equidistance. It was not: "... facts invoked by Canada do not warrant the conclusion that the U.S. Government thereby recognized the median line ..."[65]

In other words, the United States was not bound because there was no subjective intent to be (regard-

---

61   See, e.g., the argument in A. Bleckmann, *Grundprobleme und Methoden des Völkerrechts* (1982) 81, 184-89. On the tacit consent construction generally, see Koskenniemi, *supra* note 12, at 284-91.

62   See, e.g., J.P. Muller, *Vertrauenschutz im Völkerrecht* (1970); A. Martin, *L'estoppel en droit international public* (1979).

63   "[l]e principe de bonne foi est un principe moral et rien de plus." E. Zoller, *La bonne foi en droit international public* (1977) 345.

64   *Gulf of Maine* case, ICJ Reports (1984) 305 (para. 130).

65   *Id.* at 307 (para. 138).

less of considerations of good faith or equity). How did the Court arrive at this conclusion? This would have been apologist and a violation of Canadian sovereignty. The Chamber's conclusion did not concern lack of "real" intent but rather of "constructive" U.S. intent. On what principles was that construction based? Mainly on inconsistency in the facts and on the low governmental status of the authorities involved.[66] But what justified this choice of relevant facts and their ensuing interpretation? What made the Court's construction better than the Canadian one? The argument stops here. The principles of construction were left undiscussed.

In theory, the Chamber could have used two principles of construction: 1) a construction is justified if it corresponds to intent; 2) a construction is justified if it reflects non-consensual justice. These are exclusive justifications. But neither was open to the Chamber. The former was excluded by the previous argument which ruled out the possibility of knowing real U.S. intent and using it against Canada. The latter was excluded because it would have involved arguing in a fully non-consensual way against Canadian non-consensual justifications. This would have assumed the correctness of an objective justice and would have conflicted with the Chamber's previous refusal to think of acquiescence-estoppel in a fully non-consensual way. The Chamber simply took another interpretation of U.S. conduct than Canada. Why it was better was not discussed as it could not have been discussed. The decision was, on its own premises, undetermined by legal argument.

An identical argumentative structure is present in treaty interpretation. Particular interpretations are traced back either to party will or to some idea of good faith, reasonableness, etc.[67] Because "real" party will cannot be identified and justifiably opposed to a party denying such intent, and because the content of what is a just interpretation cannot be determined in a legal way, late modern doctrines usually concede the aesthetic, impressionistic character of the interpretative process.[68] Controversial points about party will clash against equally controversial points about the justice of particular interpretations.

In the case *Concerning the Interpretation of the Algerian Declaration of 19 January 1981*, the Iran-United States Claims Tribunal was to decide whether Article II of the Claims Settlement Declaration included a right for Iran to press claims against United States' nationals. The majority held that it could not be so interpreted. A "clear formulation" of that Article excluded Iranian claims from the Tribunal's jurisdiction. This clear formulation had authority because it was clearest evidence of Party consent.[69] The minority argued that a literal construction failed to give effect to the settlement's reciprocal character. According to the minority, reciprocity had been the very basis on which Iran had entered the agreement. By excluding reciprocity, the majority had violated Iranian consent and unjustifiably preferred the justice of literality to the justice of reciprocity.[70] Both sides invoke consent and justice but are unable to address each others' views directly. Neither side argues on the basis of "real consent." But while the majority sees consent manifested in the text, the minority sees consent in reciprocity. Both sides say their interpretative principle is better as it better reflects consent. But deciding the dispute on these arguments would require a means of knowing consent independently of its manifestations—a possibility excluded as reference was made to manifestations because of the assumption that real consent could not be known. Moreover, neither can the two sides argue that their justice—the justice of literality or

66 *Id.*

67 For this contrast generally, see, e.g., Zoller, supra note 63, at 205-44.

68 Sur, *supra* note 13. See also McDougal, *supra* note 23 at 149-57.

69 Iran–United States Claims Tribunal, "Interpretation of the Algerian Declaration of 19th January 1981," 62 ILR (1982) 599-600.

70 *Id.* at 603-06.

the justice of reciprocity—is better without arguing from a theory of justice which seems indefensible under the Rule of Law. Ultimately, both interpretations are unargued. A doctrine which excludes arguments from "knowing better" and natural justice has no means to decide on the superiority of conflicting interpretations.

Attempts to explain why states should be bound by unilateral declarations meet with similar problems. In the first place, as the ICJ observed in the *Nuclear Tests* case (1974) such statements might be held binding "(w)hen it is the intention of the state making the declaration that it should become bound according to its terms."[71] However, their binding force cannot be fully consensual because then the state could be freed simply by a further act of will. Therefore, the Court also noted that "(o)ne of the principles governing the creation and performance of legal obligations ... is the principle of good faith... Thus interested states may take cognizance of unilateral declarations and place confidence in them, and are entitled to require that the obligation thus created be respected."[72] Now the declaring state is bound regardless of its will, by the simple fact of the statement and others' reliance.

The necessity of making both arguments seems evident. The Court's first—consensual—argument justified holding France bound by its statements. But it was also threatening because it implied that France could modify or terminate this obligation at will. This would violate the wills and sovereignty of the Applicants (Australia and New Zealand). The second—non-consensual—argument about good faith and legitimate expectations was needed to protect the latter. The decision was consensualist and non-consensualist at the same time. It allowed basing the applicable norm on protecting the sovereignty of each state involved. Simultaneously, it seemed to give effect to what justice seemed to require.

But the decision remains also vulnerable from each perspective. How could the Court base its norm on French consent in face of French denial of such consent? It leaves unexplained how it can protect the Applicants' reliance, as they denied having relied. And it leaves unexplained its theory of justice which says that these statements and actions in these circumstances bind because that is in accordance with good faith.

The structure, importance and weaknesses of tacit consent is nowhere more visible that in the orthodox argument about customary international law.

According to this argument, binding custom exists if there is a material practice of states to that effect and that practice is motivated by the belief that it is obligatory. This "two-element theory" gives expression to the principle of liberal sociology for which the meaning—law or not law—of social action lies neither in its external appearance nor in what someone thinks about but is a combination of the two: an external (material) and an internal (psychological) element.[73] The function of the former element is to ensure that custom can be ascertained without having to rely on states' momentary, political views. The point of the latter is to distinguish custom from coercion.

The problem with the two-element theory is that neither element can be identified independently of the other. Hence, they cannot be used to prevent the appearance of Mr. Hyde in each other.

Modern lawyers have rejected fully materialistic explanations of custom as apologist, incapable of distinguishing between factual constraint and law. If the possibility is excluded that this distinction can be made by the justice of the relevant behaviour, then it can only be made by reference to the psychological element, the *opinio juris*. But, as many students of

---

71 *Nuclear Tests* cases, ICJ Reports (1974) 267 (para. 43).
72 *Id.* at 268 (para. 46).

73 See Hart, *supra* note 19, at 91. For discussion, see Koskenniemi, "The Normative Force of Habit: International Custom and Social Theory," 1 *Finnish Yearbook of International Law* (forthcoming).

the ICJ jurisprudence have shown, there are no independently applicable criteria for ascertaining the presence of the *opinio juris*. The ICJ has simply inferred its presence or absence from the extent and intensity of the material practice it has studied.[74] Moreover, it does not even seem possible to assume the existence of such criteria and that the opinio thus received could be opposed to a non-consenting state. That would be an argument about knowing better. In other words, though it seems possible to distinguish "custom" from what is actually effective only by recourse to what states believe, such beliefs do not seem capable of identification regardless of what is actually effective.

One might try to avoid the above circularity by assuming that some types of behaviour are by their character—"intrinsically"—such as to generate (or not to generate) normative custom. But attempts to single out lists of such types have been unsuccessful. A "flexible" concept of material practice has emerged: any act or statement may count as custom-generating practice if only the states wish so.[75] (Indeed, any other conclusion would manifest an illegitimate naturalism and violate the principles of liberal sociology: it would fail to have regard to the "internal aspect.") Using this criterion (what it is that states wish), however, would assume that we can know the opinio independently of the act in which it is expressed. But this possibility was already excluded by our previous argument about the need to look at material practice in the first place. Indeed, were it so that we could know state intentions regardless of what states do, the whole two-element theory would

become unnecessary: we could simply apply those intentions. Custom would coalesce with (informal) agreement. (In which case, of course, we would face the difficulty of having to interpret the content embedded in any such agreement by further reference to the parties' "real" wills or to some notion of justice, as explained above.)

Customary law doctrine remains indeterminate because it is circular. It assumes behaviour to be evidence of states' intentions (*opinio juris*) and the latter to be evidence of what behaviour is relevant as custom. To avoid apologism (relying on the state's present will), it looks at the psychological element from the perspective of the material; to avoid utopianism (making the distinction between binding and nonbinding usages by reference to what is just), it looks at the material element from the perspective of the psychological. It can occupy neither position in a permanent way without becoming vulnerable to criticism compelled by the other. The very assumptions behind customary international law provide the mechanism for its self-destruction.

For late modern international practice the standard theory is increasingly a camouflage for what is really an attempt to understand custom in terms of a bilateralized equity. The ICJ, for instance, has always been somewhat ambiguous as to the character of the rules of non-written law which it has discerned. The Court's argument about the relevant custom in the *Anglo-Norwegian Fisheries* (1951) as well as *Fisheries Jurisdiction* (1974) cases already looked upon the matter more in terms of the relevant interest at stake than trying to find some general rule to "apply."[76] The several maritime boundary cases further extended this move. The judgement in the *U.S. Military and Paramilitary Activities* case (1986) did not even seriously attempt to justify its four customary rules—non-use of force, non-intervention, respect for sovereignty and especially the relevant humani-

---

74 See, e.g., M. Sørensen, *Les sources du droit international* (1946) 108-11; Virally, "The Sources of International Law," in Sørensen (ed.), *Manual of Public International Law* (1968) 134-35; H. Günther, *Zur Entstehung von Völkergewohnheitsrecht* (1970) 70. See further, Koskenniemi, *supra* note 12, at 380-81.

75 See, e.g., Ferrari-Bravo, "La coutume internationale dans la pratique des Etats," 192 *RCDI* (1985) 243, 261 and Koskenniemi, *supra* note 12, at 383-84.

76 *Anglo-Norwegian* case, ICJ Reports (1951) 133. *Fisheries Jurisdiction* cases, Reports (1974) 30-33 (paras. 69-79).

tarian rules—in terms of material practice and the opinio juris.[77]

Many have been dissatisfied with the modern strategy of arguing every imaginable non-written standard as "custom." Sir Robert Jennings, among others, has noted that what we tend to call custom: "is not only not customary law: it does not even faintly resemble a customary law."[78] But if a non-written standard is not arguable in terms of material practices or beliefs relating to such practices then it can only exist as natural law—being defensible only by reference to the political importance of its content. In fact, much ICJ practice in the relevant respect remains *ex cathedra*: the Court has "instituted a system of decision-making in which the conclusion reached is determined by the application of rules largely treated as self-evident."[79] To be sure, often there is consensus on such rules, for instance, on the "elementary considerations of humanity" invoked by the Court in the *Corfu Channel* case (1949). But the problem is clearly less to explain why people who agree are bound than why also those should be who do not and how one should argue if interpretative controversies arise.

V. *The Politics of International Law*

The idea of an international Rule of Law has been a credible one because to strive for it implies no commitment regarding the content of the norms thereby established or the character of the society advanced. It was possible for 19th-century European powers to start thinking of their relationships in terms of legal rules because they formalized inter-sovereign

relationships and no sovereign needed to feel that his substantive policies were excluded by them it. It was possible for the UN General Assembly to accept by consensus the Declaration on the "Decade for International Law" for precisely those same reasons. This is strikingly highlighted by the fact that the Decade contained no substantive programme. The declaration merely calls for the promotion of respect for the principles of international law and the peaceful settlement of disputes and for the encouragement of the development and dissemination of international law. For what purpose the law was to be put or what kinds of rules it should promote is not addressed by it.

Modern international law is an elaborate framework for deferring substantive resolution elsewhere: into further procedure, interpretation, equity, context, and so on. The 1982 Law of the Sea Convention is the typical example: in place of a list of do's and don't's it establishes a framework for delimiting sovereign powers and allocating jurisdictions—assuming that the substantive problems of the uses of the sea can be best dealt with through allocating decision-power elsewhere, into context and usually by reference to "equitable principles."[80] The success of international law depends on this formality; this refusal to set down determining rules or ready-made resolutions to future conflict. Though there is a distinctly legal "process"—and in this sense a relatively autonomous and coherent system which can be abstracted in academic treatises—there are no determining legal standards. Let me explain this somewhat schematically.

The Rule of Law constitutes an attempt to provide communal life without giving up individual autonomy. Communal life is, of course, needed to check individualism from leading either into anarchy or tyranny. Individualism is needed because

---

77 *US Military and Paramilitary Activities* case, ICJ Reports (1986) 97-115 (paras. 183-220).

78 Jennings, "The Identification of International Law," in Cheng (ed.), *International Law, Teaching and Practice* (1982) 5.

79 Kearney, "Sources of Law and the International Court of Justice," in Gross (ed.), *The Future of the International Court of Justice* (Vol. I) (1976) 653.

80 See generally, Allott, "Power Sharing in the Law of the Sea," 77 *AJIL* (1983)1-30; Kennedy, *supra* note 16, at 201-45.

otherwise it would remain objectionable for those who feel that the kind of community provided by it does not meet their political criteria. From their perspective, the law's communitarian pretensions would turn out as totalitarian apologies.[81]

The law aims to fulfil its double task by becoming formal: by endorsing neither particular communitarian ideals nor particular sovereign policies. Or, conversely, an acceptable legal rule, argument or doctrine is one which can explain itself both from the perspective of enhancing community (because it would otherwise seem apologist) as well as safeguarding sovereignty (because its implications would otherwise remain totalitarian). The problem is that as soon as any of these justifications are advanced to support *some particular kind of communal existence or some determined limit for sovereign autonomy*, they are vulnerable from an opposing substantive perspective. So, while an advocate justifies his preferred substantive outcome by its capacity to support community, it becomes simultaneously possible for his counterpart—not sharing the same communal ideal—to challenge the very justification as totalitarian. Correspondingly, a rule, principle or solution justified by recourse to the way it protects sovereignty may—for someone drawing the limits of "sovereignty" differently—be objected as furthering egoism and anarchy.

Take the case of transfrontier pollution. Noxious fumes flow from state A into the territory of state B. State A refers to its "sovereign right to use its natural resources in accordance with its national policies." State B argues that A has to put a stop to the pollution. It interprets A's position to be an egoistic one while it makes its own argument seem communitarian. It might refer to a norm of "non-harmful use of territory," for example, and justify this by reference to analogies from rules concerning international rivers and natural resources as well as precedents and General Assembly resolutions.[82]

State A can now retort by saying that norms cannot be opposed to it in such a totalitarian fashion. A is bound only by norms which it has accepted. It has never accepted the analogies drawn by B. This would force B either to argue that its preferred norm binds irrespective of acceptance—in which case it stands to lose as its argument would seem utopian—or to change ground so as to make its position seem protective of sovereignty as well. State B might now argue that the pollution violates its own freedom and constitutes an interference in its internal affairs as Australia did in the *Nuclear Tests* case.[83] B's position would now seem both communitarian (in respect to A) and individualistic (in respect to B itself).

To counter this last argument by B, A needs to make a communitarian point. It may argue that there is a norm about friendly neighbourliness, for example such as that observed in the *Lake Lanoux* case (1957), which requires that states tolerate minor inconveniences which result from legitimate uses of neighbouring states' territories.[84] B cannot demand complete territorial integrity. A's position is now both individualistic (in respect of A itself) and communitarian (in respect of B).

The argument could be continued. Both parties could support the communitarian strand in their positions by referring to equity, general principles and the like, to deny the autonomy (egoism) of the other. And they could support the sovereignty-based arguments by further emphasis on their independence, consent, territorial integrity, self-determination, etc. to counter their adversary's communitarian (totalitarian) arguments. As a result, the case cannot be decided by simply preferring autonomy to community or vice-versa. Both arguments support

81 See further the seminal article by Kennedy, "The Structure of Blackstone's Commentaries," 18 *Buffalo L.R.* (1979) 205.

82 For both arguments, see Principle 21 of the Stockholm Declaration, *supra* note 50 and further Koskenniemi, *supra* note 51, at 100-03.

83 *Nuclear Tests* cases, ICJ Pleadings I at 14.

84 *Lake Lanoux* case, XII UNRIAA at 316.

both positions. The case cannot be solved by reference to any of the available concepts (sovereignty, non-harmful use of territory, territorial integrity, independence, good neighbourliness, equity, etc.) as each of the concepts may be so construed as to support either one of the claims. And the constructions have no *legally* determined preference. A court could say that one of the positions is better as a matter of equity, for example. Or it might attempt to "balance" the claims. But in justifying its conception of what is equitable, the court will have to assume a theory of justice—a theory, however, which it cannot justify by further reference to the legal concepts themselves.

Another example concerns the relations between a foreign investor and the host state. The view which emphasizes individualism, separation and consent may be put forward to support the host state's sovereignty—its right to nationalize the corporation without "full, prompt and adequate" compensation. But the same position can equally well be derived from communitarian points about justice, equality or solidarity or the binding character of the new international economic order, for example.[85] The home state's case may be argued in a similar way, by laying emphasis on that state's freedom, individuality and consent—as expressed in the acquired rights doctrine—or the non-consensually binding character of the *pacta sunt servanda* norm, good faith or other convenient conceptions of justice. To make a choice, the problem-solver should simply have to prefer one of the sovereignties—in which case sovereign equality is overruled—or it should use another theory of justice (or equity) which it cannot, however, justify by reference to the Rule of Law.[86]

The relationship between the principles of self-determination and territorial integrity, both having been enshrined in countless UN General Assembly Resolutions, has remained a puzzle.[87] The problem, as we now can understand it, is that neither of the conflicting principles can be preferred because they are ultimately the same. When a people call for territorial integrity, they call for respect for their identity as a self-determining entity and vice-versa. In order to solve the conflict, one should need an external principle about which types of human association entail this respect and which do not. And this seems to involve arguing on the basis of contested, political views about the type of organization the law should materially aim at.

The formality of international law makes it possible for each state to read its substantive conception of world society as well as its view of the extent of sovereign freedom into legal concepts and categories. This is no externally introduced distortion in the law. It is a necessary consequence of a view which holds that there is no naturally existing "good life," no limit to sovereign freedom which would exist by force of some historical necessity. If this kind of naturalism is rejected—and since the Enlightenment, everybody has had good reason to reject it—then to impose any substantive conception of communal life or limits of sovereignty can appear only as illegitimate constraint—preferring one state's politics to those of another.

It is impossible to make substantive decisions within the law which would imply no political choice. The late modern turn to equity in the different realms of international law is, in this sense, a healthy admission of something that is anyway there: in the end, legitimizing or criticizing state be-

---

85 Both justifications for this right may be read, for example, from the Charter of Economic Rights and Duties of States, UNGA Res. 3281 (XXIX) (12 December 1974).

86 "A solution therefore should recognize the home state's and the host state's sovereign right to the investment concerned and should endeavour to find an equitable balance between them." Seidl-Hohenveldem, "Interna-

tional Economic Law: General Course on Public International Law," 198 *RCDI* (1986) 54.

87 See UNGA Res. 1514 (XV) 14 December 1960; 2625 (XXV) 24 October 1970 and comments, e.g., in M. Pomerance, *Self-Determination in Law and Practice: The New Doctrine in the United Nations*, 43-47 and *passim*.

haviour is not a matter of applying formally neutral rules but depends on what one regards as politically right, or just.

Conclusion

Theorists of the present often explain our post-modern condition as a result of a tragedy of losses. For international lawyers, the Enlightenment signified loss of faith in a natural order among peoples, nations and sovereigns. To contain political subjectivism, 19th- and 20th-century jurists put their faith variably on logic and texts, history and power to find a secure, objective foothold. Each attempt led to disappointment. One's use of logic depended on what political axioms were inserted as the premises. Texts, facts and history were capable of being interpreted in the most varied ways. In making his interpretations the jurist was always forced to rely on conceptual matrices which could no longer be defended by the texts, facts or histories to which they provided meaning. They were—and are—arenas of political struggle.

But the way back to Victoria's or Suarez' unquestioning faith is not open to us. We cannot simply start assuming that politics—justice and equity—could be discussed so that in the end everyone should agree. This teaches us a lesson. Because the world—including lawyers' views about it—is conflictual, any grand design for a "world order" will always remain suspect. Any legal rule, principle or world order project will only seem acceptable when stated in an abstract and formal fashion. When it is applied, it will have overruled some interpretation, some collective experience, and appear apologist.

Social theorists have documented a recent modern turn in national societies away from the Rechtstaat into a society in which social conflict is increasingly met with flexible, contextually determined standards and compromises.[88] The turn

away from general principles and formal rules into contextually determined equity may reflect a similar turn in the development of international legal thought and practice. There is every reason to take this turn seriously—though this may mean that lawyers have to re-think their professional self-image. For issues of contextual justice cannot be solved by the application of ready-made rules or principles. Their solution requires venturing into fields such as politics, social and economic casuistry which were formally delimited beyond the point at which legal argument was supposed to stop in order to remain "legal." To be sure, we shall remain uncertain. Resolutions based on political acceptability cannot be made with the kind of certainty post-Enlightenment lawyers once hoped to attain. And yet, it is only by their remaining so which will prevent their use as apologies for tyranny.

* * * * *

D. NEIL MacCORMICK

"On Sovereignty and Post-Sovereignty,"* from *Questioning Sovereignty*

1. Introduction

The world of modernity owes much to the epoch of reformation and religious wars in sixteenth- and seventeenth-century Europe. Elizabeth Tudor won it a certain insular safety in her long reign in England,

---

88 See, e.g., R.M. Unger, *Law in Modern Society: Toward a Criticism of Social Theory* (1976); T. O'Hagan, *The End of Law?* (1984).

---

*   Ed. note: In his argument MacCormick frequently refers to parts of his book which are not included in this excerpt; however, these references have been left in the excerpted text in the interest of its completeness as a resource for further exploration of the full text of *Questioning Sovereignty*.

but the Sweden of the Vasa dynasty was its first and founding guarantor in Northern Europe. Not until the Peace of Westphalia in 1648 was it settled that the new order would prove durable. At a conference on argumentation in Lisbon some years ago, Stephen Toulmin made a remark that left a great impression with me. He remarked how significant was the date of birth of Gottfried Wilhelm Freiherr von Leibnitz—in 1646. So Leibnitz was just 2 years of age as the Peace of Westphalia was being signed. It is from Leibnitz, perhaps second only to Descartes, who died in Uppsala in 1650, that what is now known and often criticized as "foundationalism" in philosophy descends. Foundationalism seeks a starting point in something interpersonally certain and indubitable from which to carry forward the search for reliable forms of knowledge. Toulmin found it only too natural that a Europe weary with thirty years of religious war should be hospitable to philosophies offering some common ground of indubitable certainty, above or below the level of all the religious controversies. The persuasive character of Cartesian or Leibnitzian foundationalism was, he suggested, the outcome of that longing.

Toulmin's speculation is a pleasing one. Yet however tempting it is in relation to metaphysics, all the more plausible would be its analogue in relation to politics. Immediately, Leibnitz's older contemporary Thomas Hobbes springs to mind as candidate founding foundationalist for political theory. It is difficult to be sure whether we would better call him an absolute foundationalist or a foundational absolutist. For Hobbes, absolute state-power, absolute sovereignty, was (as remarked in Chapters 2 and 5) the necessary condition for stable politics and indeed for human safety. The fundamental question is about the founding of absolute state-power. Although this power has to be founded on the common agreement of all who are subject to it, the sovereign constituted by the foundational compact cannot be limited by its terms. For the sovereign is not one of the parties to the bargain, but the one who stands over it guar-

anteeing it with the power of the sword. "Covenants without swords are but words," we recall.

Religion, in Hobbes's view is simply an adjunct of state-power, not a coordinate base of, far less a higher source for, state authority. Uppsala, with the castle on the hill addressing its cannonry towards the Cathedral in the valley might almost have been designed to illustrate the Hobbesian thesis on church-state relationships. Perhaps Gustavus Adolphus and his clan would have found little in Hobbes's work with which to disagree.

To be sure, the odd thing about Hobbes's version of the original social contract is the way he turns it into the basis for absolute royal or parliamentary-oligarchical authority. Here, he went against contractarian predecessors, such as George Buchanan, who derived limits on the kingly power from the myth of a foundational compact. *In De Iure Regni apud Scotos*,[1] Buchanan argued that in the Baltic countries and in Scotland there uniquely survived kingdoms based on the choice and consent of the populace rather than on external conquest. In such polities, he argued, royal or governmental power is always subject to the limits expressly or impliedly put upon it by the people as, generation by generation, they confirm the title to rule of the next representative of the same old royal line.

The basic idea in Buchanan's account has had influence on posterity only via the distorting mirrors first of Locke and subsequently of Rousseau. Distinctively, it accords true sovereignty ultimately to the people on whose will depends the legitimate authority of constitutional rulers and Parliaments. In Locke's version, though, the people act to protect their natural rights to life, liberty, and estate. These rights are derived from a higher law of reason, and that higher law in turn places restrictions on the abso-

---

1   See G. Buchanan, *The Art and Science of Government among the Scots* (trans. D.H. MacNeill, Glasgow: William Maclellan and Co, 1964); there is a surprising lack of scholarly editions and translations of Buchanan's work.

luteness of any claim to legislative sovereignty, even, we must suppose, the sovereignty of the people acting collectively against any individual of their number.[2]

On the whole, and certainly in Britain, state practice seems to have owed more to the doctrine of Hobbes, through his successors such as David Hume, Jeremy Bentham, or John Austin or, in constitutional law, A.V. Dicey, than to the Lockean school. Elsewhere in Europe, Hegelian versions of state absolutism, however unfaithful to the original thought, tended to prevail in the nineteenth century and into the twentieth. In Sweden, the influence of the Uppsala school[3] no doubt brought about the abandonment of Hegelian voluntarism as well as Hegelian idealism. But the residual idea of law and indeed of morality as conformity to settled patterns of behaviour upheld by power of an ultimately physical kind was no less hospitable to the idea of an unchallengeable sovereignty in the state.

In all these traditions, the modern state has been portrayed as the stark alternative to anarchy at home and abroad. The absolute power of the sovereign state has been the foundational doctrine for political theory and practice. No doubt the French revolution was one defining moment in this process. But in the North the origins are, I suspect, older. We might not go far wrong if we located them in the form of post-reformation kingdoms that emerged with Leibnitz into the light of day at the end of the Thirty Years War.

Whenever we should date the emergence of the sovereign state, and wherever we may locate its first emergence, it seems that we may at last be witness-ing its demise in Europe, through the development of a new and not-yet-well-theorized legal and political order in the form of the European Union. If that were so, would it be a cause for concern or for satisfaction? On the side of concern, even alarm, there are two lines of thought, one nationalistic and the other democratic. The nationalistic one deplores the erosion of national independence and self-determination. The democratic one recalls the point made by contractarians about the popular sovereignty that may be taken to underlie the sovereignty of the state. In truth these two run together, for the relevant version of democracy locates the ultimate source of legitimacy in a people as in principle a pre-political entity. National self-determination similarly alludes to the people as a pre-political body, and asserts each people's right to determine its own destiny through its own processes of decision-making. The great revolutions, particularly in America and in France, gave dramatic expression to these basic ideas. The overthrow of misruling monarchs restored sovereignty to the people, who constituted themselves into a state or union of states through adopting a constitution by common consent. The sovereign state or union asserted itself as a nation state, the property of its sovereign people.

So if the sovereign state is a democratic state, concern about sovereignty is also concern for democracy. Can sovereignty be lost without abandoning popular self-government? Can it be lost without breaking the democratic faith? This fear is held in common among those Europeans, perhaps more numerous in the Nordic countries and the UK than farther south, who are sceptical of the possibility of democracy being realizable in a Europe that is not a super-state. Yet these same people are all the more repelled by the idea of such a super-state. In the same vein was the argument of the German petitioners who challenged the Maastricht treaty, in the manner discussed in the preceding chapter, as requiring an illegal abandonment of the democratic form of government guaranteed in the German constitution.

---

2   This is discussed in a more elaborate way, and with citation of source, in Ch. 2 above.

3   This is the group of philosophers and jurists who took their intellectal lead from Axel Hägerström, best known in English language sources through Karl Olivecrona's *Law as Fact*, 1st edn. (London: Humphrey Milford/Oxford University Press, 1939; 2nd edn. London: Stevens, 1971); see also Hägerström, *Inquiries into the Nature of Law and Morals*, trans. C.D. Broad, ed. K. Olivecrona (Stockholm, Almqvist & Wiksell, 1953).

The Court did not agree that the Maastricht treaty had that effect, but one of the theses it stated, not hitherto taken into account, was that there could not be a democratic European Union without the emergence of a self-determining European *demos or Volk*. Pending further evolution of popular European consciousness, there could not lawfully be any further radical transference of power to European organs.[4] The powers already transferred must be confined within the carefully delimited spheres marked out by the Union Treaty and its predecessors. In line with this, the Constitutional Court declared itself ready to draw lines beyond which decisions of the European Court of Justice would be unacceptable for implementation in Germany. In short, the Court asserted a continuing German sovereignty, and did so in the light of its particular constitutional duty to uphold the democratic character of the state constituted by the Grundgesetz, the German "Basic Law" of 1949.

Perhaps we should not be too ready, then, lightly to embrace the demise of sovereignty either as already accomplished fact or as consummation devoutly to be wished. Yet we cannot be so sure, for there is another side. The international order of sovereign states has been a bloody one, marked by struggles over the establishment and maintenance of empires. Sweden and Switzerland practically alone succeeded in holding aside from interstate violence on a catastrophic scale during the two most recent centuries. It is easy to understand a special reluctance in such countries to give up an independence so prudently exercised. Yet the example from all around does not make it seem that mere nostalgia for lost sovereignties, or zeal for establishing new ones in the old mode, is necessarily a happy posture. It is a serious issue whether it is possible to envisage a world "beyond the sovereign state" in which new types of legal and political interaction come into being that exclude claims of out-and-out sovereignty either from old states or from new communities devised to reorder economic and political coexistence. Could we advance in peace and prosperity without losing popular democracy?

The key question becomes whether there can be a loss of sovereignty at one level without its inevitable and resultant re-creation at another. Is sovereignty like property, which can be given up only when another person gains it? Or should we think of it more like virginity, something that can be lost by one without another's gaining it—and whose loss in apt circumstances can even be a matter for celebration? This book is dedicated to the latter view. The case to be made here is one welcoming the prospect of Europe beyond sovereign statehood. The idea of subsidiarity points us to better visions of democracy than all-purpose sovereignty ever did. There is a possible future reality preferable to the past of nostalgic mythology.

My argument depends on a careful analysis of basic ideas. Much of the argument up to this point has been posited on the distinction drawn between political and legal forms of power. If that distinction holds, and if sovereignty is a form of power, then there is merit in the old idea that sovereignty has both a political and a legal form, which are not necessarily the same thing. A related, but not identical, distinction is that between sovereignty internal to a country and that same country's external sovereignty *vis-à-vis* other states or relevant international entities. This distinction between external and internal sovereignty is what makes it possible to contemplate division or limitation of sovereign power. Armed with these distinctions, we can reflect on the reasons why neither member states nor the European Union of which they are members can strictly be said to enjoy sovereignty at the present time. Finally, reflection upon subsidiarity and democracy will help assuage any alarm the conclusion about sovereignty may have aroused.

4   See J.H.H. Weiler, "European Neo-constitutionalism: in Search of Foundations for the European Constitutional Order," *Political Studies*, 44 (1996), 517-33 at pp. 522-25.

2. Sovereignty, Legal and Political

What is "Sovereignty?" Let me recall an earlier quoted remark by A.V. Dicey:[5] whereas as a "merely legal conception," sovereignty is "the power of law-making unrestricted by any legal limit," by contrast "that body is "politically" sovereign or supreme in a state the will of which is ultimately obeyed by the citizens of the state." Power without restriction is on this view the key idea. Power of one kind, normative power or "authority," is conferred by law. This may be a power of law-making in a certain territory conferred by a certain constitutional order that is effectively observed in that territory. Sovereign power is that which is enjoyed, legally, by the holder of a constitutional power to make law, so long as the constitution places no restrictions on the exercise of that power (though, necessarily, the constitution must define what counts as a valid exercise of the power, and judges may have to satisfy themselves in problem cases that the validity-conditions have been satisfied, and this may involve problematic interpretation of the constitutional validity conditions).

If the constitution then confers such a power but contains no limit upon the power (other than the discretion and judgement of those who exercise the power) we may say that sovereignty is vested in the holder of the law-making power.

But what of political sovereignty? By parallel reasoning, one would be inclined to define it as political power unrestrained by higher political power. We recall the elucidation offered of political power. Political power is interpersonal power over the conditions of life in a human community or society. It is the ability to take effective decisions on whatever concerns the common well-being of the members, and on whatever affects the distribution of the economic resources available to them. The taking of such decisions has important bearing on the reasons that guide the actions of people in their social intercourse with each other.

As between human beings, power of one over another, or over others, is the ability within some determinable context to take decisions that affect that other's (or those others') interests regardless of their consent or dissent. When one has power so defined, one is also able to affect the other's reasons for action. Someone who has power over another is able to impose on that other reasons for action or inaction that would not otherwise have existed. Since people often act in accordance with the reasons they have for acting, it follows that having power means being able to get people to do things, to act as they might not otherwise have acted. Exercises of power affect the way in which it is rational for people to act.

Sovereign power is, then, territorial in character, and is power not subject to limitation by higher or coordinate power. It is material to consider which of the two species identified, political or legal sovereignty, has priority. Is ultimate political power a precondition of ultimate legal authority, or vice versa? The tradition of Hobbes, carried on by Austin,[6] reconceptualized in the Germanic tradition by Carl Schmitt, unhesitatingly ascribes primacy to the political. However it comes about that one person or group is habitually obeyed by others, thereby acquiring the power to enforce physical sanctions over any recalcitrant elements, the person or persons who hold this position are able to issue commands to others within their society, and those commands are laws.[7] Legal authority established by such commands is evidently secondary to political power. Law is then dependent on political sovereignty. Only a sovereign person or group, absolutely sovereign at home, independent of any purported external power, can be an authentic source of law. In Schmitt's version,

---

5   *Law of the Constitution*, 27, discussed above, Ch. 5. [Ed. note: Ch. 5 refers to: A.V. Dicey, *Introduction to the Study of the Law of the Constitution* (10th edn., London: Macmillan, 1964).]

6   J. Austin, *The Province of Jurisprudence Determined*, ed. H.L.A. Hart (London: Weidenfeld & Nicolson, 1954), chs. 1 and 6.

7   Ibid., as cited.

the key to the ultimate basis of law lies in the question who can exercise effective power on behalf of a whole community in states of emergency or "states of exception" when ordinary legal provisions break down or prove inadequate.[8]

Persuasive and illuminating though such accounts may be for some types of politico-legal order, they have been found wanting in respect of those situations in which there is a standing constitutional tradition. Under such a tradition, the powers of state are effectively divided according to a constitutional scheme that is respected in the practical conduct of affairs. There is then a difficulty in identifying any sovereign being or sovereign entity holding power without any legal limitation. Confronted with the example of federal states, Austin in particular was driven back to analysing such cases, in particular the USA, in terms of the sovereignty of the people (or, at least, of the actual electorate whose members can amend the constitution). The difficulty is that the account then becomes circular, since one has to assume the validity of the constitution in order to explain how the people can carry out an act of amendment as a binding and effective legal act.

For the case of the *Rechtsstaat*, law has to be explained in terms that do not presuppose the prior existence of an absolute political sovereignty. I am happy to suggest such terms. Law, as stated above, is an institutional system of rules or norms involving both duties which are required of legal subjects and powers vested in legal institutions holding legislative, executive, or judicial power. Legal systems so understood do not only and do not necessarily exist in states. There are non-state systems of law, such as for example Canon law, public international law, the specialist international law represented by the

European Convention on Human Rights, and the law of the European Union, and other less presently relevant forms of law as well. But the point of the *Rechtsstaat* is that it is a state which has law, and in which law regulates and restricts the conduct of political officials as well as citizens, presupposing no monolithic political sovereign power outside or above the law. Where a "lawstate" in this sense exists, it is presumably explicable in terms of a political practice and tradition within which a constitution and a broadly shared approach to constitutional interpretation are accepted.

This seems to show that sovereignty is neither necessary to the existence of law and state nor even desirable. A well-ordered Law-State or *Rechtsstaat* is not subordinated to any political sovereign outside or above the law, nor is it necessarily constructed around some constitutional organ which enjoys sovereignty conferred by law. Certainly, the classical theory of the British constitution ascribed sovereignty to the monarch in Parliament, or, more summarily, to Parliament itself. This was held to be a doctrine of the common law, and to be advantageous as a legal dispensation on the ground that it secured the political sovereignty of the electorate. But such supreme legal power ascribed to a single organ is not necessary even in a unitary state, and is incompatible with the very frame of government of a federal state.

Nevertheless, before dismissing sovereignty out of hand, we need to reflect on a further distinction, that between internal and external sovereignty. As was stated above, sovereignty is power not subject to limitation by higher or coordinate power, held independently over some territory. It is clear that this could apply in two different ways. If we look at a state in terms of its internal ordering, we may ask whether there is any person who enjoys power without higher power internally to the state. Either in the political or in the legal sense, we may discover that all power holders are subject to some legal or some political checks or controls. In that case, there

---

8   C. Schmitt, "Was bedeutet der Streit um den Rechtsstaat?," *ZStW* 95 (1935), 189; cf. D. Dyzenhaus, *Legality and Legitimacy: Carl Schmitt, Hans Kelsen and Hermann Heller in Weimar* (Oxford: Clarendon Press, 1997), chs. 1 and 2, esp. at p. 54.

is no single sovereign internal to the state, neither a legal nor a political sovereign.

On the other hand, we might survey the same state from the outside, considering its relations with other states and international or religious or commercial organizations. We might conclude that in this perspective a state, whatever its internal distribution of legal or political power, is a "sovereign state" in the sense that the totality of legal or political powers exercised within it is in fact subject to no higher power exercised from without. What we shall therefore call "external sovereignty" characterizes a state which is not subject to superior political power or legal authority in respect of its territory.

Politically, this enables us to distinguish a fully or substantially independent state from a mere satellite or client state which, even if legally independent, has no effective independent power of decision. In a legal sense, external sovereignty is the authority granted by international law to each state to exercise legal control over its own territory without deference to any claim of legal superiority made by another state or organization. This is coupled with the right under international law to be free from the exercise of military power or political interference by other states.

External sovereignty is thus distinct conceptually from internal sovereignty, and may be present even when in the strict sense internal sovereignty is absent.

These distinctions make it possible to account for the concept of "divided sovereignty," which some theorists, such as Austin and Schmitt, have taken to be a contradiction in terms. They were anxious to argue that nothing which has supreme power can coexist with a rival supreme power in any stable way within a single legal or political order. From their point of view, it was certainly misleading to say that the organ or institution which has the ultimate power of decision over a certain range of topics is sovereign over those topics, while other organs and institutions are sovereign for other purposes. The

doctrine of sovereignty was a doctrine of the unity of states and of the unity of governmental functions within them. As such, it was a significant element in the drive towards modernization and the development of unified territorial states in place of the more fragmentary feudal forms of ancient kingdoms and empires. For the same reason and in the same way, they were unenthusiastic both analytically and politically about the idea of limited sovereignty.

Nevertheless, the distinction of external and internal sovereignty shows that even a strict definition of sovereignty permits a sense of divided or limited sovereignty. The point is this. A state that is sovereign in the external sense may have a constitution under which no full sovereign power is possessed by any organ of state. The external sovereignty of the state may be, so to say, internally distributed among organs of state in such a way that none legally exercises plenary power, or competence finally to define its own competence. Each such organ is effectively limited by checks and controls exercised by another. Where that is so, and where constitutional stability has engendered a political system in which the limits laid down in the constitution are well respected, we can predict that there will be no internal political sovereign. Yet externally, the state may be as sovereign as it is possible to imagine. The United States, Canada, Australia, and Switzerland, all provide rather good examples of this.

A final conceptual point to be made about sovereignty concerns the issue of "popular sovereignty," "the sovereignty of the people." There are various constitutional and political traditions that promote this idea. The idea goes back at least as far as to the constitutional writings of George Buchanan. Its appeal is to the principle that all political and legal power ought to rest on the will and consent of those among or over whom power is exercised. This is a principle of political morality. It has two applications. One is in the context of an established constitutional order, and here the claim is that the constitution must always be subject to adoption, confirmation, or revision by processes involving the whole people. The other is where a group or community of people seeks to exercise self-determination by constituting itself into a legal and political rather than simply a cultural or ethnic or religious community. In either application, the principle belongs to the theory of democracy as a basis for ideal constitution-making, to some greater or lesser extent achieved in the actual constitutional experience of different states or polities.

In terms of the differentiation of external and internal sovereignty, we can now properly add that where a state is sovereign in the external sense, it makes perfect sense to say that this sovereignty belongs to the whole people of the state. Especially in the context of a *Rechtsstaat* enjoying a democratic form of internal government, there would be significant truth in the idea that the people as a whole exercises selfgovernment independently of higher power. Popular sovereignty in this sense does not imply or presuppose the existence internal to the state of any constitutional or political organ enjoying either legal or political sovereignty in the internal sense. Indeed, it is the absence of any such organ—king, president, party, or Parliament or whatever—that forces us to identify the people as the ultimate possessor of the sovereignty of their state. This does not mean that there is an entity "the people" that has an existence distinct from or prior to their constitution. On the contrary, they count as "a people" by virtue of the constitution that makes them so.

3. Beyond the Sovereign State

The argument so far has tried to elucidate the ideas of sovereignty, legal and political, and of the sovereign state and sovereign people. The next point is to discuss the relevance of contemporary developments to these concepts. I particularly wish to consider their relevance and usefulness in the context of the developing European Union evolving from the Paris and Rome Treaties, and through to the Union

Treaty of Maastricht, the Treaty of Amsterdam, and beyond.

As was discussed at some length in Chapter 7, since at least 1964,[9] it has been the doctrine of the European Court of Justice that the Community (as it now is) constitutes a new legal order, neither a subordinate part of the laws of the member states nor simply a sub-system of International law. From the point of view of a soundly pluralistic theory of law as institutional normative order, there is no difficulty about accepting this self-characterization of Community law as a distinct legal order. It owes its origin, certainly, to treaties binding under general International law. Further, from the point of view of member-state legal systems, the ground of validity of provisions of Community law is located within the state-system. Community law's validity as a high level source of law is traceable to the acts of ratification or adoption of foundational or amending treaties by appropriate modes of decision-making. The appropriateness to this end of a mode of decision-making is determined by the state constitution in question. But there has been an institutionalization of a legal order under the foundation treaties and the treaty amendments have elaborated this, always preserving the *acquis communautaire*. There are now long-established Community organs for law-making, for executive action, and for judicial law-application. That these have operated in a largely efficacious way over a substantial period of time makes it both proper and necessary to recognize that here we have a full-blown instance of an institutional normative order, and thus to confirm the Court's representation of it as a distinct legal order.

Within that legal order and from the point of view of Community organs and persons working within Community law, the criteria for recognition of the validity of Community legal provisions are now internal to this legal system. The system has acquired what Niklas Luhmann or Gunther Teub-

9   See *Costa v ENEL*, case 6/64.

ner would characterize as self-referentiality.[10] As a system, it differentiates itself from other systems by whose distinct criteria of validity Community legal provisions are also valid and applicable. This is the case within the legal orders of member states, each of whose organs acknowledge Community provisions as valid and applicable in relevant situations, in a manner coordinated with, and justifiable by, reference to the member state's own internal criteria of validity. "Community-validity" is a relevant fact when it comes to assessing member-state validity. "Member-state validity" is a relevant fact for some purposes of Community law. The situation is one of differentiation of systems subject to mutual overlap and interaction. There are institutional arrangements to resolve potential conflicts of norms or of their interpretation.

The application and enforcement of rights and obligations under Community law remain, to a considerable extent, matters for implementation by the authorities of member states, though remedies can now be awarded against states by the European Court to compensate for damages arising from state action found to have been in breach of Community obligations. Community law is and remains to a considerable extent both normatively and politically dependent on law and practice in member states. So far as concerns the validity of national legislation, legislators within state systems are now limited by the requirement to avoid conflict with valid Community law. Community decisions of various kinds can change law within state systems regardless of the operation of the normal internal legislative process. Yet the making of Community decisions depends at the highest level on the joint action of state authorities of member states acting in the Council of Ministers of the EC. Politically and economically, there

are powerful reasons deterring states from large scale unilateral defiance of Community norms or (*a fortiori*) unilateral renunciation of membership (which would clearly be invalid as a matter of Community Law, though possibly valid or subject to being validated by the law of the member state).

Given that, and given our earlier discussion of sovereignty whether as a legal or as a political concept, it is clear that absolute or unitary sovereignty is entirely absent from the legal and political setting of the European Community. Neither politically nor legally is any member state in possession of ultimate power over its own internal affairs. Politically, the Community affects vital interests, and hence exercises political power on some matters over member states. Legally, Community legislation binds member states and overrides internal state-law within the respective criteria of validity. So the states are no longer fully sovereign states externally, nor can any of their internal organs be considered to enjoy present internal sovereignty under law; nor have they any unimpaired political sovereignty. The Community on the other hand is plainly not a state. Nor does it possess sovereignty as a kind of Federation or Confederation. It is neither legally nor politically independent of its members. The German Constitutional Court in its decision on the Maastricht Treaty denied that the Union or Community and their organs of decision have the ultimate legal competence to determine their own competence. If so, this precludes sovereignty.

In one highly important sense, sovereignty has not been lost in this process. In International law, no state or other entity outside the Union has any greater power over member states individually or jointly than before, except to the extent that a similar process on a global level has brought about the formation of the World Trade Organization. Thus there is a kind of compendious legal external sovereignty towards the rest of the world; and politically it seems that the scale of the Community enhances the independence of action of its members collectively and

---

10 See N. Luhmann, "Law as a Social System," *Northwestern Univ. Law Rev.* (1989), 136 at 141-43.; G. Teubner, *Law as an Autopoietic System,* trans. R. Adler and A. Bankowska, ed. Z. Bankowski (Oxford, Basil Blackwell 1993), 13-24.

perhaps even individually for some purposes. To the extent that the terminology of "divided sovereignty" is found valuable either rhetorically or analytically, it can be applied here—the sovereignty of the Community's member states has not been lost, but subjected to a process of division and combination internally, and hence in a way enhanced externally. But the process of division and combination has taken us "beyond the sovereign state,"[11] indeed, well beyond it. Despite the rhetoric of politicians, it cannot be credibly argued that any member state of the European Union remains politically or legally a sovereign state in the strict or traditional sense of these terms. Yet it is to their traditional sense that the political rhetoricians make implicit appeal when they harangue party conferences.

4. Democracy and Subsidiarity

Western Europe's successful transcendence of the sovereign state and of state sovereignty is greatly to be welcomed. It has been and will be a condition for the security of peace and prosperity among us. Yet many are conscious of a residual unease concerning popular sovereignty. At least, in a sovereign state, with its own organs of executive and legislative government, the target for democratic activism is clear. Provided there is real popular control of sovereign government, with fair conditions for full and equal participation by all citizens, or all citizens who wish to involve themselves, democracy can be realized. There is no room for relapse into rule by a virtuous few, whether a bench of supreme court judges, or a council of ministers deliberating in private, or a bureaucracy of highly trained experts.

British Euroscepticism has in effect posed in just such terms the democratic challenge to what Eurosceptics consider the onward march of an unacceptable federalism at the European level. The British Parliament for them is the repository

11 See N. MacCormick, "Beyond the Sovereign State," *Modern Law Review*, 56 (1993), 1-18.

of legal sovereignty under the constitution, and through that legal sovereignty is secured the political sovereignty, internal and external, of the British people. European organs of legislation are immune to direct democratic control, and the European Parliament has been belittled for having neither adequate legislative power nor control over those who do have it, nor ability effectively to make accountable the members of the executive branch at Community level. To them, combined and divided state-and-community sovereignty seems the enemy of popular sovereignty, and strengthening the position of the European Parliament, as has happened in the past decade, may be as much a part of the problem as of the solution. The grounds for their concern are evident and real.

On the other hand, the record of the sovereign unitary state is not so very bright either. The highly centralized version of sovereign state presented by the United Kingdom in its classical phase itself deserves scrutiny. Here we had a proclaimedly sovereign Parliament dominated by a system of political parties with strong internal party discipline, and with an absence of proportional representation in the electoral system. This certainly did not foster anything approximating to an ideal system of popular government with fair equality of participation for all citizens or all points of view. Nor did it prevent the growth of an extensive bureaucracy, nor the enhancement of power of the executive branch of government in the modern period. So far as democracy depends not only on formal allocation of voting power to each adult citizen, but some guarantee of civil and political—perhaps also economic and social—rights to each person, to ensure continuing opportunity of participation on fair terms with others, the UK's accession to the European Human Rights Convention was a decisive step, and yet one which diminished external sovereignty. The growth of a pluralism of law and institutions in Western Europe has been in some ways problematic for democracy, but in other ways advantageous; and, to the extent that the Union

Treaty formally adopts human rights standards, the advantage is enhanced.[12]

There is another potential advantage. Concentrations of power can create opportunities for what might be called monolithic democracy. That is, if all legal or political power is concentrated at the level, say, of a single assembly with complete power over all matters in a large territory, then decisions affecting localities within the whole are as much subject to majority decision by the totality as decisions which have a broader, or even a holistic, scope. But the majority of the totality may be at odds with the majority in any particular locality. The traditional theory of internal sovereignty considers any decision-making power at local level to be the mere creature and delegate of central sovereign power. Hence it is a matter of political choice for the central power, and behind that for the holistic majority, whether to allow local-level democracy on the basis of local majority opinion, or to override local opinion and impose the solution favoured by the holistic majority.

In this light, if there is a sense of popular sovereignty ("sovereignty as self-determination," perhaps) which calls for recognition of the rights of significant groups or communities within larger wholes, the state-sovereignty version of popular sovereignty can be itself an enemy of other democratic rights. In general, any form of popular government or majoritarian democracy inevitably poses the questions: "Who are the people? Of what group must the majority be a majority?"

The great problem of nationalism in the modern world is perhaps revealed at just this point. It is graphically and tragically revealed by the strife and slaughter in former Yugoslavia. If the sovereign state is taken as the self-evident and only available framework for democracy, it becomes vital to struggle over boundaries and membership, vital to define the "nation" as possessor and master of the sovereign state, the nation-state. Inevitably there are minorities, even "national minorities." In Spain there are Catalunya and the Basque Country and others; in Belgium there are Flanders and Wallonia; in the United Kingdom, there are England, Scotland, and Wales, and the itself internally contested province of Northern Ireland. In the UK, the English majority is normally the majority of the whole.

The end of the sovereign state creates an opportunity for rethinking of problems about national identity. The nation as cultural, or linguistic, or historical, or even ethnic community is not coextensive with the (former) sovereign state, the traditional "nation-state." The cases I have mentioned all make this obvious in the highest degree. The suppression of national individualities is wrong in itself and almost inevitably a cause of bitterness and strife. But if the ideological unity of the traditional sovereign state is abandoned, new possibilities are opened.

At least one reading of the already-contested concept of "subsidiarity" points the way here. If the idea of a pluralistic legal order advanced here is an acceptable one, then it is capable of generalization and extension to what is sometimes called the "regional" level within Europe, although many people in some of the so-called regions find it important to characterize their own region and others as "nations." There can then be a basis on which to recognize further levels of system-differentiation and partial mutual independence. The doctrine of subsidiarity requires decision-making to be distributed to the most appropriate level. In that context, the best democracy—and the best interpretation of popular sovereignty—is one that insists on levels of democracy appropriate to levels of decision-making. And the tendency to over-centralize at the level of member states is as much to be countered as is any over-centralization towards Brussels. The demise of sovereignty in its classical sense truly opens opportunities for subsidiarity and democracy as essential

---

12 Cf. the excellent discussion in P. Craig and G. de Búrca, *EU Law: Text, Cases, and Materials*, 2nd edn. (Oxford: Oxford University Press, 1998), 155-59.

mutual complements. It suggests a radical hostility to any merely monolithic democracy.

It also suggests a need to reconsider some issues about democracy, or at any rate, about representative government. For the moment, at least, it is obvious that Heads of Government of Member States of the European Union enjoy considerably greater power and standing than do Governors of States in the USA. Their standing in the domestic politics of their countries remains of high significance, and electing or rejecting governments remains the basic currency of democratic politics in European States. The composition of the Commission and the Court, and their method of nomination and confirmation preclude some of the abuses of respectively party-power and presidential or governmental Court-packing that can occur in other states or federations. And yet none of what is done falls outside of some real possibility of democratic scrutiny.

It is not only our theories of law, but also our theories of democracy, that are challenged by the new forms that are evolving among us in Europe. A commitment to principles of democracy and of subsidiarity calls us to ensure the vitality of decision-making processes at many levels and in a polycentric way. It calls on us to reflect on forms of popular control that are effective at given levels, and on ensuring that those we adopt for "higher" levels do not become inimical to the vitality of politics at "lower" levels. These are questions that call for further reflection and discussion; they shall receive this in the next chapter.

◆ ◆ ◆ ◆ ◆

STUDY QUESTIONS

1. How might a legal positivist respond to Koskenniemi's claim that legal positivism and natural law theory are locked in an unending battle which neither can win?

2. Why is the tension between "apologist" and "utopian" theories of law irresolvable?

3. Have times changed sufficiently since Hart doubted the existence of a rule of recognition for international law that we can now say such a rule exists?

4. Does Grotius' natural law theory of international law contain any relevant similarities to Finnis' theory? Could Finnis' view of natural law be used to support Grotius' theory of international law?

5. How, according to MacCormick, can a state be both "post-sovereign," and have a legal system, all without simply being taken over by another state?

◆ ◆ ◆ ◆ ◆

FURTHER READINGS

Barcelona Traction, International Court of Justice Reports, 1970.

Ian Brownlie, ed. *Basic Documents in International Law*. 5th edn. Oxford: Oxford University Press, 2002.

Paul Craig and Grainne de Búrca, *EU Law, Text, Cases and Materials*. 3rd edn. Oxford: Oxford University Press, 2003.

European Union: www.europa.eu

International Criminal Court: www.icc-cpi.int

International Criminal Tribunal for Rwanda: http://69.94. 11.53/default.htm

International Criminal Tribunal for the Former Yugoslavia: www.icty.org

Journal of Philosophy of International Law

Lotus, Permanent Court of International Justice, Series A, No. 10, 1927.

North Sea Continental Shelf, International Court of Justice Reports, 1969.

R v. Secretary of State for Transport, Ex p Factortame [1990] 2 AC 85. Note that this is the first in a series of five cases known as the "Factortame litigation" treating issues of sovereignty and integration in the European Union. Online sources of "*Factortame I*" as it is called informally, will often link to reports of subsequent litigation.

Malcolm N. Shaw, *International Law.* 5th edn. Cambridge: Cambridge University Press, 2003.

United Nations international law homepage: www.un.org/law.

William Twining, *Globalisation and Legal Theory.* Evanston, IL: Northwestern University Press, 2001.

Neil Walker, "Legal Theory and the European Union: A 25th Anniversary Essay," *Oxford Journal of Legal Studies* 2005 25(4):581-601.

Stephen Weatherill, *Cases and Materials on EU Law.* 7th edn. Oxford: Oxford University Press, 2005.

GLOSSARY

This glossary contains legal, Latin, and philosophical terms which occur frequently in legal writing and in philosophical writing about law. This is not a comprehensive glossary: a complete account of philosophical and legal terms would run to several volumes. This glossary is meant to be an introductory reference and guide to help the reader bridge the gap between philosophy and law, and to bridge also some of the gaps between American, British, and Canadian usage. I have tried to offer an accurate yet concise definition of each term. Where strict accuracy might require a long explanation of different practices, I have offered a more general definition which explains a main or common sense of the term. If more precise definition of a term is required, it is best to look to a dictionary of law or philosophy which applies to the specific context in which you have found the term used.

I have relied extensively on the following excellent resources:

Bryan A. Garner, ed. *Black's Law Dictionary*, 8th edn. St. Paul, MN: Thomson West, 2004.

Elizabeth Martin and Jonathan Law, eds. *A Dictionary of Law*, 6th edn. Oxford: Oxford University Press, 2006.

J.A. Yogis, *Canadian Law Dictionary*, 5th edn. Hauppauge, NY: Barron's Educational Series, 2003.

Dennis Patterson, ed., *A Companion to the Philosophy of Law and Legal Theory*. Cambridge, MA: Blackwell, 1999.

Ab initio: (Latin) from the beginning.

Accession: the act of joining and accepting the terms of an international agreement (e.g., treaty, convention), typically used to refer to the act of joining an already established agreement.

Accused: in its most general sense, a person charged but not yet convicted of criminal wrongdoing.

Acquis communautaire: the entire body of European Union law, particularly significant for prospective members of the European Union who must accept this body of law as a condition of joining the European Union.

Acquit: in contract law, to be released from an obligation; in criminal law, to be not proven guilty and saved from further prosecution for the same crime. Note that acquittal in the criminal courts does not eliminate the possibility of a civil suit treating the same set of events.

Act: 1. intentional conduct. 2. a legislative body's written statement of a legal rule or rules, usually referred to as statute law.

Action: a legal proceeding one party has brought against another in order to have a matter of dispute resolved by a court.

Actus reus: (Latin) the conduct element of criminal wrongdoing. A criminal act is composed of legally prohibited conduct and criminal intention (*mens rea*). Some crimes involve an intentional omission or failure to act.

Adjudication: a judgment which resolves a legal dispute. A theory of adjudication accounts for what courts do (or ought to do) in order to reach a decision which resolves a legal dispute.

Affirm: an appellate court's confirmation of a lower court's decision.

Amicus curiae: (Latin) friend of the court. A representative of the public interest or some other interest relevant to the disposition of a legal action, yet otherwise unrepresented by the parties to the action. The *amicus curiae* typically presents information to the court in the form of a brief.

Analytical jurisprudence: the branch of the philosophy of law concerned mainly with description and explanation of law and legal practices.

Appeal: review by a higher court of the decision of a lower court. Appeals may be granted in order for a higher court to evaluate a party's claim that there is a need to remedy such errors of law as misapplication of law to facts, incorrect directions to a jury, or use of legally unacceptable evidence.

Appellant: the party who appeals a decision. An appeal is typically, though not necessarily, made by the party who is dissatisfied with the decision of the lower court.

Appellate court: see *Court of Appeal*.

Arraignment: a legal procedure in which the charge against an accused is read out in court and the accused is asked to enter a plea (usually guilty or not guilty).

Arrest: the legally authorized deprivation of a person's liberty in order to bring a charge against that person.

Attorney: generally, a person legally empowered to act as an agent for another; in the USA, a term used to refer to a lawyer legally authorized to practice law.

Attorney General: in Canada and England, the chief legal officer for the Crown, politically responsible for public prosecution and a source of legal advice to government. Attorneys General are elected members of Parliament or the legislative assembly of the jurisdiction for which each is responsible. In the USA, the US Attorney General is the appointed, non-elected chief legal officer of the federal government who also heads the Department of Justice, and advises the government on legal matters. A similar function is performed by the Attorneys General of individual states (elected or appointed, according to individual states' laws).

Bar: 1. the physical or imaginary division in a courtroom between public observers and the judges, lawyers, and persons formally involved in the case at trial. Bar associations comprise members of the legal profession, distinguished from Benchers, the judges who render decisions. 2. prevent. Once a case has been decided by a judge, the fact of that decision bars the parties from bringing the same matter to trial again.

Barrister: in England, a lawyer who argues cases in court. A solicitor is a lawyer who prepares cases and works outside the court in co-operation with barristers. In Canada this distinction is not made, and all lawyers may retain the designation "barrister and solicitor."

Begging the question: a fallacy (error of reasoning), consisting in circular reasoning which assumes what it sets out to prove.

Bellum omnium: (Latin) war of all against all. The state of nature in the absence of the rule of law.

Bench: generally, the court and judges. The physical seat used by judges, or the body of judges as opposed to the lawyers who argue cases and are members of the bar.

Bencher: in England, a judge or senior lawyer who is a member of the group which governs the activities of one of the Inns of Court (legal associations in London which govern the activities of barristers and perform an educational function). In Canada, a member of a provincial law society which governs activities of that law society.

Bill: most generally, a document proposing a law, and brought before a legislative body for consideration and approval.

Bill of Rights: a legislative statement of basic rights and freedoms. In England, refers to the Bill of Rights of 1689. In the USA, the first ten amendments of the United States Constitution. In Canada, the Bill of Rights of 1970 has been largely superseded by the *Charter of Rights and Freedoms* which entrenches and protects in a stronger manner the basic rights and freedoms of Canadians.

Breach: to break by action or inaction the requirements of a legal rule.

Breach of contract: failure without legal excuse by a contracting party to comply with certain provisions of a legally acceptable contract.

Brief: in the USA and Canada, a document prepared by a lawyer prior to arguing a case in court. The brief contains the facts of the case, relevant sources of law, and argument showing how the relevant legal rules apply to the facts. In England, a document prepared by a solicitor directing a barrister to argue a case in court.

Burden of proof: (Latin: *onus probandi*) generally, the duty of a party to a trial to prove the party's claims about the way a case at trial ought to be resolved. In criminal trials, it is assumed that the accused is innocent until proven guilty, and the prosecution bears the burden of proving the accused guilty beyond reasonable doubt, with certain exceptions.

By-law: local legislation by authorities who are subordinate to some higher authority. Also rules of an association or corporation.

Canon: general term for a rule, especially in the codes of conduct of professional societies.

Canon law: Roman Catholic church law, used also by the Church of England (Anglican Church), governing activities of the church and some activities of church members who are not also members of the clergy.

Case: a legal controversy to be resolved by a court, and more generally the argument offered by each party to the dispute.

Cause: the reason for some effect, or the reason for bringing a dispute to a court for resolution. Many other legal uses.

Certiorari: (Latin) to be informed. A way of causing a higher court to investigate the decision of a lower court, with the effect of cancelling the practical effects of the lower court's decision.

The higher court issues a writ to the lower court, causing the lower court to give to the higher court the records of its reasoning and decision in some matter.

Challenge: 1. to question the legal justification of some state of affairs. 2. the legal right to object to and have a potential juror or jurors removed from a jury. In Canada and the USA, each side to a dispute is allowed a set number of peremptory challenges with which a juror may be disqualified for no stated reason. Peremptory challenges were abolished in the UK by the Criminal Justice Act 1988.

Charge: in criminal law, to formally accuse a person of having committed a specific crime.

Charter: in its most general sense, a foundational document setting out the basic standards according to which a specific wide range of conduct is to be governed. In Canada, an informal way of referring to the *Canadian Charter of Rights and Freedoms*.

Civil action: legal proceeding to resolve a non-criminal dispute over a private or civil right.

Civil law: 1. law concerned with interactions between private individuals and legal persons such as corporations. Concerns rights and remedies in the context of property, family law, contracts, and torts. Distinguished from criminal law, which governs conduct which wrongs society in general. 2. Roman law which formed the basis for civil law in Louisiana, and several states in western Europe. In a form influenced by the Code Napoléon of France, civil law also forms the basis of private law in Quebec.

Civil rights: 1. personal rights protected by law. 2. in American jurisprudence, functionally synonymous with civil liberties. 3. in Canadian jurisprudence, civil rights pertain largely to interpersonal relations, and civil liberties pertain largely to relations between private persons and social institutions.

Code: generally, a systematic assembly of a particular area of law in a particular jurisdiction, e.g., the Criminal Code of Canada.

Common law: generally, the English precedent-based system of law, inherited by Commonwealth nations and the USA. More specifically, that part of the law developed by the courts in their decisions which extend the customs and principles already in place in the practices of the people. More recently, as unwritten customs have been displaced by court decisions, that part of the law developed by the courts.

Competent: generally, having authority and meeting minimum standards of rationality to take some action.

Conflict of laws: the branch of jurisprudence concerned with principled resolution of conflicts which arise when the laws of more than one jurisdiction apply to some matter. Private international law treats the ways in which a court in one jurisdiction chooses to interpret the force of laws of some other jurisdiction.

Congress: the federal legislative body of the USA, comprising the House of Representatives and the Senate.

Consideration: in contract law, the valuable thing given over as payment for some present or promised action. Valid contracts generally require consideration.

Construction: interpretation of an unclear part of some legal standard, typically according to accepted construction rules.

Contra: (Latin) against.

Contra bonos mores: (Latin) against good morals.

Contract: a legally binding agreement which gives the contracting parties specific rights or obligations which may be enforced by the courts should either party fail to comply with the conditions of the contract. Valid contracts are characterized by (1) an offer and (2) acceptance by (3) competent parties who exchange (4) consideration and aim at some (5) legal purpose.

Conveyance: a documented transfer of land between persons.

Conviction: the finding in a criminal trial that, according to the standard set by law, the accused is guilty as charged. Conviction typically also refers to the sentence which results from the finding of guilt.

Corporation: an artificial person treated by the law as a single person even though it may in fact be composed of an individual (corporation sole) or many individuals (corporation aggregate). Corporations may hold legal rights and duties.

Corpus delicti: (Latin) body of a crime. The object or the harm resulting from the *actus reus* of a crime.

Counsel: 1. generally, advice given from one to another. 2. in the USA, a general term for an attorney. In the UK, a term for a barrister or barristers. In Canada, a general term for lawyers.

Court Martial: a military court in which members of armed forces are tried for offences against service law. In the US, military courts are responsible for trial and punishment of offences against the Uniform Code of Military Justice committed by those properly subject to that code. The service law of the UK consists of a series of acts and further regulations governing each service. The service law of Canada is specified in the National Defence Act 1985.

Court of Appeal: a higher court which reviews a lower court's application of law to a case. Also referred to as "appellate courts" to mark the fact that courts which perform appeal functions need not be explicitly called "Courts of Appeal." Appellate courts evaluate a party's claim that a lower court's resolution of a legal proceeding was in error, for reasons including errors in the conduct of the trial, errors of application of law to facts, and errors in admission of evidence.

Court of King's Bench/Queen's Bench: in the UK, the highest court of common law, forming one division (Queen's Bench Division) of the High

Court's three divisions. The other divisions are Chancery and Family. In Canada, this term refers to the trial division of a province's superior or supreme court.

Crime: legally prohibited wrong against society in general.

Crown: in the UK, the office formally held by the reigning monarch as the supreme legal power. In practice, the activities of the crown are in control of the elected government and the civil service. Barring exceptional circumstances, the monarch does not exercise legal powers except on the advice of elected ministers. In Canada, the crown generally refers to the elected government and all subordinate officials.

Crown Attorney: in Canada, a lawyer appointed by an Attorney General to prosecute accused criminals on behalf of the crown. Also called Crown Prosecutor. In the UK, a prosecutor works under a regional Chief Crown Prosecutor.

Culpable: blameworthy. Culpability requires intention, recklessness, or negligence, except in instances of strict liability.

Custom: a long-held practice, standard, or usage in some place which through common acceptance is treated as law.

Damages: compensation awarded a person who has suffered a legal wrong. There are many types of damages.

Decision: used in several senses, often to refer to the formal judgment by a court which resolves a dispute brought before it.

De facto: (Latin) in fact. Often used to contrast actual practice with formal legal requirements.

Defamation: public utterance of claims which tend to harm a person's reputation according to the standards of right-thinking persons. In the USA and Canada, spoken defamation is called *slander*, and published or graphic defamation is called *libel*. In England, defamation of short duration is called *slander*, and more permanent defamation is called *libel*.

Defence: in a criminal trial, the legally acceptable reasons presented to the court in an attempt to have the accused found not guilty. In a civil trial, the legally acceptable reasons presented to the court in an attempt to reduce or eliminate the plaintiff's claim against the defendant. Also used to refer to the pleading given the court by a defendant in response to a plaintiff's claim.

Defendant: in a criminal trial, the person accused of commission of a crime. In a civil trial, the person sued by the plaintiff.

De jure: (Latin) by right, as required by law. Often contrasted with *de facto,* "matter of fact" practice.

De novo: (Latin) fresh, new. A trial *de novo* is held as if the matter had not previously been tried.

Deposition: pre-trial testimony made under oath by a witness in response to spoken or written questions, as part of the process of discovery in which each side gathers evidence for its case. In Canada and the US, depositions are typically taken in the office of the lawyer of one of the parties. In criminal trials in the UK, depositions are taken before the magistrates' court; and in civil trials an examiner of the court (an official) may take depositions.

Devolution: a central government's delegation of limited domestic authority to a regional government. Recent example: establishment of regional governments in Scotland and Wales.

Dicta/dictum: (Latin) words/word. Remarks offered by a judge in the course of resolving a dispute, but not directly connected to the reasons upon which the judge relies in reaching a judgement. *Dicta* usually do not set a binding precedent.

Diligence: many types. Generally, the standard of carefulness reasonably expected of a person in a given situation.

Discharge: generally, a release from some obligation.

Discovery: in the context of trials, the pre-trial process by which opposing parties gather information from one another in order to prepare the arguments to be heard before the court.

Discretion: generally, the power of an official to exercise official powers in accordance with the official's best judgment.

Dismiss: to end a legal dispute prior to or during a trial.

Dissent: in a judicial decision, the fact of disagreement by a judge or judges who are in the minority. A dissenting opinion consists of reasons for disagreement with the majority of the court.

Docket: generally, a record of a court's activities, including a list of disputes to be heard, and the resolution of the dispute.

Double jeopardy: the legal doctrine that an accused person cannot be tried more than once for the same charge on the same evidence.

Due process: US and Canadian doctrine of fairness in both procedural operation of law and its substantive effects.

Duress: coercive or other threat used to compel action against the actor's will.

Duty: an obligation to act or withhold from a particular course of conduct.

Eminent domain: American legal doctrine later adopted in Canada, recognizing a governmental right to take private property for public purposes.

Enlargement: in the context of the European Union, the process of growth of the Union by acceptance of more state members.

Epistemology: the branch of philosophy concerned with the foundations of knowledge and what can be known.

Equity: generally, recourse to considerations of justice or fairness, rather than the strict letter of the law.

Erga omnes: (Latin) against all.

Ergo: (Latin) therefore.

Estoppel: generally, the legal principle that bars or stops party A from denying or alleging that the truth of some matter is different from what A previously represented it to be, and was (usually) taken by B as the truth, so A cannot gain advantage over B through a new, different representation of the truth of some matter. A is bound by A's initial representation of the truth of the matter. Roughly and intuitively stated, you may not change your story now to take advantage of someone else's having relied on your prior story. There are several types of estoppel, whose interpretation must be determined with reference to the specific jurisdiction.

Et al.: (Latin) and others.

Ethics: 1. the branch of philosophy concerned with the nature of the good life and right conduct. 2. in the legal context, often used to refer to standards of professional conduct which apply to members of the legal profession. See also *moral philosophy.*

Evidence: legally acceptable matter such as testimony, documents, substantial objects used to prove or disprove the existence of some claimed fact.

Exculpatory: legally admissible evidence or other facts which tend to relieve a defendant from legal liability. See *inculpatory.*

Excuse: a legally acceptable reason for relief from legal liability. See *exculpatory.*

Ex parte: (Latin) on behalf of one side only.

Ex post facto: (Latin) after the fact.

Extradition: the process in which a person is returned to a state in which he or she is to stand trial for a criminal offence. Extradition treaties between states provide for the giving over of fugitives from other states' criminal law.

Felony: in the USA, especially serious crimes, contrasted with less serious misdemeanours. In Canada and England this term has largely fallen out of use, and carries on in England only in pre-1967 criminal statutes. Especially serious crimes are now called indictable offences, and less serious crimes are now called summary offences.

Fraud: intentional misrepresentation of the truth of some matter for the purpose of gain.

Gratis: (Latin) free.

Guilty: a plea before the court or a finding by a court that an accused has committed the crime charged.

Habeas Corpus: (Latin) you have the body. A *writ* used in the procedure of judicial determination of the legality of detention of a person. If the detention is illegal, the accused is released.

Hearing: a proceeding held to resolve issues of fact and of law. Can refer to proceedings of courts, or quasi-judicial institutions.

House of Commons: in the UK and Canada, the lower house of Parliament, composed of elected Members of Parliament who serve terms of up to five years.

House of Lords: The unelected upper house of the Parliament of the UK, composed of Lords Spiritual and Temporal. Lords Spiritual are senior Church of England officials. Lords Temporal are composed of hereditary and life-peers, as well as senior Law Lords appointed from the ranks of the legal profession to carry out the judicial functions of the House of Lords. The *Constitutional Reform Act 2005* may soon see the removal of the Law Lords from the legislature, as the Act provides for the establishment of a new Supreme Court which will take over the judicial functions previously held by the House of Lords.

House of Representatives: one-half of the United States Congress, composed of elected members who serve terms of two years.

Ibid.: abbreviation for (Latin) *ibidem*: in the same place.

I.e.: abbreviation for (Latin) *Id est*: that is.

Ignorantia legis non excusat: (Latin) ignorance of the law is no excuse.

In camera: (Latin) in private. Proceedings of courts are typically public, yet some matters warrant being considered without public observation.

Inculpatory: legally admissible evidence or other facts which tend to incriminate or contribute weight to the case aimed at proving a defendant's legal liability. See *exculpatory*.

Indictable offence: In Canada and the UK, a criminal offence involving a matter more serious (e.g., murder) than matters involved in a summary offence (e.g., assault). Typically heard by courts higher than those which deal with less serious summary offences, and typically involving the option of a trial by judge and jury. Distinction no longer clearly evident in Canada. See also *summary offence, felony*.

Indictment: a written charge of a serious criminal offence which must be proved before a court.

Infra/Supra: (Latin) below/above. *Infra* indicates a following provision of reference information; *supra* indicates previously provided reference information.

Injunction: a judicial direction to a specific party to refrain from or to carry out certain conduct.

Inter alia: (Latin) among others.

Ipso facto: (Latin) by the fact.

Judgment: a decision by a court of competent jurisdiction regarding a dispute brought before it.

Jurisdiction: 1. the area of law to which a specific court's authority extends. 2. generally, a particular legal system.

Jurist: a person knowledgeable in law.

Jury: a number of persons selected to decide the facts of a case at trial, and to render a verdict. Grand juries traditionally composed of twenty-three persons are still used in the USA to determine whether facts and charges brought by a prosecutor are sufficient for the matter to go to trial. In England and Canada, grand juries are no longer used. Trial juries are typically composed of six or twelve persons.

Jus: (Latin) law or right.

Jus belli: (Latin) law of war.

Jus cogens: (Latin) known law. Refers to the doctrine of public international law which declares invalid any new agreement which conflicts with the overriding, peremptory norms of the widely accepted body of fundamental international legal norms.

Jus gentium: (Latin) law of nations. Refers to international law generally.

Leading case: a particularly important decision which has resolved a dispute in a way which is later relied upon as a strong guide for similar cases.

Leading question: a question which suggests to the witness the answer desired by the questioner, typically a "yes" or "no" answer. Usually allowed only in cross-examination or examination of a witness hostile to the questioner.

Legislation: generally, written law enacted by an authoritative body.

Liability: term broadly used to include obligation, duty, responsibility, in civil and criminal contexts.

Libel: generally, defamation of longer duration, typically printed, written, or graphic as opposed to verbally issued defamation. May include cartoons, sketches, sculpture, films, or audio recordings.

Litigants: the persons engaged in a civil dispute brought before a court.

Litigation: generally, the activity of bringing a civil dispute before a court for resolution.

Locus poenitentiae: (Latin) place for repentance. An opportunity for a change of mind prior to completion of some act.

Logic: the branch of philosophy concerned with the characteristics of good and bad arguments.

Malum in se: (Latin) evil or wrong in itself. Evil according to the standard of civilized society even in the absence of specific limiting legislation.

Malum prohibitum: (Latin) evil or wrong because it is prohibited.

Martial law: government of civilians by military authorities in a time of emergency.

Material: important, necessary, substantially relevant.

Mens rea: (Latin) guilty mind. The mental element of the type of crime which requires for its commission both *mens rea* and the actual criminal conduct, called *actus reus*. The *mens rea* requirement for particular crimes is specified by legislation or precedent as intention, recklessness, or negligence. Strict liability criminal offences have no *mens rea* requirement. See *strict liability*.

Mercantile law: the body of law regarding commercial transactions.

Metaphysics: the branch of philosophy which examines the nature of what is real.

Misdemeanor: in the USA, a crime less serious than a felony. Distinction eliminated from English and Canadian law.

Mistrial: a failure of a trial for a fundamental reason.

Moral philosophy: the branch of philosophy which examines the nature of the good life and right conduct. See also *ethics*.

Natural justice: generally, principles of procedural fairness which prohibit bias on the part of the judge, and require that both sides to a dispute be heard.

Necessity defence: a defence against a criminal charge on the ground that no alternative legally permissible course of action was available to the defendant.

Negligence: conduct which is assessed careless when measured against the standard of what a reasonable person could be expected to do or not do. Aspect of *mens rea*.

Non-performance: the failure of a contracting party to adhere to the terms of a contract.

Non sequitur: (Latin) it does not follow. A conclusion which does not follow from the premises or reasons given.

Normative jurisprudence: the branch of philosophy of law concerned mainly with evaluation and justification of law and legal practices.

Nota bene: (Latin) note well. Abbreviated N.B.

Not guilty: a plea made by the accused to deny charges, and a verdict which indicates that the case against the accused was not proven beyond reasonable doubt.

Nulla poena sine lege: (Latin) no punishment without law. The principle that no punishment shall be given unless the punishment is set by law.

Offence: generally, a crime.

Ontology: the branch of philosophy which examines questions about the existence of things.

Opinion: a judge's or court's reasons for a decision regarding a dispute.

Overrule: the overturning of a decision in a particular case by the same court or a higher court of the same jurisdiction.

Pacta sunt servanda: (Latin) agreements must be served. General legal principle that what is agreed must be carried out.

Parliamentary sovereignty: legal doctrine that Parliament is supreme and can make or eliminate any law.

Party: persons with a direct interest in a legal proceeding.

Per curiam: (Latin) by the court.

Performance: the carrying out of an obligation, e.g., the terms of a contract.

Perjury: knowingly giving false testimony while under oath to give true testimony.

Person: an individual human or a group of persons such as a corporation or a union.

Plaintiff: a person bringing civil suit or action against another before a court.

Plea bargaining: a practice of negotiating a reduction in charges or sentence in exchange for the accused pleading guilty to agreed charges.

Pleadings: written statements of fact given by each party to the opponent reporting facts used in support of each party's case, used to make plain the issues to be resolved at trial.

Positive law: law actually put into place by an authority for government of a law-governed society.

Positive morality: the actual current moral beliefs of a particular society.

Precedent: legal doctrine by which previously decided cases are authoritative sources for settlement of later similar cases. See also *stare decisis*.

Preponderance of evidence: more probable than not. The standard of proof used in civil law, contrasted with the higher standard of reasonable doubt used in criminal law.

Prima facie: (Latin) on its face. On initial appearance or examination.

Private international law: see *conflict of laws*.

Pro bono: (Latin) for the good. Often used to refer to legal work undertaken by lawyers on an unpaid, voluntary basis.

Proceeding: generally, the form and manner of operations before a court, and the steps in the course of judicial resolution of a dispute.

Prosecutorial discretion: the power of a prosecutor to rely on his or her best judgment as to whether criminal charges ought to be laid.

Question of fact: a dispute over facts, decided by a jury.

Question of law: a dispute over a matter of law, decided by a judge.

Ratio decidendi: (Latin) reason for decision. The *ratio* of a case binds lower courts by the doctrine of precedent.

Reasonable doubt: the standard of proof used in criminal trial. A person guilty of a crime must be guilty beyond reasonable doubt, according to the standard of the reasonable person.

Rechtsstaat: (German) a state under the rule of law. This complex term expresses the ideal of a state whose nature and existence is intrinsically tied to a commitment to the principles of the rule of law.

Reckless: heedless, rash conduct which is indifferent to the existence of recognized danger. More serious than negligence. Aspect of *mens rea*.

Remedy: a means to enforce a right or to redress violation of a right.

Repeal: a legislative act which eliminates a previous law.

Reversal: the overturning of the decision of a lower court by a higher court.

Senate: in the USA, one-half of the United States Congress (the other half being the House of Representatives). Senators are elected to six-year terms. In Canada, the upper house of Parliament, composed of appointed members who serve until age seventy-five.

Sentence: the punishment given a defendant upon conviction of criminal wrongdoing.

Slander: spoken defamation. See also *defamation*.

Sovereign immunity: legal doctrine which prevents a suit against the government without the consent of the government.

Stare decisis: (Latin) stand by decided matters. The doctrine that courts follow precedent, and lower courts treat decisions of higher courts of the same jurisdiction as binding, and decisions of higher courts in other jurisdictions as only persuasive.

Statute: a written legislative act by an authoritative body.

Strict liability: a type of offence in which responsibility is assigned without a finding of fault. Strict liability offences are typically matters where the value of efficient regulation and nominal penalties outweigh the danger of omitting an assessment of fault.

Subsidiarity: the principle of European Union law which, together with principles of proportionality and necessity, requires that decisions should be made at the level closest to the citizen whenever possible, thereby balancing the need and importance of local control with the need and importance of shared European laws.

Summary offence: In Canada and the UK, a criminal offence involving a matter less serious (e.g., assault) than matters involved in an indictable offence (e.g., murder). Typically heard by a single judge in a lower court for speedy resolution of the charge. See also *indictable offence, felony*.

Supra: (Latin) above. Often used in legal writing to indicate that a full reference to some source of information has already been given, and may be found in an earlier part of the work. E.g., *supra* n. 17 means that a fuller reference may be found in note 17 which occurs in the preceding text.

Testimony: a witness's statement of evidence, given under oath.

Tort: a civil wrong remedied by an award of damages.

Tortfeasor: a person who commits a tort, called a "tortious" act.

Ultra vires: (Latin) outside of or beyond the powers. An action beyond the authorized power of the actor.

Unconstitutional: refers to a law which is inconsistent with provisions of a constitution.

Viz.: abbreviation for (Latin) *videlicet*: namely.

Volenti non fit injuria: (Latin) no injury or wrong is done to a consenting person. Defence in tort law which claims that plaintiff consented to damage or risk of damage suffered.

Writ: generally, a written court order giving authority and direction to carry out some act.

SOURCES

Austin, John. Excerpts from *Austin: The Province of Jurisprudence Determined*. Ed. W.E. Rumble. New York: Cambridge, 1995. Copyright © 1995. Reprinted by permission of Cambridge University Press.

Delgado, Richard. "About Your Masthead: A Preliminary Inquiry into the Compatibility of Civil Rights and Civil Liberties," from *Civil Rights—Civil Liberties Law Review* 39.1 (2004): 1-15. Reprinted by permission of CRCL.

Devlin, Patrick. "Morals and the Criminal Law," from *The Enforcement of Morals*. Oxford: Oxford University Press, 1965. Reprinted by permission of Oxford University Press.

Duff, R.A. "Choice, Character and Action," from *Criminal Attempts*. Oxford: Clarendon Press, 1997. Copyright © 1996 by Antony Duff. Reprinted by permission of Oxford University Press.

Dworkin, Gerald. "Paternalism," from *Morality, Harm and the Law*. Boulder: Westview Press, 1994. Copyright © 1994 by Westview Press. Reprinted by permission of Westview Press, a member of Perseus Books, L.L.C.

Dworkin, Ronald. "Integrity in Law," from *Law's Empire*. Cambridge, MA: The Belknap Press of Harvard University Press, 1986. Copyright © 1986 by Ronald Dworkin. Reprinted by permission of Harvard University Press; "The Model of Rules I," from *Taking Rights Seriously, Second Edition*. Cambridge, MA: The Belknap Press of Harvard University Press, 1977. Copyright © 1977, 1978 by Ronald Dworkin. Reprinted by permission of Harvard University Press.

Finnis, John. Excerpts from *Natural Law and Natural Rights*. Oxford: Oxford University Press, 1979. Copyright © 1979 by OUP. Reprinted by permission of Oxford University Press.

Frank, Jerome. "Preface to Sixth Printing." *Law and the Modern Mind*. Gloucester, MA: Peter Smith, 1970.

——. "Legal Realism." Chapter V of *Law and the Modern Mind*. Gloucester, MA: Peter Smith, 1970.

Grotius, Hugo. "Prolegomena," from *De Jure Belli Ac Pacis Libri Tres* (1625) in *The Classics of International Law*, ed. J.B. Scott. Oxford: Clarendon Press, 1925.

Hart, H.L.A. Excerpts from *Punishment and Responsibility*. Oxford: Oxford University Press, 1968. Reprinted by permission of Oxford University Press; Excerpts from *Law, Liberty and Morality*. Stanford, California: Stanford University Press, 1972. Copyright © 1963 by the Board of Trustees of the Leland Stanford Junior University. Reprinted by permission of Stanford University Press; "Law as the Union of Primary and Secondary Rules" and "International Law," from *The Concept of Law*. Oxford: Oxford University Press, 1961. Copyright © 1961, 1994 Oxford University Press. Reprinted by permission of Oxford University Press; "Positivism and the Separation of Law and Morals." *The Harvard Law Review* Vol. 71 (1959): 593-629. Reprinted by permission of the Harvard Law Review Association and William S. Hein Company.

Holmes, Oliver Wendell. "The Path of the Law." *The Common Law*. Boston: Little & Brown, 1897.

Koskenniemi, Martti. "The Politics of International Law." *European Journal of International Law* Vol. 1 (1990): 4-32. Reprinted by permission of Oxford University Press.

LIST
of products used:

2,215 lb(s) of Rolland Enviro100 Print
100% post-consumer

RESULTS
Based on the Cascades products you selected
compared to products in the industry made with
100% virgin fiber, your savings are:

19 trees
1 tennis court

18,325 gal. US of water
198 days of water consumption

2,316 lbs of waste
21 waste containers

6,021 lbs CO2
11,418 miles driven

29 MMBTU
142,000 60W light bulbs for one
hour

18 lbs NOx
emissions of one truck during 25
days